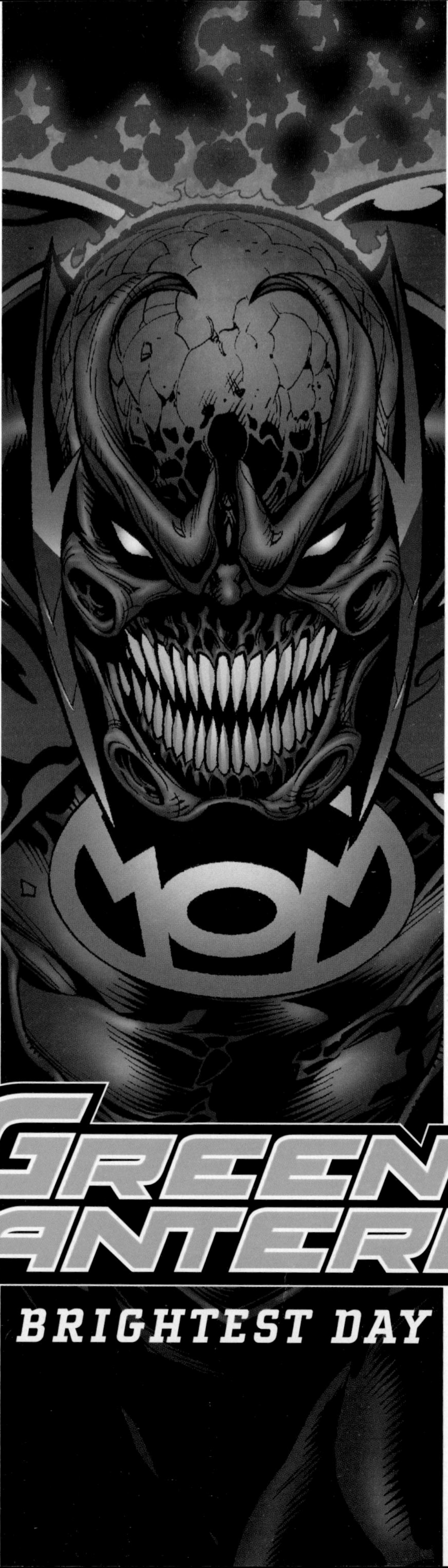

GREEN LANTERN

BRIGHTEST DAY

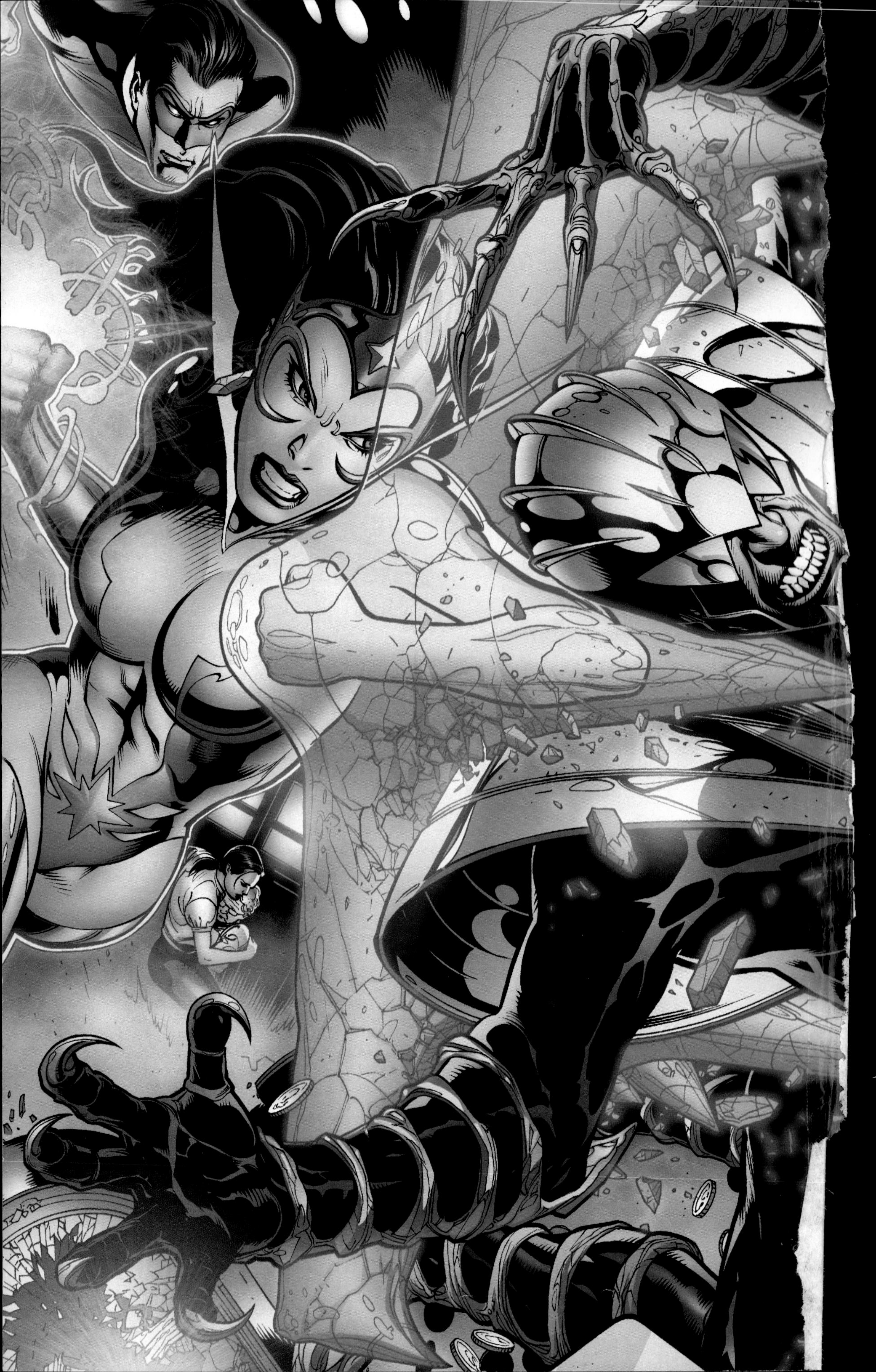

GREEN LANTERN

BRIGHTEST DAY

Geoff Johns
Writer

THE NEW GUARDIANS
Doug Mahnke
Art

**Christian Alamy, Keith Champagne, Mark Irwin, Doug Mahnke,
Tom Nguyen, Shawn Moll**
Inks

Randy Mayor, Gabe Eltaeb, Carrie Strachan, Rod Reis
Colors

TALES OF THE RED LANTERN CORPS: DEX-STARR
Shawn Davis
Art

Jamie Grant
Colors

Nick J. Napolitano, Steve Wands
Letters

DEX-STARR Created by Geoff Johns and Shane Davis

Eddie Berganza Adam Schlagman Brian Cunningham   Editor-Original Series
Ian Sattler   Director, Editorial-Archival Editions
Robbin Brosterman   Design Director-Books

Eddie Berganza   Executive Editor
Bob Harras   VP-Editor in Chief

Diane Nelson   President
Dan DiDio and Jim Lee   Co-Publishers
Geoff Johns   Chief Creative Officer
John Rood   Executive VP-Sales, Marketing and Business Development
Amy Genkins   Senior VP, Business and Legal Affairs
Nairi Gardiner   Senior VP-Finance
Jeff Boison   VP-Publishing Operations
Mark Chiarello   VP-Art Direction and Design
John Cunningham   VP-Marketing
Terri Cunningham   VP-Talent Relations and Services
Alison Gill   Senior VP-Manufacturing and Operations
David Hyde   VP-Publicity
Hank Kanalz   Senior VP-Digital
Jay Kogan   VP-Business and Legal Affairs, Publishing
Jack Mahan   VP-Business Affairs, Talent
Nick Napolitano   VP-Manufacturing Administration
Ron Perazza   VP-Online
Sue Pohja   VP-Book Sales
Courtney Simmons   Senior VP-Publicity
Bob Wayne   Senior VP, Sales

Cover by Doug Mahnke and Randy Mayor

GREEN LANTERN: BRIGHTEST DAY

DC Comics, 1700 Broadway, New York, NY 10019
A Warner Bros. Entertainment Company
Printed by Quad/Graphics, Versailles, KY. 5/13/11. First printing.
HC ISBN: 978-1-4012-3181-1
SC ISBN: 978-1-4012-3141-5

SUSTAINABLE
FORESTRY
INITIATIVE
Certified Chain of Custody
Promoting Sustainable
Forest Management
www.sfiprogram.org
Fiber used in this product line meets the
sourcing requirements of the SFI program.
www.sfiprogram.org SGS-SFICOC-0130

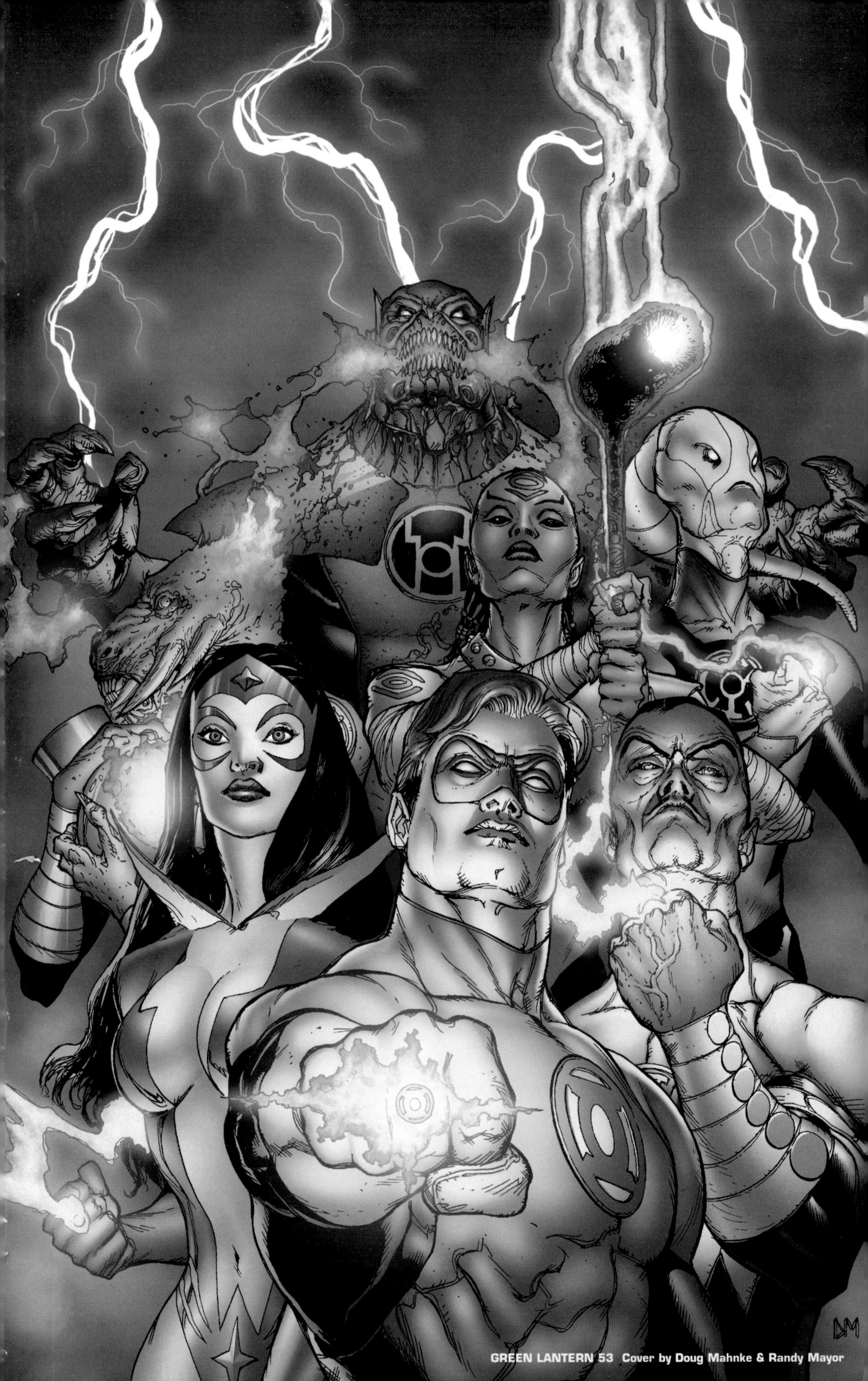

GREEN LANTERN 53 Cover by Doug Mahnke & Randy Mayor

THE NEW GUARDIANS
CHAPTER ONE

Doug Mahnke Pencils
Christian Alamy, Keith Champagne, Mark Irwin & Doug Mahnke Inks

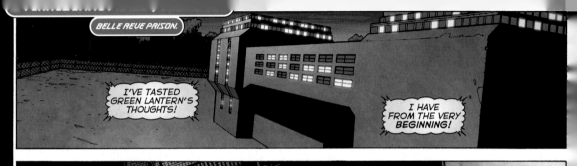

BELLE REVE PRISON.

I'VE TASTED GREEN LANTERN'S THOUGHTS!

I HAVE FROM THE VERY BEGINNING!

AND WHEN I DID IT WAS *ME* WHO GOT THE EMERALD RING AND LOVELY GIRLS!

ME WHO FLEW JETS ACROSS THE SKY AND SAVED THE UNIVERSE FROM THE *BLACKEST NIGHT!*

BUT, OH, IT WASN'T REALLY ME. ONLY THOUGHTS AND MEMORIES OF HIS GREAT ADVENTURES. BECAUSE I'M NOT HAL JORDAN.

I'M NOT HANDSOME.

THERE IS MORE TO EXISTENCE THAN HAL JORDAN, HECTOR HAMMOND.

OH, LEAVE ME ALONE!

YOU'RE AFRAID.

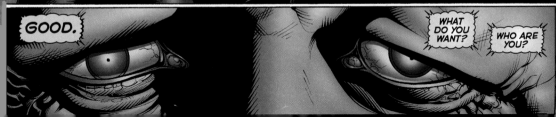

GOOD.

WHAT DO YOU WANT?

WHO ARE YOU?

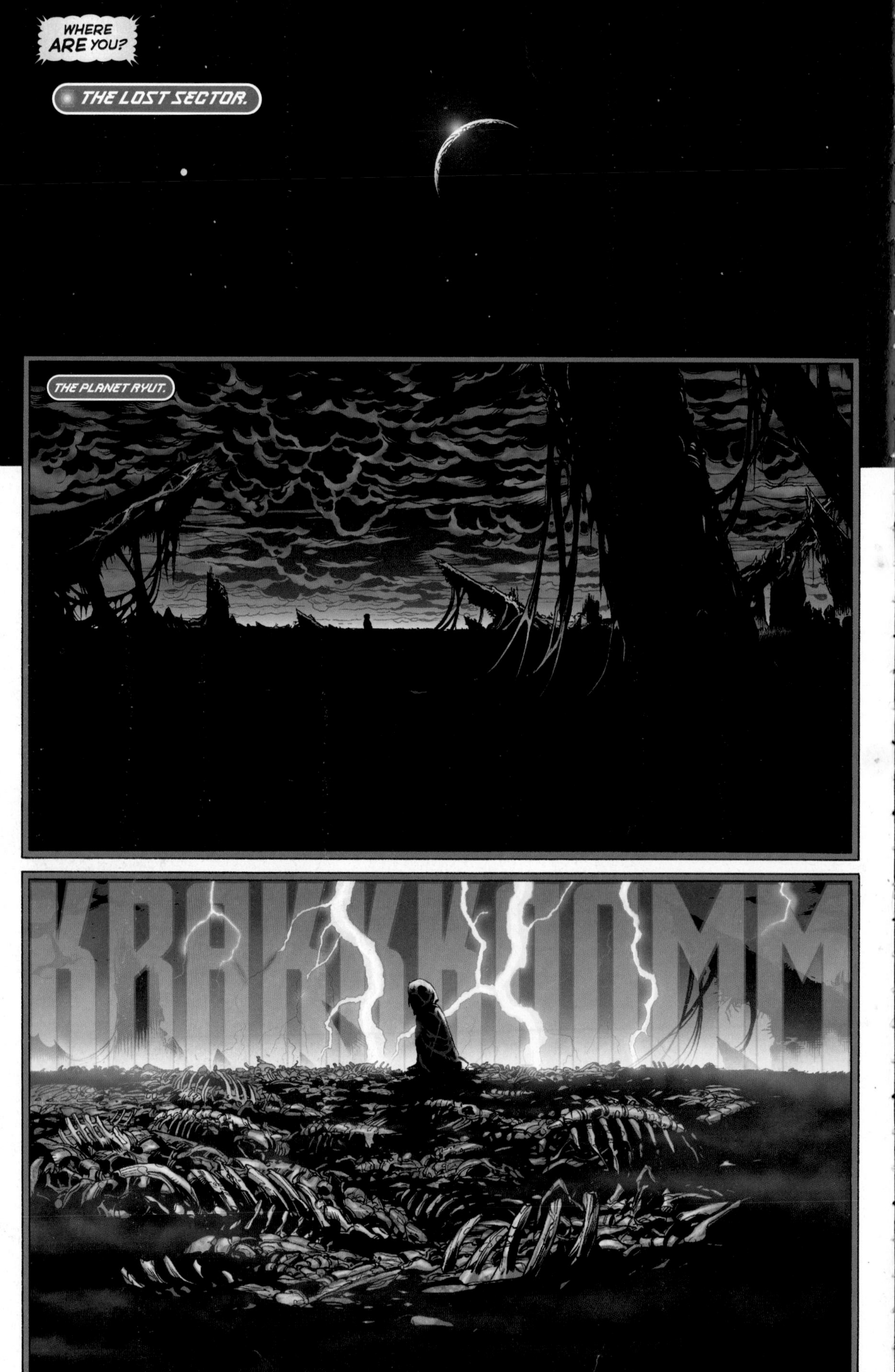

WHERE ARE YOU?
THE LOST SECTOR.
THE PLANET RYUT.
KRAKKOOMM

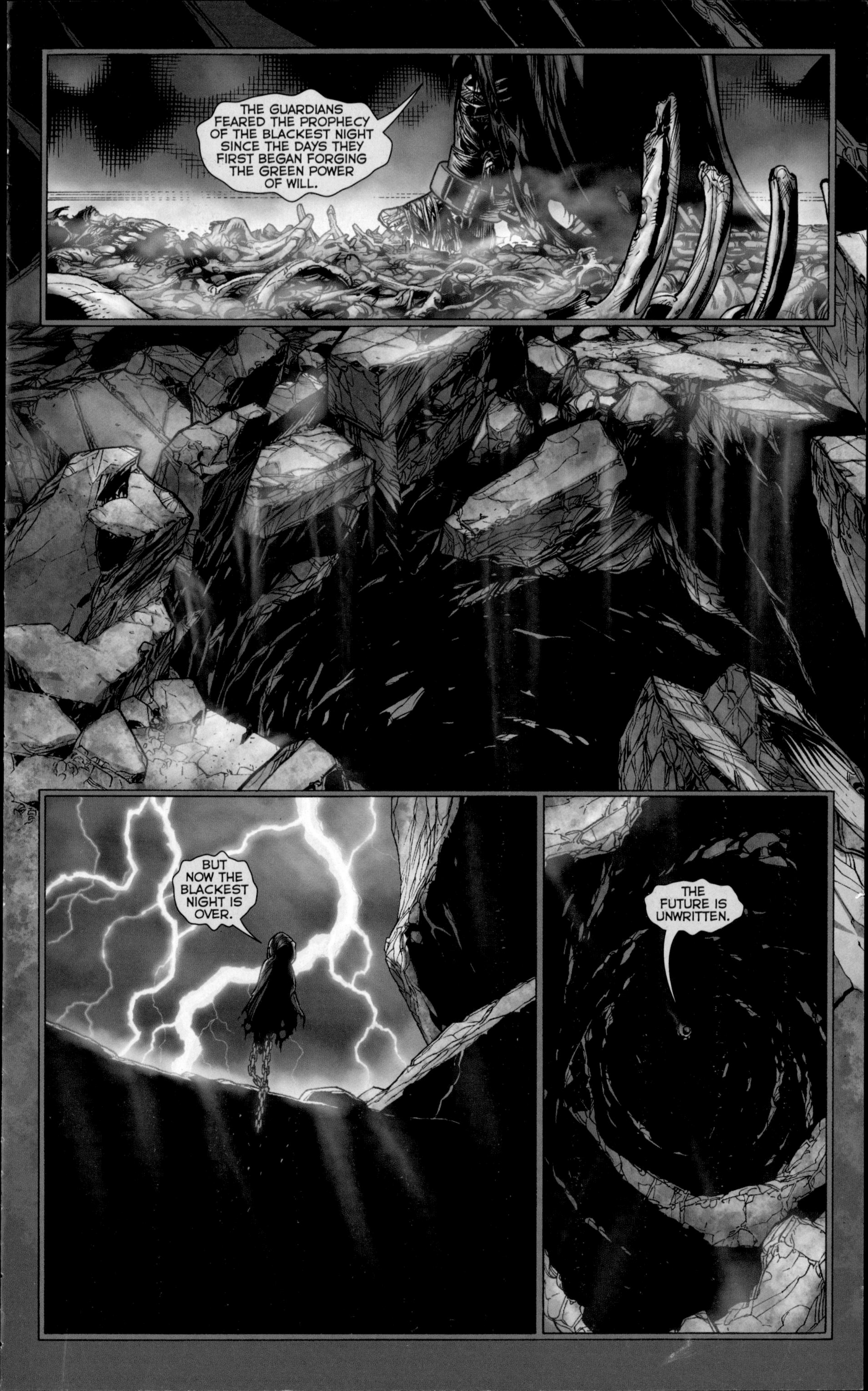
THE GUARDIANS FEARED THE PROPHECY OF THE BLACKEST NIGHT SINCE THE DAYS THEY FIRST BEGAN FORGING THE GREEN POWER OF WILL.
BUT NOW THE BLACKEST NIGHT IS OVER.
THE FUTURE IS UNWRITTEN.

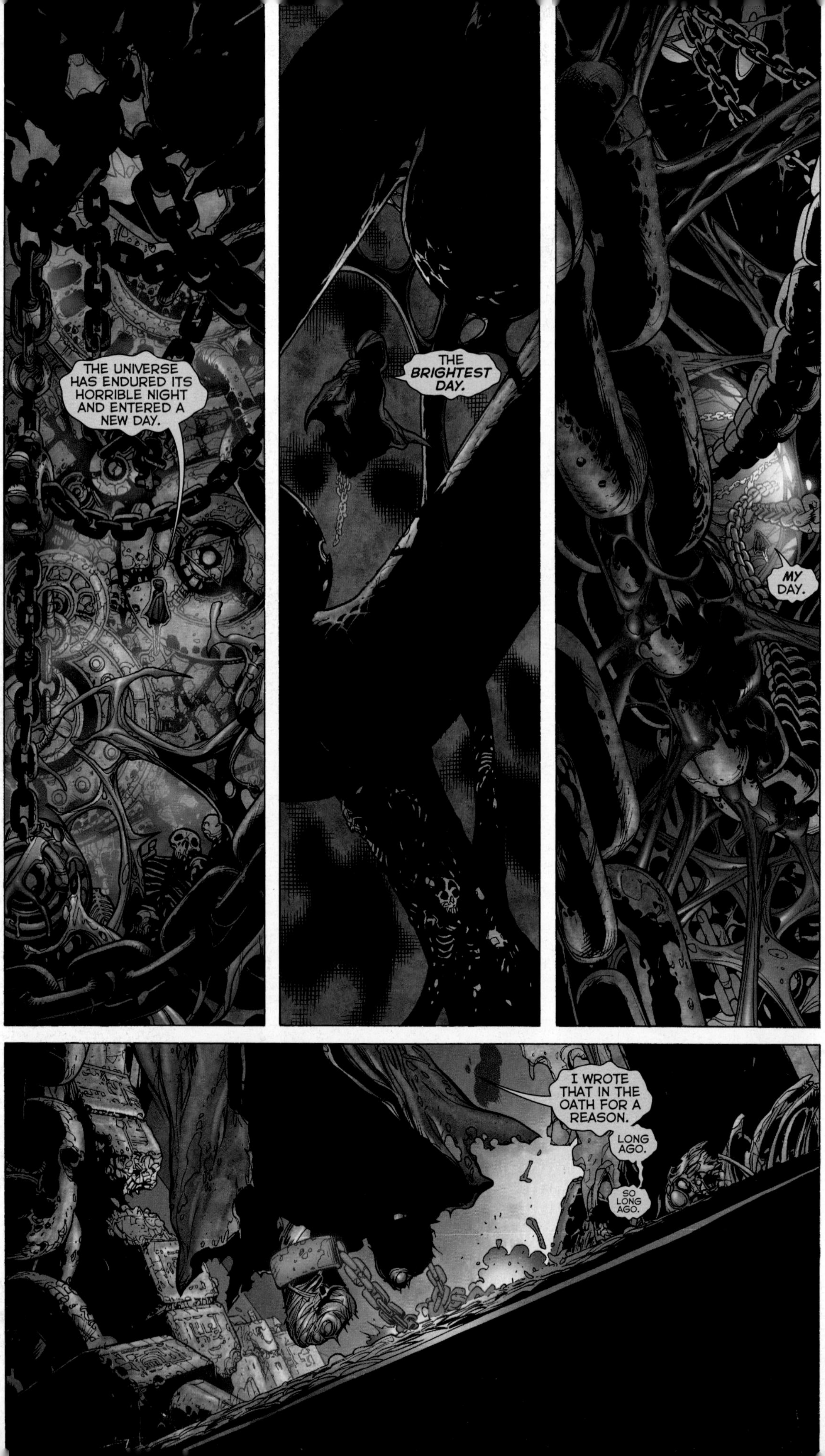
THE UNIVERSE HAS ENDURED ITS HORRIBLE NIGHT AND ENTERED A NEW DAY.
THE *BRIGHTEST* DAY.
MY DAY.
I WROTE THAT IN THE OATH FOR A REASON.
LONG AGO.
SO LONG AGO.

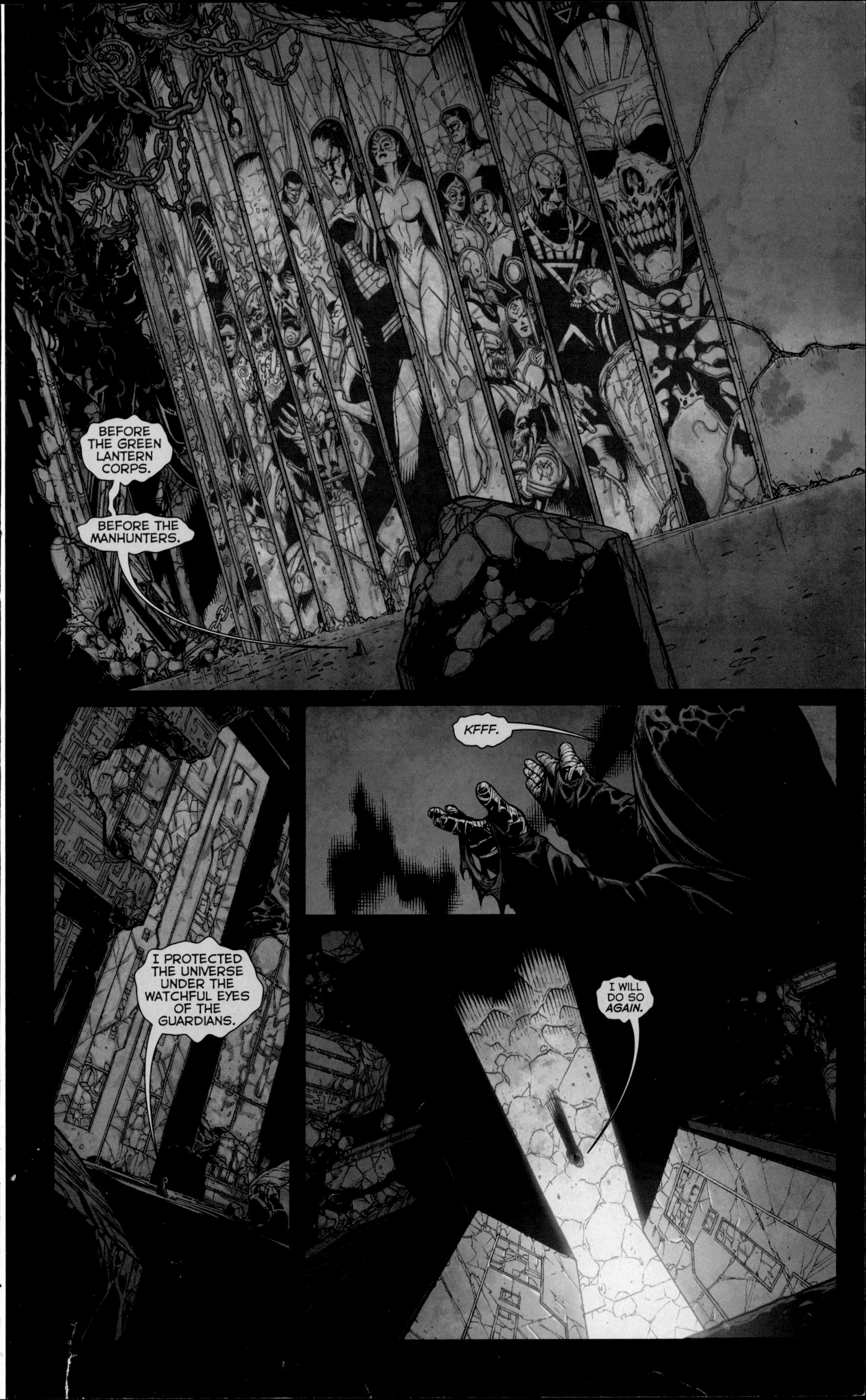
BEFORE THE GREEN LANTERN CORPS.
BEFORE THE MANHUNTERS.
I PROTECTED THE UNIVERSE UNDER THE WATCHFUL EYES OF THE GUARDIANS.
KFFF.
I WILL DO SO AGAIN.

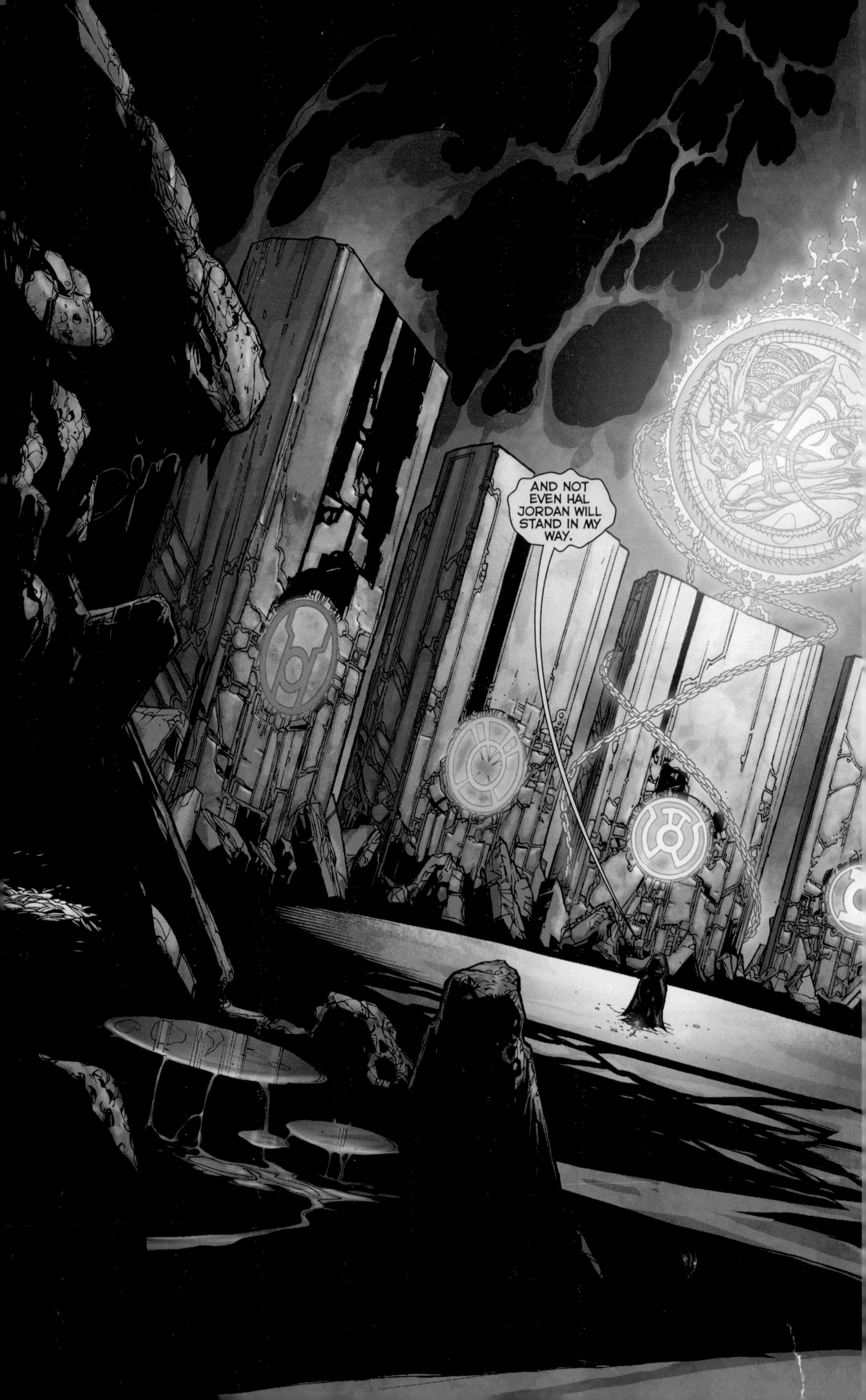
AND NOT EVEN HAL JORDAN WILL STAND IN MY WAY.

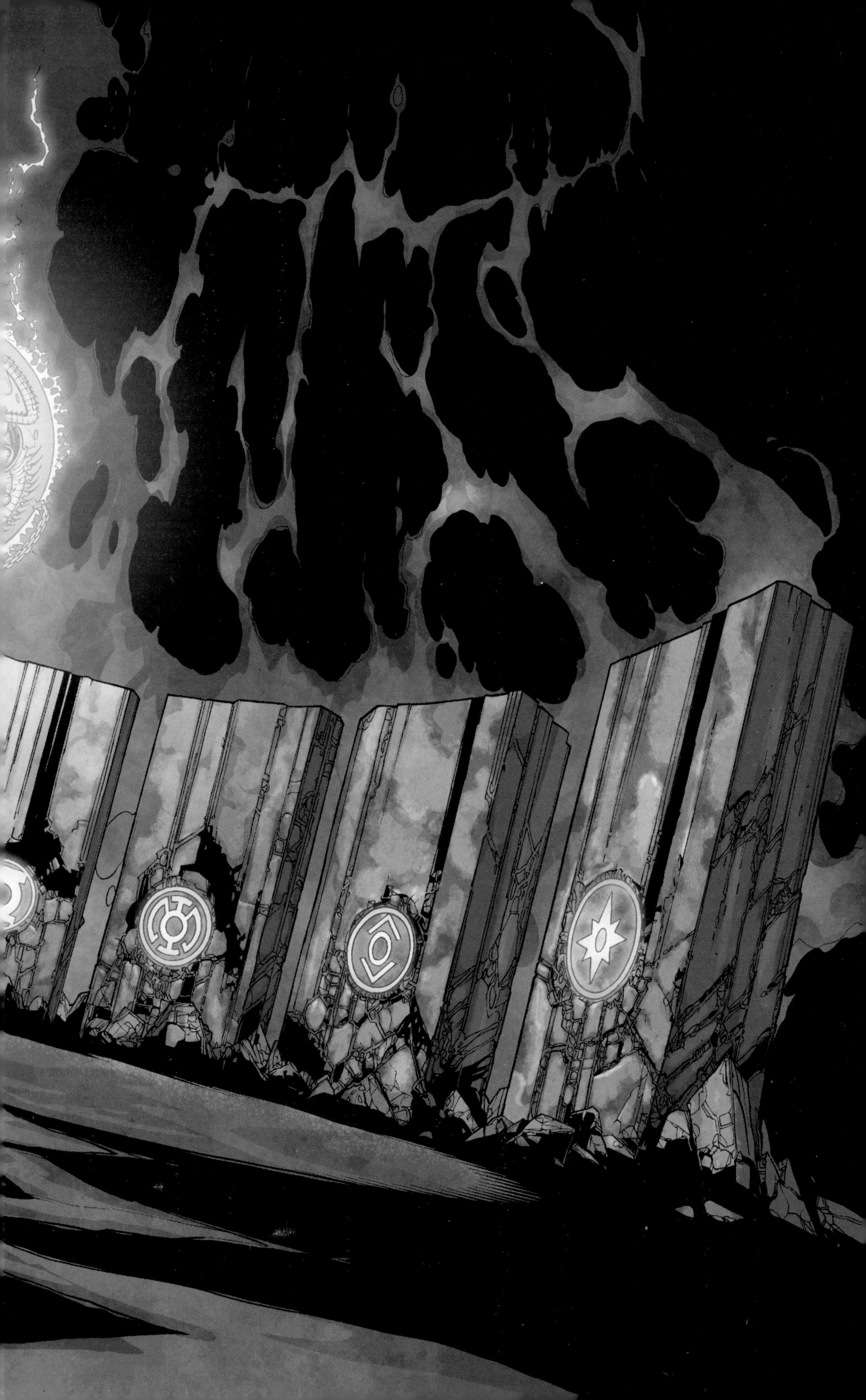

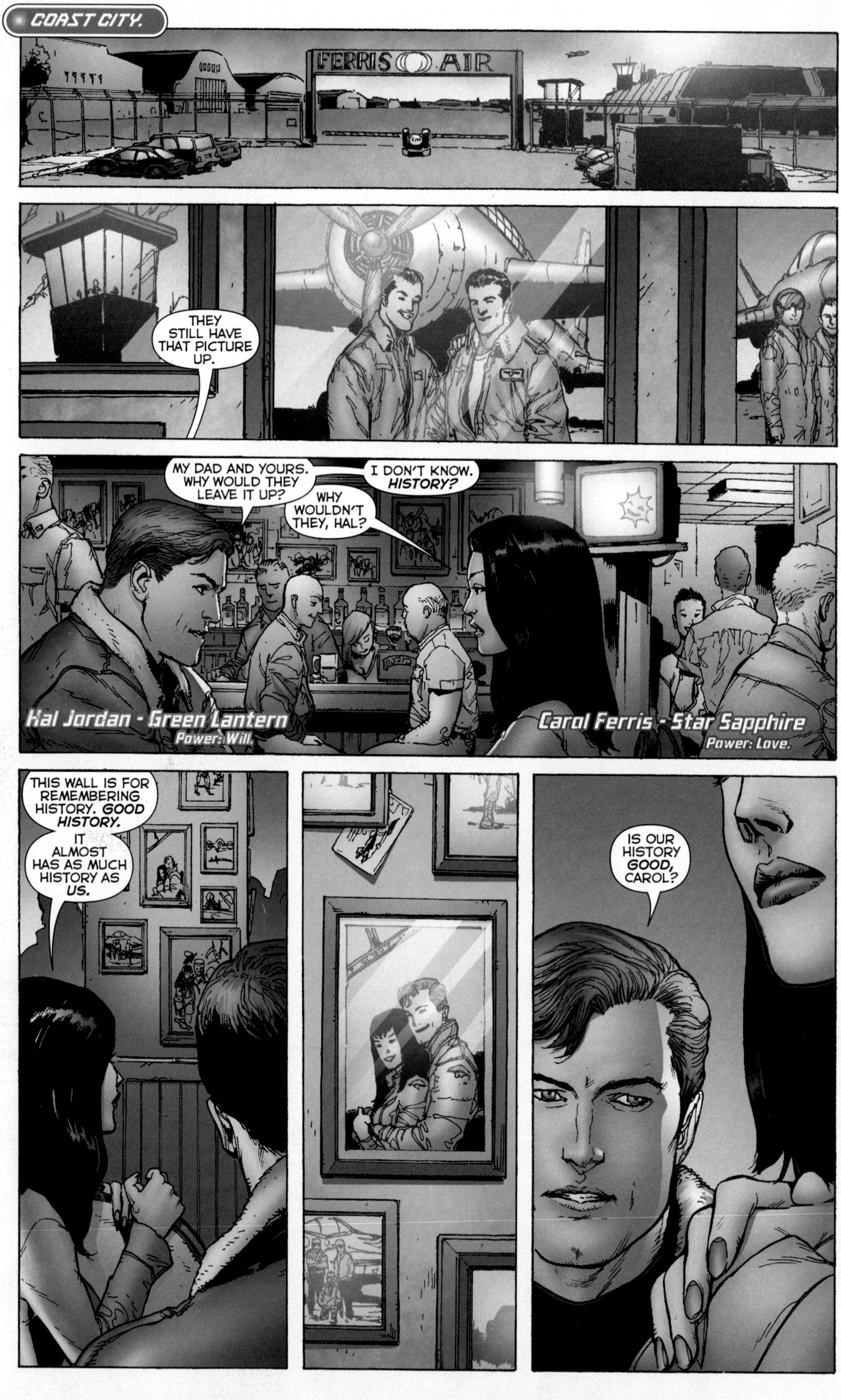
COAST CITY.
FERRIS AIR
THEY STILL HAVE THAT PICTURE UP.
MY DAD AND YOURS. WHY WOULD THEY LEAVE IT UP?
I DON'T KNOW. HISTORY?
WHY WOULDN'T THEY, HAL?
Hal Jordan - Green Lantern
Power: Will.
Carol Ferris - Star Sapphire
Power: Love.
THIS WALL IS FOR REMEMBERING HISTORY. GOOD HISTORY.
IT ALMOST HAS AS MUCH HISTORY AS US.
IS OUR HISTORY GOOD, CAROL?

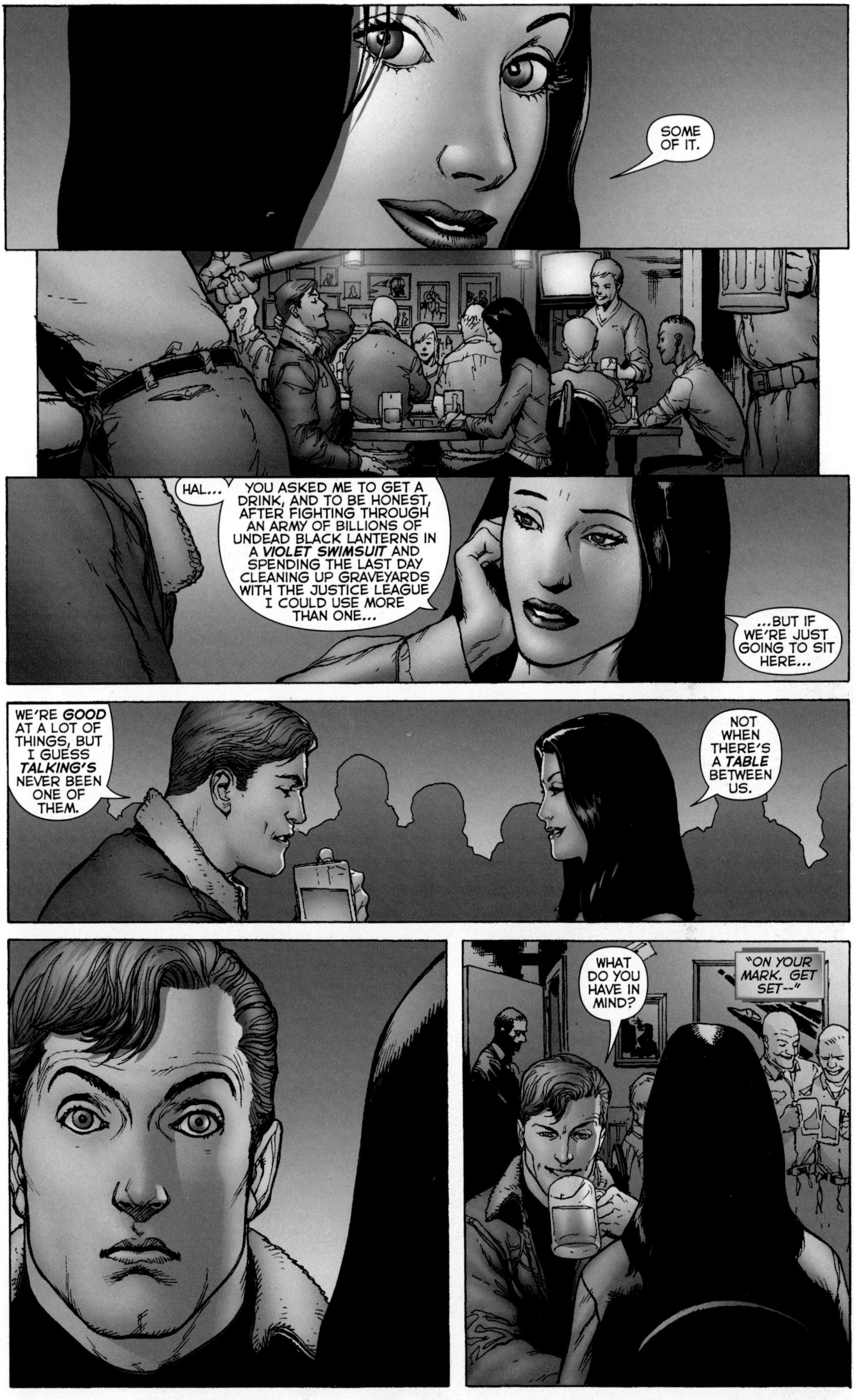
SOME OF IT.
HAL...
YOU ASKED ME TO GET A DRINK, AND TO BE HONEST, AFTER FIGHTING THROUGH AN ARMY OF BILLIONS OF UNDEAD BLACK LANTERNS IN A *VIOLET SWIMSUIT* AND SPENDING THE LAST DAY CLEANING UP GRAVEYARDS WITH THE JUSTICE LEAGUE I COULD USE MORE THAN ONE...
...BUT IF WE'RE JUST GOING TO SIT HERE...
WE'RE *GOOD* AT A LOT OF THINGS, BUT I GUESS *TALKING'S* NEVER BEEN ONE OF THEM.
NOT WHEN THERE'S A *TABLE* BETWEEN US.
WHAT DO YOU HAVE IN MIND?
"ON YOUR MARK. GET SET--"

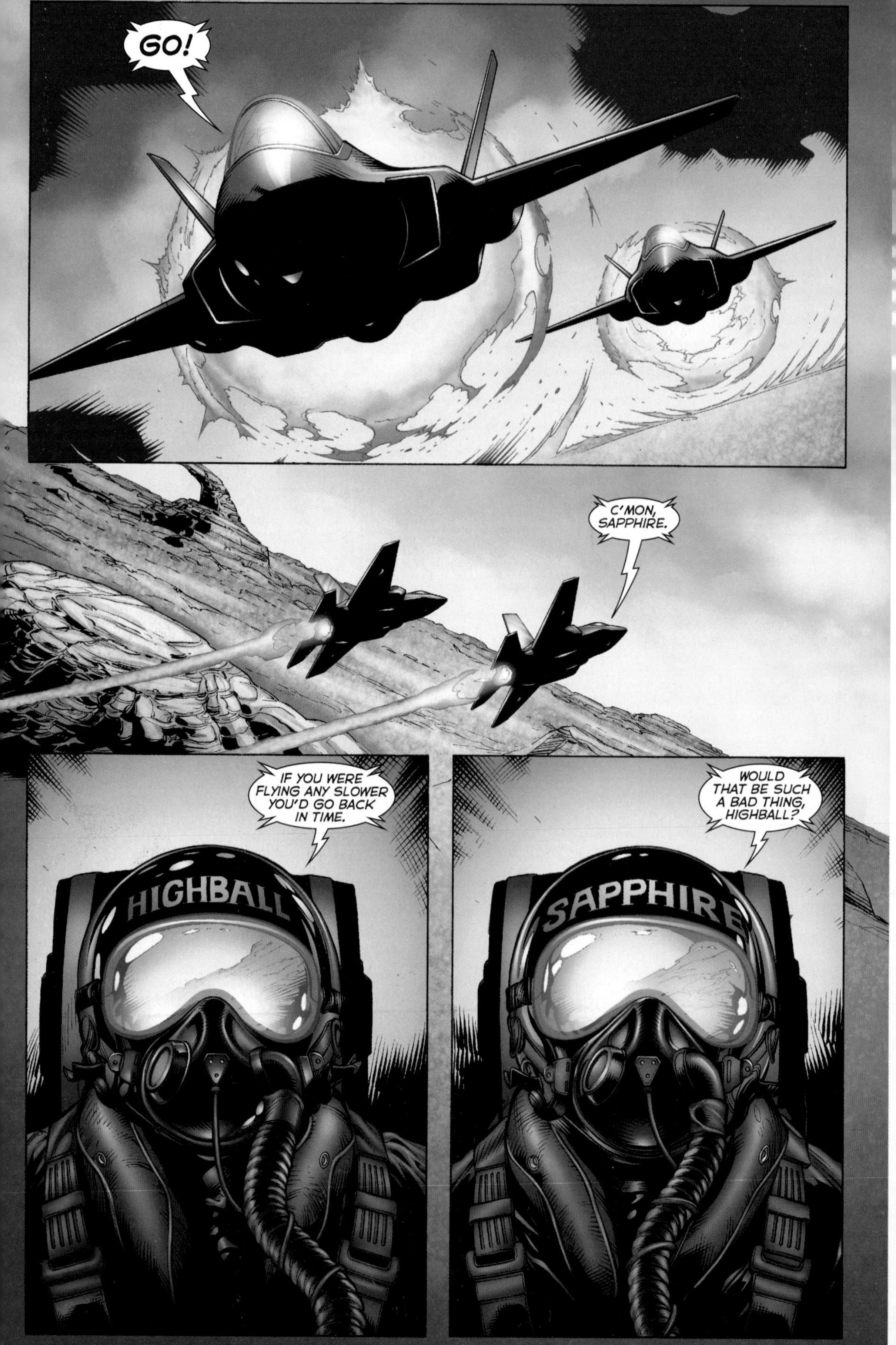
GO!
C'MON, SAPPHIRE.
IF YOU WERE FLYING ANY SLOWER YOU'D GO BACK IN TIME.
HIGHBALL
WOULD THAT BE SUCH A BAD THING, HIGHBALL?
SAPPHIRE

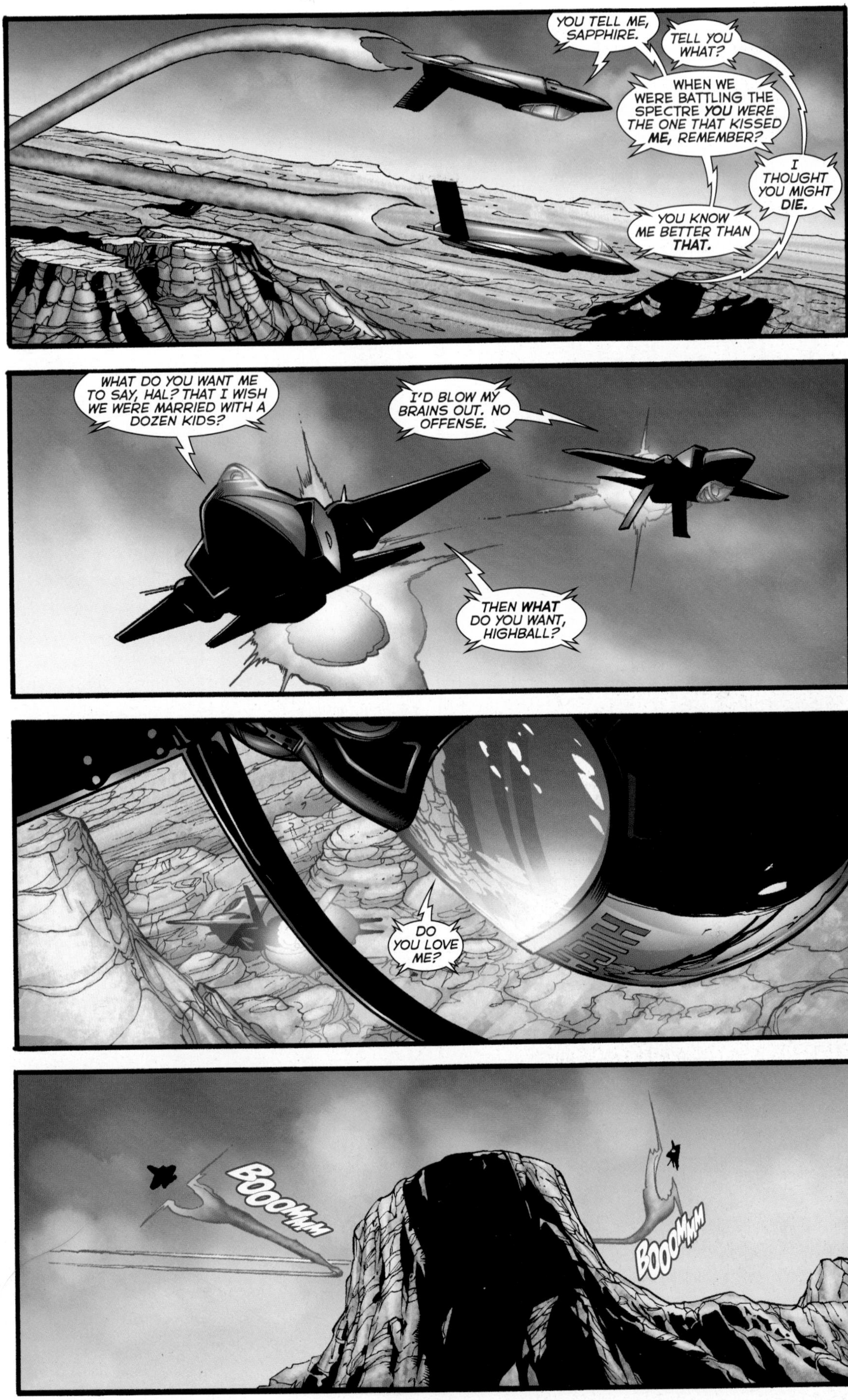
YOU TELL ME, SAPPHIRE.
TELL YOU WHAT?
WHEN WE WERE BATTLING THE SPECTRE YOU WERE THE ONE THAT KISSED ME, REMEMBER?
I THOUGHT YOU MIGHT DIE.
YOU KNOW ME BETTER THAN THAT.
WHAT DO YOU WANT ME TO SAY, HAL? THAT I WISH WE WERE MARRIED WITH A DOZEN KIDS?
I'D BLOW MY BRAINS OUT. NO OFFENSE.
THEN WHAT DO YOU WANT, HIGHBALL?
DO YOU LOVE ME?
BOOOMMMM
BOOOMMMM

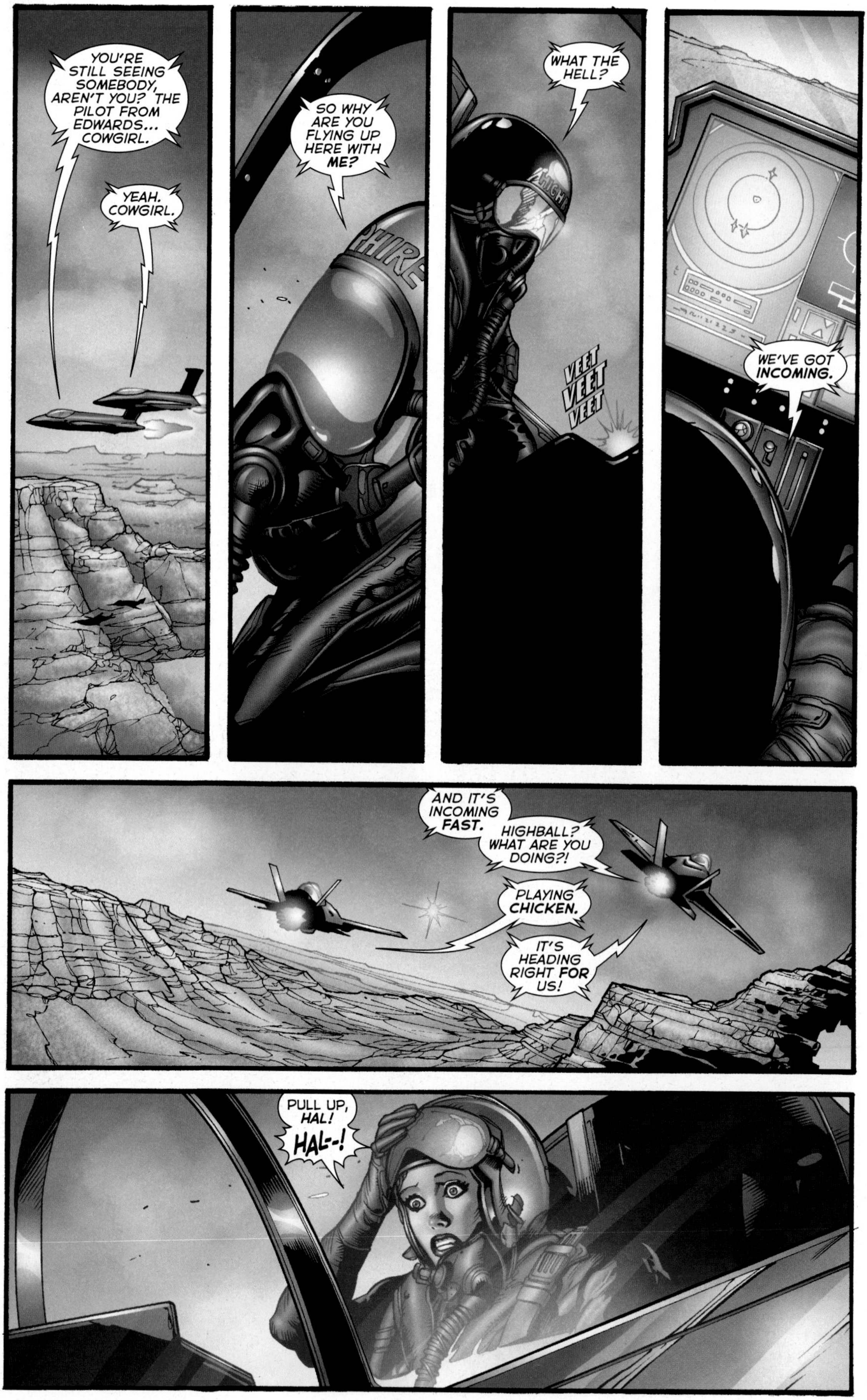
YOU'RE STILL SEEING SOMEBODY, AREN'T YOU? THE PILOT FROM EDWARDS... COWGIRL.
YEAH. COWGIRL.
SO WHY ARE YOU FLYING UP HERE WITH ME?
WHAT THE HELL?
VEET VEET VEET
WE'VE GOT INCOMING.
AND IT'S INCOMING FAST.
HIGHBALL? WHAT ARE YOU DOING?!
PLAYING CHICKEN.
IT'S HEADING RIGHT FOR US!
PULL UP, HAL!
HAL--!

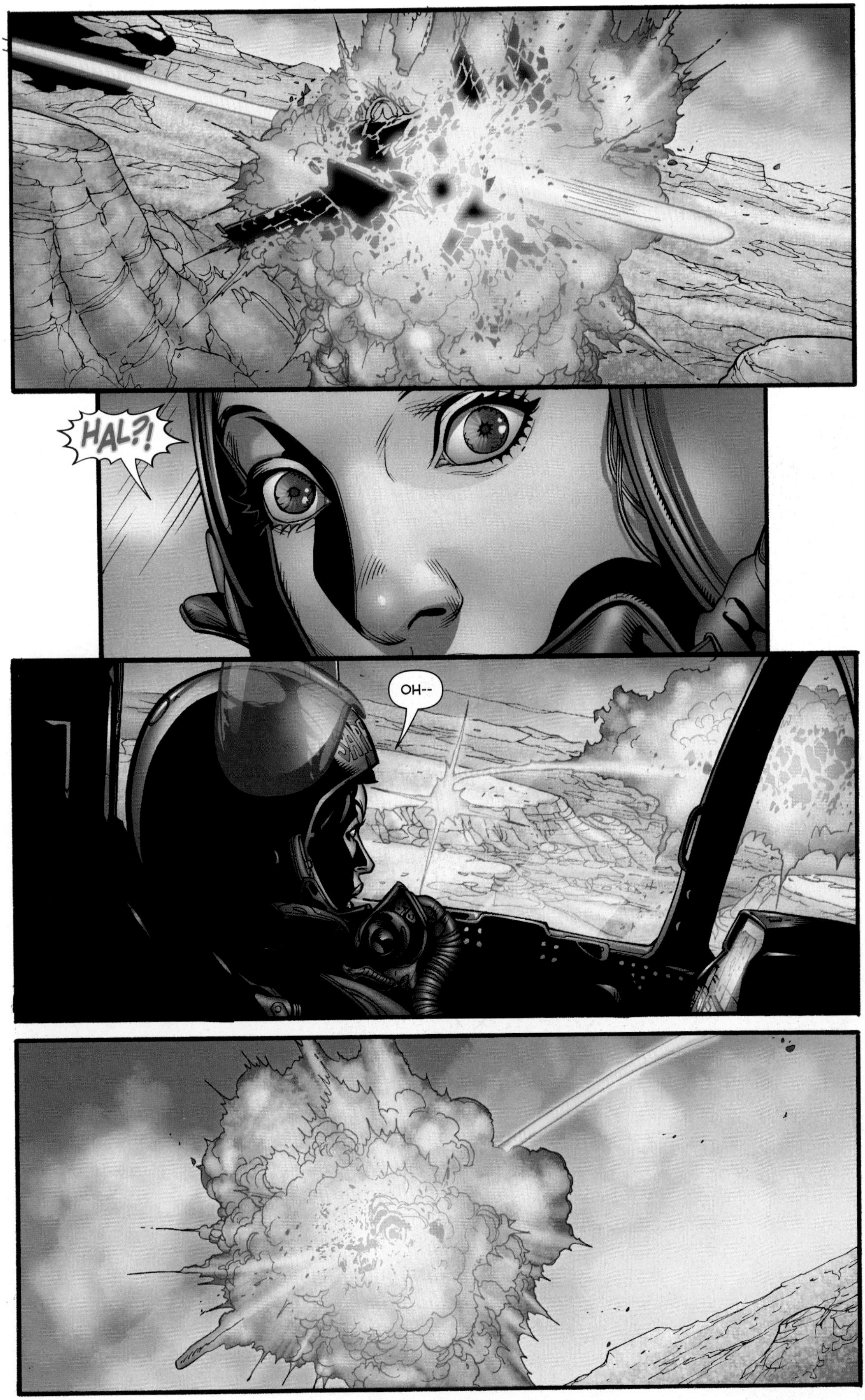
HAL?!
OH--

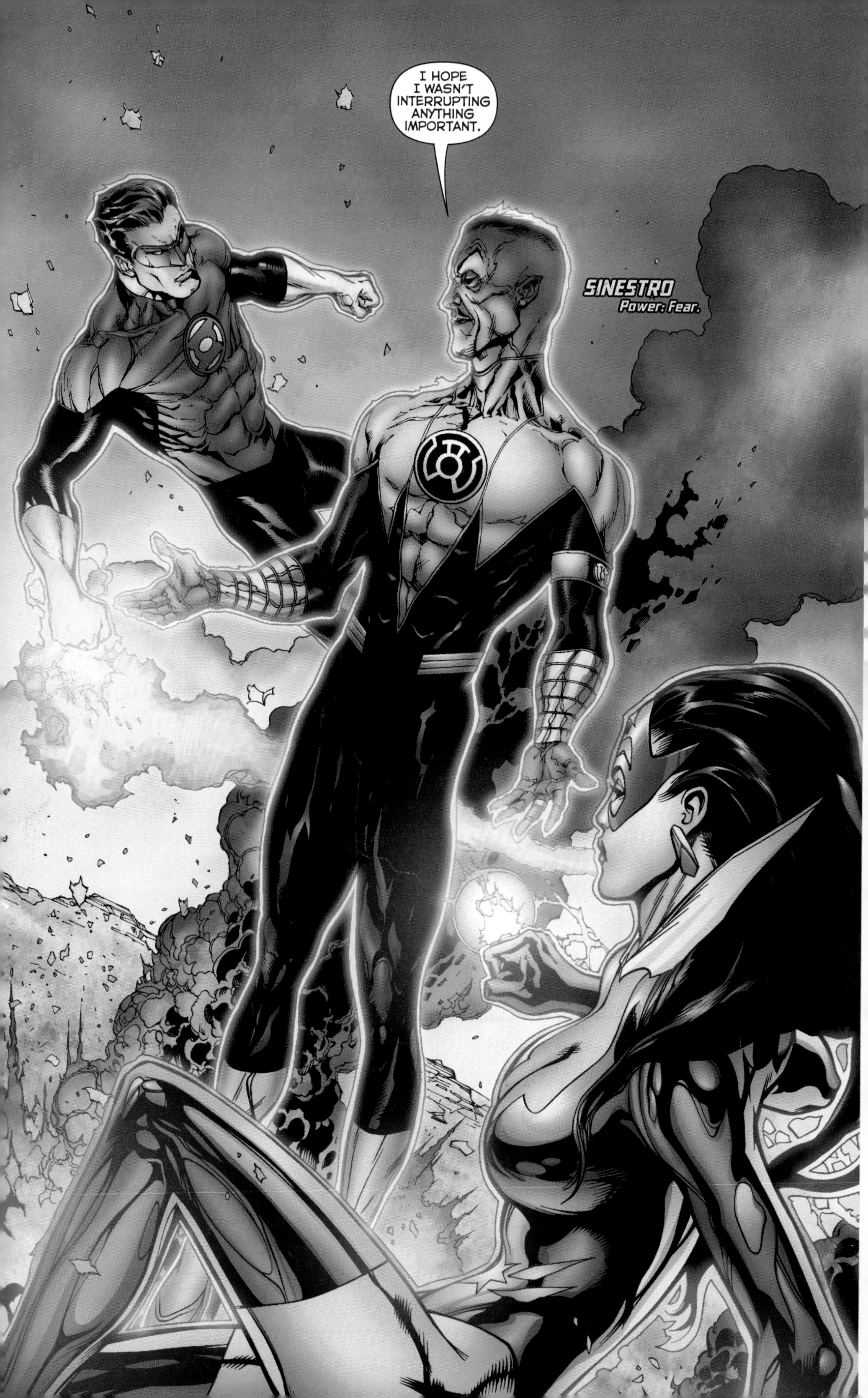
I HOPE I WASN'T INTERRUPTING ANYTHING IMPORTANT.
SINESTRO
Power: Fear.

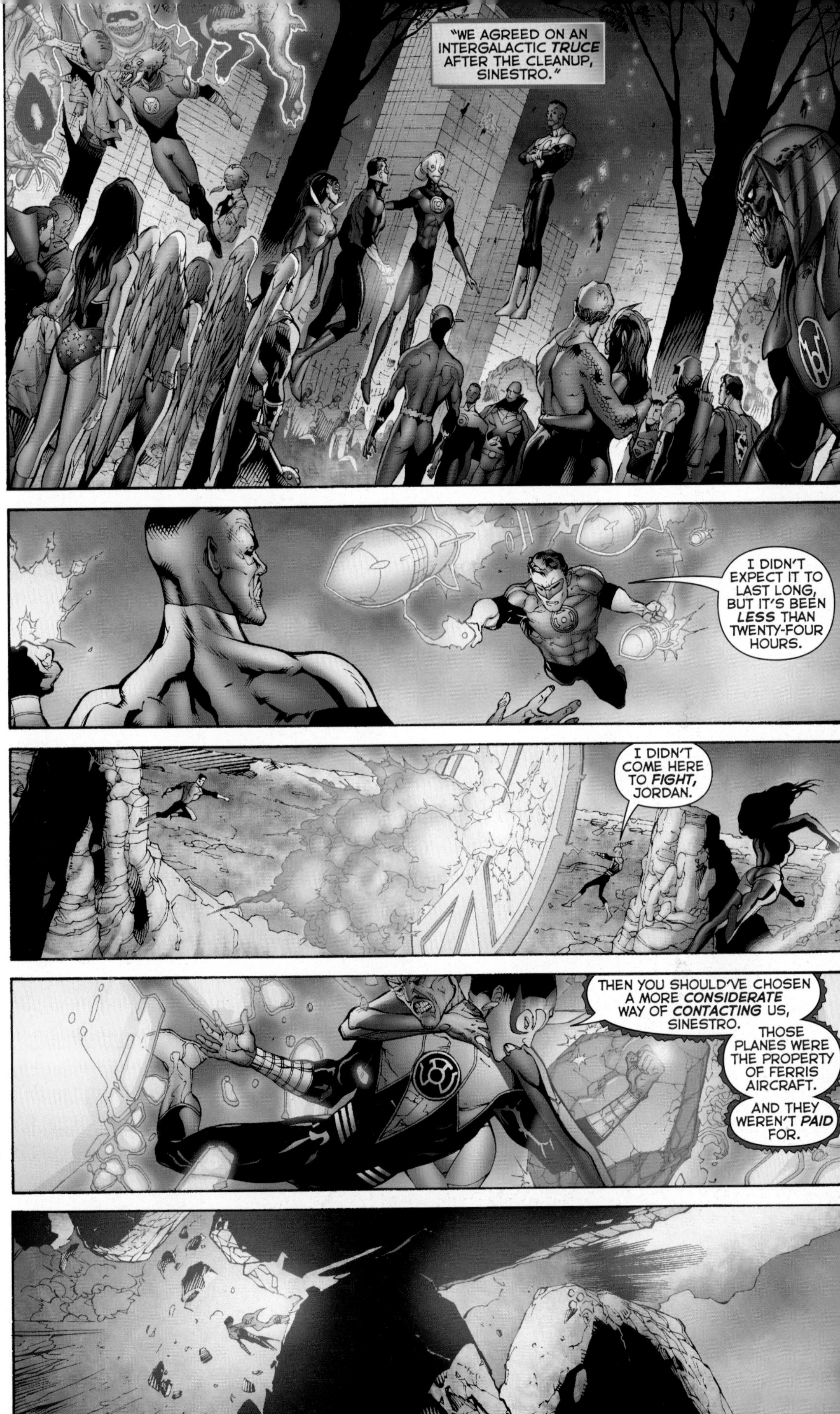
"WE AGREED ON AN INTERGALACTIC TRUCE AFTER THE CLEANUP, SINESTRO."
I DIDN'T EXPECT IT TO LAST LONG, BUT IT'S BEEN LESS THAN TWENTY-FOUR HOURS.
I DIDN'T COME HERE TO FIGHT, JORDAN.
THEN YOU SHOULD'VE CHOSEN A MORE CONSIDERATE WAY OF CONTACTING US, SINESTRO.
THOSE PLANES WERE THE PROPERTY OF FERRIS AIRCRAFT.
AND THEY WEREN'T PAID FOR.

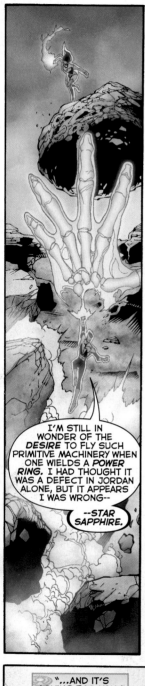

I'M STILL IN WONDER OF THE *DESIRE* TO FLY SUCH *PRIMITIVE* MACHINERY WHEN ONE WIELDS A *POWER RING.* I HAD THOUGHT IT WAS A DEFECT IN JORDAN ALONE, BUT IT APPEARS I WAS WRONG--

--*STAR SAPPHIRE.*

YOU WERE INSISTENT THAT YOUR ALLIANCE WITH THE LOVE-OBSESSED ZAMARONS AND THEIR FEMALE SOLDIERS WAS *TEMPORARY.*

IT IS.

YET YOU STILL WEAR THEIR RING.

AND I'M GOING TO ASSUME YOU *KNEW* CAROL STILL HAD IT WHEN YOU FLEW THROUGH HER PLANE.

ASSUME AWAY IF IT MAKES YOU MORE OPEN TO CONVERSATION.

THE *TRUCE* STILL *STANDS.*

AS MUCH AS I'D RATHER HAVE MY OWN EYEBALLS SUCKED OUT OF THEIR SOCKETS BY THE SPIDER GUILD, I NEED *YOU,* JORDAN.

AFTER SCOURING THIS WORLD, I'VE *LOCATED* THE ENTITY...

"...AND IT'S ASKING FOR *YOU.*"

ALL RIGHT, RUSSELL... LET'S TRY THIS AGAIN.

"...SEVERAL OF THE BLACK LANTERNS, MOST NOTABLY AQUAMAN AND MARTIAN MANHUNTER, WERE FULLY *RESTORED* AND *RESURRECTED* BY THE AS YET UNIDENTIFIED *WHITE LIGHT* THAT TRIGGERED NEKRON'S DESTRUCTION."

HOWEVER, THE MILLIONS, IF NOT BILLIONS, OF *REMAINING* BLACK LANTERNS ACROSS OUR WORLD AND COUNTLESS OTHERS SPONTANEOUSLY COMBUSTED.

ONLY THE REMNANTS OF A FEW *THOUSAND* BLACK LANTERNS WERE LEFT BEHIND.

THESE REMAINS WERE IDENTIFIED BY THE FLASH AND INTERRED BY THE JUSTICE LEAGUE.

ALTHOUGH MANY HAVE ATTEMPTED TO RECOVER A BLACK RING...*NONE* HAVE BEEN FOUND.

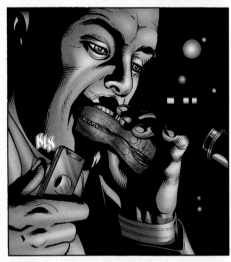

BUT I *WANT* ONE.

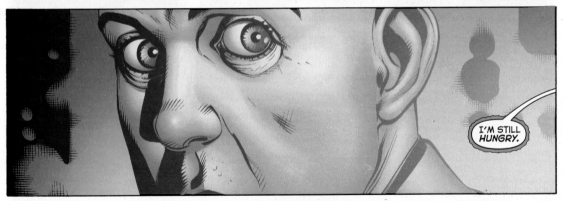

I'M STILL *HUNGRY.*

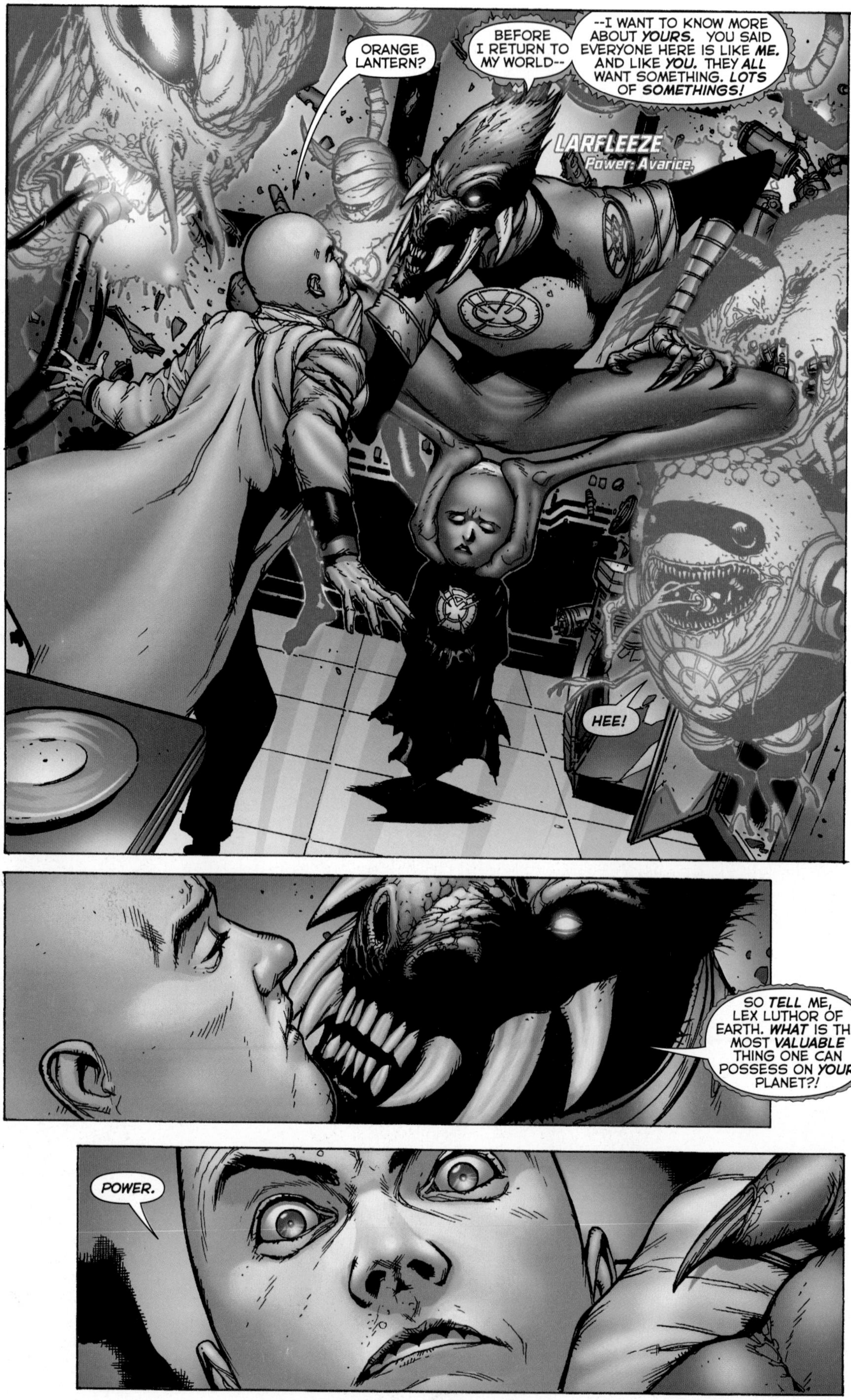
ORANGE LANTERN?
BEFORE I RETURN TO MY WORLD--
--I WANT TO KNOW MORE ABOUT YOURS. YOU SAID EVERYONE HERE IS LIKE ME. AND LIKE YOU. THEY ALL WANT SOMETHING. LOTS OF SOMETHINGS!
LARFLEEZE
Power: Avarice.
HEE!
SO TELL ME, LEX LUTHOR OF EARTH. WHAT IS THE MOST VALUABLE THING ONE CAN POSSESS ON YOUR PLANET?!
POWER.

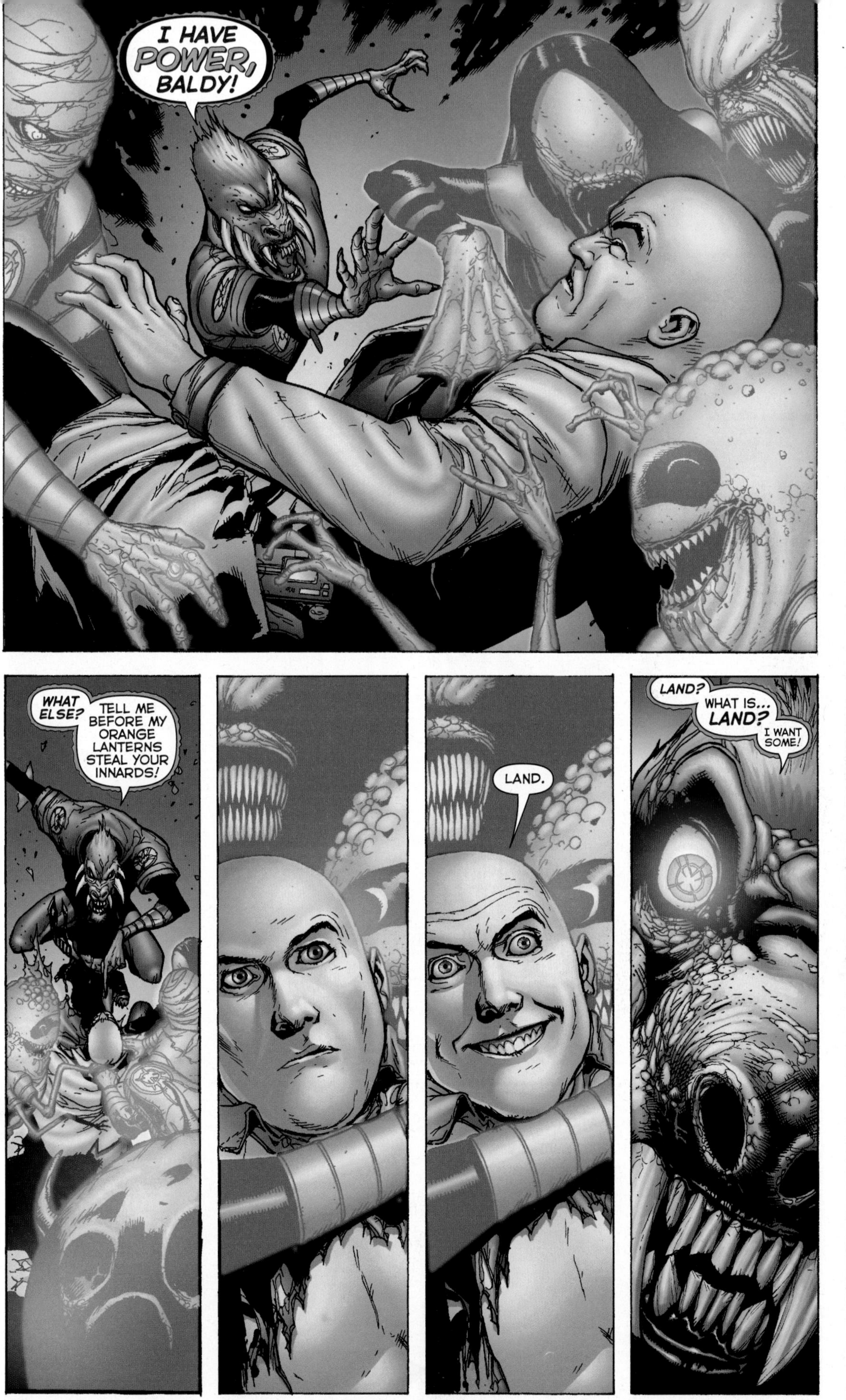
I HAVE POWER, BALDY!
WHAT ELSE?
TELL ME BEFORE MY ORANGE LANTERNS STEAL YOUR INNARDS!
LAND.
LAND? WHAT IS... LAND?
I WANT SOME!

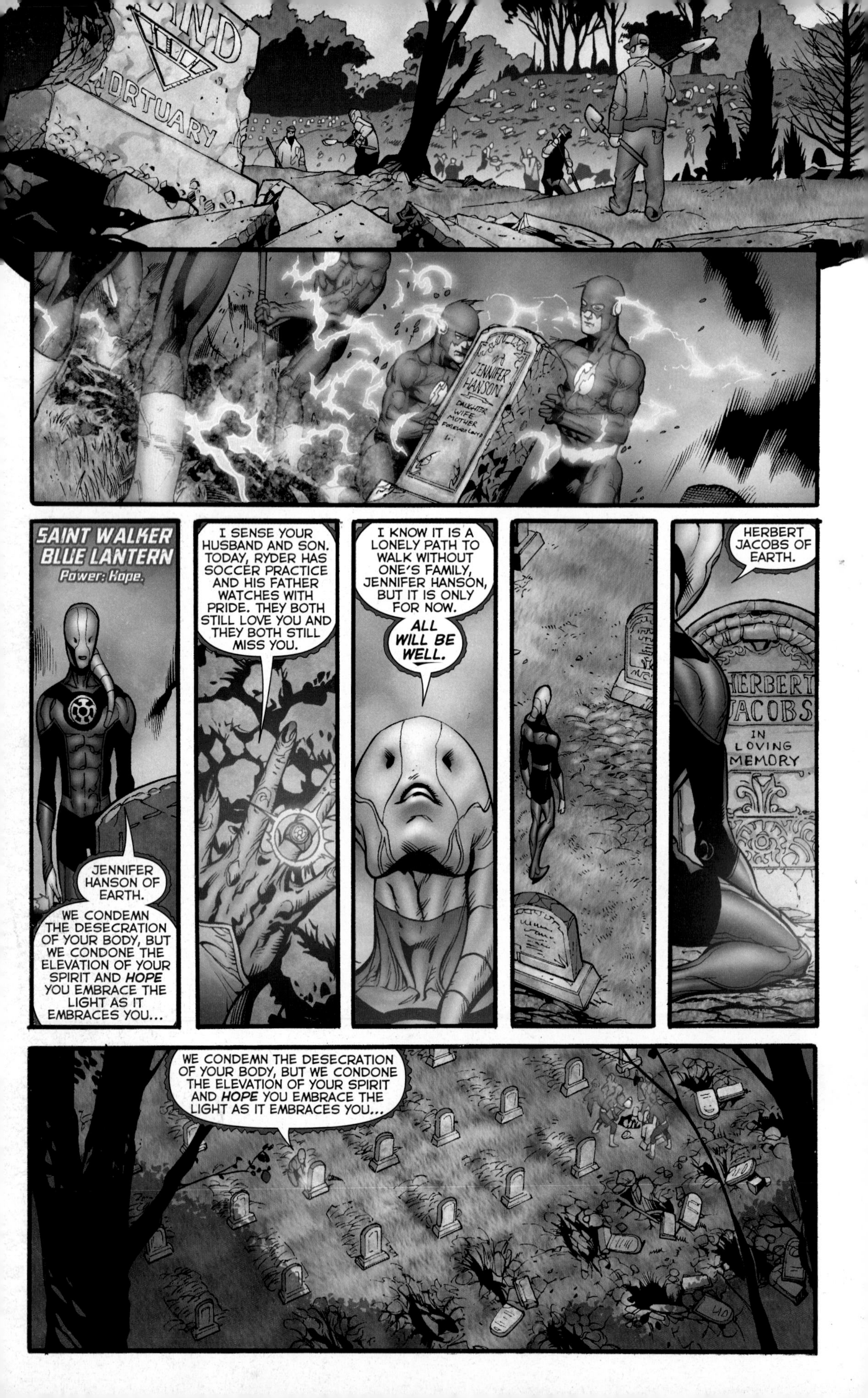
IND
MORTUARY
JENNIFER HANSON
DAUGHTER WIFE MOTHER
SAINT WALKER BLUE LANTERN
Power: Hope.
JENNIFER HANSON OF EARTH.
WE CONDEMN THE DESECRATION OF YOUR BODY, BUT WE CONDONE THE ELEVATION OF YOUR SPIRIT AND HOPE YOU EMBRACE THE LIGHT AS IT EMBRACES YOU...
I SENSE YOUR HUSBAND AND SON. TODAY, RYDER HAS SOCCER PRACTICE AND HIS FATHER WATCHES WITH PRIDE. THEY BOTH STILL LOVE YOU AND THEY BOTH STILL MISS YOU.
I KNOW IT IS A LONELY PATH TO WALK WITHOUT ONE'S FAMILY, JENNIFER HANSON, BUT IT IS ONLY FOR NOW.
ALL WILL BE WELL.
HERBERT JACOBS OF EARTH.
HERBERT JACOBS IN LOVING MEMORY
WE CONDEMN THE DESECRATION OF YOUR BODY, BUT WE CONDONE THE ELEVATION OF YOUR SPIRIT AND HOPE YOU EMBRACE THE LIGHT AS IT EMBRACES YOU...

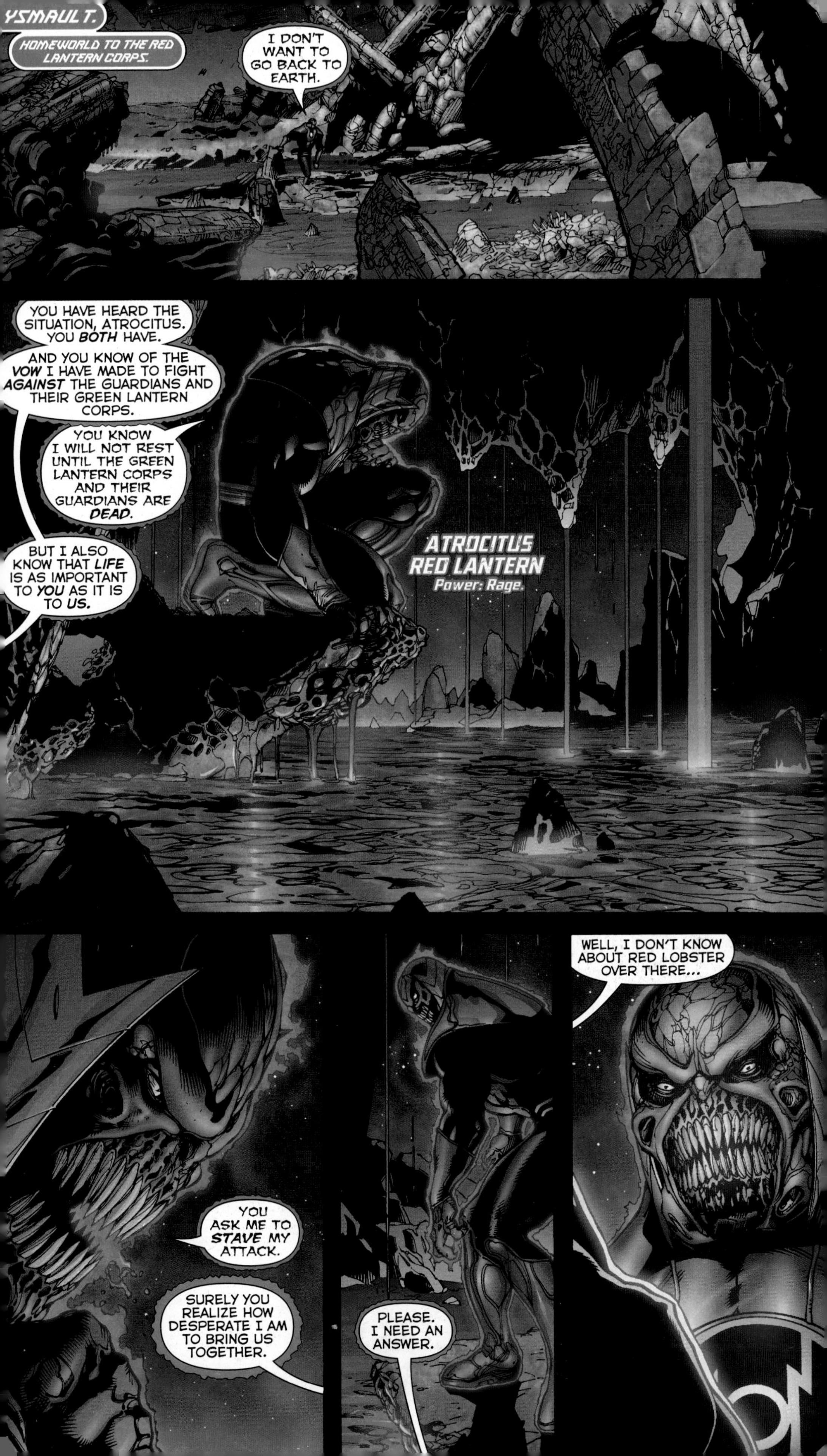
YSMAULT.
HOMEWORLD TO THE RED LANTERN CORPS.
I DON'T WANT TO GO BACK TO EARTH.
YOU HAVE HEARD THE SITUATION, ATROCITUS. YOU BOTH HAVE.
AND YOU KNOW OF THE VOW I HAVE MADE TO FIGHT AGAINST THE GUARDIANS AND THEIR GREEN LANTERN CORPS.
YOU KNOW I WILL NOT REST UNTIL THE GREEN LANTERN CORPS AND THEIR GUARDIANS ARE DEAD.
BUT I ALSO KNOW THAT LIFE IS AS IMPORTANT TO YOU AS IT IS TO US.
ATROCITUS RED LANTERN
Power: Rage.
YOU ASK ME TO STAVE MY ATTACK.
SURELY YOU REALIZE HOW DESPERATE I AM TO BRING US TOGETHER.
PLEASE. I NEED AN ANSWER.
WELL, I DON'T KNOW ABOUT RED LOBSTER OVER THERE...

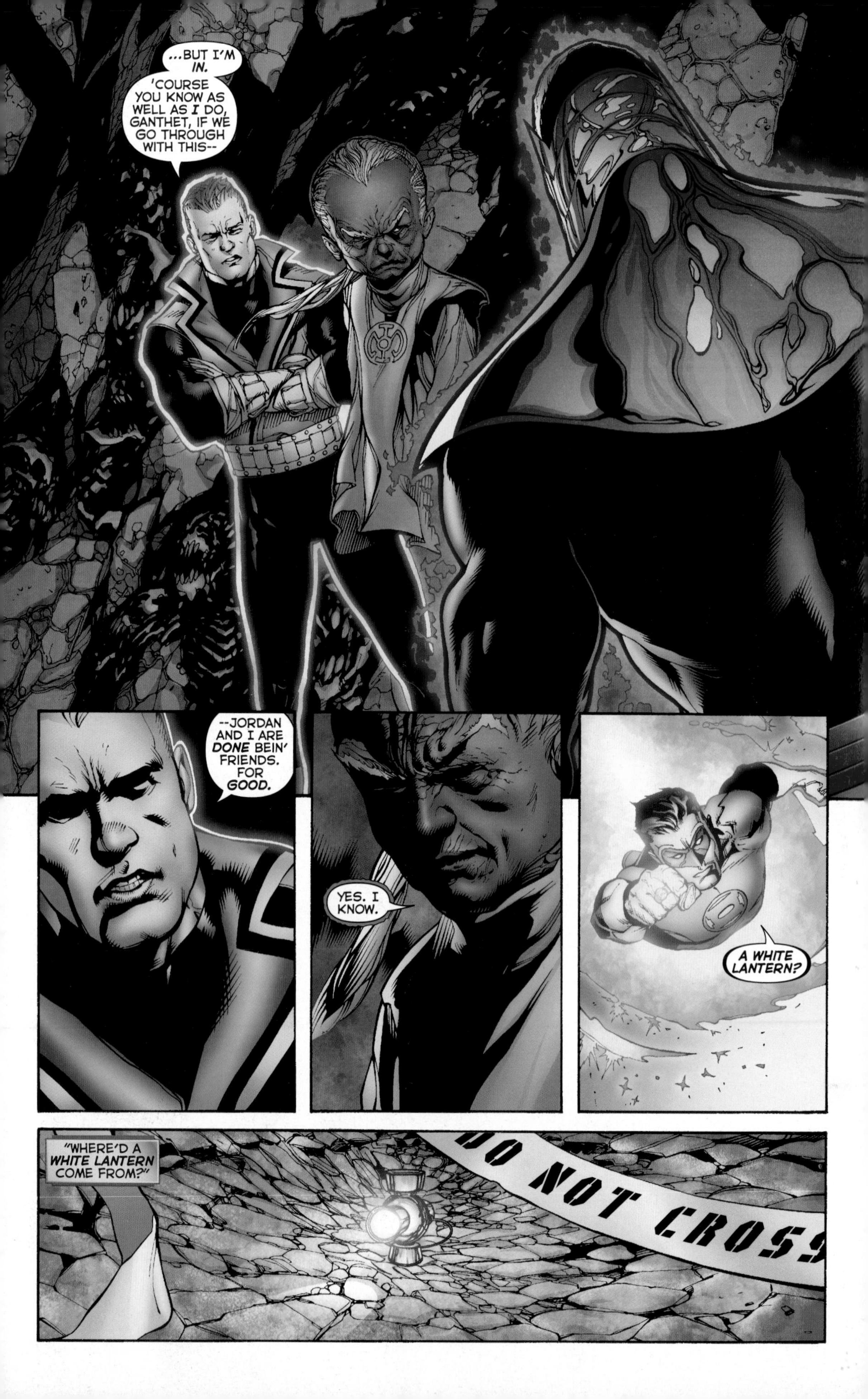
...BUT I'M IN. 'COURSE YOU KNOW AS WELL AS I DO, GANTHET, IF WE GO THROUGH WITH THIS--
--JORDAN AND I ARE DONE BEIN' FRIENDS. FOR GOOD.
YES. I KNOW.
A WHITE LANTERN?
"WHERE'D A WHITE LANTERN COME FROM?"
DO NOT CROSS

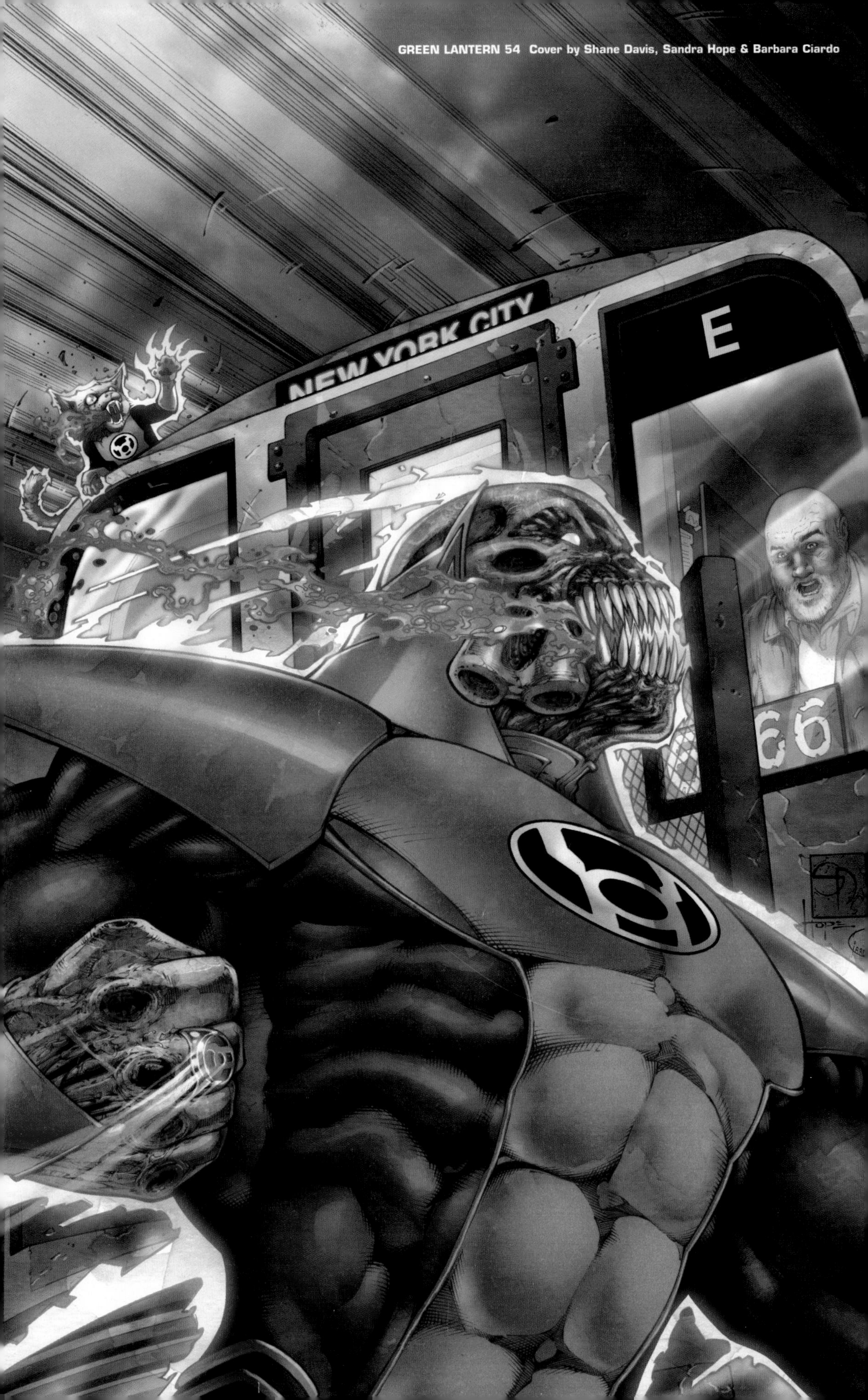
NEW YORK CITY
E
66
GREEN LANTERN 54 Cover by Shane Davis, Sandra Hope & Barbara Ciardo

THE NEW GUARDIANS
CHAPTER TWO

Doug Mahnke Pencils
Christian Alamy, Tom Nguyen, Keith Champagne & Doug Mahnke Inks

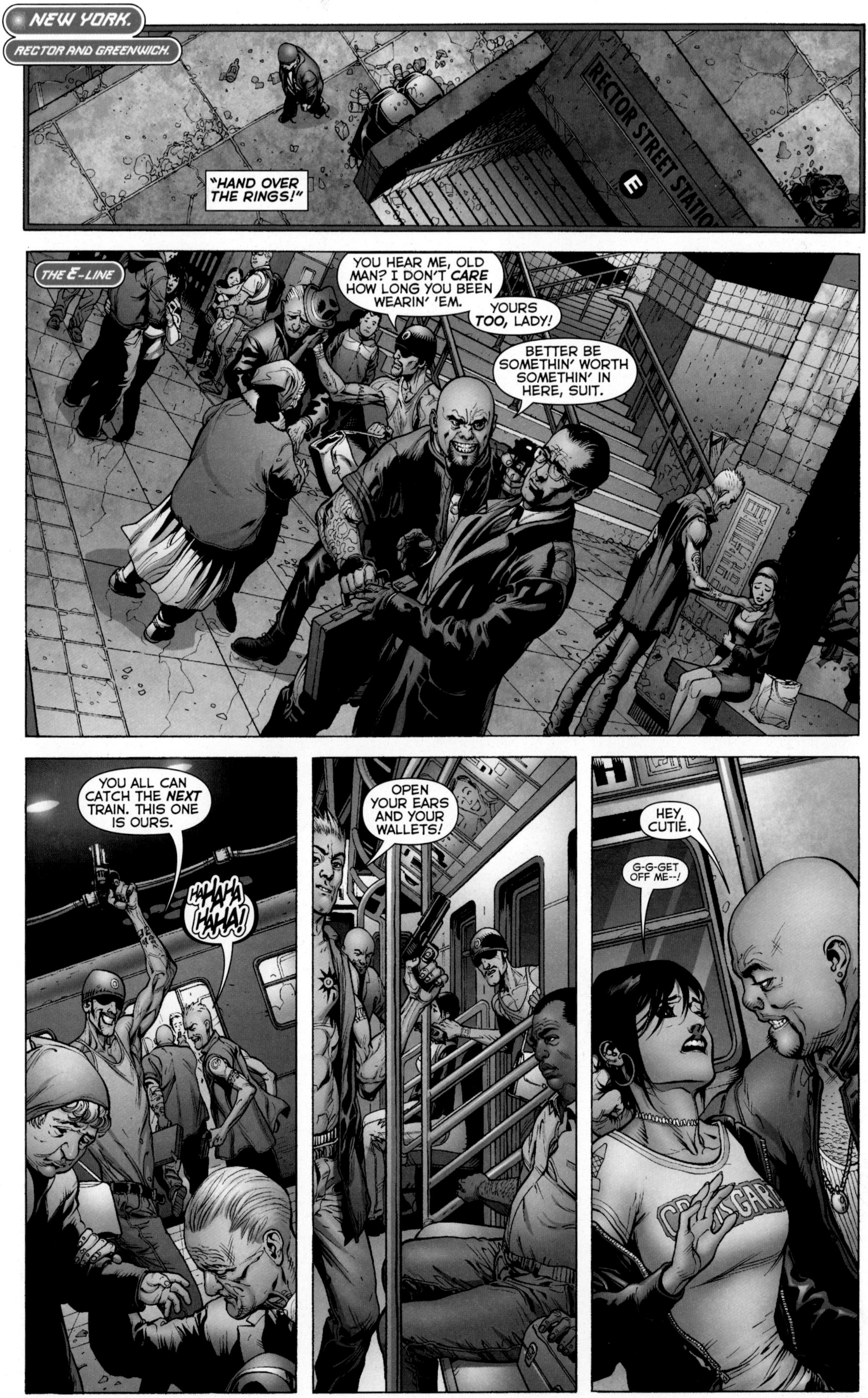
NEW YORK.
RECTOR AND GREENWICH.
"HAND OVER THE RINGS!"
RECTOR STREET STATION
E
THE E-LINE
YOU HEAR ME, OLD MAN? I DON'T CARE HOW LONG YOU BEEN WEARIN' 'EM.
YOURS TOO, LADY!
BETTER BE SOMETHIN' WORTH SOMETHIN' IN HERE, SUIT.
YOU ALL CAN CATCH THE NEXT TRAIN. THIS ONE IS OURS.
HAHAHA HAHA!
OPEN YOUR EARS AND YOUR WALLETS!
HEY, CUTIE.
G-G-GET OFF ME--!

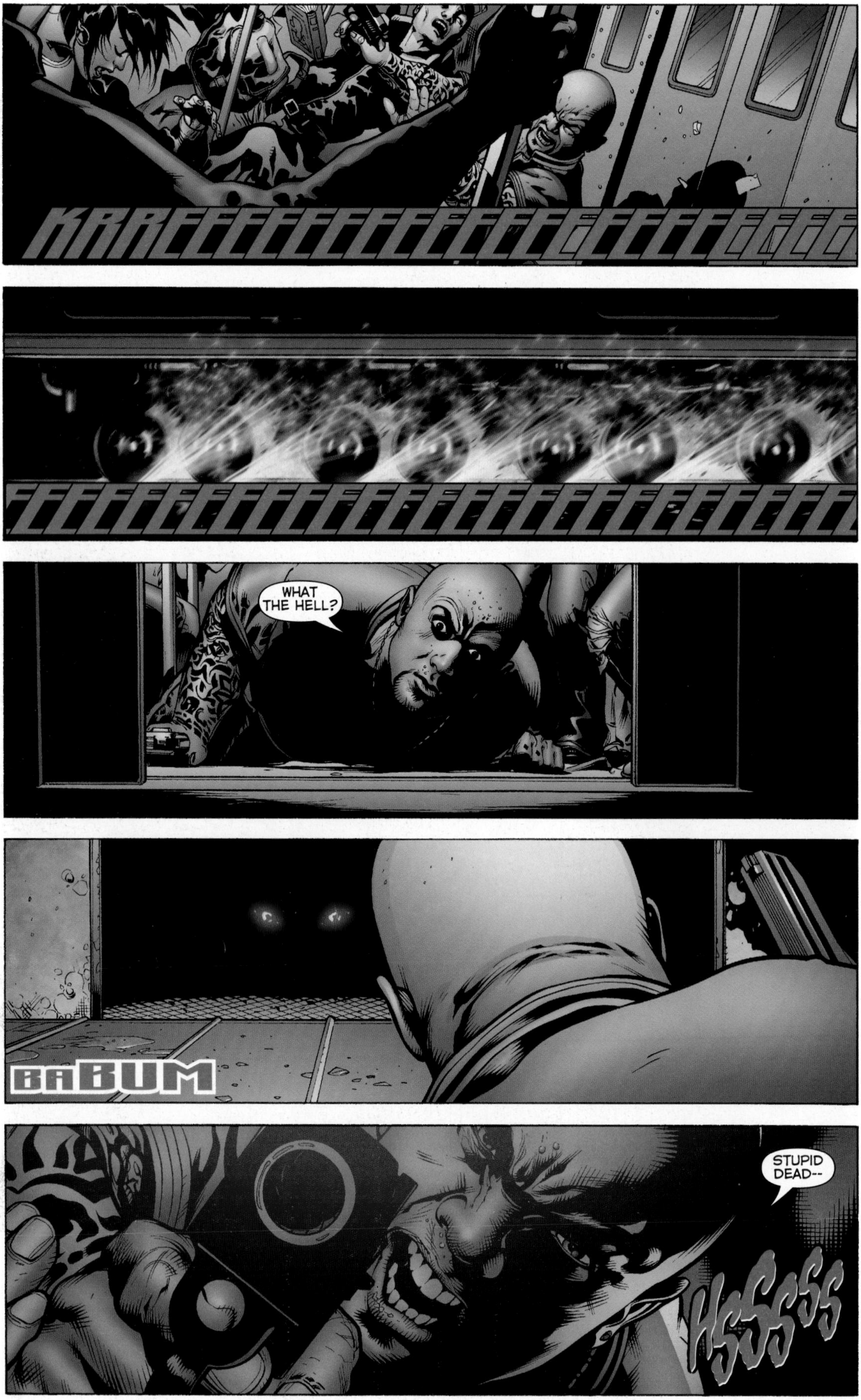
KRREEEEEEEEEEEEEEEEEEEEEEEE
WHAT THE HELL?
BABUM
STUPID DEAD--
HSSSSS

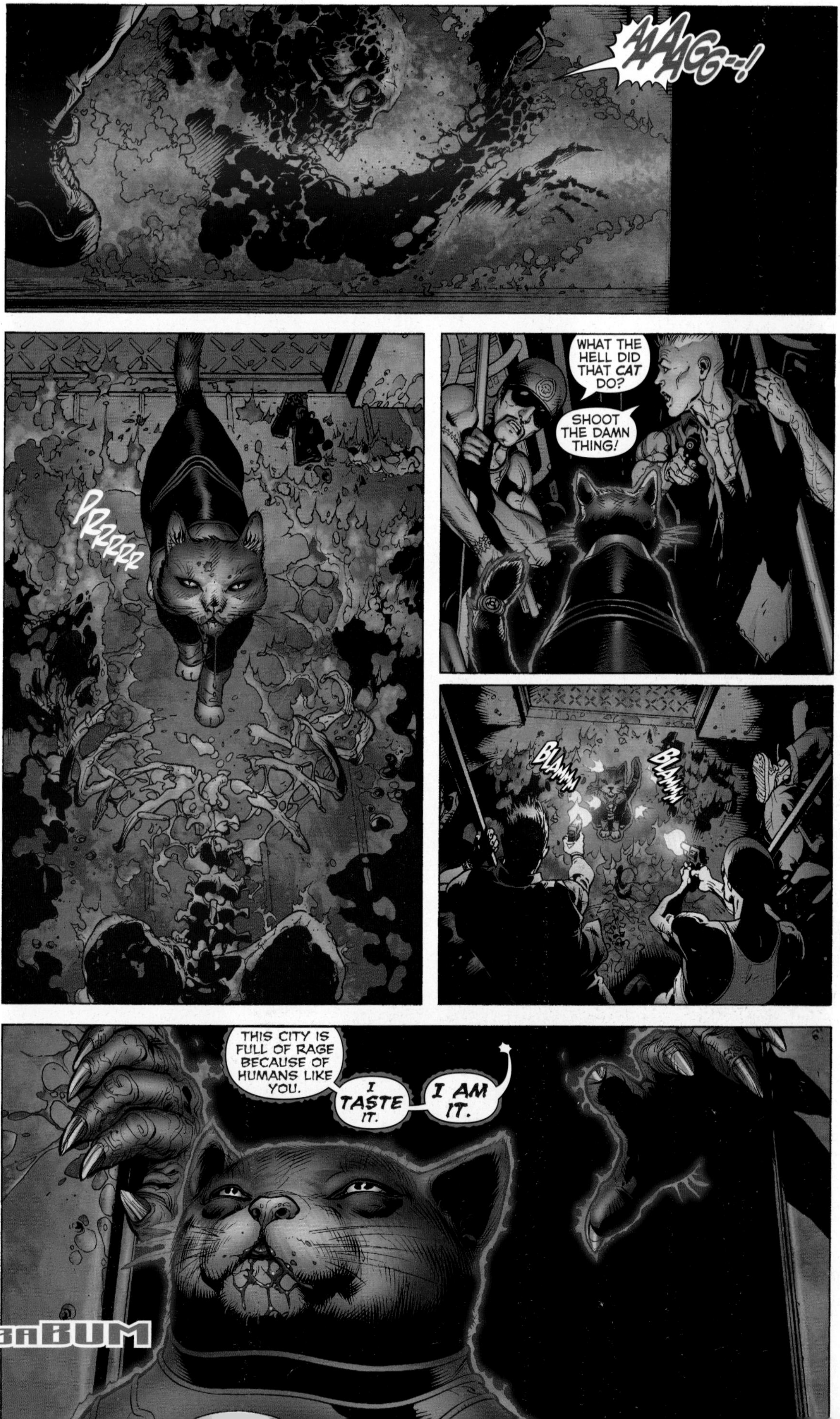
AAAAGG--!
PRRRRR
WHAT THE HELL DID THAT CAT DO?
SHOOT THE DAMN THING!
BLAMM
BLAMM
THIS CITY IS FULL OF RAGE BECAUSE OF HUMANS LIKE YOU.
I TASTE IT.
I AM IT.
BABUM

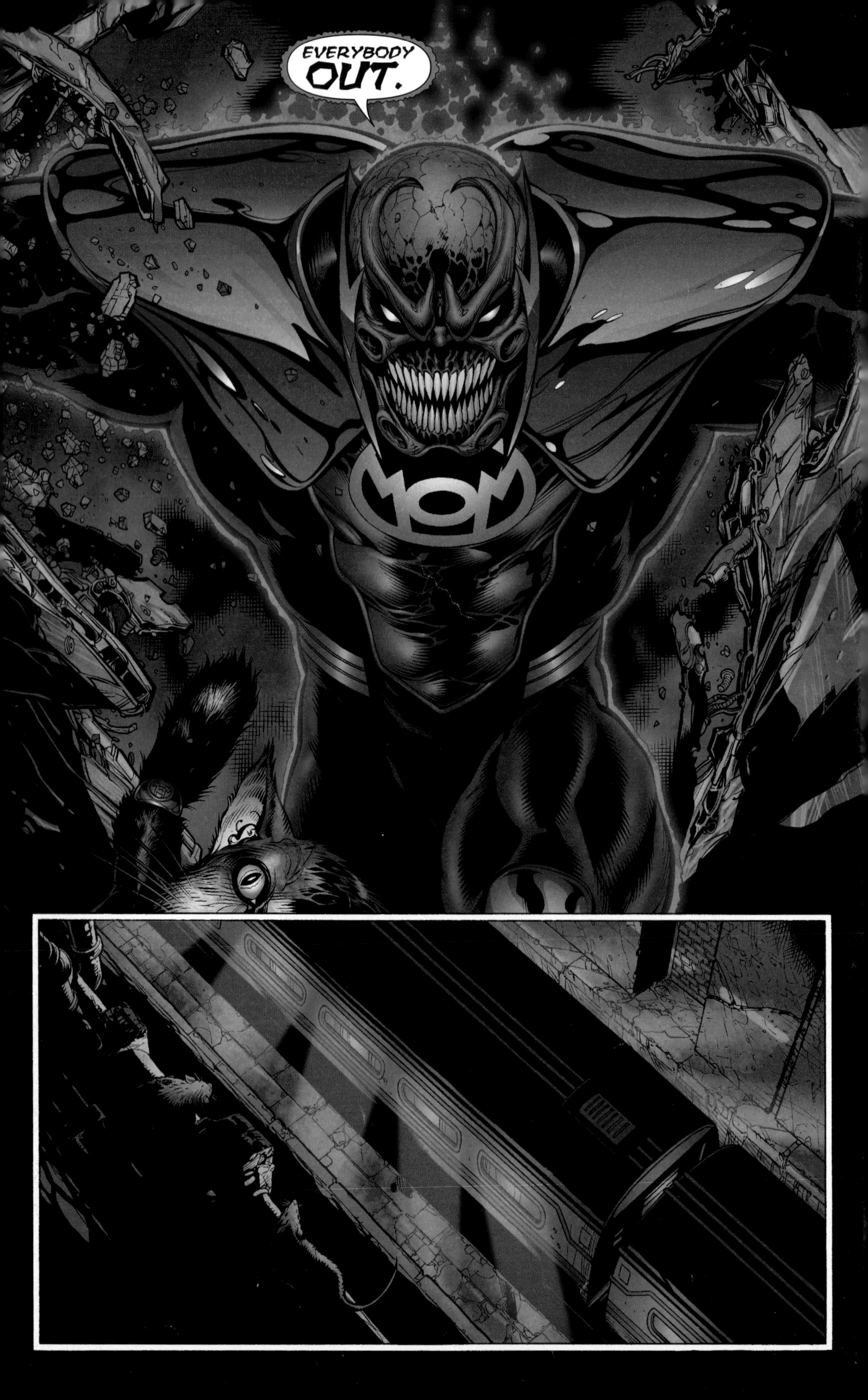
EVERYBODY OUT.

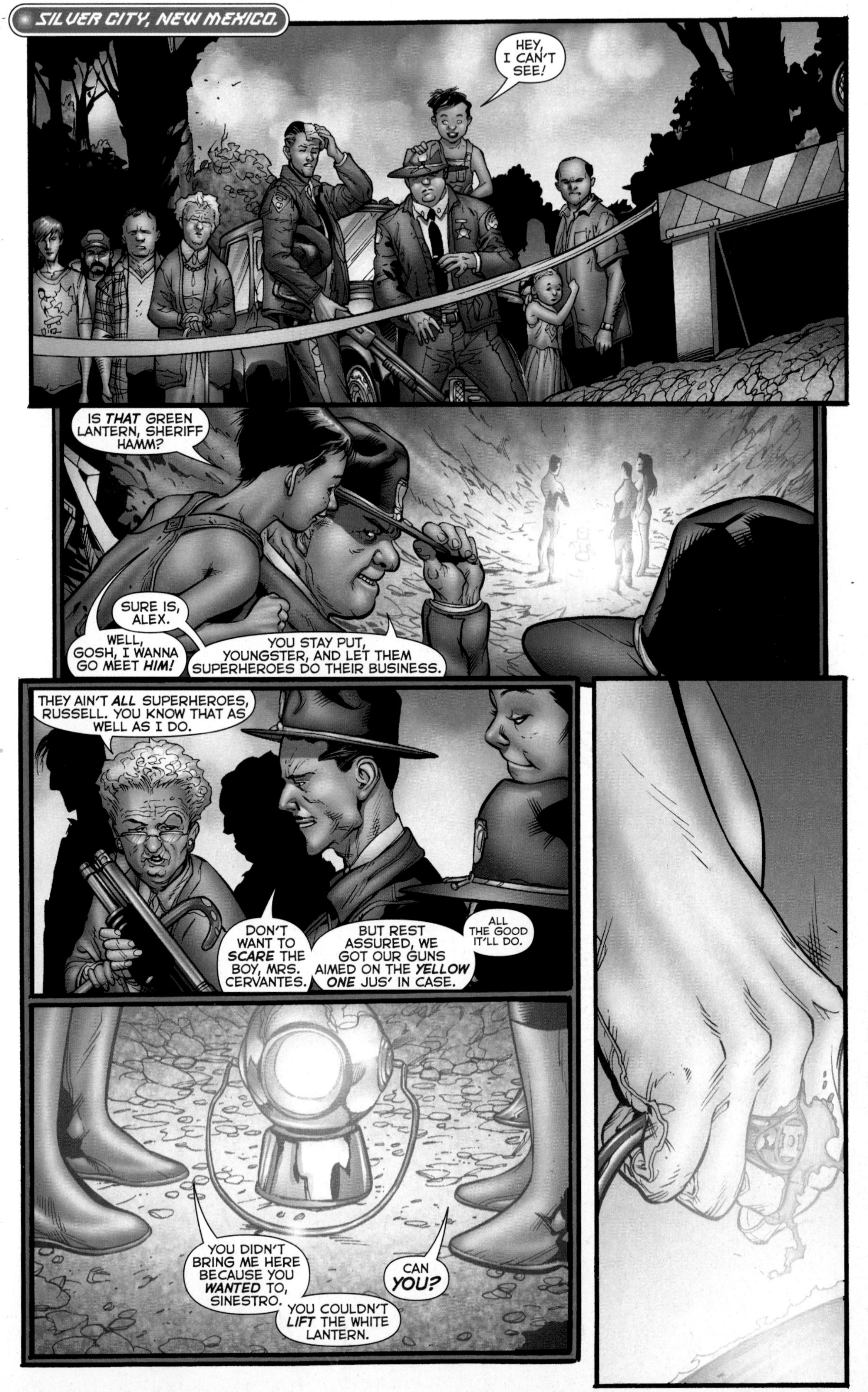
SILVER CITY, NEW MEXICO.
HEY, I CAN'T SEE!
IS *THAT* GREEN LANTERN, SHERIFF HAMM?
SURE IS, ALEX.
WELL, GOSH, I WANNA GO MEET *HIM!*
YOU STAY PUT, YOUNGSTER, AND LET THEM SUPERHEROES DO THEIR BUSINESS.
THEY AIN'T *ALL* SUPERHEROES, RUSSELL. YOU KNOW THAT AS WELL AS I DO.
DON'T WANT TO *SCARE* THE BOY, MRS. CERVANTES.
BUT REST ASSURED, WE GOT OUR GUNS AIMED ON THE *YELLOW ONE* JUS' IN CASE.
ALL THE GOOD IT'LL DO.
YOU DIDN'T BRING ME HERE BECAUSE YOU *WANTED* TO, SINESTRO.
YOU COULDN'T *LIFT* THE WHITE LANTERN.
CAN *YOU?*

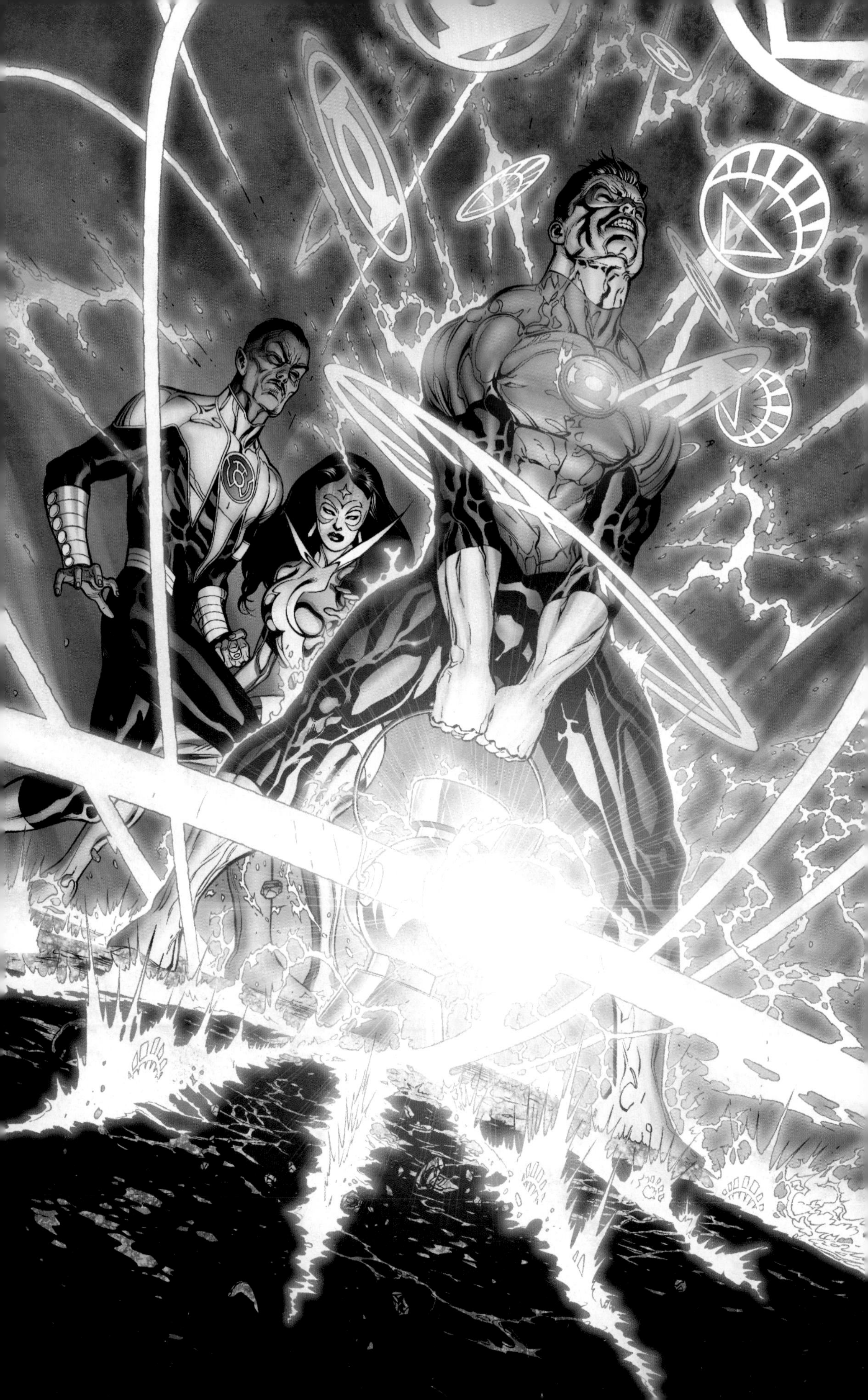

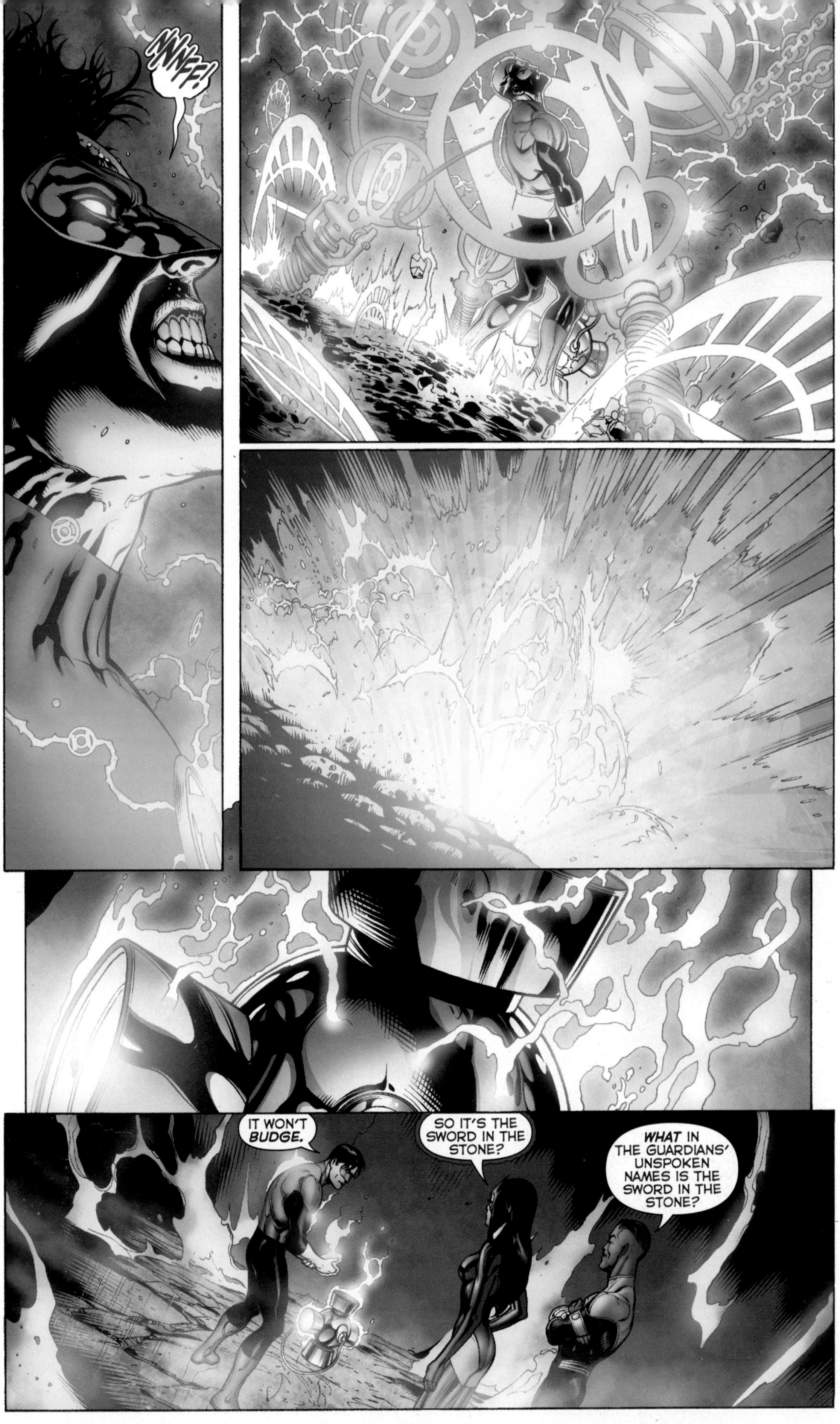
NNNFF!
IT WON'T *BUDGE.*
SO IT'S THE SWORD IN THE STONE?
WHAT IN THE GUARDIANS' UNSPOKEN NAMES IS THE SWORD IN THE STONE?

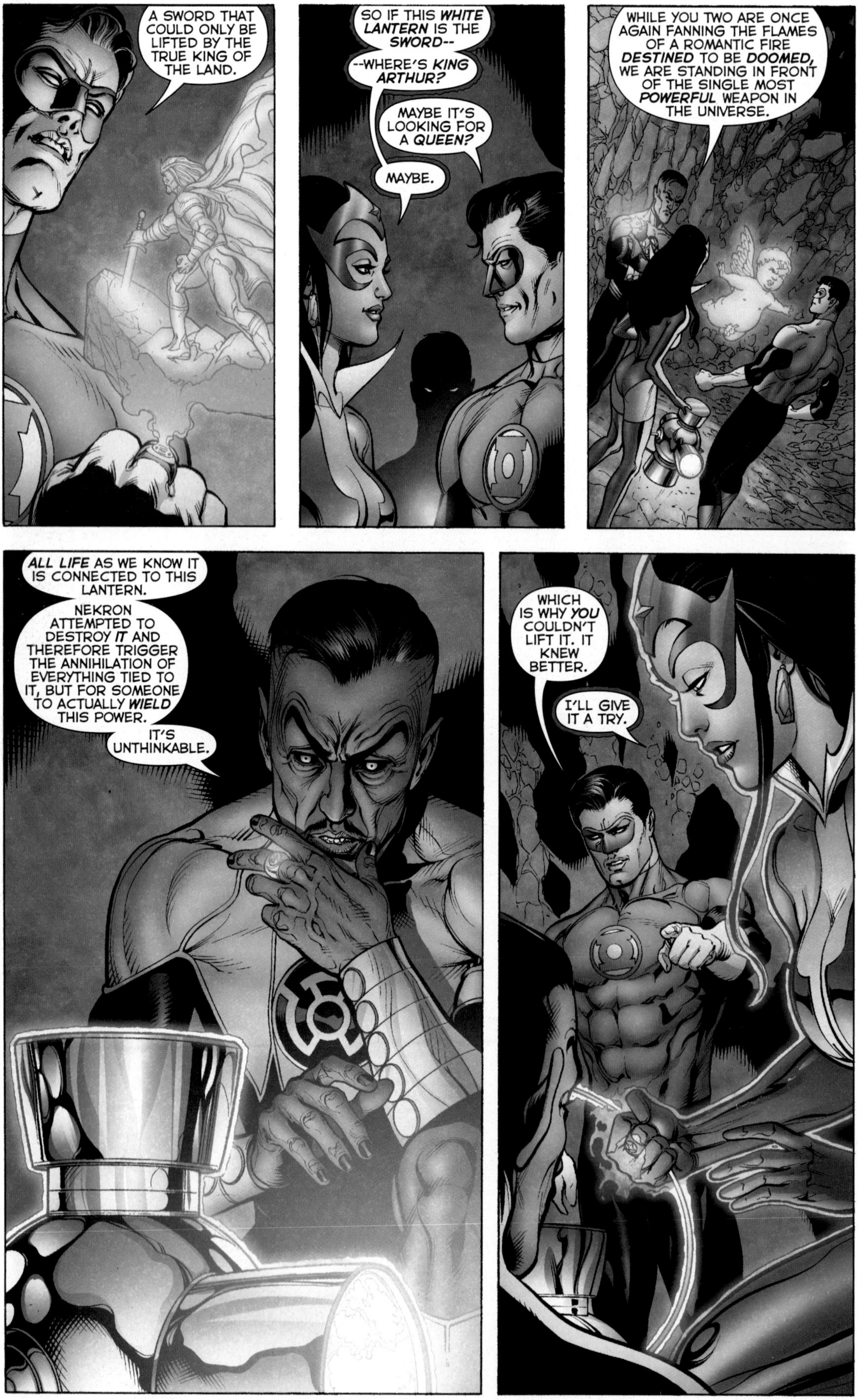

A SWORD THAT COULD ONLY BE LIFTED BY THE TRUE KING OF THE LAND.
SO IF THIS WHITE LANTERN IS THE SWORD--
--WHERE'S KING ARTHUR?
MAYBE IT'S LOOKING FOR A QUEEN?
MAYBE.
WHILE YOU TWO ARE ONCE AGAIN FANNING THE FLAMES OF A ROMANTIC FIRE DESTINED TO BE DOOMED, WE ARE STANDING IN FRONT OF THE SINGLE MOST POWERFUL WEAPON IN THE UNIVERSE.
ALL LIFE AS WE KNOW IT IS CONNECTED TO THIS LANTERN.
NEKRON ATTEMPTED TO DESTROY IT AND THEREFORE TRIGGER THE ANNIHILATION OF EVERYTHING TIED TO IT, BUT FOR SOMEONE TO ACTUALLY WIELD THIS POWER.
IT'S UNTHINKABLE.
WHICH IS WHY YOU COULDN'T LIFT IT. IT KNEW BETTER.
I'LL GIVE IT A TRY.

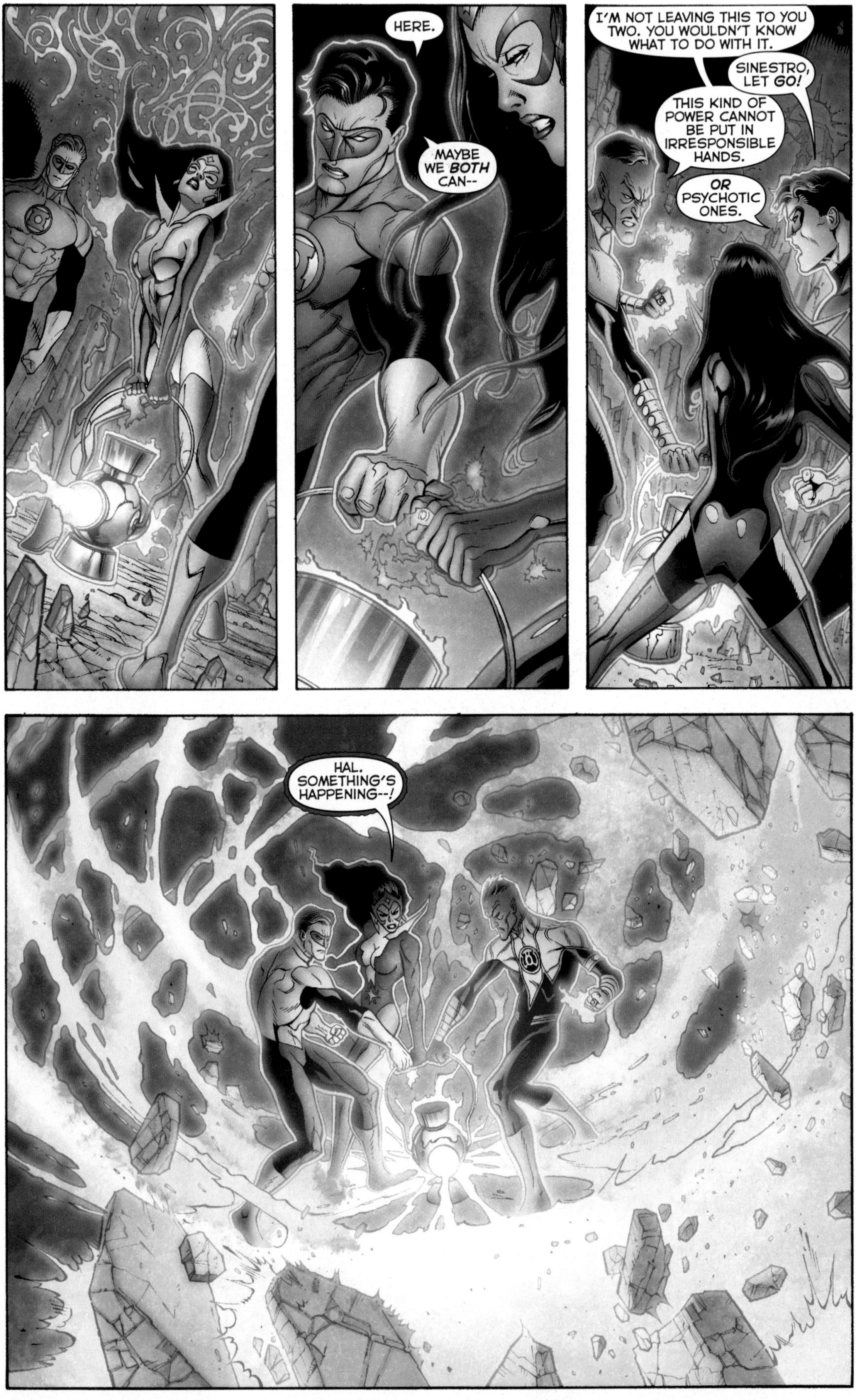
HERE.
MAYBE WE BOTH CAN--
I'M NOT LEAVING THIS TO YOU TWO. YOU WOULDN'T KNOW WHAT TO DO WITH IT.
SINESTRO, LET GO!
THIS KIND OF POWER CANNOT BE PUT IN IRRESPONSIBLE HANDS.
OR PSYCHOTIC ONES.
HAL. SOMETHING'S HAPPENING--!

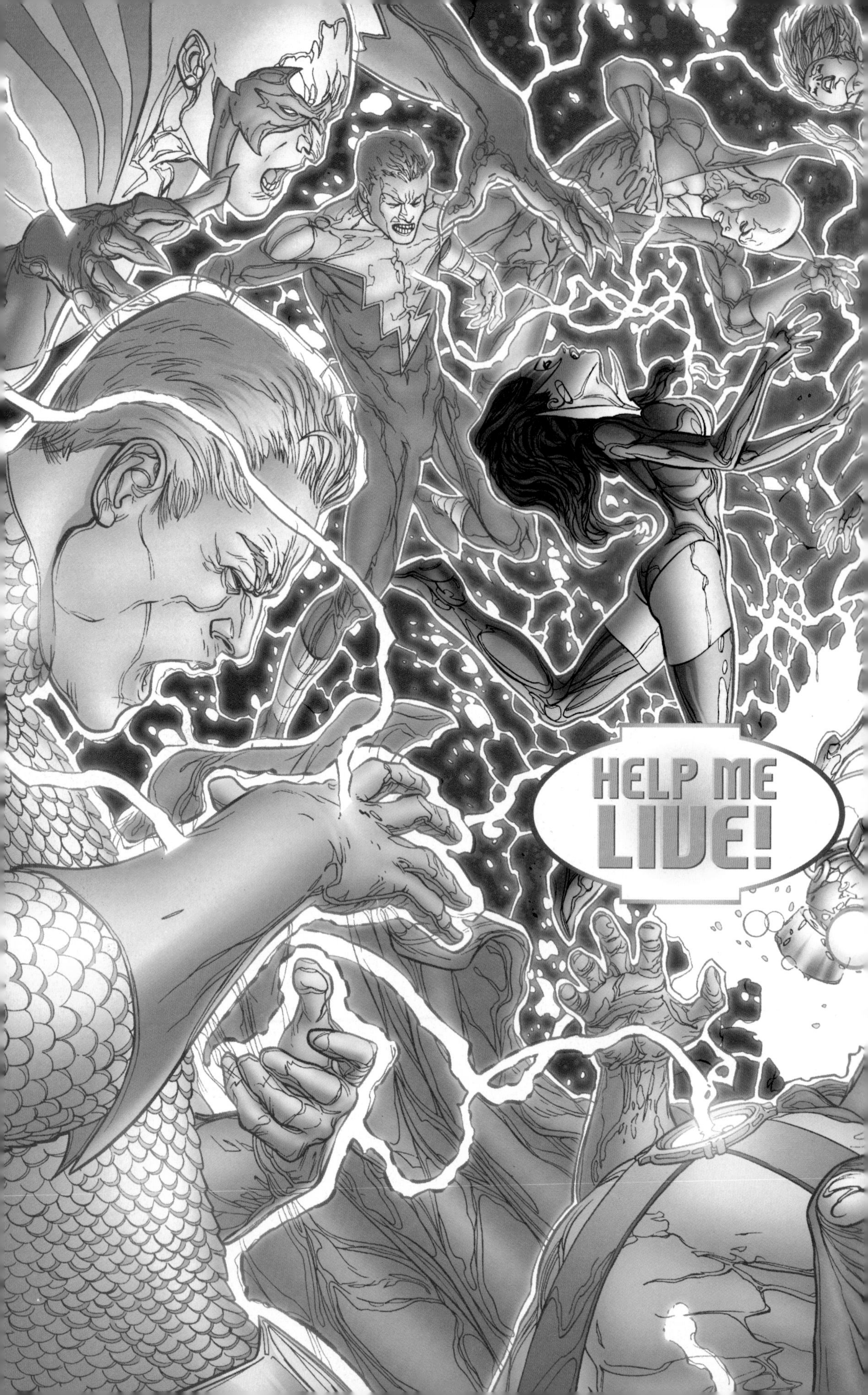
HELP ME
LIVE!

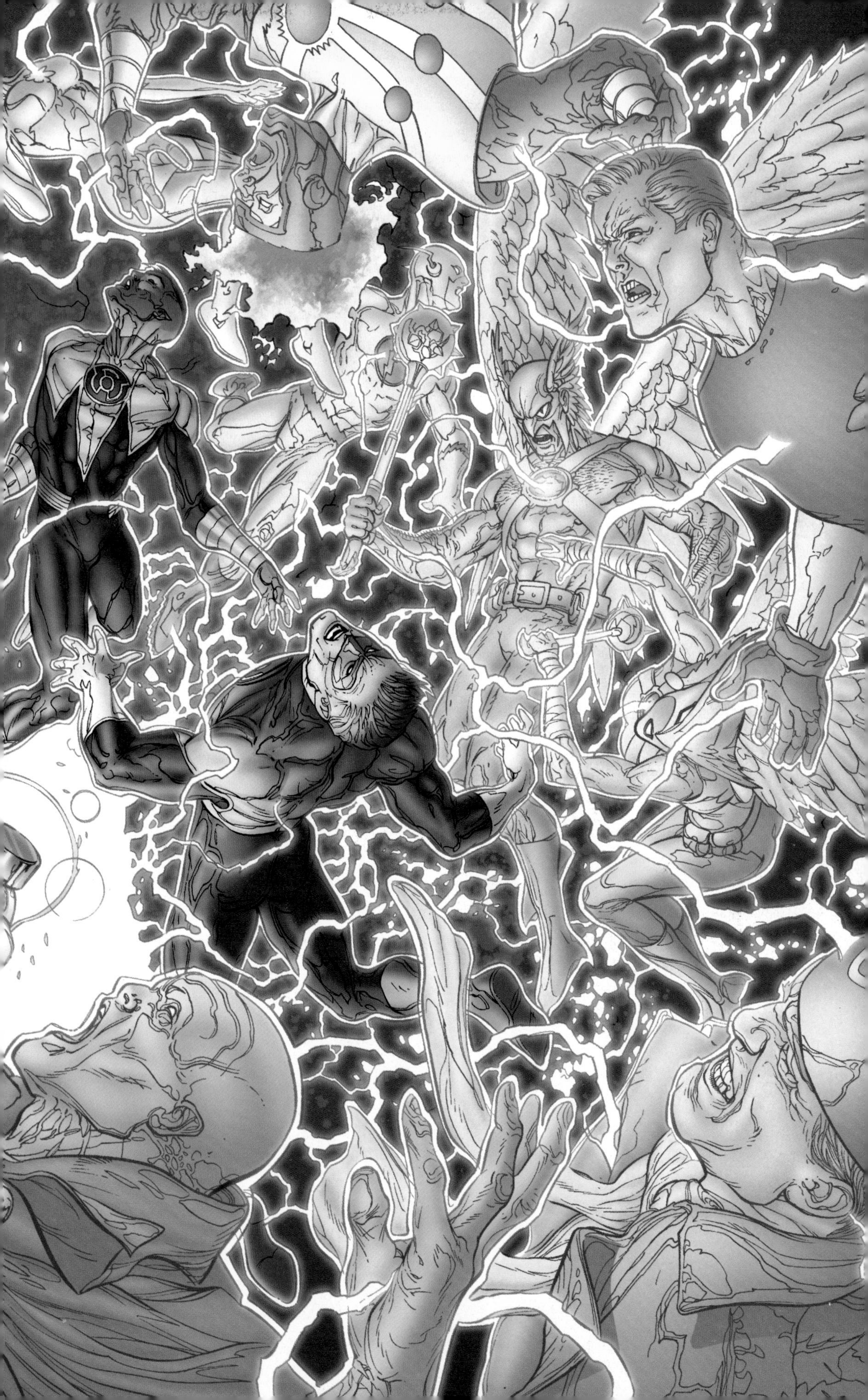

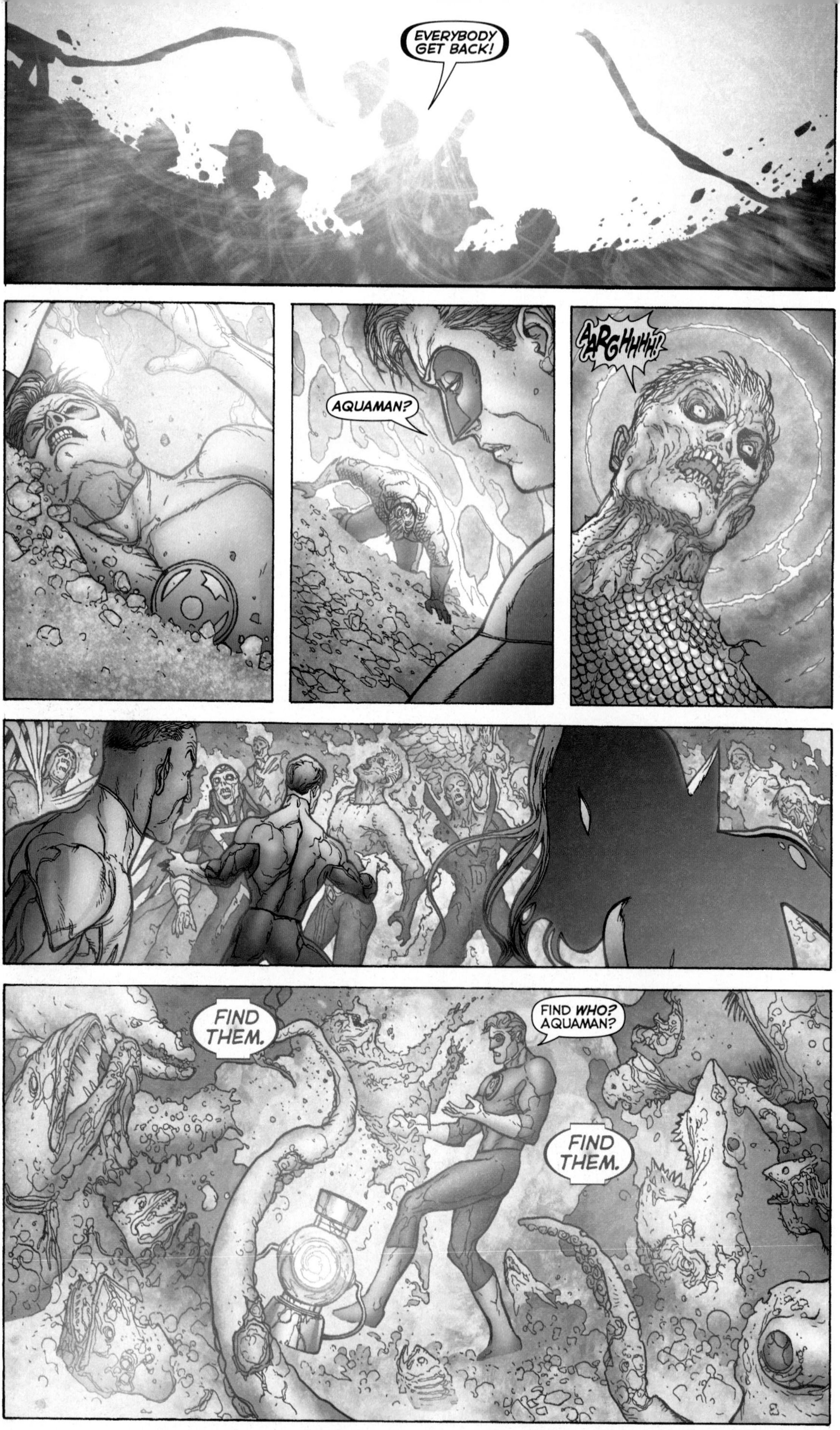
EVERYBODY GET BACK!
AQUAMAN?
AARGHHHH!
FIND THEM.
FIND WHO? AQUAMAN?
FIND THEM.

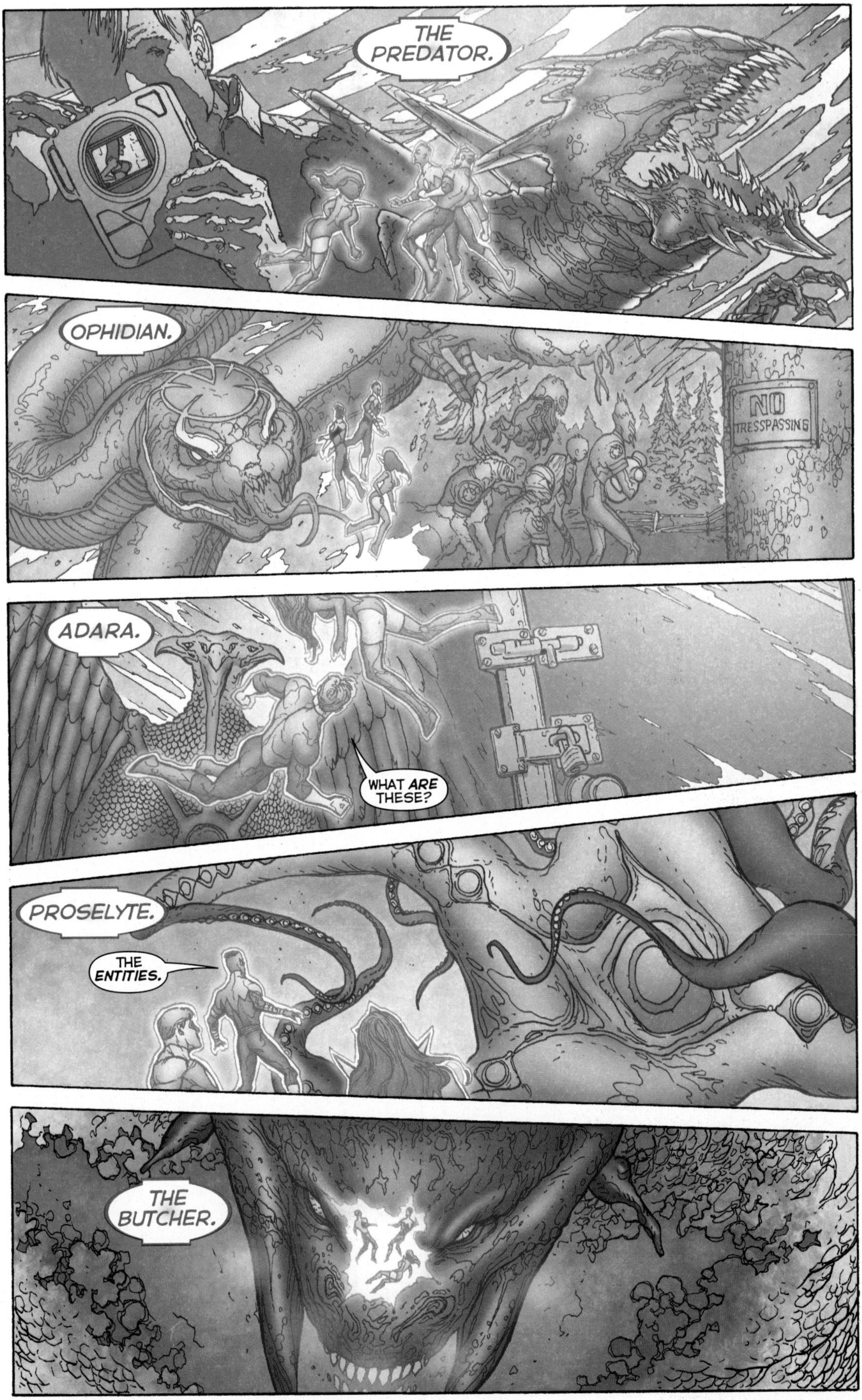
THE PREDATOR.
OPHIDIAN.
NO TRESSPASSING
ADARA.
WHAT ARE THESE?
PROSELYTE.
THE ENTITIES.
THE BUTCHER.

"ION."

SPACE SECTOR 1760.

THE PLANET DAXAM
AND ITS SUN.

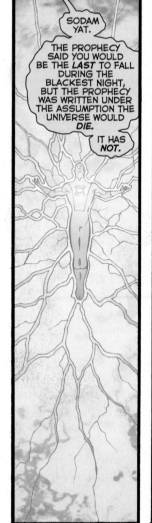

SODAM YAT.

THE PROPHECY SAID YOU WOULD BE THE LAST TO FALL DURING THE BLACKEST NIGHT, BUT THE PROPHECY WAS WRITTEN UNDER THE ASSUMPTION THE UNIVERSE WOULD DIE.

IT HAS NOT.

AND WITH ME TO PROTECT IT, IT WILL NOT.

YOU UNDERSTAND, DON'T YOU?

KRAKKK

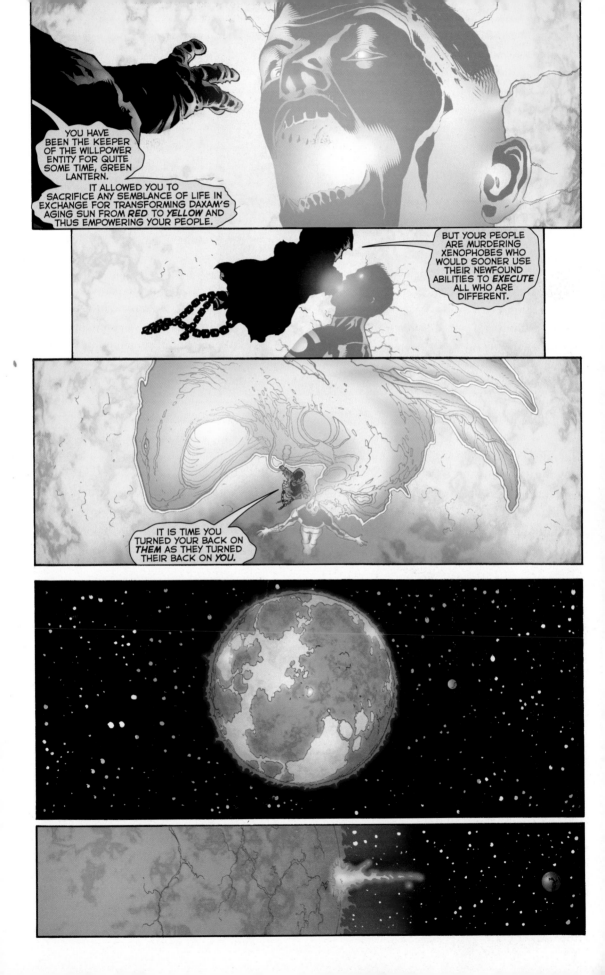

YOU HAVE BEEN THE KEEPER OF THE WILLPOWER ENTITY FOR QUITE SOME TIME, GREEN LANTERN.

IT ALLOWED YOU TO SACRIFICE ANY SEMBLANCE OF LIFE IN EXCHANGE FOR TRANSFORMING DAXAM'S AGING SUN FROM *RED* TO *YELLOW* AND THUS EMPOWERING YOUR PEOPLE.

BUT YOUR PEOPLE ARE MURDERING XENOPHOBES WHO WOULD SOONER USE THEIR NEWFOUND ABILITIES TO *EXECUTE* ALL WHO ARE DIFFERENT.

IT IS TIME YOU TURNED YOUR BACK ON *THEM* AS THEY TURNED THEIR BACK ON *YOU.*

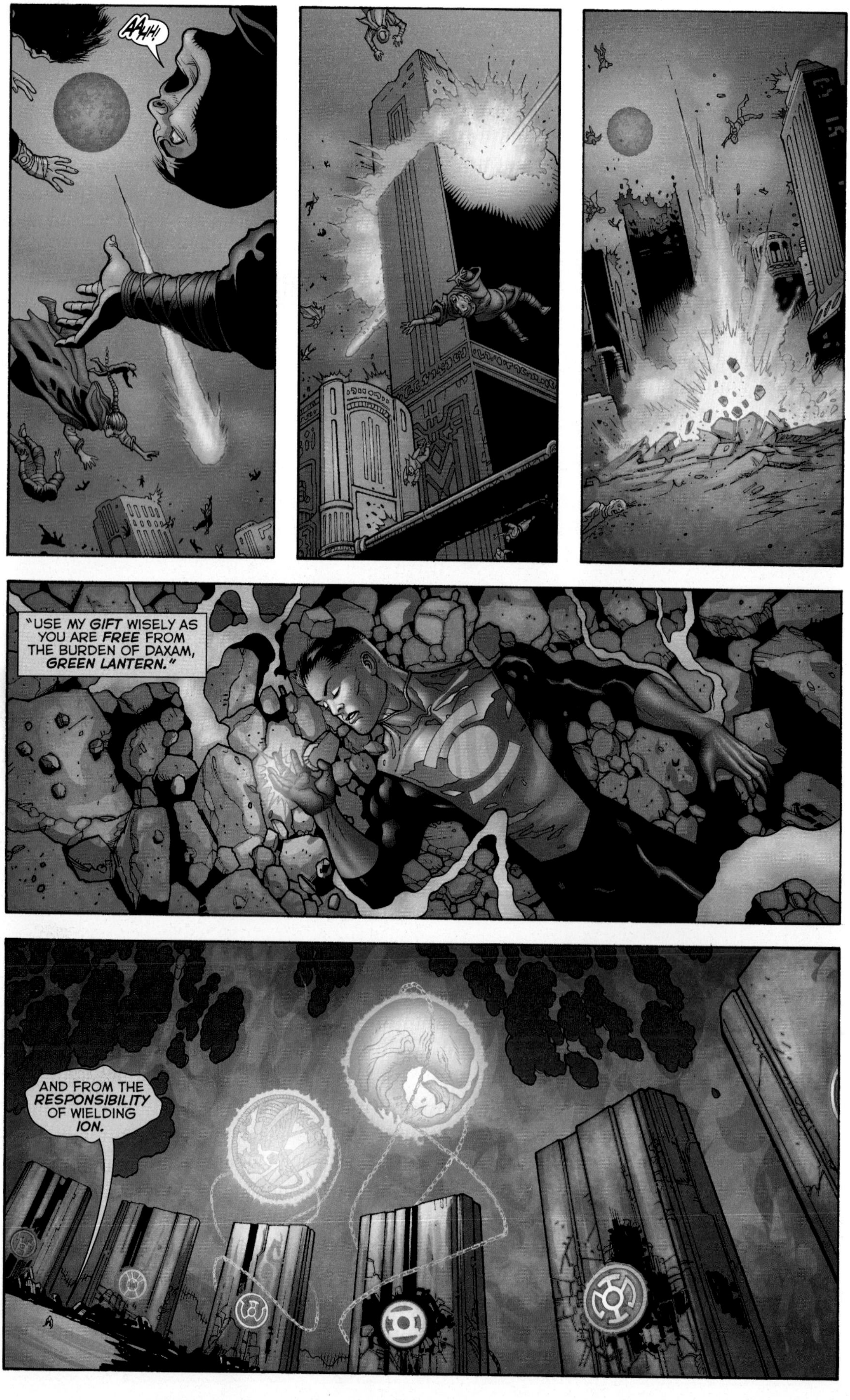
AAHH!
"USE MY GIFT WISELY AS YOU ARE FREE FROM THE BURDEN OF DAXAM, GREEN LANTERN."
AND FROM THE RESPONSIBILITY OF WIELDING ION.

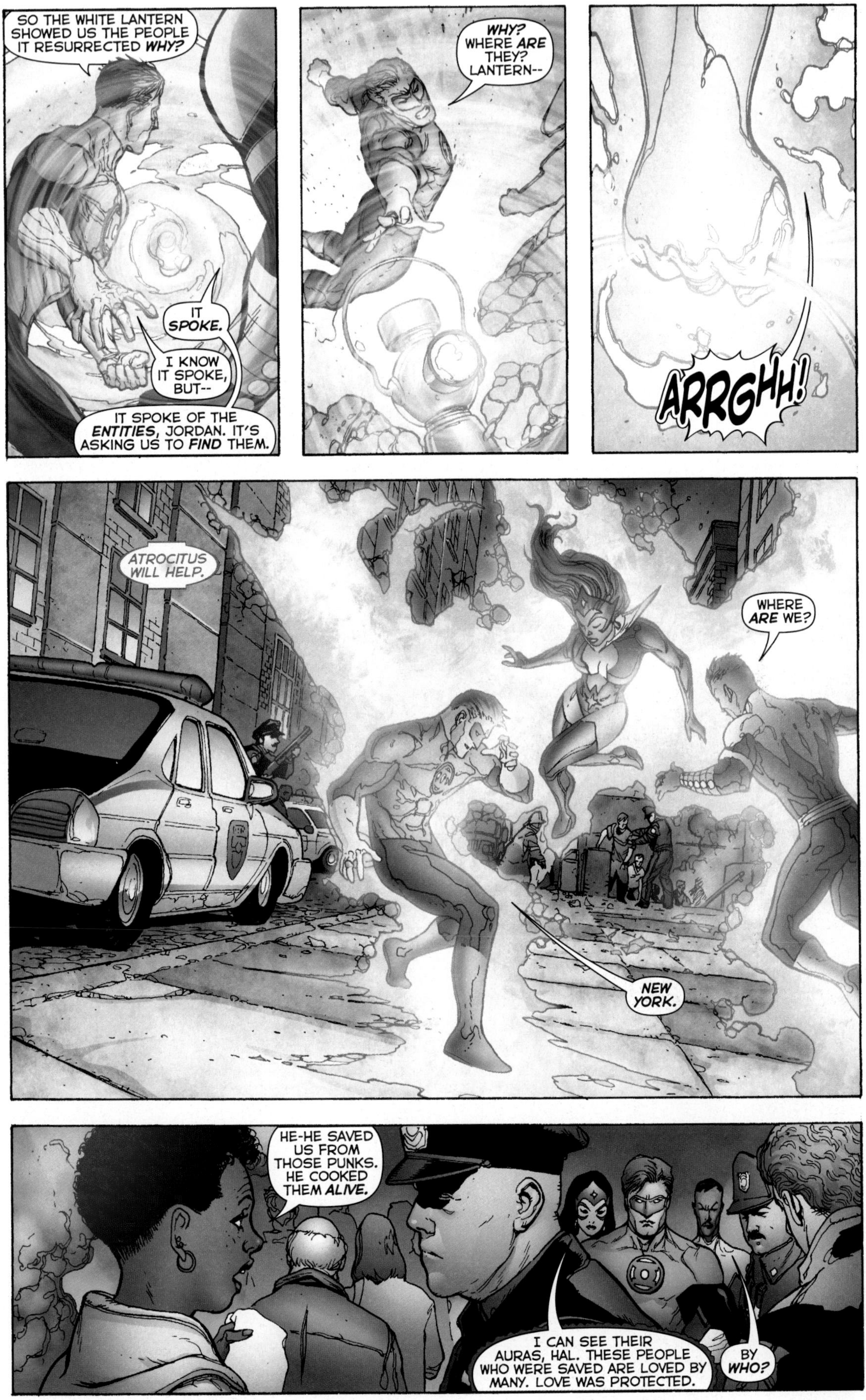
SO THE WHITE LANTERN SHOWED US THE PEOPLE IT RESURRECTED *WHY?*
IT *SPOKE.*
I KNOW IT SPOKE, BUT--
IT SPOKE OF THE *ENTITIES*, JORDAN. IT'S ASKING US TO *FIND* THEM.
WHY? WHERE *ARE* THEY? LANTERN--
ARRGHH!
ATROCITUS WILL HELP.
WHERE *ARE* WE?
NEW YORK.
HE-HE SAVED US FROM THOSE PUNKS. HE COOKED THEM *ALIVE.*
I CAN SEE THEIR AURAS, HAL. THESE PEOPLE WHO WERE SAVED ARE LOVED BY MANY. LOVE WAS PROTECTED.
BY *WHO?*

RRRFFF.

I SACRIFICE THE LIQUID OF LIFE TO YOU, UNIVERSE, AGAIN ASKING YOU TO SHOW ME WHAT IS NOT SHOWN.

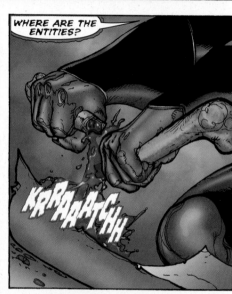

WHERE ARE THE ENTITIES?

KRRAAATCHH

PARALLAX... ION...THEY AREN'T HERE--

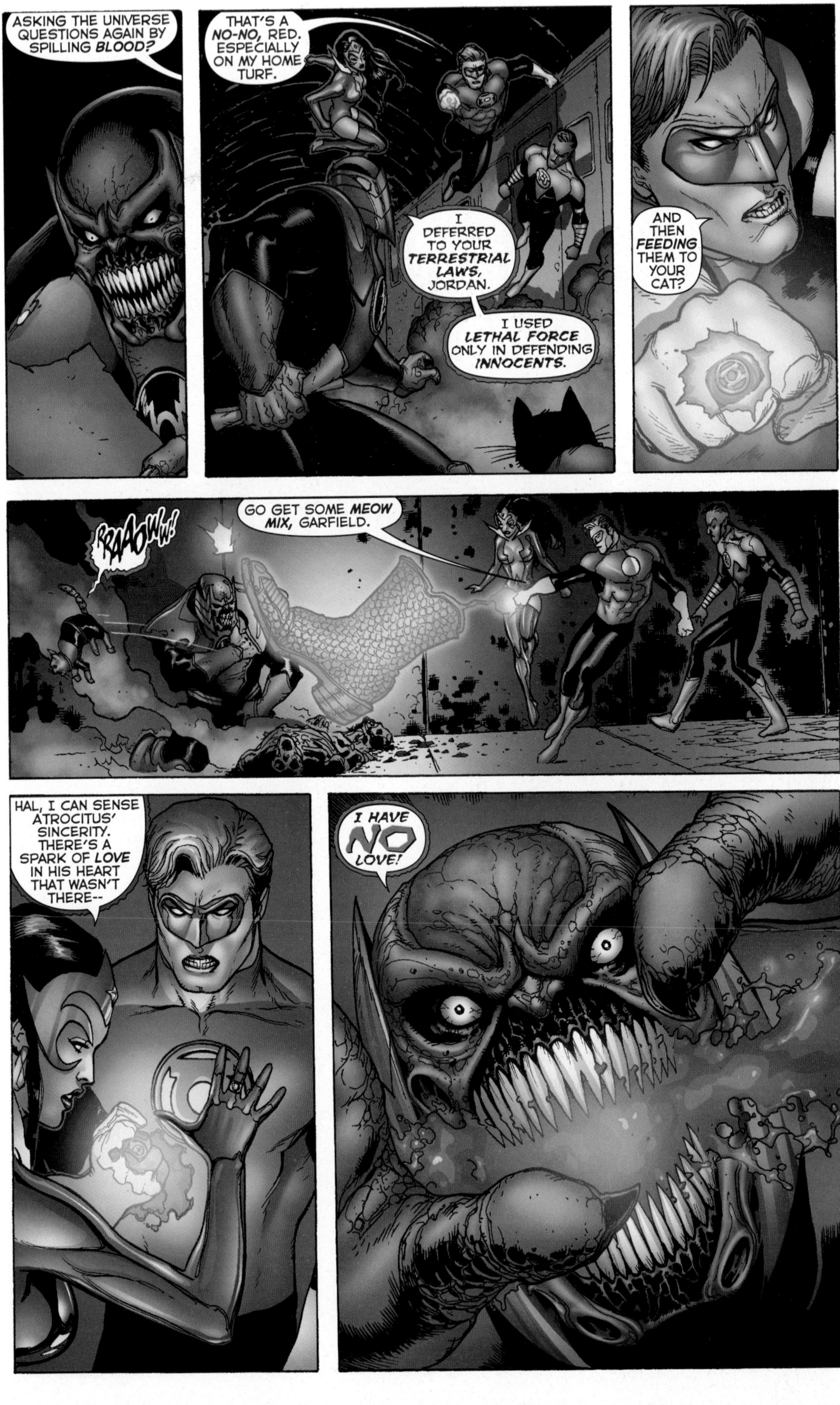
ASKING THE UNIVERSE QUESTIONS AGAIN BY SPILLING BLOOD?
THAT'S A NO-NO, RED. ESPECIALLY ON MY HOME TURF.
I DEFERRED TO YOUR TERRESTRIAL LAWS, JORDAN.
I USED LETHAL FORCE ONLY IN DEFENDING INNOCENTS.
AND THEN FEEDING THEM TO YOUR CAT?
RRAAOWW!
GO GET SOME MEOW MIX, GARFIELD.
HAL, I CAN SENSE ATROCITUS' SINCERITY. THERE'S A SPARK OF LOVE IN HIS HEART THAT WASN'T THERE--
I HAVE NO LOVE!

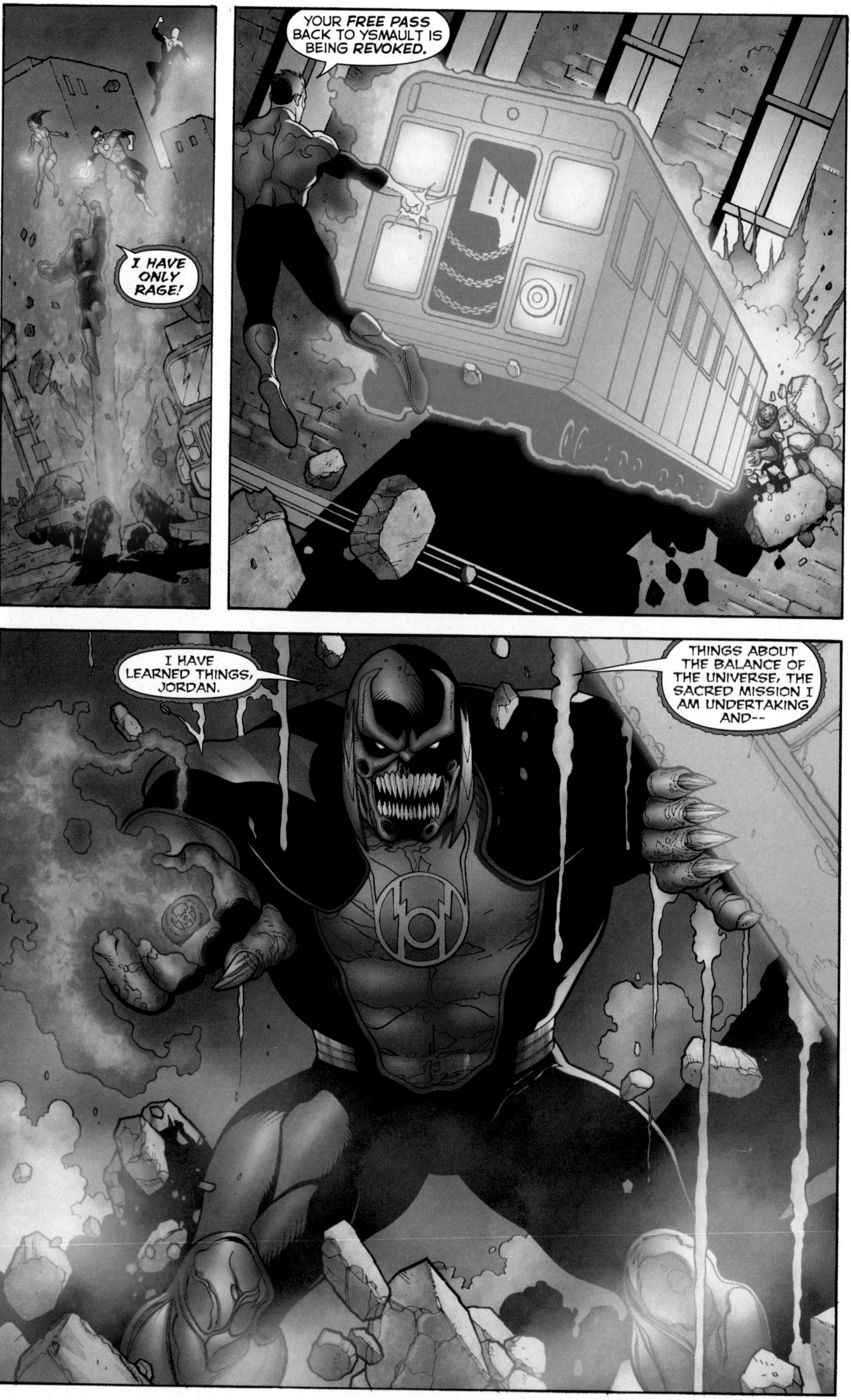
I HAVE ONLY RAGE!
YOUR FREE PASS BACK TO YSMAULT IS BEING REVOKED.
I HAVE LEARNED THINGS, JORDAN.
THINGS ABOUT THE BALANCE OF THE UNIVERSE, THE SACRED MISSION I AM UNDERTAKING AND--

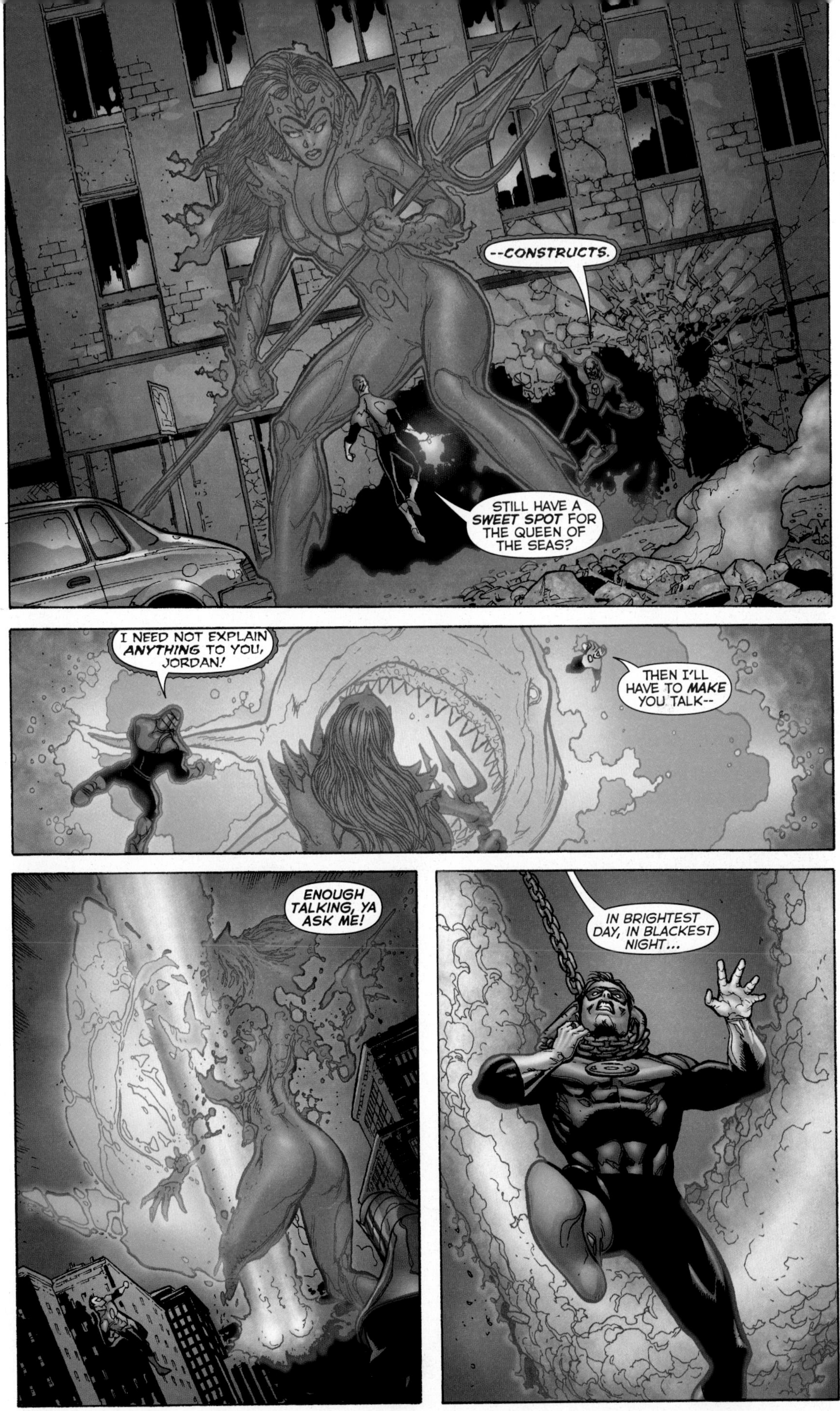
--CONSTRUCTS.
STILL HAVE A SWEET SPOT FOR THE QUEEN OF THE SEAS?
I NEED NOT EXPLAIN ANYTHING TO YOU, JORDAN!
THEN I'LL HAVE TO MAKE YOU TALK--
ENOUGH TALKING, YA ASK ME!
IN BRIGHTEST DAY, IN BLACKEST NIGHT...

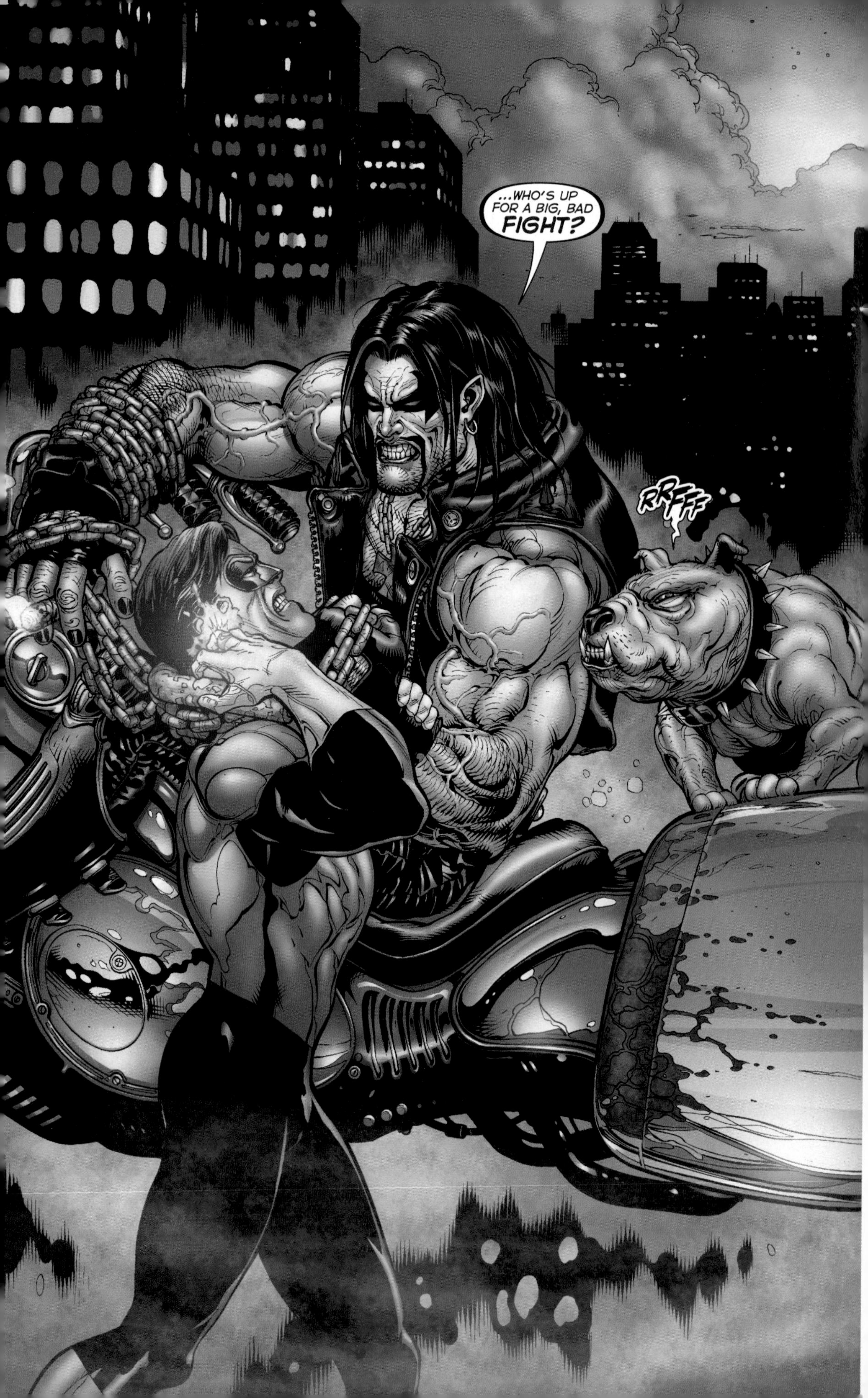
...WHO'S UP FOR A BIG, BAD FIGHT?
RRFFF

GREEN LANTERN 55 Cover by Doug Mahnke, Christian Alamy & Randy Mayor

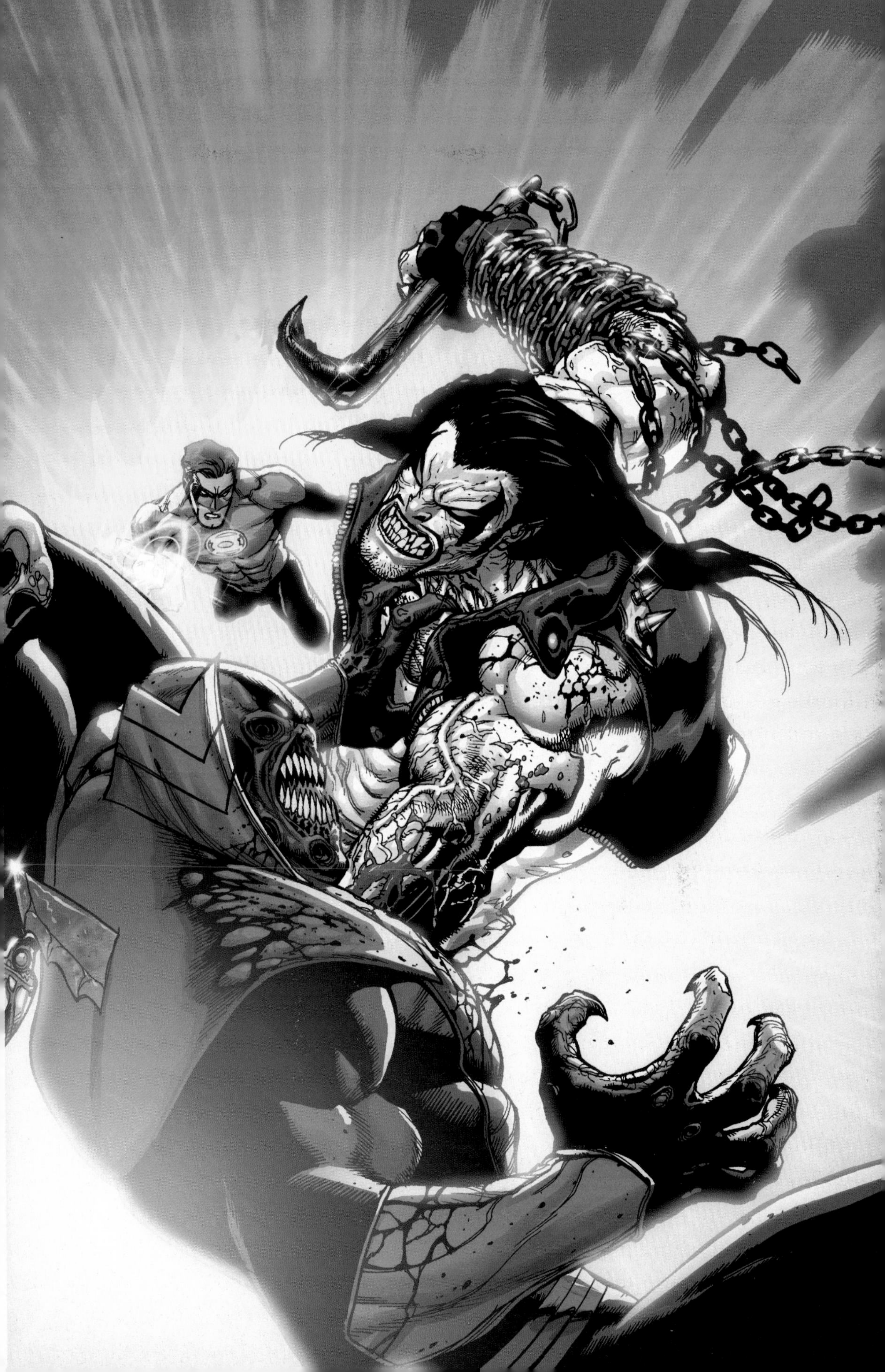

THE NEW GUARDIANS
CHAPTER THREE

Doug Mahnke Pencils

Christian Alamy, Tom Nguyen, Keith Champagne & Doug Mahnke Inks

GRASS RANGE, MONTANA.

STAY AWAY!

FWOOOSH!!

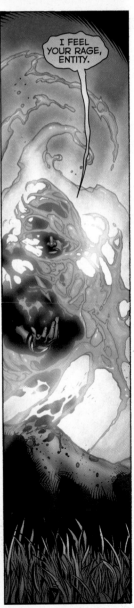

I FEEL YOUR RAGE, ENTITY.

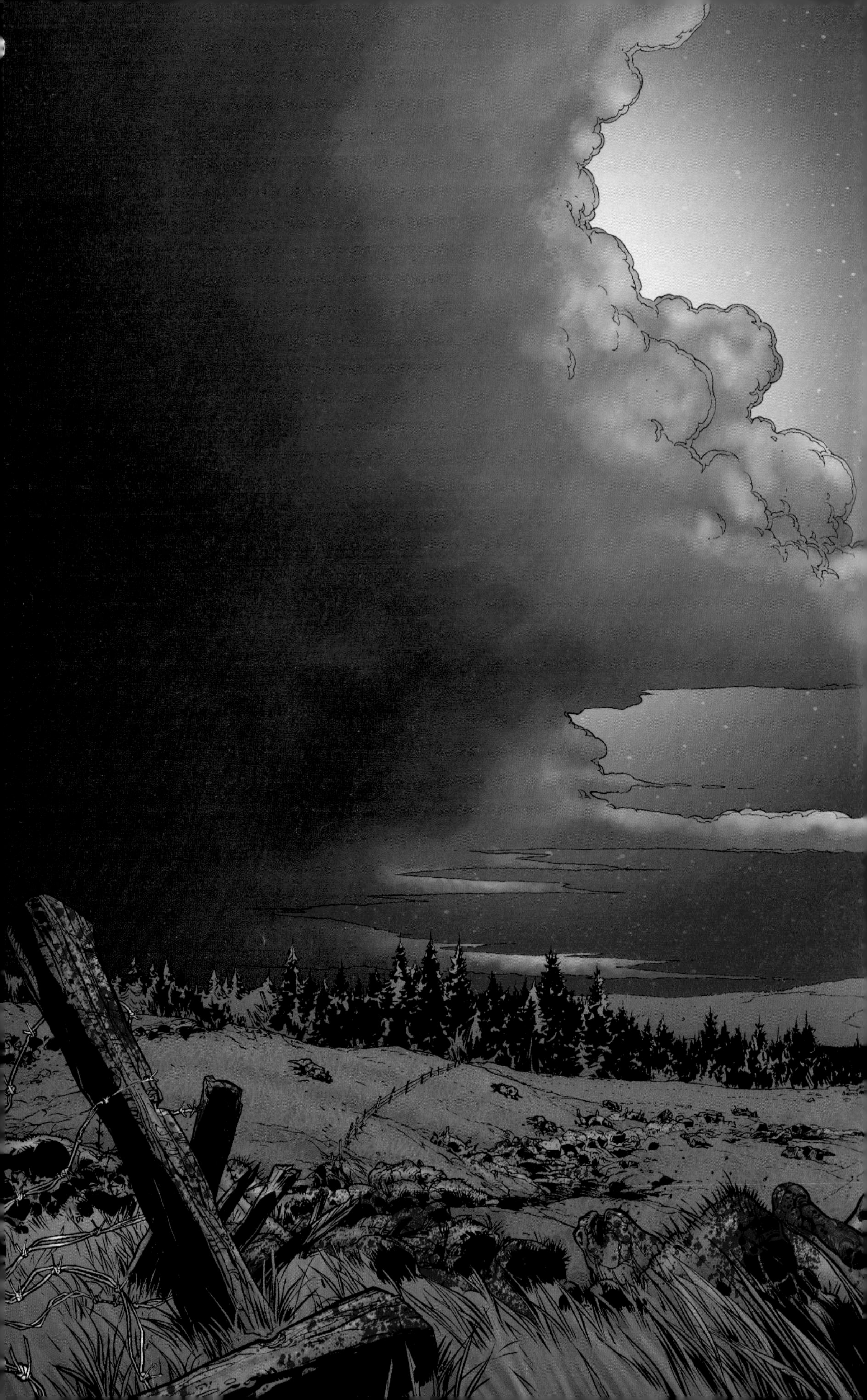

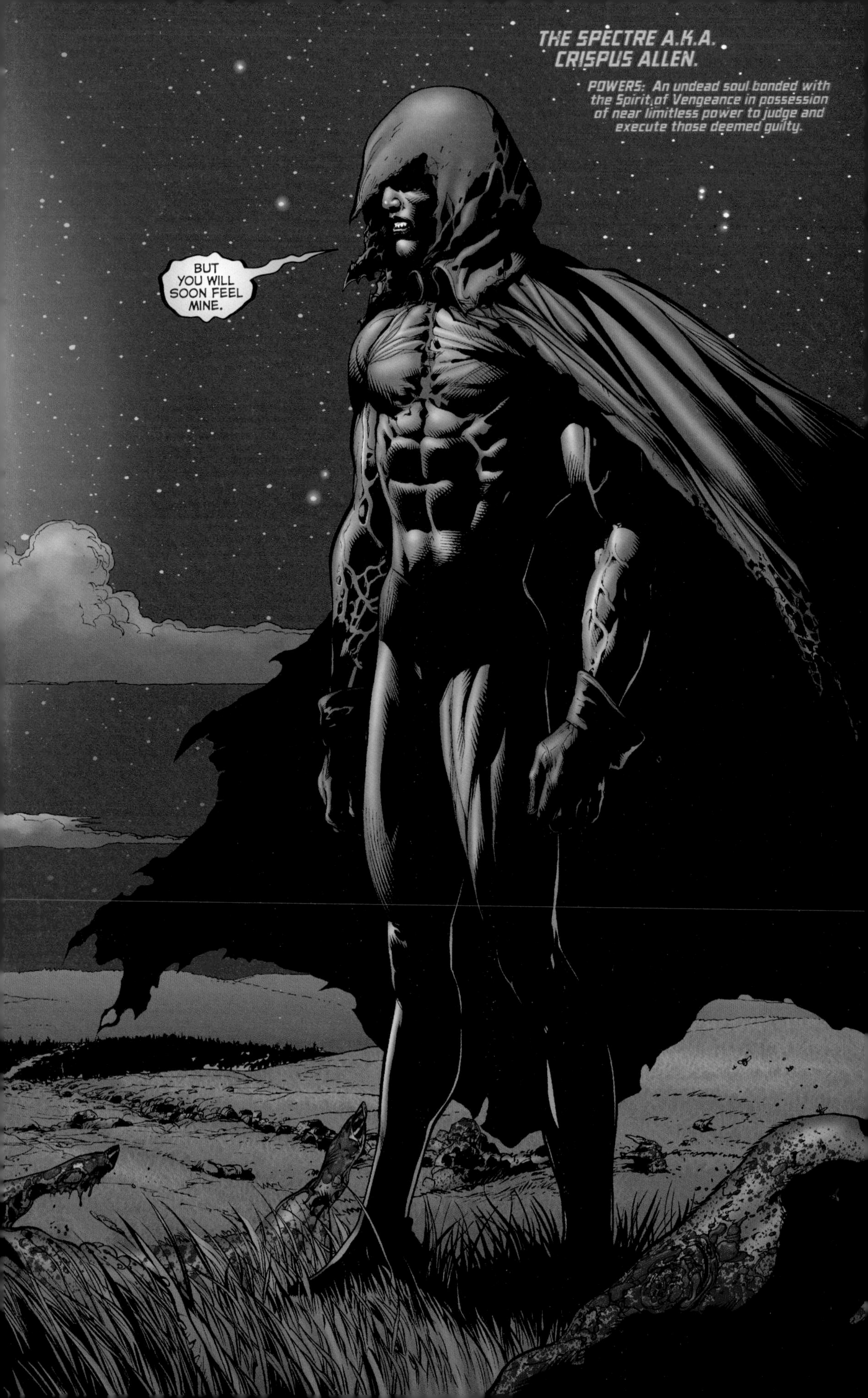
THE SPECTRE A.K.A. CRISPUS ALLEN.
POWERS: An undead soul bonded with the Spirit of Vengeance in possession of near limitless power to judge and execute those deemed guilty.
BUT YOU WILL SOON FEEL MINE.

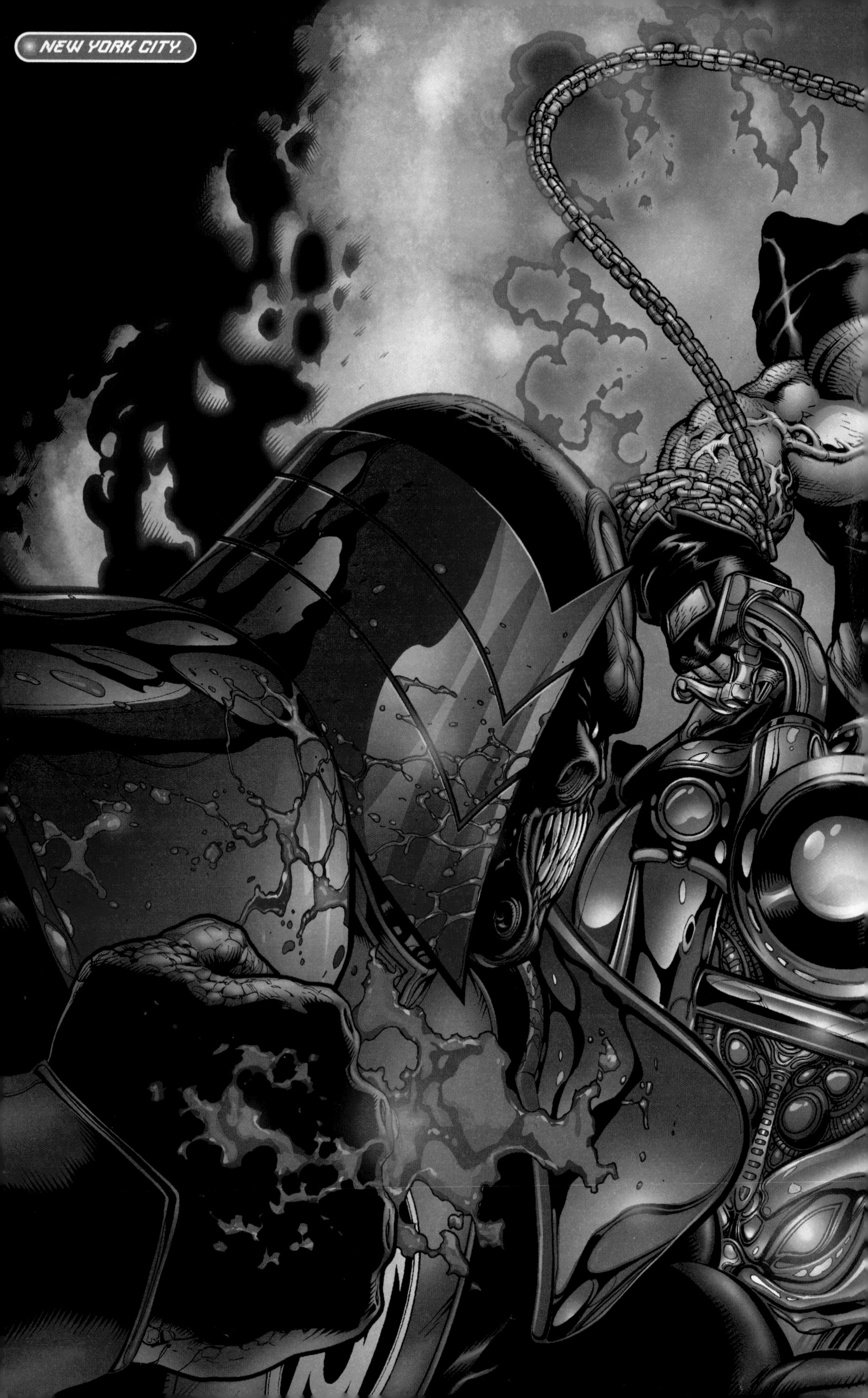
NEW YORK CITY.

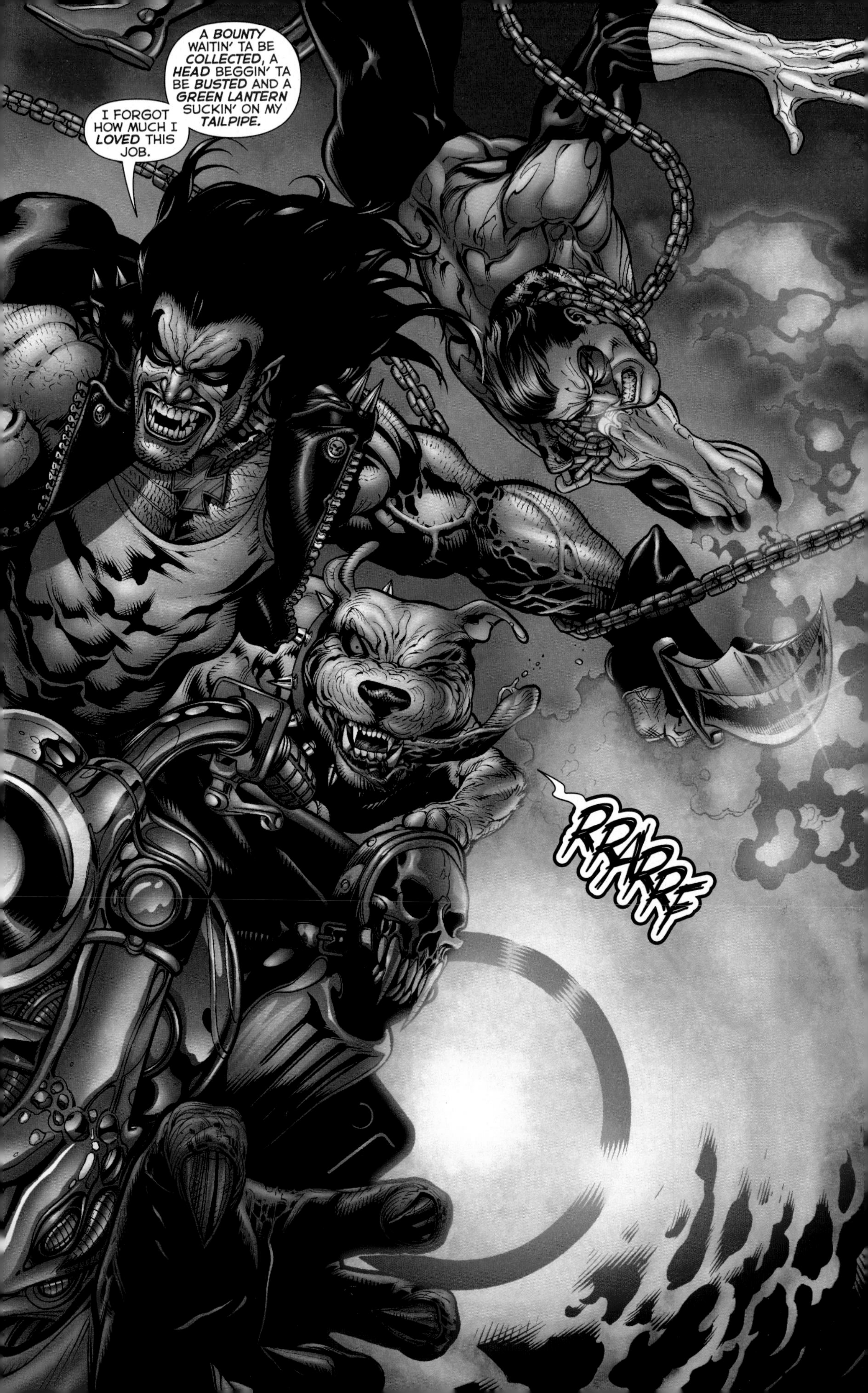
I FORGOT HOW MUCH I LOVED THIS JOB.
A BOUNTY WAITIN' TA BE COLLECTED, A HEAD BEGGIN' TA BE BUSTED AND A GREEN LANTERN SUCKIN' ON MY TAILPIPE.
RRAARRE

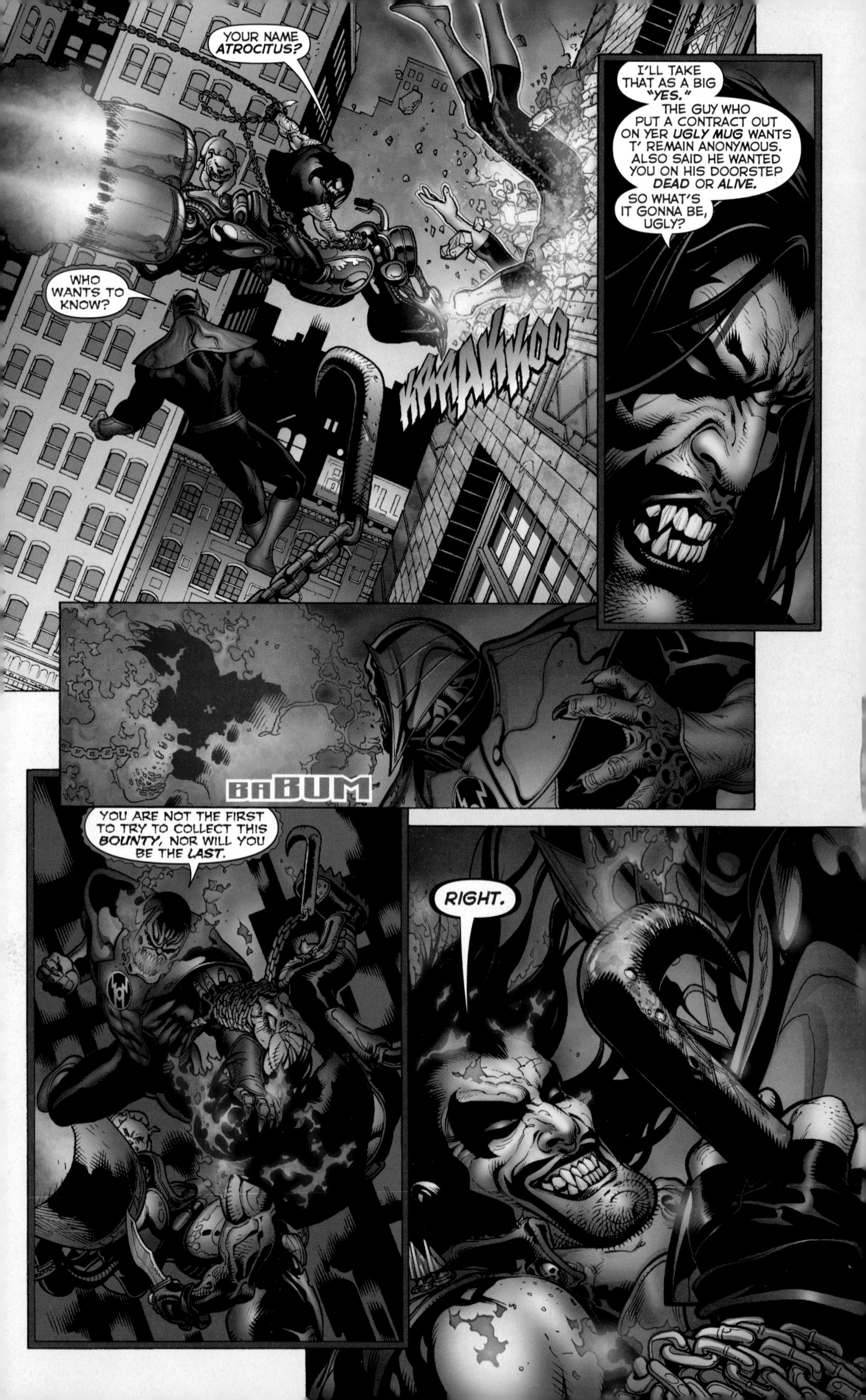

YOUR NAME ATROCITUS?
WHO WANTS TO KNOW?
KRAAKKOO
I'LL TAKE THAT AS A BIG "YES."
THE GUY WHO PUT A CONTRACT OUT ON YER UGLY MUG WANTS T' REMAIN ANONYMOUS. ALSO SAID HE WANTED YOU ON HIS DOORSTEP DEAD OR ALIVE.
SO WHAT'S IT GONNA BE, UGLY?
BABUM
YOU ARE NOT THE FIRST TO TRY TO COLLECT THIS BOUNTY, NOR WILL YOU BE THE LAST.
RIGHT.

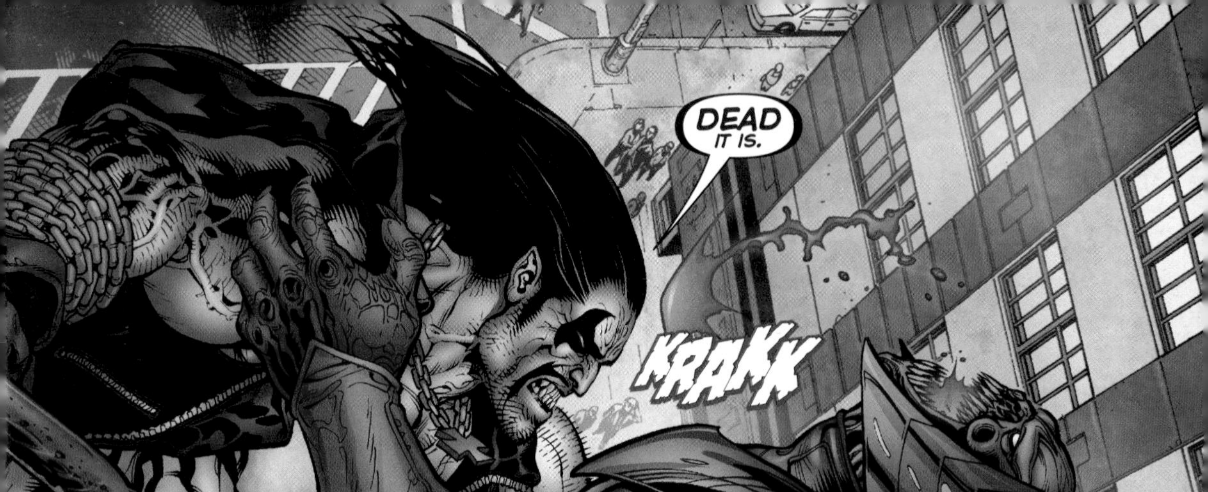
DEAD IT IS.
KRAKK

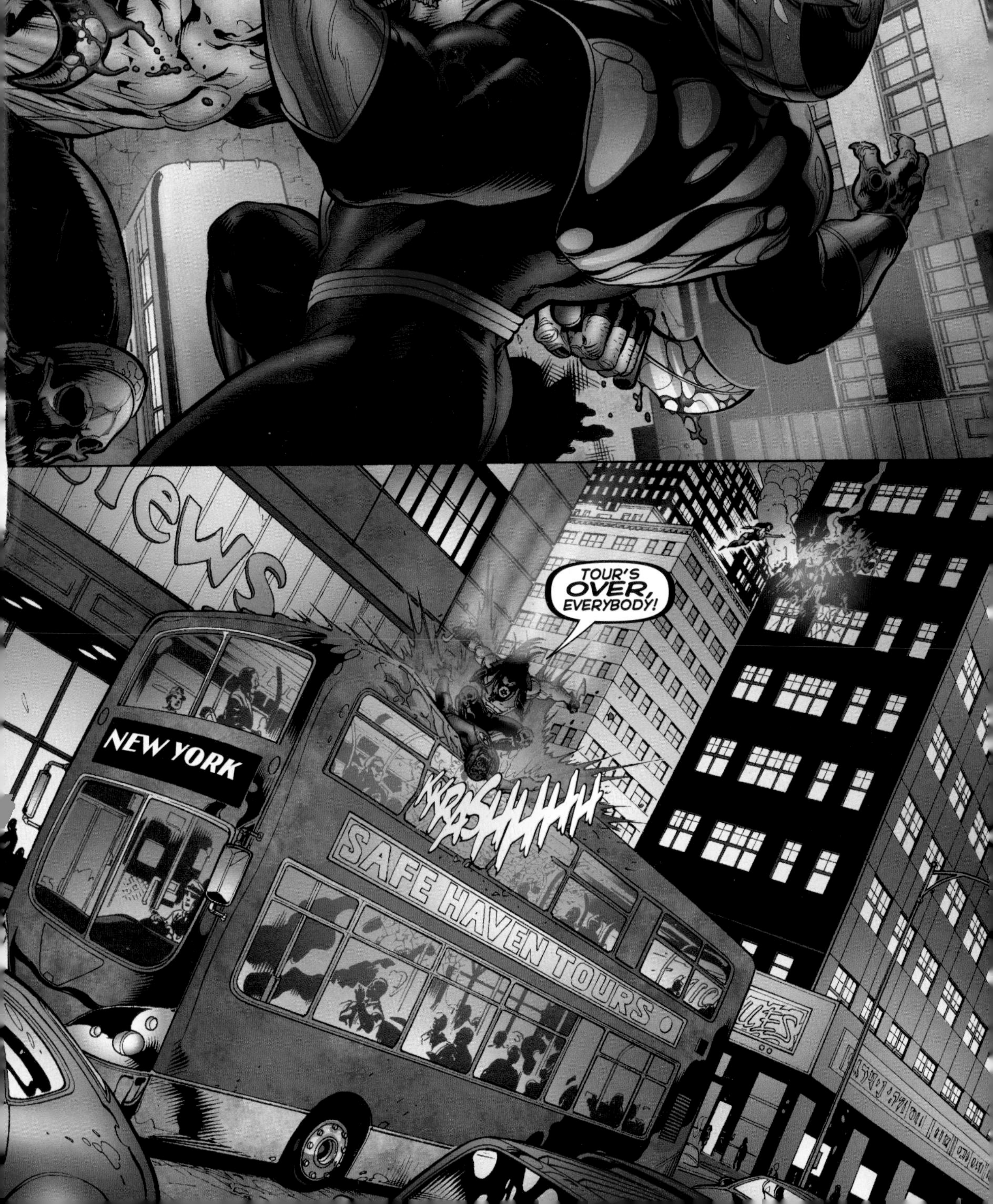
TOUR'S OVER, EVERYBODY!
NEW YORK
SAFE HAVEN TOURS

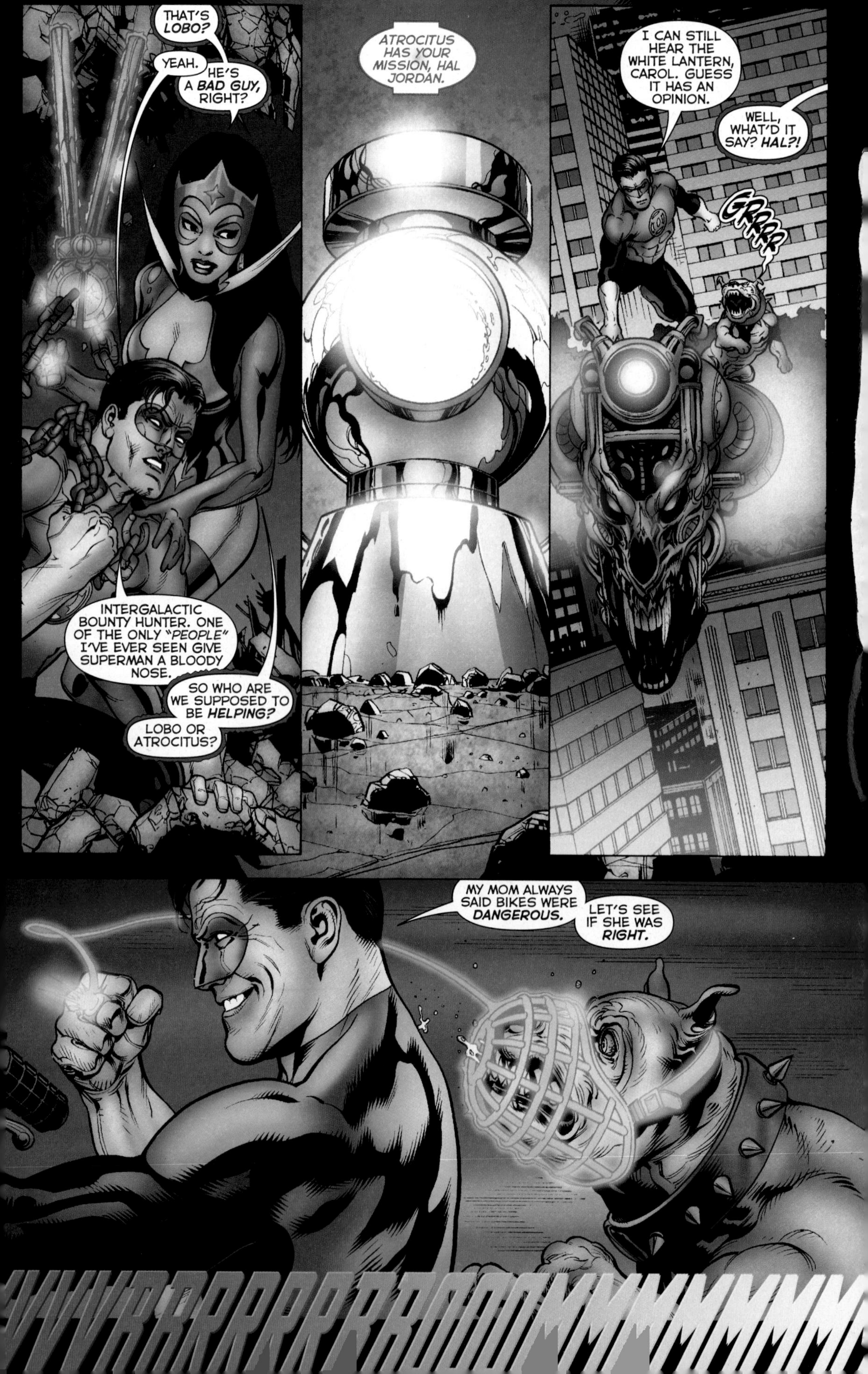
THAT'S LOBO?
YEAH.
HE'S A BAD GUY, RIGHT?
INTERGALACTIC BOUNTY HUNTER. ONE OF THE ONLY "PEOPLE" I'VE EVER SEEN GIVE SUPERMAN A BLOODY NOSE.
SO WHO ARE WE SUPPOSED TO BE HELPING?
LOBO OR ATROCITUS?
ATROCITUS HAS YOUR MISSION, HAL JORDAN.
I CAN STILL HEAR THE WHITE LANTERN, CAROL. GUESS IT HAS AN OPINION.
WELL, WHAT'D IT SAY? HAL?!
GRRRR
MY MOM ALWAYS SAID BIKES WERE DANGEROUS.
LET'S SEE IF SHE WAS RIGHT.
VVVRRRRRRRRROOOMMMMMMM

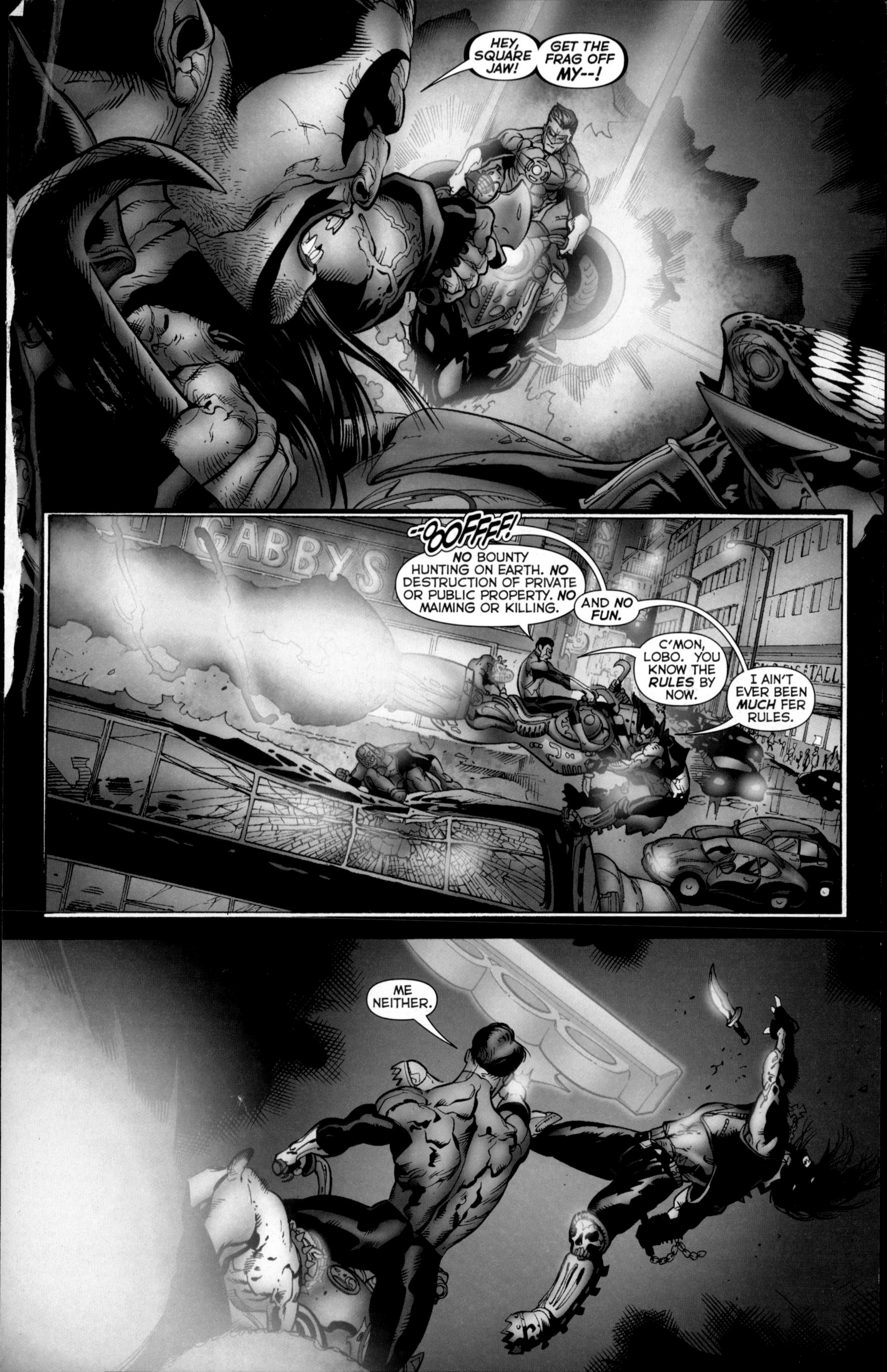
HEY, SQUARE JAW!
GET THE FRAG OFF MY--!
GABBY'S
-OOFFFF!
NO BOUNTY HUNTING ON EARTH. NO DESTRUCTION OF PRIVATE OR PUBLIC PROPERTY. NO MAIMING OR KILLING.
AND NO FUN.
C'MON, LOBO. YOU KNOW THE RULES BY NOW.
I AIN'T EVER BEEN MUCH FER RULES.
ME NEITHER.

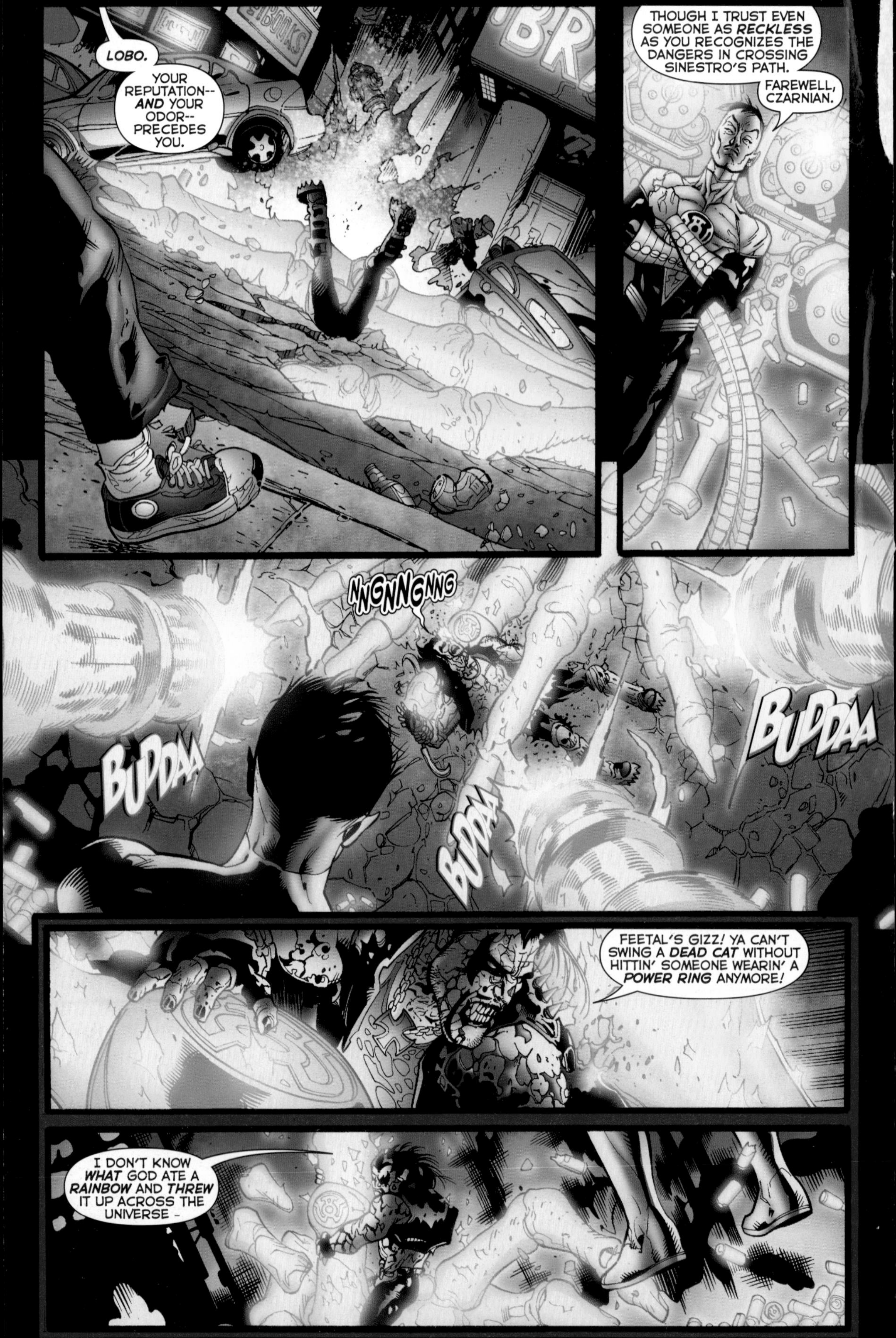
LOBO.
YOUR REPUTATION-- AND YOUR ODOR-- PRECEDES YOU.
THOUGH I TRUST EVEN SOMEONE AS RECKLESS AS YOU RECOGNIZES THE DANGERS IN CROSSING SINESTRO'S PATH.
FAREWELL, CZARNIAN.
NNGNNGNNG
BUDDAA
BUDDAA
BUDDAA
FEETAL'S GIZZ! YA CAN'T SWING A DEAD CAT WITHOUT HITTIN' SOMEONE WEARIN' A POWER RING ANYMORE!
I DON'T KNOW WHAT GOD ATE A RAINBOW AND THREW IT UP ACROSS THE UNIVERSE -

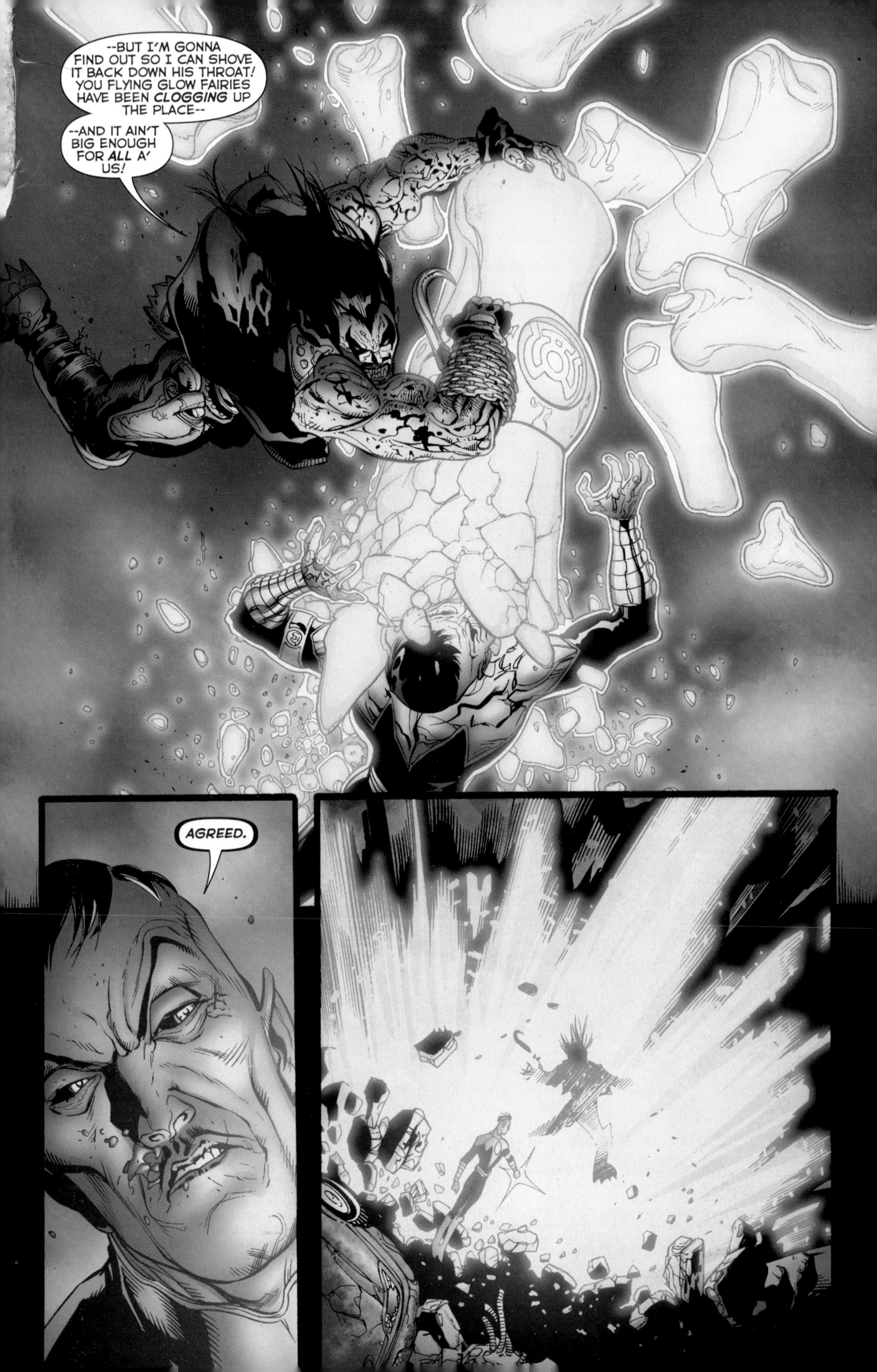
--BUT I'M GONNA FIND OUT SO I CAN SHOVE IT BACK DOWN HIS THROAT! YOU FLYING GLOW FAIRIES HAVE BEEN **CLOGGING** UP THE PLACE--
--AND IT AIN'T BIG ENOUGH FOR **ALL** A' US!
AGREED.

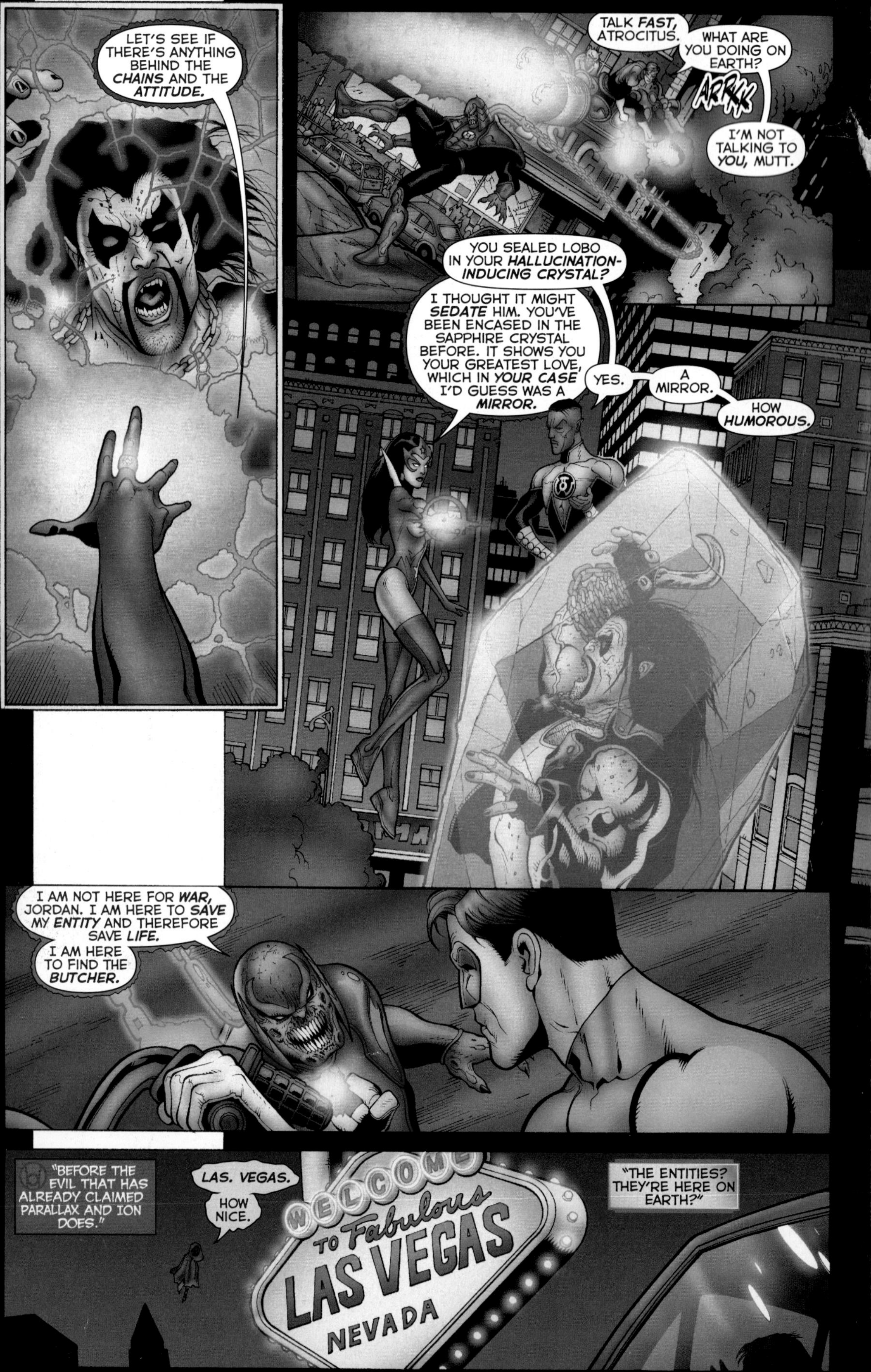
LET'S SEE IF THERE'S ANYTHING BEHIND THE CHAINS AND THE ATTITUDE.
TALK FAST, ATROCITUS.
WHAT ARE YOU DOING ON EARTH?
ARRKK
I'M NOT TALKING TO YOU, MUTT.
YOU SEALED LOBO IN YOUR HALLUCINATION-INDUCING CRYSTAL?
I THOUGHT IT MIGHT SEDATE HIM. YOU'VE BEEN ENCASED IN THE SAPPHIRE CRYSTAL BEFORE. IT SHOWS YOU YOUR GREATEST LOVE, WHICH IN YOUR CASE I'D GUESS WAS A MIRROR.
YES.
A MIRROR.
HOW HUMOROUS.
I AM NOT HERE FOR WAR, JORDAN. I AM HERE TO SAVE MY ENTITY AND THEREFORE SAVE LIFE.
I AM HERE TO FIND THE BUTCHER.
"BEFORE THE EVIL THAT HAS ALREADY CLAIMED PARALLAX AND ION DOES."
LAS. VEGAS.
HOW NICE.
WELCOME to Fabulous LAS VEGAS NEVADA
"THE ENTITIES? THEY'RE HERE ON EARTH?"

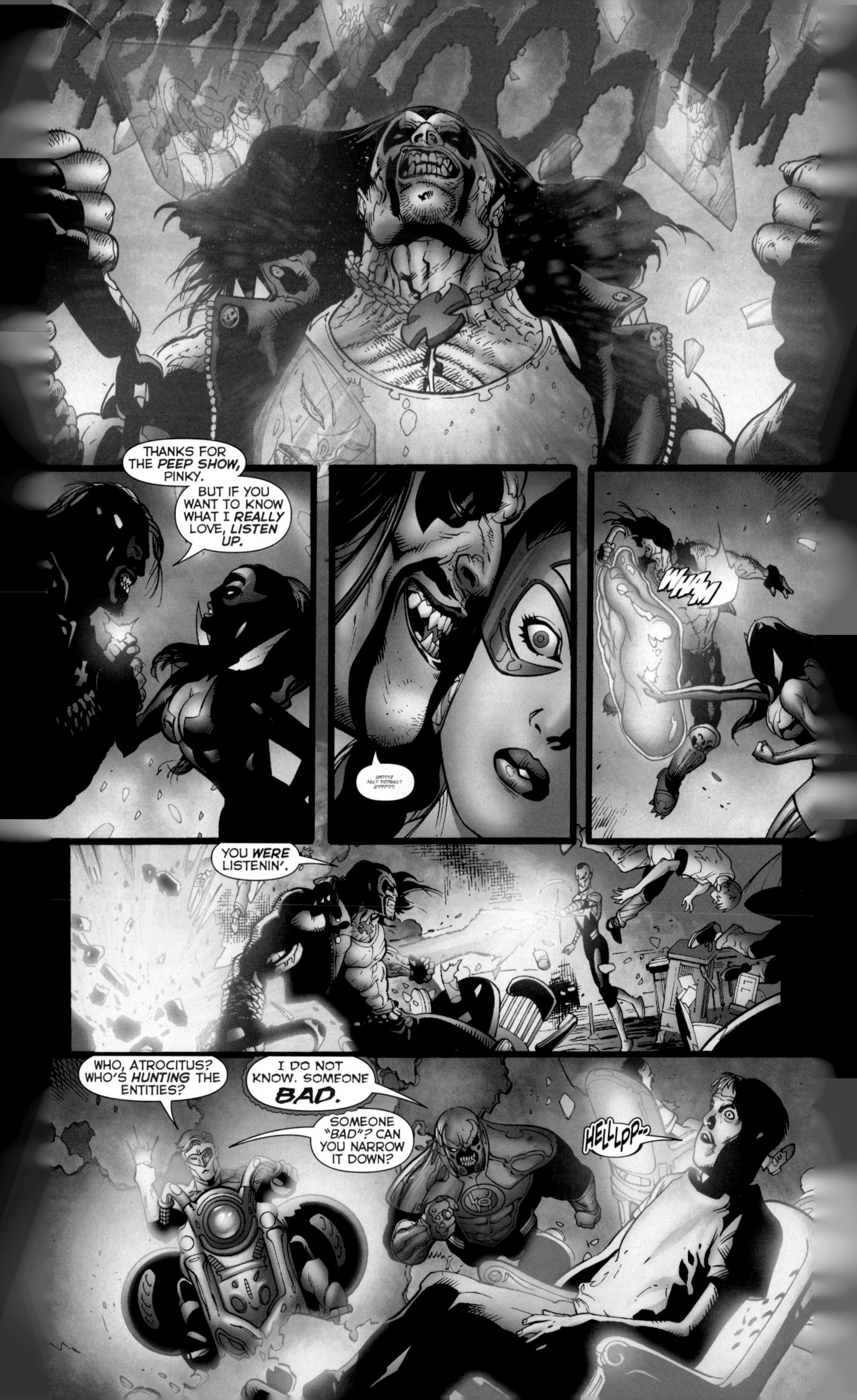
THANKS FOR THE PEEP SHOW, PINKY.
BUT IF YOU WANT TO KNOW WHAT I REALLY LOVE, LISTEN UP.
WHAM
YOU WERE LISTENIN'.
WHO, ATROCITUS? WHO'S HUNTING THE ENTITIES?
I DO NOT KNOW. SOMEONE BAD.
SOMEONE "BAD"? CAN YOU NARROW IT DOWN?
HELLLPP--

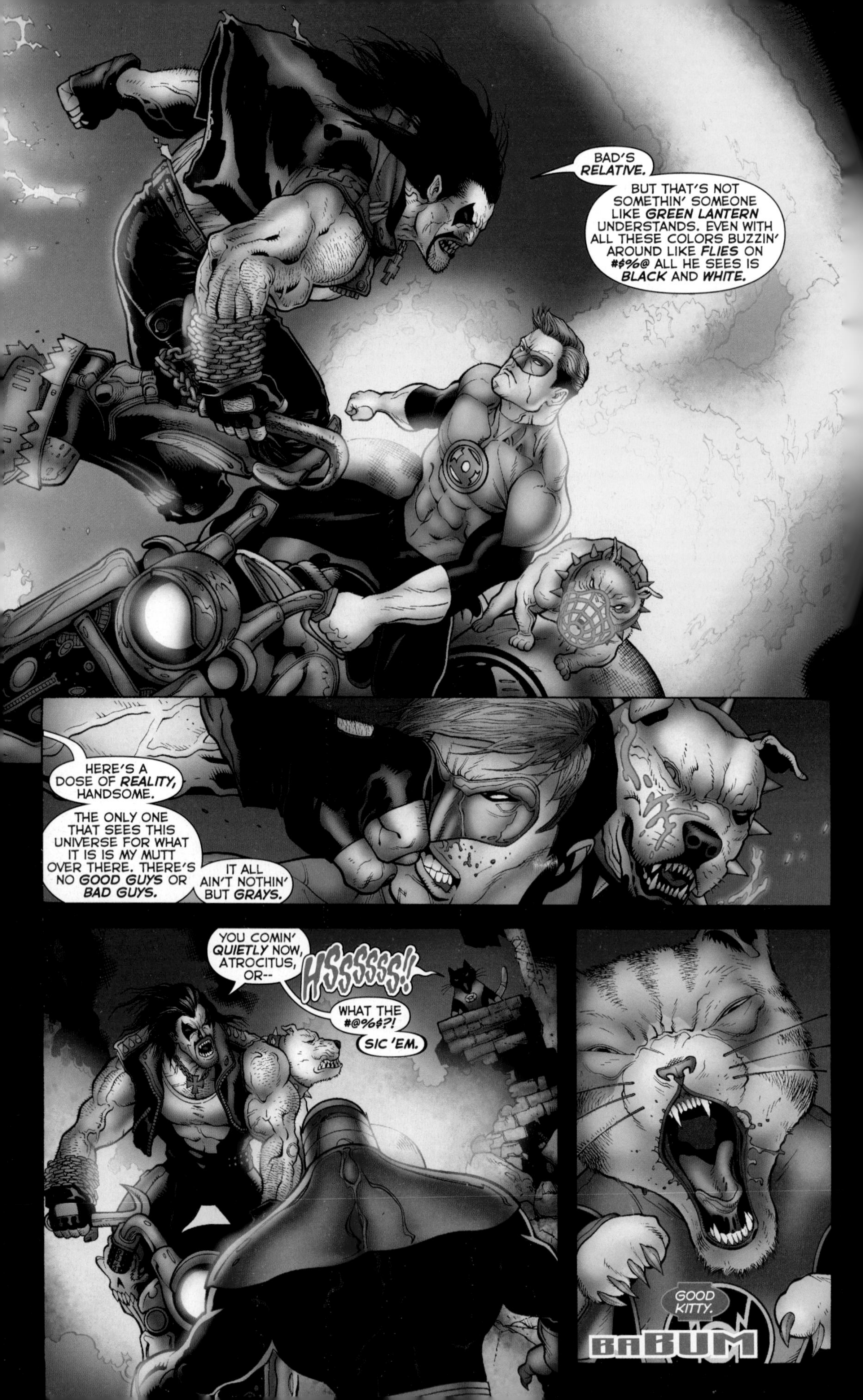
BAD'S RELATIVE.
BUT THAT'S NOT SOMETHIN' SOMEONE LIKE GREEN LANTERN UNDERSTANDS. EVEN WITH ALL THESE COLORS BUZZIN' AROUND LIKE FLIES ON #$%@ ALL HE SEES IS BLACK AND WHITE.
HERE'S A DOSE OF REALITY, HANDSOME.
THE ONLY ONE THAT SEES THIS UNIVERSE FOR WHAT IT IS IS MY MUTT OVER THERE. THERE'S NO GOOD GUYS OR BAD GUYS.
IT ALL AIN'T NOTHIN' BUT GRAYS.
YOU COMIN' QUIETLY NOW, ATROCITUS, OR--
HSSSSSS!!
WHAT THE #@%$?!
SIC 'EM.
GOOD KITTY.
BABUM

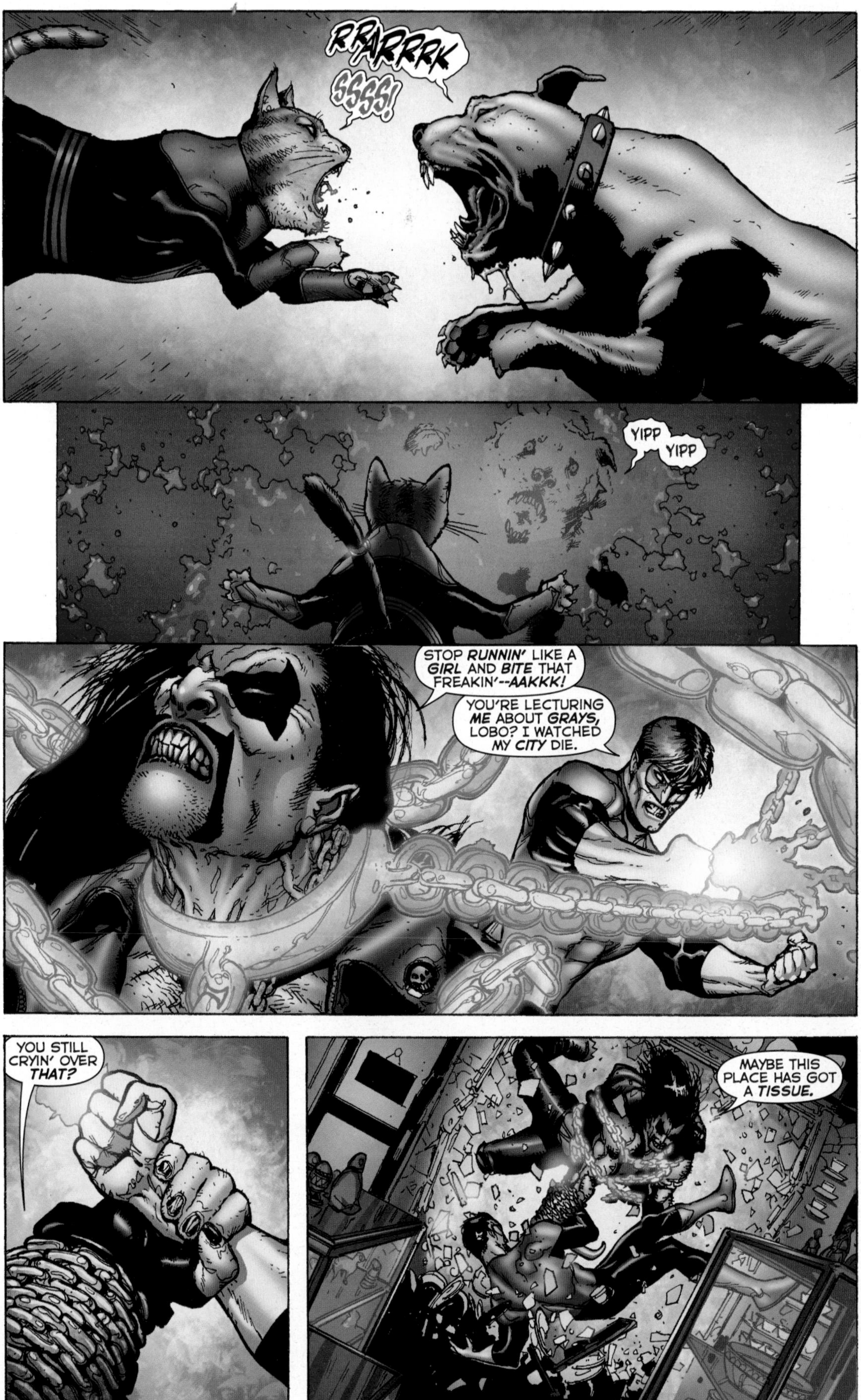
RRARRRK
SSSS!
YIPP YIPP
STOP RUNNIN' LIKE A GIRL AND BITE THAT FREAKIN'--AAKKK!
YOU'RE LECTURING ME ABOUT GRAYS, LOBO? I WATCHED MY CITY DIE.
YOU STILL CRYIN' OVER THAT?
MAYBE THIS PLACE HAS GOT A TISSUE.

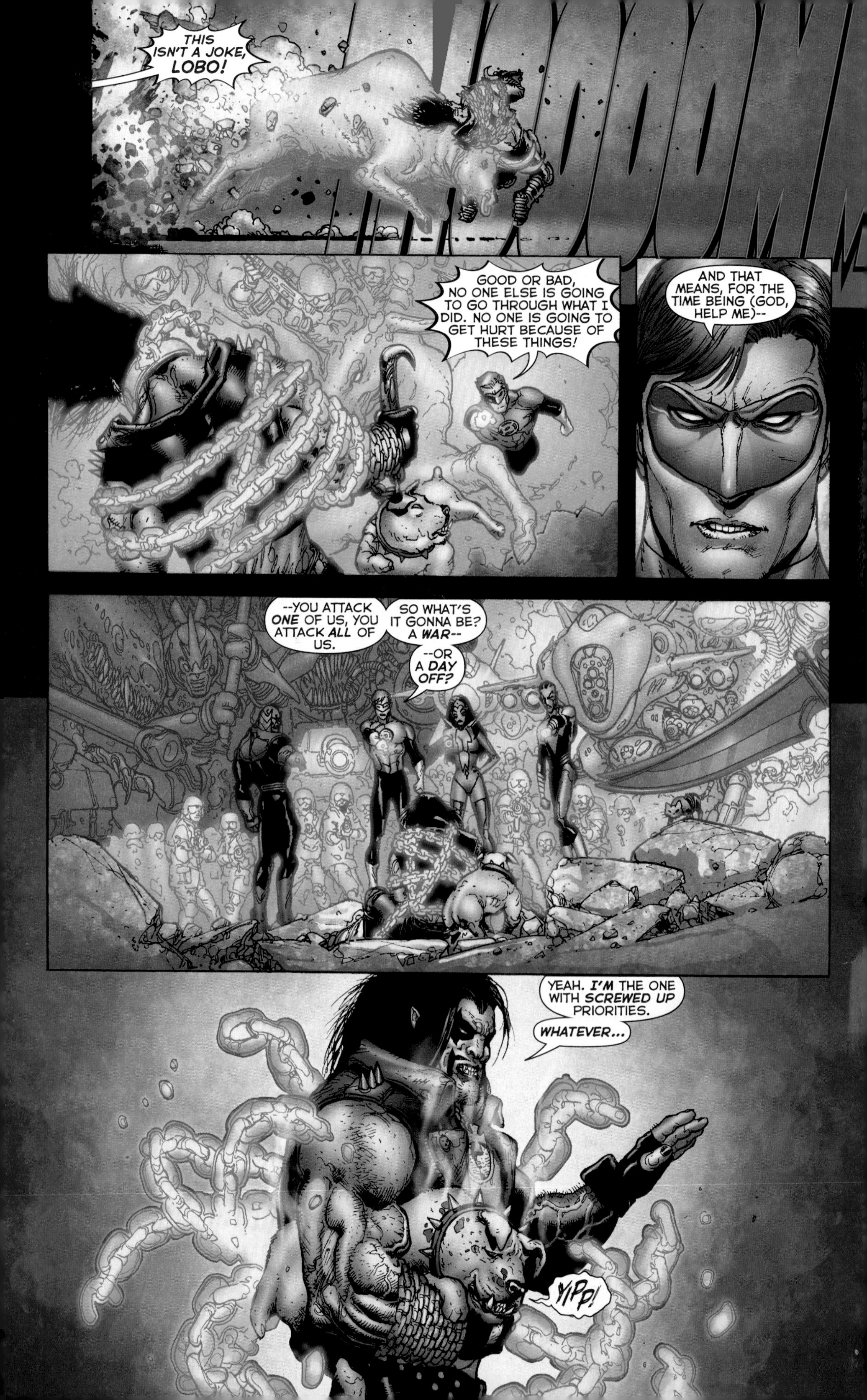
THIS ISN'T A JOKE, LOBO!
GOOD OR BAD, NO ONE ELSE IS GOING TO GO THROUGH WHAT I DID. NO ONE IS GOING TO GET HURT BECAUSE OF THESE THINGS!
AND THAT MEANS, FOR THE TIME BEING (GOD, HELP ME)--
--YOU ATTACK ONE OF US, YOU ATTACK ALL OF US.
SO WHAT'S IT GONNA BE? A WAR--
--OR A DAY OFF?
YEAH. I'M THE ONE WITH SCREWED UP PRIORITIES.
WHATEVER...
YIPP!

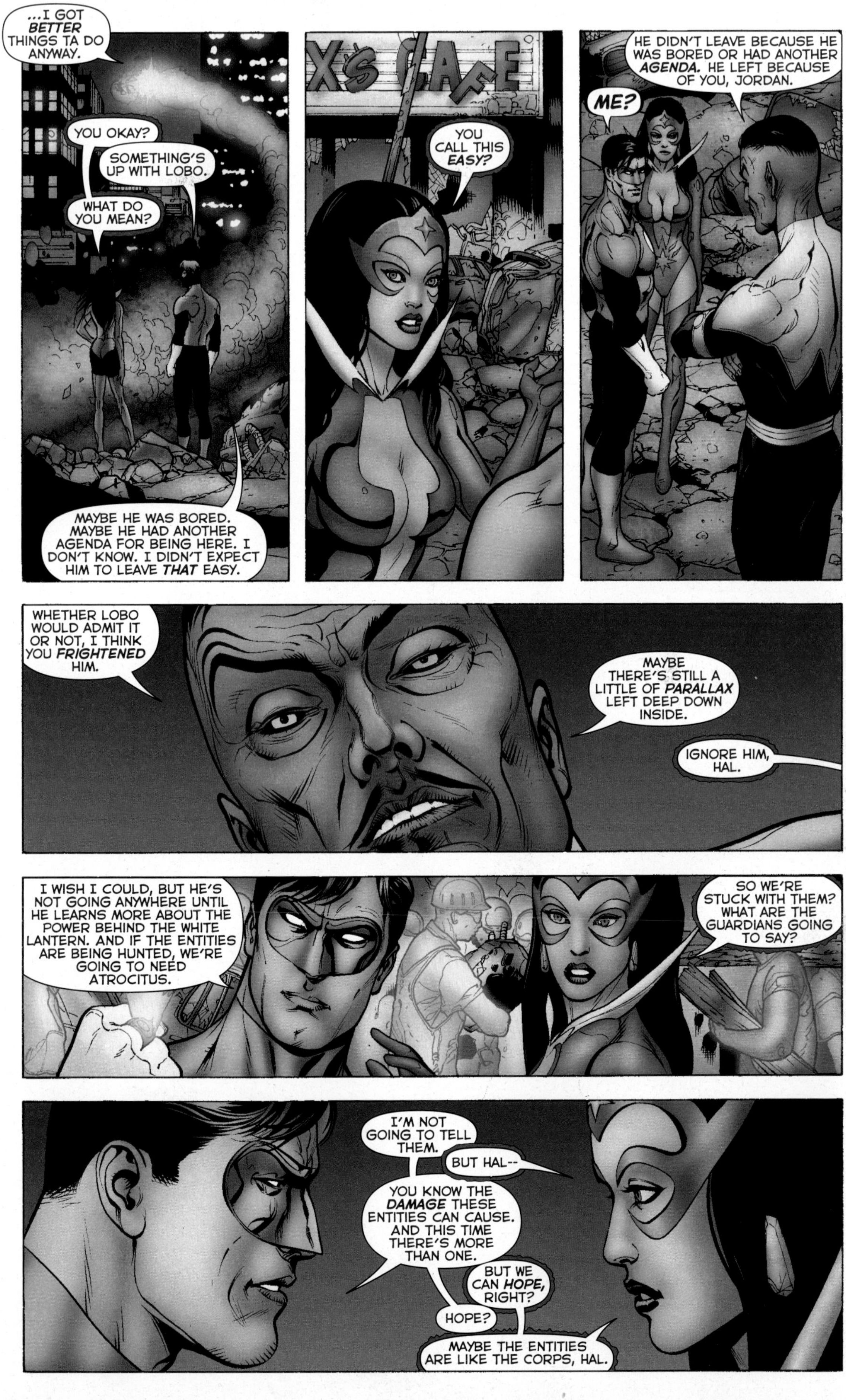
...I GOT BETTER THINGS TA DO ANYWAY.
YOU OKAY?
SOMETHING'S UP WITH LOBO.
WHAT DO YOU MEAN?
MAYBE HE WAS BORED. MAYBE HE HAD ANOTHER AGENDA FOR BEING HERE. I DON'T KNOW. I DIDN'T EXPECT HIM TO LEAVE THAT EASY.
X'S CAFE
YOU CALL THIS EASY?
HE DIDN'T LEAVE BECAUSE HE WAS BORED OR HAD ANOTHER AGENDA. HE LEFT BECAUSE OF YOU, JORDAN.
ME?
WHETHER LOBO WOULD ADMIT IT OR NOT, I THINK YOU FRIGHTENED HIM.
MAYBE THERE'S STILL A LITTLE OF PARALLAX LEFT DEEP DOWN INSIDE.
IGNORE HIM, HAL.
I WISH I COULD, BUT HE'S NOT GOING ANYWHERE UNTIL HE LEARNS MORE ABOUT THE POWER BEHIND THE WHITE LANTERN. AND IF THE ENTITIES ARE BEING HUNTED, WE'RE GOING TO NEED ATROCITUS.
SO WE'RE STUCK WITH THEM? WHAT ARE THE GUARDIANS GOING TO SAY?
I'M NOT GOING TO TELL THEM.
BUT HAL--
YOU KNOW THE DAMAGE THESE ENTITIES CAN CAUSE. AND THIS TIME THERE'S MORE THAN ONE.
BUT WE CAN HOPE, RIGHT?
HOPE?
MAYBE THE ENTITIES ARE LIKE THE CORPS, HAL.

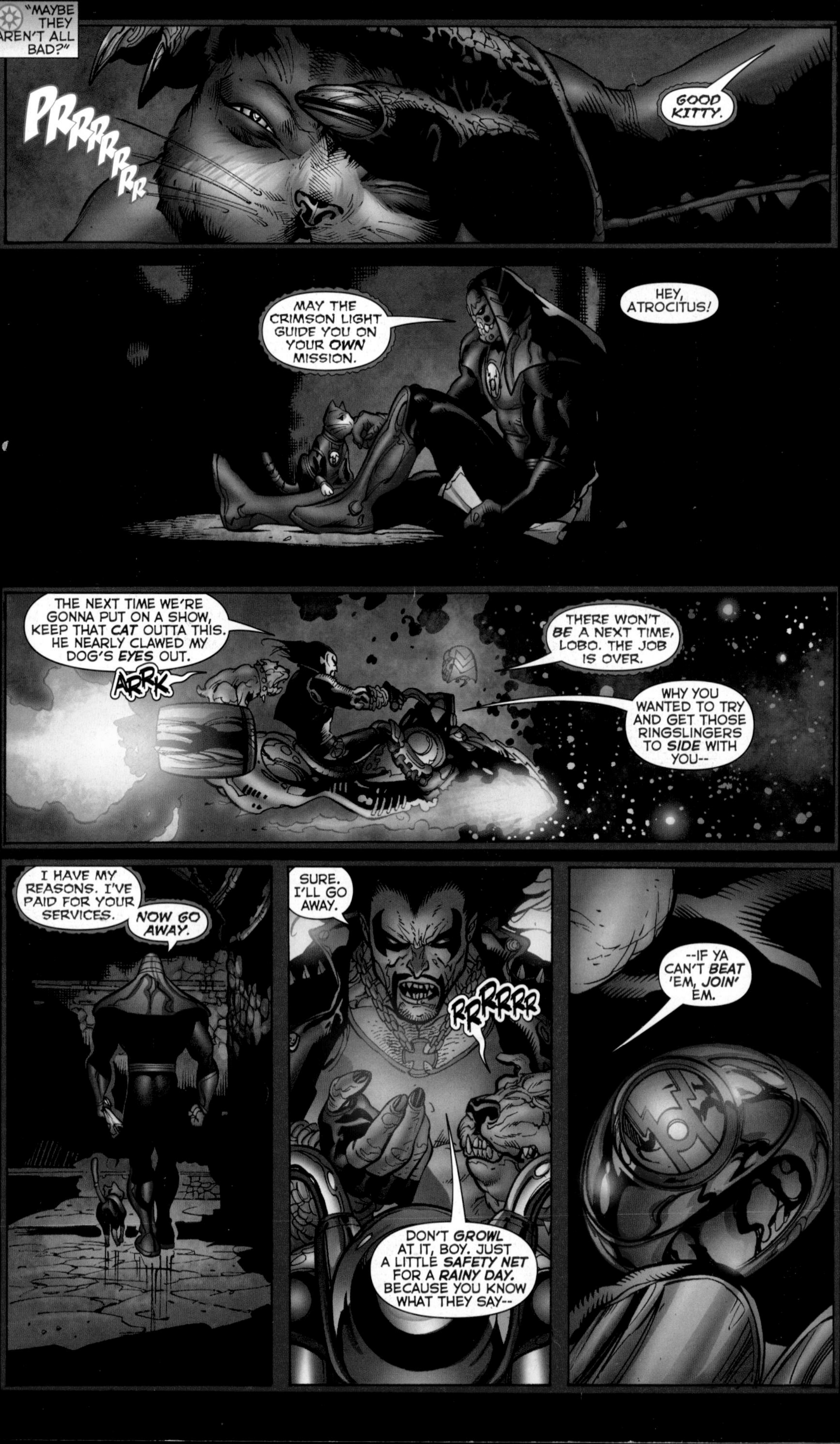
"MAYBE THEY AREN'T ALL BAD?"
PRRRRRRR
GOOD KITTY.
MAY THE CRIMSON LIGHT GUIDE YOU ON YOUR OWN MISSION.
HEY, ATROCITUS!
THE NEXT TIME WE'RE GONNA PUT ON A SHOW, KEEP THAT CAT OUTTA THIS. HE NEARLY CLAWED MY DOG'S EYES OUT.
ARRK
THERE WON'T BE A NEXT TIME, LOBO. THE JOB IS OVER.
WHY YOU WANTED TO TRY AND GET THOSE RINGSLINGERS TO SIDE WITH YOU--
I HAVE MY REASONS. I'VE PAID FOR YOUR SERVICES.
NOW GO AWAY.
SURE. I'LL GO AWAY.
RRRRRR
DON'T GROWL AT IT, BOY. JUST A LITTLE SAFETY NET FOR A RAINY DAY. BECAUSE YOU KNOW WHAT THEY SAY--
--IF YA CAN'T BEAT 'EM, JOIN' EM.

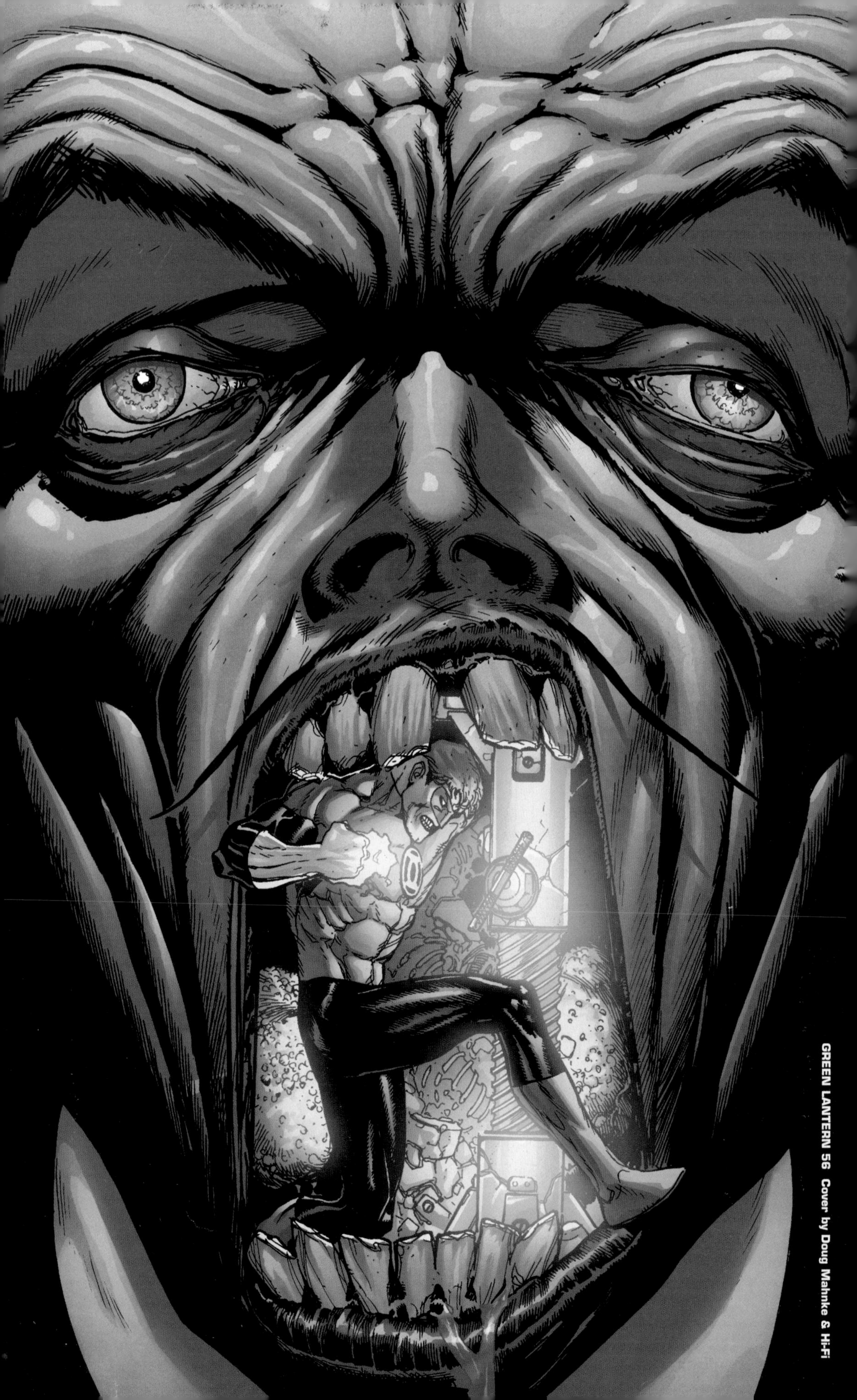
GREEN LANTERN 56 Cover by Doug Mahnke & Hi-Fi

THE NEW GUARDIANS
CHAPTER FOUR

Doug Mahnke Pencils
Christian Alamy, Tom Nguyen, Keith Champagne & Doug Mahnke Inks

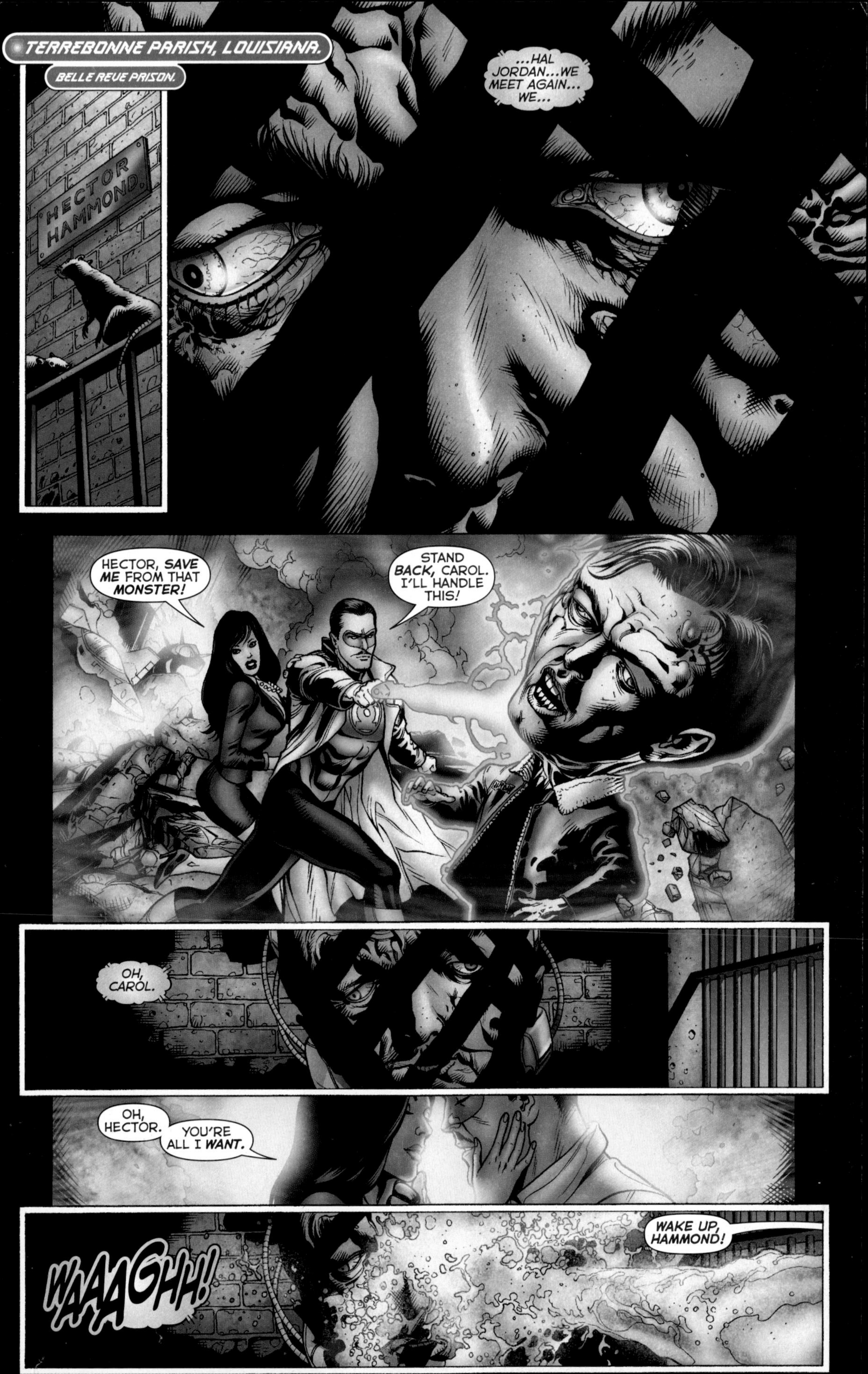
TERREBONNE PARISH, LOUISIANA.
BELLE REVE PRISON.
HECTOR HAMMOND
...HAL JORDAN...WE MEET AGAIN... WE...
HECTOR, SAVE ME FROM THAT MONSTER!
STAND BACK, CAROL. I'LL HANDLE THIS!
OH, CAROL.
OH, HECTOR.
YOU'RE ALL I WANT.
WAKE UP, HAMMOND!
WAAAGHH!

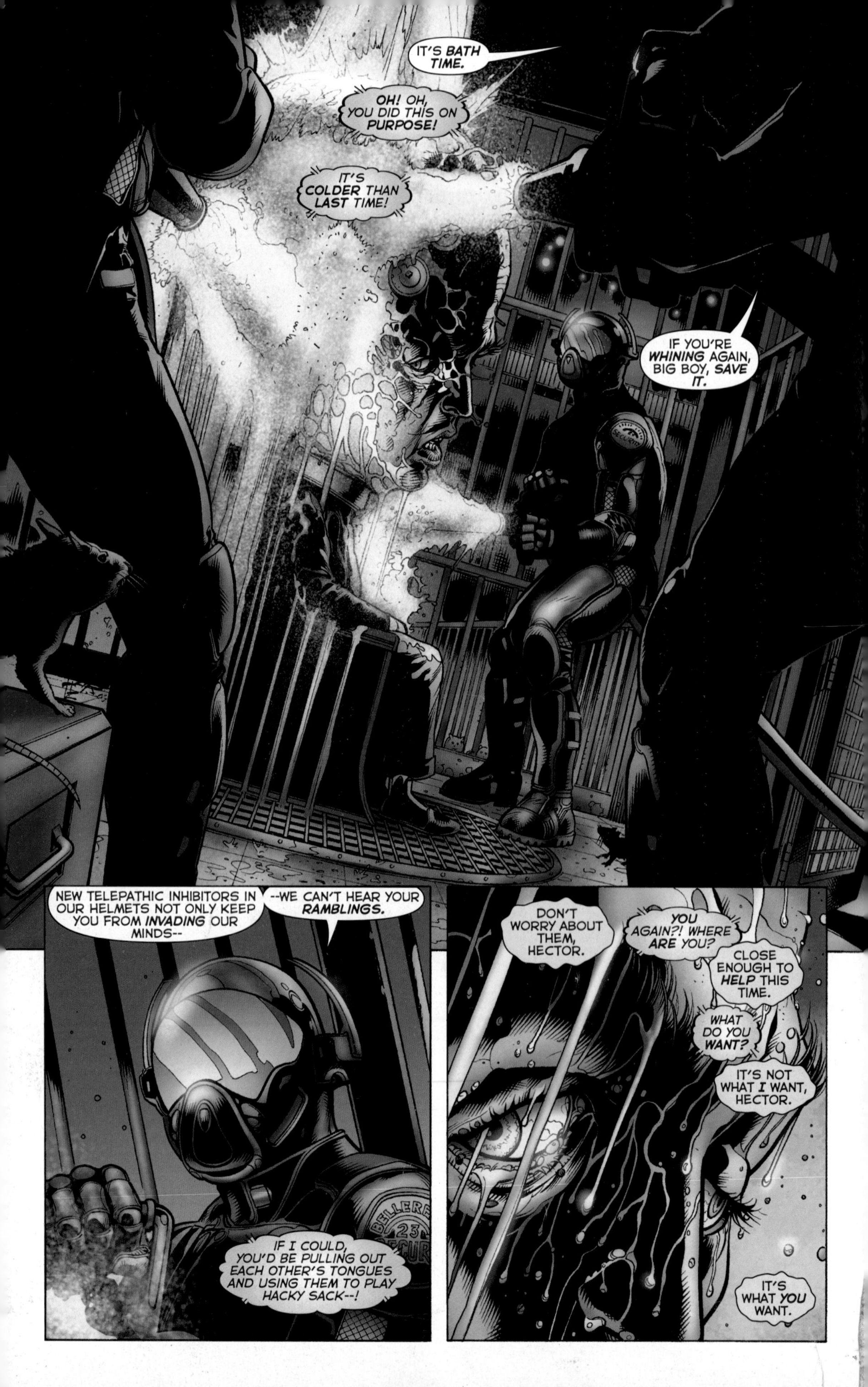
IT'S BATH TIME.
OH! OH, YOU DID THIS ON PURPOSE!
IT'S COLDER THAN LAST TIME!
IF YOU'RE WHINING AGAIN, BIG BOY, SAVE IT.
NEW TELEPATHIC INHIBITORS IN OUR HELMETS NOT ONLY KEEP YOU FROM INVADING OUR MINDS--
--WE CAN'T HEAR YOUR RAMBLINGS.
IF I COULD, YOU'D BE PULLING OUT EACH OTHER'S TONGUES AND USING THEM TO PLAY HACKY SACK--!
DON'T WORRY ABOUT THEM, HECTOR.
YOU AGAIN?! WHERE ARE YOU?
CLOSE ENOUGH TO HELP THIS TIME.
WHAT DO YOU WANT?
IT'S NOT WHAT I WANT, HECTOR.
IT'S WHAT YOU WANT.

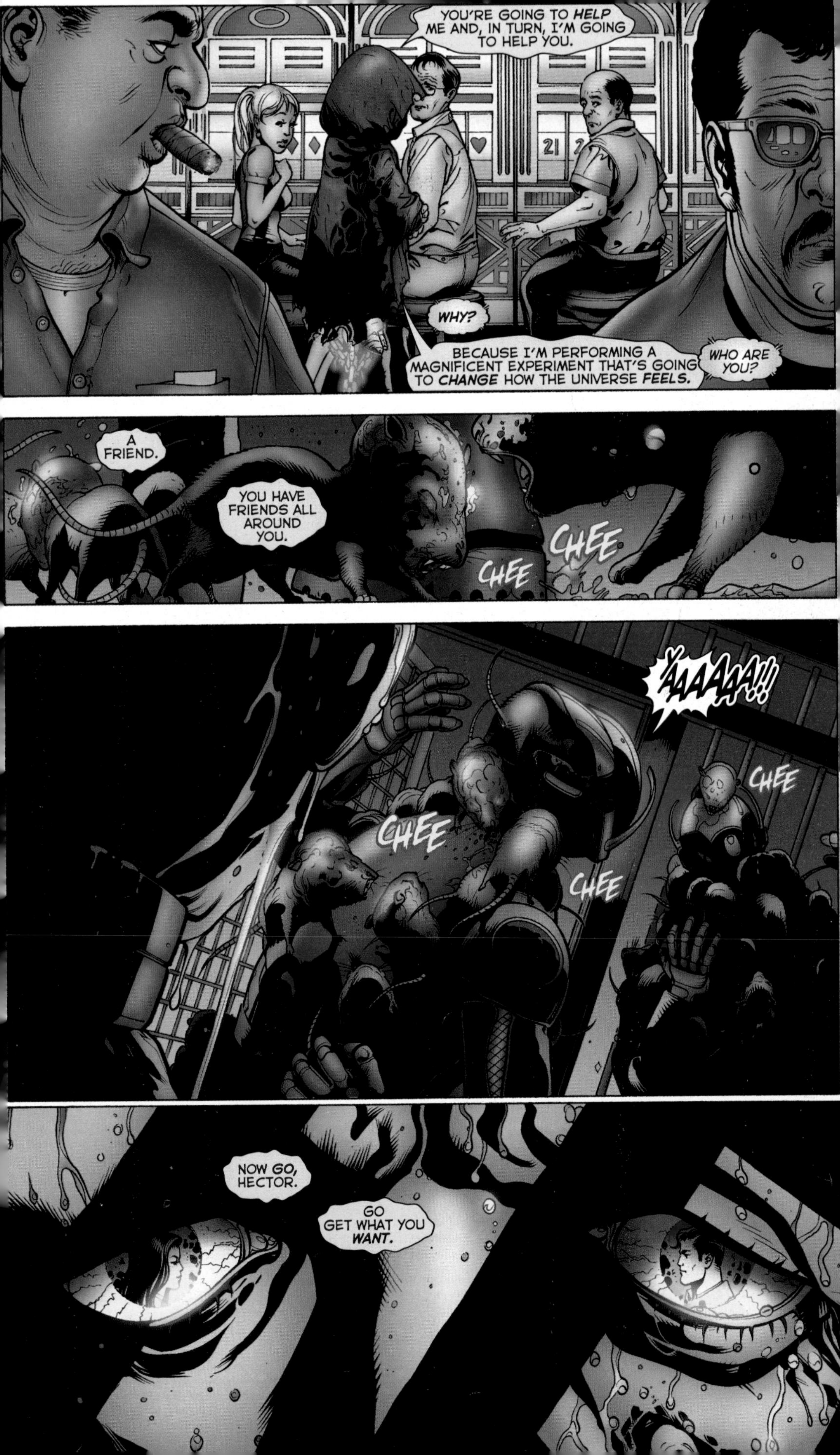

YOU'RE GOING TO HELP ME AND, IN TURN, I'M GOING TO HELP YOU.
WHY?
BECAUSE I'M PERFORMING A MAGNIFICENT EXPERIMENT THAT'S GOING TO CHANGE HOW THE UNIVERSE FEELS.
WHO ARE YOU?
A FRIEND.
YOU HAVE FRIENDS ALL AROUND YOU.
CHEE
CHEE
YAAAAAA!!
CHEE
CHEE
CHEE
NOW GO, HECTOR.
GO GET WHAT YOU WANT.

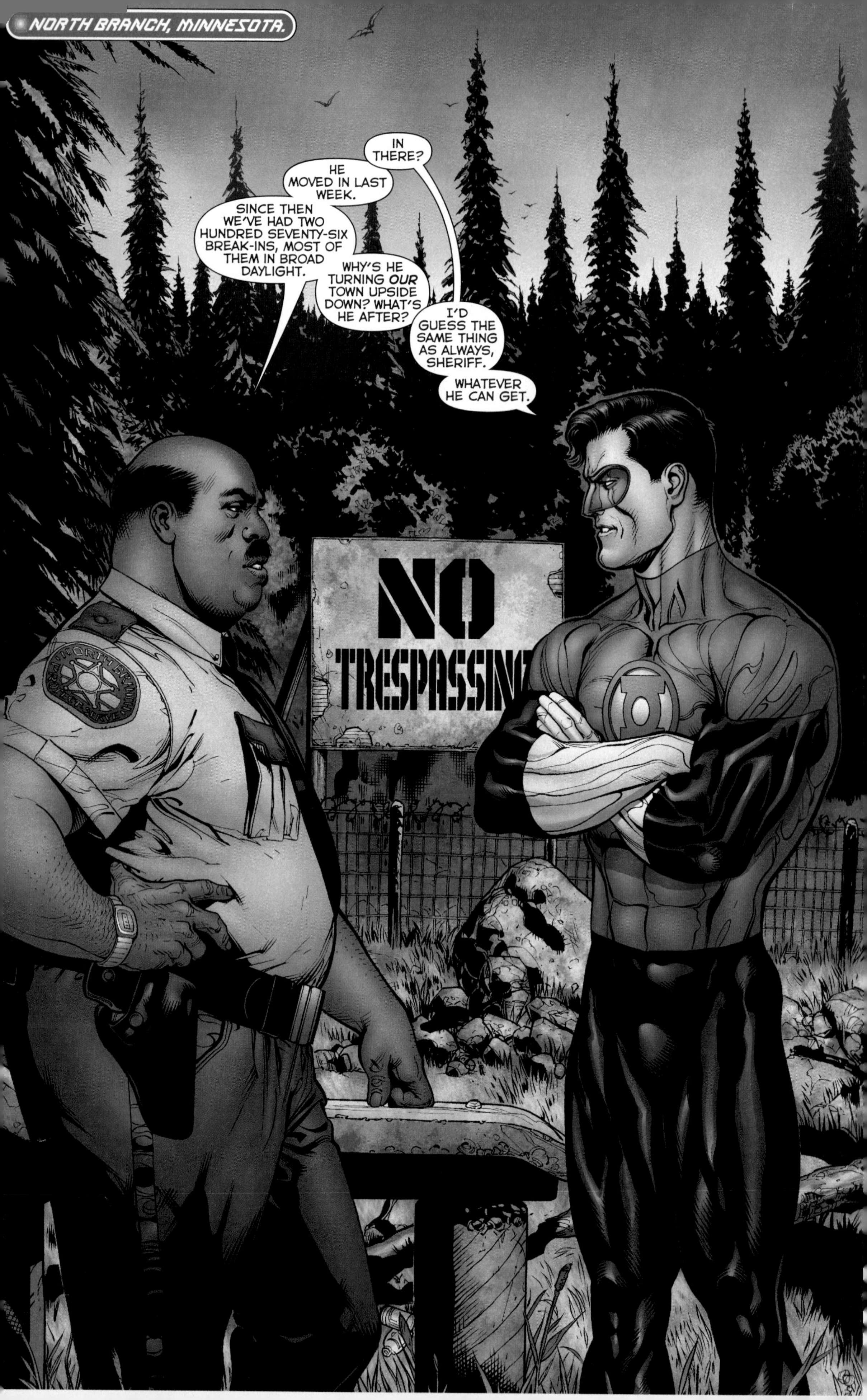
NORTH BRANCH, MINNESOTA.
IN THERE?
HE MOVED IN LAST WEEK.
SINCE THEN WE'VE HAD TWO HUNDRED SEVENTY-SIX BREAK-INS, MOST OF THEM IN BROAD DAYLIGHT.
WHY'S HE TURNING OUR TOWN UPSIDE DOWN? WHAT'S HE AFTER?
I'D GUESS THE SAME THING AS ALWAYS, SHERIFF.
WHATEVER HE CAN GET.
NO TRESPASSING

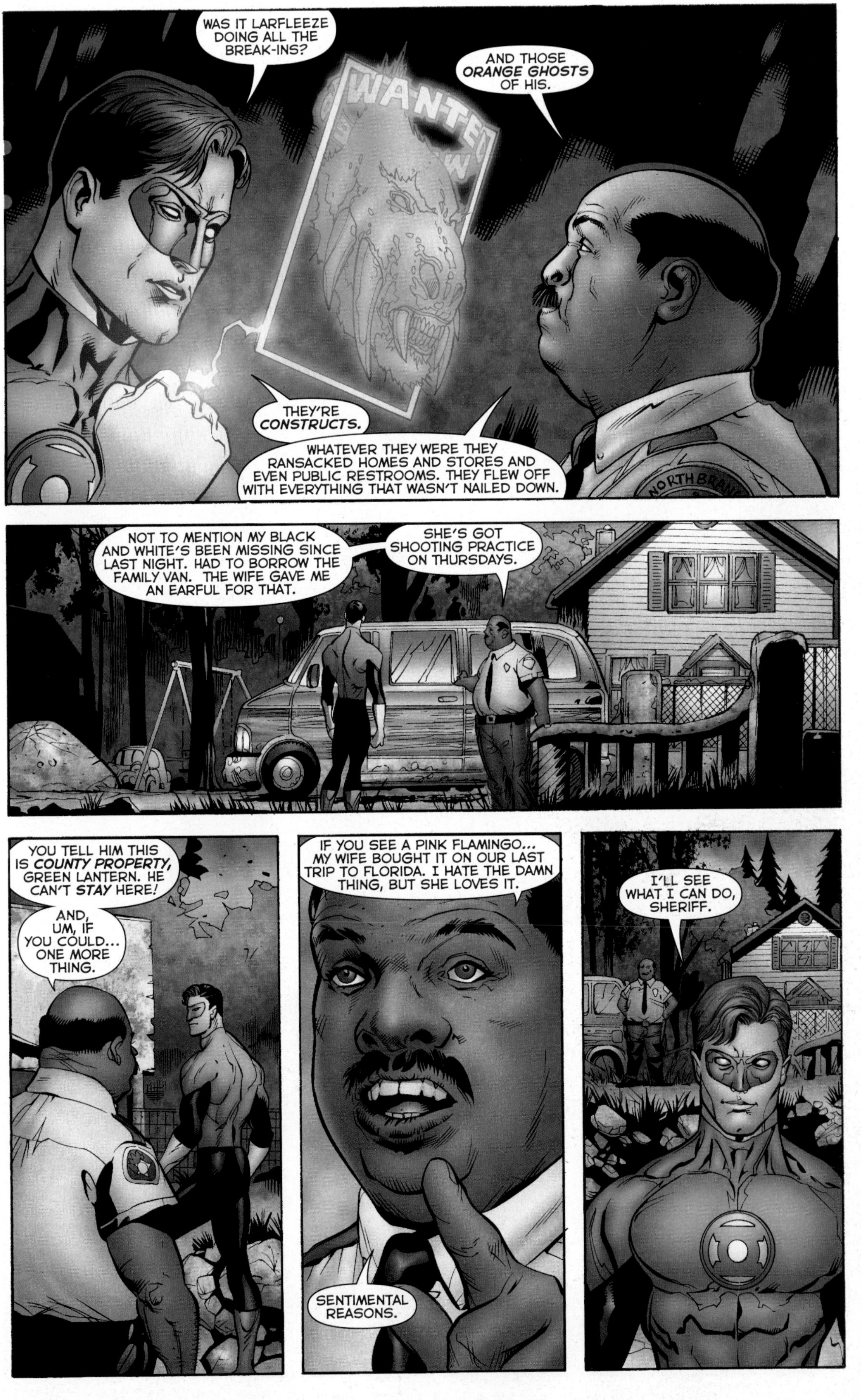

WAS IT LARFLEEZE DOING ALL THE BREAK-INS?
AND THOSE ORANGE GHOSTS OF HIS.
WANTED
THEY'RE CONSTRUCTS.
WHATEVER THEY WERE THEY RANSACKED HOMES AND STORES AND EVEN PUBLIC RESTROOMS. THEY FLEW OFF WITH EVERYTHING THAT WASN'T NAILED DOWN.
NOT TO MENTION MY BLACK AND WHITE'S BEEN MISSING SINCE LAST NIGHT. HAD TO BORROW THE FAMILY VAN. THE WIFE GAVE ME AN EARFUL FOR THAT.
SHE'S GOT SHOOTING PRACTICE ON THURSDAYS.
YOU TELL HIM THIS IS COUNTY PROPERTY, GREEN LANTERN. HE CAN'T STAY HERE!
AND, UM, IF YOU COULD... ONE MORE THING.
IF YOU SEE A PINK FLAMINGO... MY WIFE BOUGHT IT ON OUR LAST TRIP TO FLORIDA. I HATE THE DAMN THING, BUT SHE LOVES IT.
SENTIMENTAL REASONS.
I'LL SEE WHAT I CAN DO, SHERIFF.

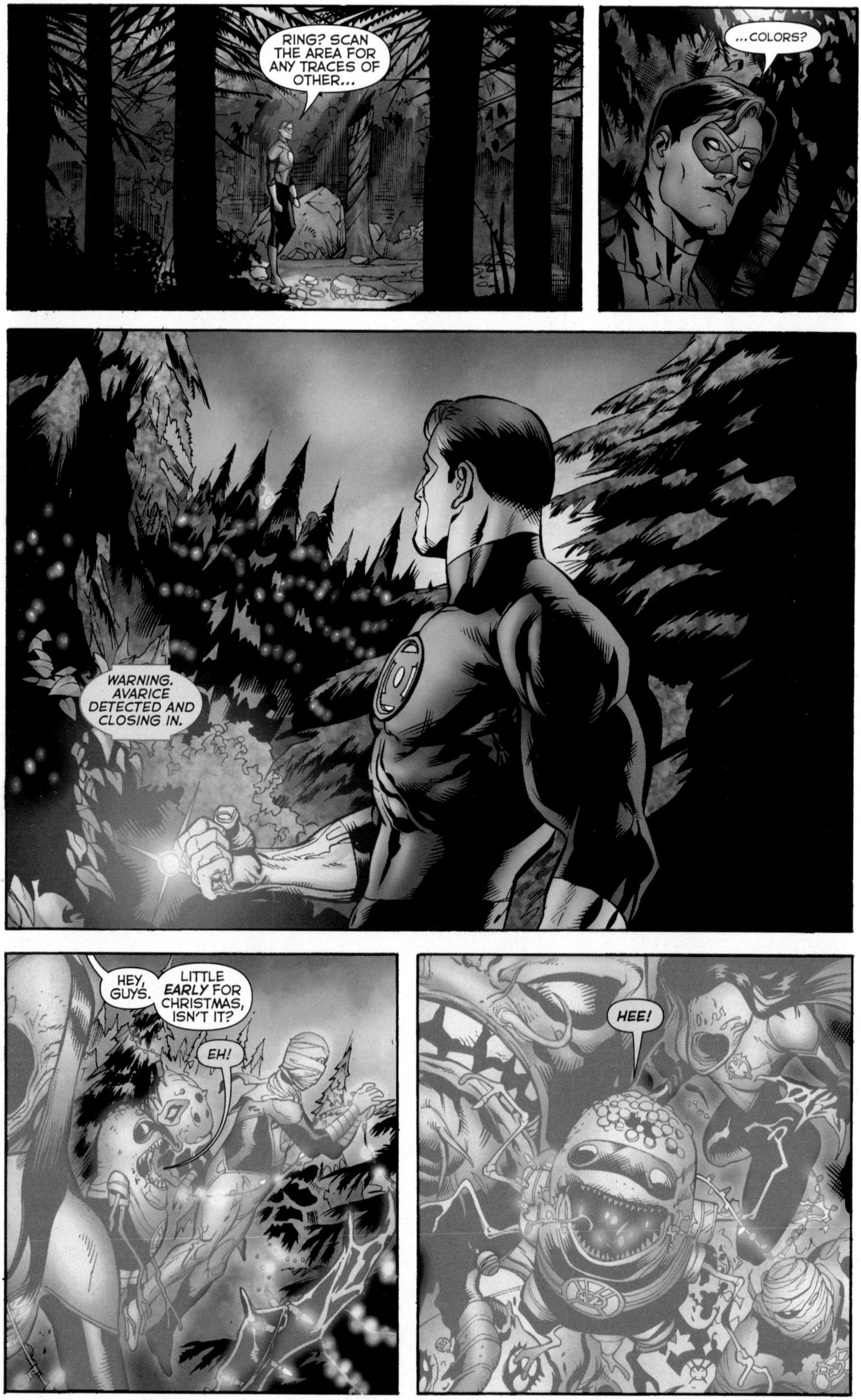

RING? SCAN THE AREA FOR ANY TRACES OF OTHER...
...COLORS?
WARNING. AVARICE DETECTED AND CLOSING IN.
HEY, GUYS.
LITTLE EARLY FOR CHRISTMAS, ISN'T IT?
EH!
HEE!

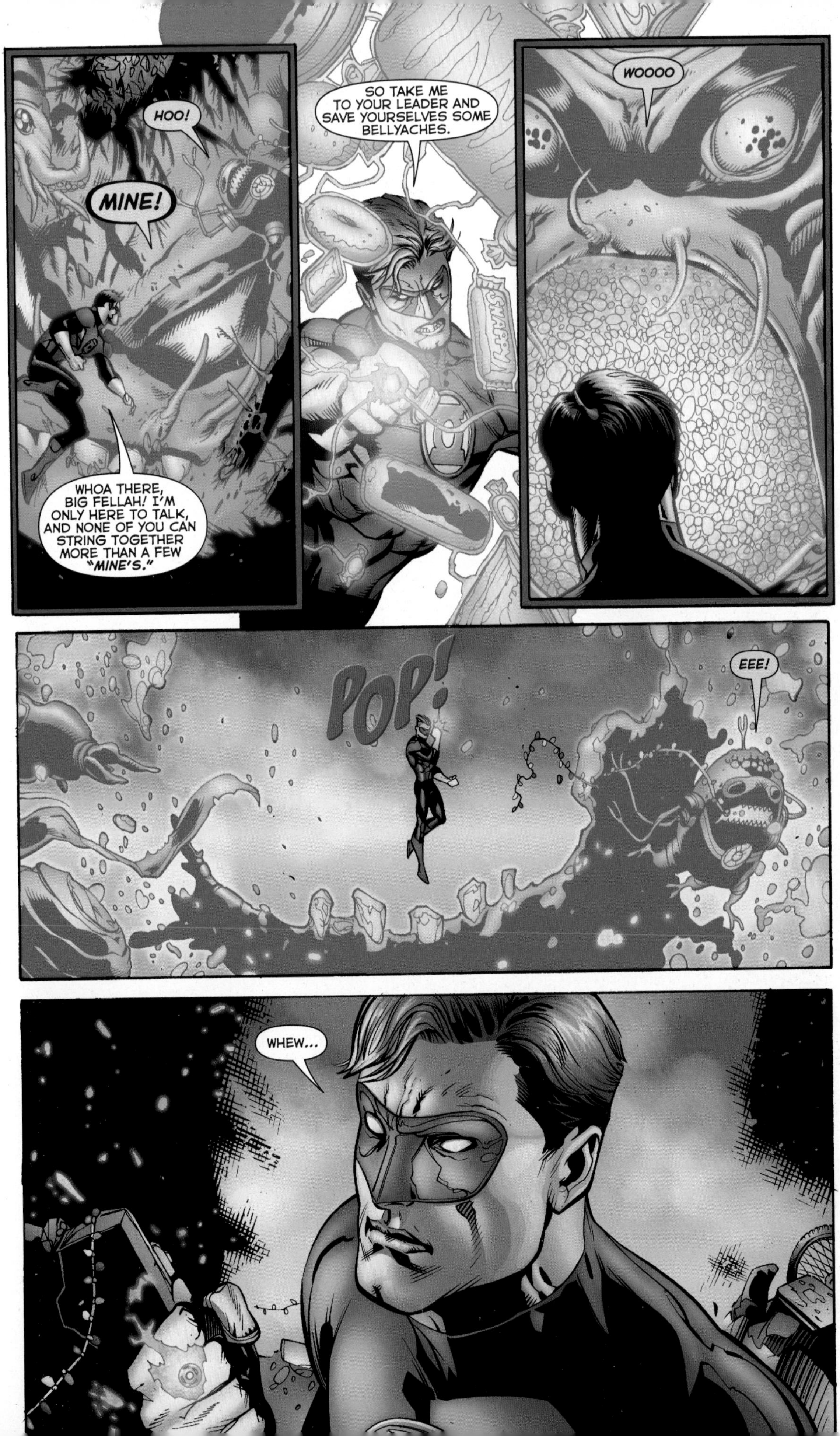
HOO!
MINE!
WHOA THERE, BIG FELLAH! I'M ONLY HERE TO TALK, AND NONE OF YOU CAN STRING TOGETHER MORE THAN A FEW "MINE'S."
SO TAKE ME TO YOUR LEADER AND SAVE YOURSELVES SOME BELLYACHES.
WOOOO
POP!
EEE!
WHEW...

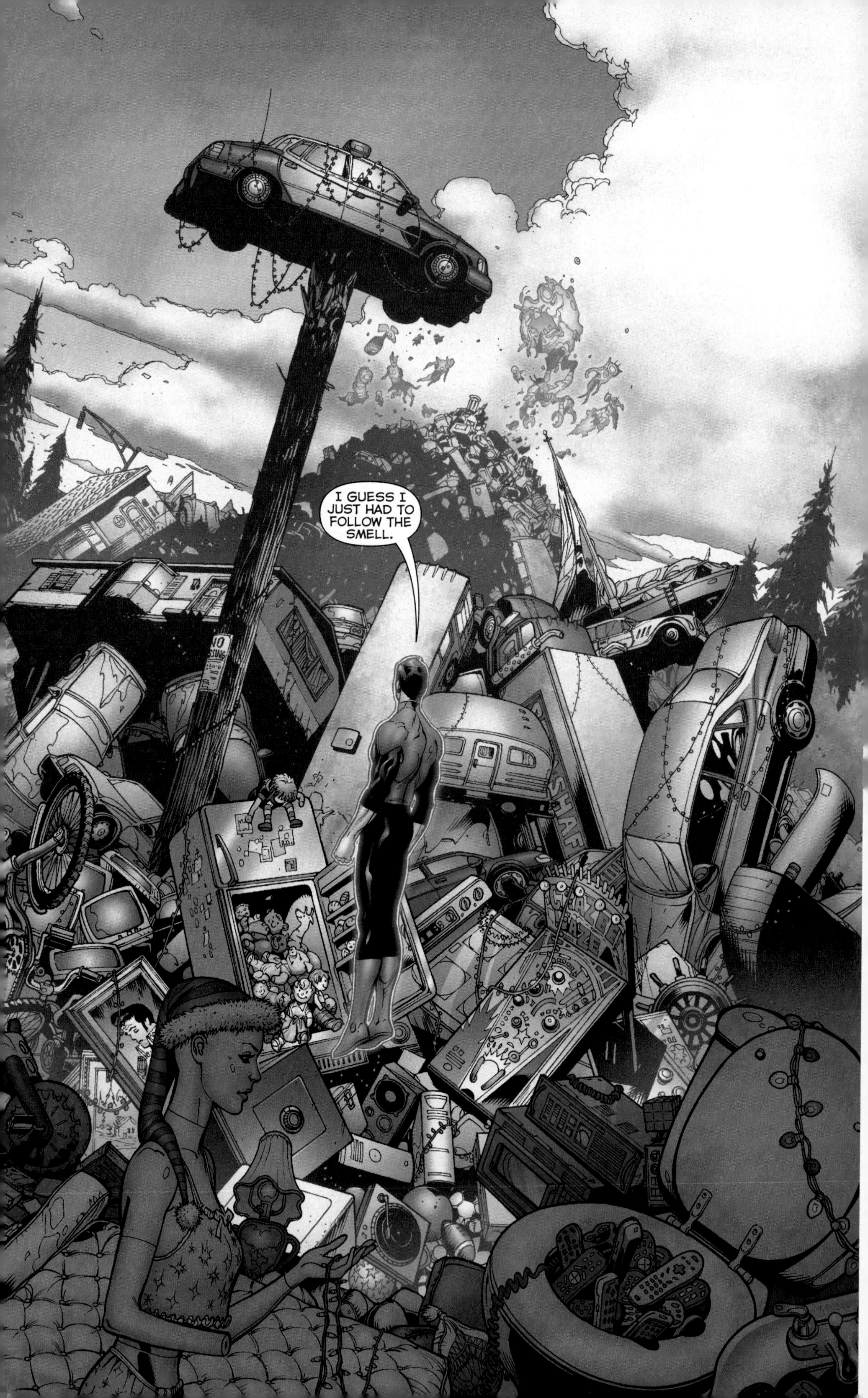
I GUESS I JUST HAD TO FOLLOW THE SMELL.

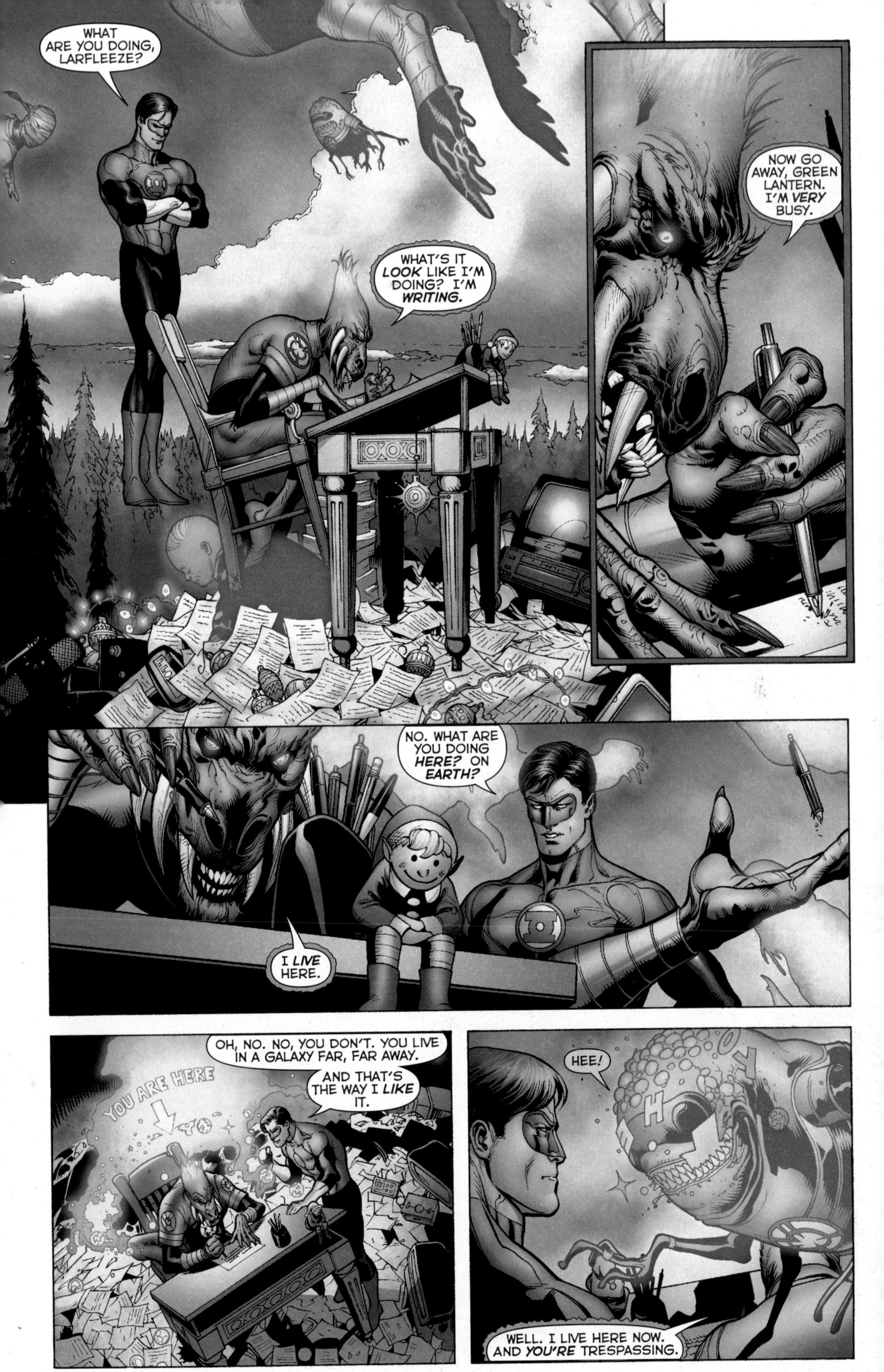
WHAT ARE YOU DOING, LARFLEEZE?
WHAT'S IT LOOK LIKE I'M DOING? I'M WRITING.
NOW GO AWAY, GREEN LANTERN. I'M VERY BUSY.
NO. WHAT ARE YOU DOING HERE? ON EARTH?
I LIVE HERE.
OH, NO. NO, YOU DON'T. YOU LIVE IN A GALAXY FAR, FAR AWAY.
AND THAT'S THE WAY I LIKE IT.
YOU ARE HERE
HEE!
WELL. I LIVE HERE NOW. AND YOU'RE TRESPASSING.

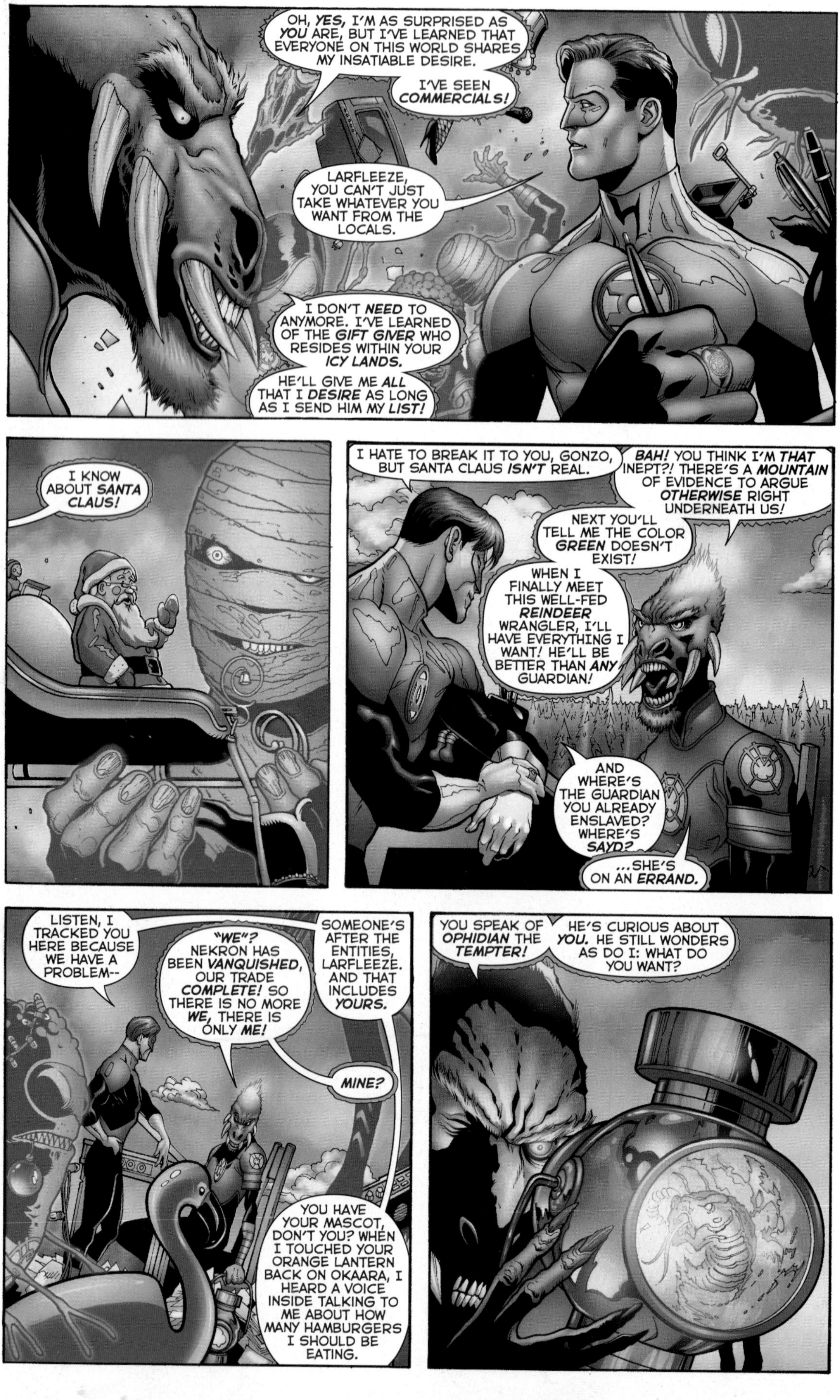

OH, YES, I'M AS SURPRISED AS YOU ARE, BUT I'VE LEARNED THAT EVERYONE ON THIS WORLD SHARES MY INSATIABLE DESIRE.
I'VE SEEN COMMERCIALS!
LARFLEEZE, YOU CAN'T JUST TAKE WHATEVER YOU WANT FROM THE LOCALS.
I DON'T NEED TO ANYMORE. I'VE LEARNED OF THE GIFT GIVER WHO RESIDES WITHIN YOUR ICY LANDS.
HE'LL GIVE ME ALL THAT I DESIRE AS LONG AS I SEND HIM MY LIST!
I KNOW ABOUT SANTA CLAUS!
I HATE TO BREAK IT TO YOU, GONZO, BUT SANTA CLAUS ISN'T REAL.
BAH! YOU THINK I'M THAT INEPT?! THERE'S A MOUNTAIN OF EVIDENCE TO ARGUE OTHERWISE RIGHT UNDERNEATH US!
NEXT YOU'LL TELL ME THE COLOR GREEN DOESN'T EXIST!
WHEN I FINALLY MEET THIS WELL-FED REINDEER WRANGLER, I'LL HAVE EVERYTHING I WANT! HE'LL BE BETTER THAN ANY GUARDIAN!
AND WHERE'S THE GUARDIAN YOU ALREADY ENSLAVED? WHERE'S SAYD?
...SHE'S ON AN ERRAND.
LISTEN, I TRACKED YOU HERE BECAUSE WE HAVE A PROBLEM--
"WE"? NEKRON HAS BEEN VANQUISHED, OUR TRADE COMPLETE! SO THERE IS NO MORE WE, THERE IS ONLY ME!
SOMEONE'S AFTER THE ENTITIES, LARFLEEZE. AND THAT INCLUDES YOURS.
MINE?
YOU HAVE YOUR MASCOT, DON'T YOU? WHEN I TOUCHED YOUR ORANGE LANTERN BACK ON OKAARA, I HEARD A VOICE INSIDE TALKING TO ME ABOUT HOW MANY HAMBURGERS I SHOULD BE EATING.
YOU SPEAK OF OPHIDIAN THE TEMPTER!
HE'S CURIOUS ABOUT YOU. HE STILL WONDERS AS DO I: WHAT DO YOU WANT?

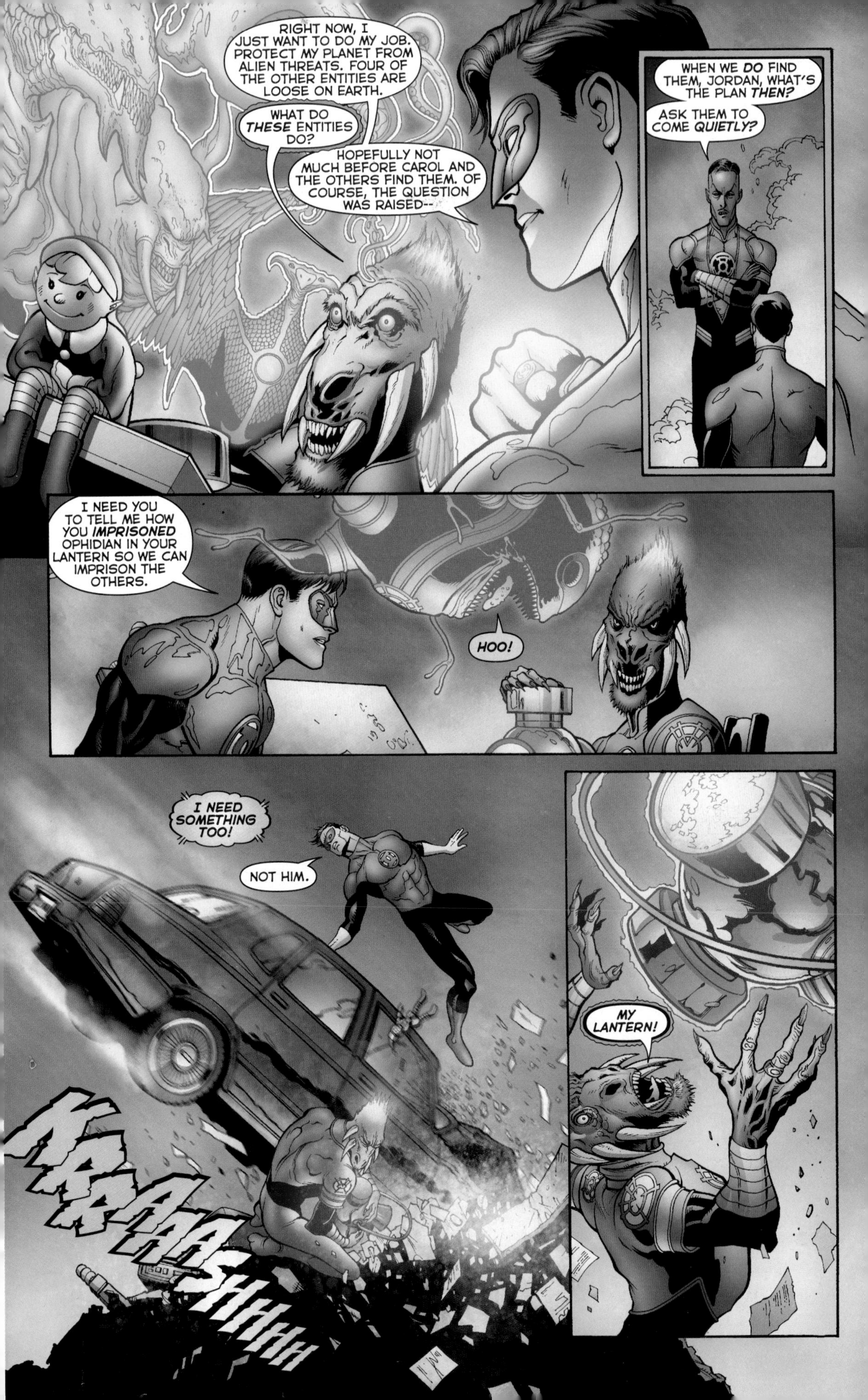
RIGHT NOW, I JUST WANT TO DO MY JOB. PROTECT MY PLANET FROM ALIEN THREATS. FOUR OF THE OTHER ENTITIES ARE LOOSE ON EARTH.
WHAT DO *THESE* ENTITIES DO?
HOPEFULLY NOT MUCH BEFORE CAROL AND THE OTHERS FIND THEM. OF COURSE, THE QUESTION WAS RAISED--
WHEN WE *DO* FIND THEM, JORDAN, WHAT'S THE PLAN *THEN?*
ASK THEM TO COME *QUIETLY?*
I NEED YOU TO TELL ME HOW YOU *IMPRISONED* OPHIDIAN IN YOUR LANTERN SO WE CAN IMPRISON THE OTHERS.
HOO!
I NEED SOMETHING TOO!
NOT HIM.
KRAASHHHH
MY LANTERN!

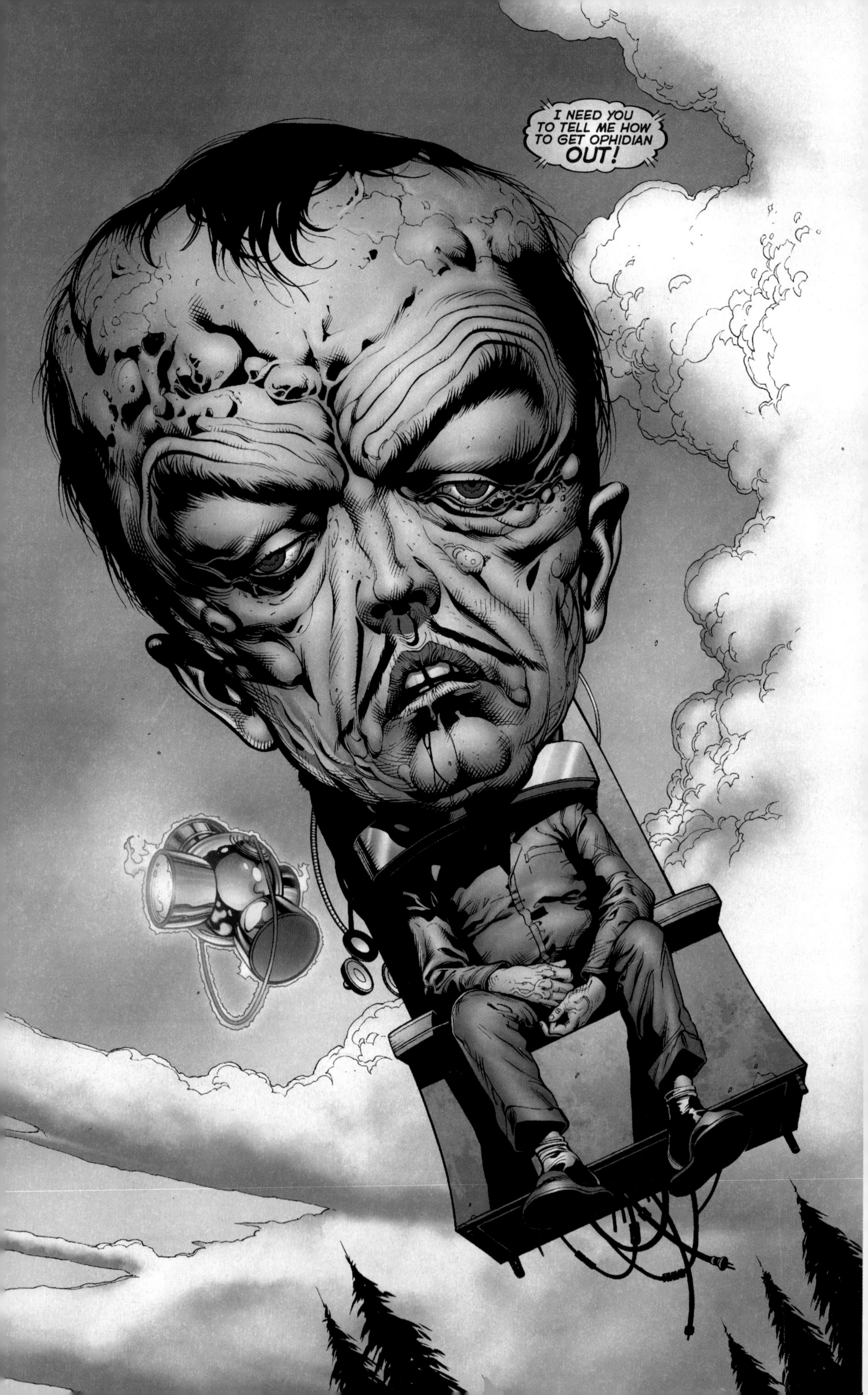
I NEED YOU TO TELL ME HOW TO GET OPHIDIAN OUT!

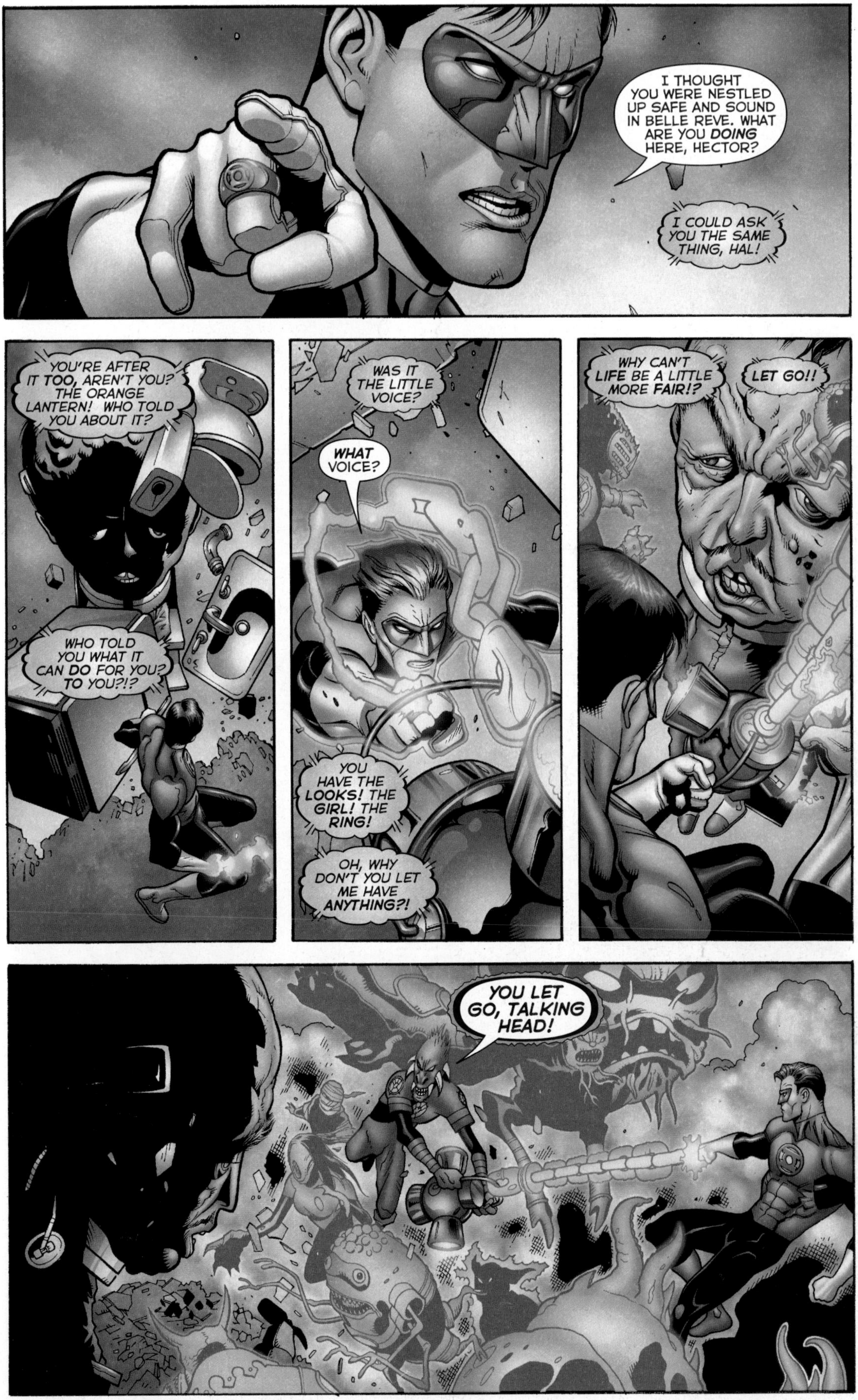
I THOUGHT YOU WERE NESTLED UP SAFE AND SOUND IN BELLE REVE. WHAT ARE YOU DOING HERE, HECTOR?
I COULD ASK YOU THE SAME THING, HAL!
YOU'RE AFTER IT TOO, AREN'T YOU? THE ORANGE LANTERN! WHO TOLD YOU ABOUT IT?
WHO TOLD YOU WHAT IT CAN DO FOR YOU? TO YOU?!?
WAS IT THE LITTLE VOICE?
WHAT VOICE?
YOU HAVE THE LOOKS! THE GIRL! THE RING!
OH, WHY DON'T YOU LET ME HAVE ANYTHING?!
WHY CAN'T LIFE BE A LITTLE MORE FAIR!?
LET GO!!
YOU LET GO, TALKING HEAD!

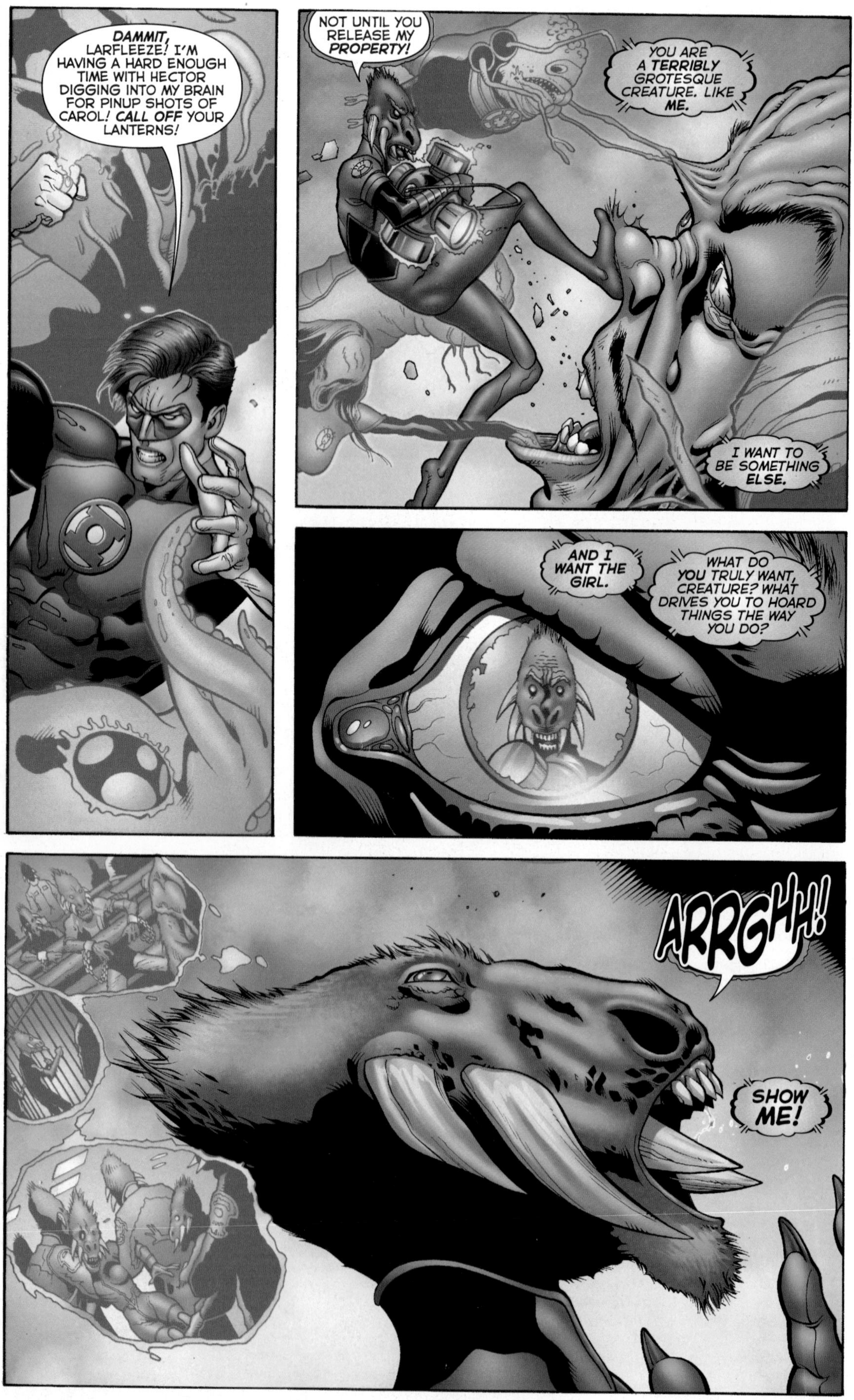
DAMMIT, LARFLEEZE! I'M HAVING A HARD ENOUGH TIME WITH HECTOR DIGGING INTO MY BRAIN FOR PINUP SHOTS OF CAROL! CALL OFF YOUR LANTERNS!
NOT UNTIL YOU RELEASE MY PROPERTY!
YOU ARE A TERRIBLY GROTESQUE CREATURE. LIKE ME.
I WANT TO BE SOMETHING ELSE.
AND I WANT THE GIRL.
WHAT DO YOU TRULY WANT, CREATURE? WHAT DRIVES YOU TO HOARD THINGS THE WAY YOU DO?
ARRGHH!
SHOW ME!

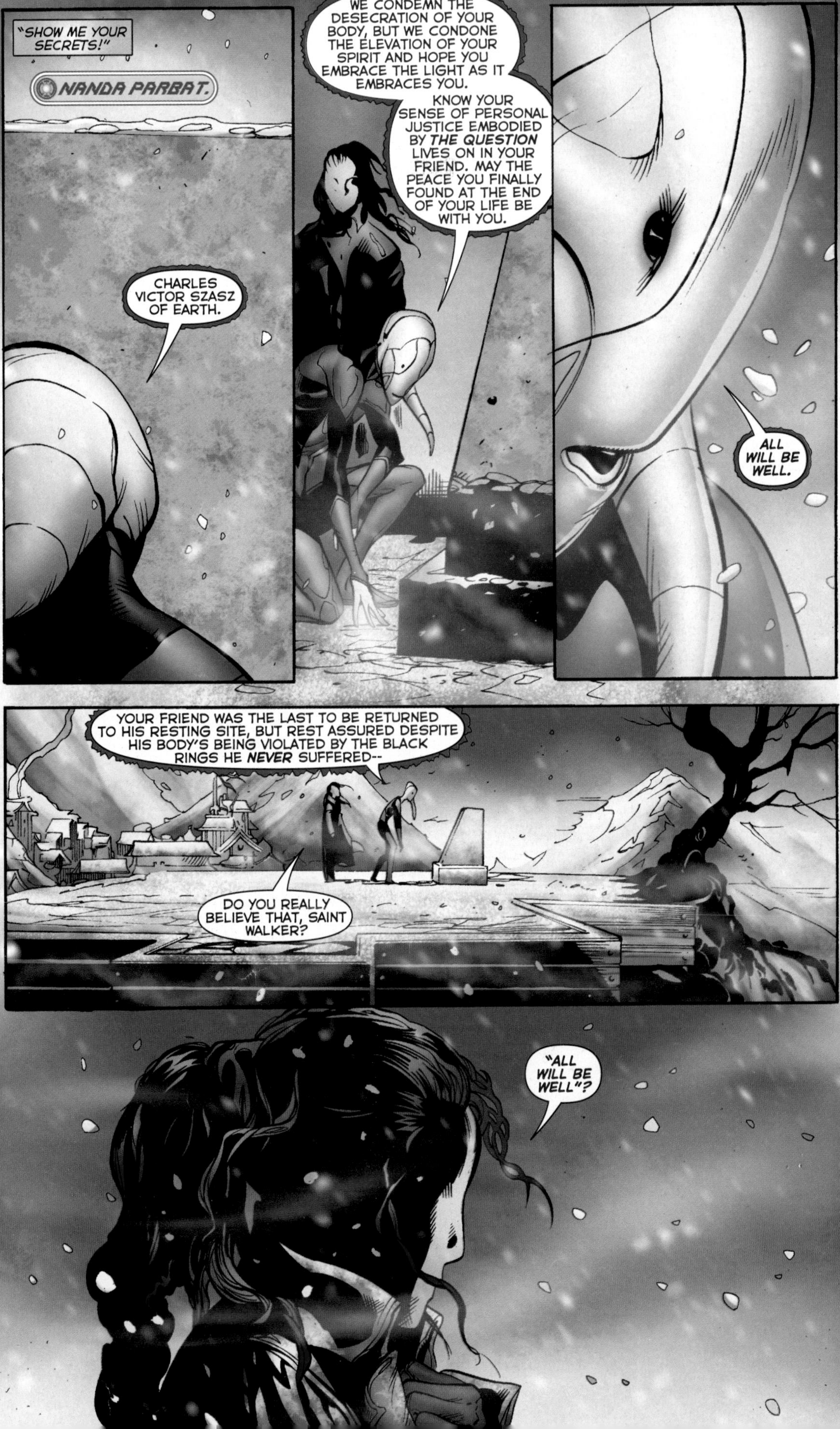
"SHOW ME YOUR SECRETS!"
NANDA PARBAT.
CHARLES VICTOR SZASZ OF EARTH.
WE CONDEMN THE DESECRATION OF YOUR BODY, BUT WE CONDONE THE ELEVATION OF YOUR SPIRIT AND HOPE YOU EMBRACE THE LIGHT AS IT EMBRACES YOU.
KNOW YOUR SENSE OF PERSONAL JUSTICE EMBODIED BY THE QUESTION LIVES ON IN YOUR FRIEND. MAY THE PEACE YOU FINALLY FOUND AT THE END OF YOUR LIFE BE WITH YOU.
ALL WILL BE WELL.
YOUR FRIEND WAS THE LAST TO BE RETURNED TO HIS RESTING SITE, BUT REST ASSURED DESPITE HIS BODY'S BEING VIOLATED BY THE BLACK RINGS HE NEVER SUFFERED--
DO YOU REALLY BELIEVE THAT, SAINT WALKER?
"ALL WILL BE WELL"?

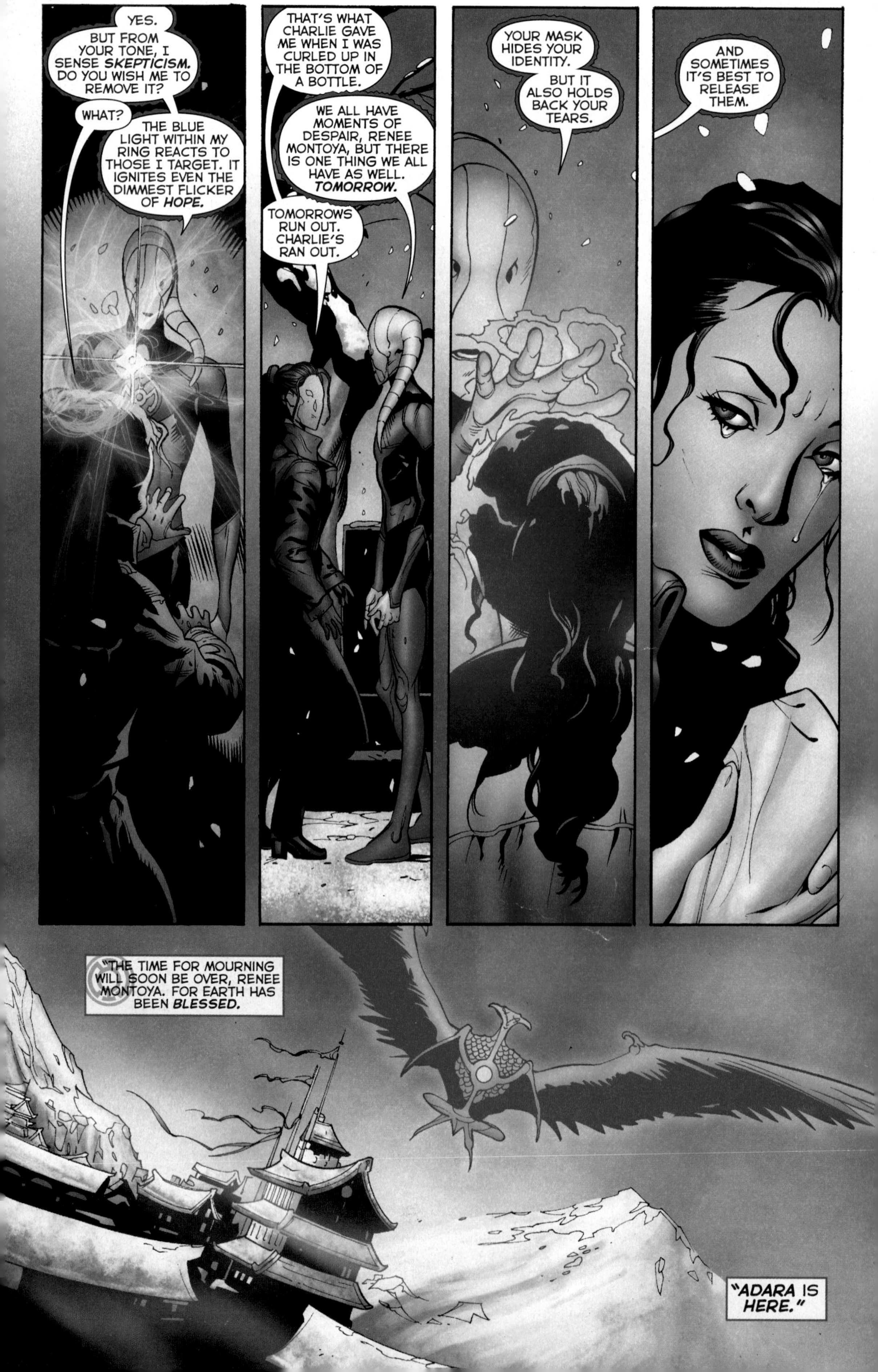

YES. BUT FROM YOUR TONE, I SENSE SKEPTICISM. DO YOU WISH ME TO REMOVE IT?
WHAT?
THE BLUE LIGHT WITHIN MY RING REACTS TO THOSE I TARGET. IT IGNITES EVEN THE DIMMEST FLICKER OF HOPE.
THAT'S WHAT CHARLIE GAVE ME WHEN I WAS CURLED UP IN THE BOTTOM OF A BOTTLE.
WE ALL HAVE MOMENTS OF DESPAIR, RENEE MONTOYA, BUT THERE IS ONE THING WE ALL HAVE AS WELL. TOMORROW.
TOMORROWS RUN OUT. CHARLIE'S RAN OUT.
YOUR MASK HIDES YOUR IDENTITY.
BUT IT ALSO HOLDS BACK YOUR TEARS.
AND SOMETIMES IT'S BEST TO RELEASE THEM.
"THE TIME FOR MOURNING WILL SOON BE OVER, RENEE MONTOYA. FOR EARTH HAS BEEN BLESSED.
"ADARA IS HERE."

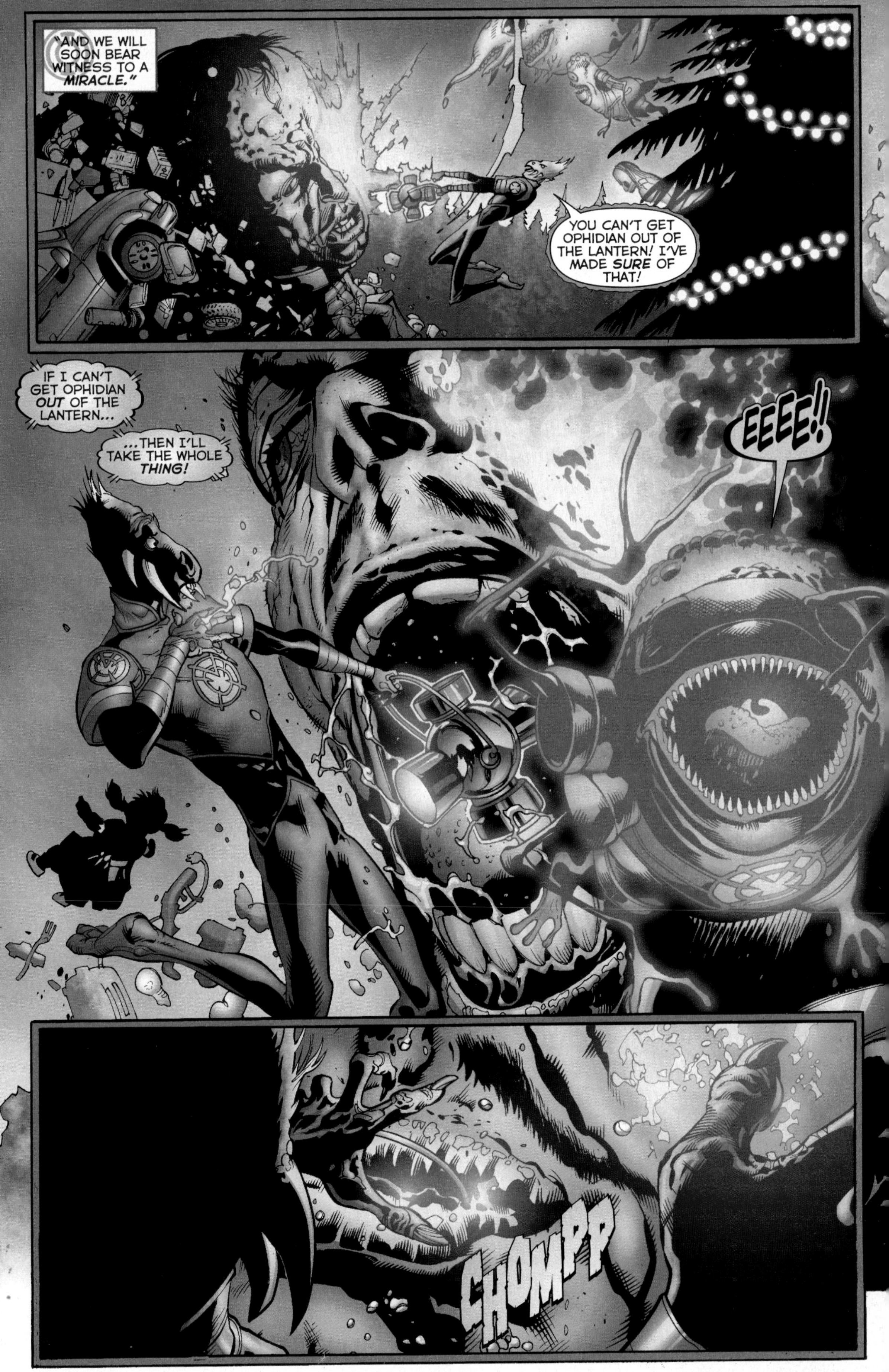
"AND WE WILL SOON BEAR WITNESS TO A *MIRACLE.*"
YOU CAN'T GET OPHIDIAN OUT OF THE LANTERN! I'VE MADE *SURE* OF THAT!
IF I CAN'T GET OPHIDIAN *OUT* OF THE LANTERN...
...THEN I'LL TAKE THE WHOLE *THING!*
EEEE!!
CHOMPP

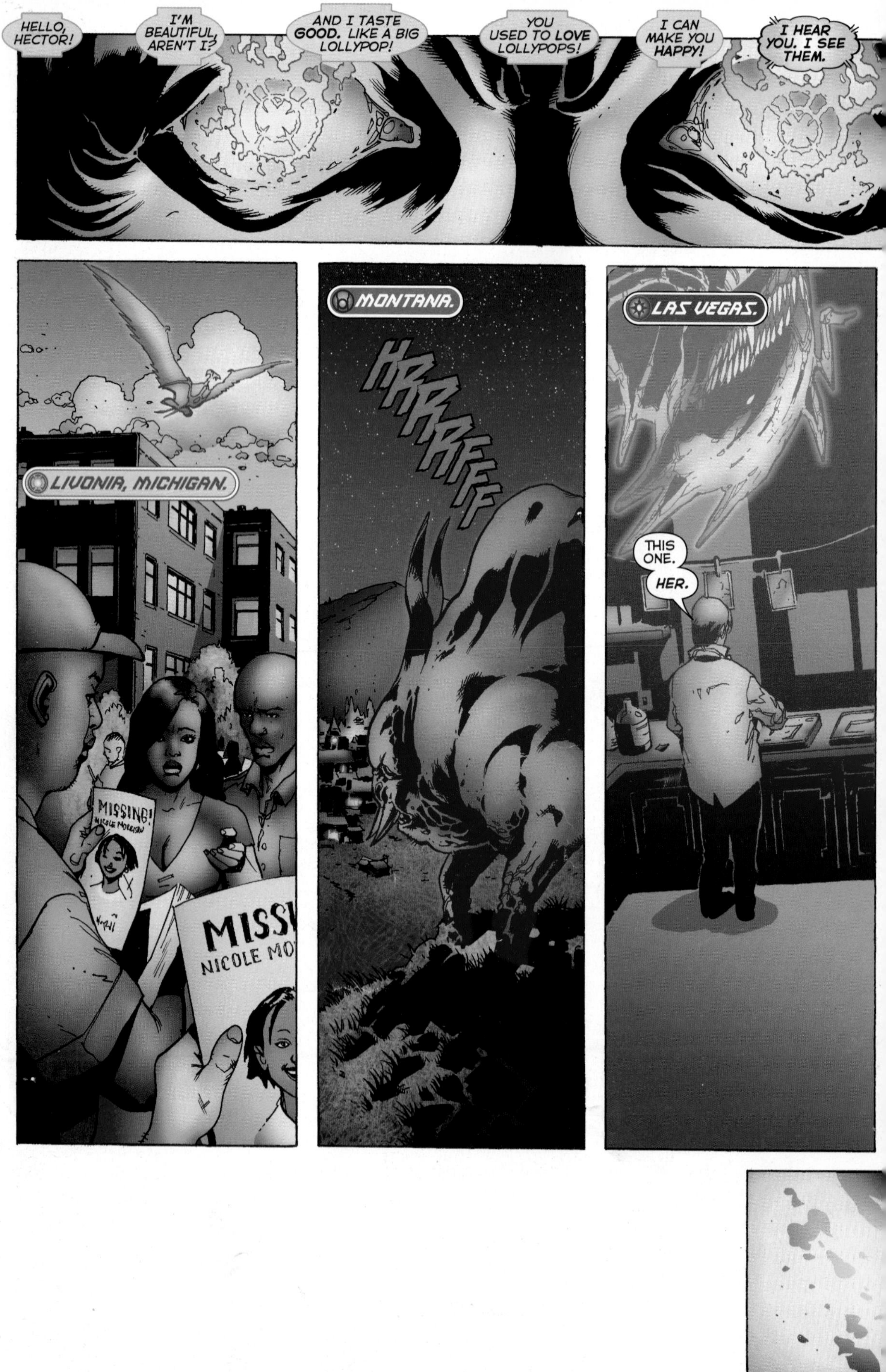
HELLO, HECTOR!
I'M BEAUTIFUL, AREN'T I?
AND I TASTE GOOD. LIKE A BIG LOLLYPOP!
YOU USED TO LOVE LOLLYPOPS!
I CAN MAKE YOU HAPPY!
I HEAR YOU. I SEE THEM.
LIVONIA, MICHIGAN.
MISSING!
NICOLE MORRISON
MISS
NICOLE MO
MONTANA.
HRRRFFF
LAS VEGAS.
THIS ONE.
HER.

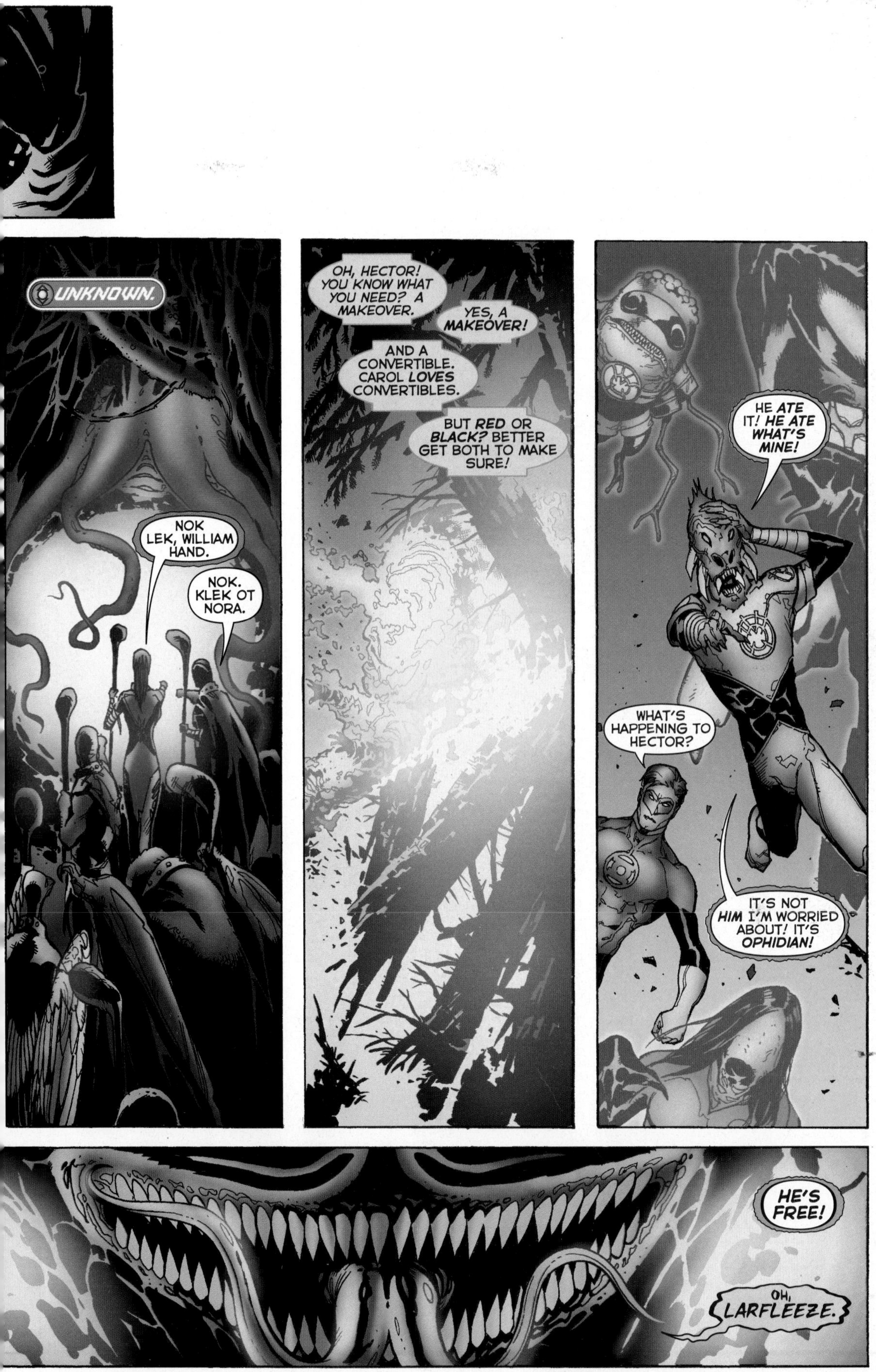
UNKNOWN.
NOK LEK, WILLIAM HAND.
NOK. KLEK OT NORA.
OH, HECTOR! YOU KNOW WHAT YOU NEED? A MAKEOVER.
YES, A MAKEOVER!
AND A CONVERTIBLE. CAROL LOVES CONVERTIBLES.
BUT RED OR BLACK? BETTER GET BOTH TO MAKE SURE!
HE ATE IT! HE ATE WHAT'S MINE!
WHAT'S HAPPENING TO HECTOR?
IT'S NOT HIM I'M WORRIED ABOUT! IT'S OPHIDIAN!
HE'S FREE!
OH, LARFLEEZE.

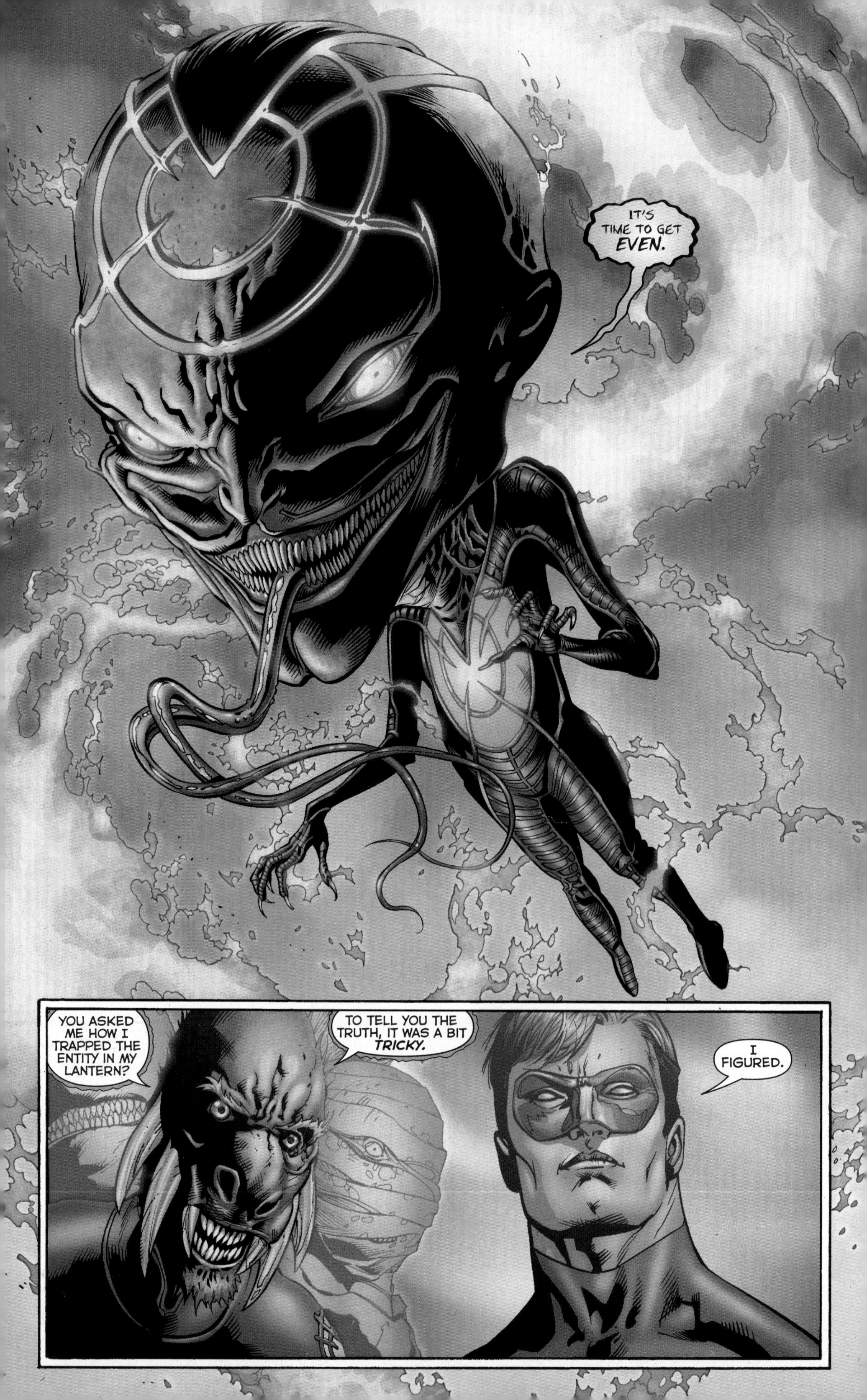
IT'S TIME TO GET EVEN.
YOU ASKED ME HOW I TRAPPED THE ENTITY IN MY LANTERN?
TO TELL YOU THE TRUTH, IT WAS A BIT TRICKY.
I FIGURED.

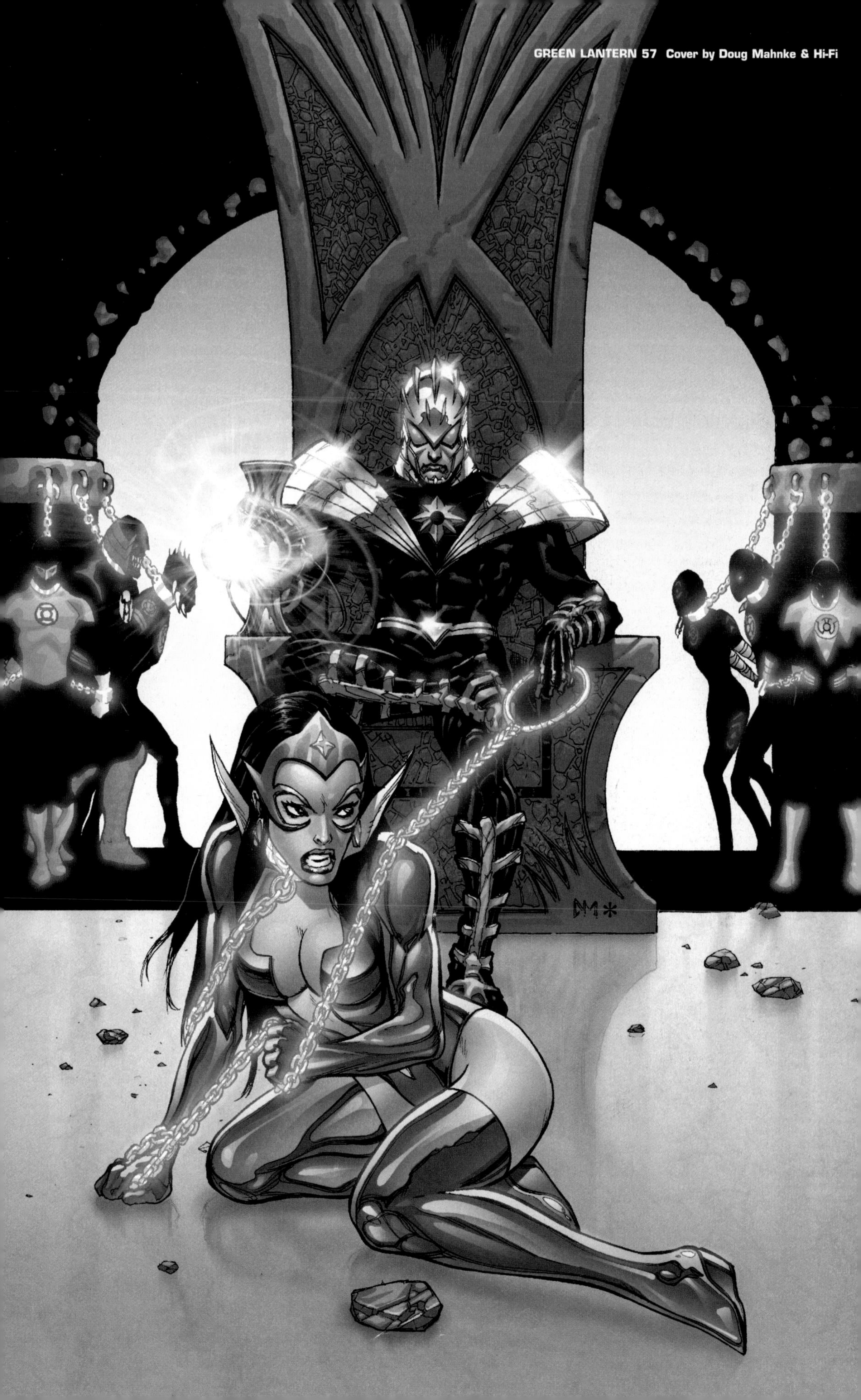
GREEN LANTERN 57 Cover by Doug Mahnke & Hi-Fi

THE NEW GUARDIANS
CHAPTER FIVE

Doug Mahnke Pencils
Christian Alamy, Tom Nguyen, Keith Champagne & Doug Mahnke Inks

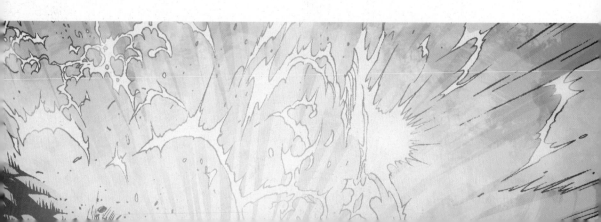

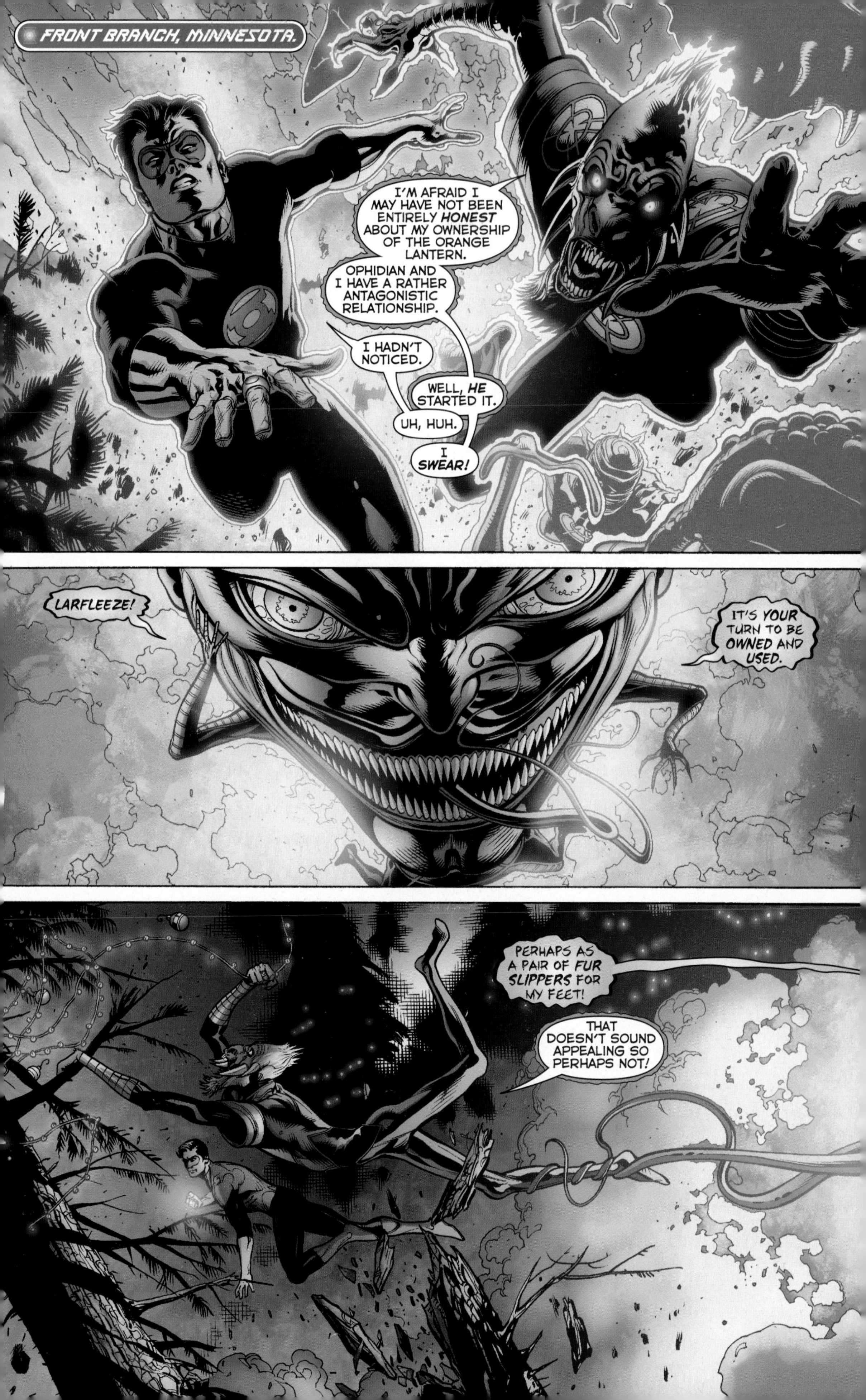
FRONT BRANCH, MINNESOTA.
I'M AFRAID I MAY HAVE NOT BEEN ENTIRELY HONEST ABOUT MY OWNERSHIP OF THE ORANGE LANTERN.
OPHIDIAN AND I HAVE A RATHER ANTAGONISTIC RELATIONSHIP.
I HADN'T NOTICED.
WELL, HE STARTED IT.
UH, HUH.
I SWEAR!
LARFLEEZE!
IT'S YOUR TURN TO BE OWNED AND USED.
PERHAPS AS A PAIR OF FUR SLIPPERS FOR MY FEET!
THAT DOESN'T SOUND APPEALING SO PERHAPS NOT!

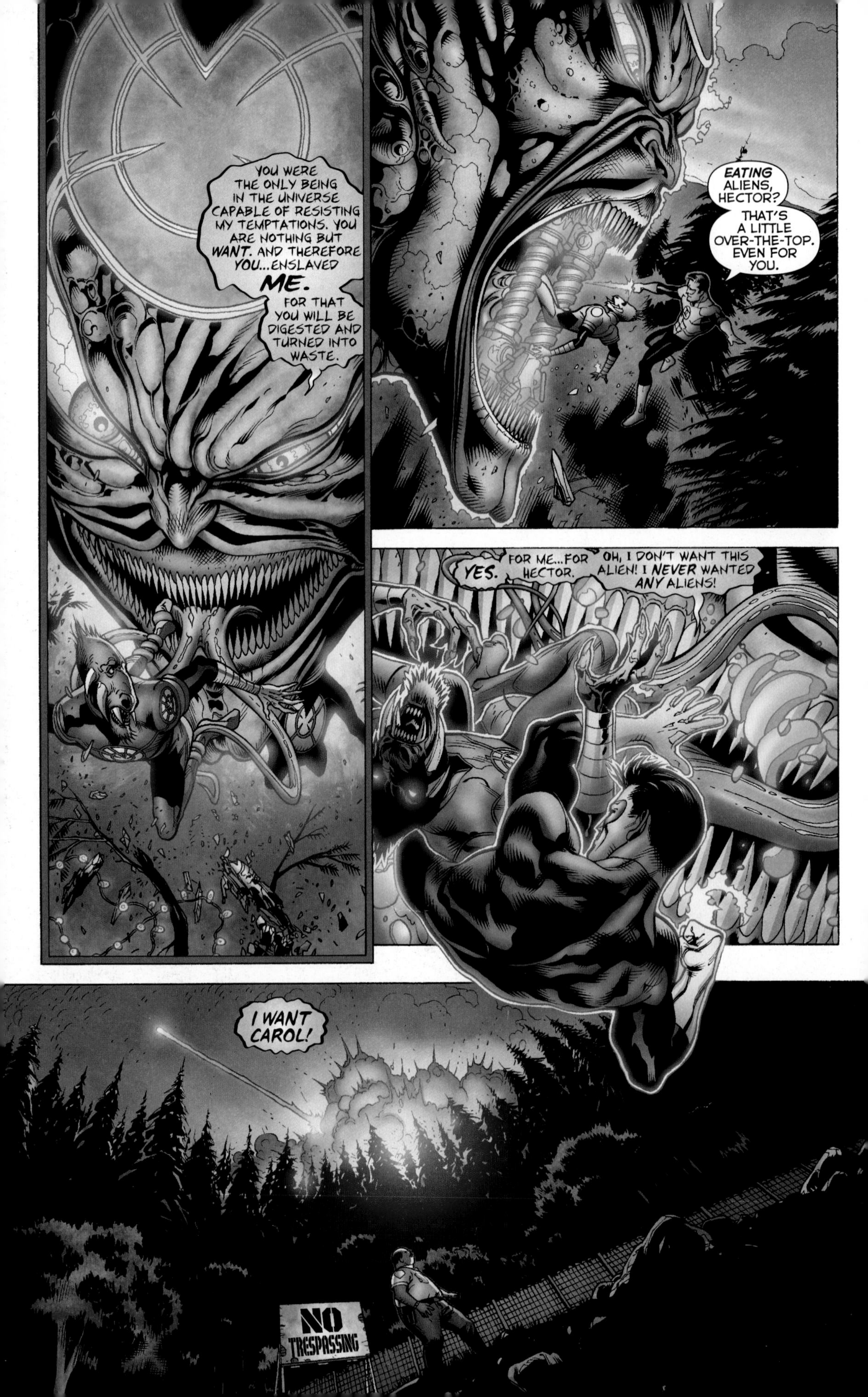

YOU WERE THE ONLY BEING IN THE UNIVERSE CAPABLE OF RESISTING MY TEMPTATIONS. YOU ARE NOTHING BUT WANT. AND THEREFORE YOU...ENSLAVED ME.
FOR THAT YOU WILL BE DIGESTED AND TURNED INTO WASTE.
EATING ALIENS, HECTOR?
THAT'S A LITTLE OVER-THE-TOP. EVEN FOR YOU.
YES.
FOR ME...FOR HECTOR.
OH, I DON'T WANT THIS ALIEN! I NEVER WANTED ANY ALIENS!
I WANT CAROL!
NO TRESPASSING

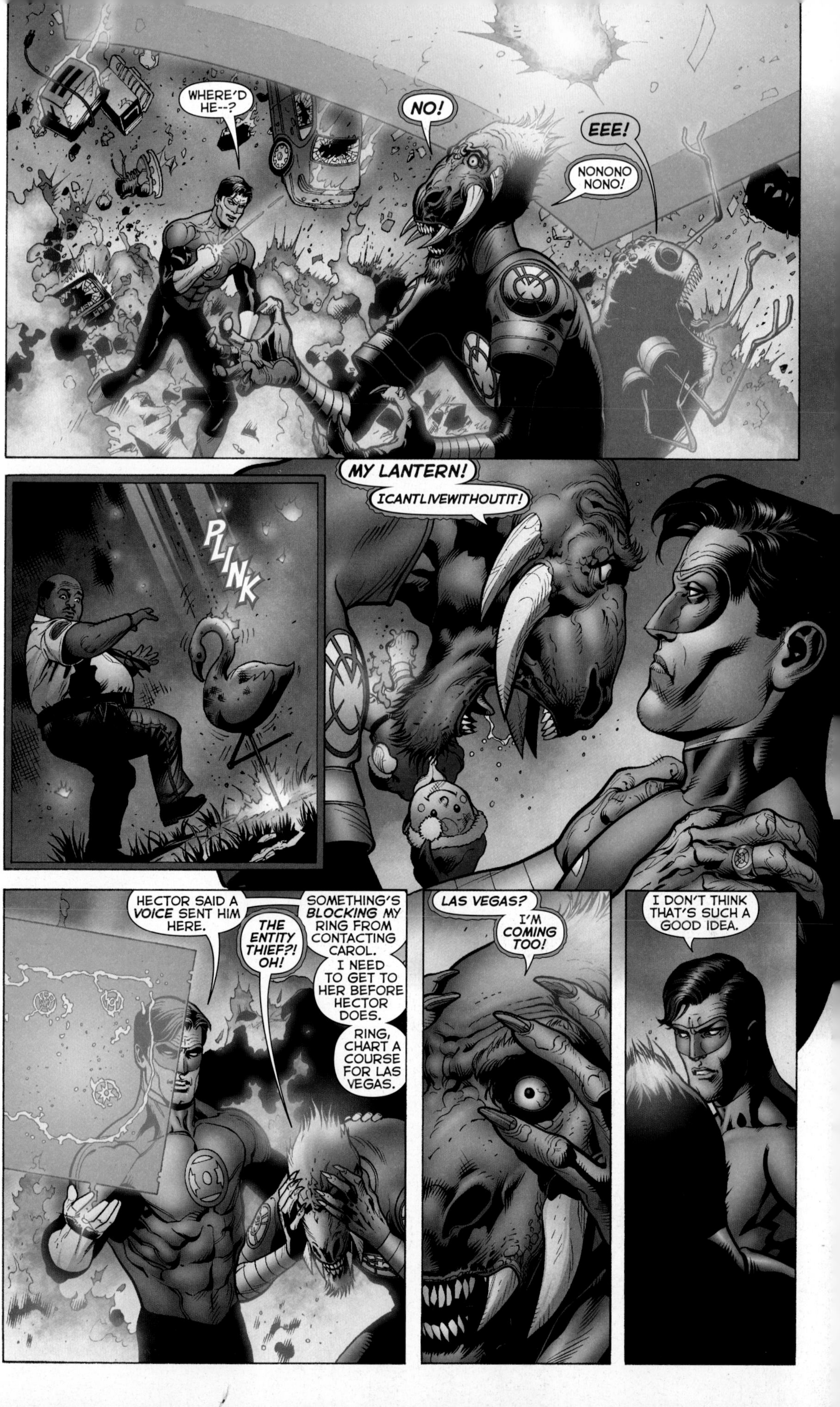

WHERE'D HE--?
NO!
EEE!
NONONO NONO!
PLINK
MY LANTERN!
ICANTLIVEWITHOUTIT!
HECTOR SAID A VOICE SENT HIM HERE.
THE ENTITY THIEF?! OH!
SOMETHING'S BLOCKING MY RING FROM CONTACTING CAROL.
I NEED TO GET TO HER BEFORE HECTOR DOES.
RING, CHART A COURSE FOR LAS VEGAS.
LAS VEGAS?
I'M COMING TOO!
I DON'T THINK THAT'S SUCH A GOOD IDEA.

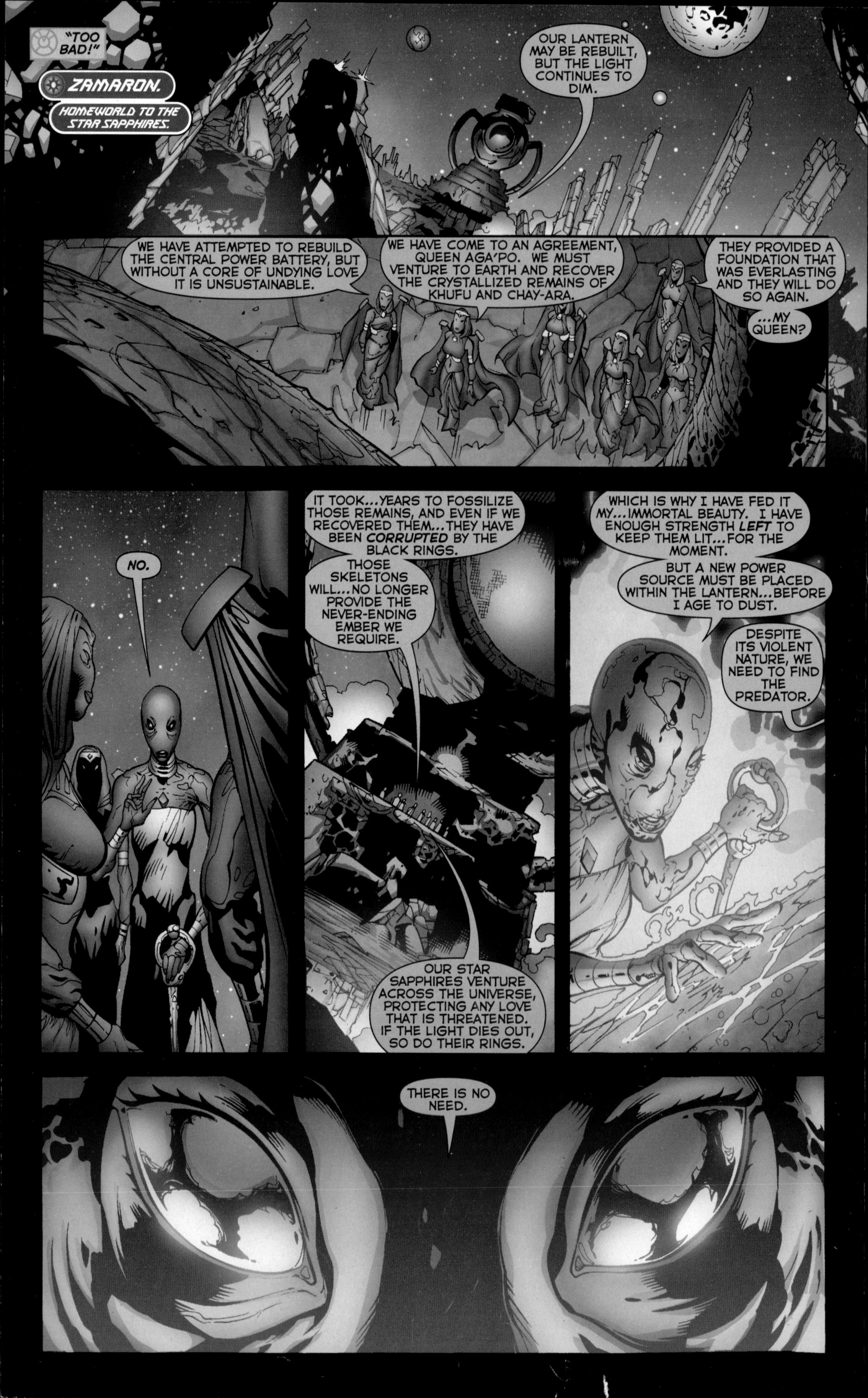
"TOO BAD!"
ZAMARON.
HOMEWORLD TO THE STAR SAPPHIRES.
OUR LANTERN MAY BE REBUILT, BUT THE LIGHT CONTINUES TO DIM.
WE HAVE ATTEMPTED TO REBUILD THE CENTRAL POWER BATTERY, BUT WITHOUT A CORE OF UNDYING LOVE IT IS UNSUSTAINABLE.
WE HAVE COME TO AN AGREEMENT, QUEEN AGA'PO. WE MUST VENTURE TO EARTH AND RECOVER THE CRYSTALLIZED REMAINS OF KHUFU AND CHAY-ARA.
THEY PROVIDED A FOUNDATION THAT WAS EVERLASTING AND THEY WILL DO SO AGAIN.
...MY QUEEN?
NO.
IT TOOK...YEARS TO FOSSILIZE THOSE REMAINS, AND EVEN IF WE RECOVERED THEM...THEY HAVE BEEN CORRUPTED BY THE BLACK RINGS.
THOSE SKELETONS WILL...NO LONGER PROVIDE THE NEVER-ENDING EMBER WE REQUIRE.
OUR STAR SAPPHIRES VENTURE ACROSS THE UNIVERSE, PROTECTING ANY LOVE THAT IS THREATENED. IF THE LIGHT DIES OUT, SO DO THEIR RINGS.
WHICH IS WHY I HAVE FED IT MY...IMMORTAL BEAUTY. I HAVE ENOUGH STRENGTH LEFT TO KEEP THEM LIT...FOR THE MOMENT.
BUT A NEW POWER SOURCE MUST BE PLACED WITHIN THE LANTERN...BEFORE I AGE TO DUST.
DESPITE ITS VIOLENT NATURE, WE NEED TO FIND THE PREDATOR.
THERE IS NO NEED.

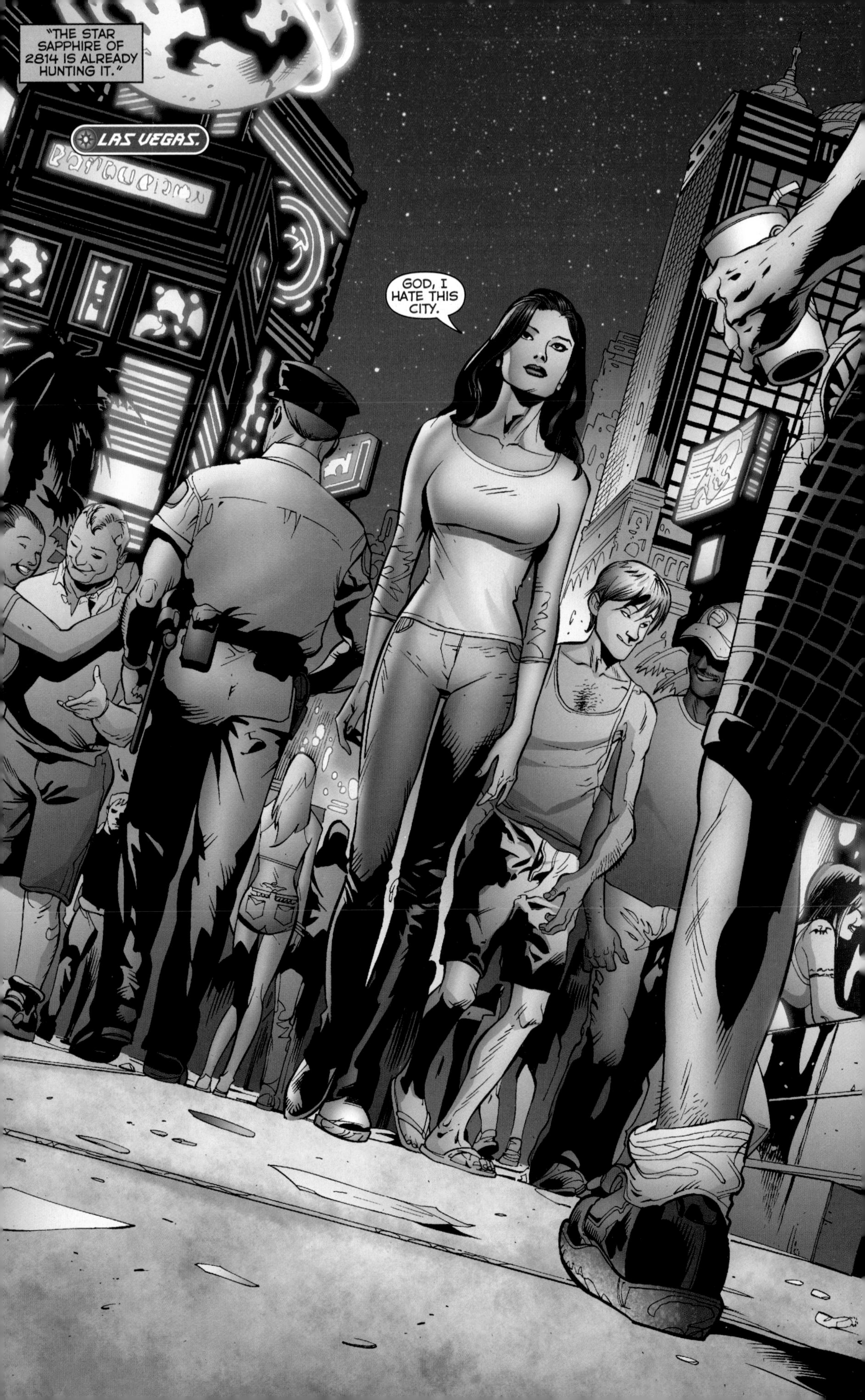
"THE STAR SAPPHIRE OF 2814 IS ALREADY HUNTING IT."
LAS VEGAS.
GOD, I HATE THIS CITY.

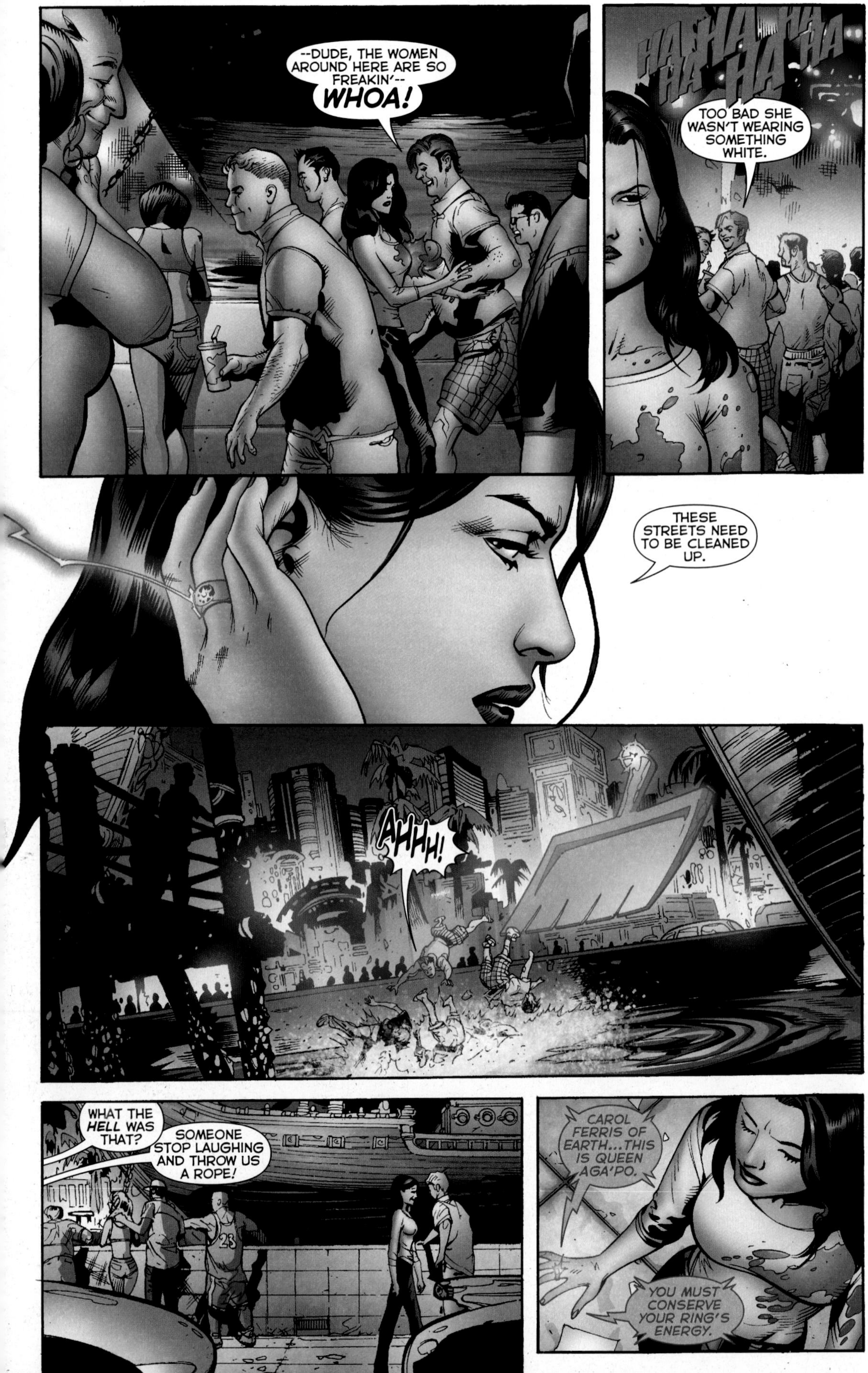
--DUDE, THE WOMEN AROUND HERE ARE SO FREAKIN'-- WHOA!
HA HA HA HA HA HA HA
TOO BAD SHE WASN'T WEARING SOMETHING WHITE.
THESE STREETS NEED TO BE CLEANED UP.
AHHH!
WHAT THE HELL WAS THAT?
SOMEONE STOP LAUGHING AND THROW US A ROPE!
CAROL FERRIS OF EARTH...THIS IS QUEEN AGA'PO.
YOU MUST CONSERVE YOUR RING'S ENERGY.

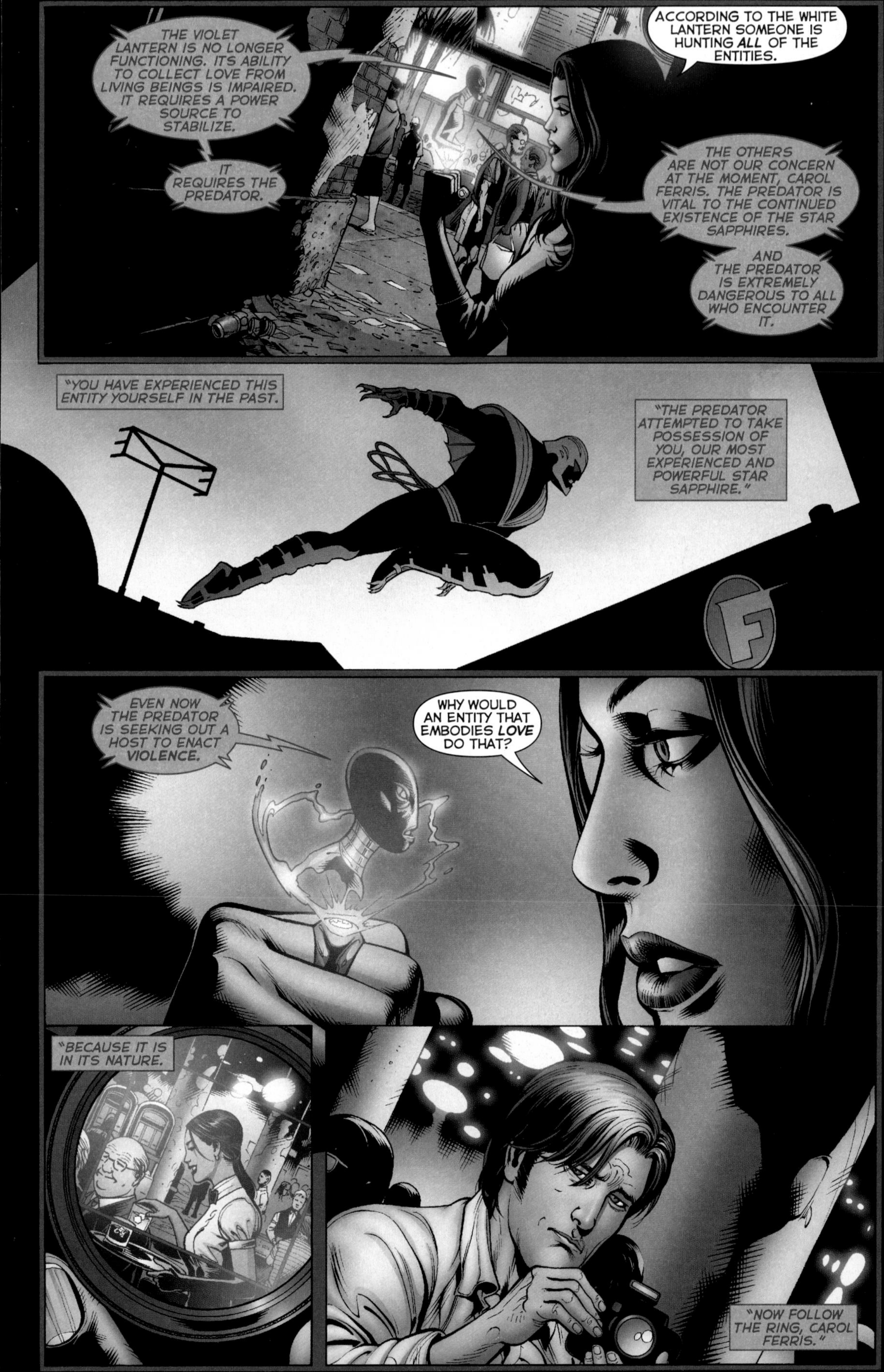
THE VIOLET LANTERN IS NO LONGER FUNCTIONING. ITS ABILITY TO COLLECT LOVE FROM LIVING BEINGS IS IMPAIRED. IT REQUIRES A POWER SOURCE TO STABILIZE.
IT REQUIRES THE PREDATOR.
ACCORDING TO THE WHITE LANTERN SOMEONE IS HUNTING ALL OF THE ENTITIES.
THE OTHERS ARE NOT OUR CONCERN AT THE MOMENT, CAROL FERRIS. THE PREDATOR IS VITAL TO THE CONTINUED EXISTENCE OF THE STAR SAPPHIRES.
AND THE PREDATOR IS EXTREMELY DANGEROUS TO ALL WHO ENCOUNTER IT.
"YOU HAVE EXPERIENCED THIS ENTITY YOURSELF IN THE PAST.
"THE PREDATOR ATTEMPTED TO TAKE POSSESSION OF YOU, OUR MOST EXPERIENCED AND POWERFUL STAR SAPPHIRE."
F
EVEN NOW THE PREDATOR IS SEEKING OUT A HOST TO ENACT VIOLENCE.
WHY WOULD AN ENTITY THAT EMBODIES LOVE DO THAT?
"BECAUSE IT IS IN ITS NATURE.
"NOW FOLLOW THE RING, CAROL FERRIS."

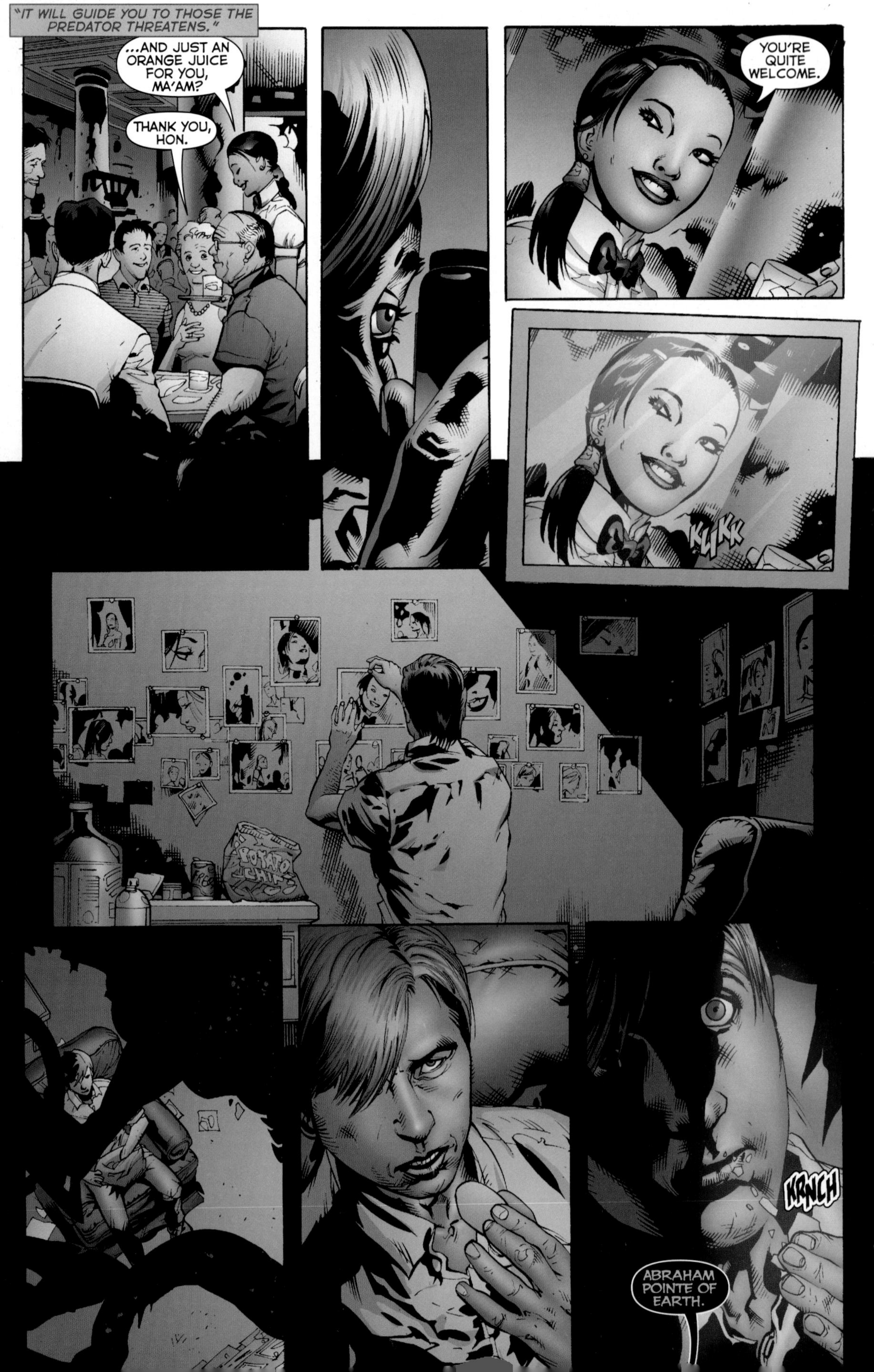
"IT WILL GUIDE YOU TO THOSE THE PREDATOR THREATENS."
...AND JUST AN ORANGE JUICE FOR YOU, MA'AM?
THANK YOU, HON.
YOU'RE QUITE WELCOME.
KLIKK
POTATO CHIPS
KRNCH
ABRAHAM POINTE OF EARTH.

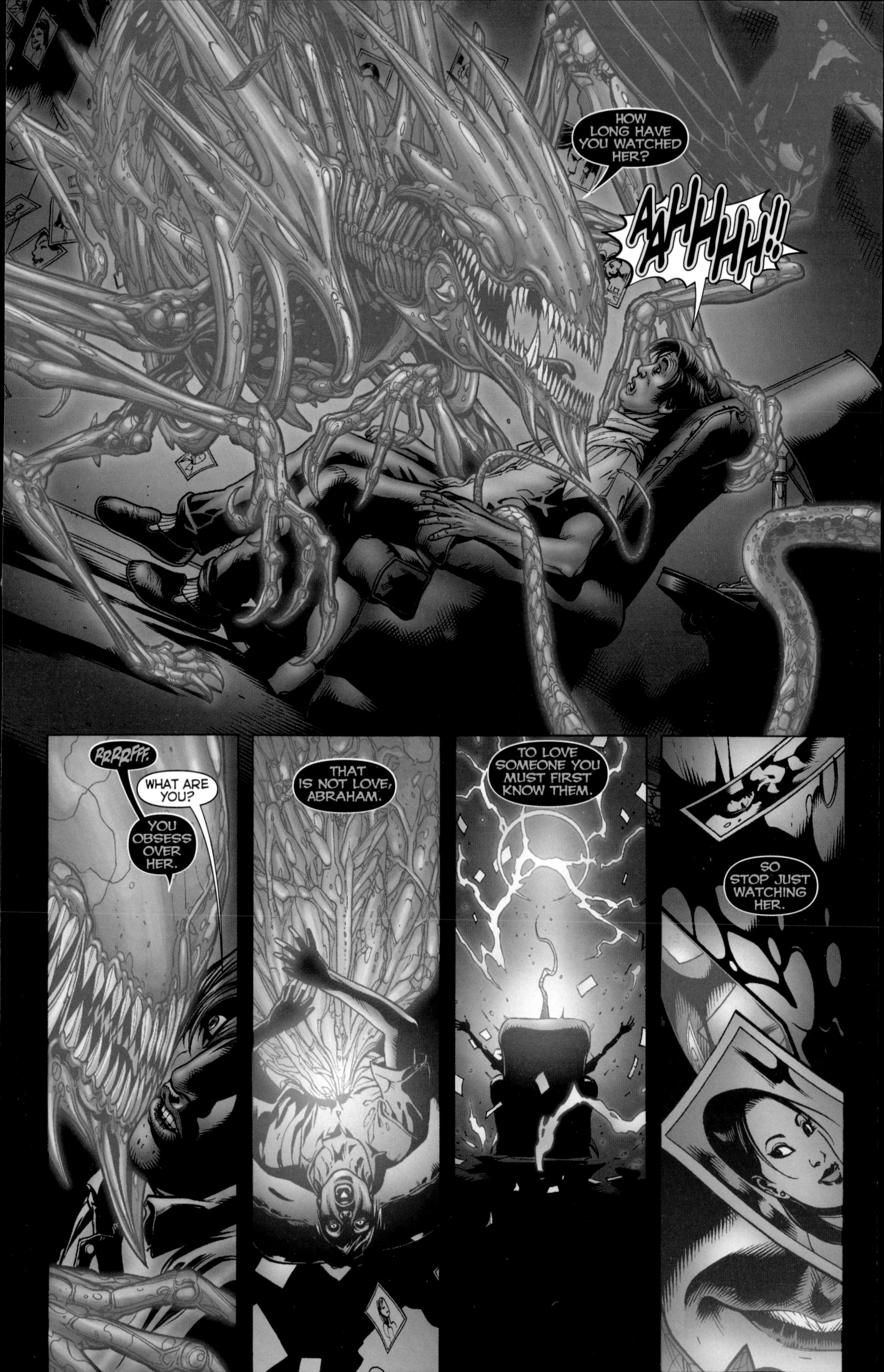
HOW LONG HAVE YOU WATCHED HER?
AHHHHH!!
RRRRFFF.
WHAT ARE YOU?
YOU OBSESS OVER HER.
THAT IS NOT LOVE, ABRAHAM.
TO LOVE SOMEONE YOU MUST FIRST KNOW THEM.
SO STOP JUST WATCHING HER.

"AND LET'S **DO** SOMETHING **ABOUT** IT TOGETHER!"

WARNING. THE PREDATOR IS IN THE VICINITY.

WHAT THE HELL IS THAT?!

OUTTA MY WAY!

AIIEEE!

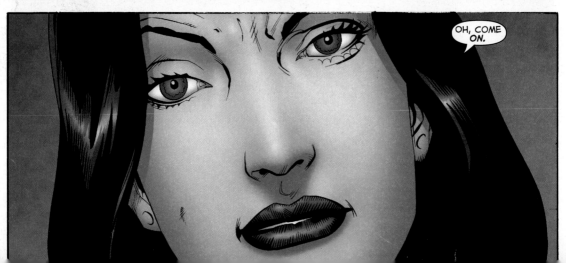

OH, COME ON.

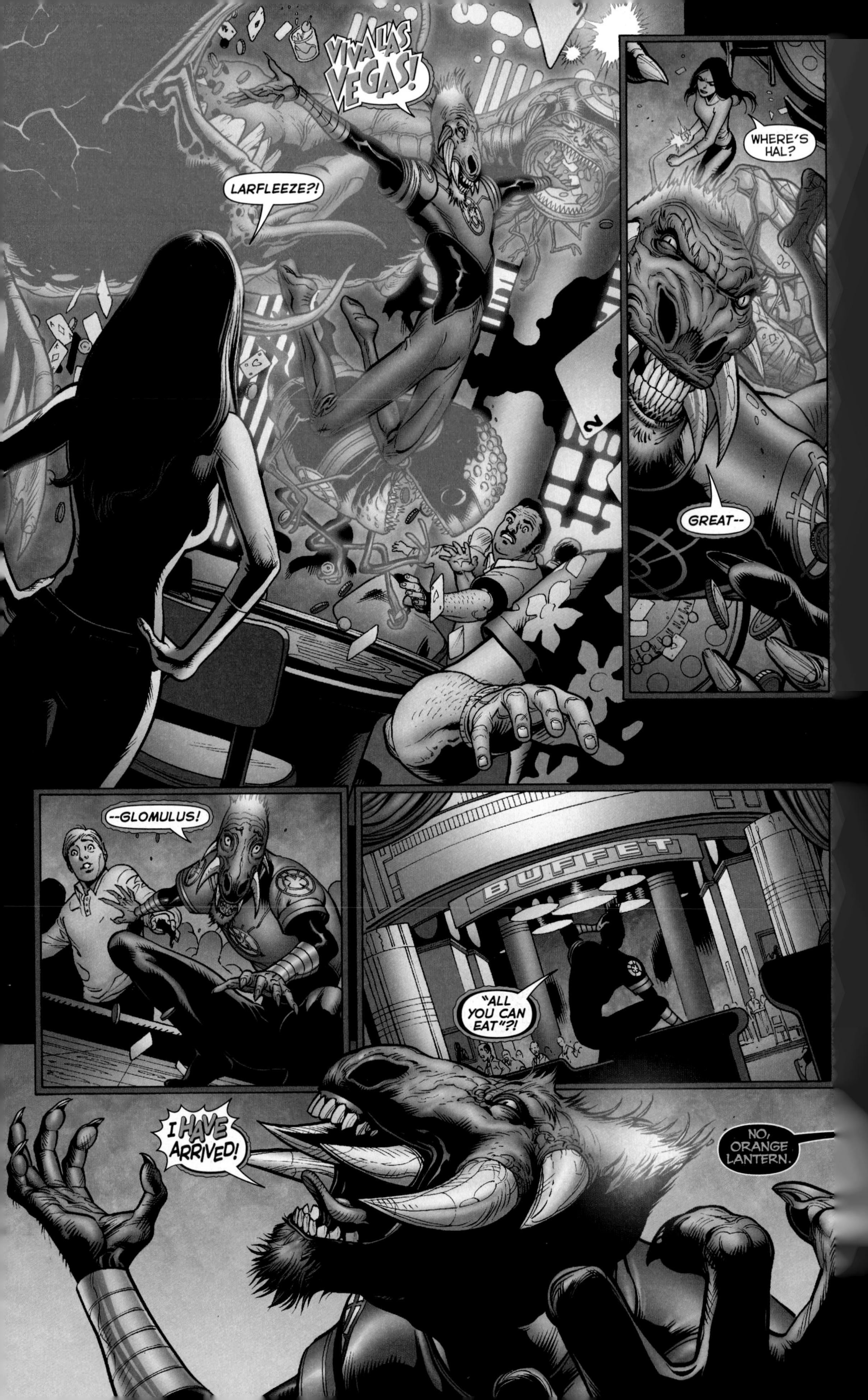
VIVA LAS VEGAS!
LARFLEEZE?!
WHERE'S HAL?
GREAT--
--GLOMULUS!
BUFFET
"ALL YOU CAN EAT"?!
I HAVE ARRIVED!
NO, ORANGE LANTERN.

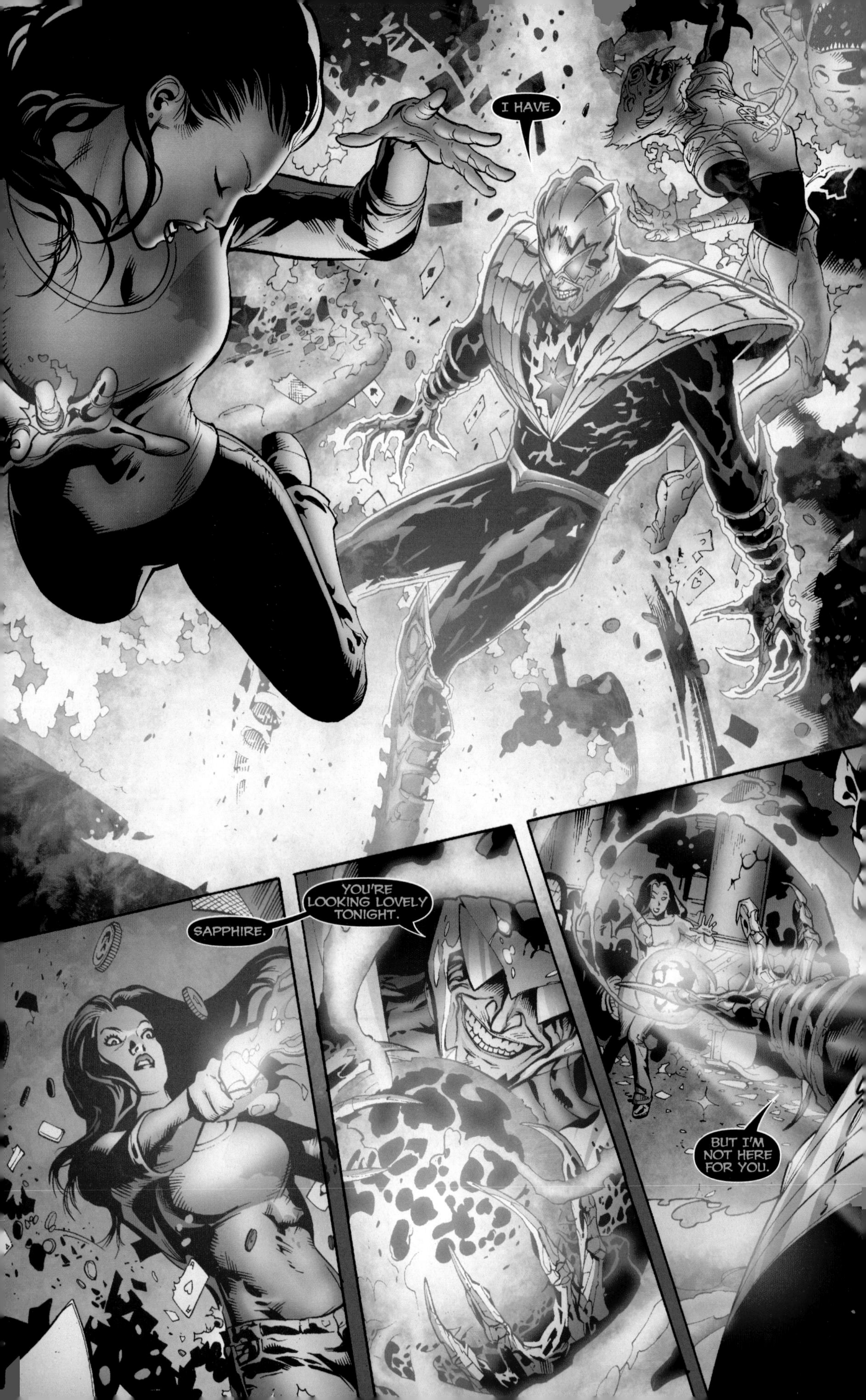
I HAVE.
SAPPHIRE.
YOU'RE LOOKING LOVELY TONIGHT.
BUT I'M NOT HERE FOR YOU.

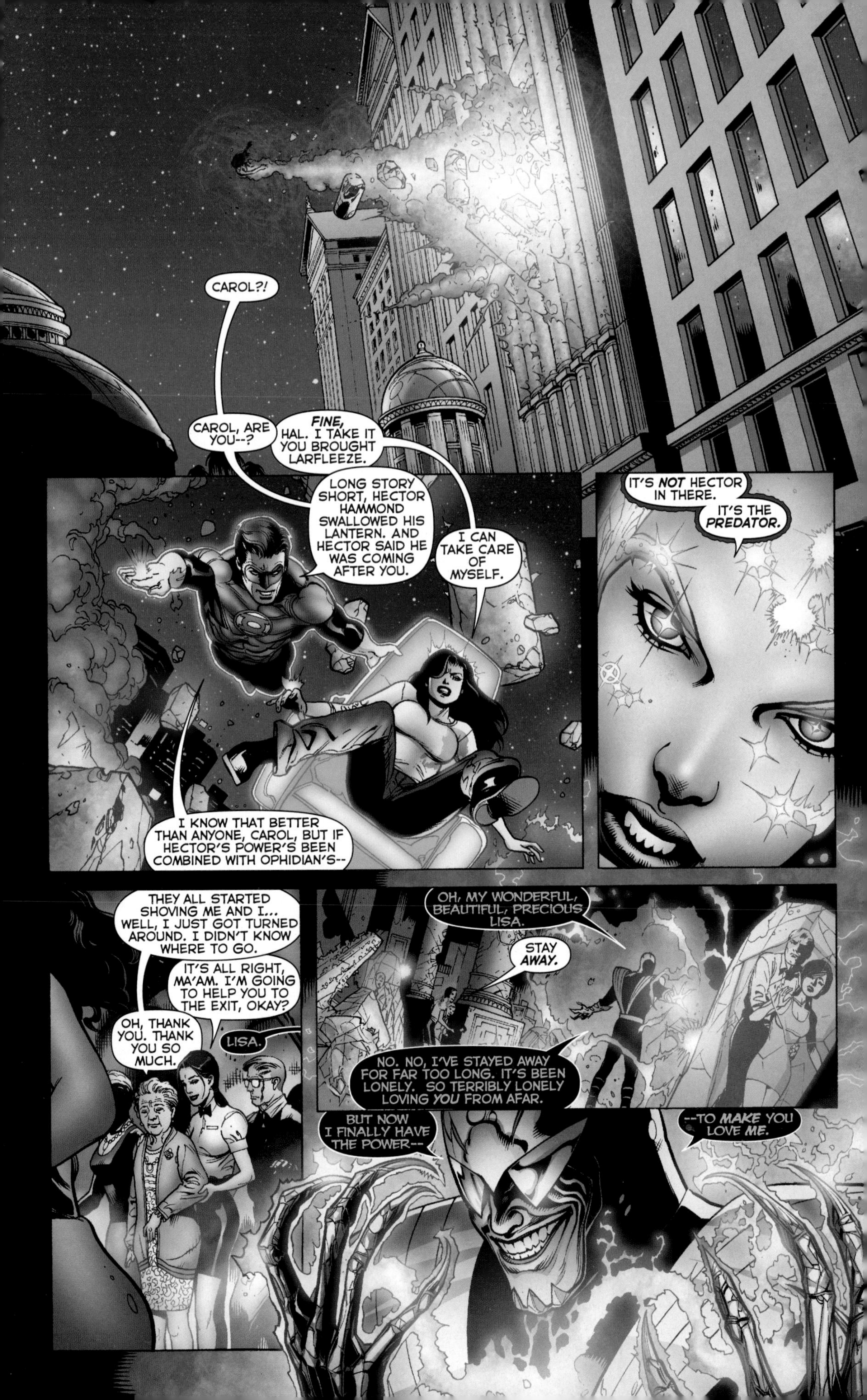
CAROL?!
CAROL, ARE YOU--?
FINE, HAL. I TAKE IT YOU BROUGHT LARFLEEZE.
LONG STORY SHORT, HECTOR HAMMOND SWALLOWED HIS LANTERN. AND HECTOR SAID HE WAS COMING AFTER YOU.
I CAN TAKE CARE OF MYSELF.
I KNOW THAT BETTER THAN ANYONE, CAROL, BUT IF HECTOR'S POWER'S BEEN COMBINED WITH OPHIDIAN'S--
IT'S NOT HECTOR IN THERE.
IT'S THE PREDATOR.
THEY ALL STARTED SHOVING ME AND I... WELL, I JUST GOT TURNED AROUND. I DIDN'T KNOW WHERE TO GO.
IT'S ALL RIGHT, MA'AM. I'M GOING TO HELP YOU TO THE EXIT, OKAY?
OH, THANK YOU. THANK YOU SO MUCH.
LISA.
OH, MY WONDERFUL, BEAUTIFUL, PRECIOUS LISA.
STAY AWAY.
NO. NO, I'VE STAYED AWAY FOR FAR TOO LONG. IT'S BEEN LONELY. SO TERRIBLY LONELY LOVING YOU FROM AFAR.
BUT NOW I FINALLY HAVE THE POWER--
--TO MAKE YOU LOVE ME.

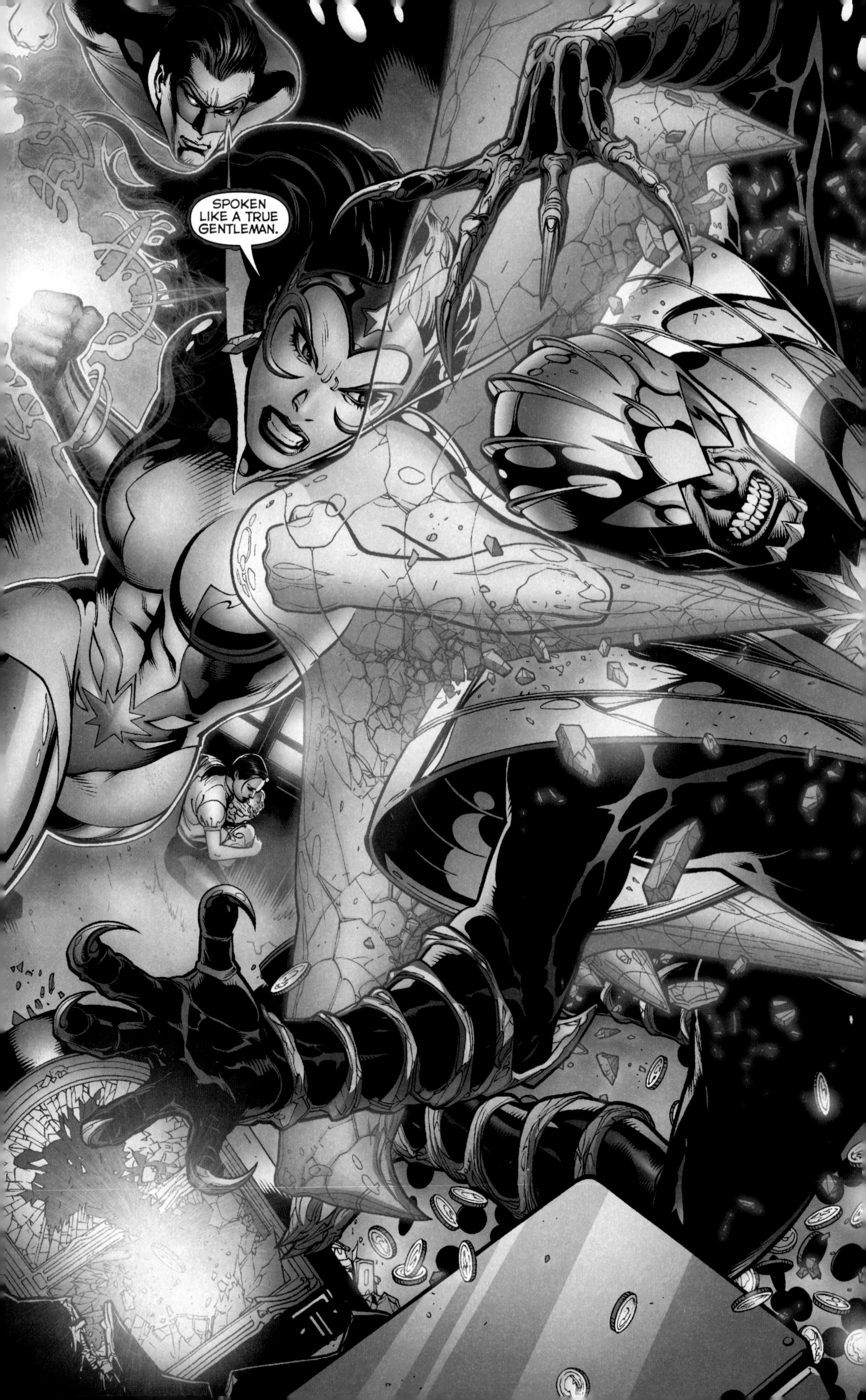
SPOKEN LIKE A TRUE GENTLEMAN.

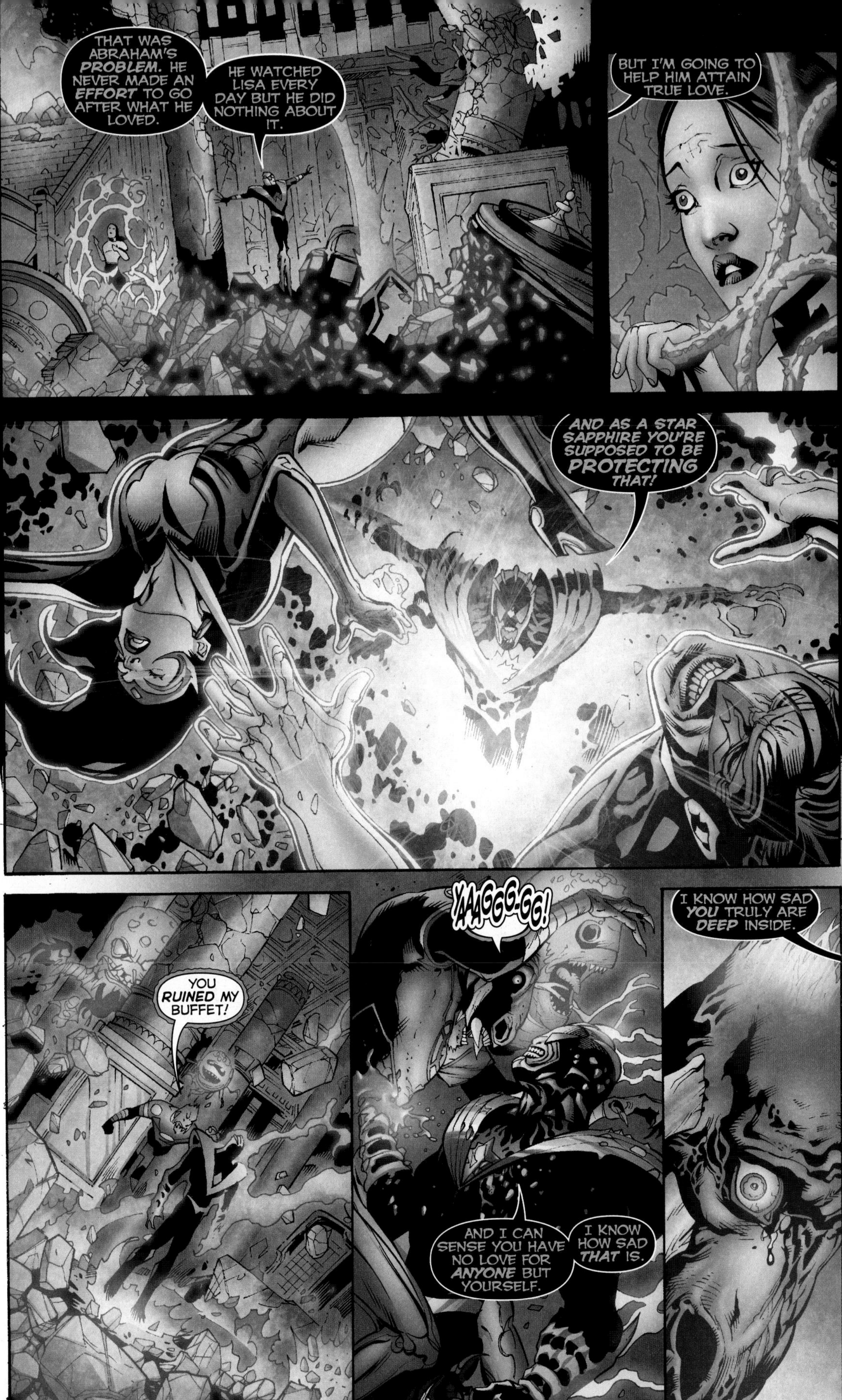
THAT WAS ABRAHAM'S PROBLEM. HE NEVER MADE AN EFFORT TO GO AFTER WHAT HE LOVED.
HE WATCHED LISA EVERY DAY BUT HE DID NOTHING ABOUT IT.
BUT I'M GOING TO HELP HIM ATTAIN TRUE LOVE.
AND AS A STAR SAPPHIRE YOU'RE SUPPOSED TO BE PROTECTING THAT!
YOU RUINED MY BUFFET!
YAAGGG-GG!
AND I CAN SENSE YOU HAVE NO LOVE FOR ANYONE BUT YOURSELF.
I KNOW HOW SAD THAT IS.
I KNOW HOW SAD YOU TRULY ARE DEEP INSIDE.

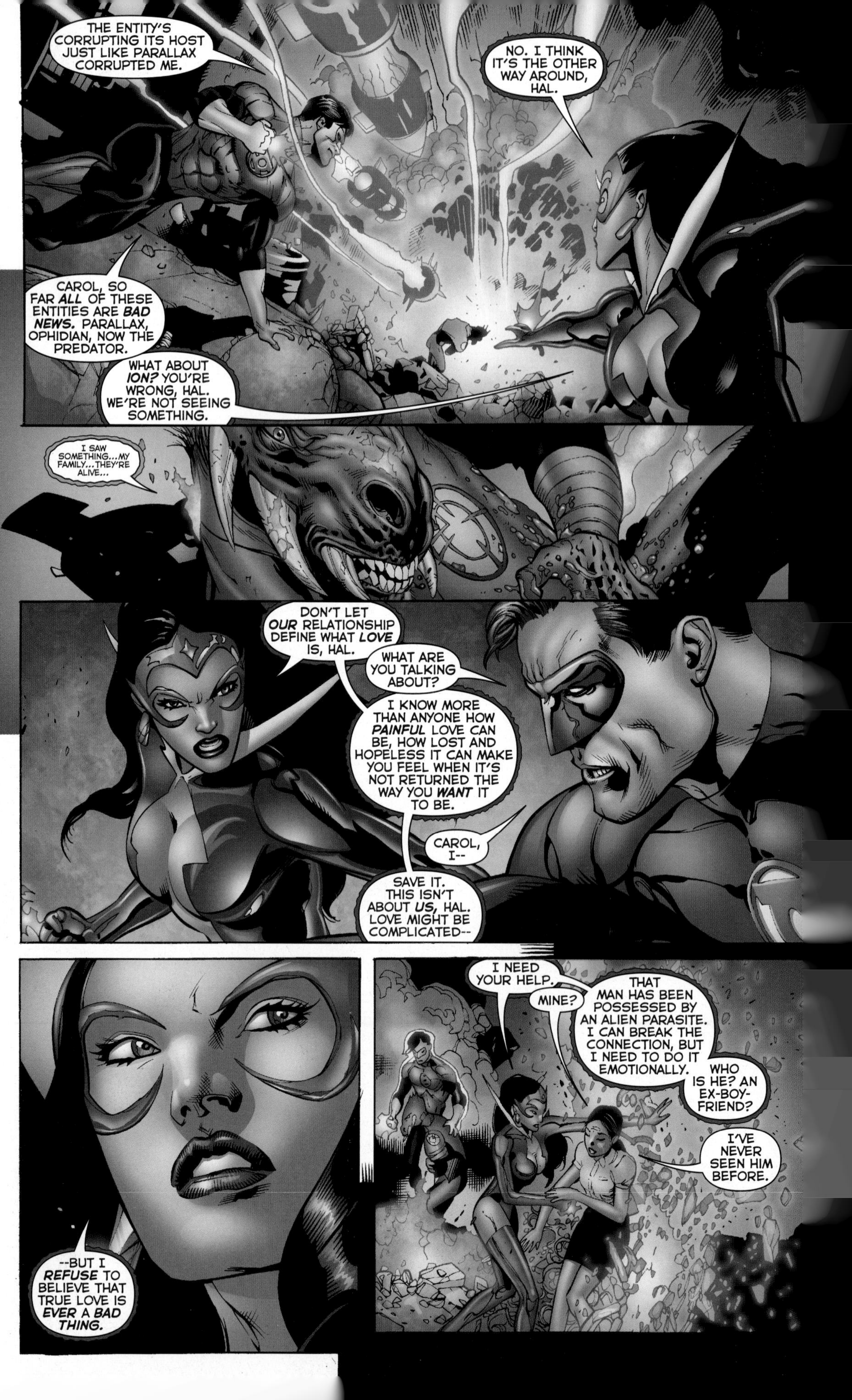

THE ENTITY'S CORRUPTING ITS HOST JUST LIKE PARALLAX CORRUPTED ME.
NO. I THINK IT'S THE OTHER WAY AROUND, HAL.
CAROL, SO FAR ALL OF THESE ENTITIES ARE BAD NEWS. PARALLAX, OPHIDIAN, NOW THE PREDATOR.
WHAT ABOUT ION? YOU'RE WRONG, HAL. WE'RE NOT SEEING SOMETHING.
I SAW SOMETHING...MY FAMILY...THEY'RE ALIVE...
DON'T LET OUR RELATIONSHIP DEFINE WHAT LOVE IS, HAL.
WHAT ARE YOU TALKING ABOUT?
I KNOW MORE THAN ANYONE HOW PAINFUL LOVE CAN BE, HOW LOST AND HOPELESS IT CAN MAKE YOU FEEL WHEN IT'S NOT RETURNED THE WAY YOU WANT IT TO BE.
CAROL, I--
SAVE IT. THIS ISN'T ABOUT US, HAL. LOVE MIGHT BE COMPLICATED--
--BUT I REFUSE TO BELIEVE THAT TRUE LOVE IS EVER A BAD THING.
I NEED YOUR HELP.
MINE?
THAT MAN HAS BEEN POSSESSED BY AN ALIEN PARASITE. I CAN BREAK THE CONNECTION, BUT I NEED TO DO IT EMOTIONALLY.
WHO IS HE? AN EX-BOY-FRIEND?
I'VE NEVER SEEN HIM BEFORE.

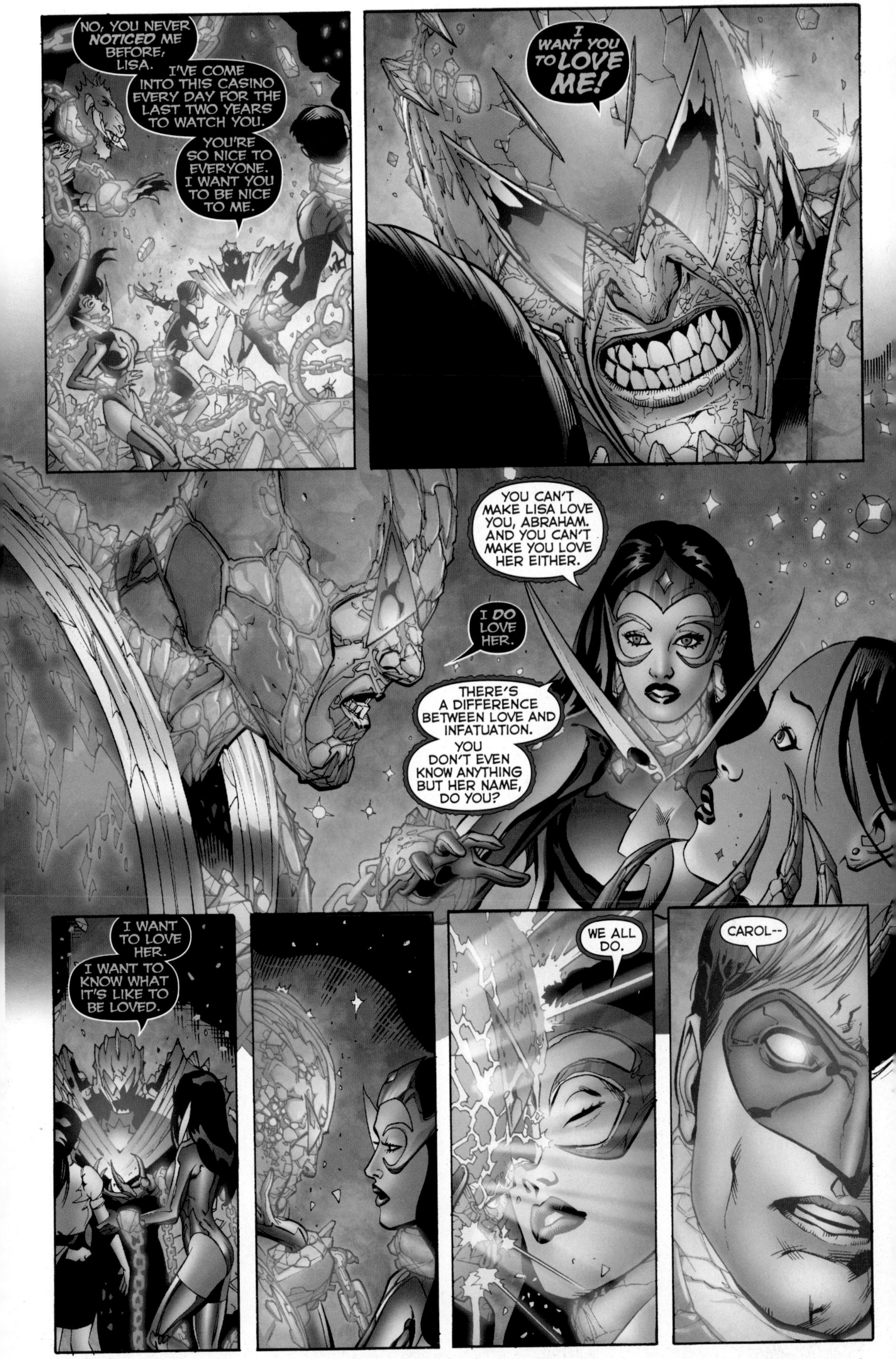
NO, YOU NEVER NOTICED ME BEFORE, LISA.
I'VE COME INTO THIS CASINO EVERY DAY FOR THE LAST TWO YEARS TO WATCH YOU.
YOU'RE SO NICE TO EVERYONE. I WANT YOU TO BE NICE TO ME.
I WANT YOU TO LOVE ME!
YOU CAN'T MAKE LISA LOVE YOU, ABRAHAM. AND YOU CAN'T MAKE YOU LOVE HER EITHER.
I DO LOVE HER.
THERE'S A DIFFERENCE BETWEEN LOVE AND INFATUATION.
YOU DON'T EVEN KNOW ANYTHING BUT HER NAME, DO YOU?
I WANT TO LOVE HER.
I WANT TO KNOW WHAT IT'S LIKE TO BE LOVED.
WE ALL DO.
CAROL--

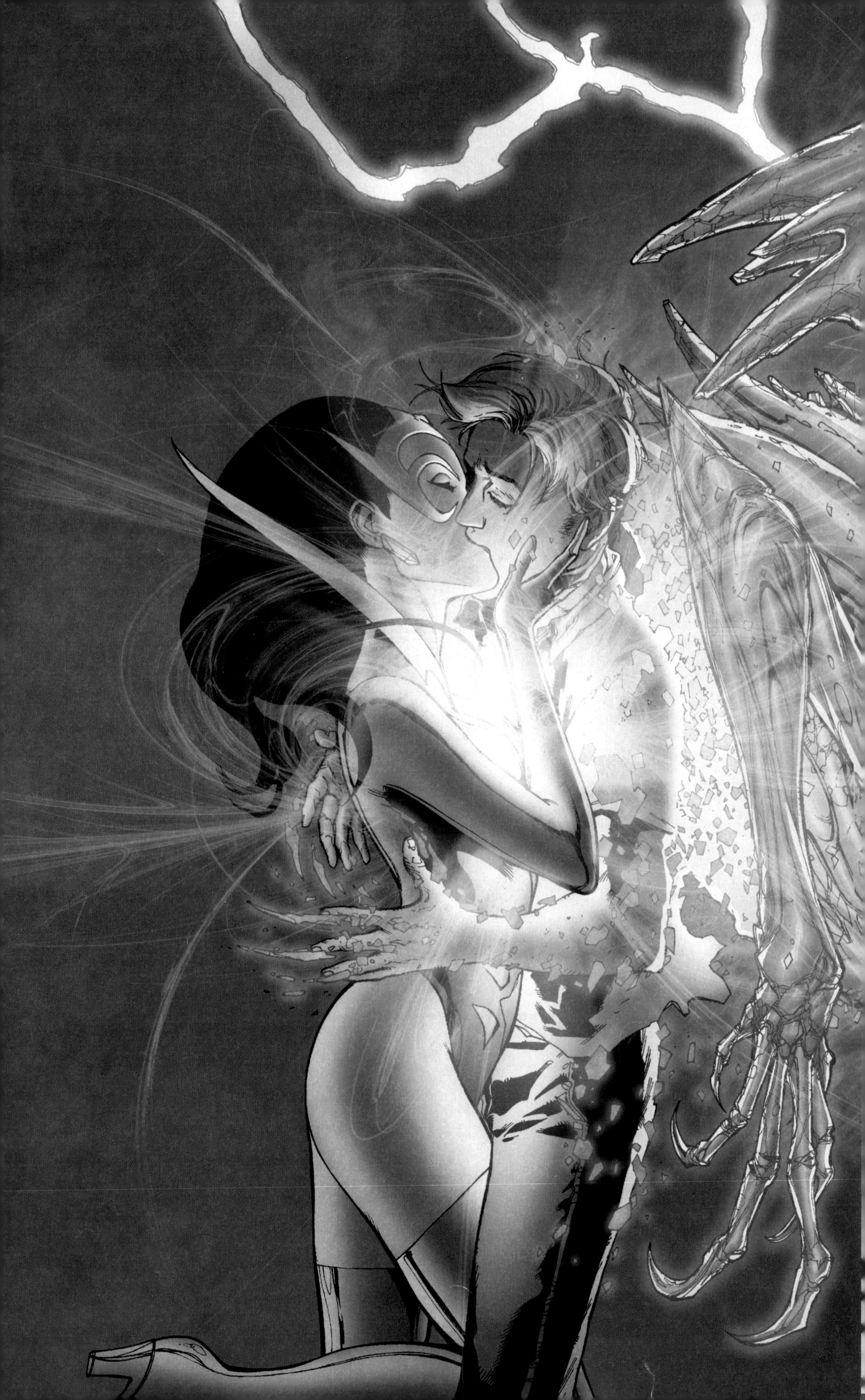

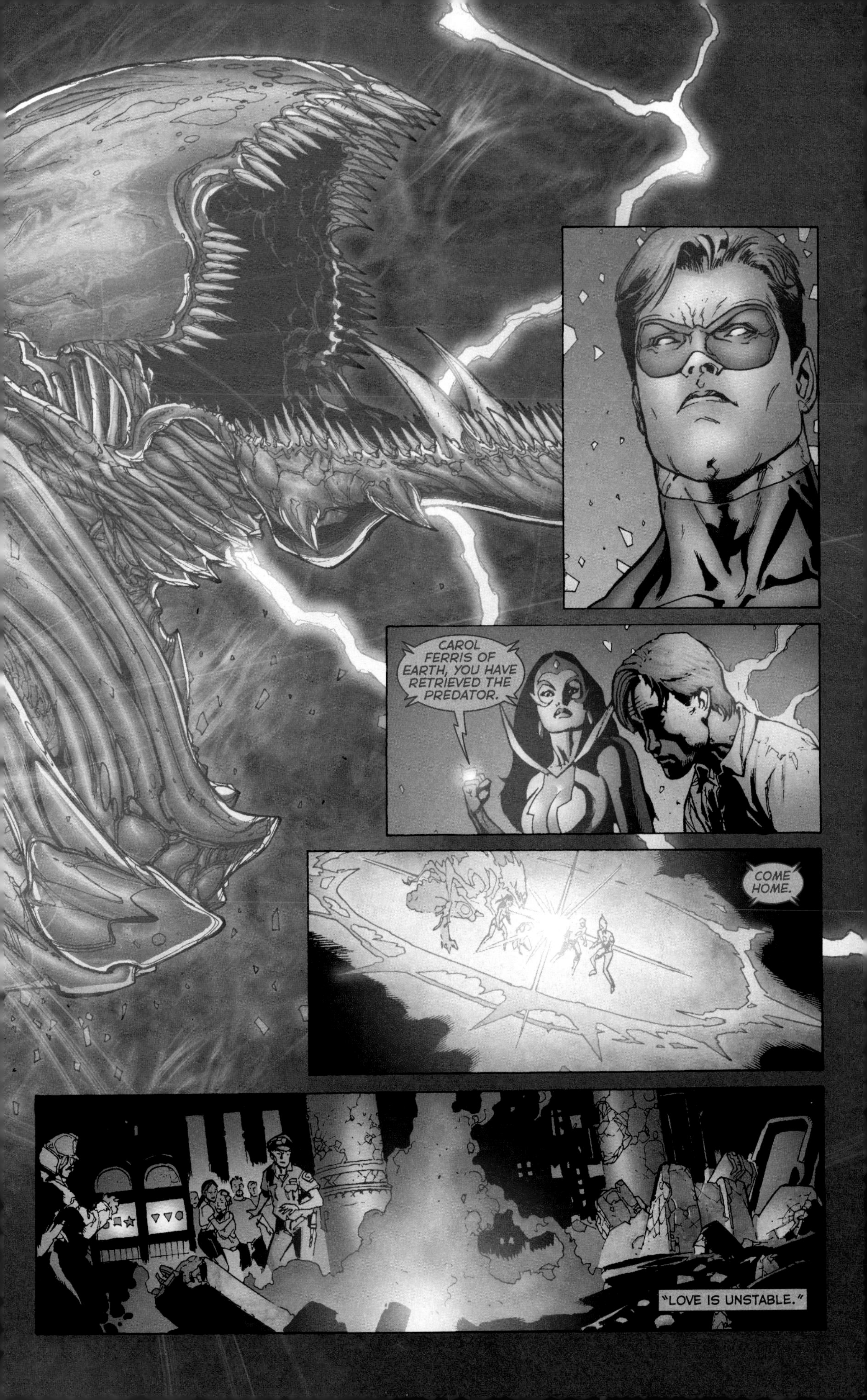

CAROL FERRIS OF EARTH, YOU HAVE RETRIEVED THE PREDATOR.
COME HOME.
"LOVE IS UNSTABLE."

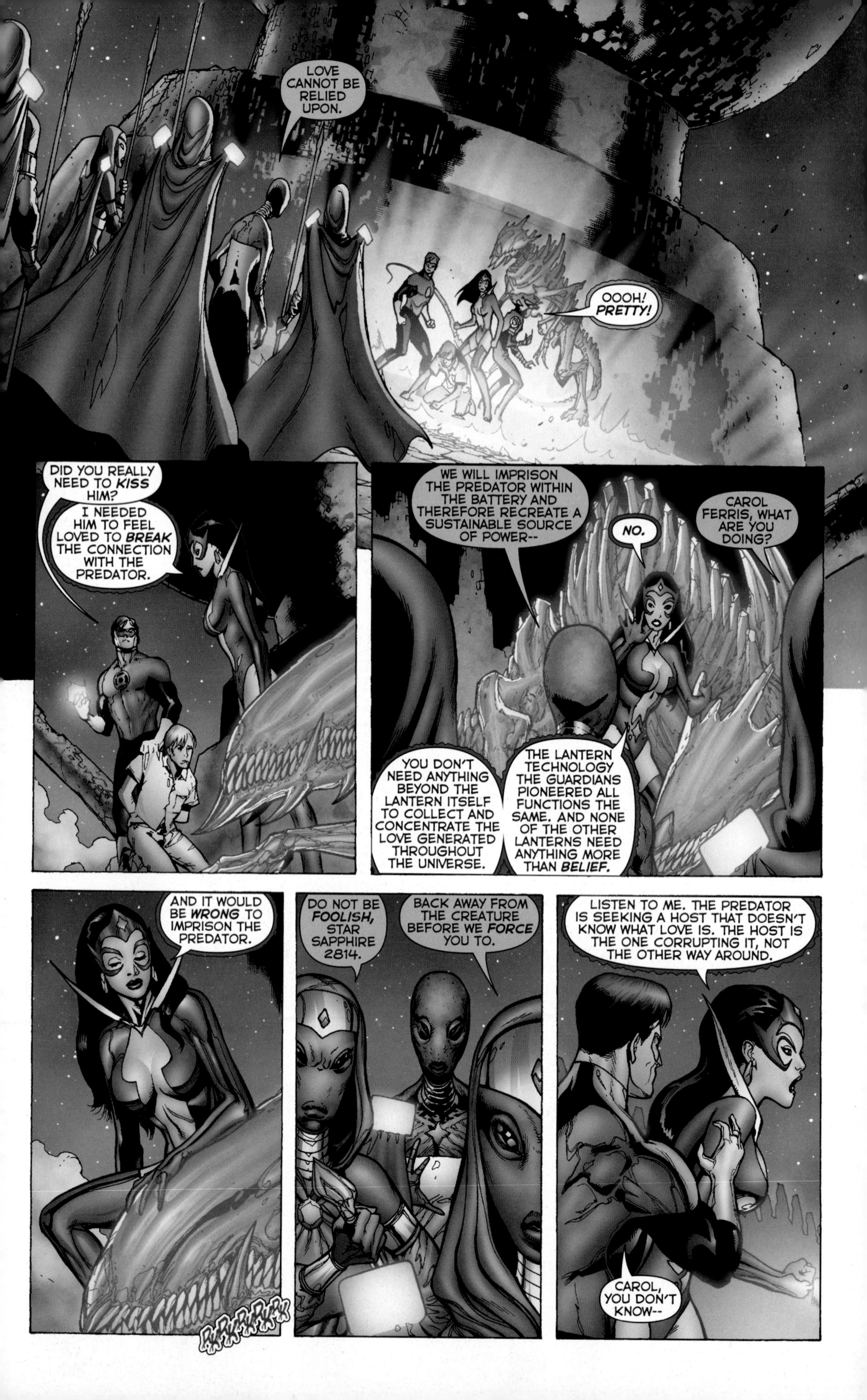

LOVE CANNOT BE RELIED UPON.
OOOH! PRETTY!
DID YOU REALLY NEED TO KISS HIM?
I NEEDED HIM TO FEEL LOVED TO BREAK THE CONNECTION WITH THE PREDATOR.
WE WILL IMPRISON THE PREDATOR WITHIN THE BATTERY AND THEREFORE RECREATE A SUSTAINABLE SOURCE OF POWER--
NO.
CAROL FERRIS, WHAT ARE YOU DOING?
YOU DON'T NEED ANYTHING BEYOND THE LANTERN ITSELF TO COLLECT AND CONCENTRATE THE LOVE GENERATED THROUGHOUT THE UNIVERSE.
THE LANTERN TECHNOLOGY THE GUARDIANS PIONEERED ALL FUNCTIONS THE SAME. AND NONE OF THE OTHER LANTERNS NEED ANYTHING MORE THAN BELIEF.
AND IT WOULD BE WRONG TO IMPRISON THE PREDATOR.
DO NOT BE FOOLISH, STAR SAPPHIRE 2814.
BACK AWAY FROM THE CREATURE BEFORE WE FORCE YOU TO.
LISTEN TO ME. THE PREDATOR IS SEEKING A HOST THAT DOESN'T KNOW WHAT LOVE IS. THE HOST IS THE ONE CORRUPTING IT, NOT THE OTHER WAY AROUND.
CAROL, YOU DON'T KNOW--

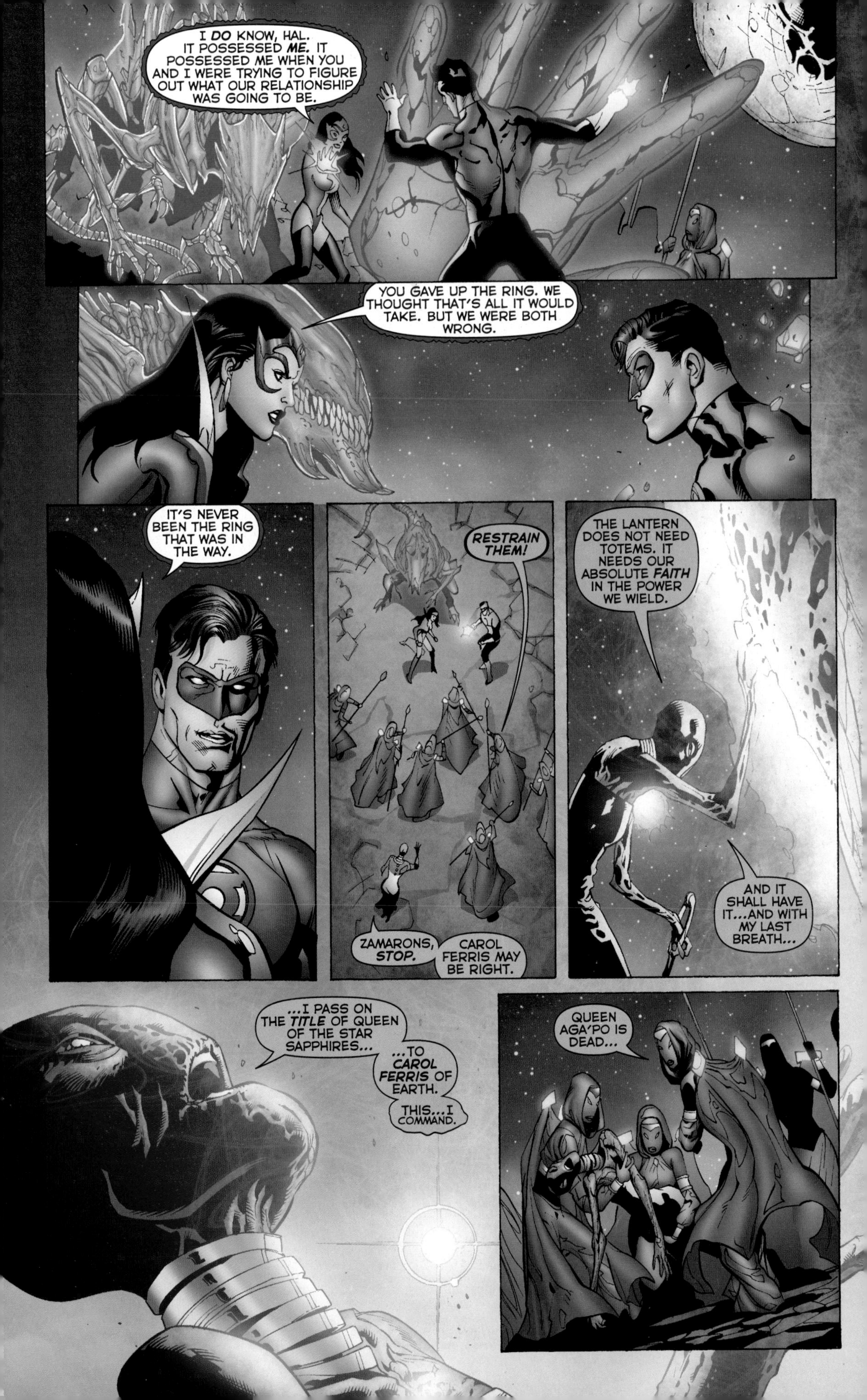
I DO KNOW, HAL. IT POSSESSED ME. IT POSSESSED ME WHEN YOU AND I WERE TRYING TO FIGURE OUT WHAT OUR RELATIONSHIP WAS GOING TO BE.
YOU GAVE UP THE RING. WE THOUGHT THAT'S ALL IT WOULD TAKE. BUT WE WERE BOTH WRONG.
IT'S NEVER BEEN THE RING THAT WAS IN THE WAY.
RESTRAIN THEM!
ZAMARONS, STOP.
CAROL FERRIS MAY BE RIGHT.
THE LANTERN DOES NOT NEED TOTEMS. IT NEEDS OUR ABSOLUTE FAITH IN THE POWER WE WIELD.
AND IT SHALL HAVE IT...AND WITH MY LAST BREATH...
...I PASS ON THE TITLE OF QUEEN OF THE STAR SAPPHIRES...
...TO CAROL FERRIS OF EARTH.
THIS...I COMMAND.
QUEEN AGA'PO IS DEAD...

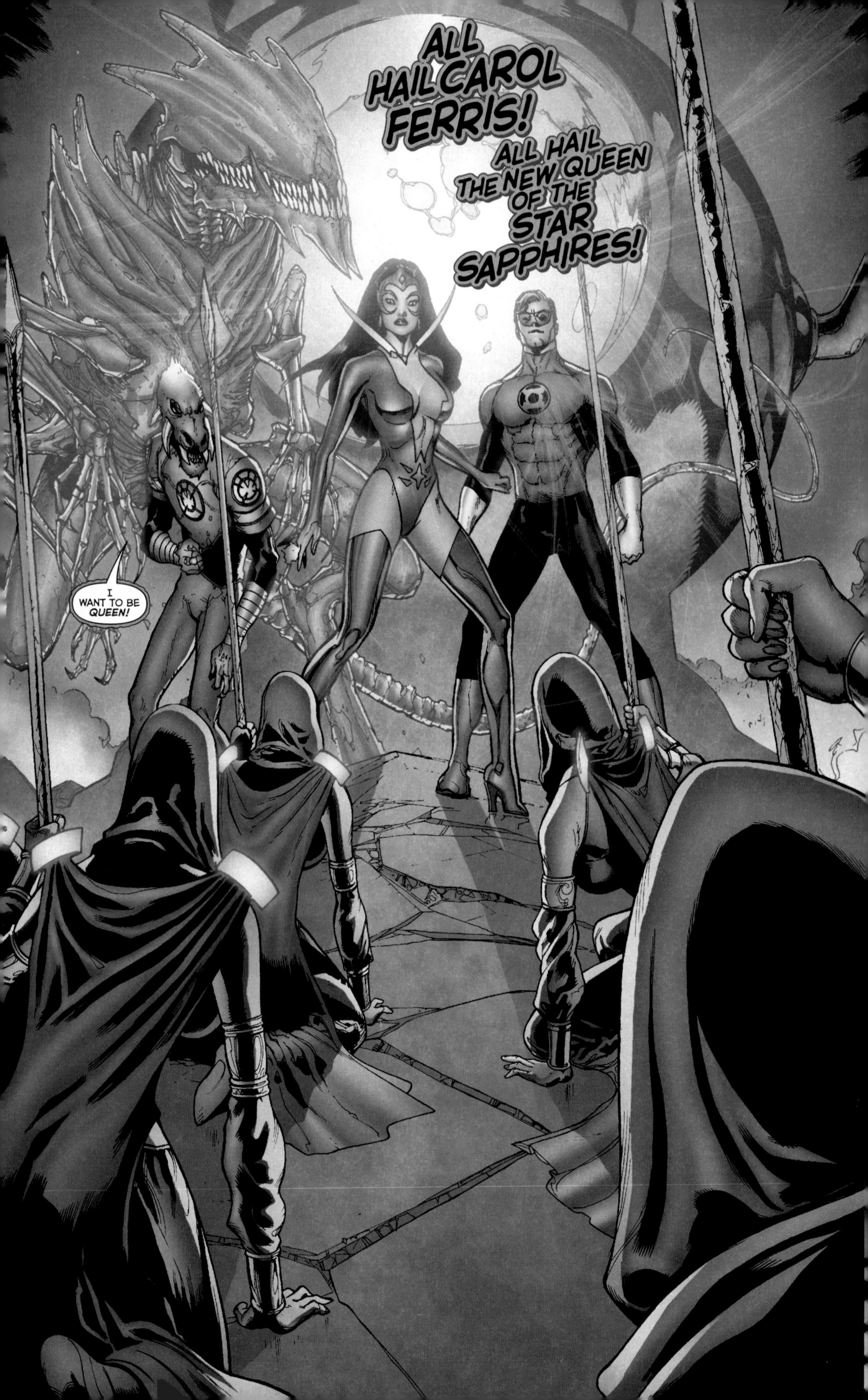
ALL HAIL CAROL FERRIS!
ALL HAIL THE NEW QUEEN OF THE STAR SAPPHIRES!
I WANT TO BE QUEEN!

GREEN LANTERN 58 Cover by Doug Mahnke, Christian Alamy & Randy Mayor

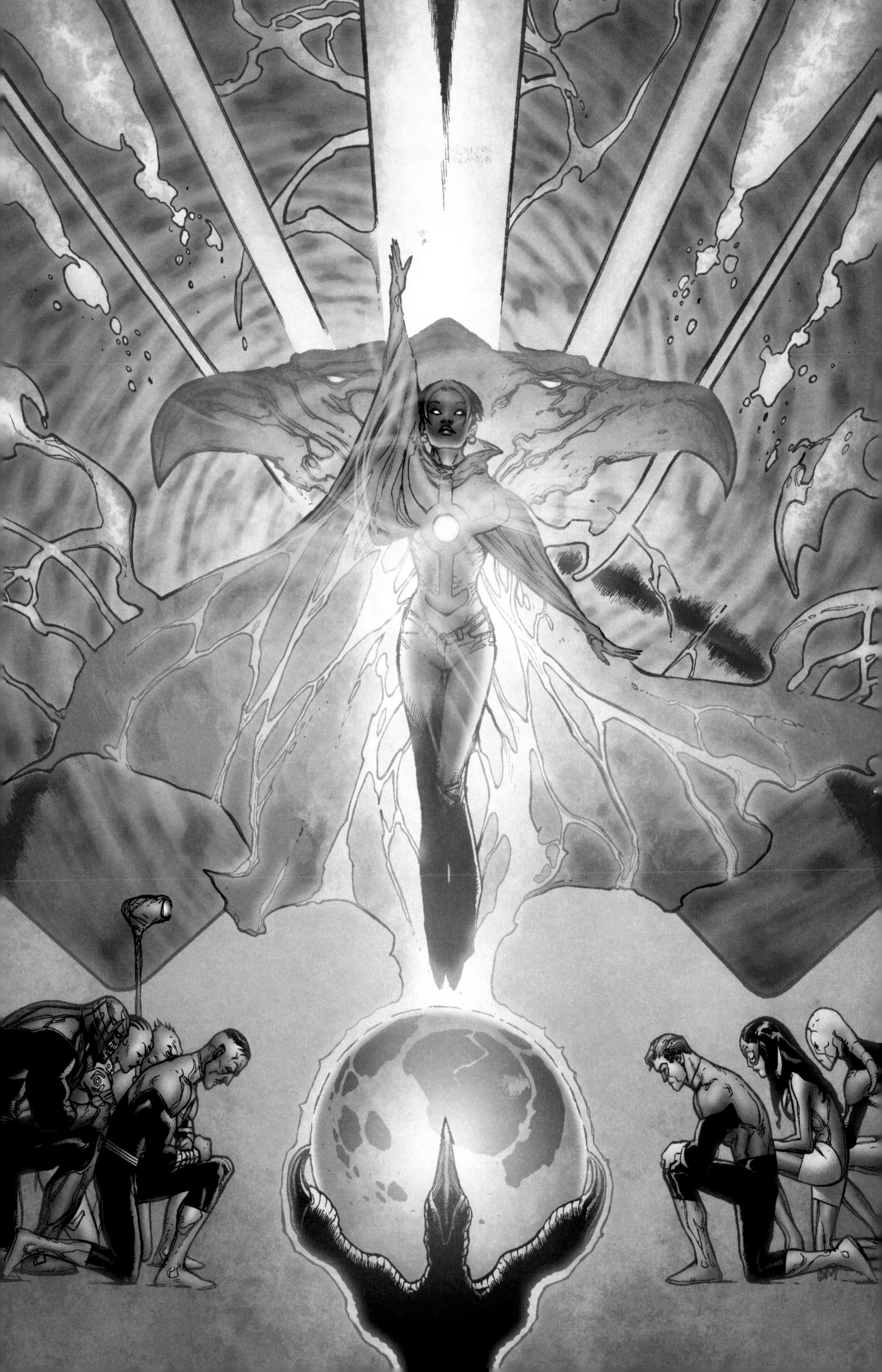

THE NEW GUARDIANS
CHAPTER SIX

Doug Mahnke Pencils
Christian Alamy, Keith Champagne & Doug Mahnke Inks

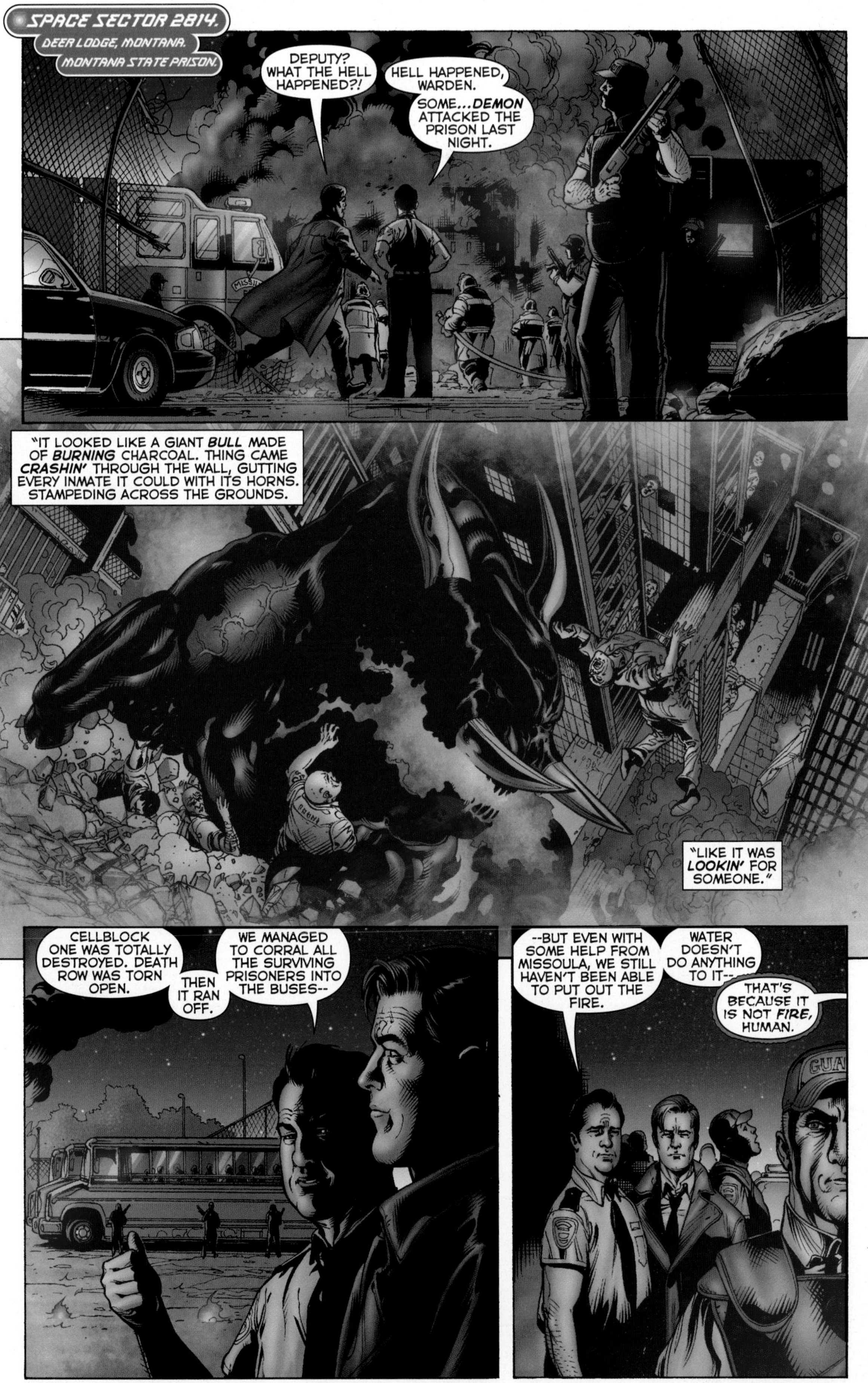
SPACE SECTOR 2814.
DEER LODGE, MONTANA.
MONTANA STATE PRISON.
DEPUTY? WHAT THE HELL HAPPENED?!
HELL HAPPENED, WARDEN.
SOME...DEMON ATTACKED THE PRISON LAST NIGHT.
"IT LOOKED LIKE A GIANT BULL MADE OF BURNING CHARCOAL. THING CAME CRASHIN' THROUGH THE WALL, GUTTING EVERY INMATE IT COULD WITH ITS HORNS. STAMPEDING ACROSS THE GROUNDS.
"LIKE IT WAS LOOKIN' FOR SOMEONE."
CELLBLOCK ONE WAS TOTALLY DESTROYED. DEATH ROW WAS TORN OPEN.
THEN IT RAN OFF.
WE MANAGED TO CORRAL ALL THE SURVIVING PRISONERS INTO THE BUSES--
--BUT EVEN WITH SOME HELP FROM MISSOULA, WE STILL HAVEN'T BEEN ABLE TO PUT OUT THE FIRE.
WATER DOESN'T DO ANYTHING TO IT--
THAT'S BECAUSE IT IS NOT FIRE, HUMAN.

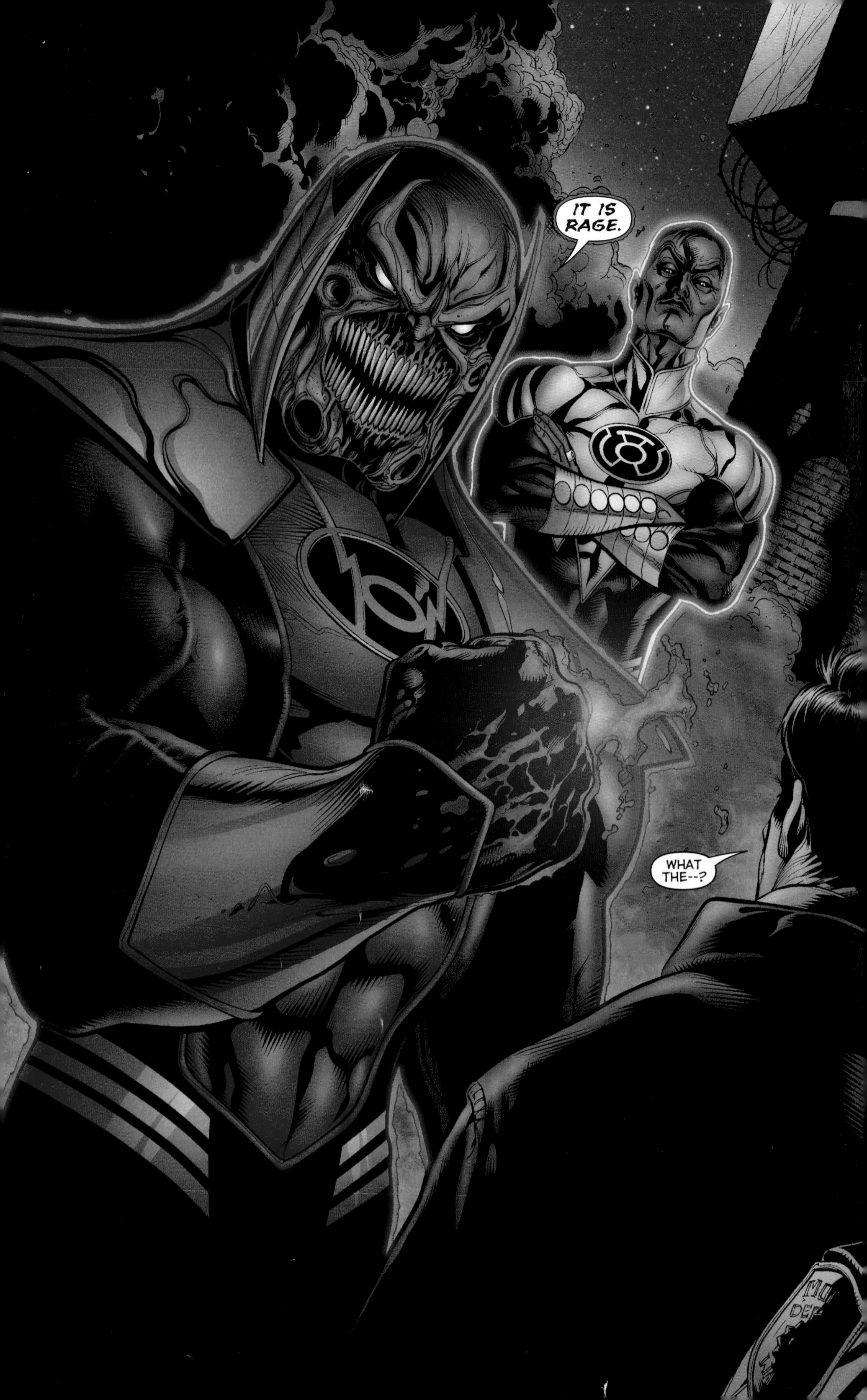
IT IS RAGE.
WHAT THE--?

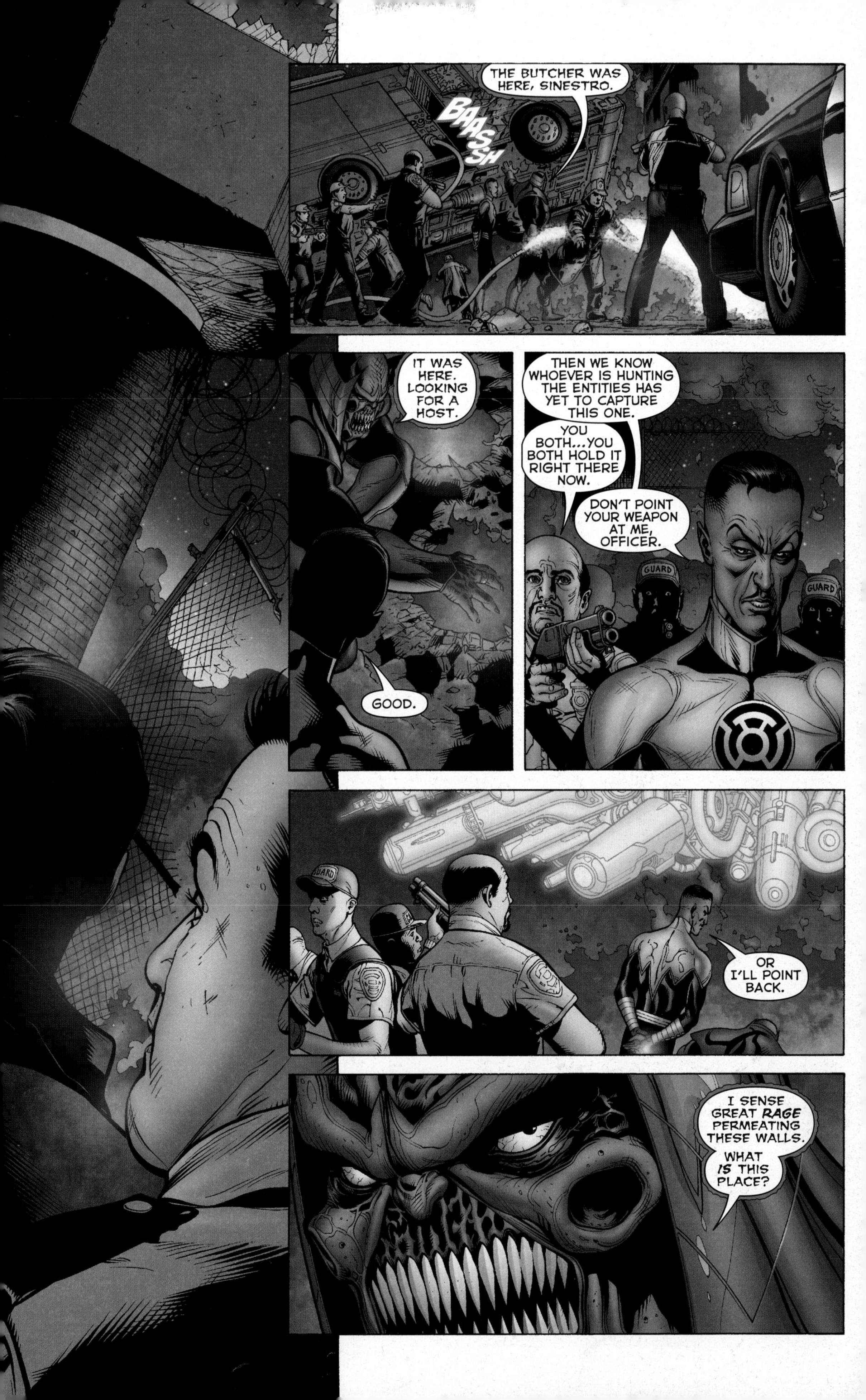
THE BUTCHER WAS HERE, SINESTRO.
BAASH
IT WAS HERE. LOOKING FOR A HOST.
GOOD.
THEN WE KNOW WHOEVER IS HUNTING THE ENTITIES HAS YET TO CAPTURE THIS ONE.
YOU BOTH...YOU BOTH HOLD IT RIGHT THERE NOW.
DON'T POINT YOUR WEAPON AT ME, OFFICER.
GUARD
GUARD
OR I'LL POINT BACK.
I SENSE GREAT RAGE PERMEATING THESE WALLS.
WHAT IS THIS PLACE?

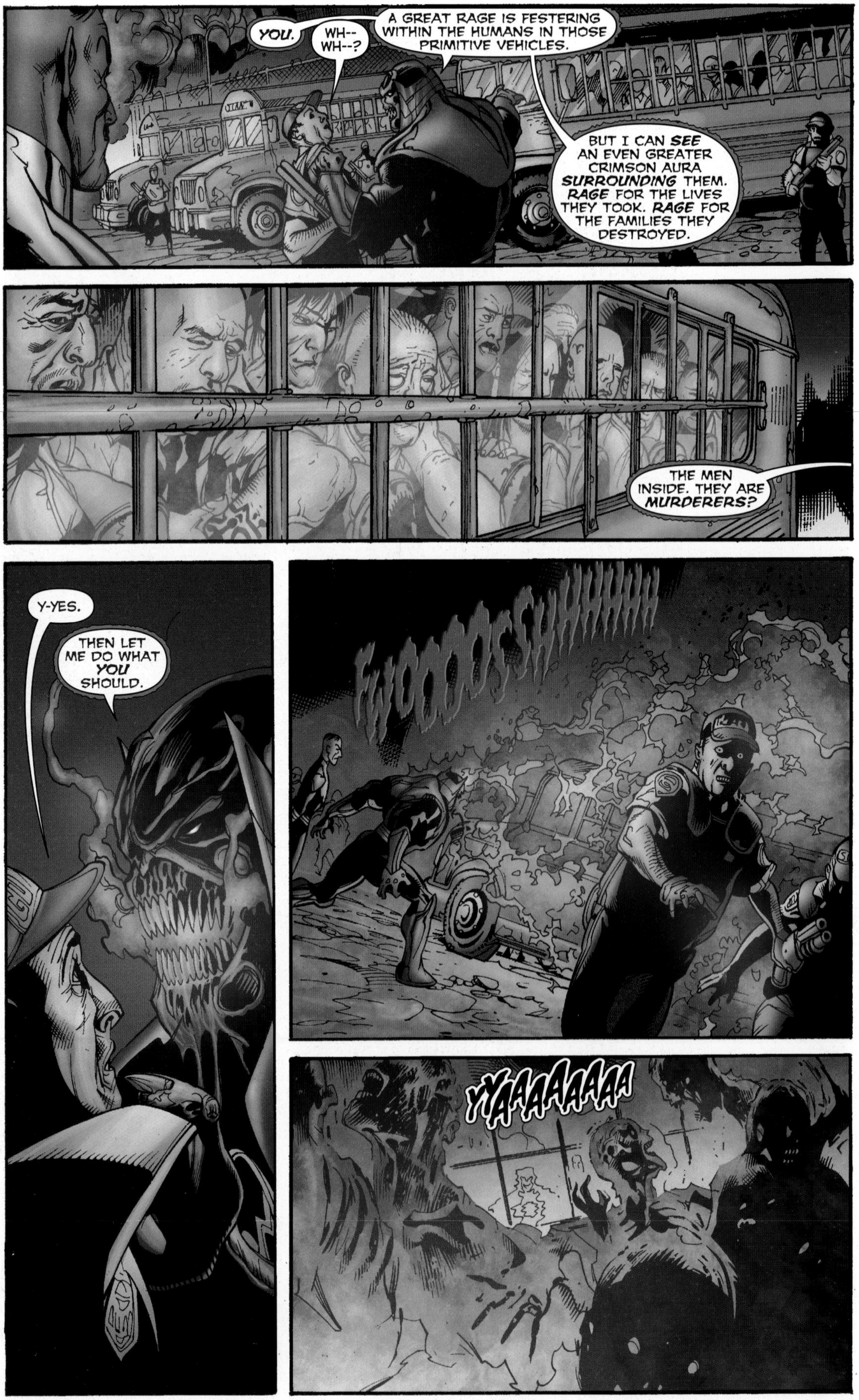
YOU.
WH-- WH--?
A GREAT RAGE IS FESTERING WITHIN THE HUMANS IN THOSE PRIMITIVE VEHICLES.
BUT I CAN SEE AN EVEN GREATER CRIMSON AURA SURROUNDING THEM. RAGE FOR THE LIVES THEY TOOK. RAGE FOR THE FAMILIES THEY DESTROYED.
THE MEN INSIDE. THEY ARE MURDERERS?
Y-YES.
THEN LET ME DO WHAT YOU SHOULD.
FWOOOOSHHHHHH
YYAAAAAAA

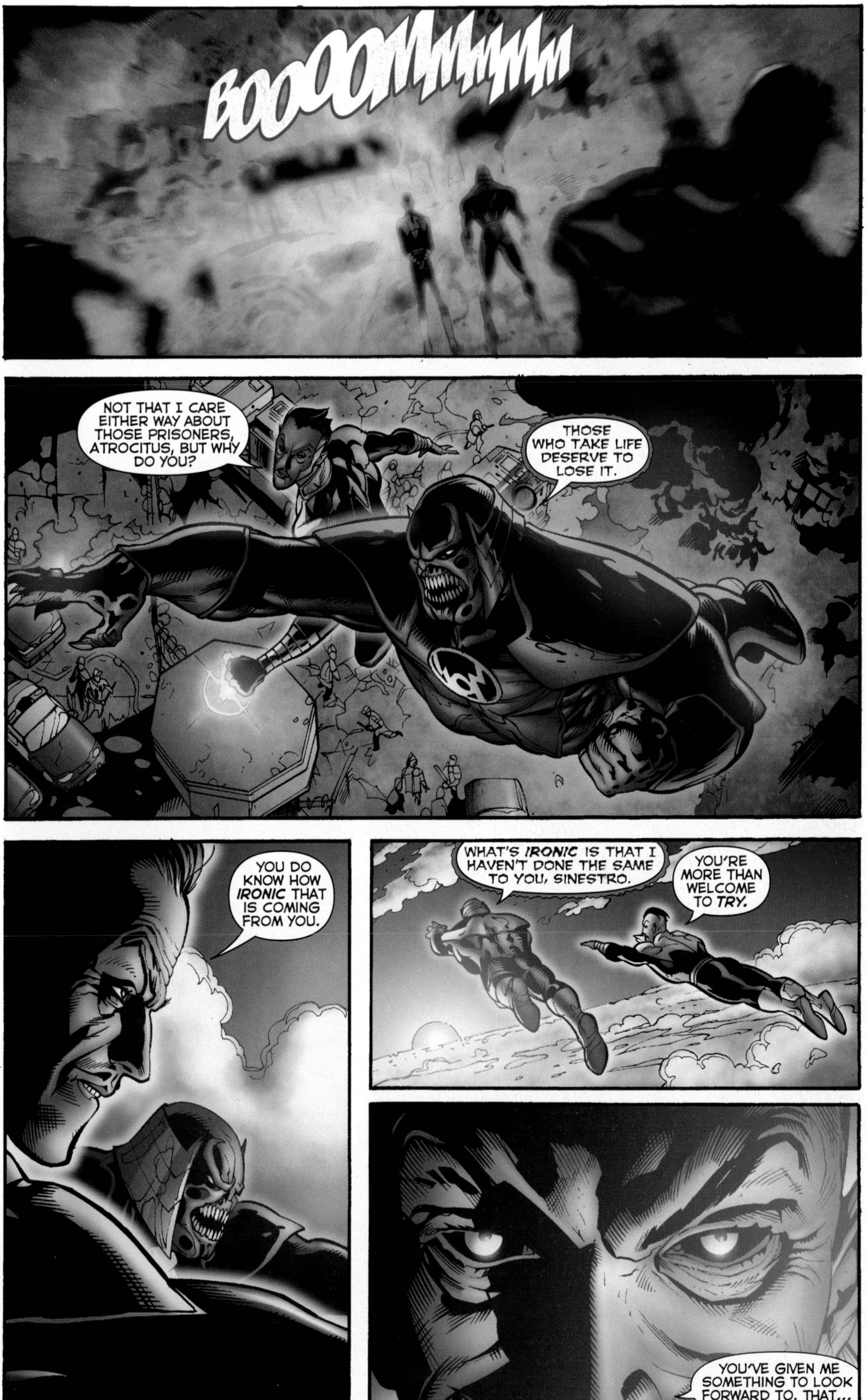
BOOOOMMMMM
NOT THAT I CARE EITHER WAY ABOUT THOSE PRISONERS, ATROCITUS, BUT WHY DO YOU?
THOSE WHO TAKE LIFE DESERVE TO LOSE IT.
YOU DO KNOW HOW IRONIC THAT IS COMING FROM YOU.
WHAT'S IRONIC IS THAT I HAVEN'T DONE THE SAME TO YOU, SINESTRO.
YOU'RE MORE THAN WELCOME TO TRY.
YOU'VE GIVEN ME SOMETHING TO LOOK FORWARD TO. THAT...

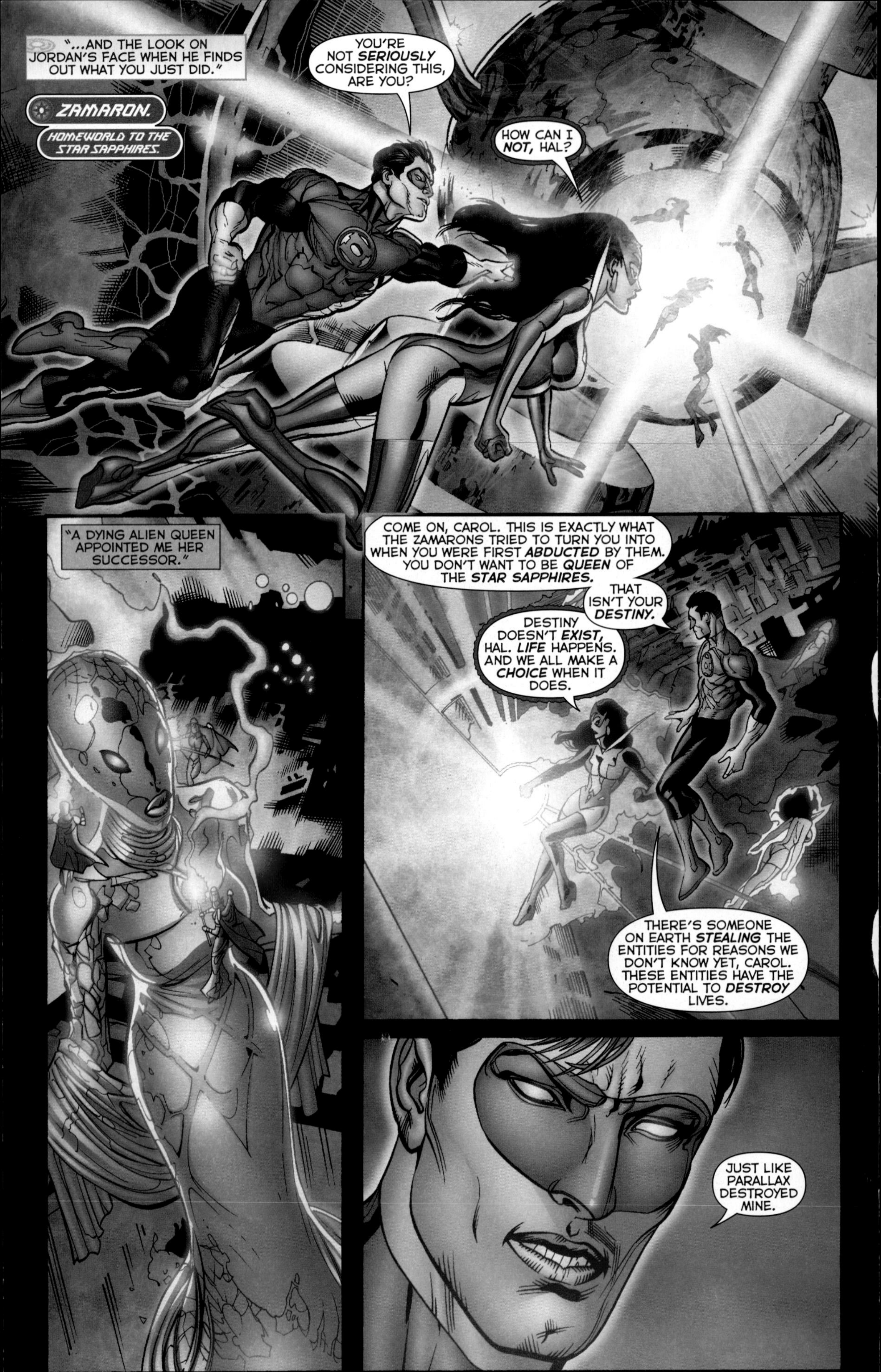
"...AND THE LOOK ON JORDAN'S FACE WHEN HE FINDS OUT WHAT YOU JUST DID."
ZAMARON.
HOMEWORLD TO THE STAR SAPPHIRES.
YOU'RE NOT SERIOUSLY CONSIDERING THIS, ARE YOU?
HOW CAN I NOT, HAL?
"A DYING ALIEN QUEEN APPOINTED ME HER SUCCESSOR."
COME ON, CAROL. THIS IS EXACTLY WHAT THE ZAMARONS TRIED TO TURN YOU INTO WHEN YOU WERE FIRST ABDUCTED BY THEM. YOU DON'T WANT TO BE QUEEN OF THE STAR SAPPHIRES.
THAT ISN'T YOUR DESTINY.
DESTINY DOESN'T EXIST, HAL. LIFE HAPPENS. AND WE ALL MAKE A CHOICE WHEN IT DOES.
THERE'S SOMEONE ON EARTH STEALING THE ENTITIES FOR REASONS WE DON'T KNOW YET, CAROL. THESE ENTITIES HAVE THE POTENTIAL TO DESTROY LIVES.
JUST LIKE PARALLAX DESTROYED MINE.

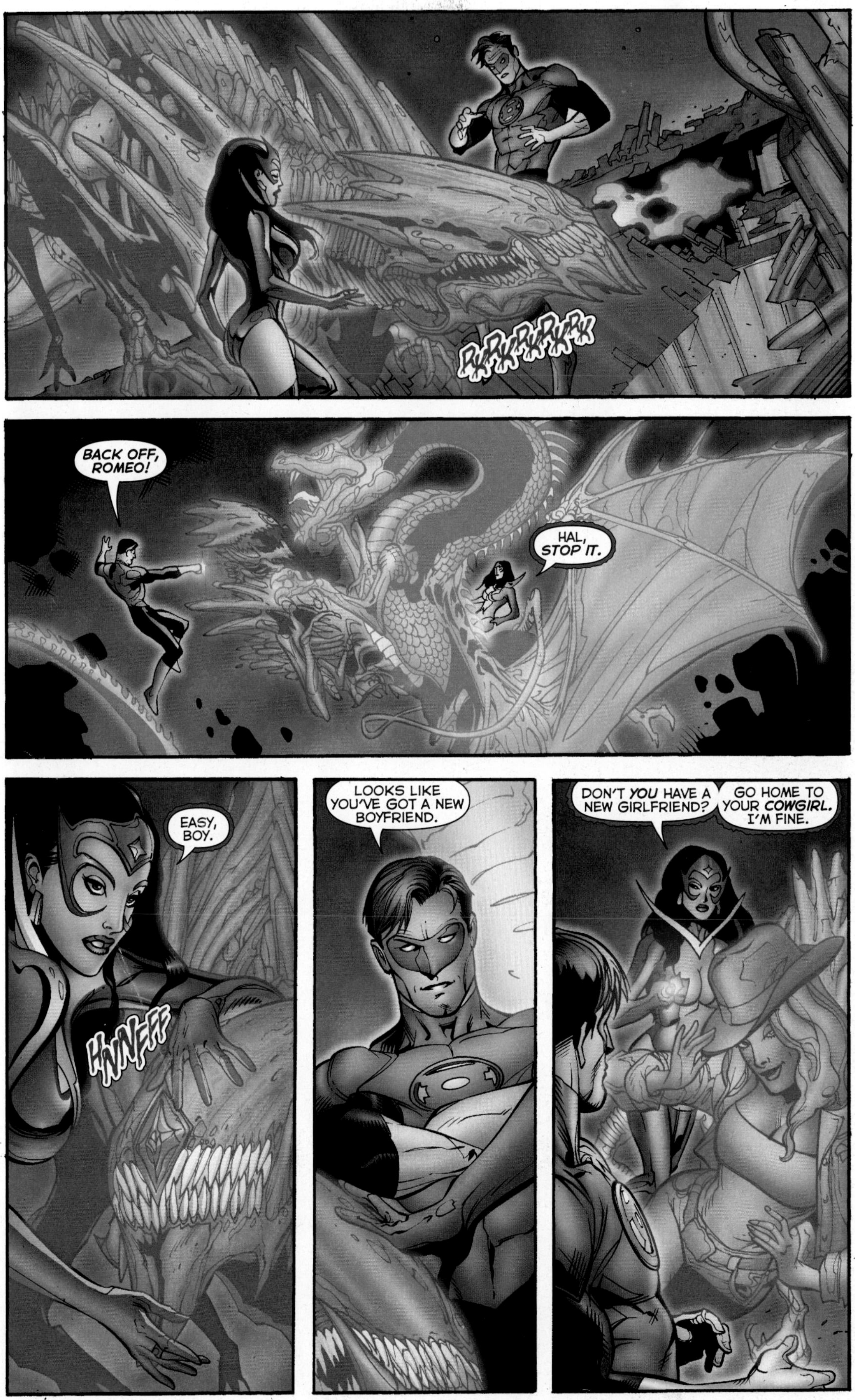
DRRRRRRRRRR
BACK OFF, ROMEO!
HAL, STOP IT.
EASY, BOY.
HNNEFF
LOOKS LIKE YOU'VE GOT A NEW BOYFRIEND.
DON'T *YOU* HAVE A NEW GIRLFRIEND?
GO HOME TO YOUR *COWGIRL.* I'M FINE.

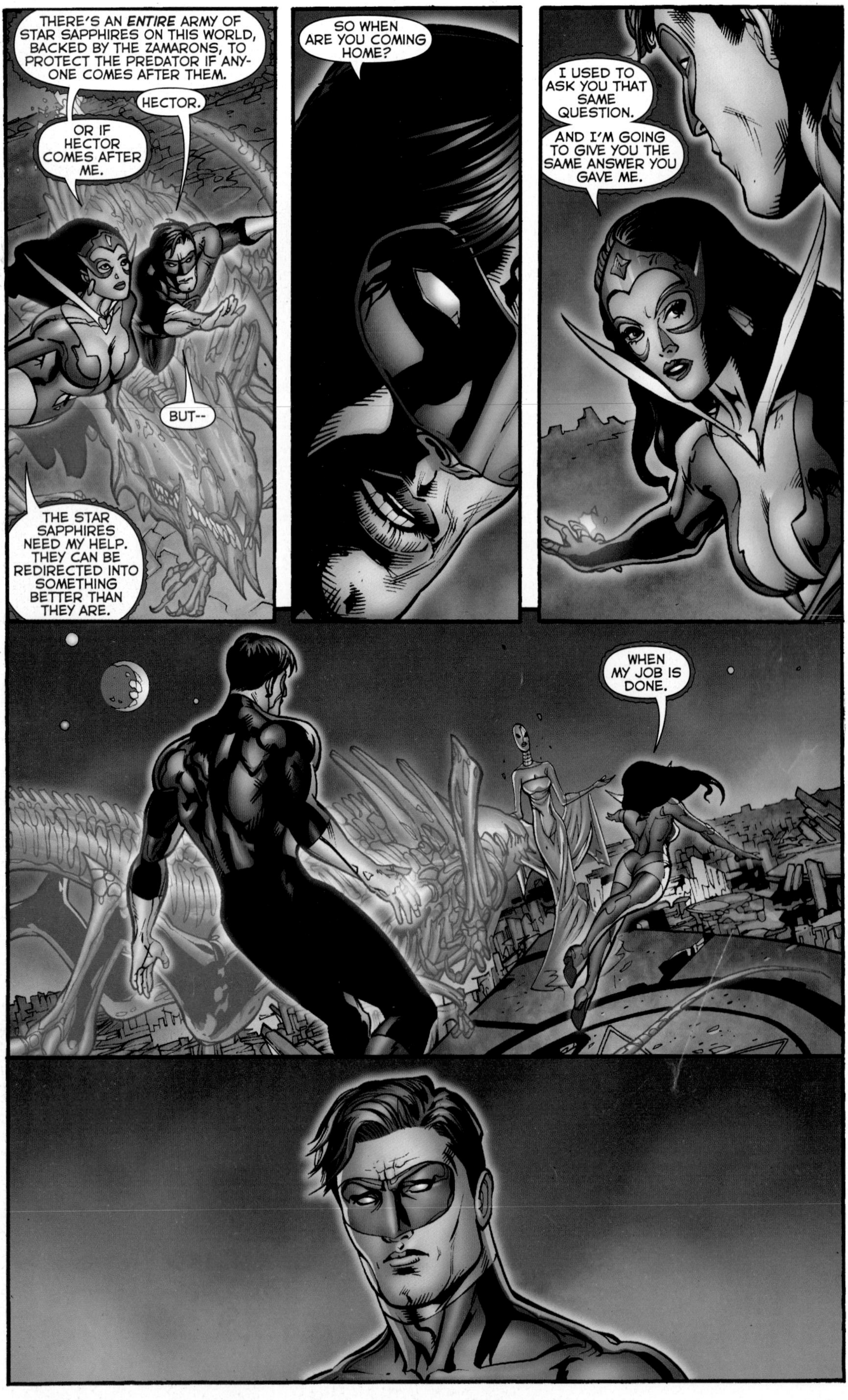
THERE'S AN ENTIRE ARMY OF STAR SAPPHIRES ON THIS WORLD, BACKED BY THE ZAMARONS, TO PROTECT THE PREDATOR IF ANYONE COMES AFTER THEM.
HECTOR.
OR IF HECTOR COMES AFTER ME.
BUT--
THE STAR SAPPHIRES NEED MY HELP. THEY CAN BE REDIRECTED INTO SOMETHING BETTER THAN THEY ARE.
SO WHEN ARE YOU COMING HOME?
I USED TO ASK YOU THAT SAME QUESTION.
AND I'M GOING TO GIVE YOU THE SAME ANSWER YOU GAVE ME.
WHEN MY JOB IS DONE.

...CONTINUING DAY TWO OF THE SEARCH FOR FOURTEEN-YEAR-OLD NICOLE MORRISON.

NICOLE WAS LAST SEEN TUESDAY AFTERNOON LEAVING BATES HAMBURGERS AT 5 MILE AND FARMINGTON.

SINCE THEN, HUNDREDS HAVE VOLUNTEERED AND HAVE BEEN SEARCHING THE AREA. EARLIER THIS MORNING, NICOLE'S BACKPACK WAS FOUND IN A DUMPSTER IN WARREN.

MY DAUGHTER IS STRONG AND SHE'S FIGHTING WHOEVER TOOK HER.

I KNOW SHE IS.

AND I...

...I....

...I WANT MY DAUGHTER BACK.

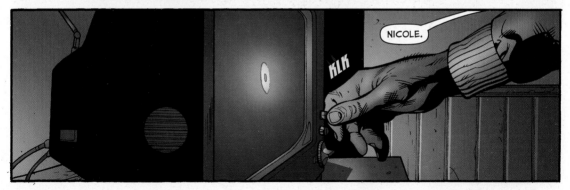

NICOLE.

KLK

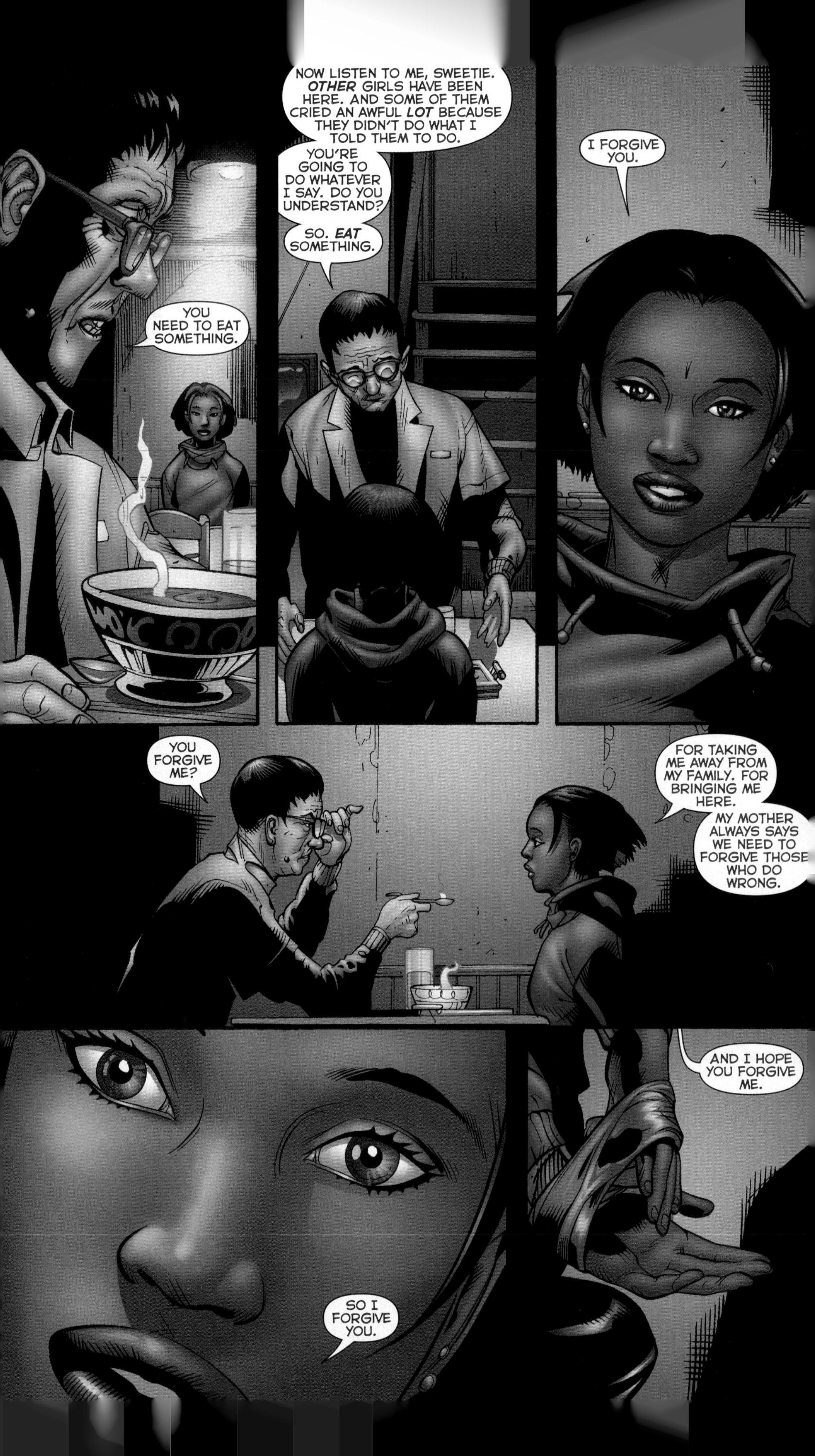
YOU NEED TO EAT SOMETHING.
NOW LISTEN TO ME, SWEETIE. OTHER GIRLS HAVE BEEN HERE. AND SOME OF THEM CRIED AN AWFUL LOT BECAUSE THEY DIDN'T DO WHAT I TOLD THEM TO DO.
YOU'RE GOING TO DO WHATEVER I SAY. DO YOU UNDERSTAND?
SO. EAT SOMETHING.
I FORGIVE YOU.
YOU FORGIVE ME?
FOR TAKING ME AWAY FROM MY FAMILY. FOR BRINGING ME HERE.
MY MOTHER ALWAYS SAYS WE NEED TO FORGIVE THOSE WHO DO WRONG.
SO I FORGIVE YOU.
AND I HOPE YOU FORGIVE ME.

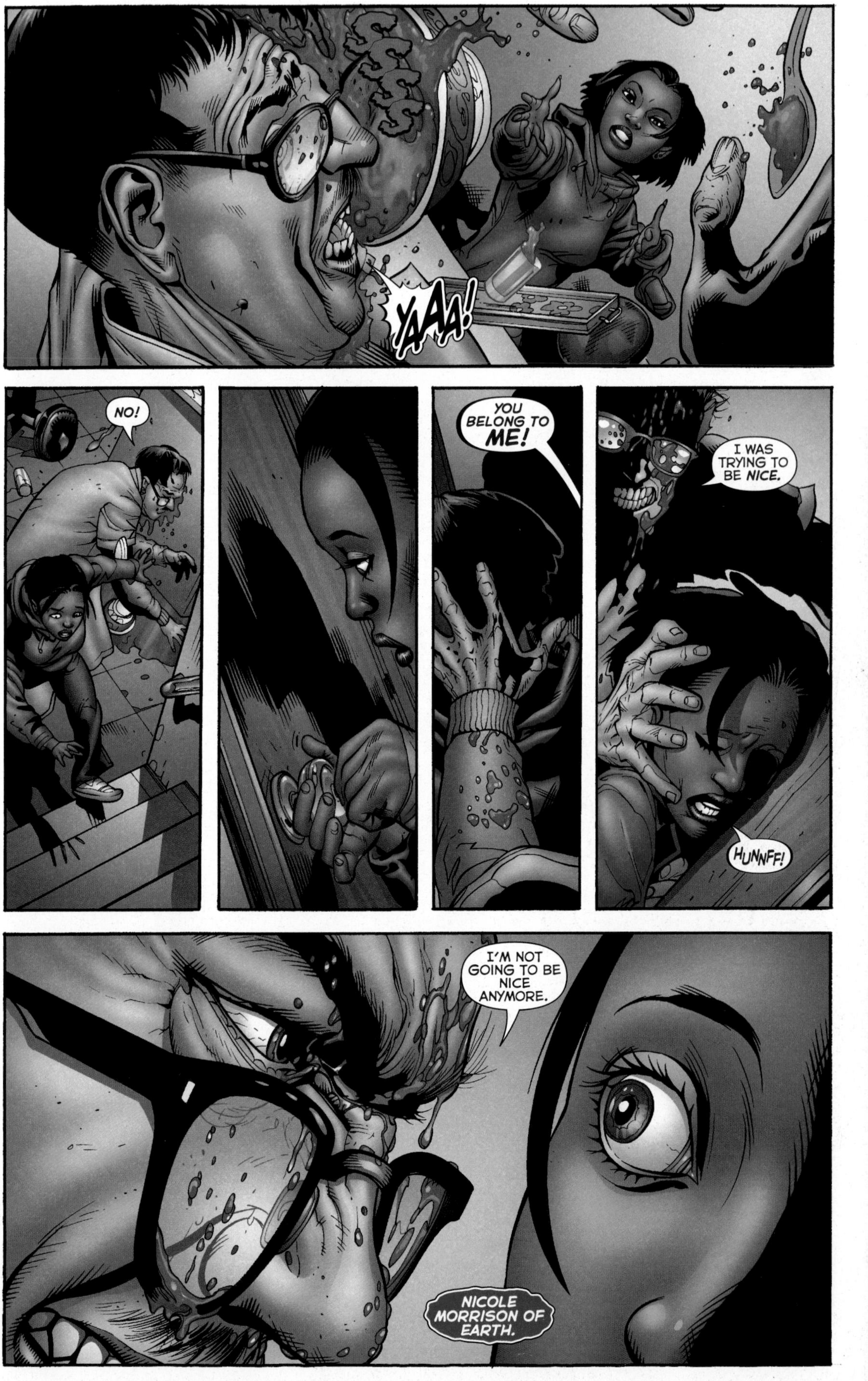
SSSS
YAAA!
NO!
YOU BELONG TO ME!
I WAS TRYING TO BE NICE.
HUNNFF!
I'M NOT GOING TO BE NICE ANYMORE.
NICOLE MORRISON OF EARTH.

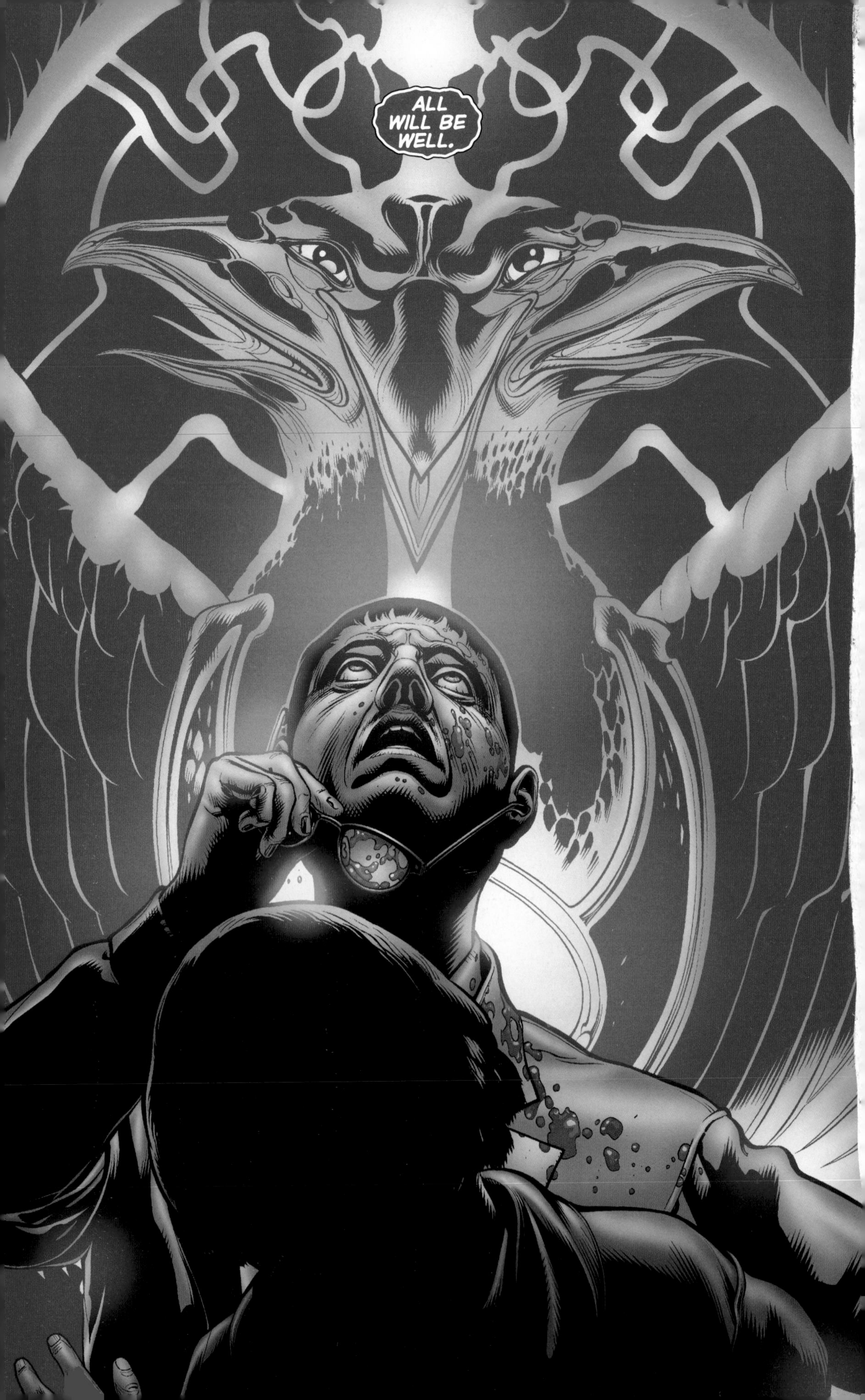
ALL WILL BE WELL.

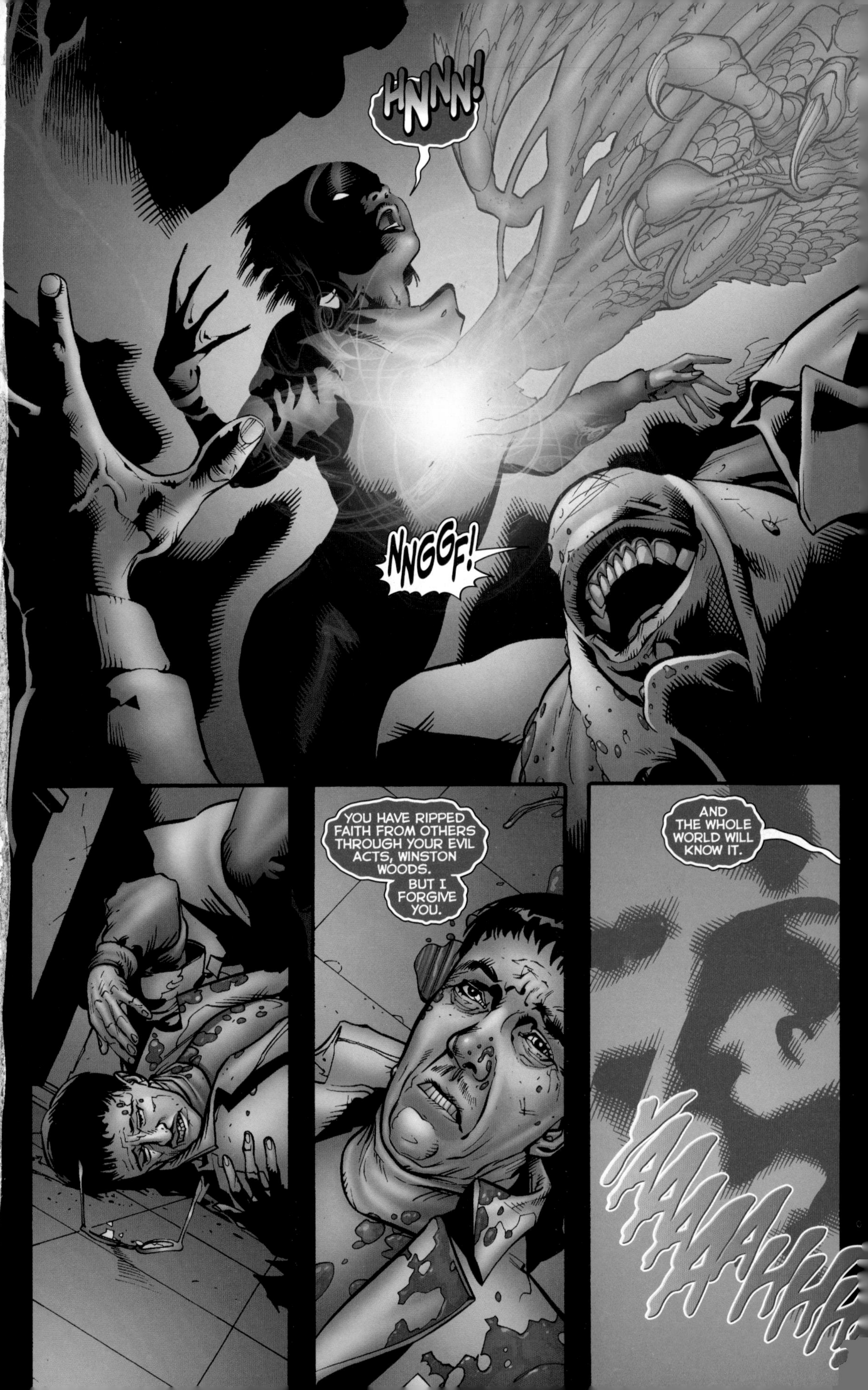
HNNN!
NNGGF!
YOU HAVE RIPPED FAITH FROM OTHERS THROUGH YOUR EVIL ACTS, WINSTON WOODS.
BUT I FORGIVE YOU.
AND THE WHOLE WORLD WILL KNOW IT.

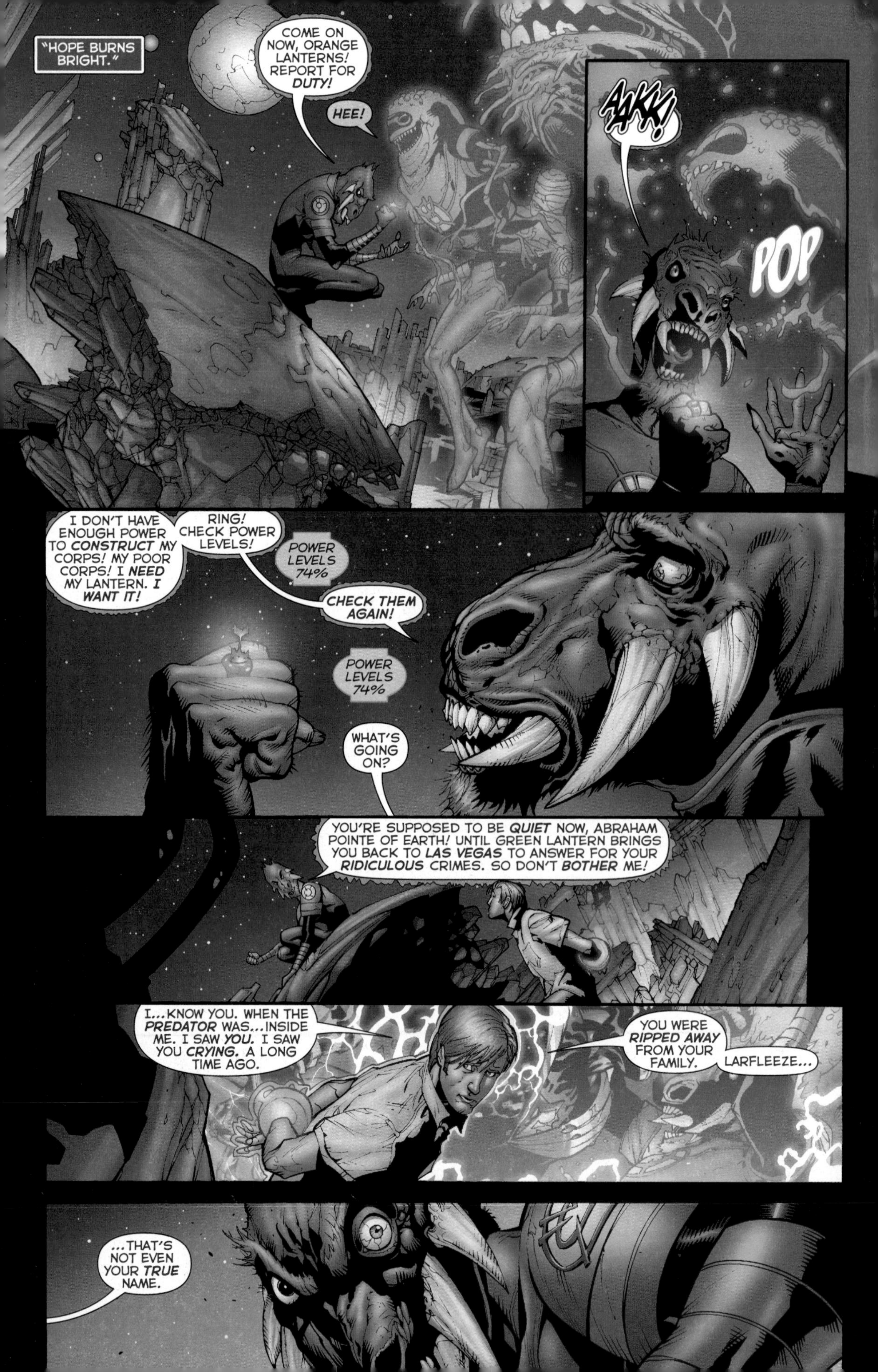
"HOPE BURNS BRIGHT."
COME ON NOW, ORANGE LANTERNS! REPORT FOR DUTY!
HEE!
AAKK!
POP
I DON'T HAVE ENOUGH POWER TO CONSTRUCT MY CORPS! MY POOR CORPS! I NEED MY LANTERN. I WANT IT!
RING! CHECK POWER LEVELS!
POWER LEVELS 74%
CHECK THEM AGAIN!
POWER LEVELS 74%
WHAT'S GOING ON?
YOU'RE SUPPOSED TO BE QUIET NOW, ABRAHAM POINTE OF EARTH! UNTIL GREEN LANTERN BRINGS YOU BACK TO LAS VEGAS TO ANSWER FOR YOUR RIDICULOUS CRIMES. SO DON'T BOTHER ME!
I...KNOW YOU. WHEN THE PREDATOR WAS...INSIDE ME. I SAW YOU. I SAW YOU CRYING. A LONG TIME AGO.
YOU WERE RIPPED AWAY FROM YOUR FAMILY.
LARFLEEZE...
...THAT'S NOT EVEN YOUR TRUE NAME.

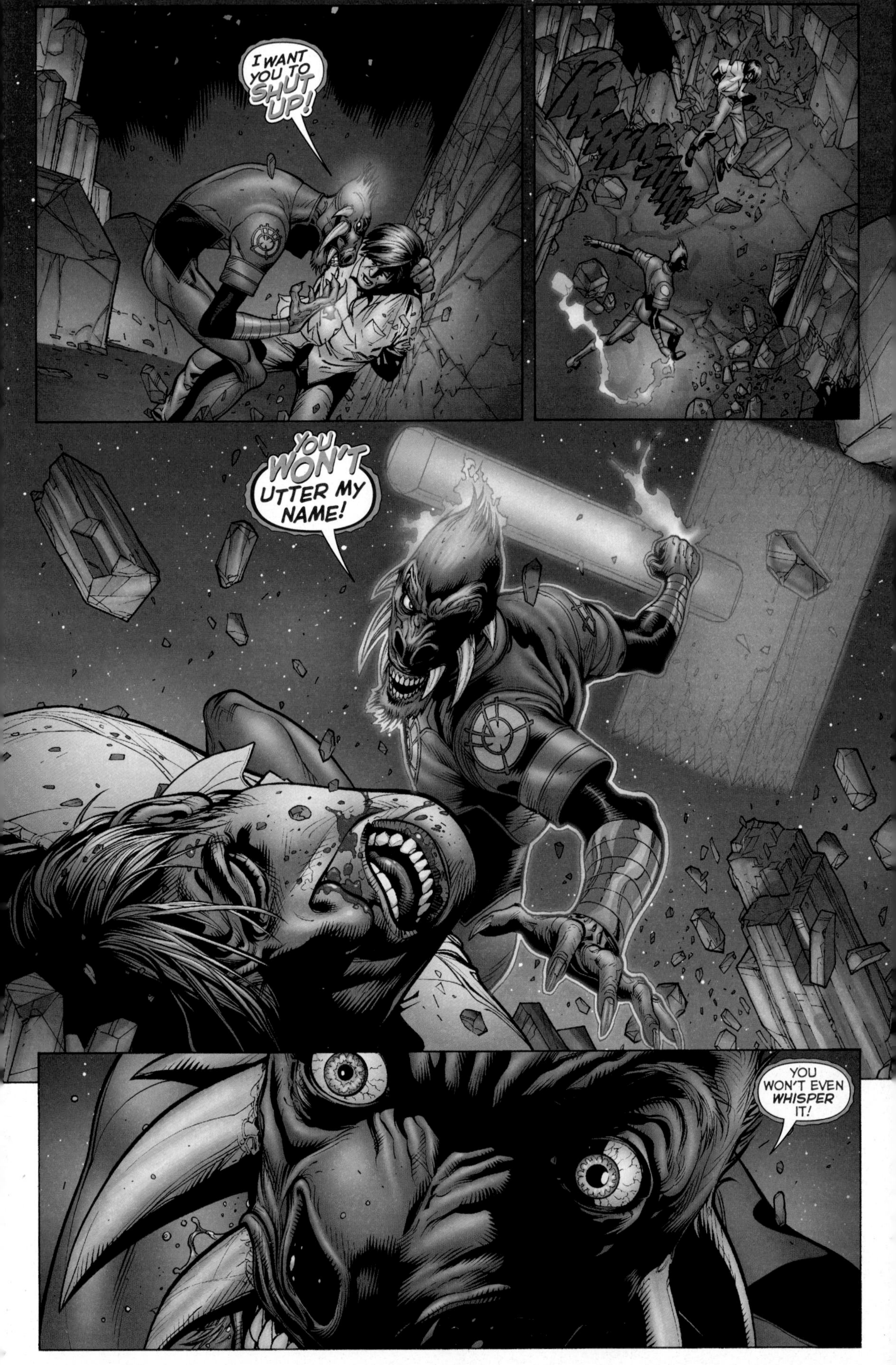
I WANT YOU TO SHUT UP!
YOU WON'T UTTER MY NAME!
YOU WON'T EVEN WHISPER IT!

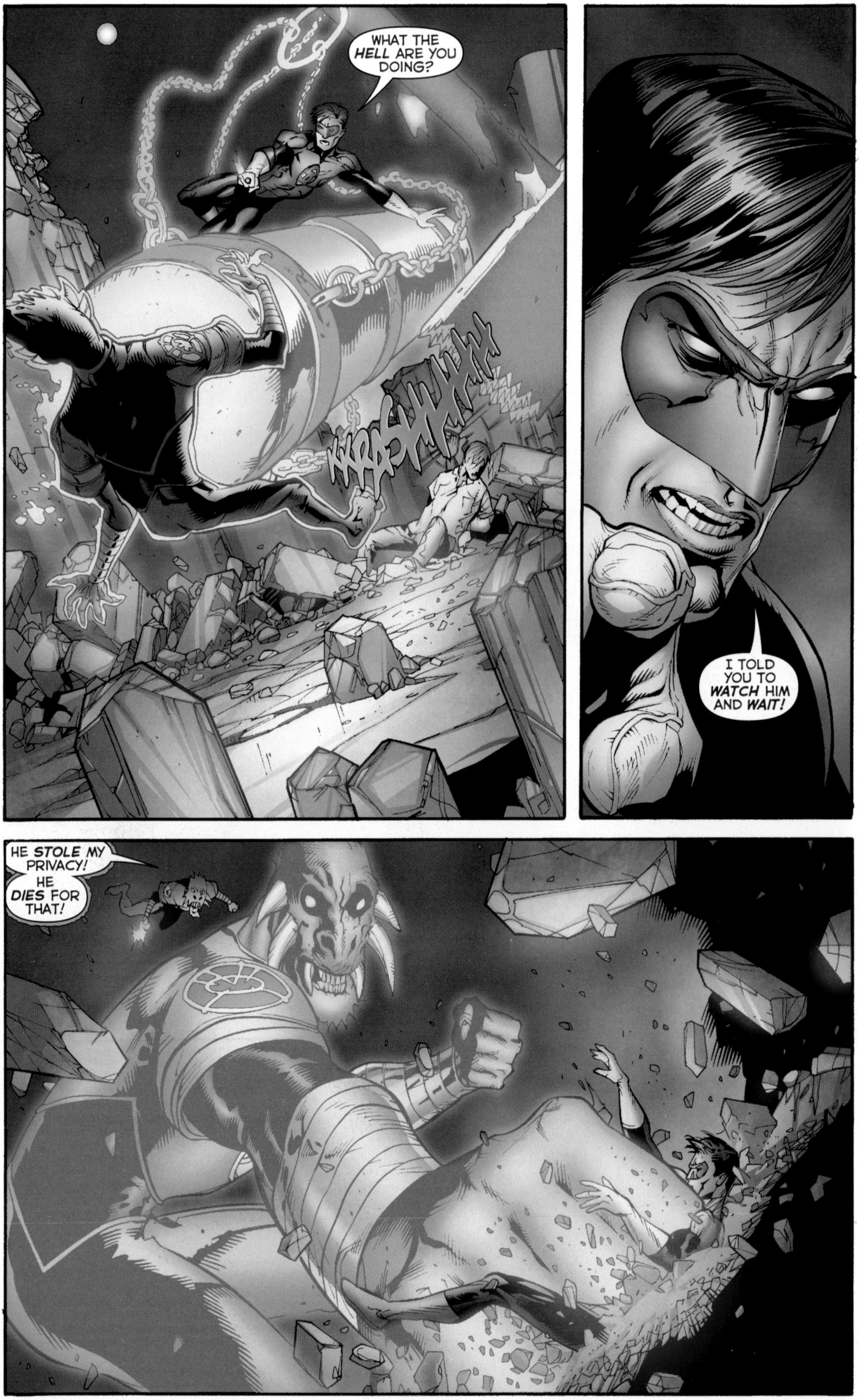
WHAT THE HELL ARE YOU DOING?
I TOLD YOU TO WATCH HIM AND WAIT!
HE STOLE MY PRIVACY! HE DIES FOR THAT!

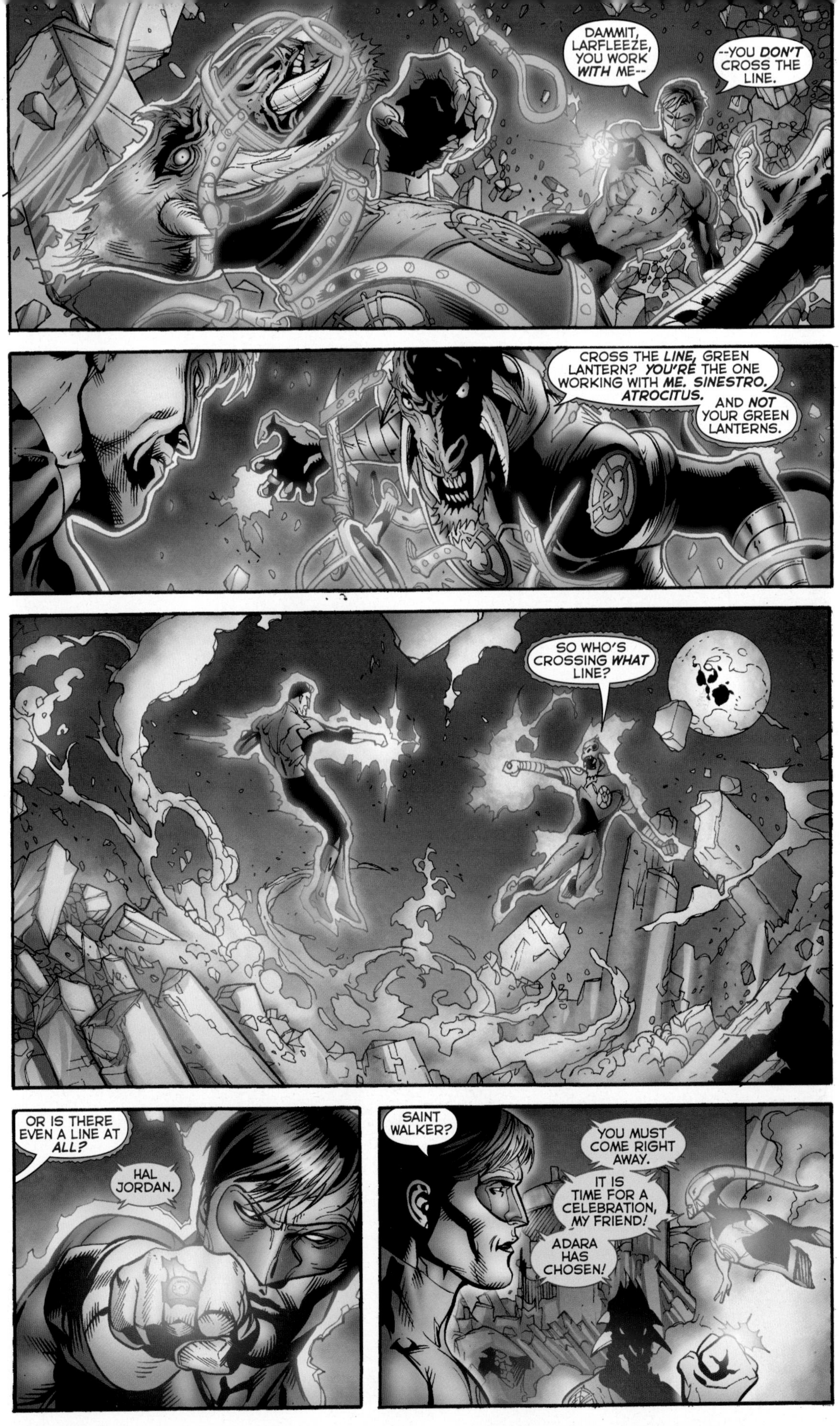

DAMMIT, LARFLEEZE, YOU WORK WITH ME--
--YOU DON'T CROSS THE LINE.
CROSS THE LINE, GREEN LANTERN? YOU'RE THE ONE WORKING WITH ME. SINESTRO. ATROCITUS.
AND NOT YOUR GREEN LANTERNS.
SO WHO'S CROSSING WHAT LINE?
OR IS THERE EVEN A LINE AT ALL?
HAL JORDAN.
SAINT WALKER?
YOU MUST COME RIGHT AWAY.
IT IS TIME FOR A CELEBRATION, MY FRIEND!
ADARA HAS CHOSEN!

OA.
THE CENTRAL PRECINCT OF THE GREEN LANTERN CORPS.
"HOPE IS HERE!"
WHAT IS IT, SALAAK? MORE PRISONERS TO HOUSE IN THE SCIENCE CELLS?
QUITE THE CONTRARY, VOX.
HAL JORDAN'S RING HASN'T LOGGED ANY ARRESTS, OR A SINGLE CONFRONTATION, SINCE THE DAY AFTER WE DEFEATED NEKRON AND HIS BLACK LANTERNS.
HE'S DOING WHAT MOST HUMANS DO AFTER A LONG STRETCH OF WORK, SALAAK!
AND WHAT IS THAT, LARVOX?
TAKING SOME WELL-DESERVED "R & R!"
"R & R"?
REST AND RELAXATION. YOU SHOULD DO THAT YOURSELF SOMETIME. IT'S REALLY RATHER PLEASANT!
SINCE WHEN HAS HAL JORDAN EVER TAKEN R & R?
HM.
I AM BEGINNING TO SUSPECT HAL JORDAN'S RING IS EITHER MALFUNCTIONING--

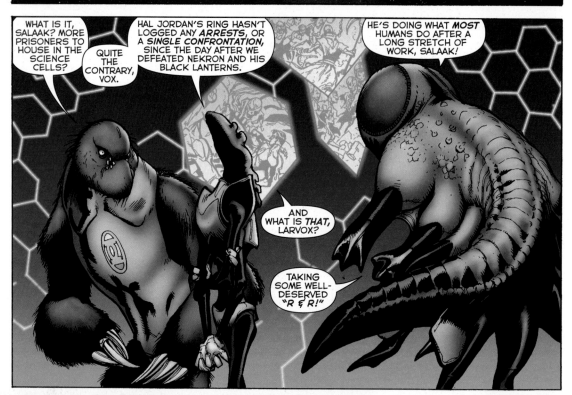

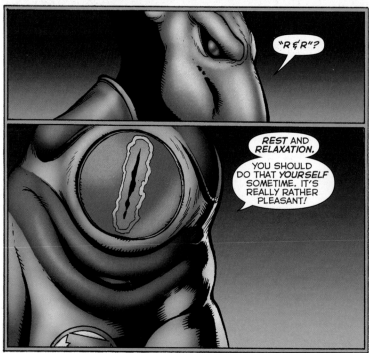

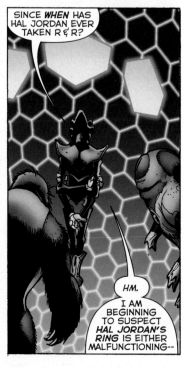

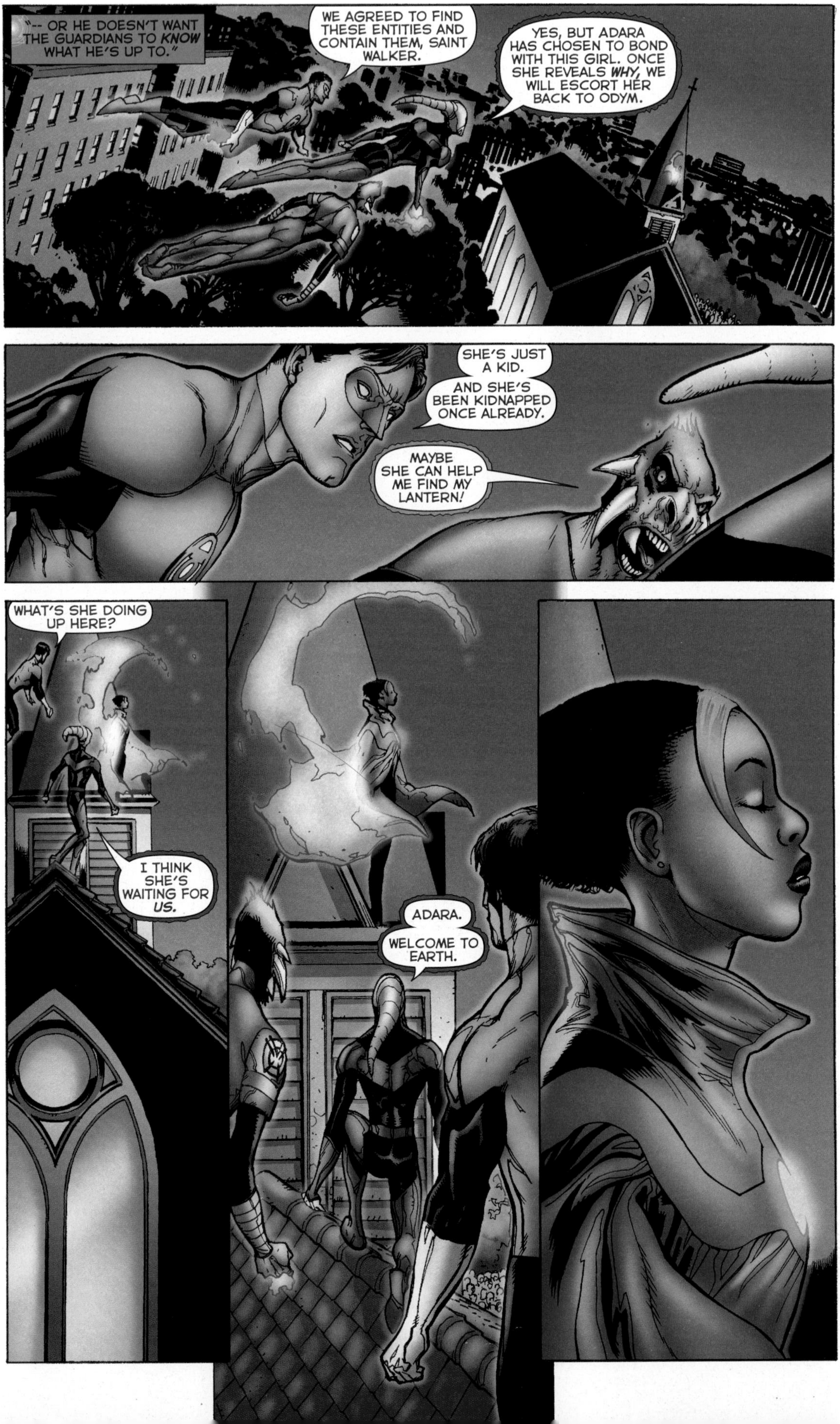
"-- OR HE DOESN'T WANT THE GUARDIANS TO KNOW WHAT HE'S UP TO."
WE AGREED TO FIND THESE ENTITIES AND CONTAIN THEM, SAINT WALKER.
YES, BUT ADARA HAS CHOSEN TO BOND WITH THIS GIRL. ONCE SHE REVEALS WHY, WE WILL ESCORT HER BACK TO ODYM.
SHE'S JUST A KID.
AND SHE'S BEEN KIDNAPPED ONCE ALREADY.
MAYBE SHE CAN HELP ME FIND MY LANTERN!
WHAT'S SHE DOING UP HERE?
I THINK SHE'S WAITING FOR US.
ADARA.
WELCOME TO EARTH.

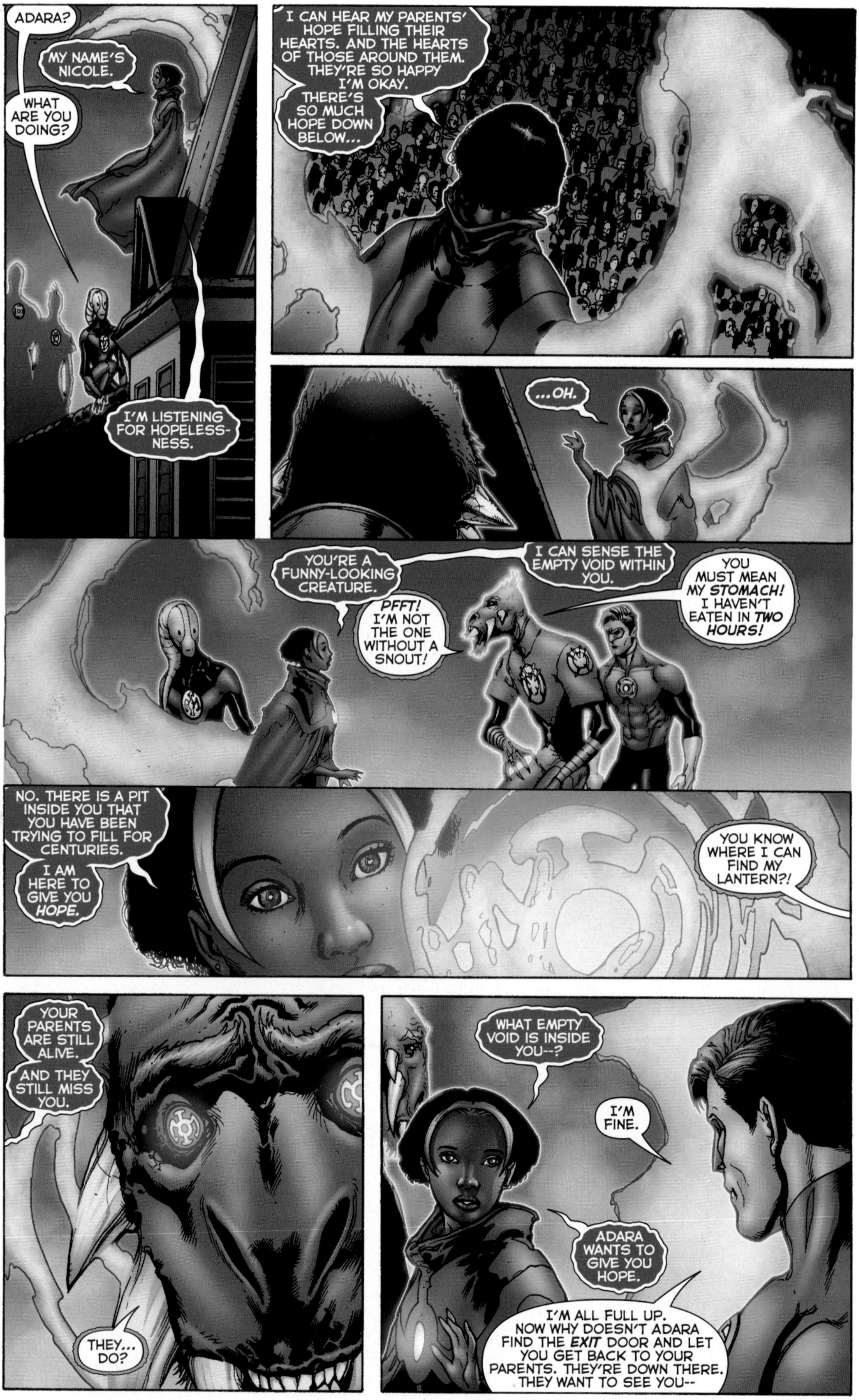
ADARA?
MY NAME'S NICOLE.
WHAT ARE YOU DOING?
I'M LISTENING FOR HOPELESS-NESS.
I CAN HEAR MY PARENTS' HOPE FILLING THEIR HEARTS. AND THE HEARTS OF THOSE AROUND THEM. THEY'RE SO HAPPY I'M OKAY.
THERE'S SO MUCH HOPE DOWN BELOW...
...OH.
YOU'RE A FUNNY-LOOKING CREATURE.
PFFT! I'M NOT THE ONE WITHOUT A SNOUT!
I CAN SENSE THE EMPTY VOID WITHIN YOU.
YOU MUST MEAN MY STOMACH! I HAVEN'T EATEN IN TWO HOURS!
NO. THERE IS A PIT INSIDE YOU THAT YOU HAVE BEEN TRYING TO FILL FOR CENTURIES.
I AM HERE TO GIVE YOU HOPE.
YOU KNOW WHERE I CAN FIND MY LANTERN?!
YOUR PARENTS ARE STILL ALIVE.
AND THEY STILL MISS YOU.
THEY... DO?
WHAT EMPTY VOID IS INSIDE YOU--?
I'M FINE.
ADARA WANTS TO GIVE YOU HOPE.
I'M ALL FULL UP. NOW WHY DOESN'T ADARA FIND THE EXIT DOOR AND LET YOU GET BACK TO YOUR PARENTS. THEY'RE DOWN THERE. THEY WANT TO SEE YOU--

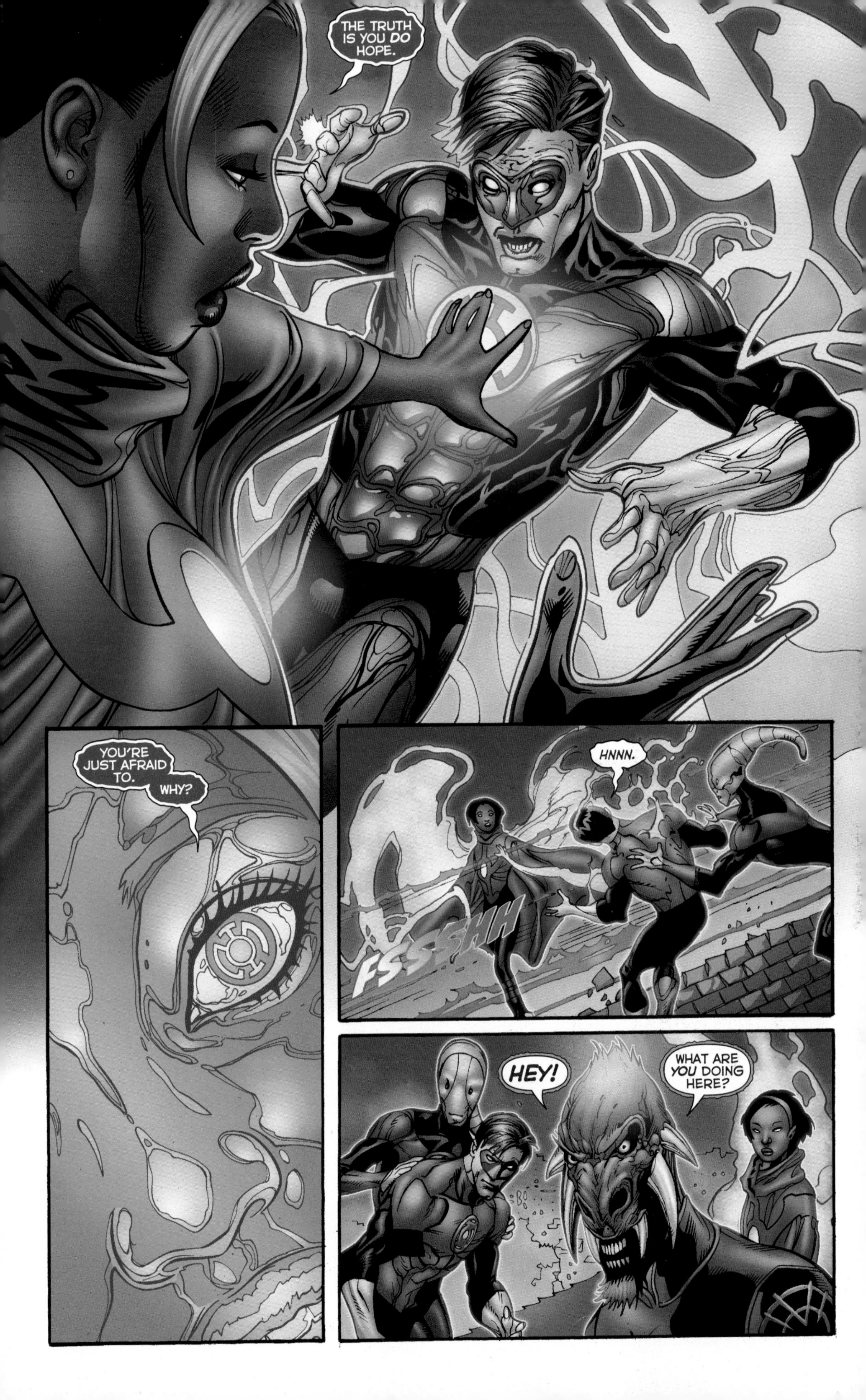
THE TRUTH IS YOU *DO* HOPE.
YOU'RE JUST AFRAID TO.
WHY?
HNNN.
FSSSHH
HEY!
WHAT ARE *YOU* DOING HERE?

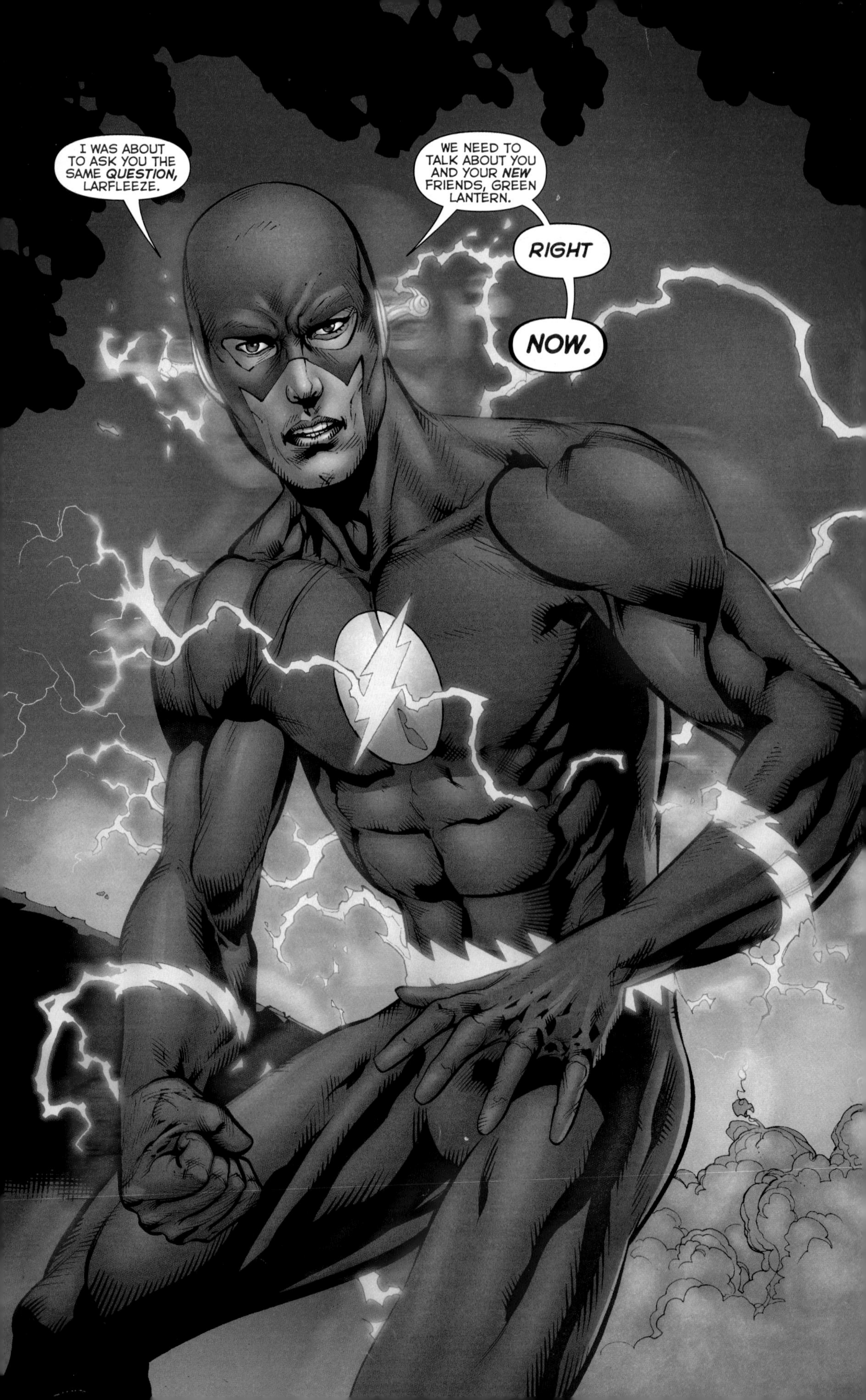

I WAS ABOUT TO ASK YOU THE SAME *QUESTION,* LARFLEEZE.
WE NEED TO TALK ABOUT YOU AND YOUR *NEW* FRIENDS, GREEN LANTERN.
RIGHT
NOW.

GREEN LANTERN 59 Cover by Doug Mahnke, Christian Alamy & Randy Mayor

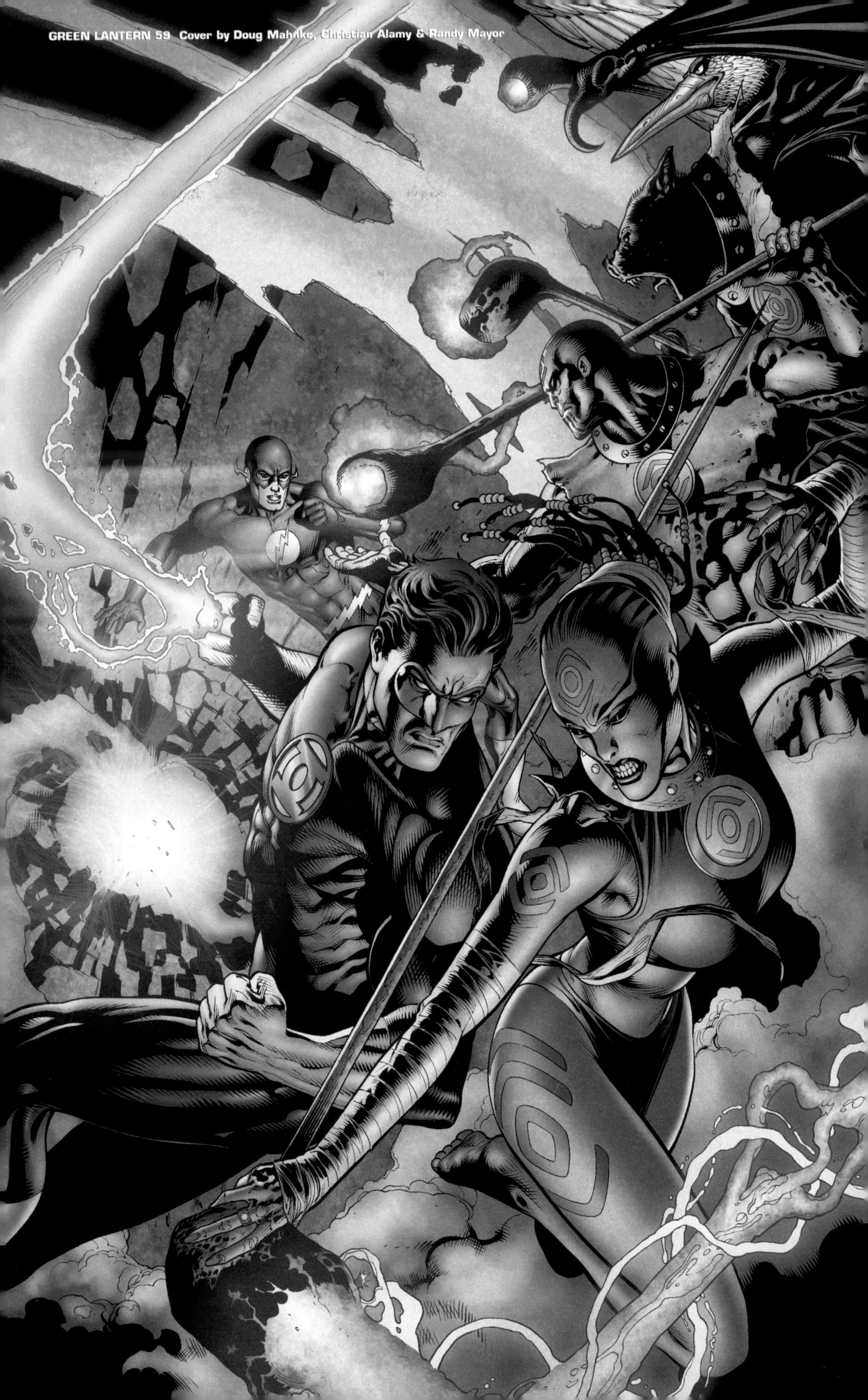

THE NEW GUARDIANS
CHAPTER SEVEN

Doug Mahnke Pencils
Christian Alamy, Keith Champagne & Doug Mahnke Inks

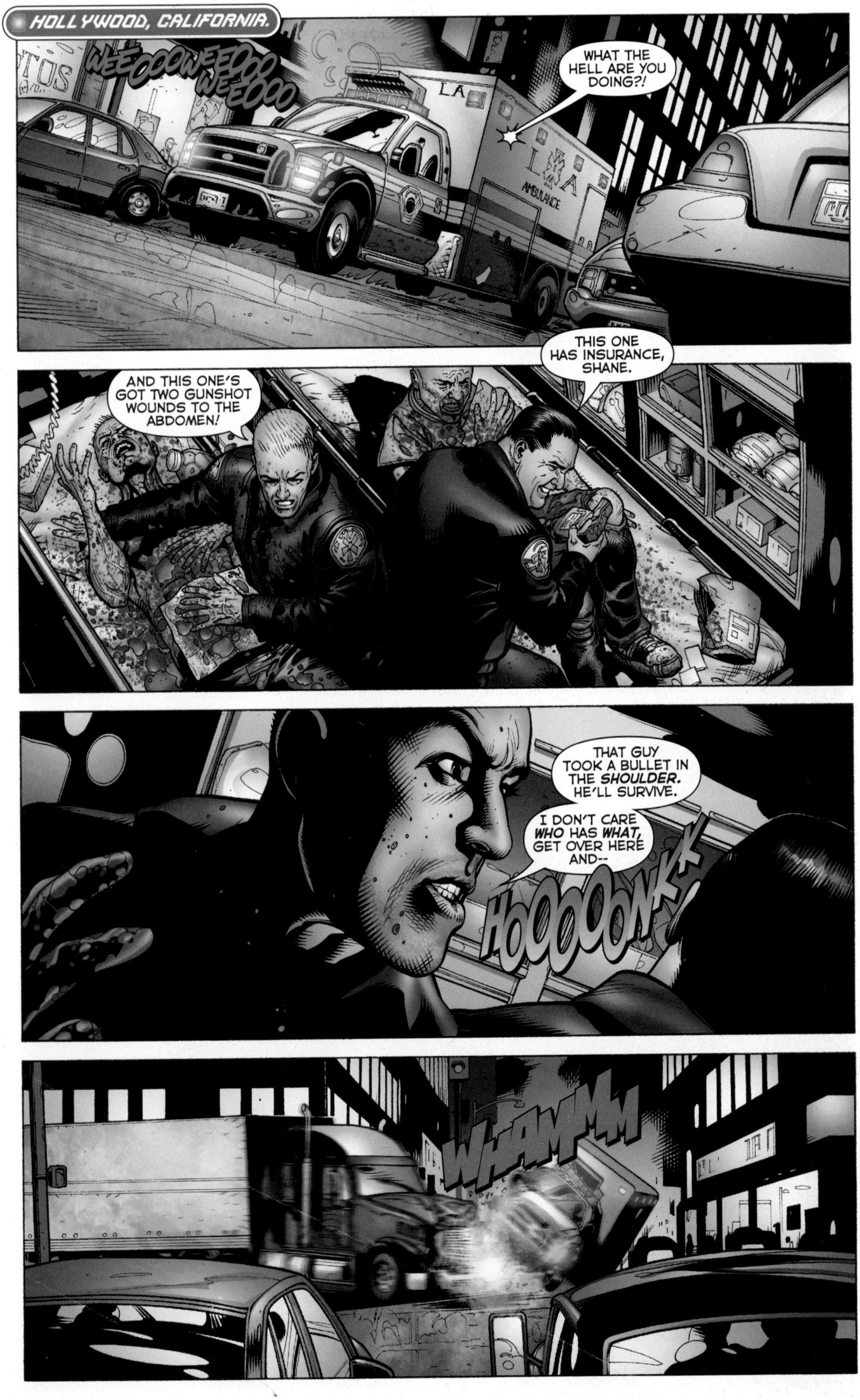
HOLLYWOOD, CALIFORNIA.
WEEOOOWEEOOO WEEOOO
WHAT THE HELL ARE YOU DOING?!
THIS ONE HAS INSURANCE, SHANE.
AND THIS ONE'S GOT TWO GUNSHOT WOUNDS TO THE ABDOMEN!
THAT GUY TOOK A BULLET IN THE SHOULDER. HE'LL SURVIVE.
I DON'T CARE WHO HAS WHAT, GET OVER HERE AND--
HOOOOONKK
WHAMMMM

KKRRAAANNKKK
BAMM BAMM
THOOM
KKKFFF
N-NO...
...HAVE TO S-SAVE THEM...
PLEASE.
NOK.

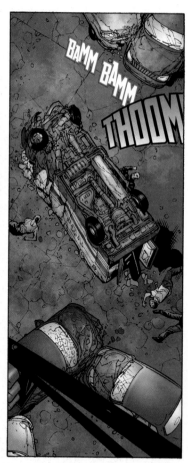

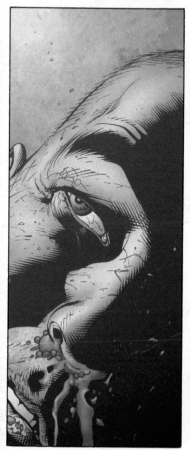

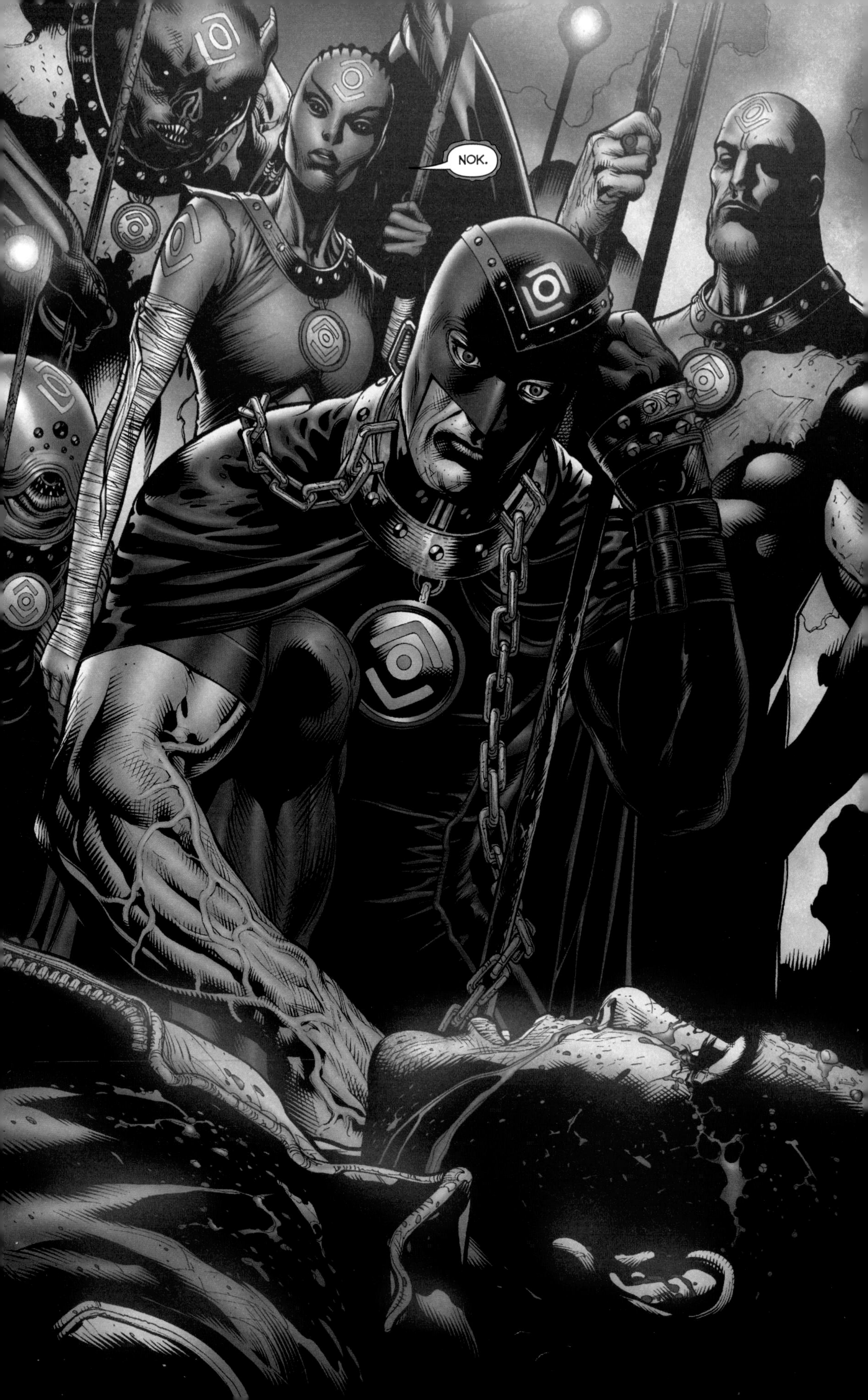
NOK.

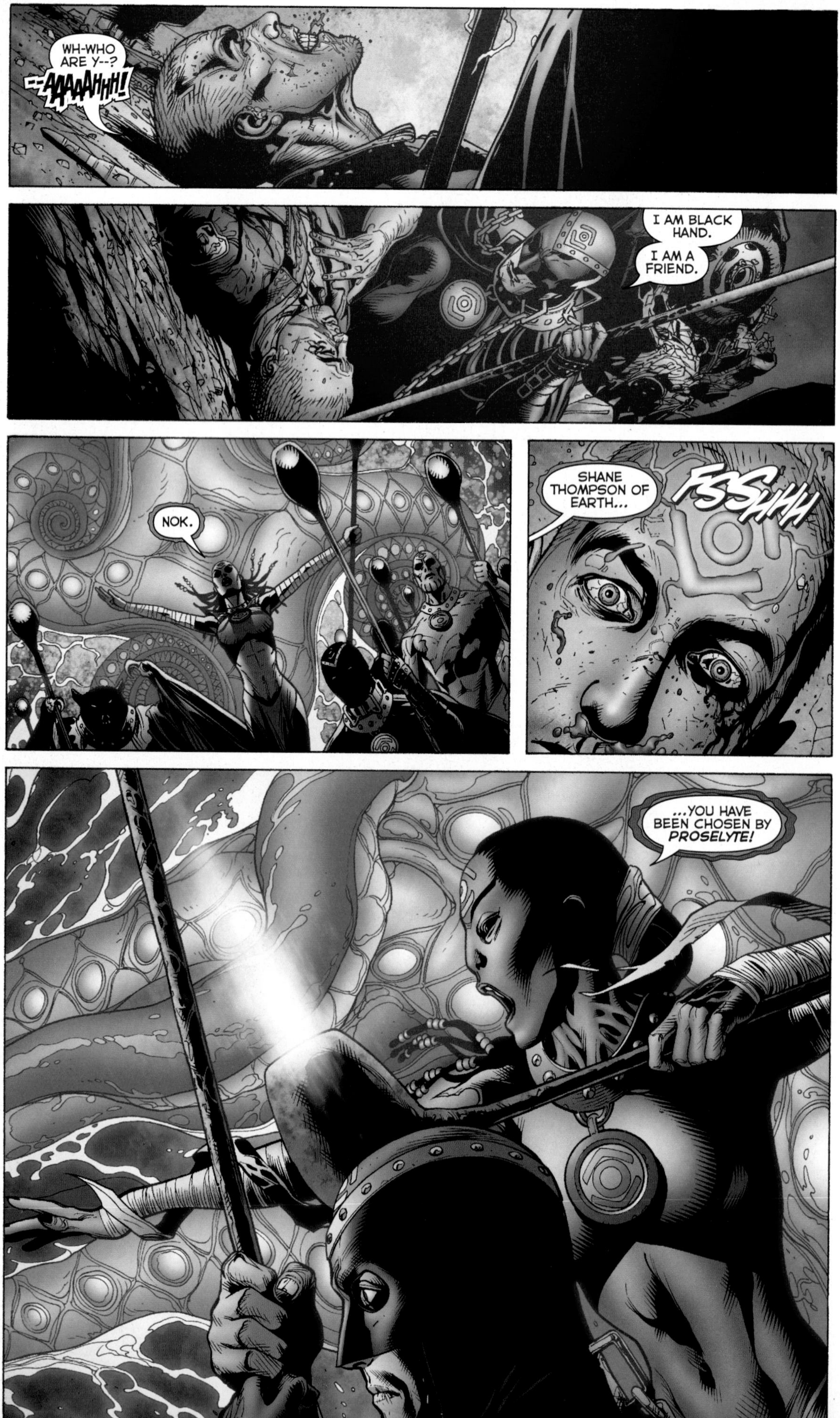
WH-WHO ARE Y--?
--AAAAAHHH!
I AM BLACK HAND.
I AM A FRIEND.
NOK.
SHANE THOMPSON OF EARTH...
FSSHHH
...YOU HAVE BEEN CHOSEN BY PROSELYTE!

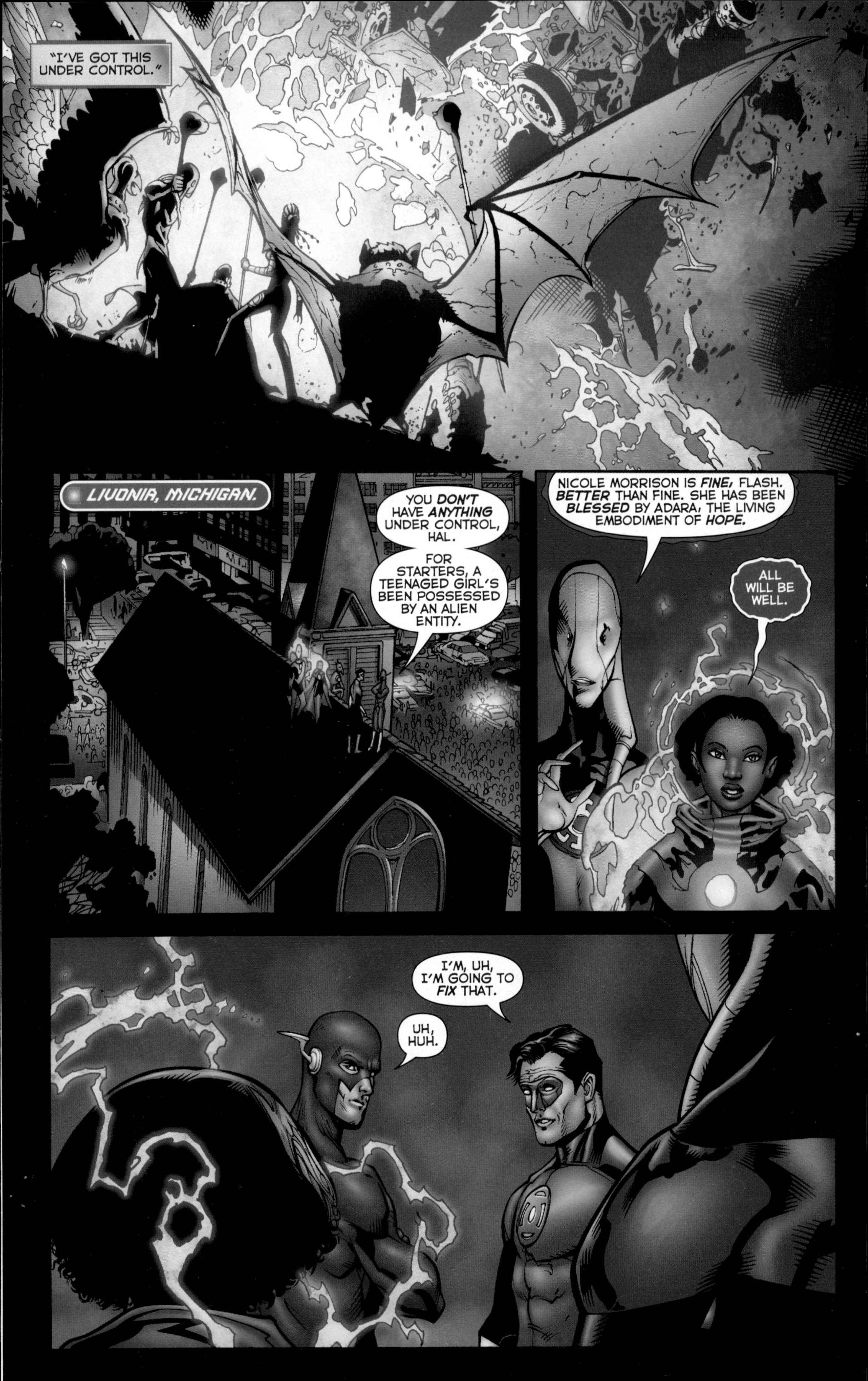
"I'VE GOT THIS UNDER CONTROL."
LIVONIA, MICHIGAN.
YOU DON'T HAVE ANYTHING UNDER CONTROL, HAL.
FOR STARTERS, A TEENAGED GIRL'S BEEN POSSESSED BY AN ALIEN ENTITY.
NICOLE MORRISON IS FINE, FLASH. BETTER THAN FINE. SHE HAS BEEN BLESSED BY ADARA, THE LIVING EMBODIMENT OF HOPE.
ALL WILL BE WELL.
I'M, UH, I'M GOING TO FIX THAT.
UH, HUH.

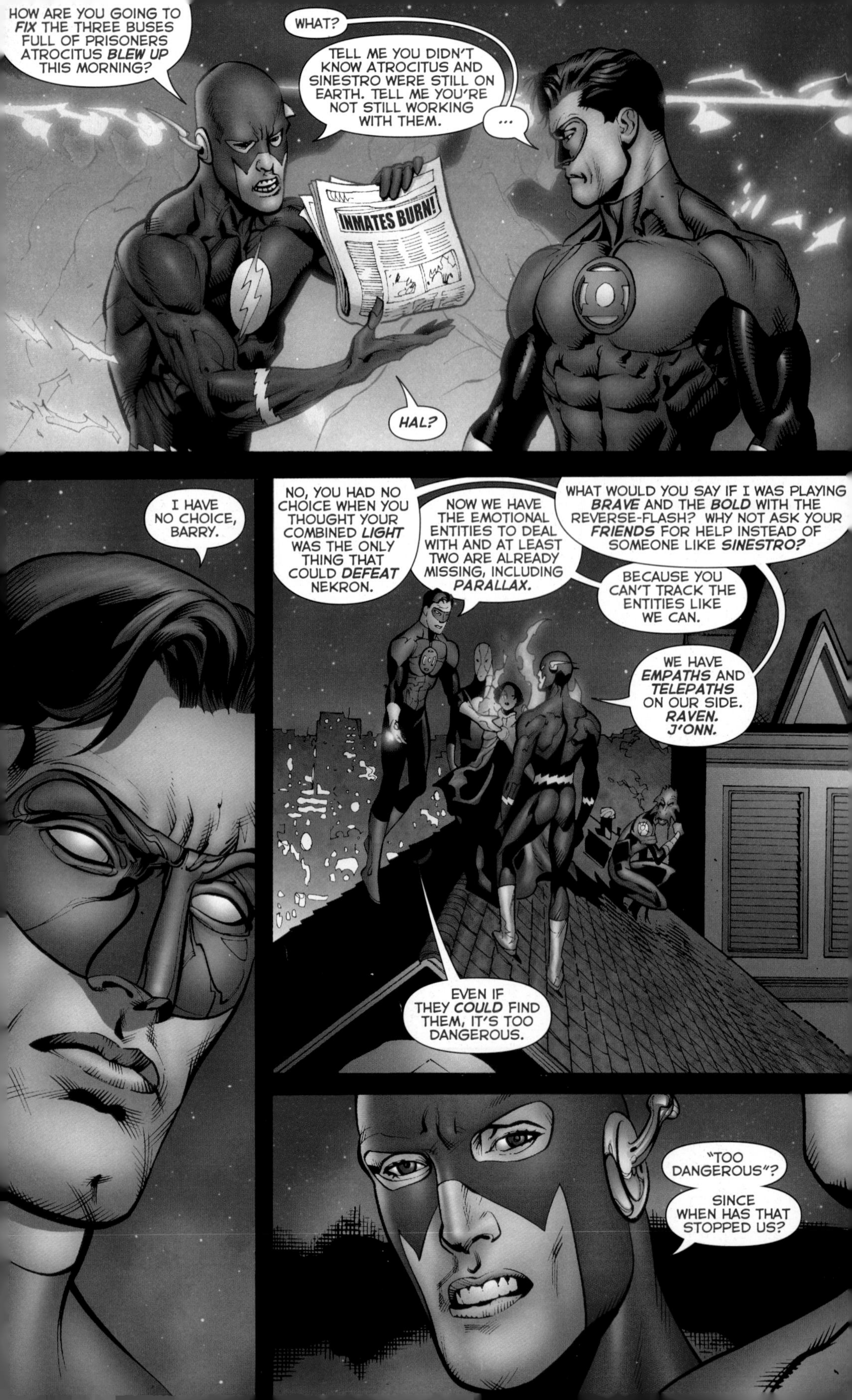
HOW ARE YOU GOING TO FIX THE THREE BUSES FULL OF PRISONERS ATROCITUS BLEW UP THIS MORNING?
WHAT?
TELL ME YOU DIDN'T KNOW ATROCITUS AND SINESTRO WERE STILL ON EARTH. TELL ME YOU'RE NOT STILL WORKING WITH THEM.
...
INMATES BURN!
HAL?
I HAVE NO CHOICE, BARRY.
NO, YOU HAD NO CHOICE WHEN YOU THOUGHT YOUR COMBINED LIGHT WAS THE ONLY THING THAT COULD DEFEAT NEKRON.
NOW WE HAVE THE EMOTIONAL ENTITIES TO DEAL WITH AND AT LEAST TWO ARE ALREADY MISSING, INCLUDING PARALLAX.
WHAT WOULD YOU SAY IF I WAS PLAYING BRAVE AND THE BOLD WITH THE REVERSE-FLASH? WHY NOT ASK YOUR FRIENDS FOR HELP INSTEAD OF SOMEONE LIKE SINESTRO?
BECAUSE YOU CAN'T TRACK THE ENTITIES LIKE WE CAN.
WE HAVE EMPATHS AND TELEPATHS ON OUR SIDE. RAVEN. J'ONN.
EVEN IF THEY COULD FIND THEM, IT'S TOO DANGEROUS.
"TOO DANGEROUS"?
SINCE WHEN HAS THAT STOPPED US?

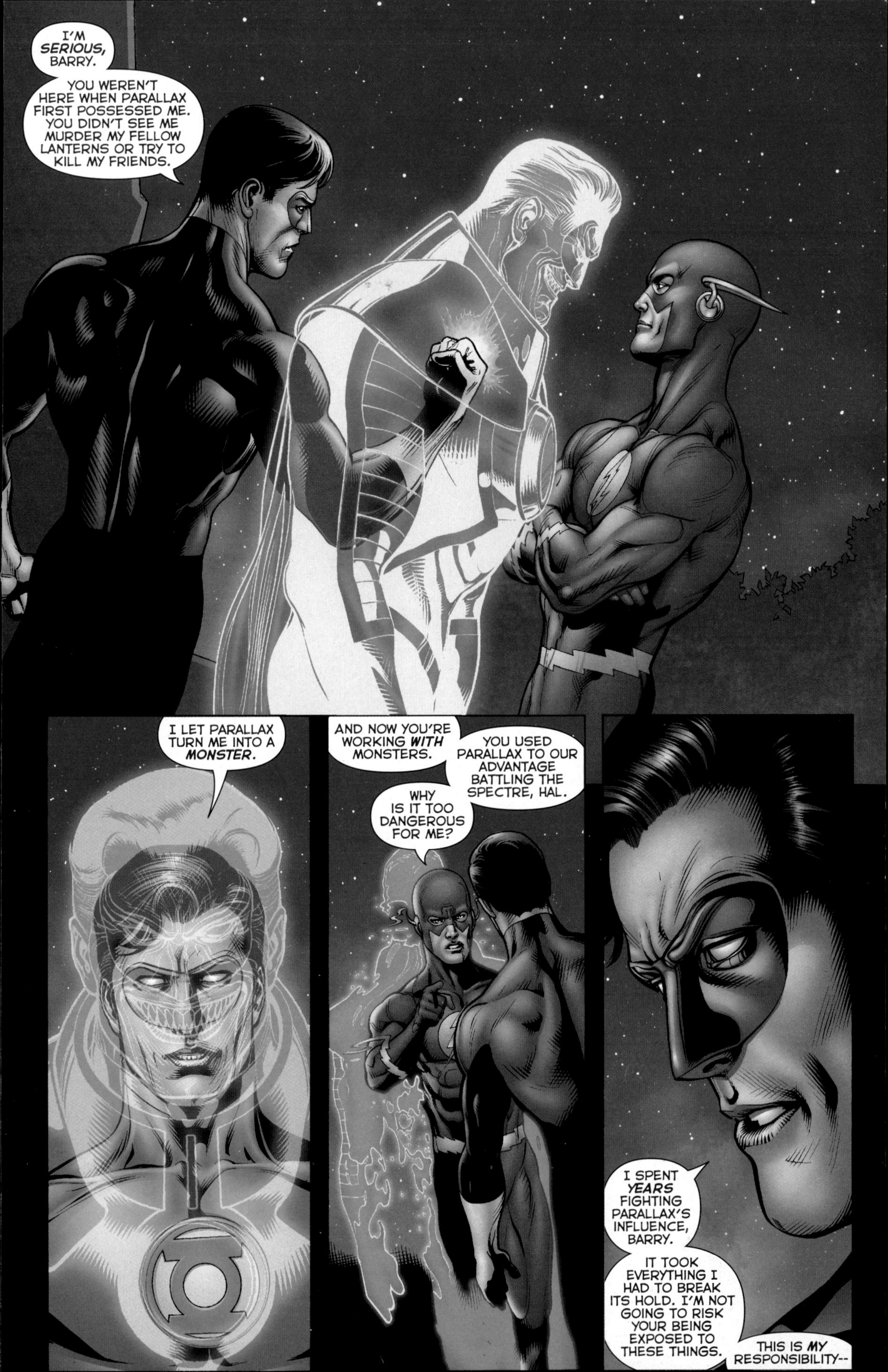
I'M SERIOUS, BARRY.
YOU WEREN'T HERE WHEN PARALLAX FIRST POSSESSED ME. YOU DIDN'T SEE ME MURDER MY FELLOW LANTERNS OR TRY TO KILL MY FRIENDS.
I LET PARALLAX TURN ME INTO A MONSTER.
AND NOW YOU'RE WORKING WITH MONSTERS.
YOU USED PARALLAX TO OUR ADVANTAGE BATTLING THE SPECTRE, HAL.
WHY IS IT TOO DANGEROUS FOR ME?
I SPENT YEARS FIGHTING PARALLAX'S INFLUENCE, BARRY.
IT TOOK EVERYTHING I HAD TO BREAK ITS HOLD. I'M NOT GOING TO RISK YOUR BEING EXPOSED TO THESE THINGS.
THIS IS MY RESPONSIBILITY--

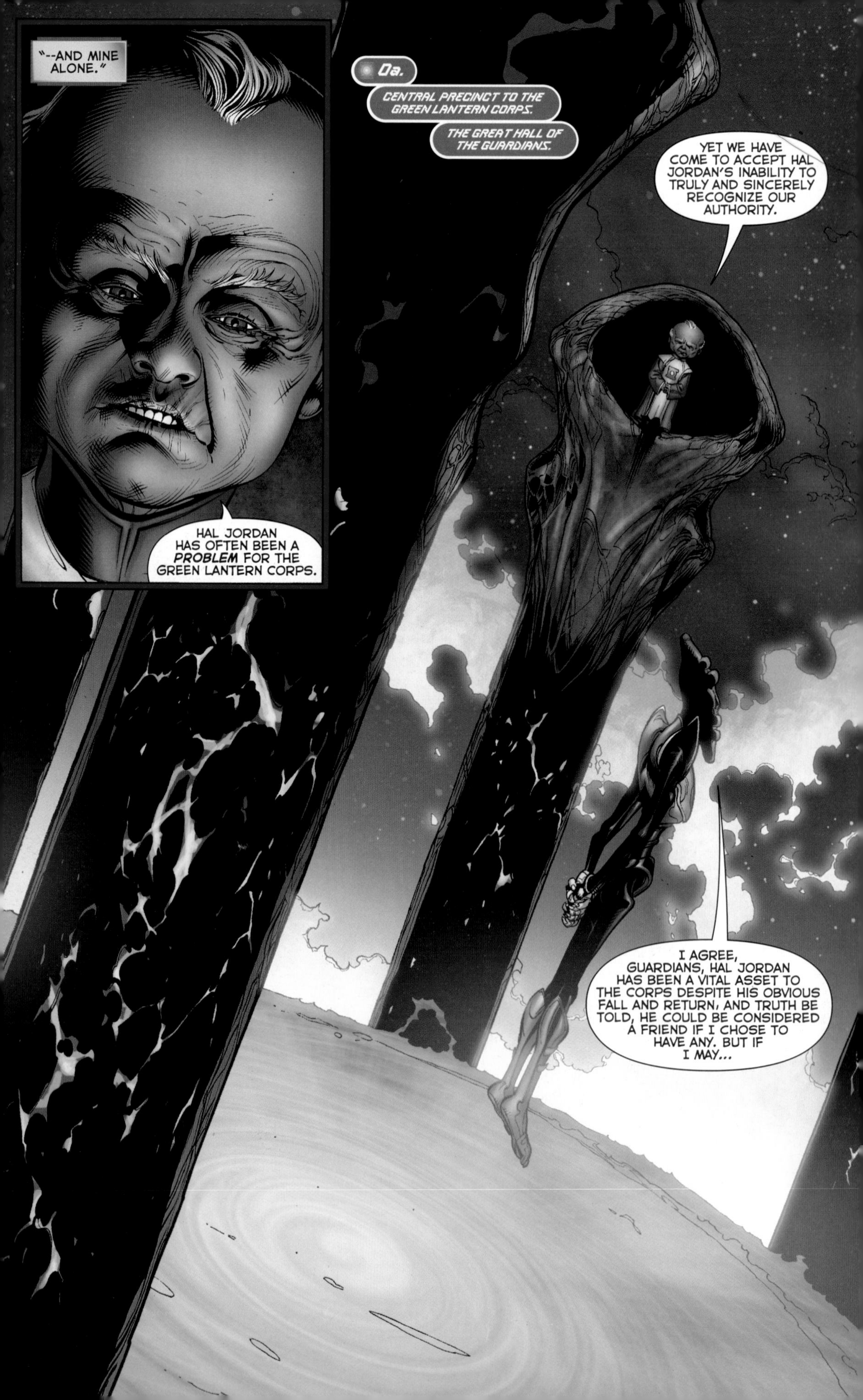
"--AND MINE ALONE."
HAL JORDAN HAS OFTEN BEEN A PROBLEM FOR THE GREEN LANTERN CORPS.
Oa.
CENTRAL PRECINCT TO THE GREEN LANTERN CORPS.
THE GREAT HALL OF THE GUARDIANS.
YET WE HAVE COME TO ACCEPT HAL JORDAN'S INABILITY TO TRULY AND SINCERELY RECOGNIZE OUR AUTHORITY.
I AGREE, GUARDIANS, HAL JORDAN HAS BEEN A VITAL ASSET TO THE CORPS DESPITE HIS OBVIOUS FALL AND RETURN, AND TRUTH BE TOLD, HE COULD BE CONSIDERED A FRIEND IF I CHOSE TO HAVE ANY. BUT IF I MAY...

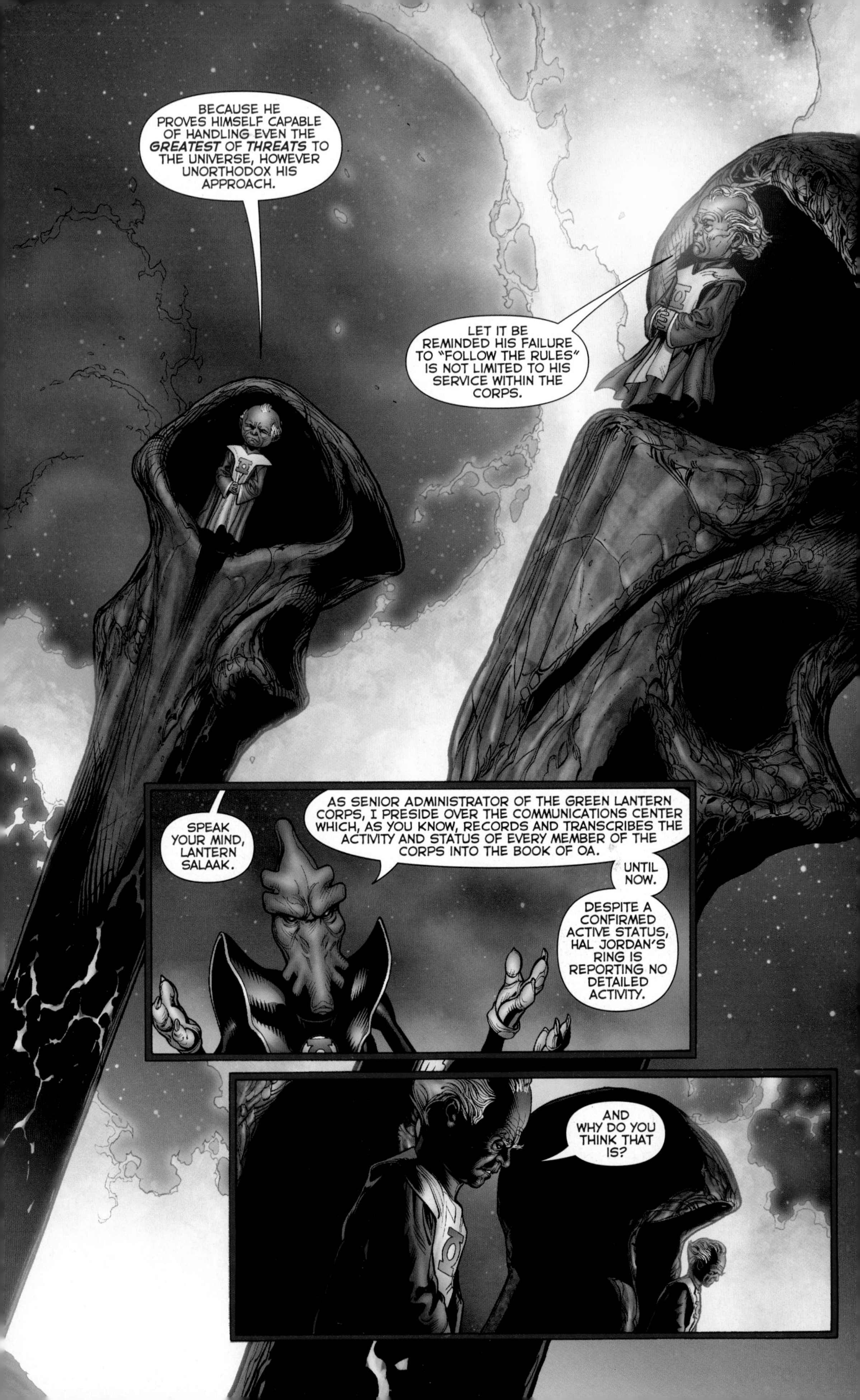
BECAUSE HE PROVES HIMSELF CAPABLE OF HANDLING EVEN THE ***GREATEST*** OF ***THREATS*** TO THE UNIVERSE, HOWEVER UNORTHODOX HIS APPROACH.
LET IT BE REMINDED HIS FAILURE TO "FOLLOW THE RULES" IS NOT LIMITED TO HIS SERVICE WITHIN THE CORPS.
SPEAK YOUR MIND, LANTERN SALAAK.
AS SENIOR ADMINISTRATOR OF THE GREEN LANTERN CORPS, I PRESIDE OVER THE COMMUNICATIONS CENTER WHICH, AS YOU KNOW, RECORDS AND TRANSCRIBES THE ACTIVITY AND STATUS OF EVERY MEMBER OF THE CORPS INTO THE BOOK OF OA.
UNTIL NOW.
DESPITE A CONFIRMED ACTIVE STATUS, HAL JORDAN'S RING IS REPORTING NO DETAILED ACTIVITY.
AND WHY DO YOU THINK THAT IS?

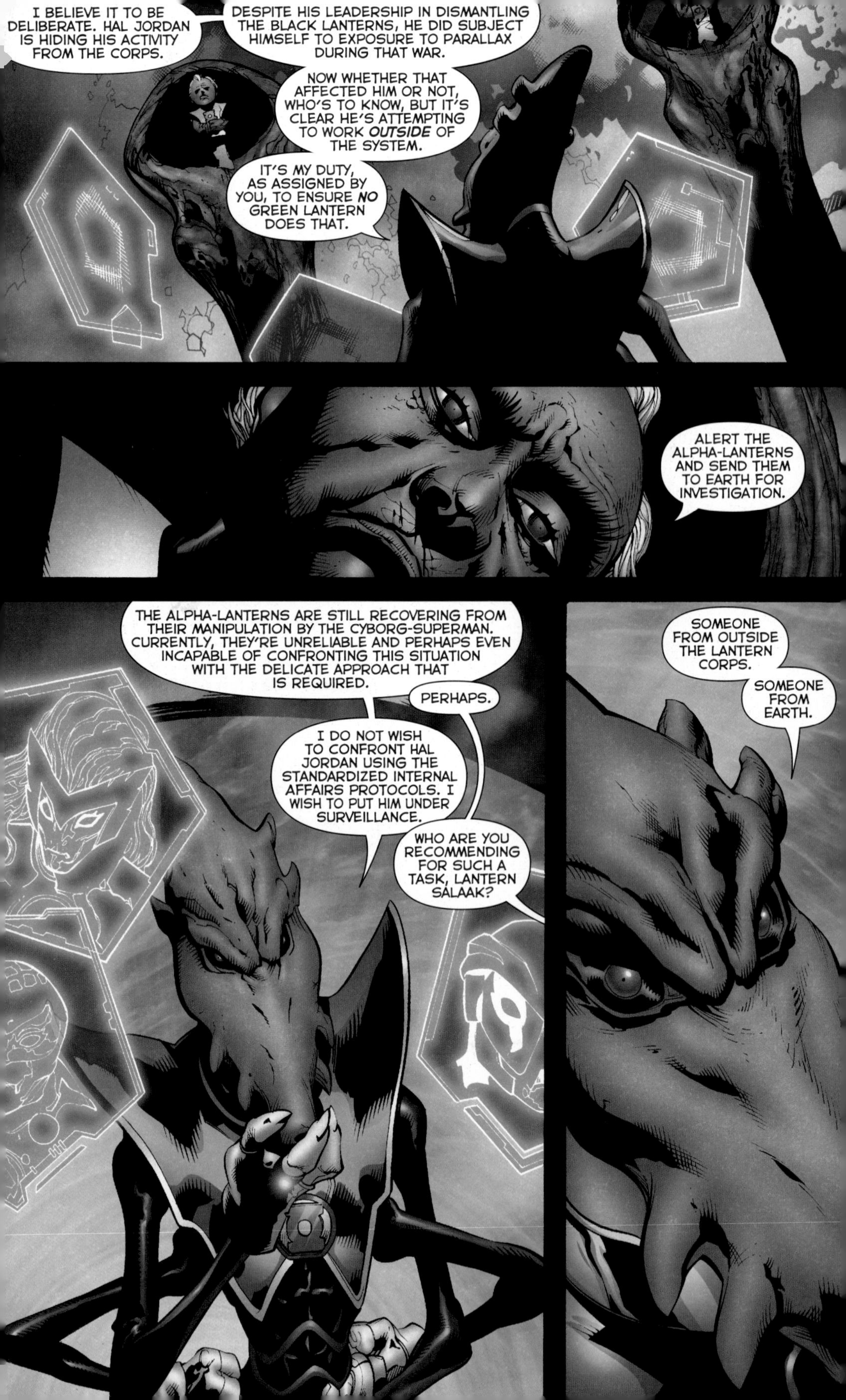
I BELIEVE IT TO BE DELIBERATE. HAL JORDAN IS HIDING HIS ACTIVITY FROM THE CORPS.
DESPITE HIS LEADERSHIP IN DISMANTLING THE BLACK LANTERNS, HE DID SUBJECT HIMSELF TO EXPOSURE TO PARALLAX DURING THAT WAR.
NOW WHETHER THAT AFFECTED HIM OR NOT, WHO'S TO KNOW, BUT IT'S CLEAR HE'S ATTEMPTING TO WORK *OUTSIDE* OF THE SYSTEM.
IT'S MY DUTY, AS ASSIGNED BY YOU, TO ENSURE *NO* GREEN LANTERN DOES THAT.
ALERT THE ALPHA-LANTERNS AND SEND THEM TO EARTH FOR INVESTIGATION.
THE ALPHA-LANTERNS ARE STILL RECOVERING FROM THEIR MANIPULATION BY THE CYBORG-SUPERMAN. CURRENTLY, THEY'RE UNRELIABLE AND PERHAPS EVEN INCAPABLE OF CONFRONTING THIS SITUATION WITH THE DELICATE APPROACH THAT IS REQUIRED.
PERHAPS.
I DO NOT WISH TO CONFRONT HAL JORDAN USING THE STANDARDIZED INTERNAL AFFAIRS PROTOCOLS. I WISH TO PUT HIM UNDER SURVEILLANCE.
WHO ARE YOU RECOMMENDING FOR SUCH A TASK, LANTERN SALAAK?
SOMEONE FROM OUTSIDE THE LANTERN CORPS.
SOMEONE FROM EARTH.

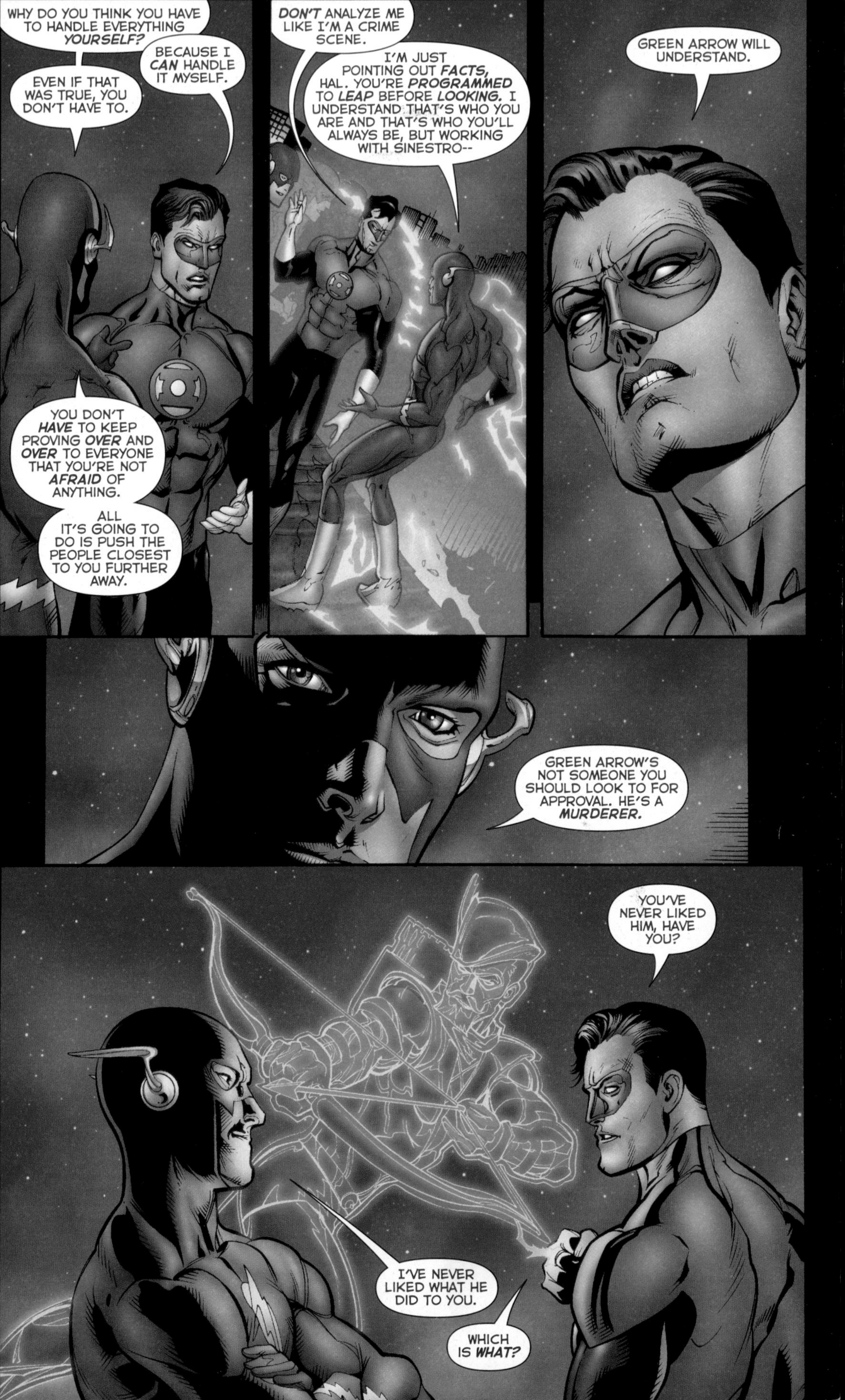
WHY DO YOU THINK YOU HAVE TO HANDLE EVERYTHING *YOURSELF?*
BECAUSE I *CAN* HANDLE IT MYSELF.
EVEN IF THAT WAS TRUE, YOU DON'T HAVE TO.
YOU DON'T *HAVE* TO KEEP PROVING *OVER* AND *OVER* TO EVERYONE THAT YOU'RE NOT *AFRAID* OF ANYTHING.
ALL IT'S GOING TO DO IS PUSH THE PEOPLE CLOSEST TO YOU FURTHER AWAY.
DON'T ANALYZE ME LIKE I'M A CRIME SCENE.
I'M JUST POINTING OUT *FACTS,* HAL. YOU'RE *PROGRAMMED* TO *LEAP* BEFORE *LOOKING.* I UNDERSTAND THAT'S WHO YOU ARE AND THAT'S WHO YOU'LL ALWAYS BE, BUT WORKING WITH SINESTRO--
GREEN ARROW WILL UNDERSTAND.
GREEN ARROW'S NOT SOMEONE YOU SHOULD LOOK TO FOR APPROVAL. HE'S A *MURDERER.*
YOU'VE NEVER LIKED HIM, HAVE YOU?
I'VE NEVER LIKED WHAT HE DID TO YOU.
WHICH IS *WHAT?*

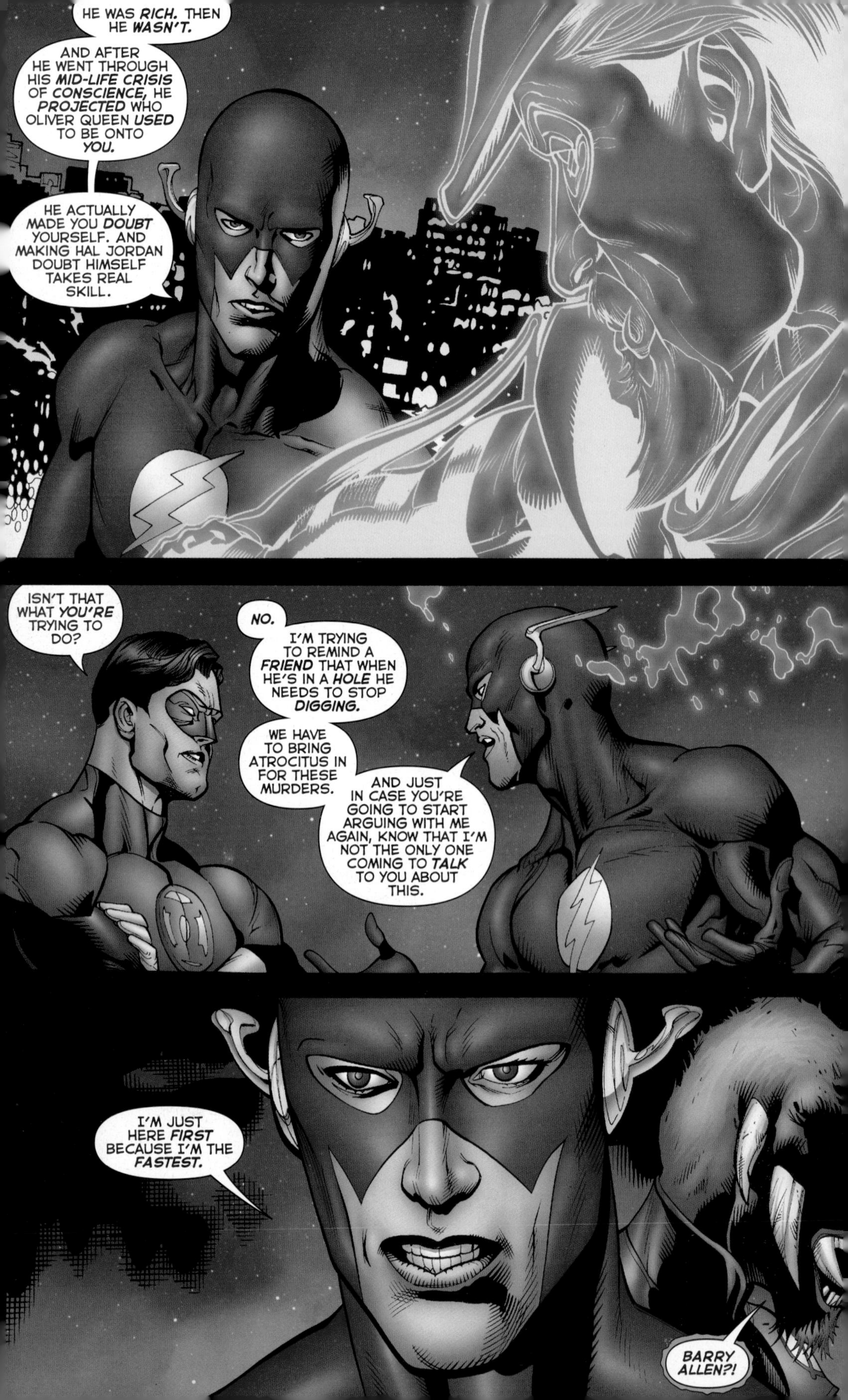
HE WAS RICH. THEN HE WASN'T.
AND AFTER HE WENT THROUGH HIS MID-LIFE CRISIS OF CONSCIENCE, HE PROJECTED WHO OLIVER QUEEN USED TO BE ONTO YOU.
HE ACTUALLY MADE YOU DOUBT YOURSELF. AND MAKING HAL JORDAN DOUBT HIMSELF TAKES REAL SKILL.
ISN'T THAT WHAT YOU'RE TRYING TO DO?
NO.
I'M TRYING TO REMIND A FRIEND THAT WHEN HE'S IN A HOLE HE NEEDS TO STOP DIGGING.
WE HAVE TO BRING ATROCITUS IN FOR THESE MURDERS.
AND JUST IN CASE YOU'RE GOING TO START ARGUING WITH ME AGAIN, KNOW THAT I'M NOT THE ONLY ONE COMING TO TALK TO YOU ABOUT THIS.
I'M JUST HERE FIRST BECAUSE I'M THE FASTEST.
BARRY ALLEN?!

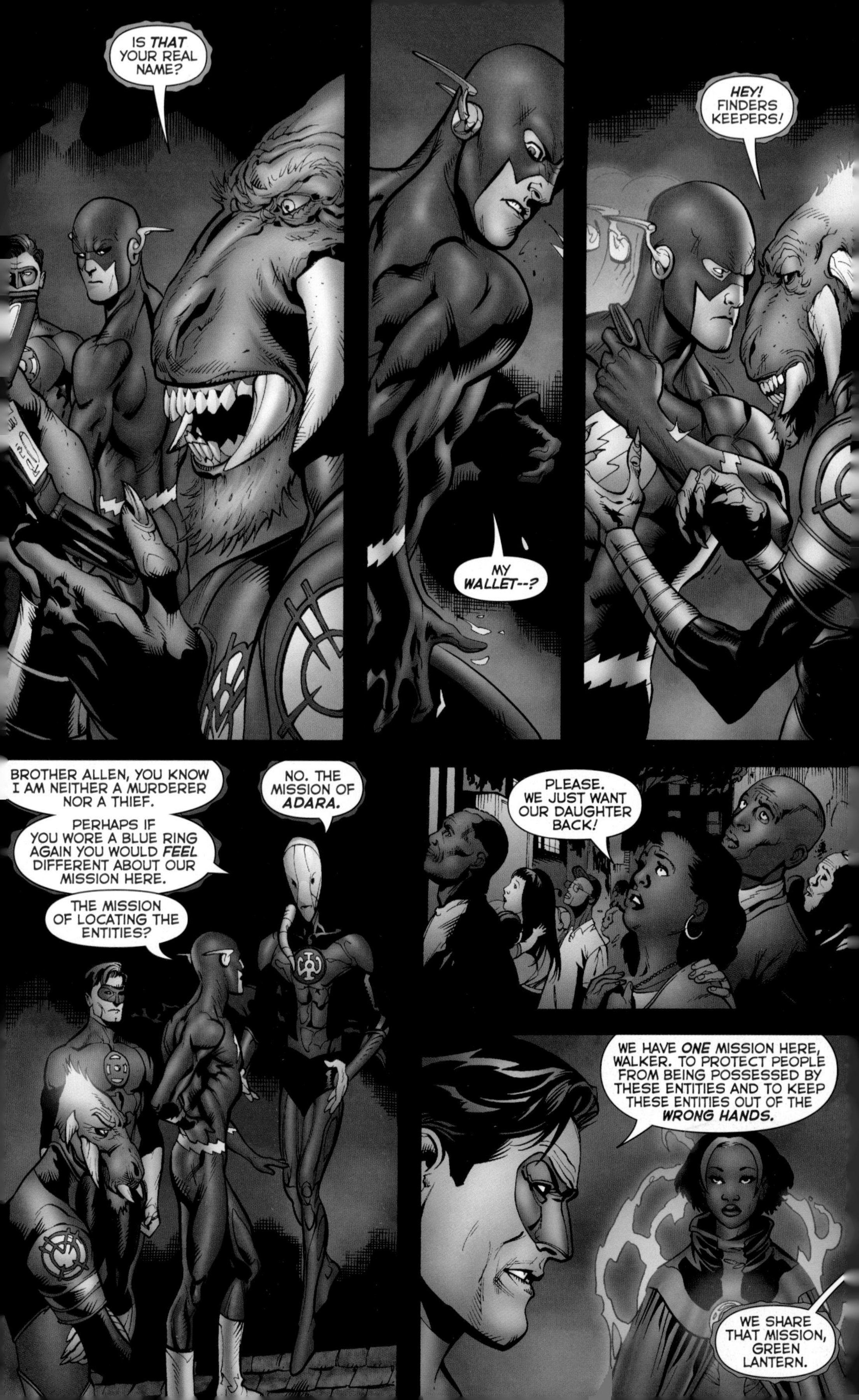
IS *THAT* YOUR REAL NAME?
MY *WALLET*--?
HEY! FINDERS KEEPERS!
BROTHER ALLEN, YOU KNOW I AM NEITHER A MURDERER NOR A THIEF.
PERHAPS IF YOU WORE A BLUE RING AGAIN YOU WOULD *FEEL* DIFFERENT ABOUT OUR MISSION HERE.
THE MISSION OF LOCATING THE ENTITIES?
NO. THE MISSION OF ***ADARA.***
PLEASE. WE JUST WANT OUR DAUGHTER BACK!
WE HAVE *ONE* MISSION HERE, WALKER. TO PROTECT PEOPLE FROM BEING POSSESSED BY THESE ENTITIES AND TO KEEP THESE ENTITIES OUT OF THE ***WRONG HANDS.***
WE SHARE THAT MISSION, GREEN LANTERN.

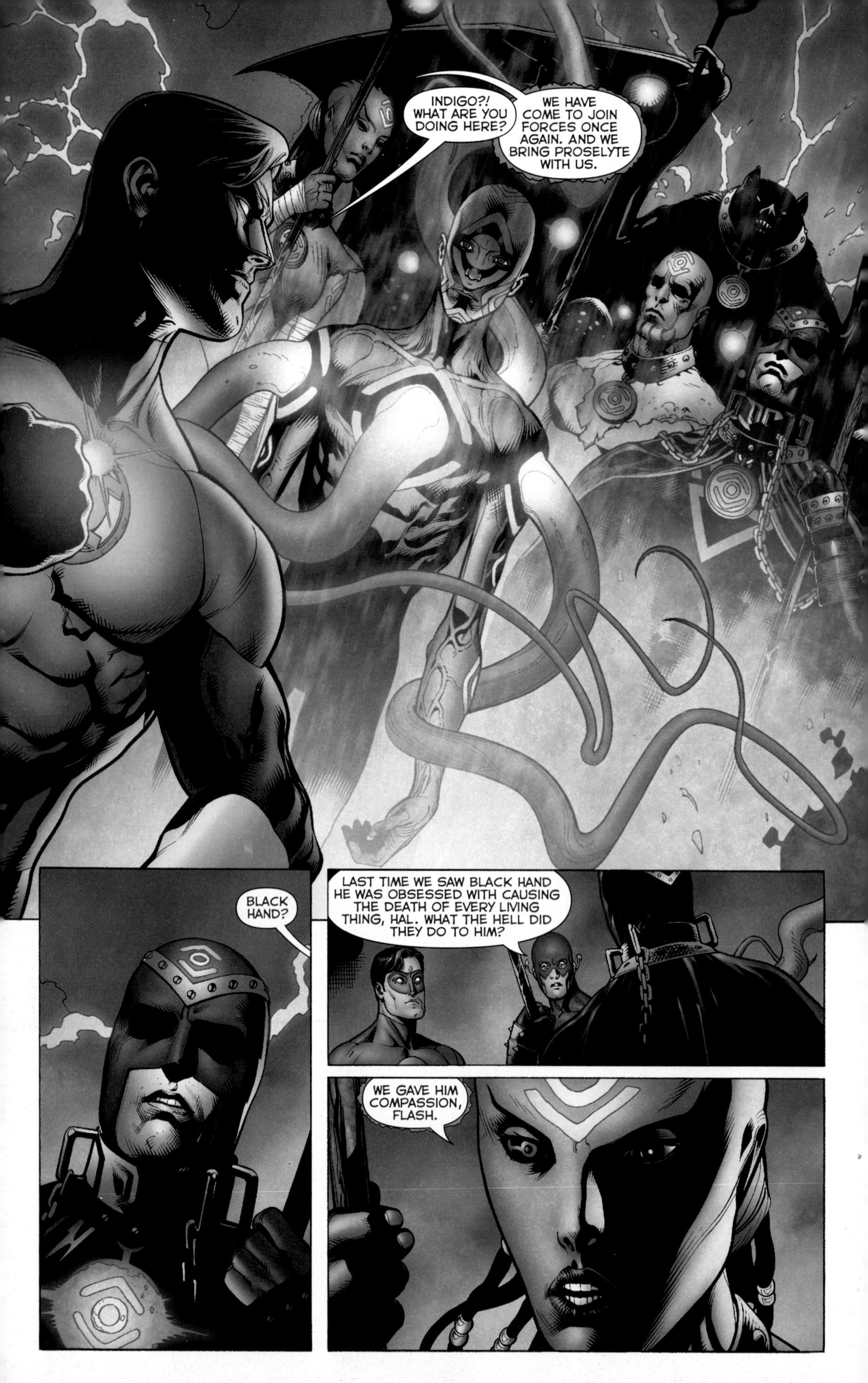
INDIGO?! WHAT ARE YOU DOING HERE?
WE HAVE COME TO JOIN FORCES ONCE AGAIN. AND WE BRING PROSELYTE WITH US.
BLACK HAND?
LAST TIME WE SAW BLACK HAND HE WAS OBSESSED WITH CAUSING THE DEATH OF EVERY LIVING THING, HAL. WHAT THE HELL DID THEY DO TO HIM?
WE GAVE HIM COMPASSION, FLASH.

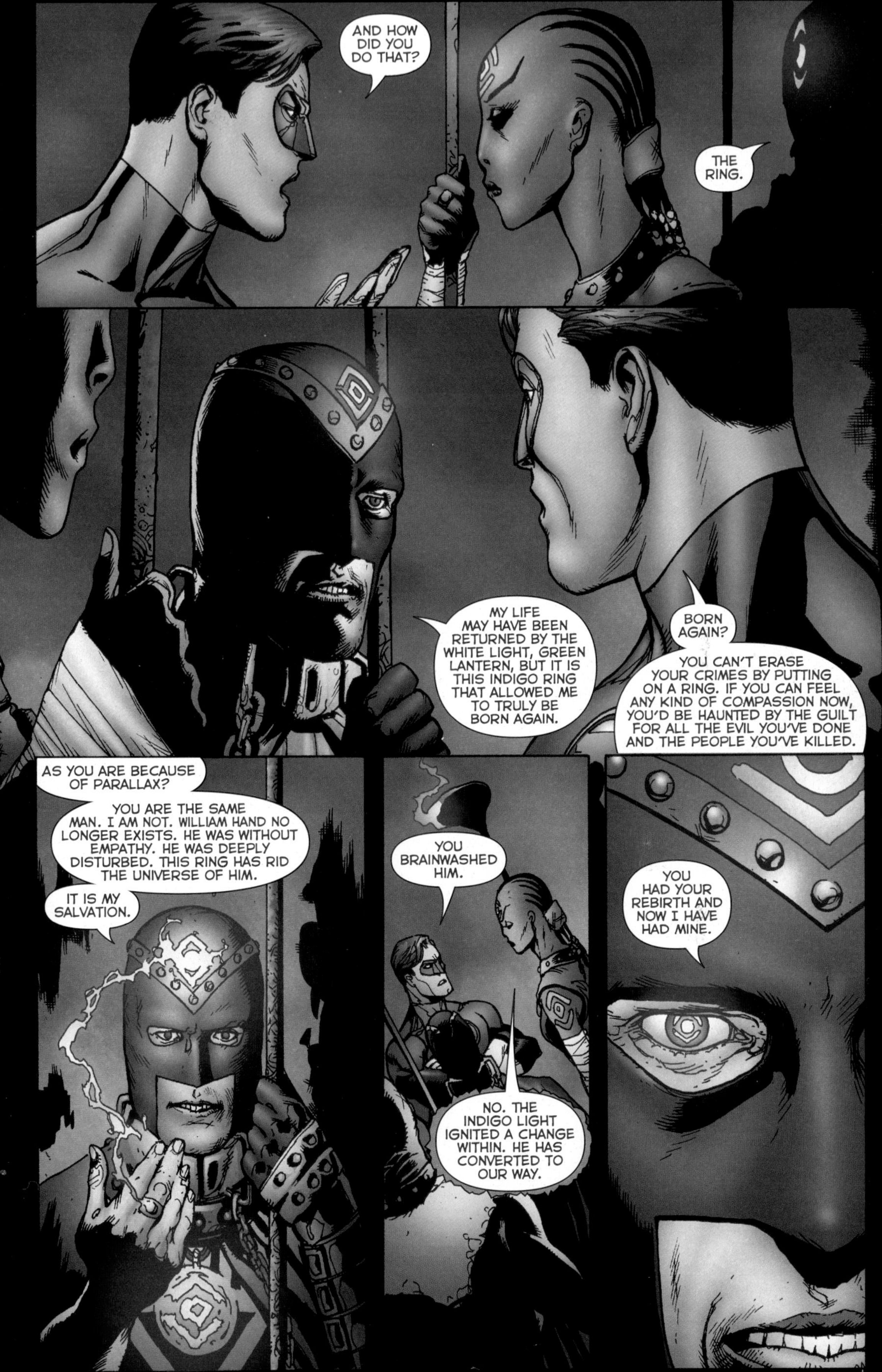
AND HOW DID YOU DO THAT?
THE RING.
MY LIFE MAY HAVE BEEN RETURNED BY THE WHITE LIGHT, GREEN LANTERN, BUT IT IS THIS INDIGO RING THAT ALLOWED ME TO TRULY BE BORN AGAIN.
BORN AGAIN?
YOU CAN'T ERASE YOUR CRIMES BY PUTTING ON A RING. IF YOU CAN FEEL ANY KIND OF COMPASSION NOW, YOU'D BE HAUNTED BY THE GUILT FOR ALL THE EVIL YOU'VE DONE AND THE PEOPLE YOU'VE KILLED.
AS YOU ARE BECAUSE OF PARALLAX?
YOU ARE THE SAME MAN. I AM NOT. WILLIAM HAND NO LONGER EXISTS. HE WAS WITHOUT EMPATHY. HE WAS DEEPLY DISTURBED. THIS RING HAS RID THE UNIVERSE OF HIM.
IT IS MY SALVATION.
YOU BRAINWASHED HIM.
NO. THE INDIGO LIGHT IGNITED A CHANGE WITHIN. HE HAS CONVERTED TO OUR WAY.
YOU HAD YOUR REBIRTH AND NOW I HAVE HAD MINE.

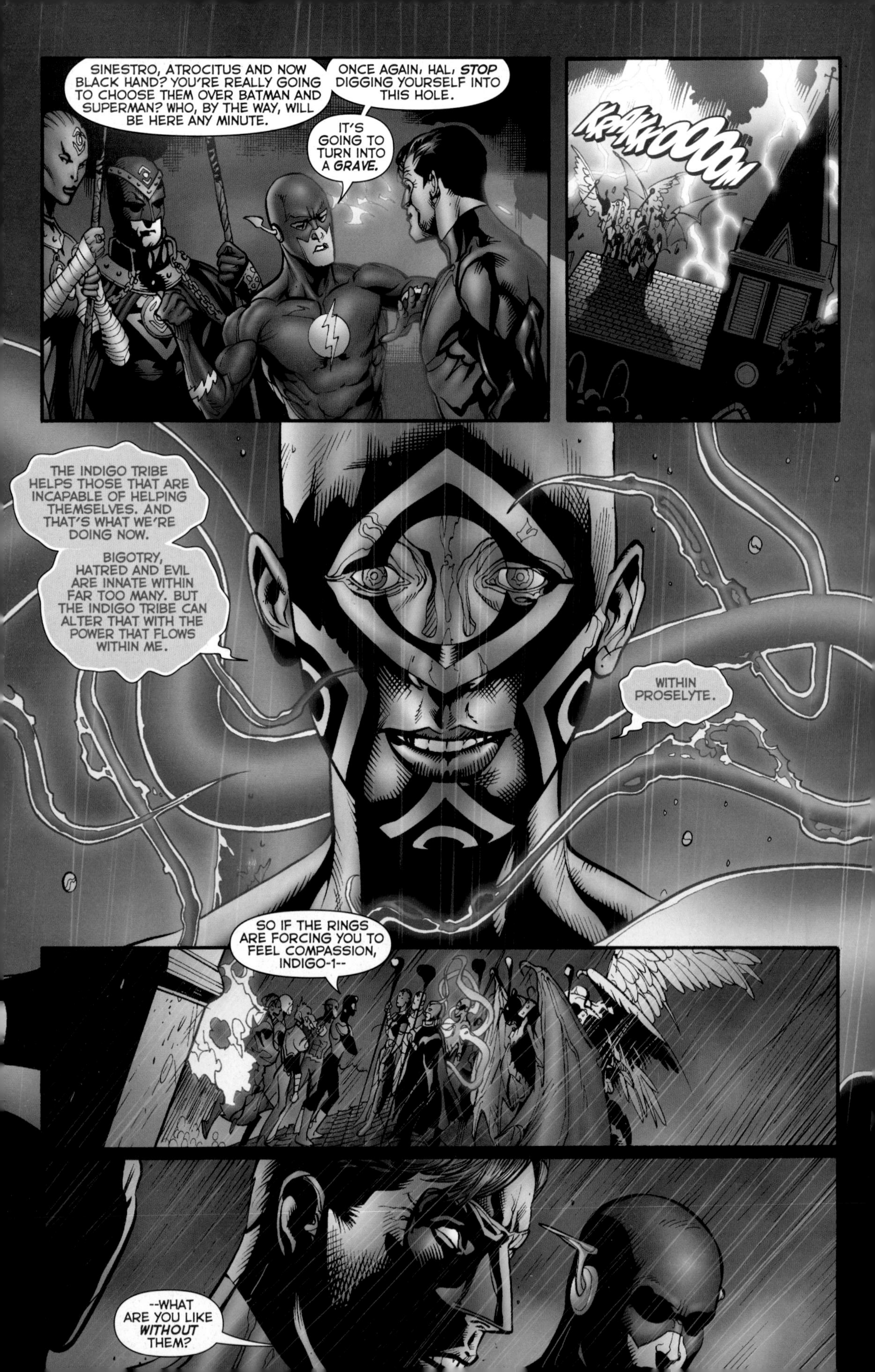
SINESTRO, ATROCITUS AND NOW BLACK HAND? YOU'RE REALLY GOING TO CHOOSE THEM OVER BATMAN AND SUPERMAN? WHO, BY THE WAY, WILL BE HERE ANY MINUTE.
ONCE AGAIN, HAL, STOP DIGGING YOURSELF INTO THIS HOLE.
IT'S GOING TO TURN INTO A GRAVE.
KRAKKOOOOOM
THE INDIGO TRIBE HELPS THOSE THAT ARE INCAPABLE OF HELPING THEMSELVES. AND THAT'S WHAT WE'RE DOING NOW.
BIGOTRY, HATRED AND EVIL ARE INNATE WITHIN FAR TOO MANY. BUT THE INDIGO TRIBE CAN ALTER THAT WITH THE POWER THAT FLOWS WITHIN ME.
WITHIN PROSELYTE.
SO IF THE RINGS ARE FORCING YOU TO FEEL COMPASSION, INDIGO-1--
--WHAT ARE YOU LIKE WITHOUT THEM?

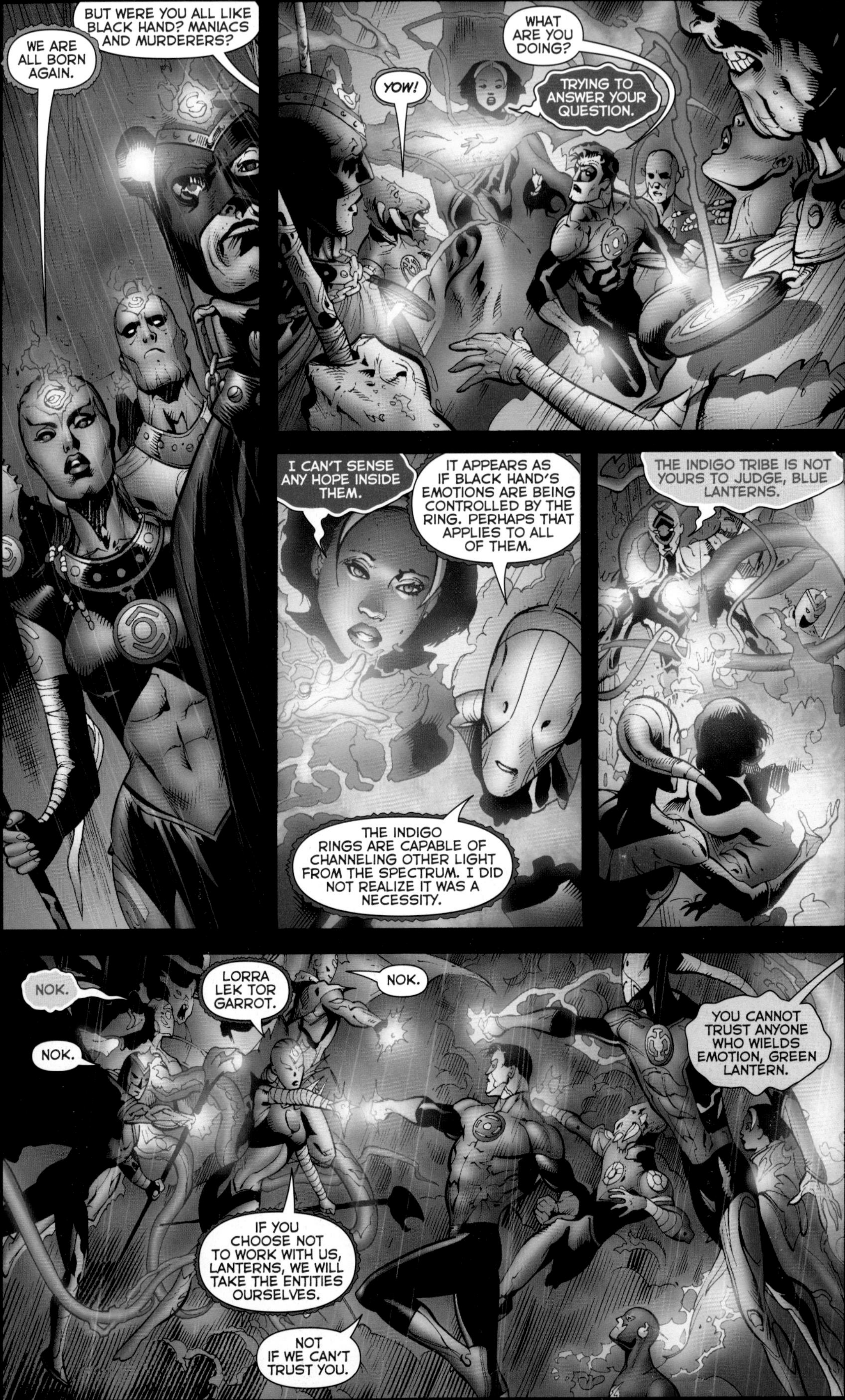

BUT WERE YOU ALL LIKE BLACK HAND? MANIACS AND MURDERERS?
WE ARE ALL BORN AGAIN.
WHAT ARE YOU DOING?
YOW!
TRYING TO ANSWER YOUR QUESTION.
I CAN'T SENSE ANY HOPE INSIDE THEM.
IT APPEARS AS IF BLACK HAND'S EMOTIONS ARE BEING CONTROLLED BY THE RING. PERHAPS THAT APPLIES TO ALL OF THEM.
THE INDIGO RINGS ARE CAPABLE OF CHANNELING OTHER LIGHT FROM THE SPECTRUM. I DID NOT REALIZE IT WAS A NECESSITY.
THE INDIGO TRIBE IS NOT YOURS TO JUDGE, BLUE LANTERNS.
NOK.
LORRA LEK TOR GARROT.
NOK.
NOK.
YOU CANNOT TRUST ANYONE WHO WIELDS EMOTION, GREEN LANTERN.
IF YOU CHOOSE NOT TO WORK WITH US, LANTERNS, WE WILL TAKE THE ENTITIES OURSELVES.
NOT IF WE CAN'T TRUST YOU.

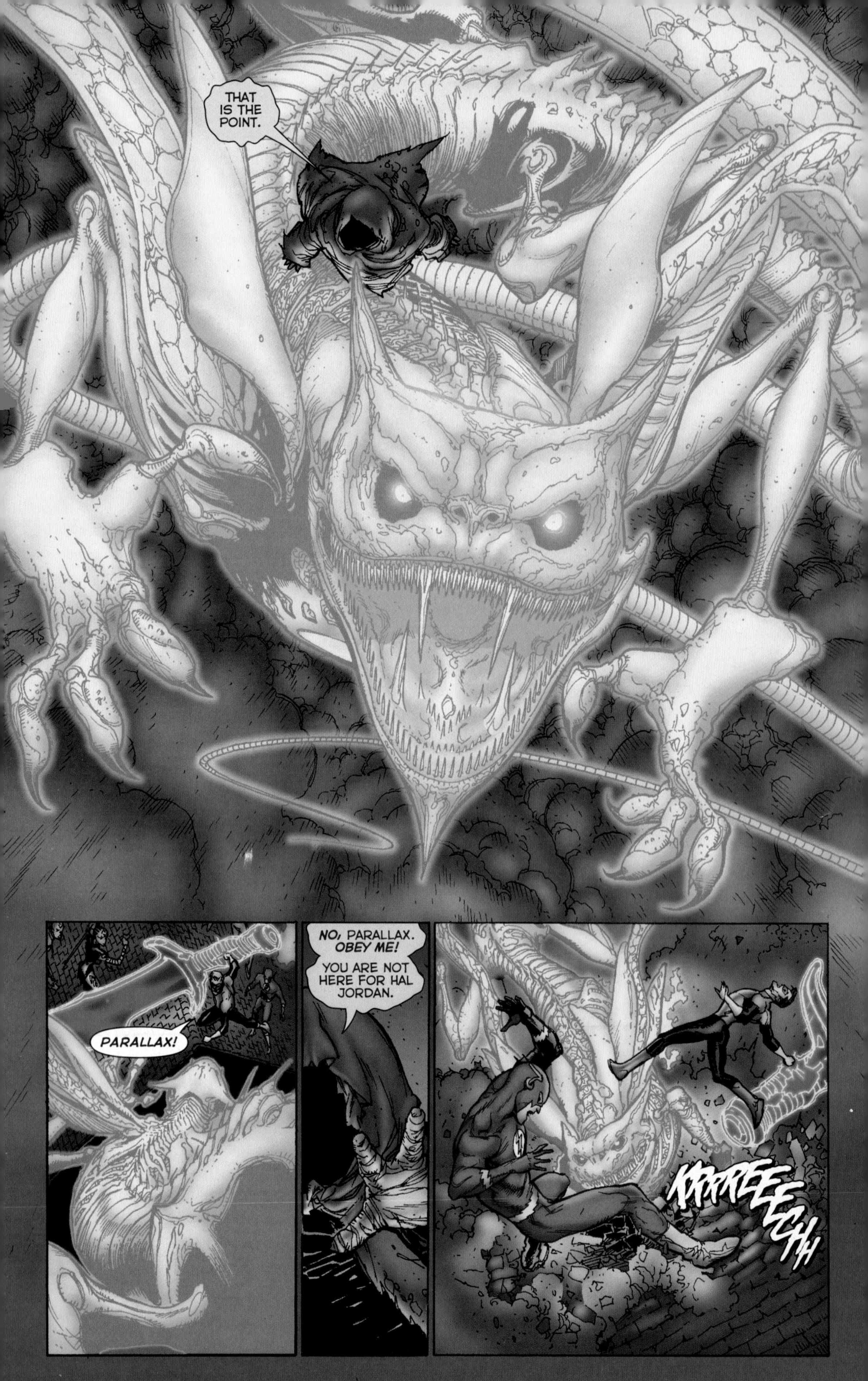
THAT IS THE POINT.
PARALLAX!
NO, PARALLAX. OBEY ME!
YOU ARE NOT HERE FOR HAL JORDAN.
KRRREEEECHH

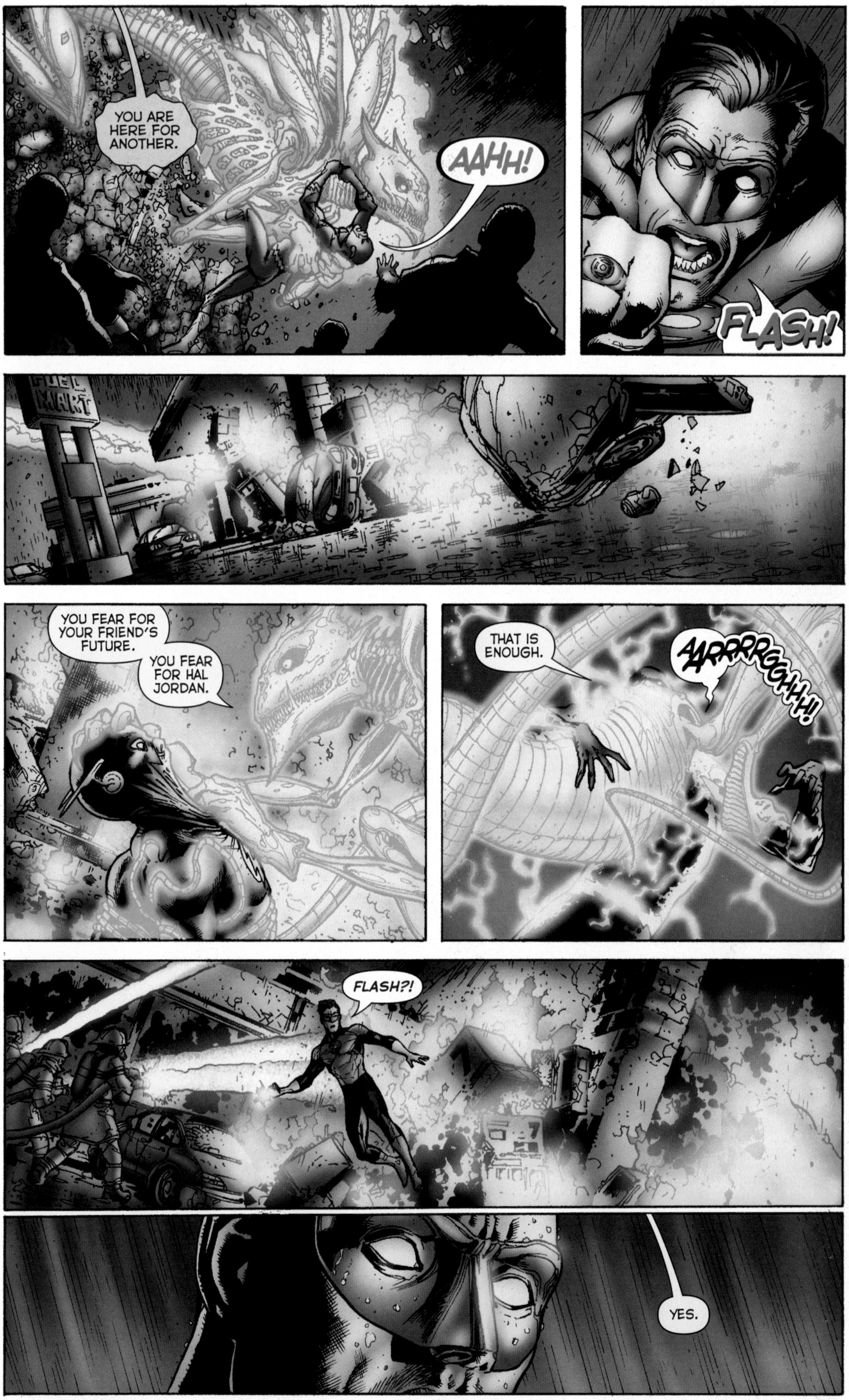
YOU ARE HERE FOR ANOTHER.
AAHH!
FLASH!
YOU FEAR FOR YOUR FRIEND'S FUTURE.
YOU FEAR FOR HAL JORDAN.
THAT IS ENOUGH.
AARRRRGHHH!
FLASH?!
YES.

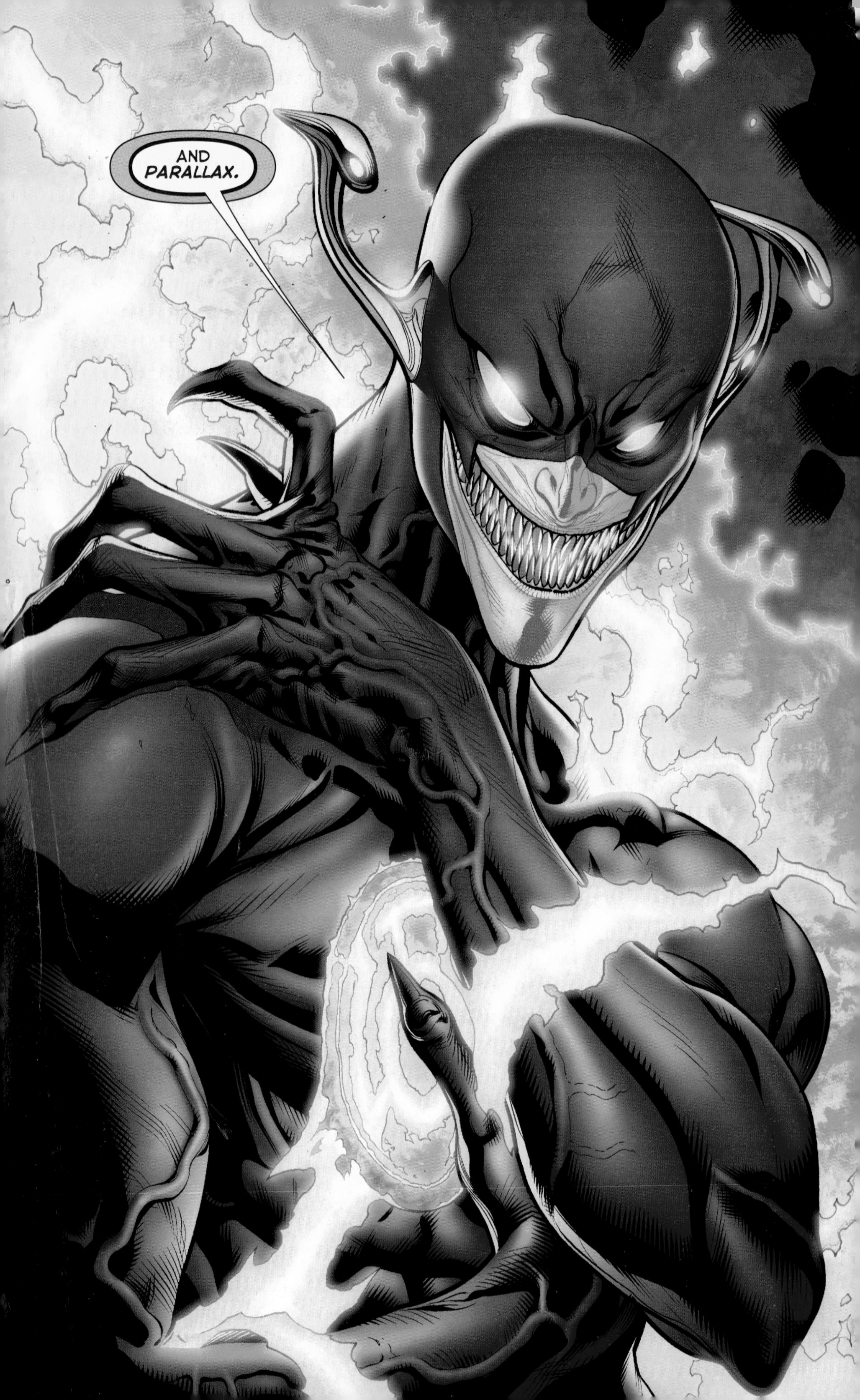
AND PARALLAX.

GREEN LANTERN 60 Cover by Gary Frank & Nathan Eyring

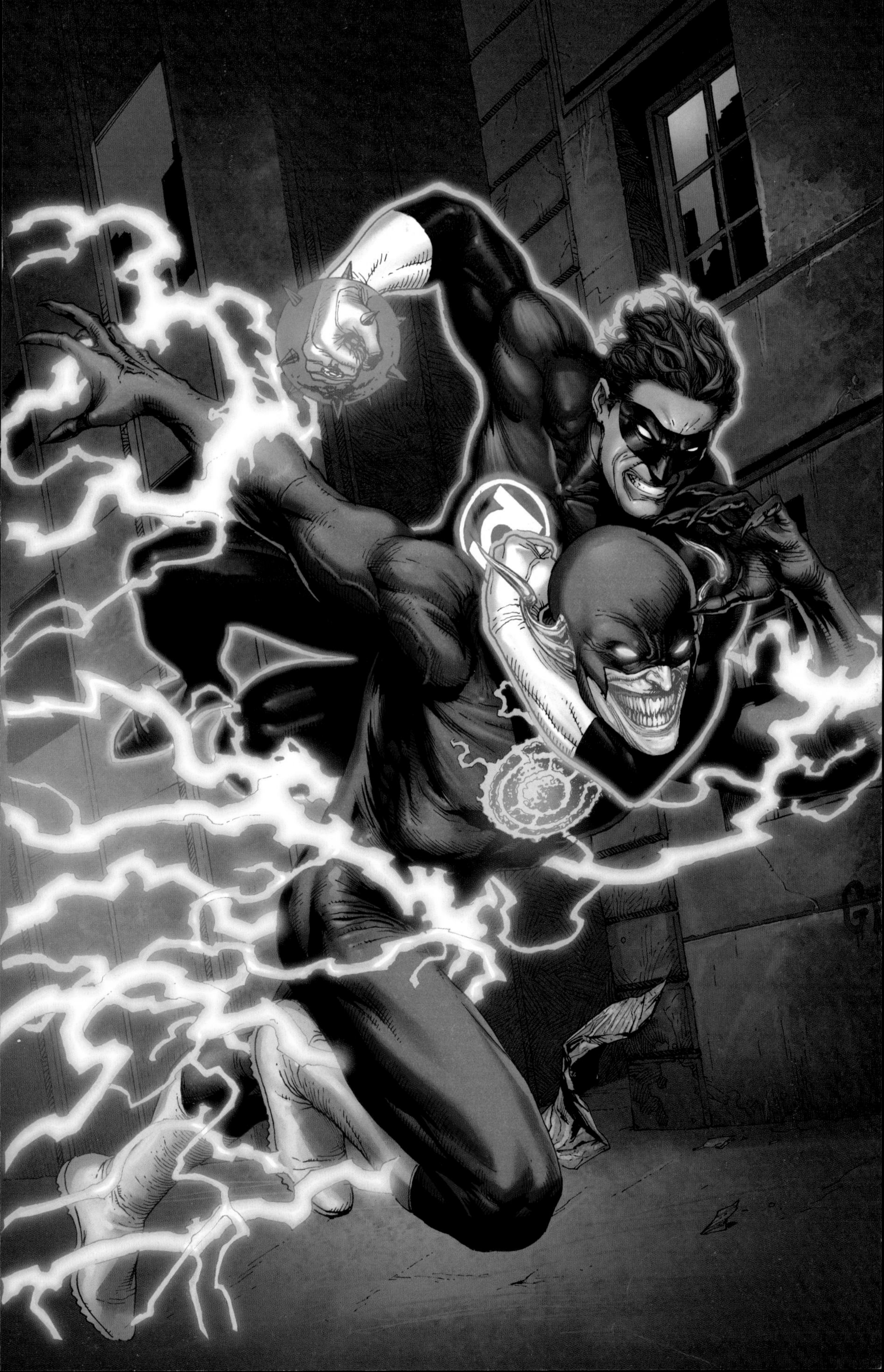

THE NEW GUARDIANS
CHAPTER EIGHT

Doug Mahnke Pencils
Keith Champagne, Christian Alamy, Doug Mahnke & Shawn Moll Inks

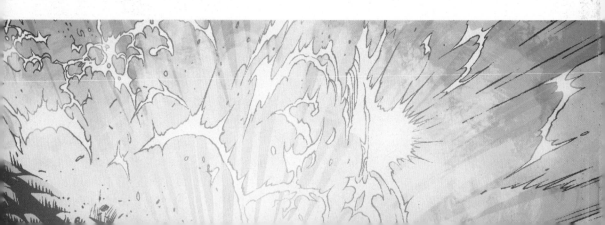

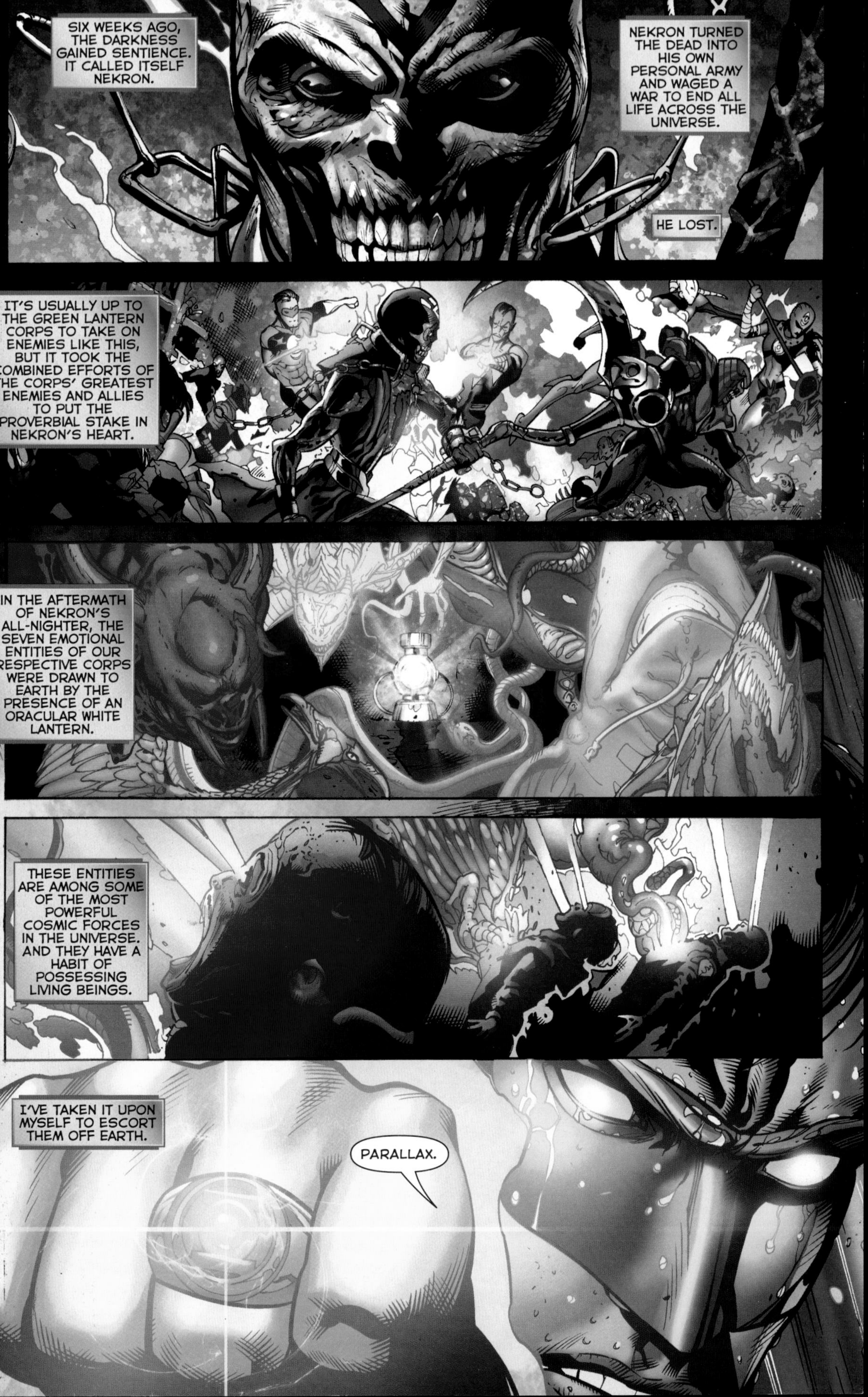
SIX WEEKS AGO, THE DARKNESS GAINED SENTIENCE. IT CALLED ITSELF NEKRON.
NEKRON TURNED THE DEAD INTO HIS OWN PERSONAL ARMY AND WAGED A WAR TO END ALL LIFE ACROSS THE UNIVERSE.
HE LOST.
IT'S USUALLY UP TO THE GREEN LANTERN CORPS TO TAKE ON ENEMIES LIKE THIS, BUT IT TOOK THE COMBINED EFFORTS OF THE CORPS' GREATEST ENEMIES AND ALLIES TO PUT THE PROVERBIAL STAKE IN NEKRON'S HEART.
IN THE AFTERMATH OF NEKRON'S ALL-NIGHTER, THE SEVEN EMOTIONAL ENTITIES OF OUR RESPECTIVE CORPS WERE DRAWN TO EARTH BY THE PRESENCE OF AN ORACULAR WHITE LANTERN.
THESE ENTITIES ARE AMONG SOME OF THE MOST POWERFUL COSMIC FORCES IN THE UNIVERSE. AND THEY HAVE A HABIT OF POSSESSING LIVING BEINGS.
I'VE TAKEN IT UPON MYSELF TO ESCORT THEM OFF EARTH.
PARALLAX.

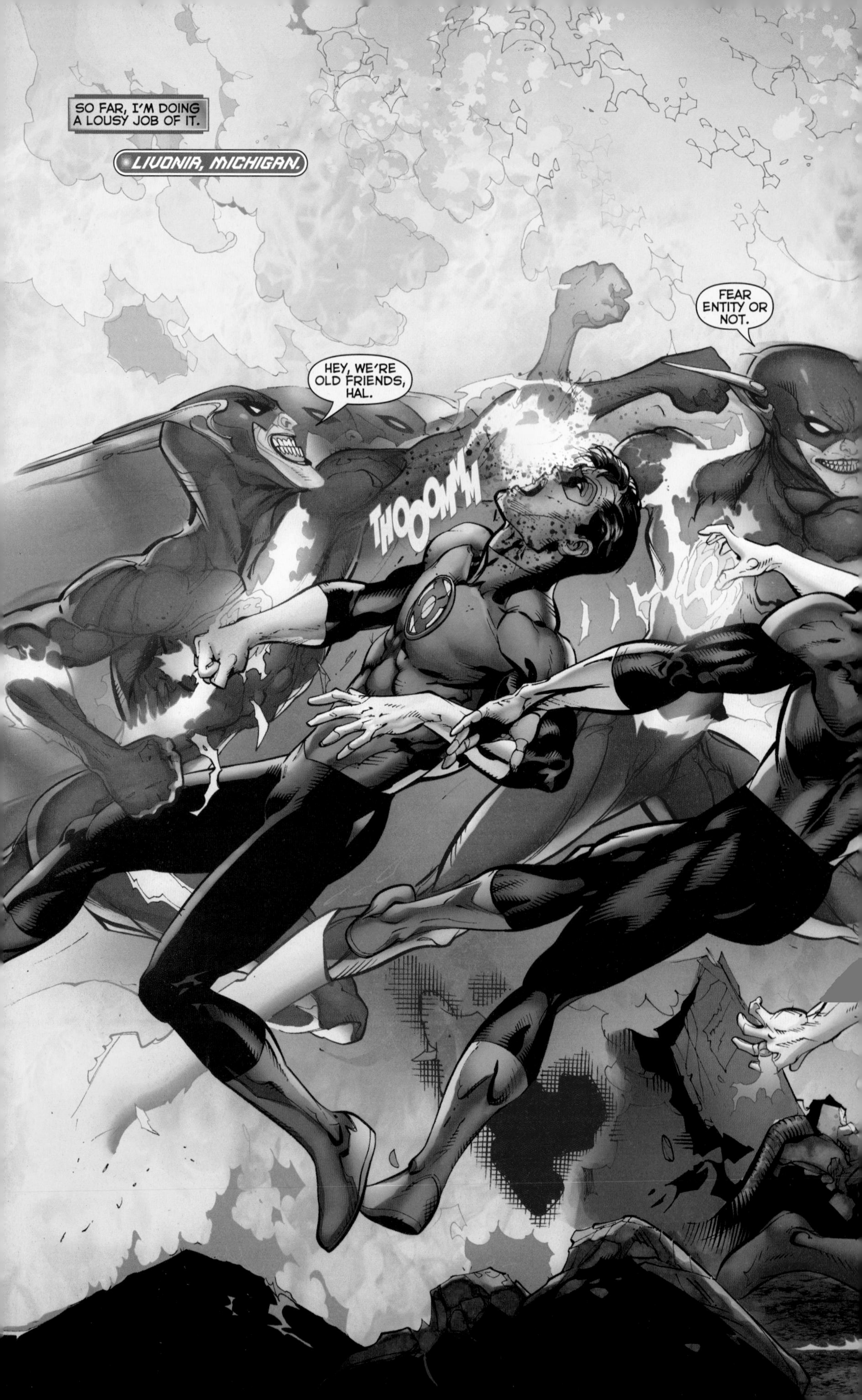
SO FAR, I'M DOING A LOUSY JOB OF IT.
LIVONIA, MICHIGAN.
HEY, WE'RE OLD FRIENDS, HAL.
FEAR ENTITY OR NOT.
THOOOMM

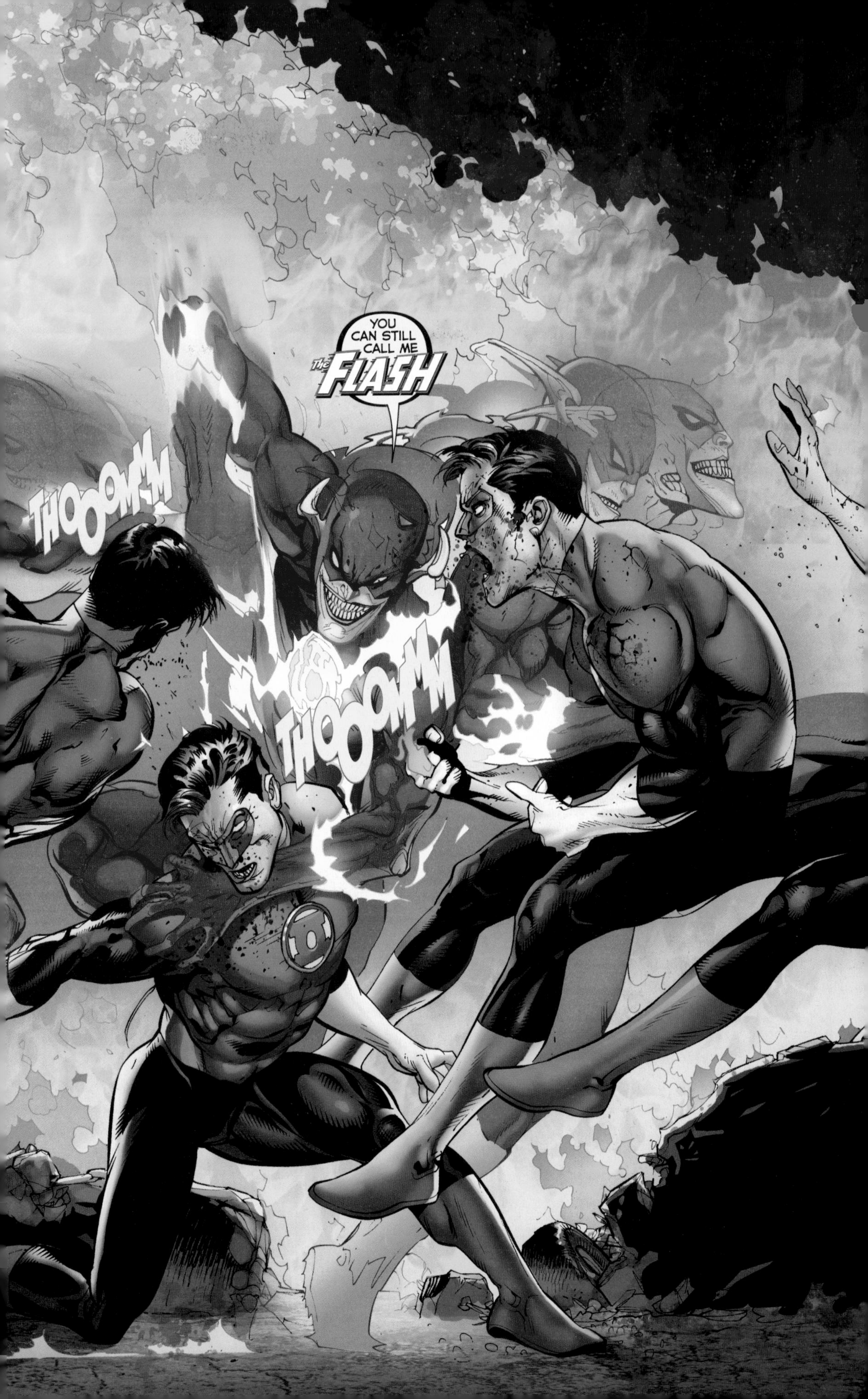
YOU CAN STILL CALL ME THE FLASH
THOOOMMM
THOOOMMM

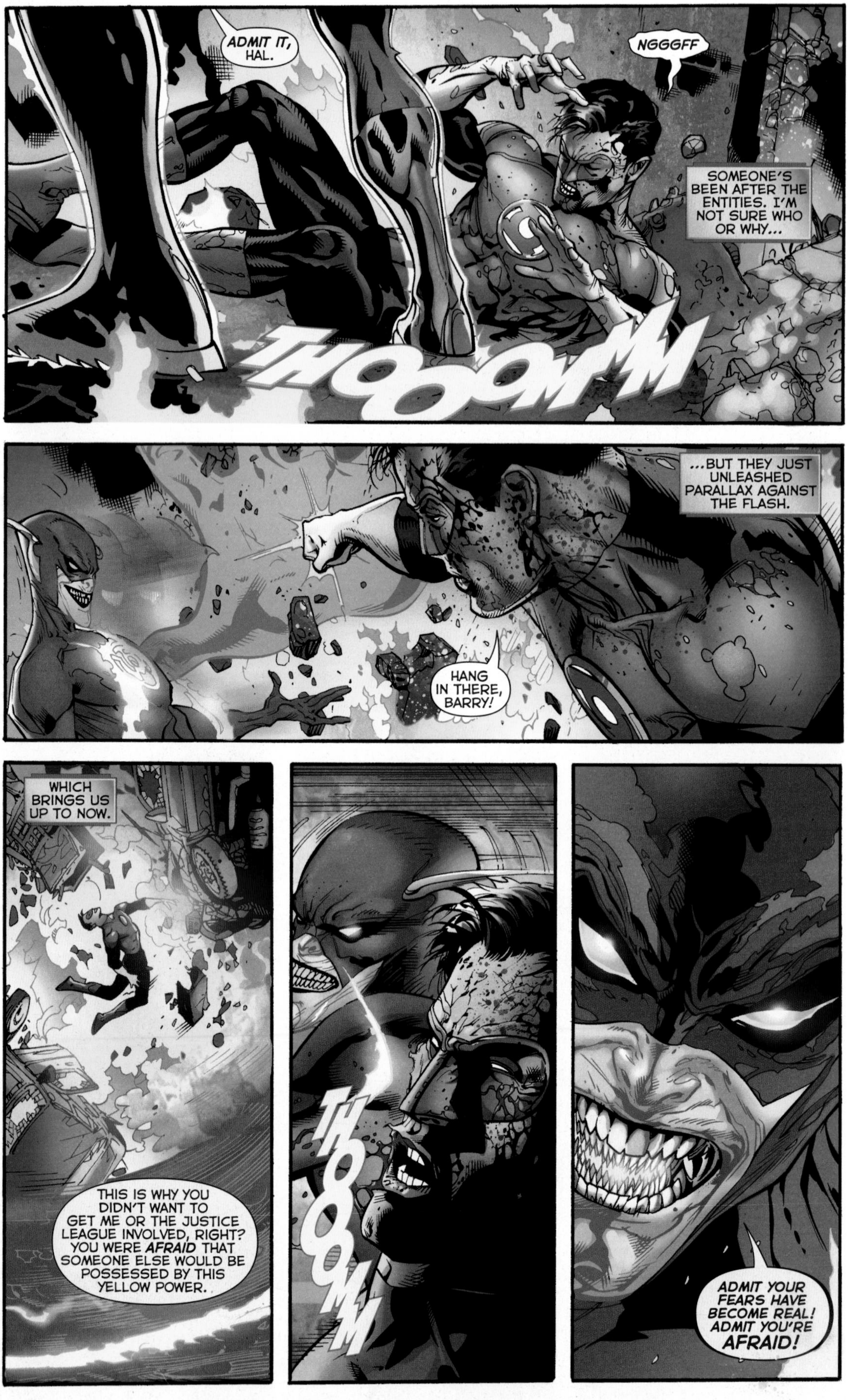
ADMIT IT, HAL.
NGGGFF
SOMEONE'S BEEN AFTER THE ENTITIES. I'M NOT SURE WHO OR WHY...
THOOOMMM
...BUT THEY JUST UNLEASHED PARALLAX AGAINST THE FLASH.
HANG IN THERE, BARRY!
WHICH BRINGS US UP TO NOW.
THIS IS WHY YOU DIDN'T WANT TO GET ME OR THE JUSTICE LEAGUE INVOLVED, RIGHT? YOU WERE AFRAID THAT SOMEONE ELSE WOULD BE POSSESSED BY THIS YELLOW POWER.
THOOOMM
ADMIT YOUR FEARS HAVE BECOME REAL! ADMIT YOU'RE AFRAID!

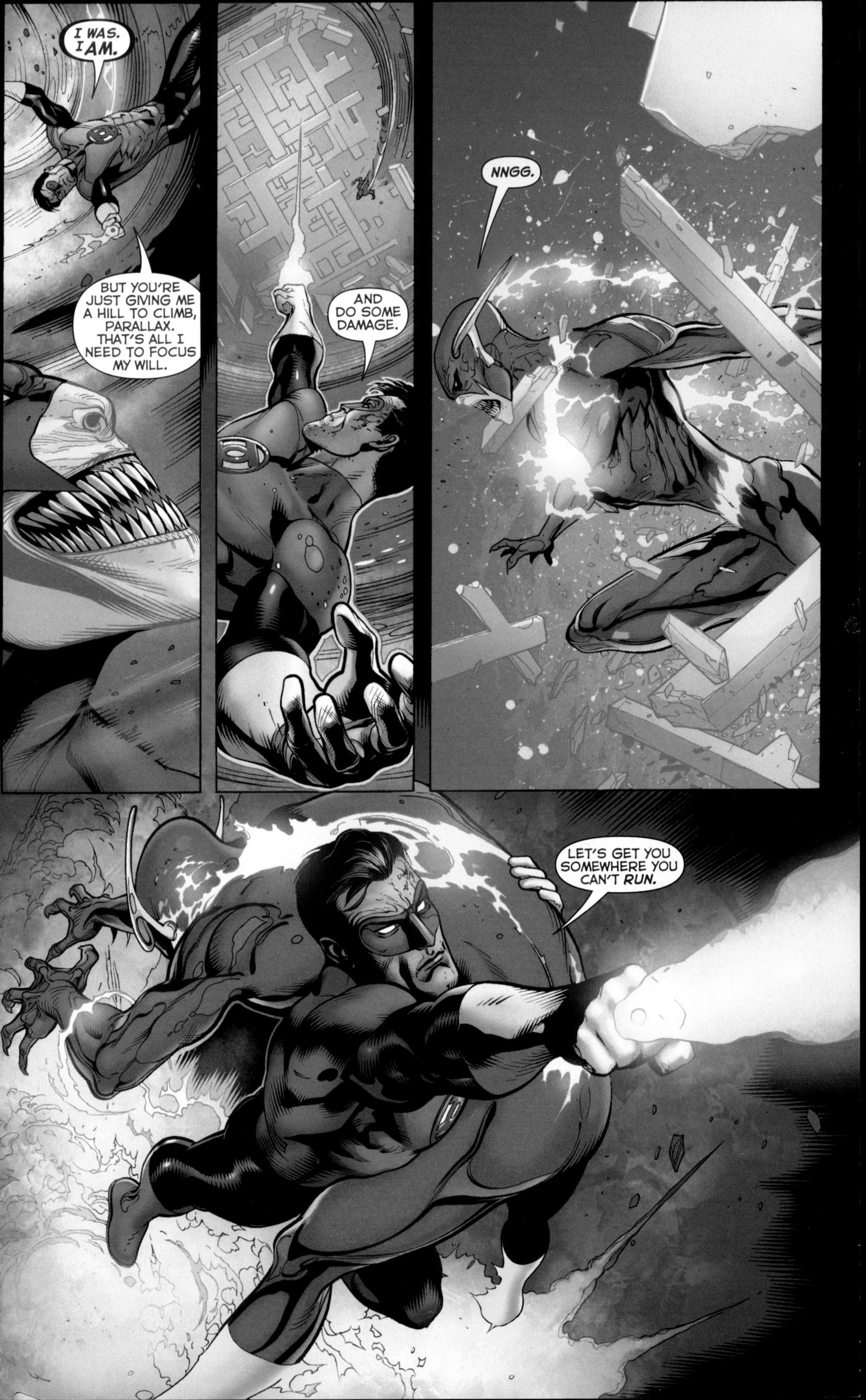
I WAS. I AM.
BUT YOU'RE JUST GIVING ME A HILL TO CLIMB, PARALLAX. THAT'S ALL I NEED TO FOCUS MY WILL.
AND DO SOME DAMAGE.
NNGG.
LET'S GET YOU SOMEWHERE YOU CAN'T RUN.

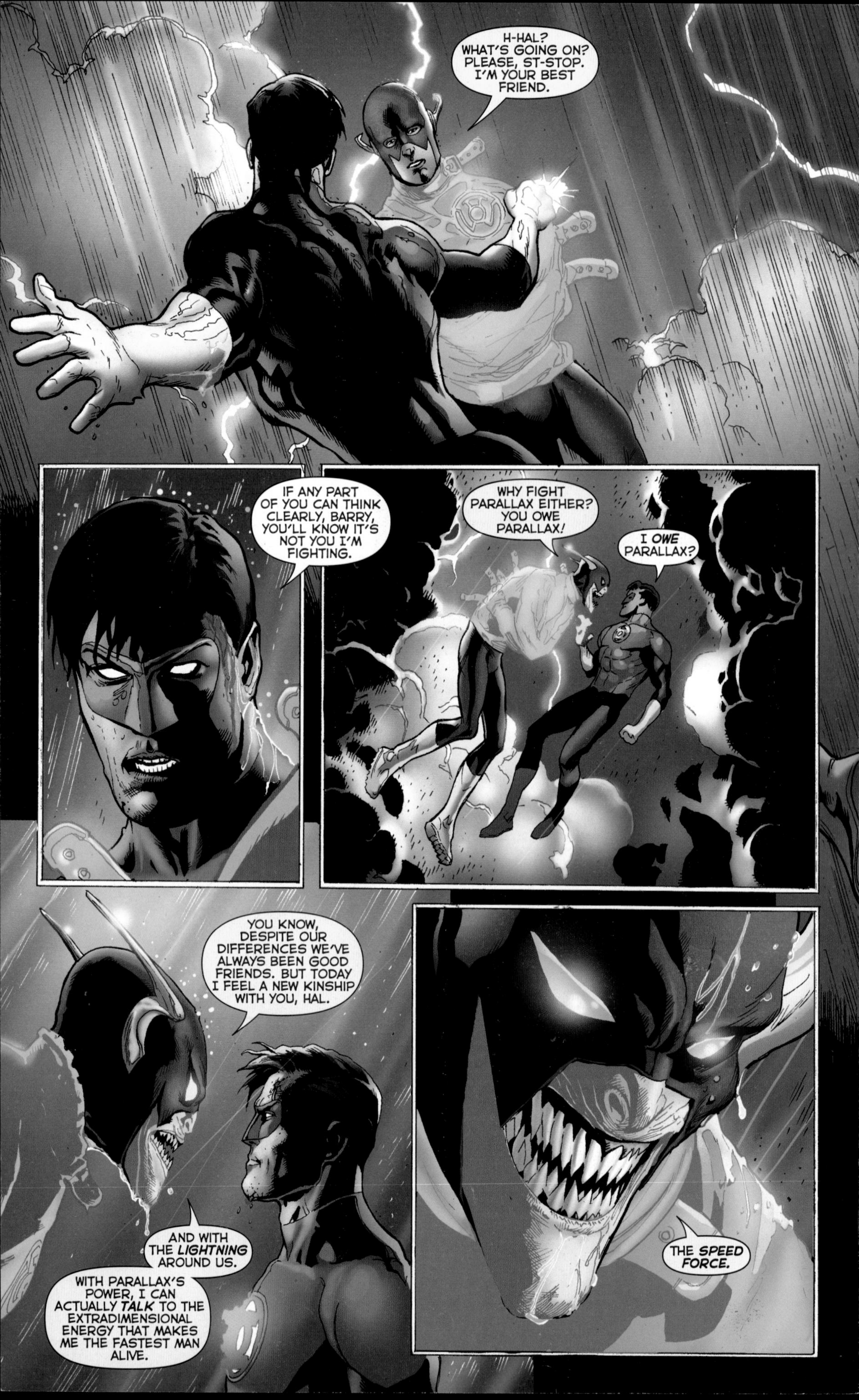
H-HAL? WHAT'S GOING ON? PLEASE, ST-STOP. I'M YOUR BEST FRIEND.
IF ANY PART OF YOU CAN THINK CLEARLY, BARRY, YOU'LL KNOW IT'S NOT YOU I'M FIGHTING.
WHY FIGHT PARALLAX EITHER? YOU OWE PARALLAX!
I *OWE* PARALLAX?
YOU KNOW, DESPITE OUR DIFFERENCES WE'VE ALWAYS BEEN GOOD FRIENDS. BUT TODAY I FEEL A NEW KINSHIP WITH YOU, HAL.
AND WITH THE *LIGHTNING* AROUND US.
WITH PARALLAX'S POWER, I CAN ACTUALLY *TALK* TO THE EXTRADIMENSIONAL ENERGY THAT MAKES ME THE FASTEST MAN ALIVE.
THE *SPEED FORCE.*

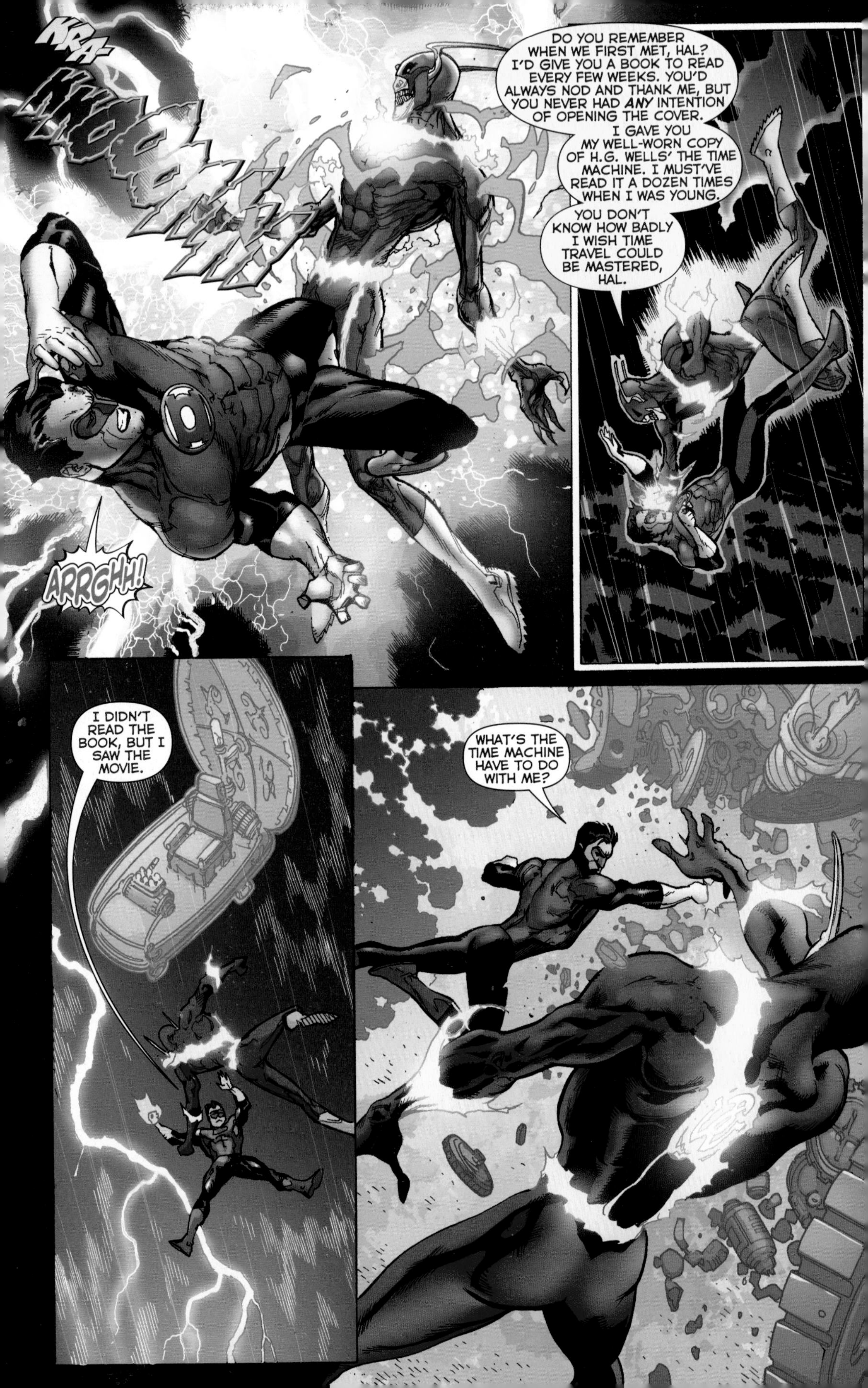
KRA-KOOOOOM
DO YOU REMEMBER WHEN WE FIRST MET, HAL? I'D GIVE YOU A BOOK TO READ EVERY FEW WEEKS. YOU'D ALWAYS NOD AND THANK ME, BUT YOU NEVER HAD ANY INTENTION OF OPENING THE COVER.
I GAVE YOU MY WELL-WORN COPY OF H.G. WELLS' THE TIME MACHINE. I MUST'VE READ IT A DOZEN TIMES WHEN I WAS YOUNG.
YOU DON'T KNOW HOW BADLY I WISH TIME TRAVEL COULD BE MASTERED, HAL.
ARRGHH!
I DIDN'T READ THE BOOK, BUT I SAW THE MOVIE.
WHAT'S THE TIME MACHINE HAVE TO DO WITH ME?

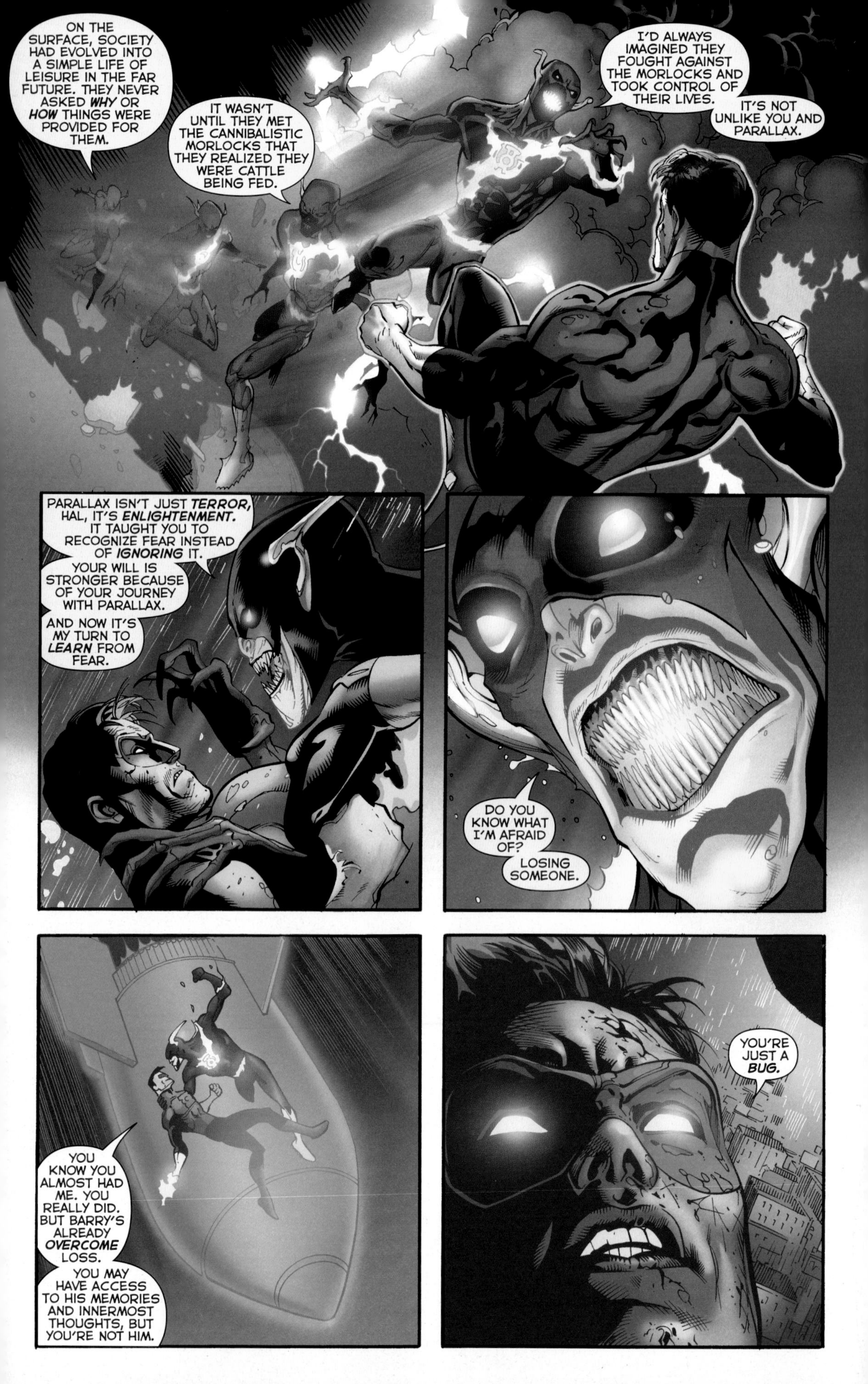
ON THE SURFACE, SOCIETY HAD EVOLVED INTO A SIMPLE LIFE OF LEISURE IN THE FAR FUTURE. THEY NEVER ASKED WHY OR HOW THINGS WERE PROVIDED FOR THEM.
IT WASN'T UNTIL THEY MET THE CANNIBALISTIC MORLOCKS THAT THEY REALIZED THEY WERE CATTLE BEING FED.
I'D ALWAYS IMAGINED THEY FOUGHT AGAINST THE MORLOCKS AND TOOK CONTROL OF THEIR LIVES.
IT'S NOT UNLIKE YOU AND PARALLAX.
PARALLAX ISN'T JUST TERROR, HAL, IT'S ENLIGHTENMENT. IT TAUGHT YOU TO RECOGNIZE FEAR INSTEAD OF IGNORING IT.
YOUR WILL IS STRONGER BECAUSE OF YOUR JOURNEY WITH PARALLAX.
AND NOW IT'S MY TURN TO LEARN FROM FEAR.
DO YOU KNOW WHAT I'M AFRAID OF?
LOSING SOMEONE.
YOU KNOW YOU ALMOST HAD ME. YOU REALLY DID. BUT BARRY'S ALREADY OVERCOME LOSS.
YOU MAY HAVE ACCESS TO HIS MEMORIES AND INNERMOST THOUGHTS, BUT YOU'RE NOT HIM.
YOU'RE JUST A BUG.

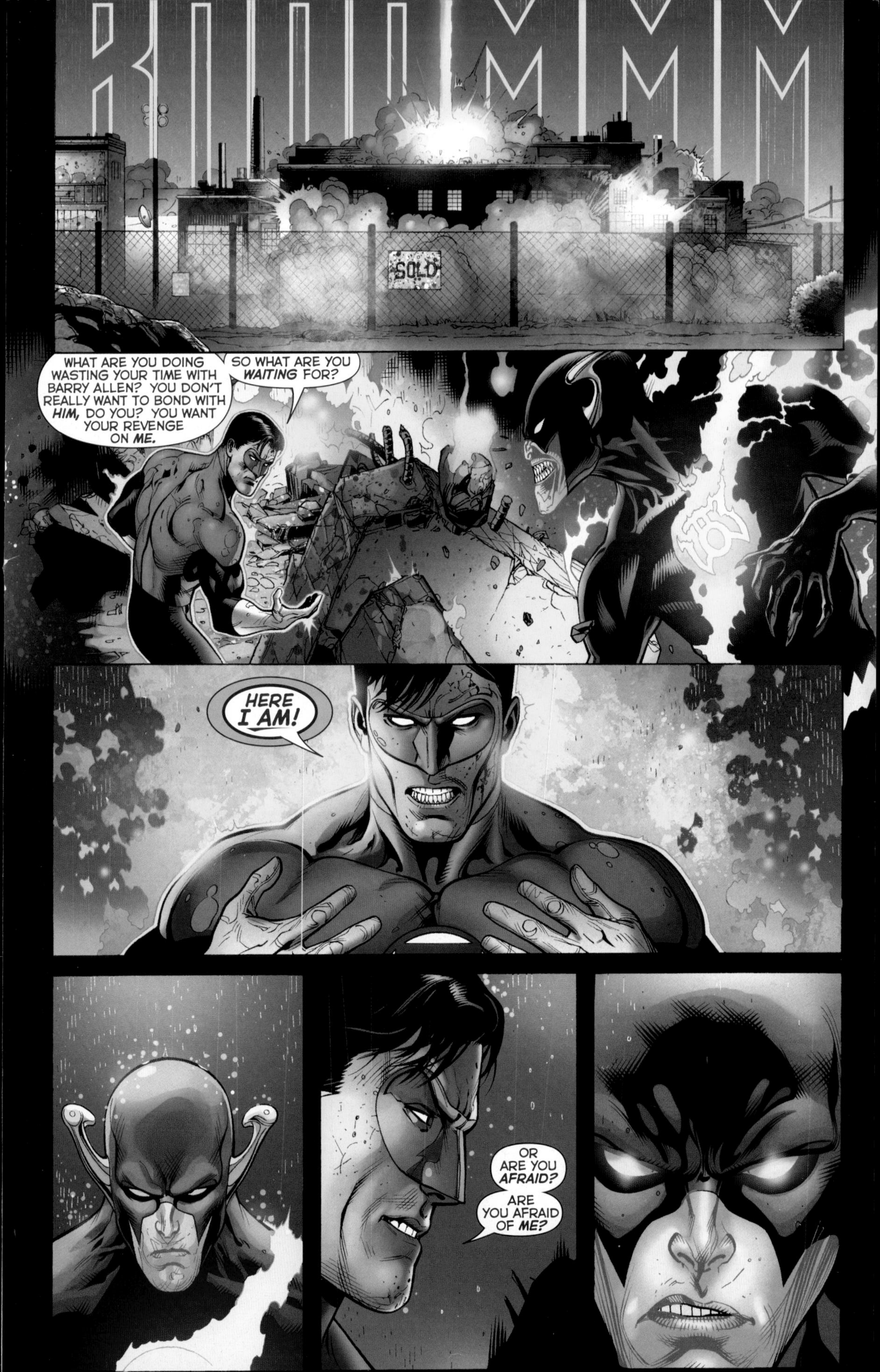

KROOOMMM
SOLD
WHAT ARE YOU DOING WASTING YOUR TIME WITH BARRY ALLEN? YOU DON'T REALLY WANT TO BOND WITH HIM, DO YOU? YOU WANT YOUR REVENGE ON ME.
SO WHAT ARE YOU WAITING FOR?
HERE I AM!
OR ARE YOU AFRAID?
ARE YOU AFRAID OF ME?

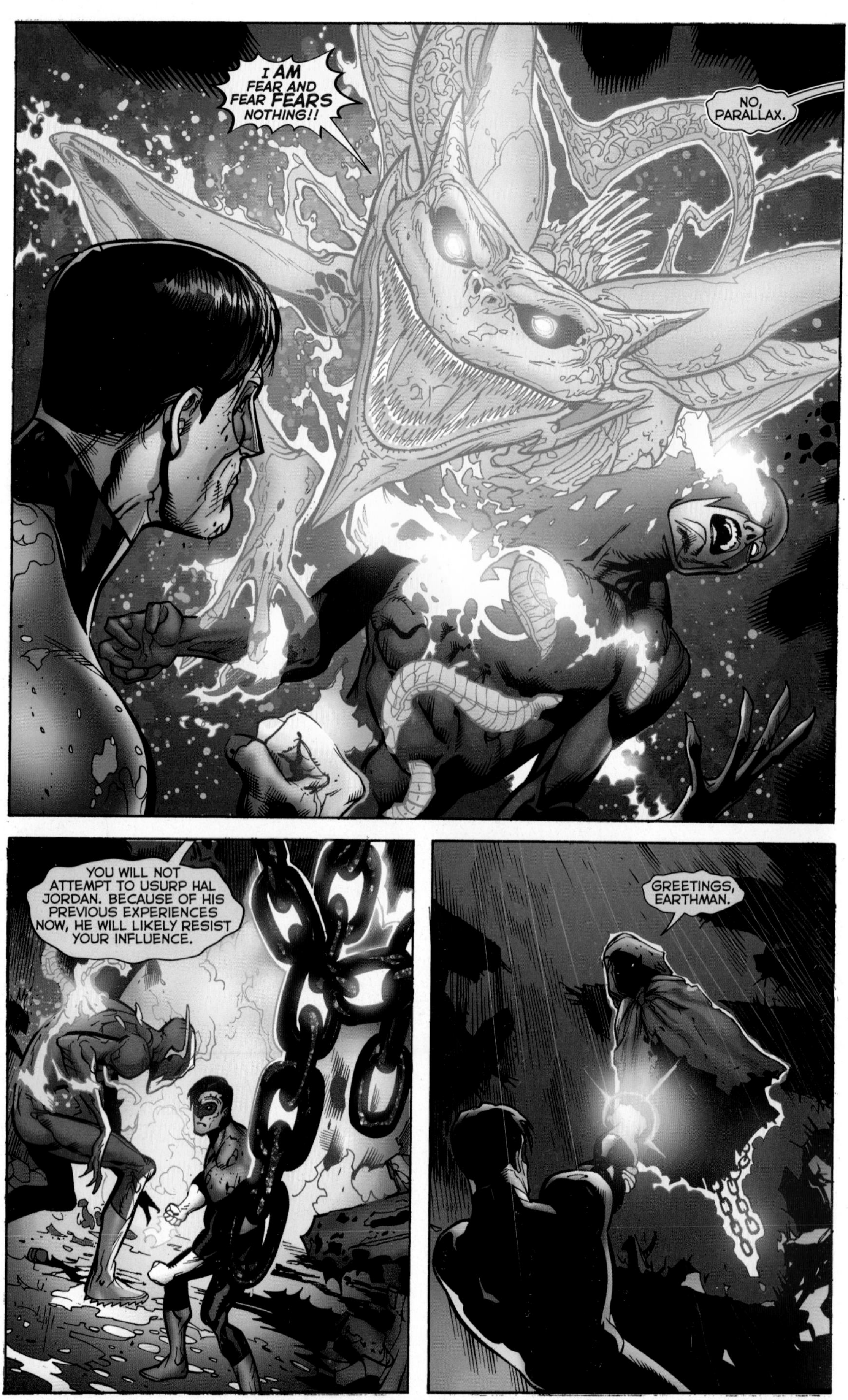
I AM FEAR AND FEAR FEARS NOTHING!!
NO, PARALLAX.
YOU WILL NOT ATTEMPT TO USURP HAL JORDAN. BECAUSE OF HIS PREVIOUS EXPERIENCES NOW, HE WILL LIKELY RESIST YOUR INFLUENCE.
GREETINGS, EARTHMAN.

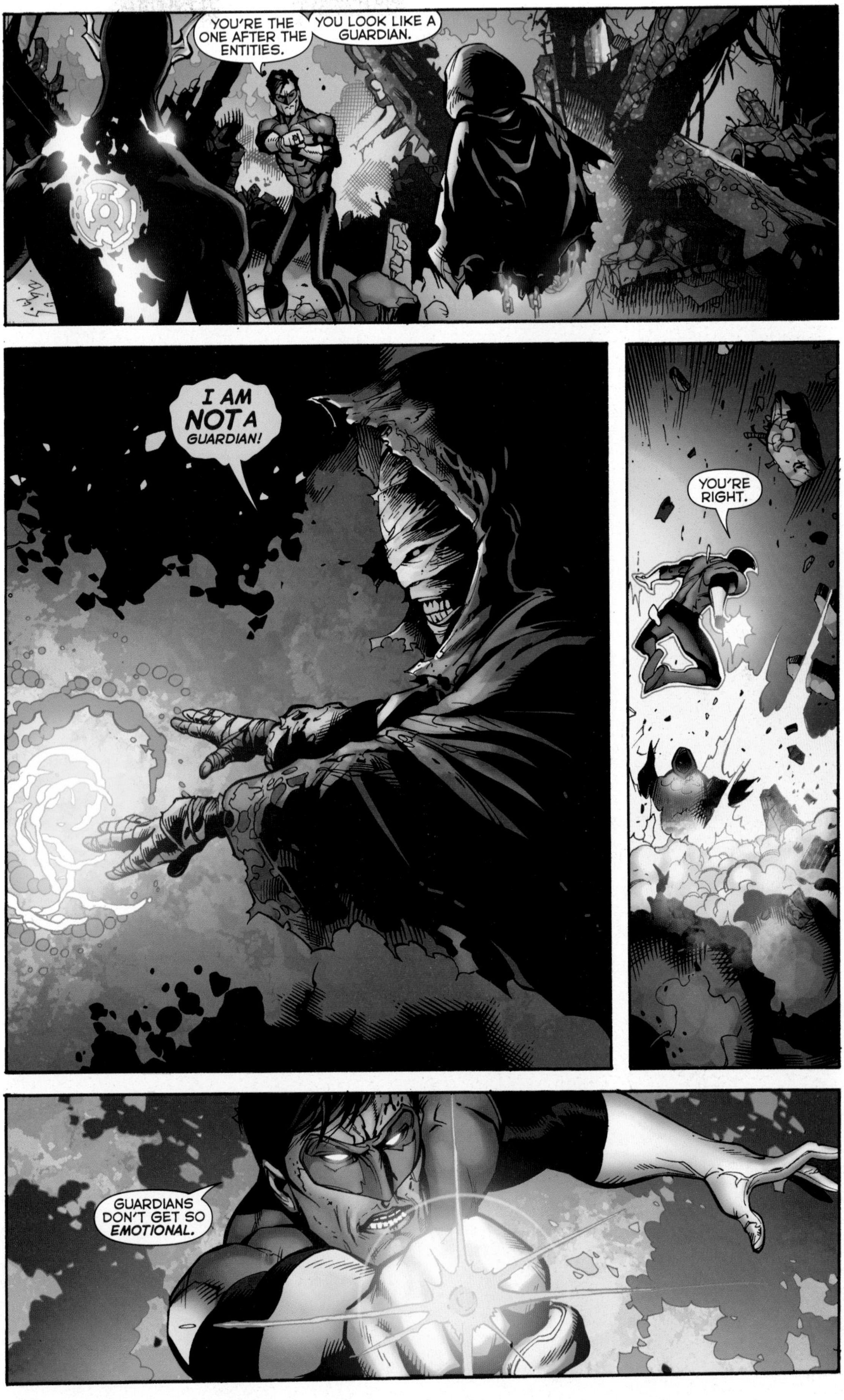
YOU'RE THE ONE AFTER THE ENTITIES.
YOU LOOK LIKE A GUARDIAN.
I AM *NOT* A GUARDIAN!
YOU'RE RIGHT.
GUARDIANS DON'T GET SO *EMOTIONAL*.

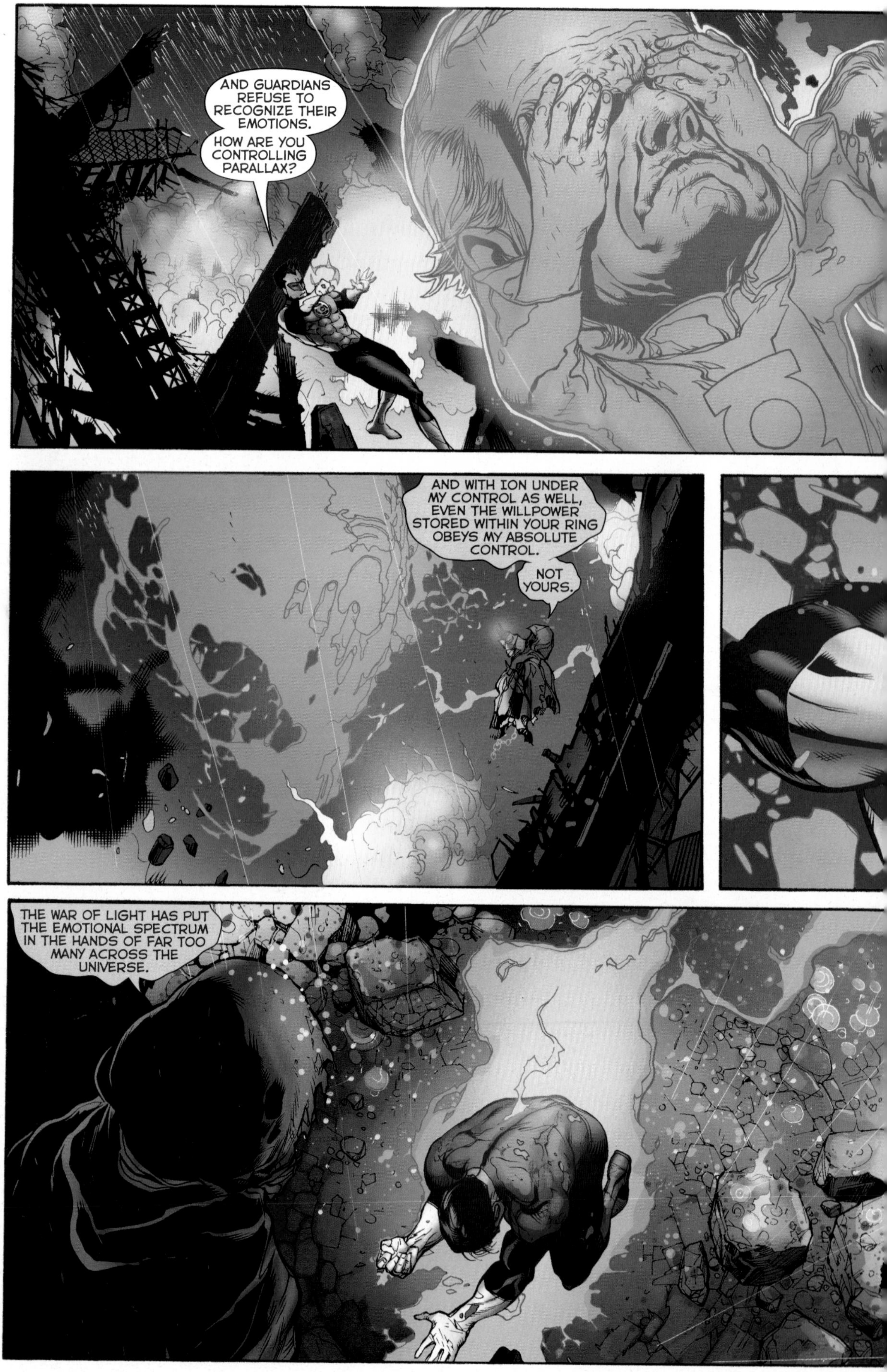
AND GUARDIANS REFUSE TO RECOGNIZE THEIR EMOTIONS.
HOW ARE YOU CONTROLLING PARALLAX?
AND WITH ION UNDER MY CONTROL AS WELL, EVEN THE WILLPOWER STORED WITHIN YOUR RING OBEYS MY ABSOLUTE CONTROL.
NOT YOURS.
THE WAR OF LIGHT HAS PUT THE EMOTIONAL SPECTRUM IN THE HANDS OF FAR TOO MANY ACROSS THE UNIVERSE.

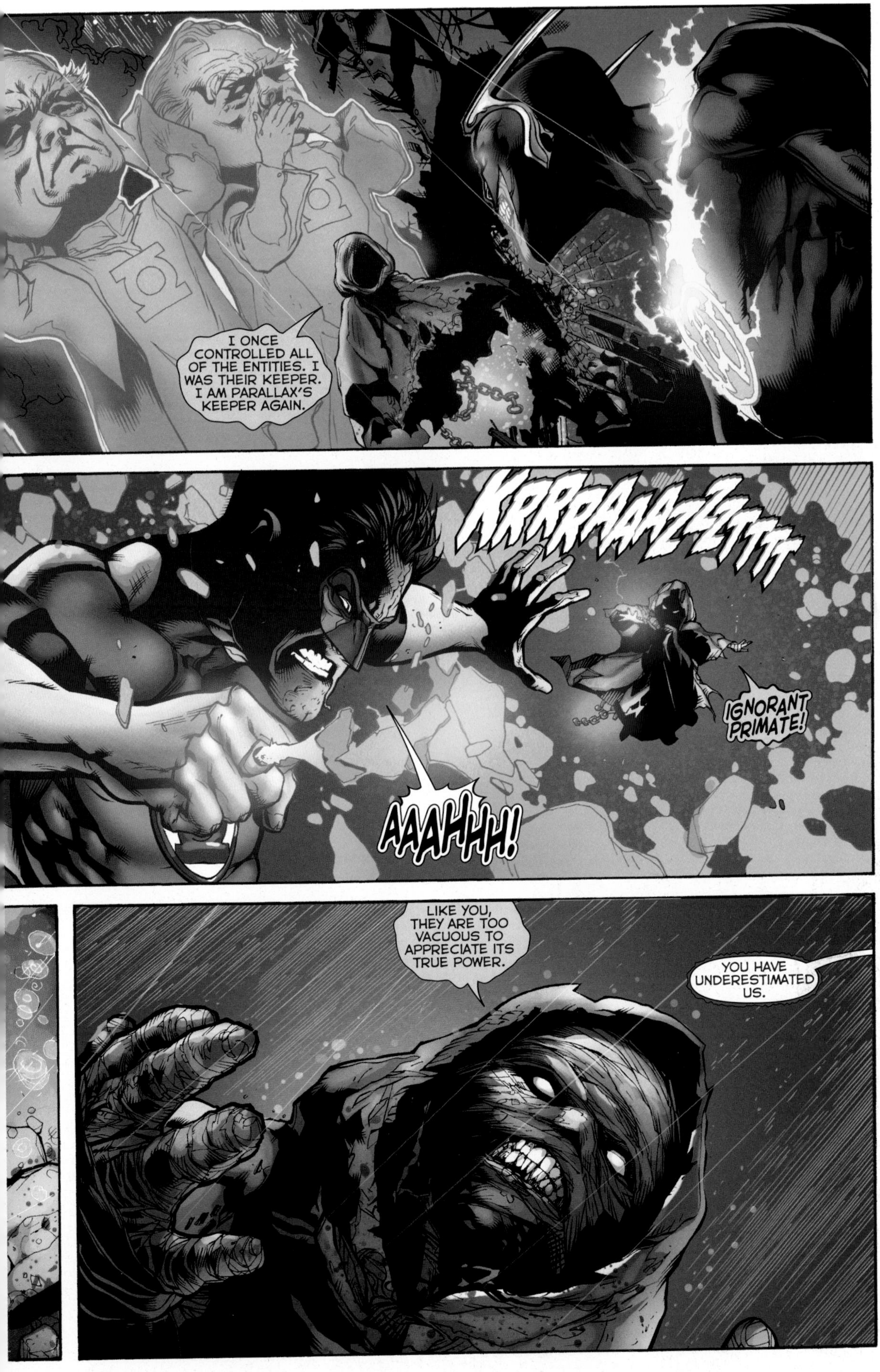

I ONCE CONTROLLED ALL OF THE ENTITIES. I WAS THEIR KEEPER. I AM PARALLAX'S KEEPER AGAIN.
KRRRAAAZZZTTTT
IGNORANT PRIMATE!
AAAHHH!
LIKE YOU, THEY ARE TOO VACUOUS TO APPRECIATE ITS TRUE POWER.
YOU HAVE UNDERESTIMATED US.

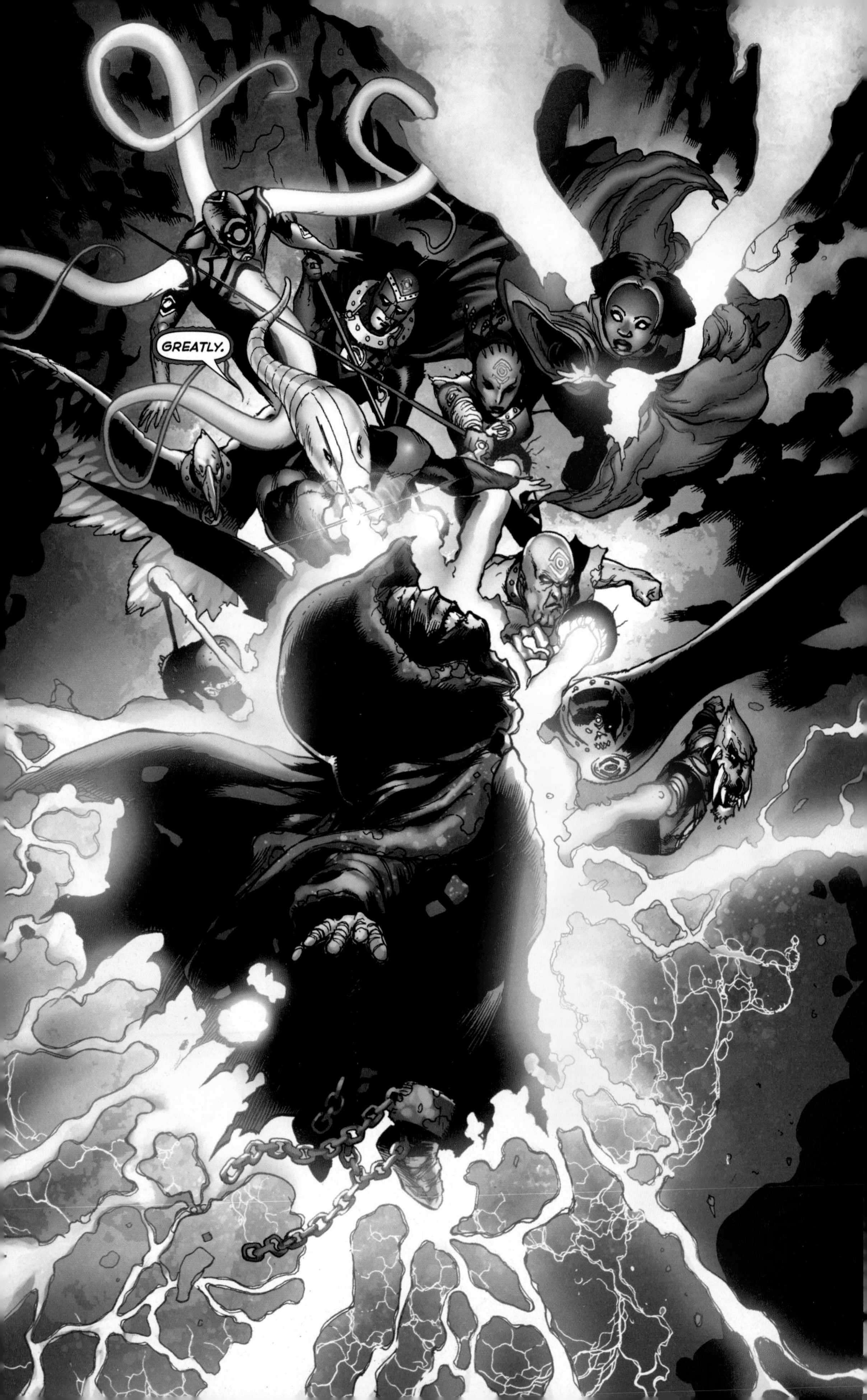
GREATLY.

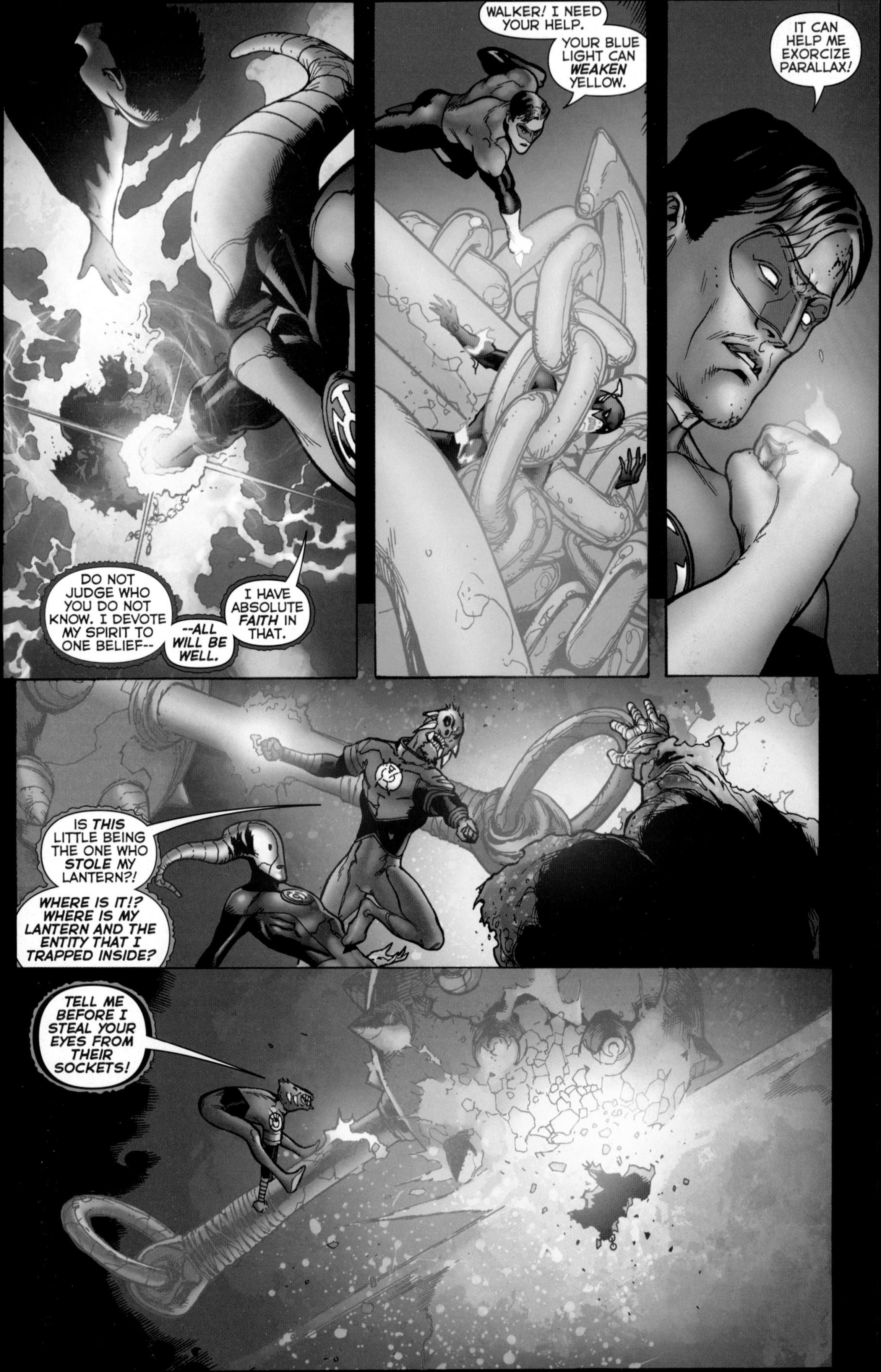
DO NOT JUDGE WHO YOU DO NOT KNOW. I DEVOTE MY SPIRIT TO ONE BELIEF--
--ALL WILL BE WELL.
I HAVE ABSOLUTE FAITH IN THAT.
WALKER! I NEED YOUR HELP.
YOUR BLUE LIGHT CAN WEAKEN YELLOW.
IT CAN HELP ME EXORCIZE PARALLAX!
IS THIS LITTLE BEING THE ONE WHO STOLE MY LANTERN?!
WHERE IS IT!? WHERE IS MY LANTERN AND THE ENTITY THAT I TRAPPED INSIDE?
TELL ME BEFORE I STEAL YOUR EYES FROM THEIR SOCKETS!

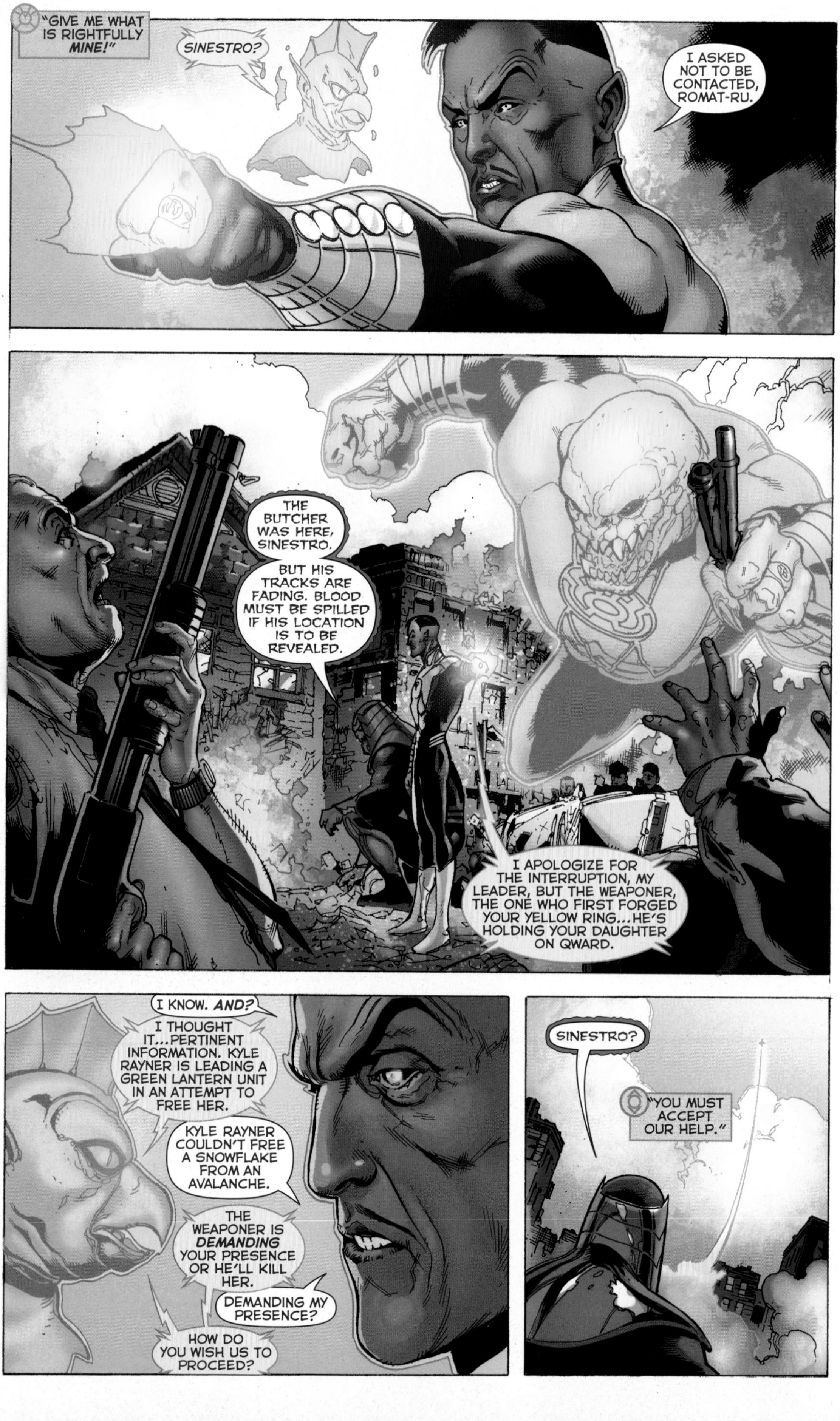
"GIVE ME WHAT IS RIGHTFULLY *MINE!*"
SINESTRO?
I ASKED NOT TO BE CONTACTED, ROMAT-RU.
THE BUTCHER WAS HERE, SINESTRO.
BUT HIS TRACKS ARE FADING. BLOOD MUST BE SPILLED IF HIS LOCATION IS TO BE REVEALED.
I APOLOGIZE FOR THE INTERRUPTION, MY LEADER, BUT THE WEAPONER, THE ONE WHO FIRST FORGED YOUR YELLOW RING...HE'S HOLDING YOUR DAUGHTER ON QWARD.
I KNOW. *AND?*
I THOUGHT IT...PERTINENT INFORMATION. KYLE RAYNER IS LEADING A GREEN LANTERN UNIT IN AN ATTEMPT TO FREE HER.
KYLE RAYNER COULDN'T FREE A SNOWFLAKE FROM AN AVALANCHE.
THE WEAPONER IS *DEMANDING* YOUR PRESENCE OR HE'LL KILL HER.
DEMANDING MY PRESENCE?
HOW DO YOU WISH US TO PROCEED?
SINESTRO?
"YOU MUST ACCEPT OUR HELP."

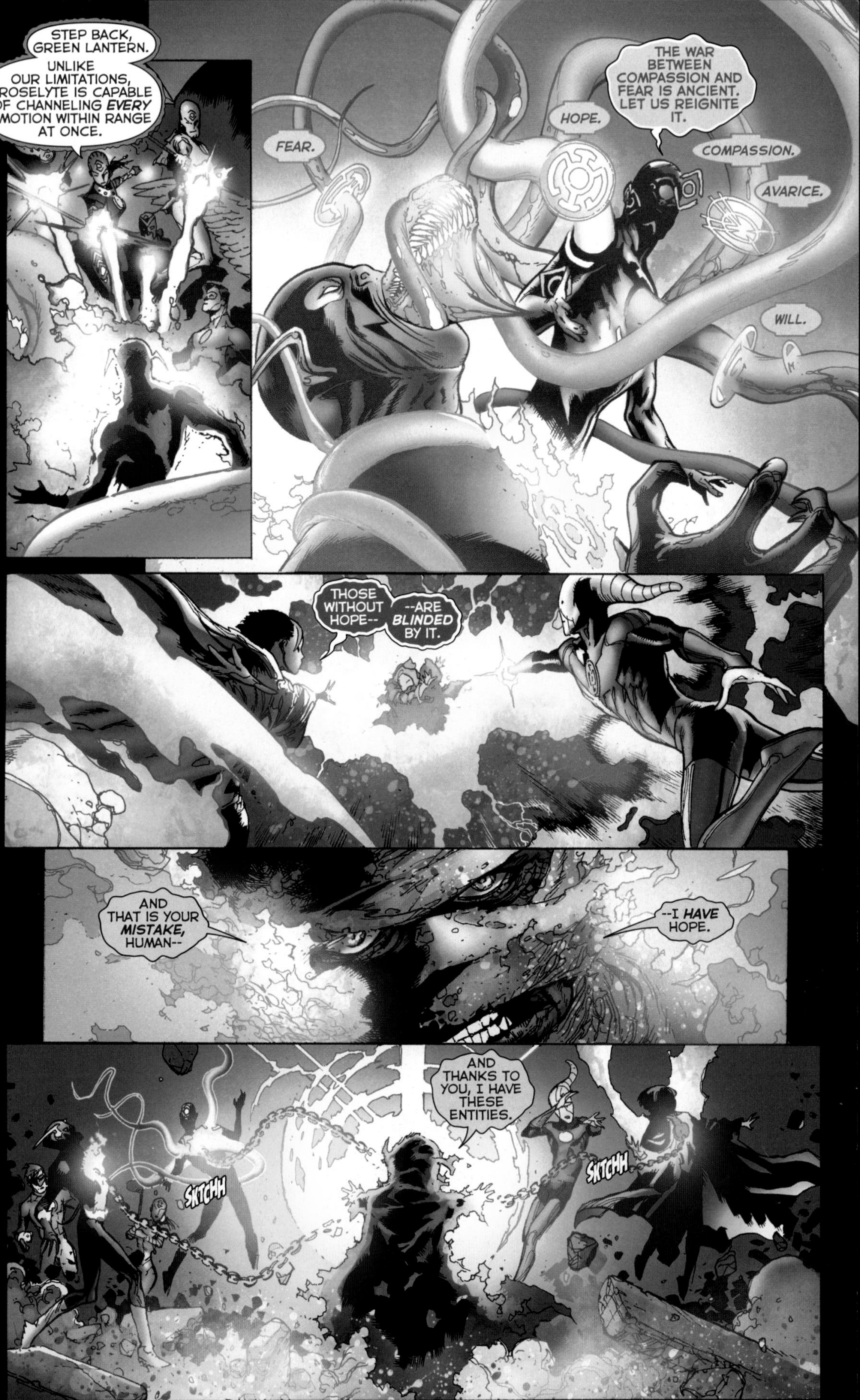
STEP BACK, GREEN LANTERN.
UNLIKE OUR LIMITATIONS, PROSELYTE IS CAPABLE OF CHANNELING EVERY EMOTION WITHIN RANGE AT ONCE.
THE WAR BETWEEN COMPASSION AND FEAR IS ANCIENT. LET US REIGNITE IT.
FEAR.
HOPE.
COMPASSION.
AVARICE.
WILL.
THOSE WITHOUT HOPE--
--ARE BLINDED BY IT.
AND THAT IS YOUR MISTAKE, HUMAN--
--I HAVE HOPE.
AND THANKS TO YOU, I HAVE THESE ENTITIES.
SKTCHH
SKTCHH

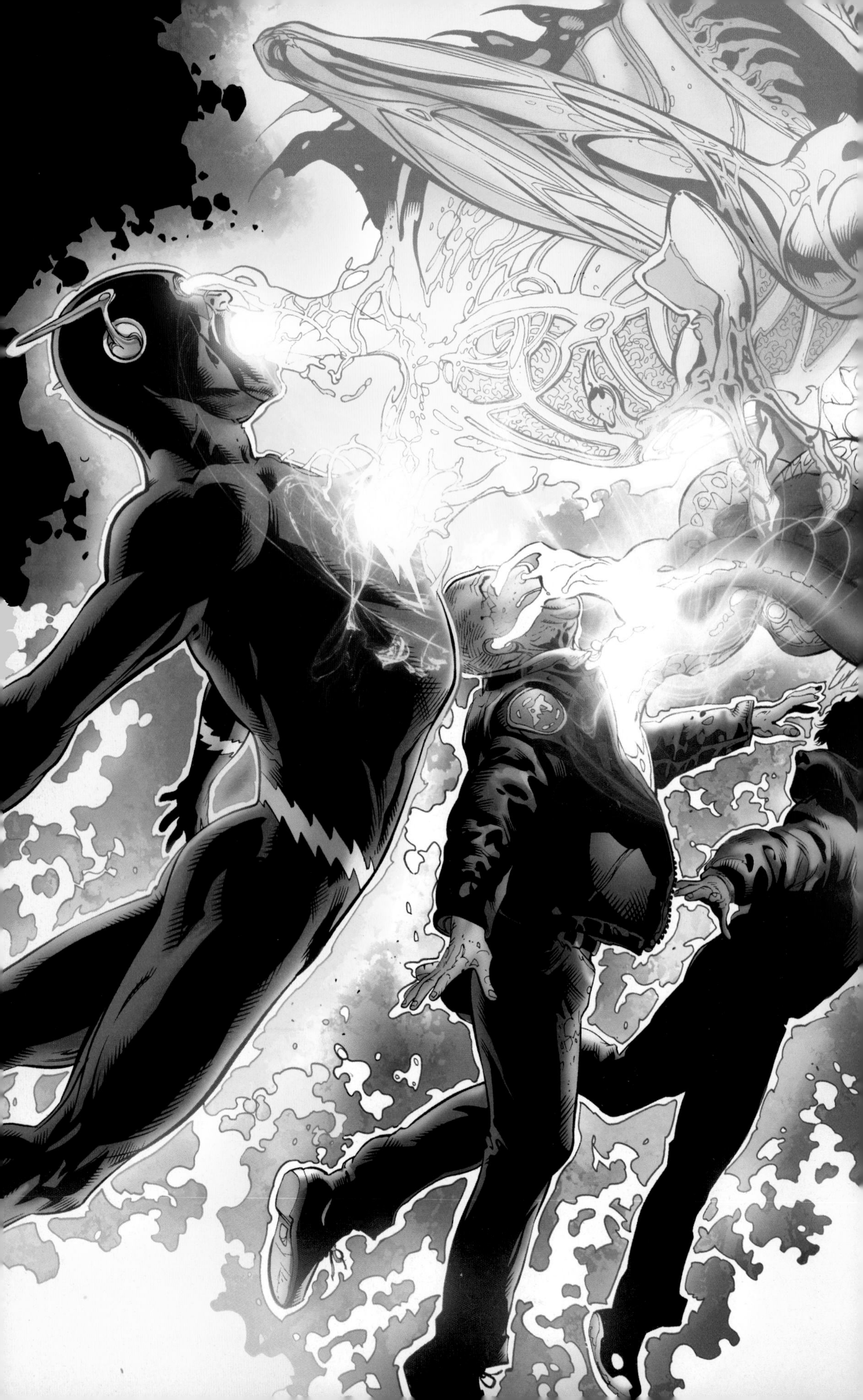

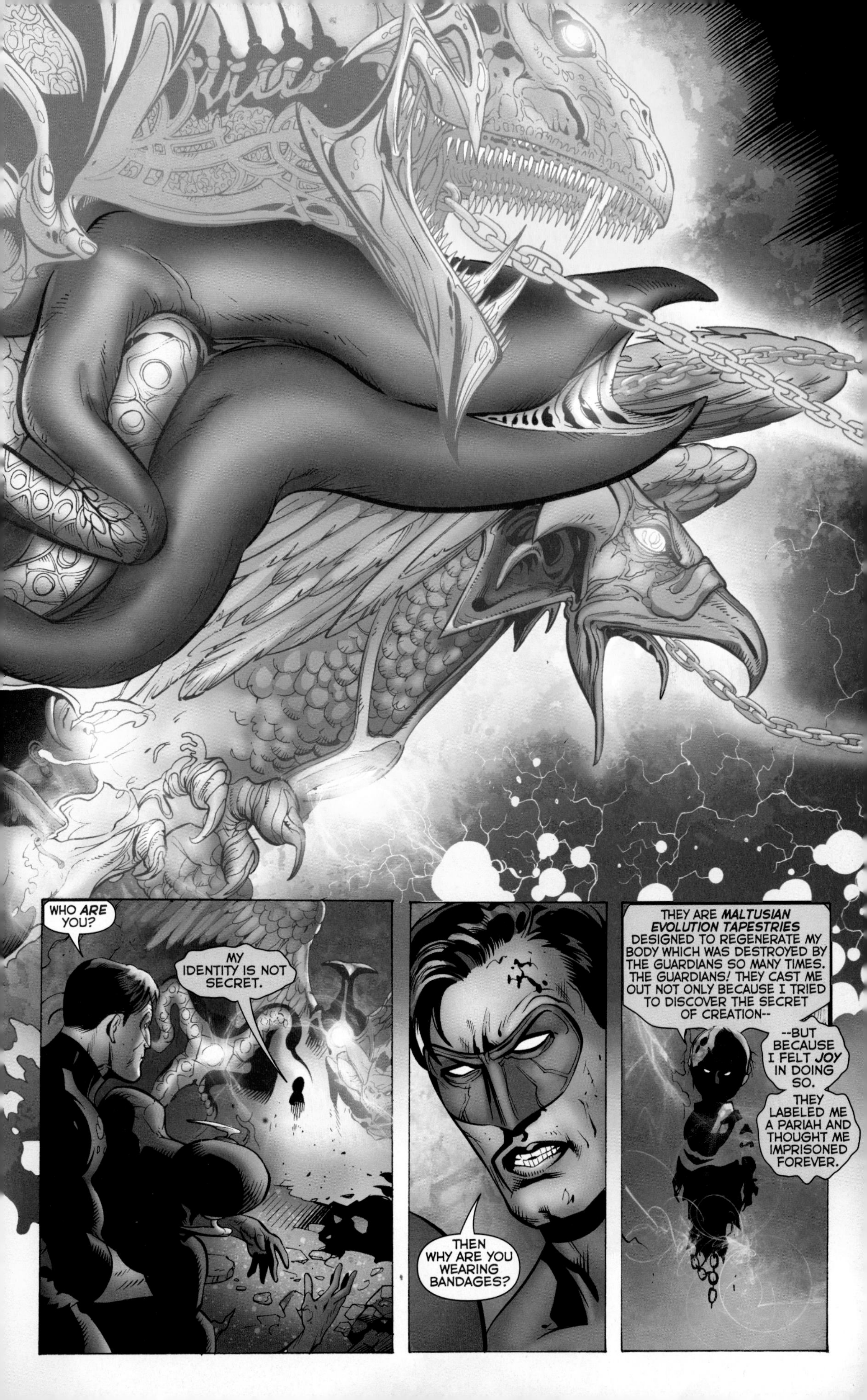

WHO *ARE* YOU?
MY IDENTITY IS NOT SECRET.
THEN WHY ARE YOU WEARING BANDAGES?
THEY ARE *MALTUSIAN EVOLUTION TAPESTRIES* DESIGNED TO REGENERATE MY BODY WHICH WAS DESTROYED BY THE GUARDIANS SO MANY TIMES. THE GUARDIANS! THEY CAST ME OUT NOT ONLY BECAUSE I TRIED TO DISCOVER THE SECRET OF CREATION--
--BUT BECAUSE I FELT *JOY* IN DOING SO.
THEY LABELED ME A PARIAH AND THOUGHT ME IMPRISONED FOREVER.

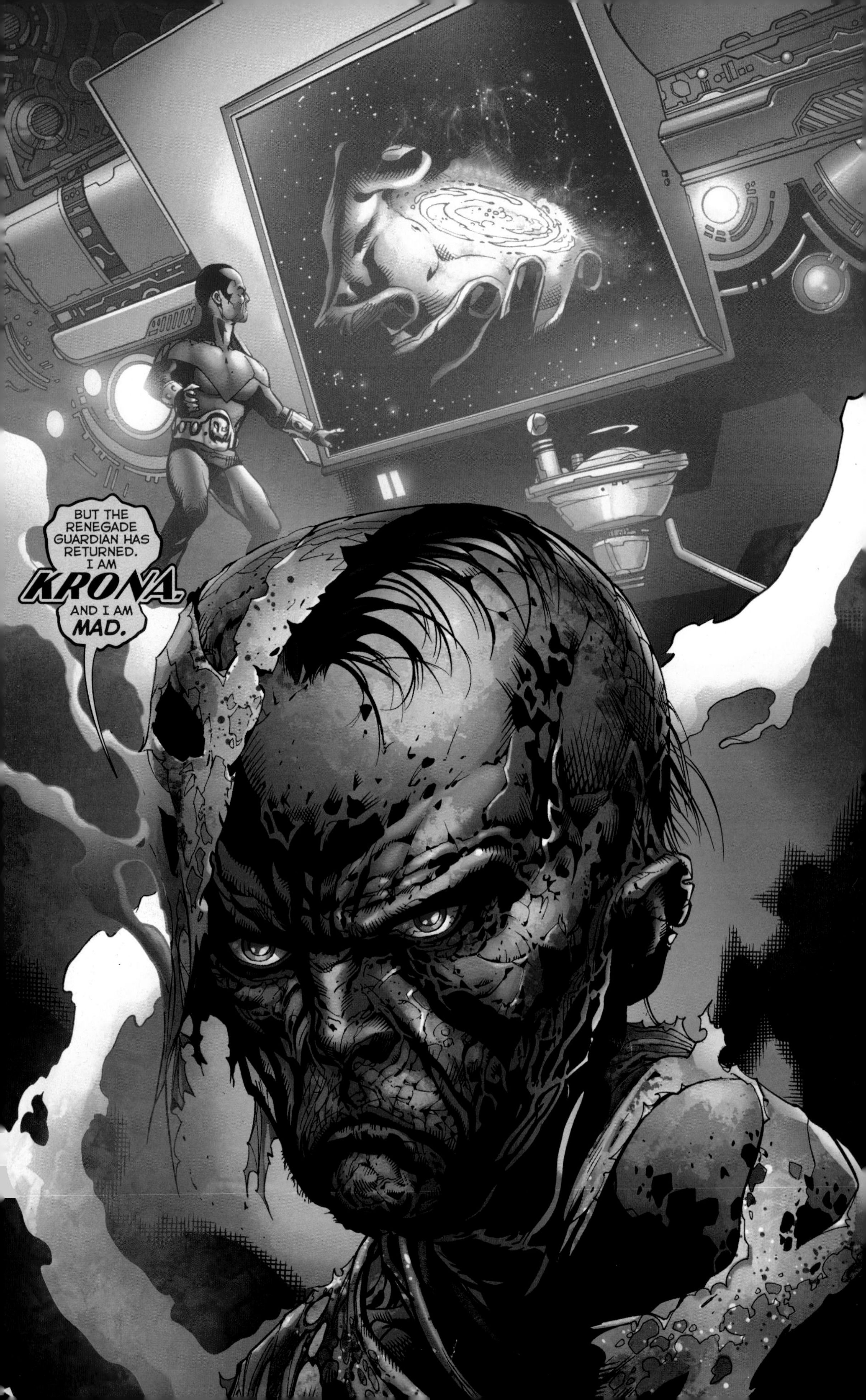
BUT THE RENEGADE GUARDIAN HAS RETURNED. I AM KRONA. AND I AM MAD.

GREEN LANTERN 61 Cover by Gary Frank & Randy Mayor

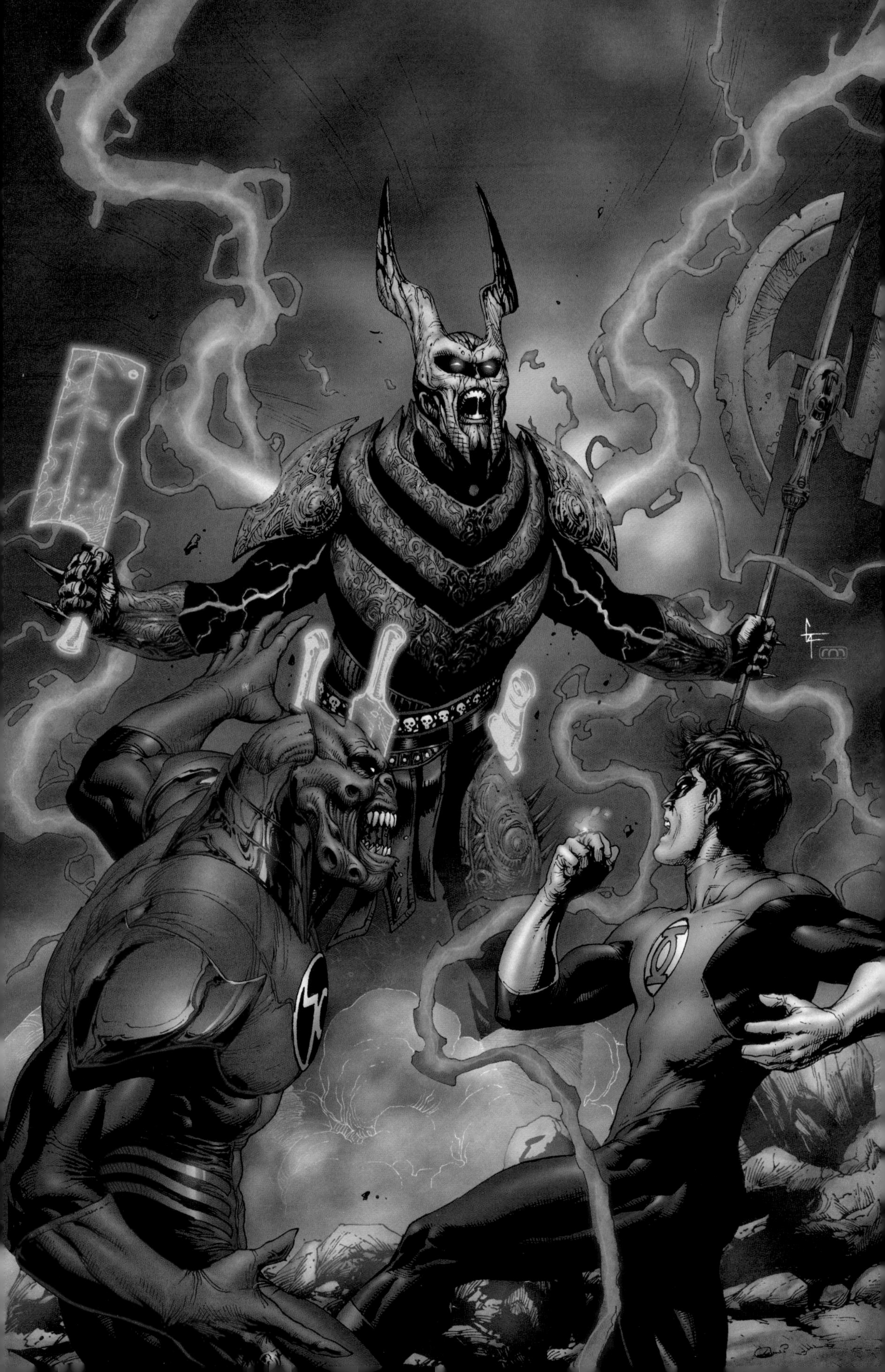

THE NEW GUARDIANS
CHAPTER NINE

Doug Mahnke Pencils
Keith Champagne, Christian Alamy, Tom Nguyen & Mark Irwin Inks

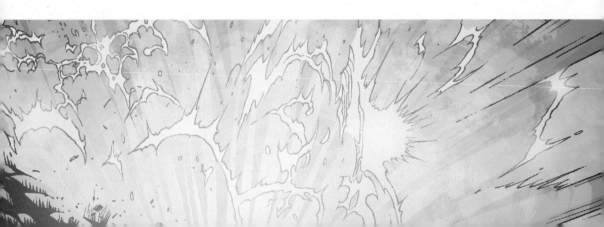

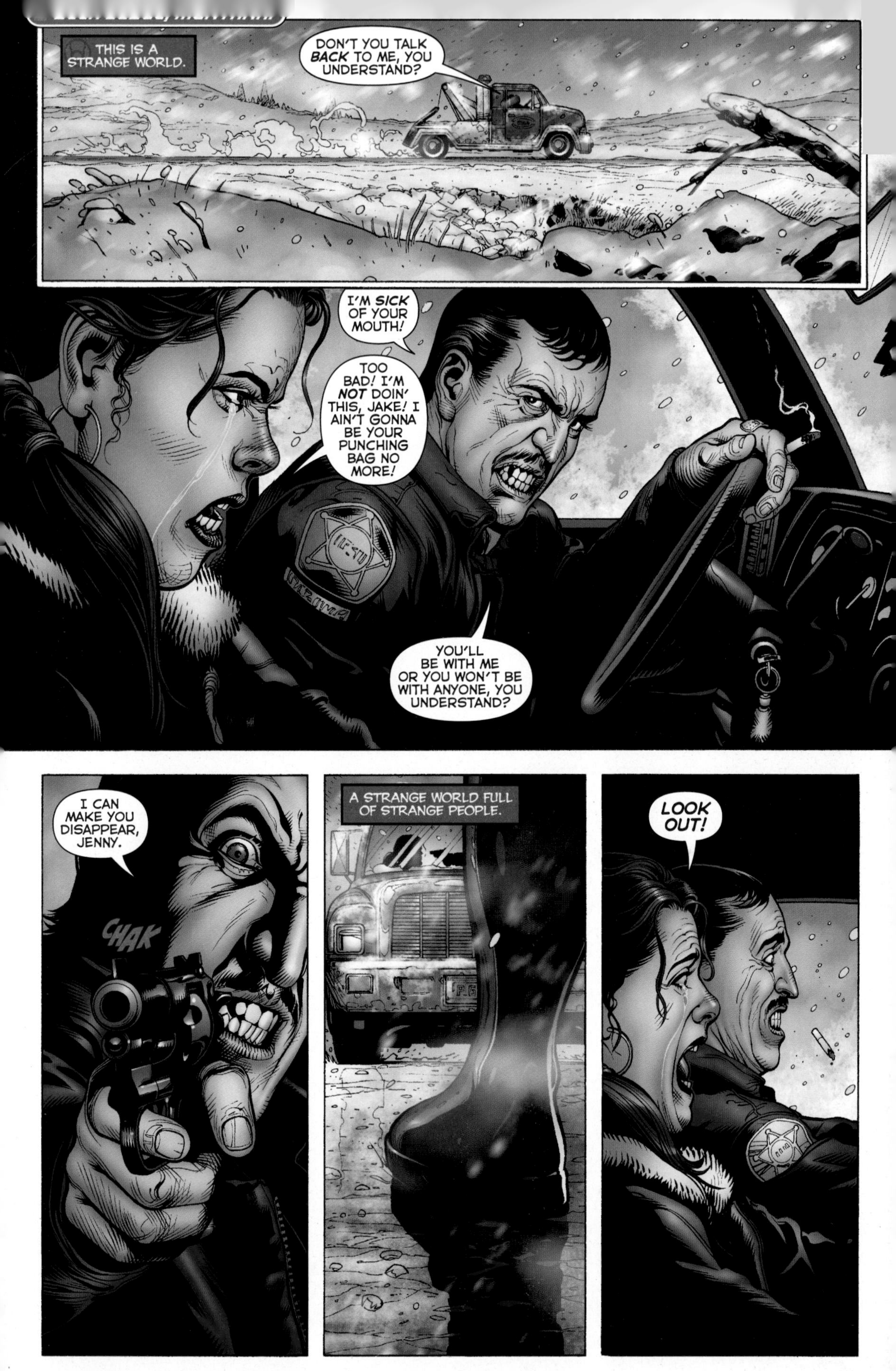
THIS IS A STRANGE WORLD.
DON'T YOU TALK BACK TO ME, YOU UNDERSTAND?
I'M SICK OF YOUR MOUTH!
TOO BAD! I'M NOT DOIN' THIS, JAKE! I AIN'T GONNA BE YOUR PUNCHING BAG NO MORE!
YOU'LL BE WITH ME OR YOU WON'T BE WITH ANYONE, YOU UNDERSTAND?
I CAN MAKE YOU DISAPPEAR, JENNY.
CHAK
A STRANGE WORLD FULL OF STRANGE PEOPLE.
LOOK OUT!

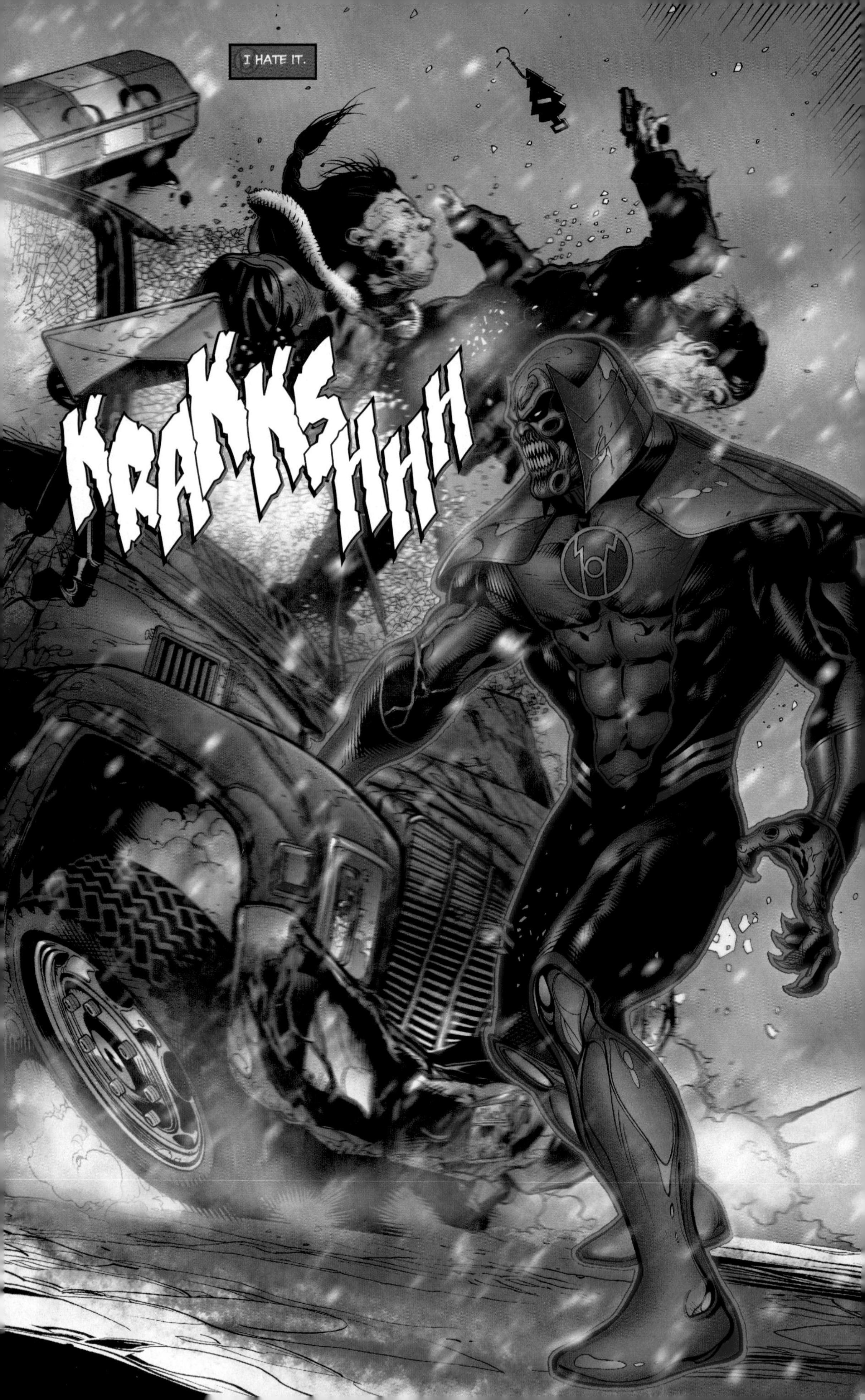
I HATE IT.
KRAKKSHHH

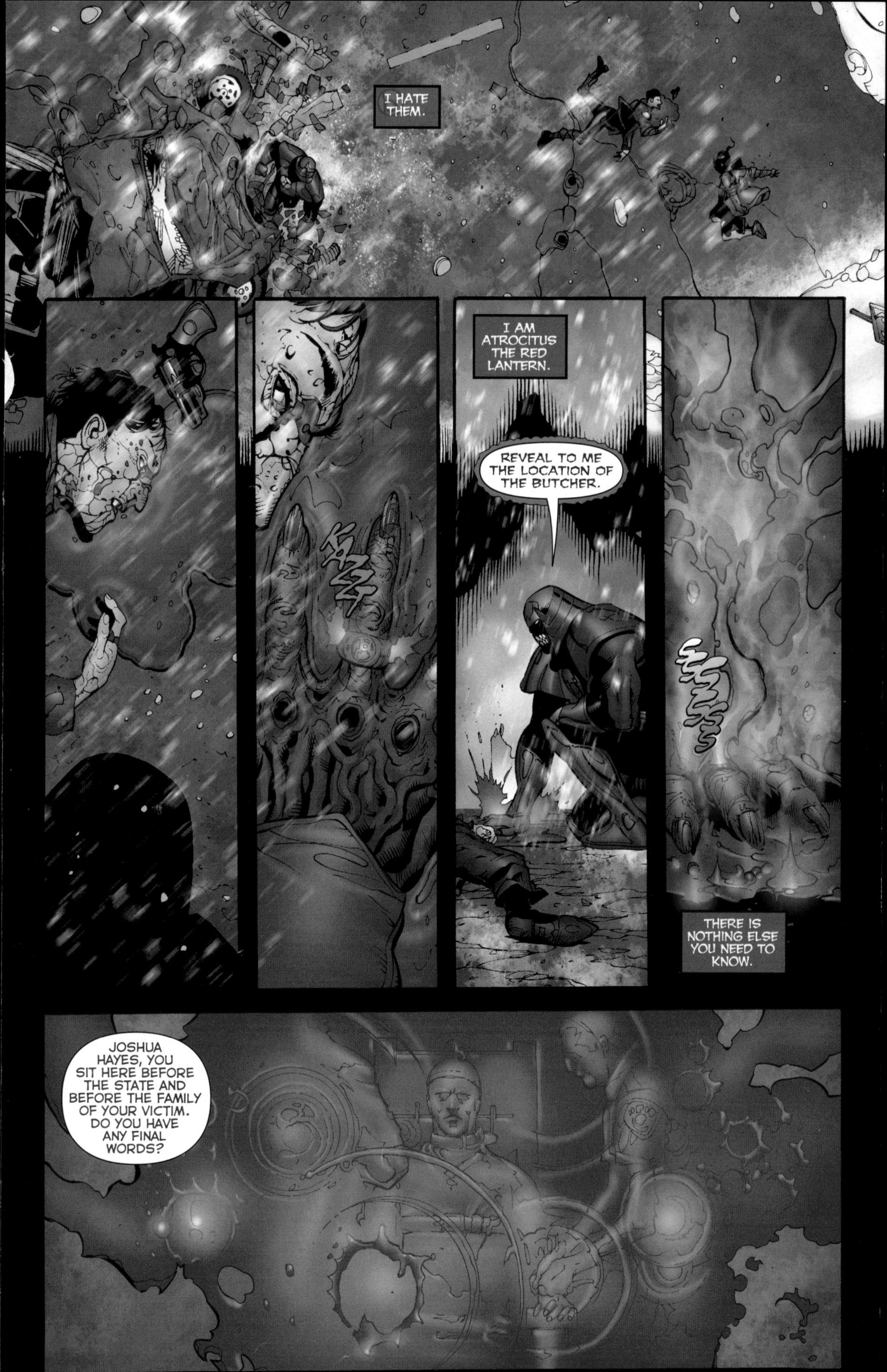
I HATE THEM.
I AM ATROCITUS THE RED LANTERN.
REVEAL TO ME THE LOCATION OF THE BUTCHER.
THERE IS NOTHING ELSE YOU NEED TO KNOW.
JOSHUA HAYES, YOU SIT HERE BEFORE THE STATE AND BEFORE THE FAMILY OF YOUR VICTIM. DO YOU HAVE ANY FINAL WORDS?

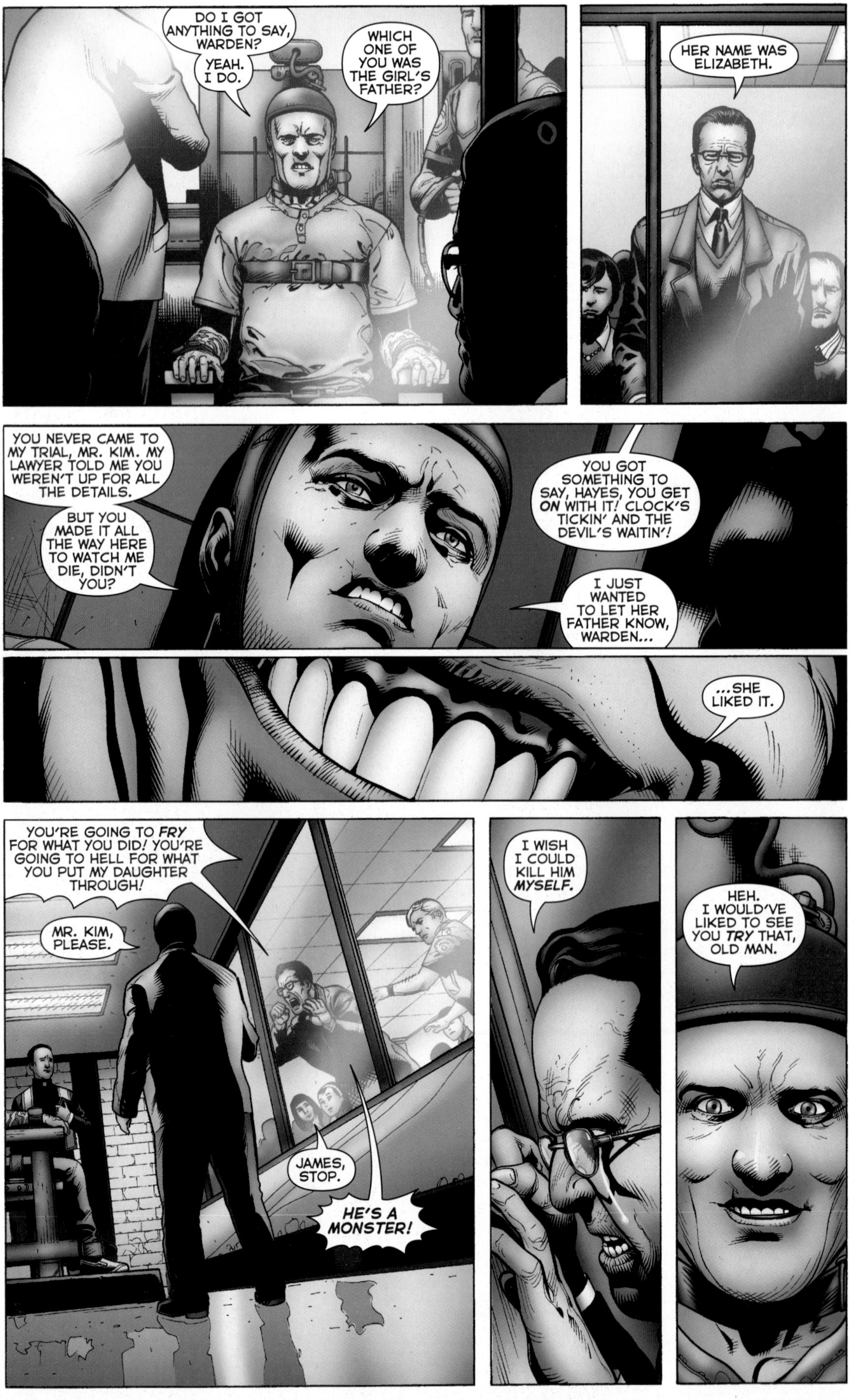
DO I GOT ANYTHING TO SAY, WARDEN?
YEAH. I DO.
WHICH ONE OF YOU WAS THE GIRL'S FATHER?
HER NAME WAS ELIZABETH.
YOU NEVER CAME TO MY TRIAL, MR. KIM. MY LAWYER TOLD ME YOU WEREN'T UP FOR ALL THE DETAILS.
BUT YOU MADE IT ALL THE WAY HERE TO WATCH ME DIE, DIDN'T YOU?
YOU GOT SOMETHING TO SAY, HAYES, YOU GET ON WITH IT! CLOCK'S TICKIN' AND THE DEVIL'S WAITIN'!
I JUST WANTED TO LET HER FATHER KNOW, WARDEN...
...SHE LIKED IT.
YOU'RE GOING TO FRY FOR WHAT YOU DID! YOU'RE GOING TO HELL FOR WHAT YOU PUT MY DAUGHTER THROUGH!
MR. KIM, PLEASE.
JAMES, STOP.
HE'S A MONSTER!
I WISH I COULD KILL HIM MYSELF.
HEH. I WOULD'VE LIKED TO SEE YOU TRY THAT, OLD MAN.

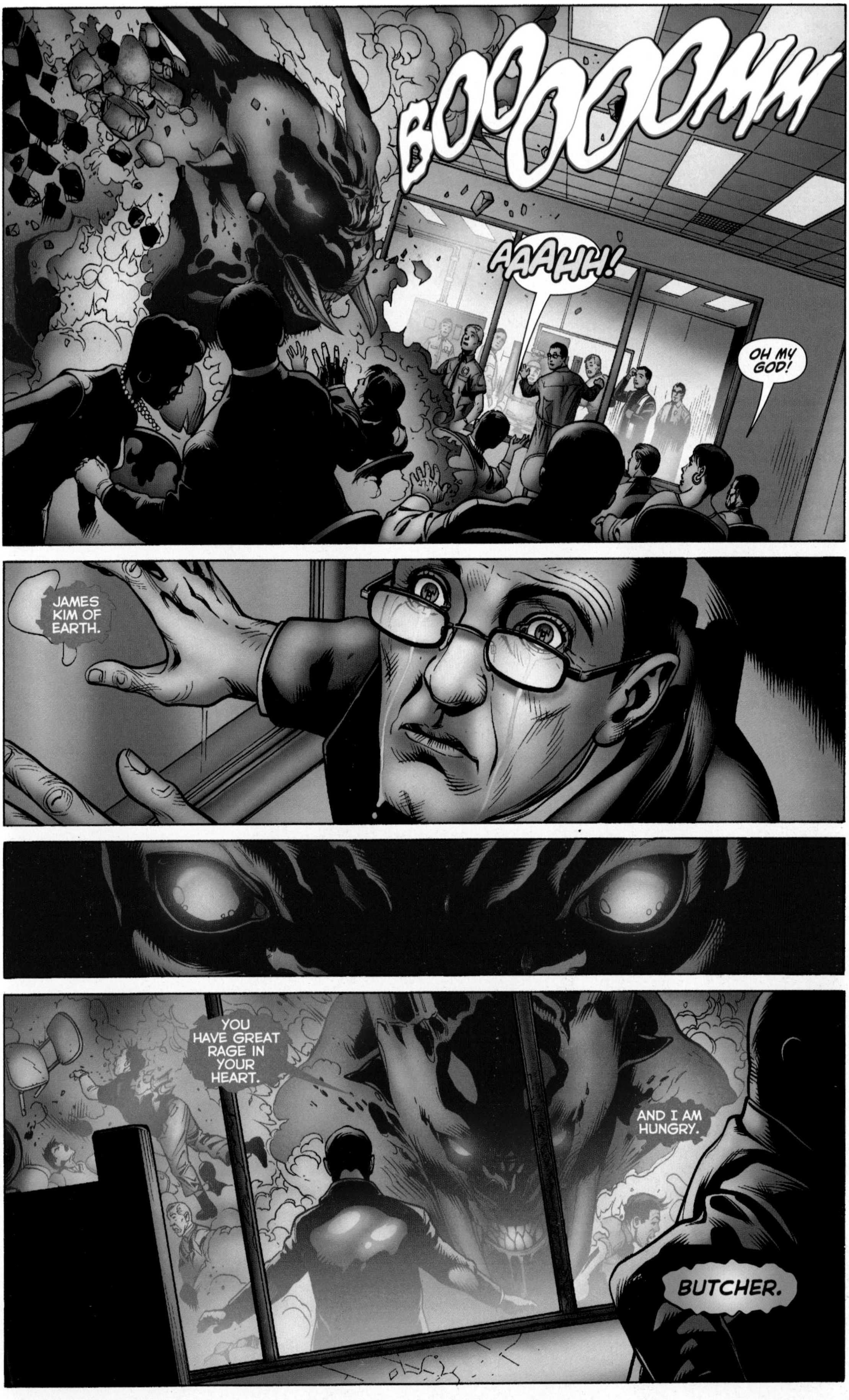
BOOOOOMM
AAAHH!
OH MY GOD!
JAMES KIM OF EARTH.
YOU HAVE GREAT RAGE IN YOUR HEART.
AND I AM HUNGRY.
BUTCHER.

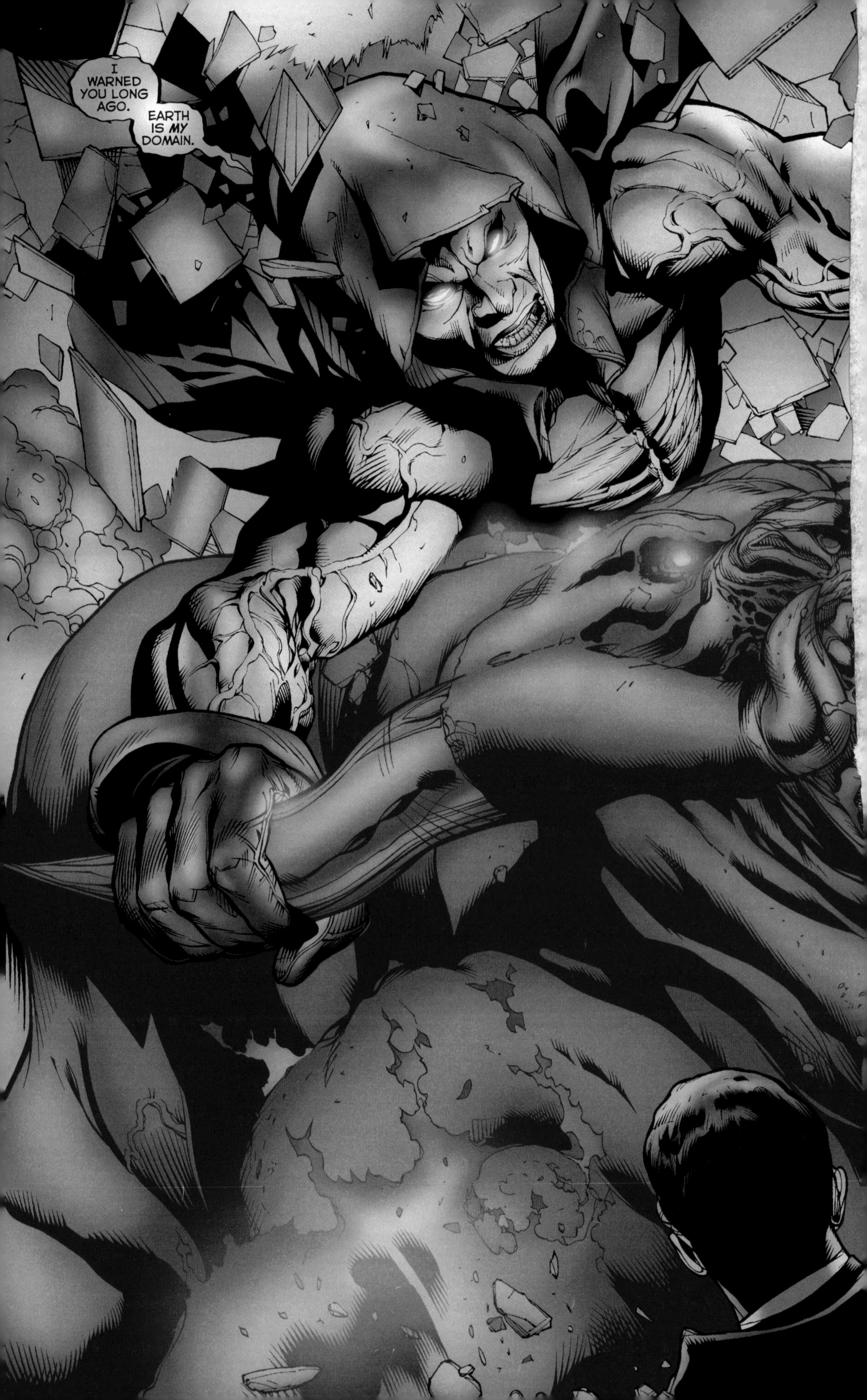
I WARNED YOU LONG AGO.
EARTH IS MY DOMAIN.

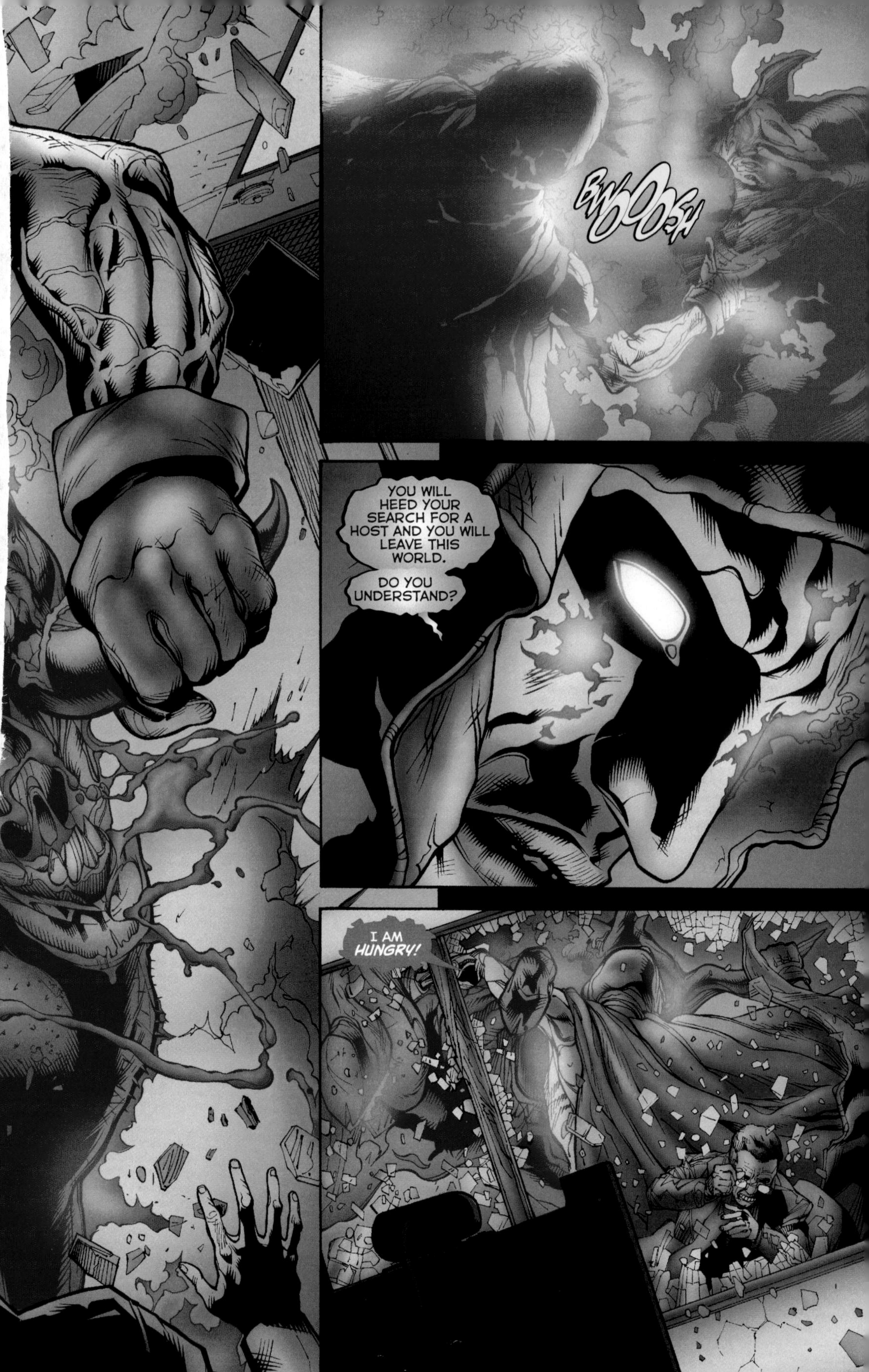
BWOOOOSH
YOU WILL HEED YOUR SEARCH FOR A HOST AND YOU WILL LEAVE THIS WORLD.
DO YOU UNDERSTAND?
I AM HUNGRY!

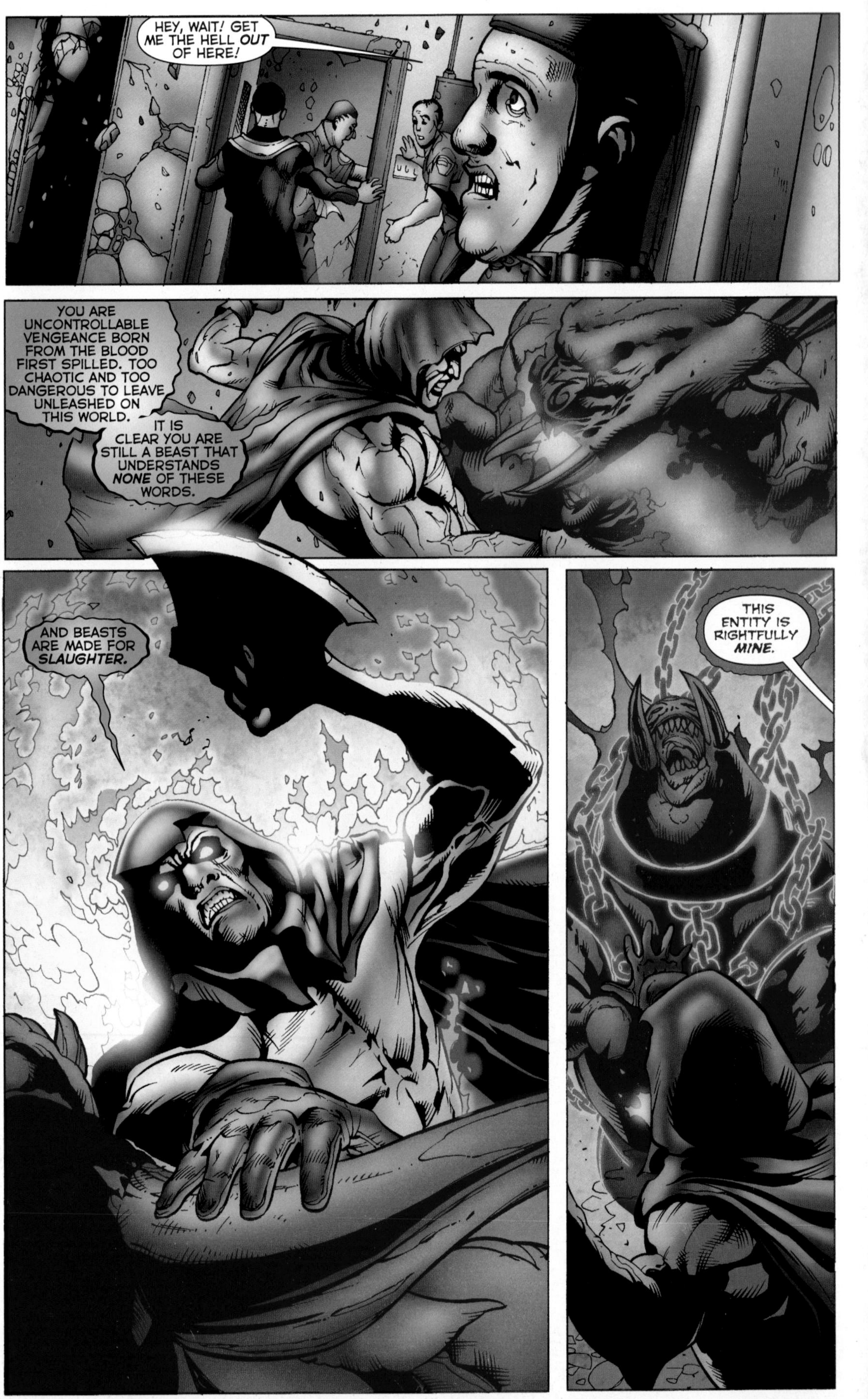
HEY, WAIT! GET ME THE HELL *OUT* OF HERE!
YOU ARE UNCONTROLLABLE VENGEANCE BORN FROM THE BLOOD FIRST SPILLED. TOO CHAOTIC AND TOO DANGEROUS TO LEAVE UNLEASHED ON THIS WORLD.
IT IS CLEAR YOU ARE STILL A BEAST THAT UNDERSTANDS *NONE* OF THESE WORDS.
AND BEASTS ARE MADE FOR *SLAUGHTER.*
THIS ENTITY IS RIGHTFULLY *MINE.*

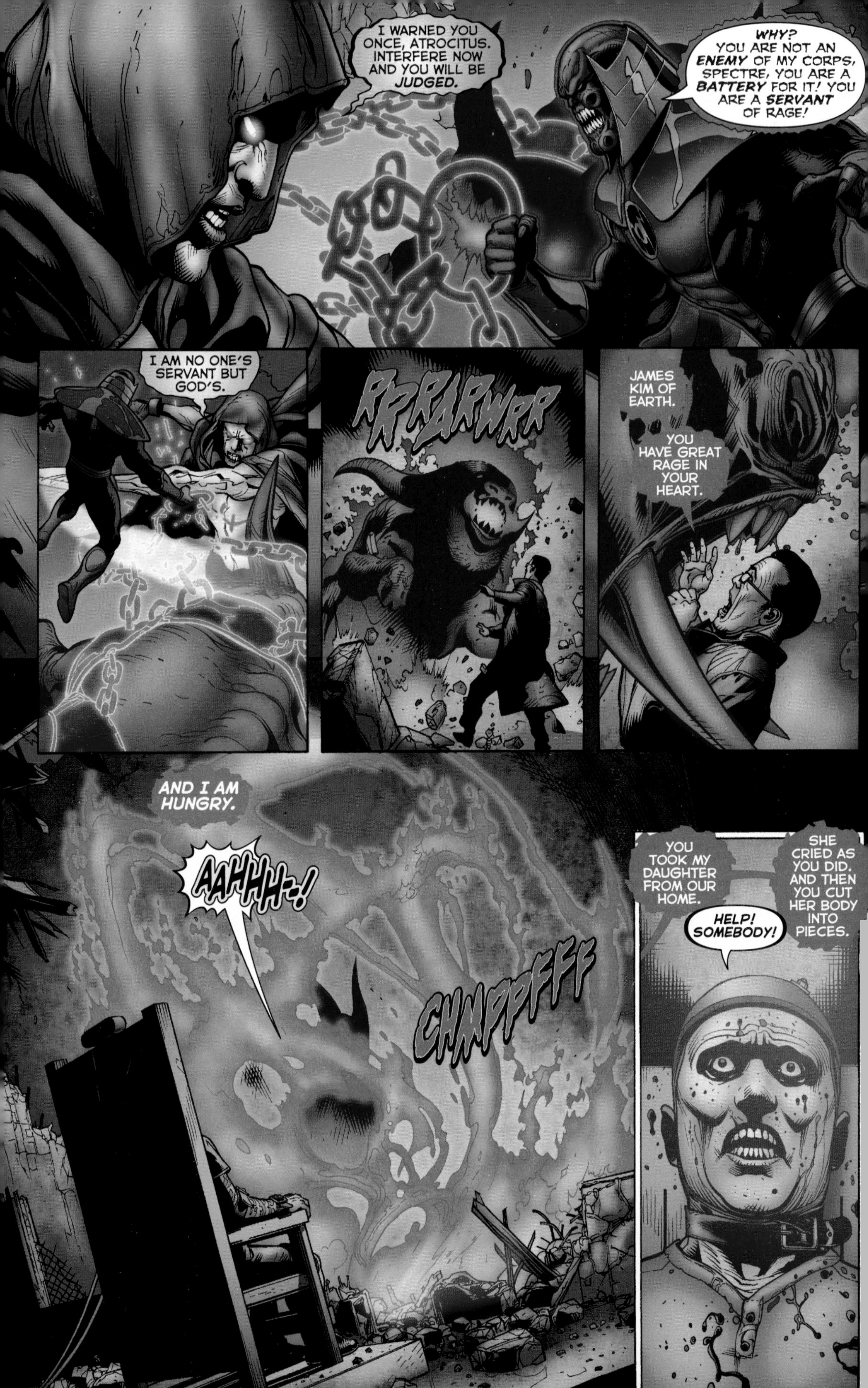
I WARNED YOU ONCE, ATROCITUS. INTERFERE NOW AND YOU WILL BE JUDGED.
WHY? YOU ARE NOT AN ENEMY OF MY CORPS, SPECTRE, YOU ARE A BATTERY FOR IT! YOU ARE A SERVANT OF RAGE!
I AM NO ONE'S SERVANT BUT GOD'S.
RRRARWRR
JAMES KIM OF EARTH.
YOU HAVE GREAT RAGE IN YOUR HEART.
AND I AM HUNGRY.
AAHHH--!
CHMPFFF
YOU TOOK MY DAUGHTER FROM OUR HOME.
SHE CRIED AS YOU DID. AND THEN YOU CUT HER BODY INTO PIECES.
HELP! SOMEBODY!

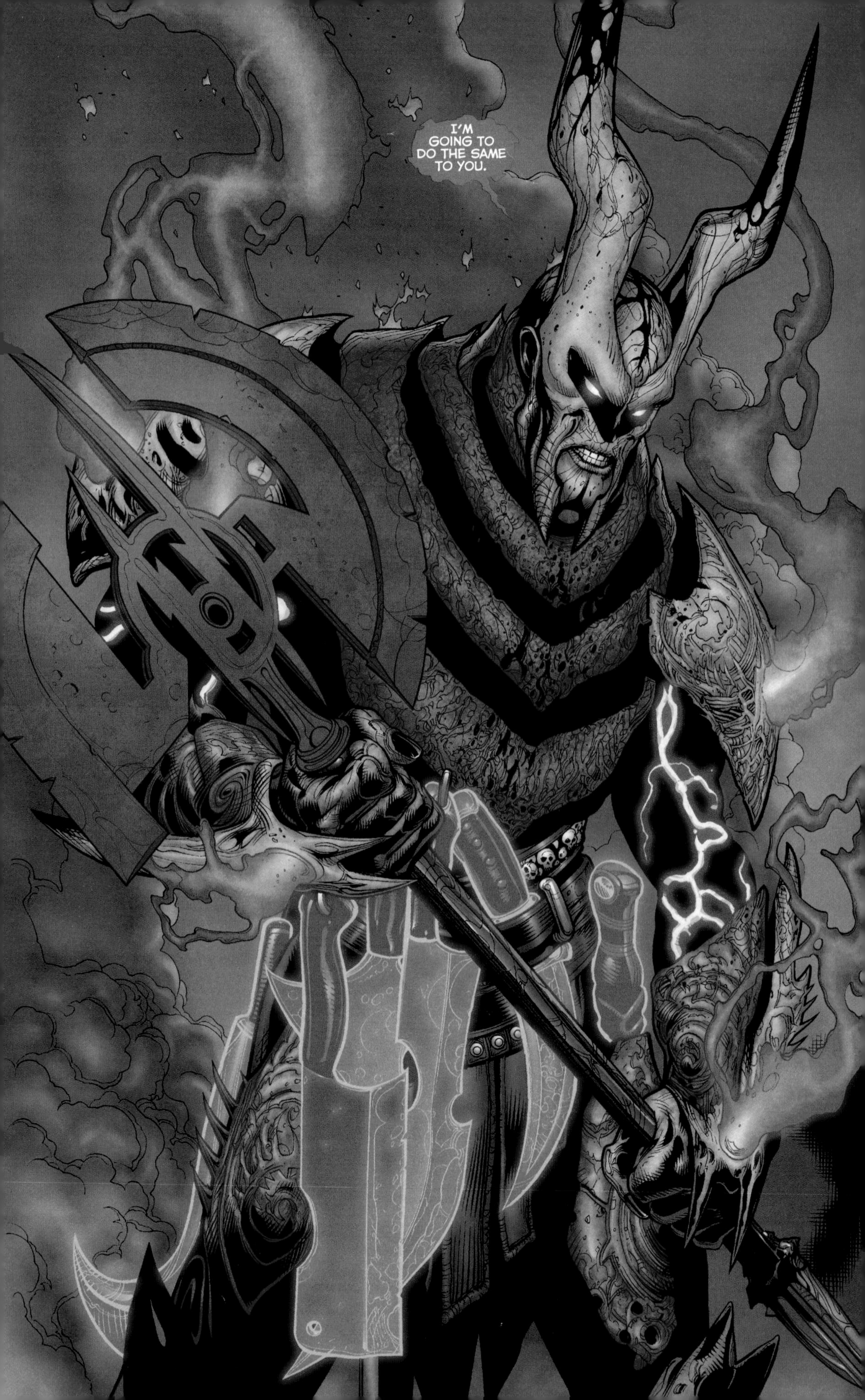
I'M GOING TO DO THE SAME TO YOU.

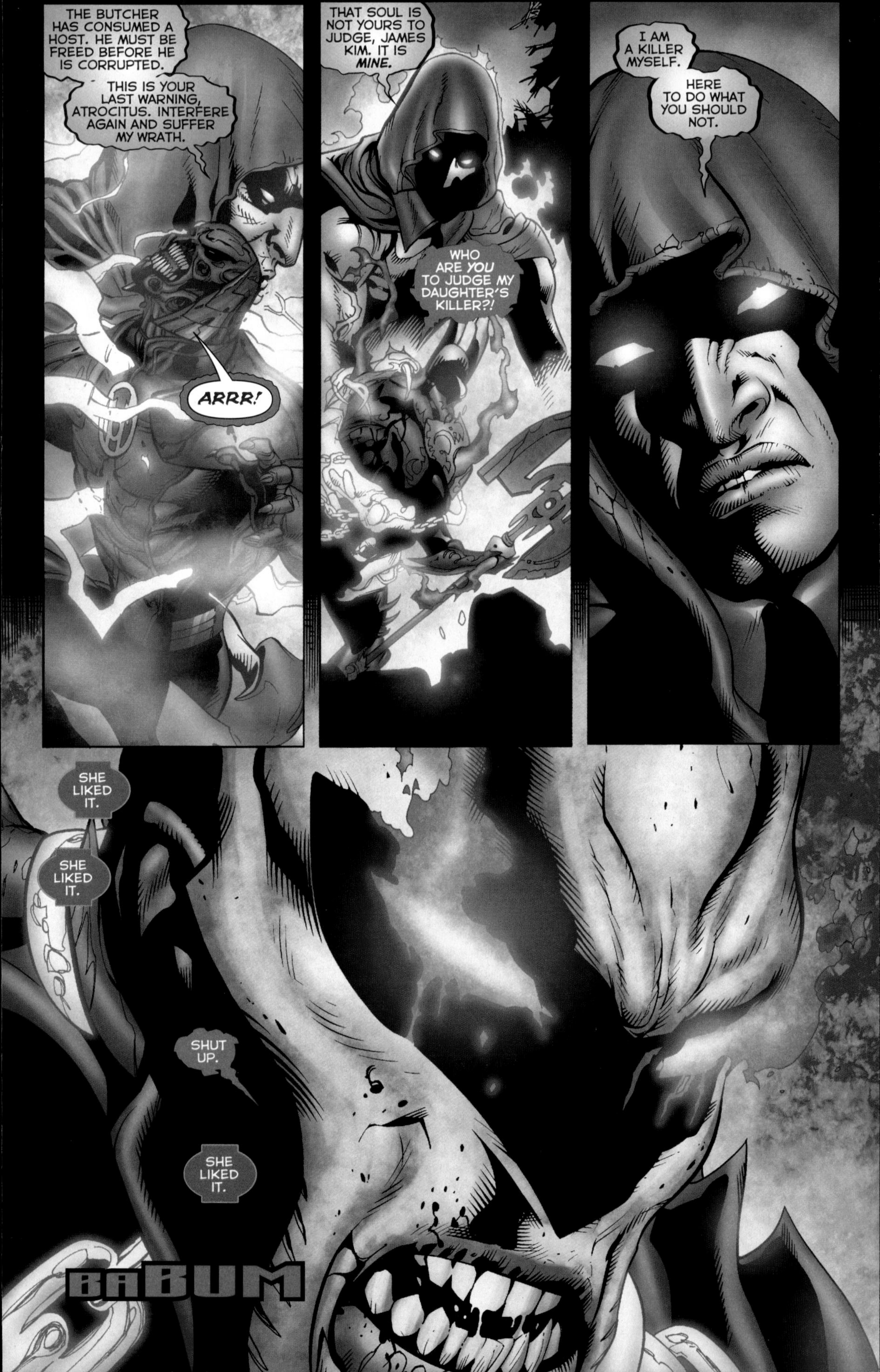
THE BUTCHER HAS CONSUMED A HOST. HE MUST BE FREED BEFORE HE IS CORRUPTED.
THIS IS YOUR LAST WARNING, ATROCITUS. INTERFERE AGAIN AND SUFFER MY WRATH.
ARRR!
THAT SOUL IS NOT YOURS TO JUDGE, JAMES KIM. IT IS *MINE.*
WHO ARE *YOU* TO JUDGE MY DAUGHTER'S KILLER?!
I AM A KILLER MYSELF.
HERE TO DO WHAT YOU SHOULD NOT.
SHE LIKED IT.
SHE LIKED IT.
SHUT UP.
SHE LIKED IT.
BABUM

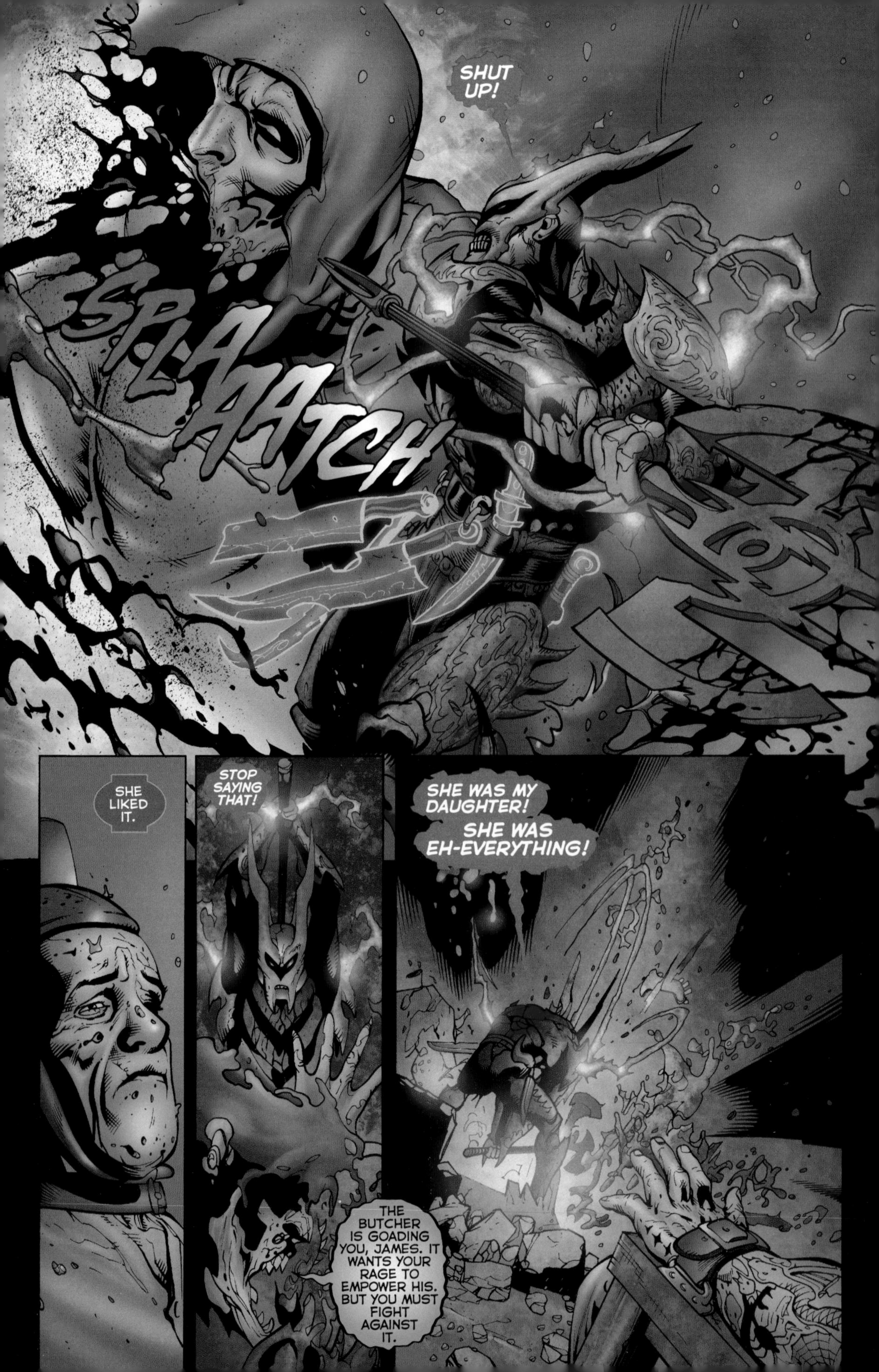
SHUT UP!
SPLAAATCH
SHE LIKED IT.
STOP SAYING THAT!
SHE WAS MY DAUGHTER!
SHE WAS EH-EVERYTHING!
THE BUTCHER IS GOADING YOU, JAMES. IT WANTS YOUR RAGE TO EMPOWER HIS. BUT YOU MUST FIGHT AGAINST IT.

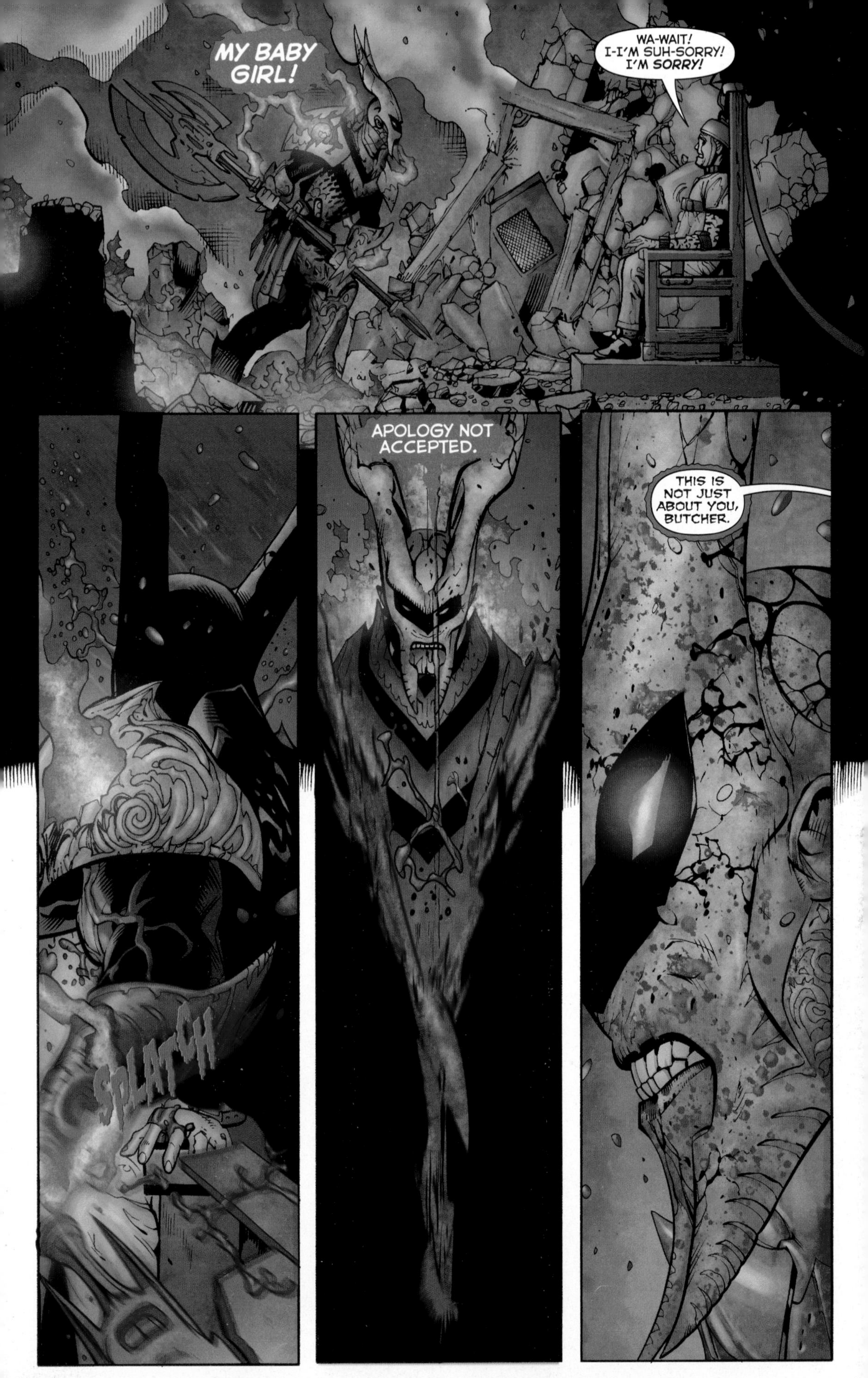
MY BABY GIRL!
WA-WAIT! I-I'M SUH-SORRY! I'M SORRY!
SPLATCH
APOLOGY NOT ACCEPTED.
THIS IS NOT JUST ABOUT YOU, BUTCHER.

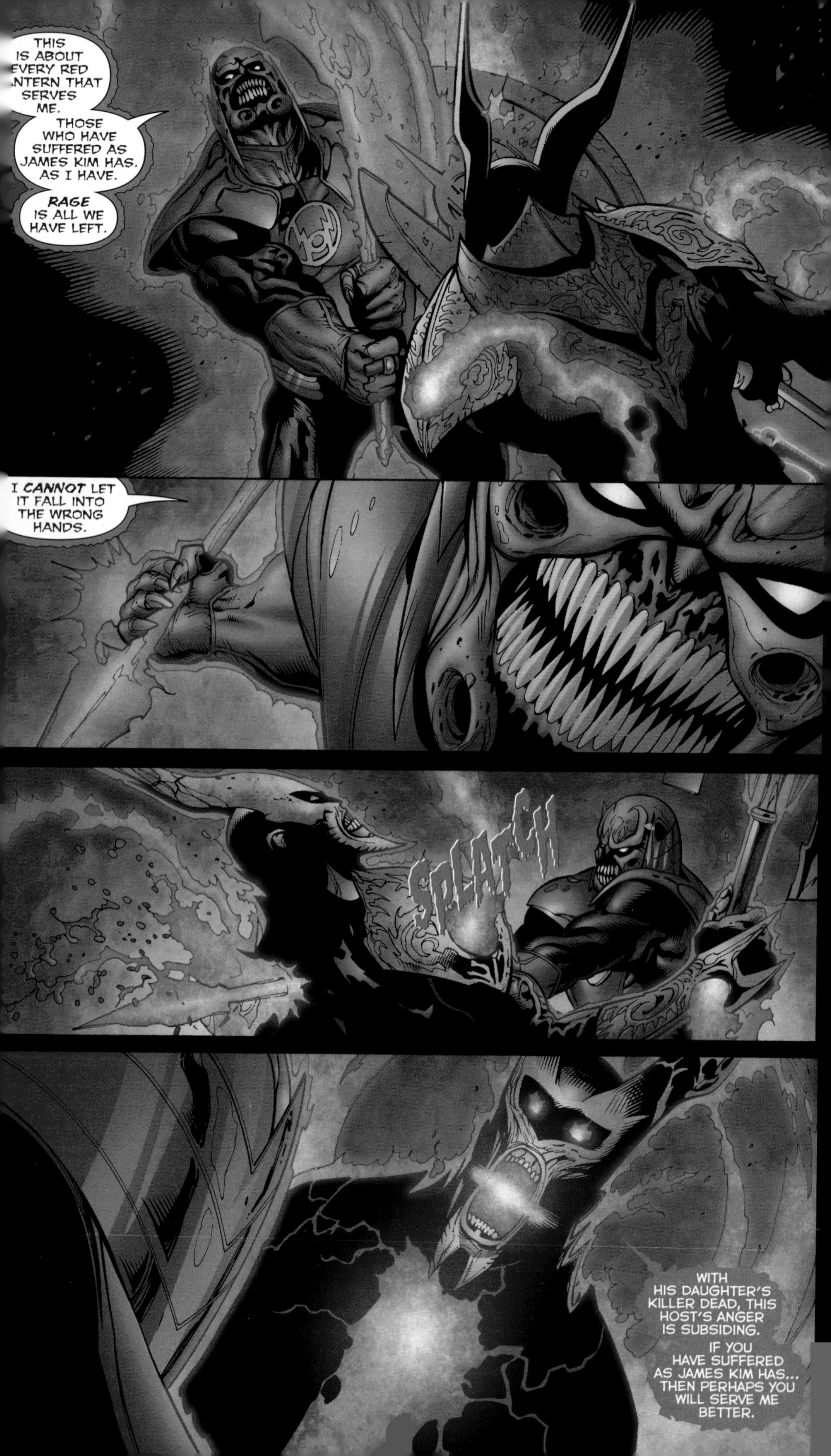

THIS IS ABOUT EVERY RED LANTERN THAT SERVES ME.
THOSE WHO HAVE SUFFERED AS JAMES KIM HAS. AS I HAVE.
RAGE IS ALL WE HAVE LEFT.
I CANNOT LET IT FALL INTO THE WRONG HANDS.
SPLATCH
WITH HIS DAUGHTER'S KILLER DEAD, THIS HOST'S ANGER IS SUBSIDING.
IF YOU HAVE SUFFERED AS JAMES KIM HAS... THEN PERHAPS YOU WILL SERVE ME BETTER.

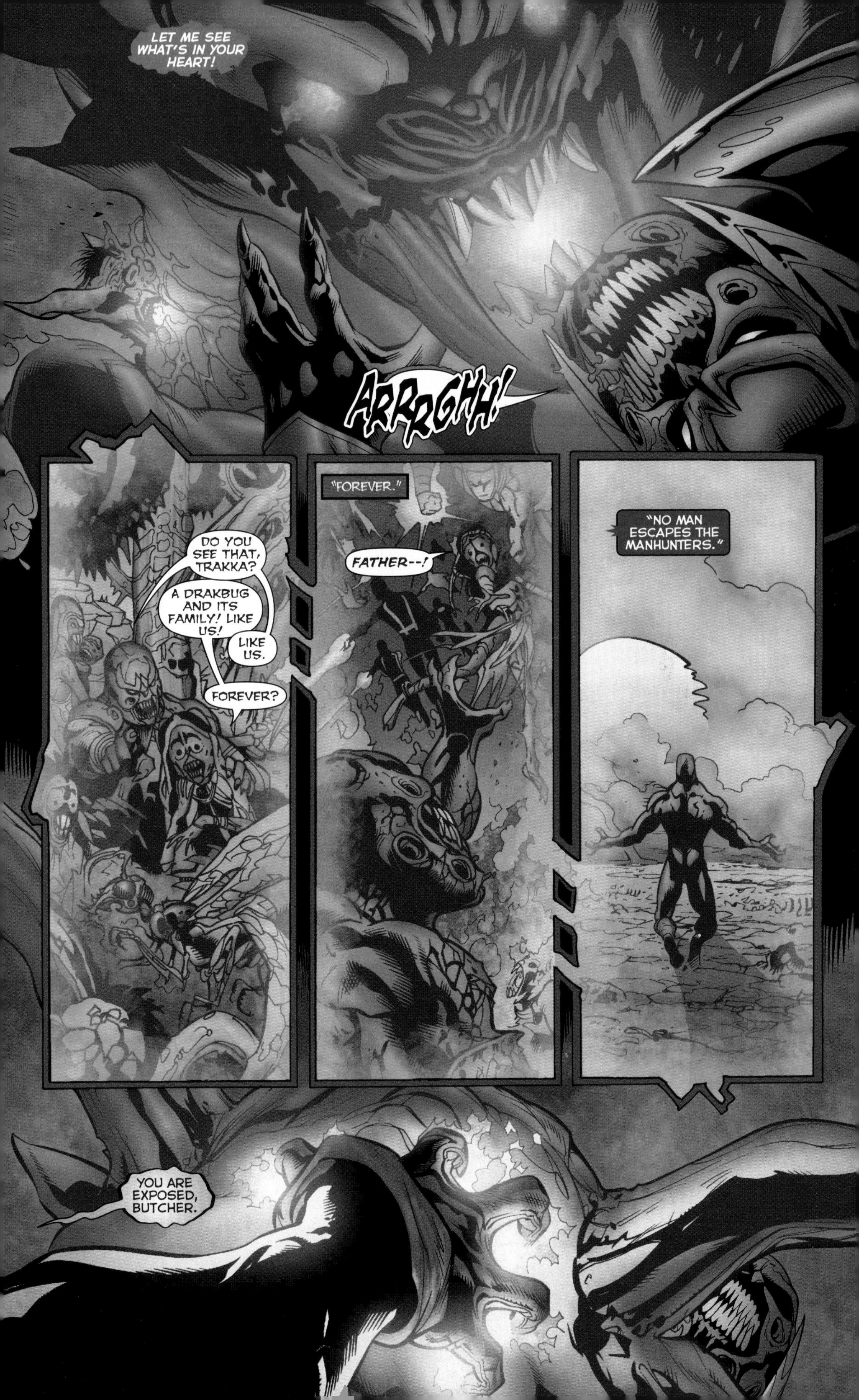
LET ME SEE WHAT'S IN YOUR HEART!
ARRRGHH!
DO YOU SEE THAT, TRAKKA?
A DRAKBUG AND ITS FAMILY! LIKE US!
LIKE US.
FOREVER?
"FOREVER."
FATHER--!
"NO MAN ESCAPES THE MANHUNTERS."
YOU ARE EXPOSED, BUTCHER.

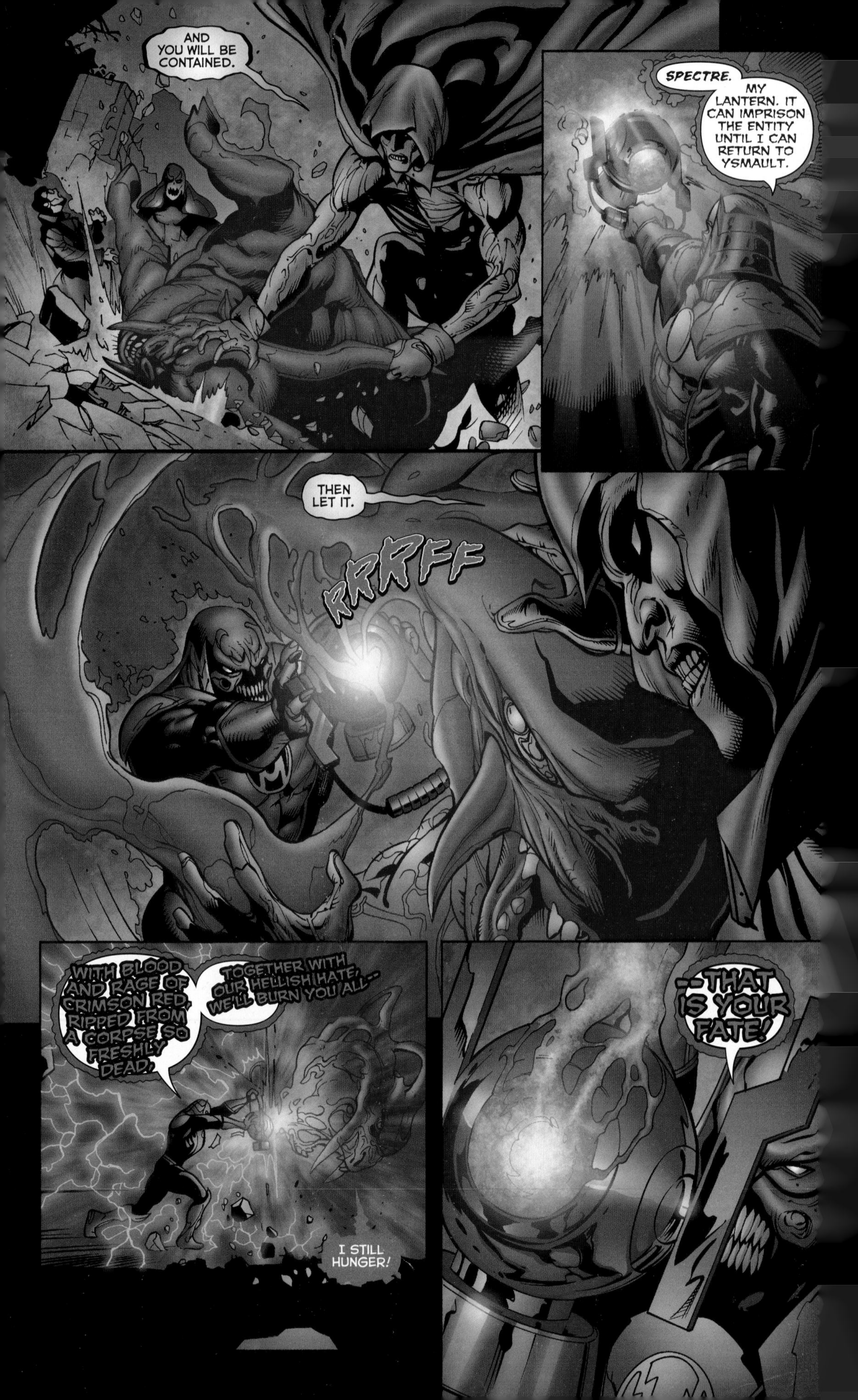
AND YOU WILL BE CONTAINED.
SPECTRE.
MY LANTERN. IT CAN IMPRISON THE ENTITY UNTIL I CAN RETURN TO YSMAULT.
THEN LET IT.
RRRFF
WITH BLOOD AND RAGE OF CRIMSON RED, RIPPED FROM A CORPSE SO FRESHLY DEAD.
TOGETHER WITH OUR HELLISH HATE, WE'LL BURN YOU ALL--
I STILL HUNGER!
--THAT IS YOUR FATE!

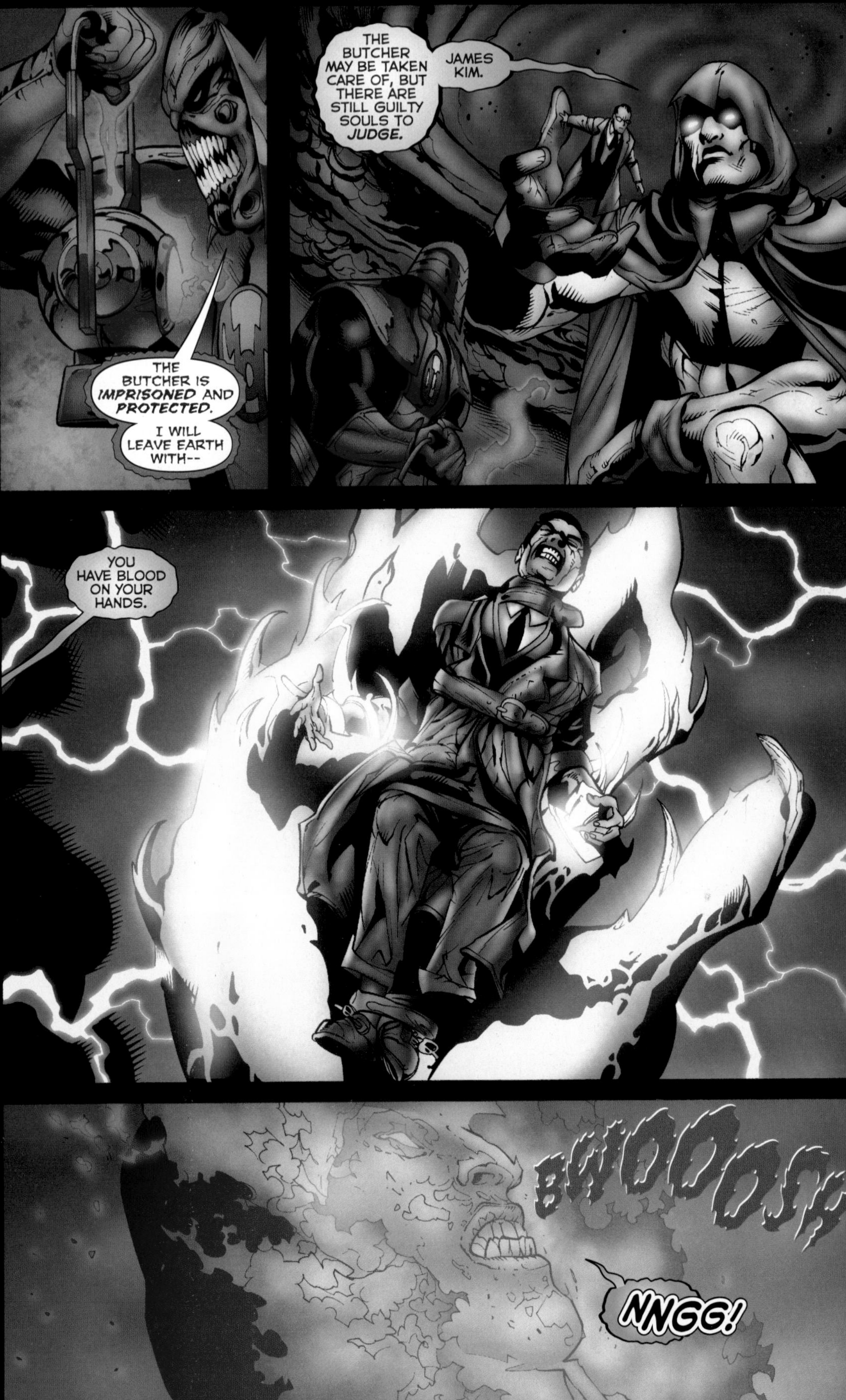
THE BUTCHER IS IMPRISONED AND PROTECTED.
I WILL LEAVE EARTH WITH--
THE BUTCHER MAY BE TAKEN CARE OF, BUT THERE ARE STILL GUILTY SOULS TO JUDGE.
JAMES KIM.
YOU HAVE BLOOD ON YOUR HANDS.
BWOOOSH
NNGG!

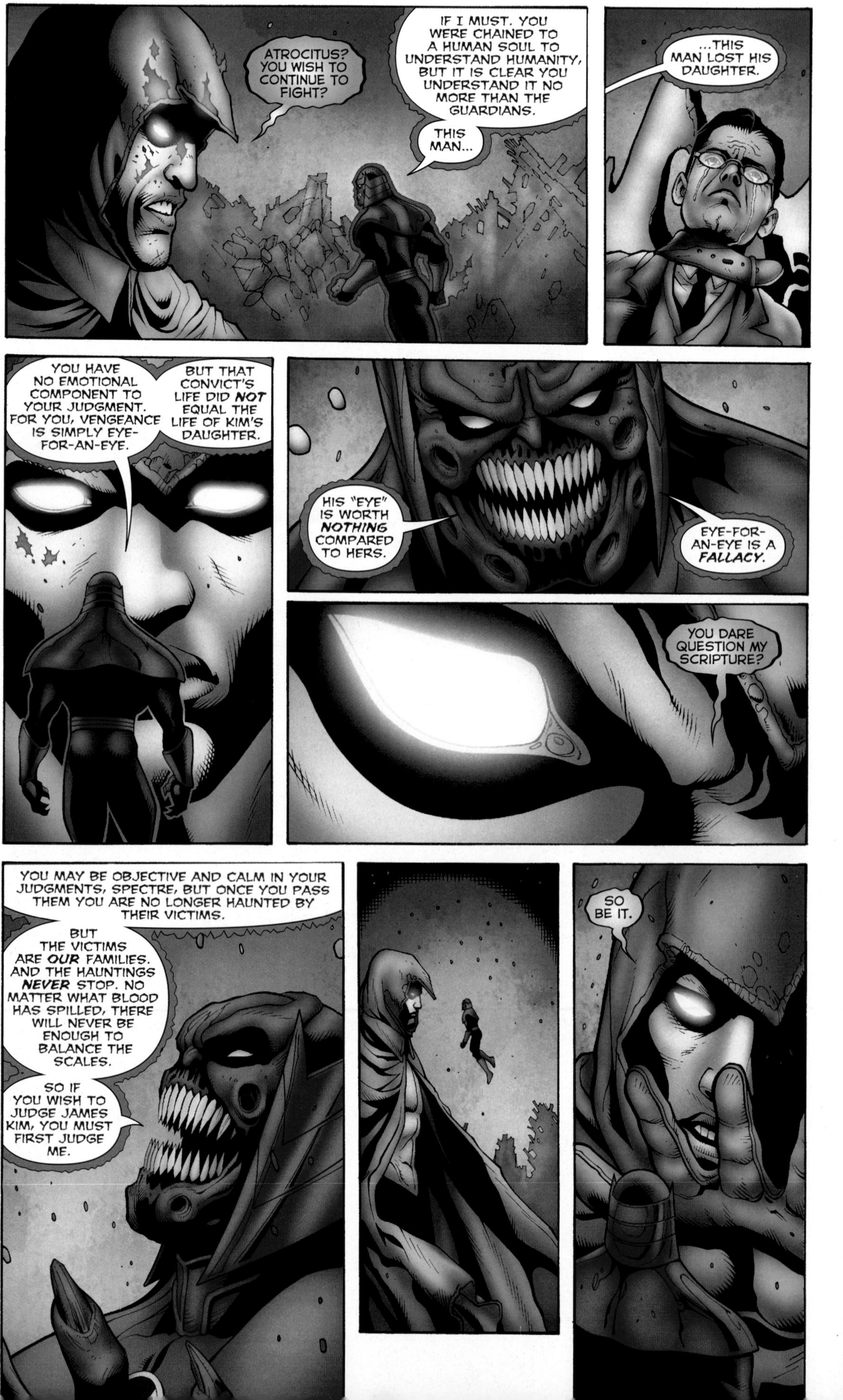
ATROCITUS? YOU WISH TO CONTINUE TO FIGHT?
IF I MUST. YOU WERE CHAINED TO A HUMAN SOUL TO UNDERSTAND HUMANITY, BUT IT IS CLEAR YOU UNDERSTAND IT NO MORE THAN THE GUARDIANS.
THIS MAN...
...THIS MAN LOST HIS DAUGHTER.
YOU HAVE NO EMOTIONAL COMPONENT TO YOUR JUDGMENT. FOR YOU, VENGEANCE IS SIMPLY EYE-FOR-AN-EYE.
BUT THAT CONVICT'S LIFE DID NOT EQUAL THE LIFE OF KIM'S DAUGHTER.
HIS "EYE" IS WORTH NOTHING COMPARED TO HERS.
EYE-FOR-AN-EYE IS A FALLACY.
YOU DARE QUESTION MY SCRIPTURE?
YOU MAY BE OBJECTIVE AND CALM IN YOUR JUDGMENTS, SPECTRE, BUT ONCE YOU PASS THEM YOU ARE NO LONGER HAUNTED BY THEIR VICTIMS.
BUT THE VICTIMS ARE OUR FAMILIES. AND THE HAUNTINGS NEVER STOP. NO MATTER WHAT BLOOD HAS SPILLED, THERE WILL NEVER BE ENOUGH TO BALANCE THE SCALES.
SO IF YOU WISH TO JUDGE JAMES KIM, YOU MUST FIRST JUDGE ME.
SO BE IT.

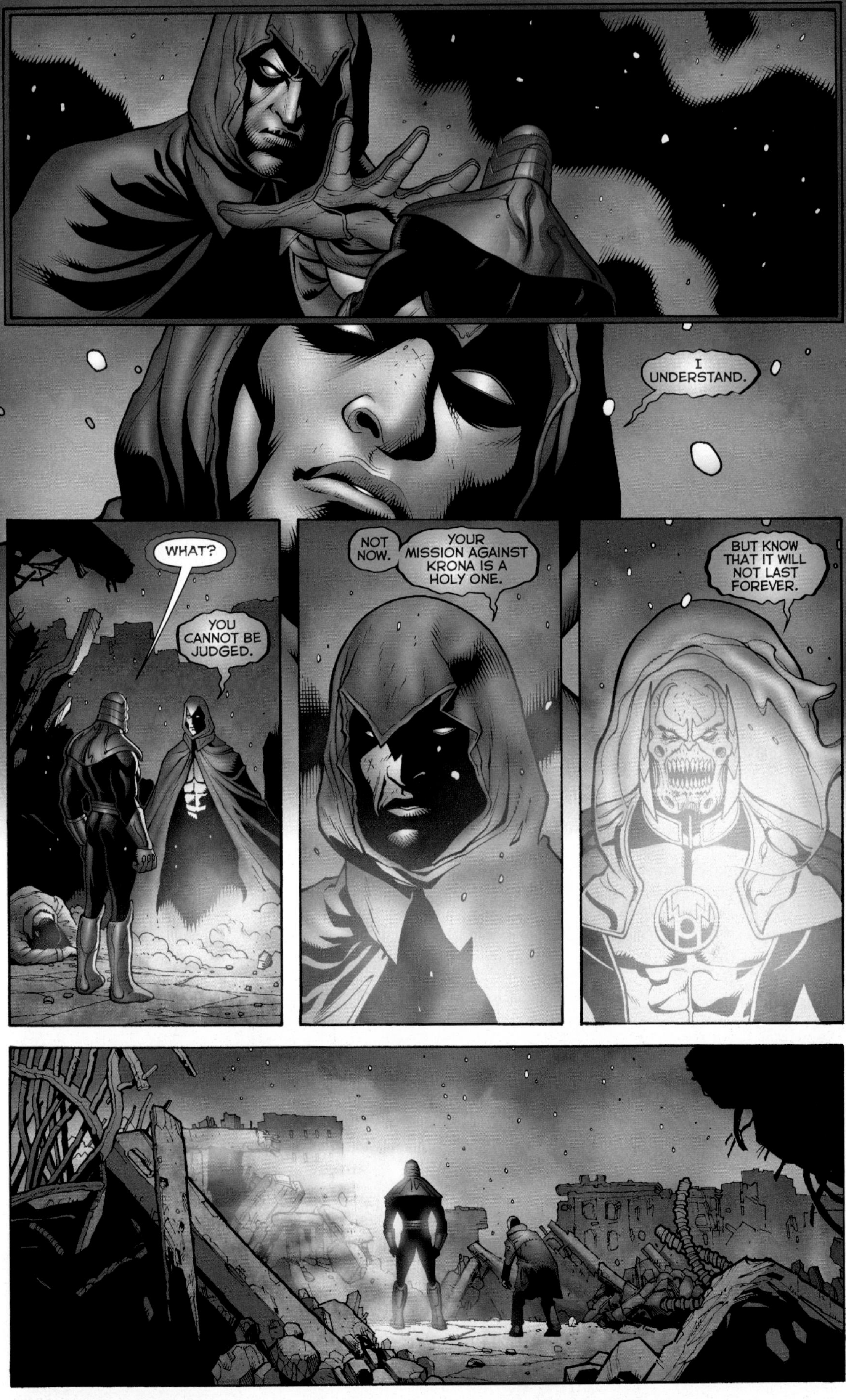
I UNDERSTAND.
WHAT?
YOU CANNOT BE JUDGED.
NOT NOW.
YOUR MISSION AGAINST KRONA IS A HOLY ONE.
BUT KNOW THAT IT WILL NOT LAST FOREVER.

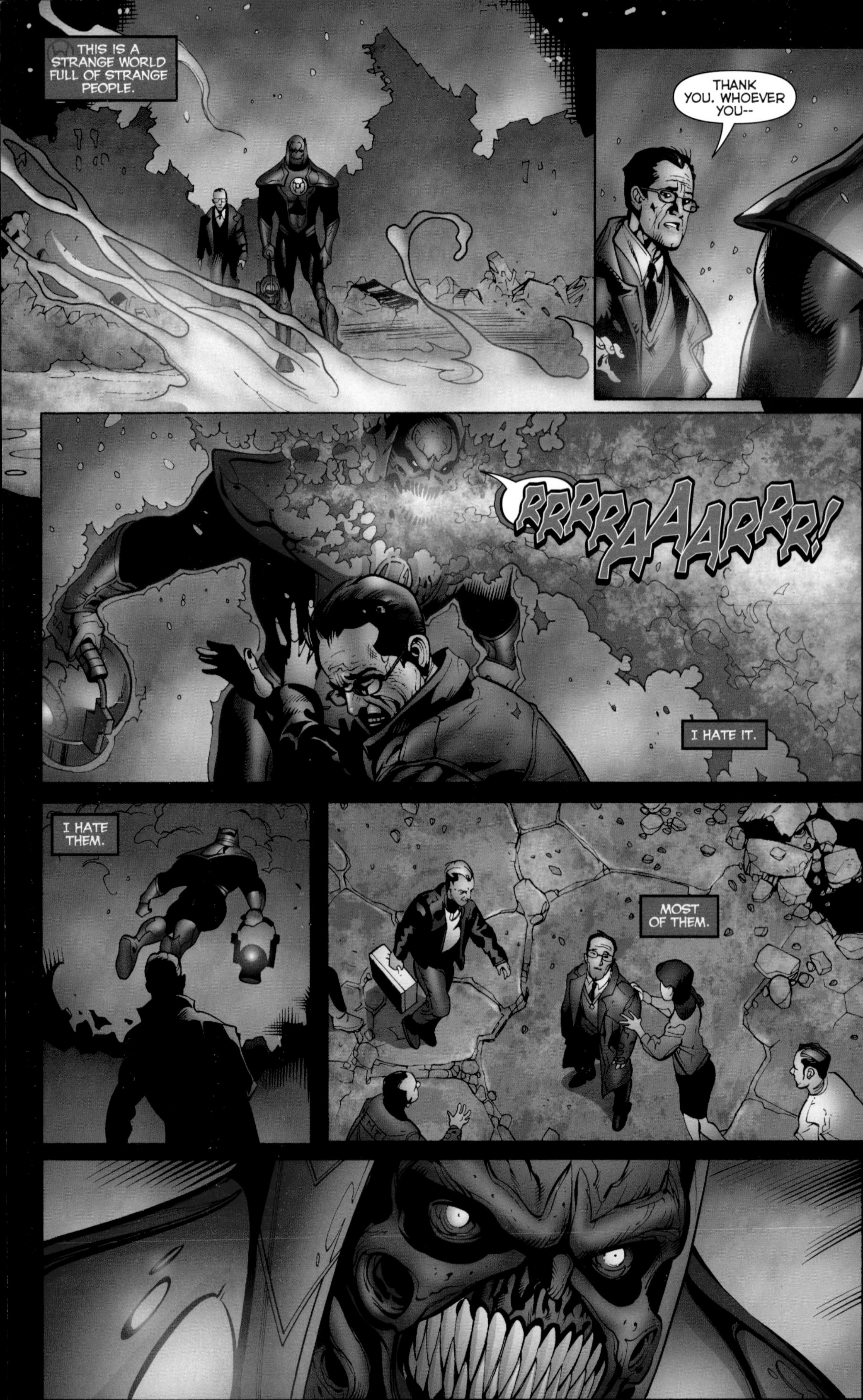
THIS IS A STRANGE WORLD FULL OF STRANGE PEOPLE.
THANK YOU. WHOEVER YOU--
RRRRAAARRRR!
I HATE IT.
I HATE THEM.
MOST OF THEM.

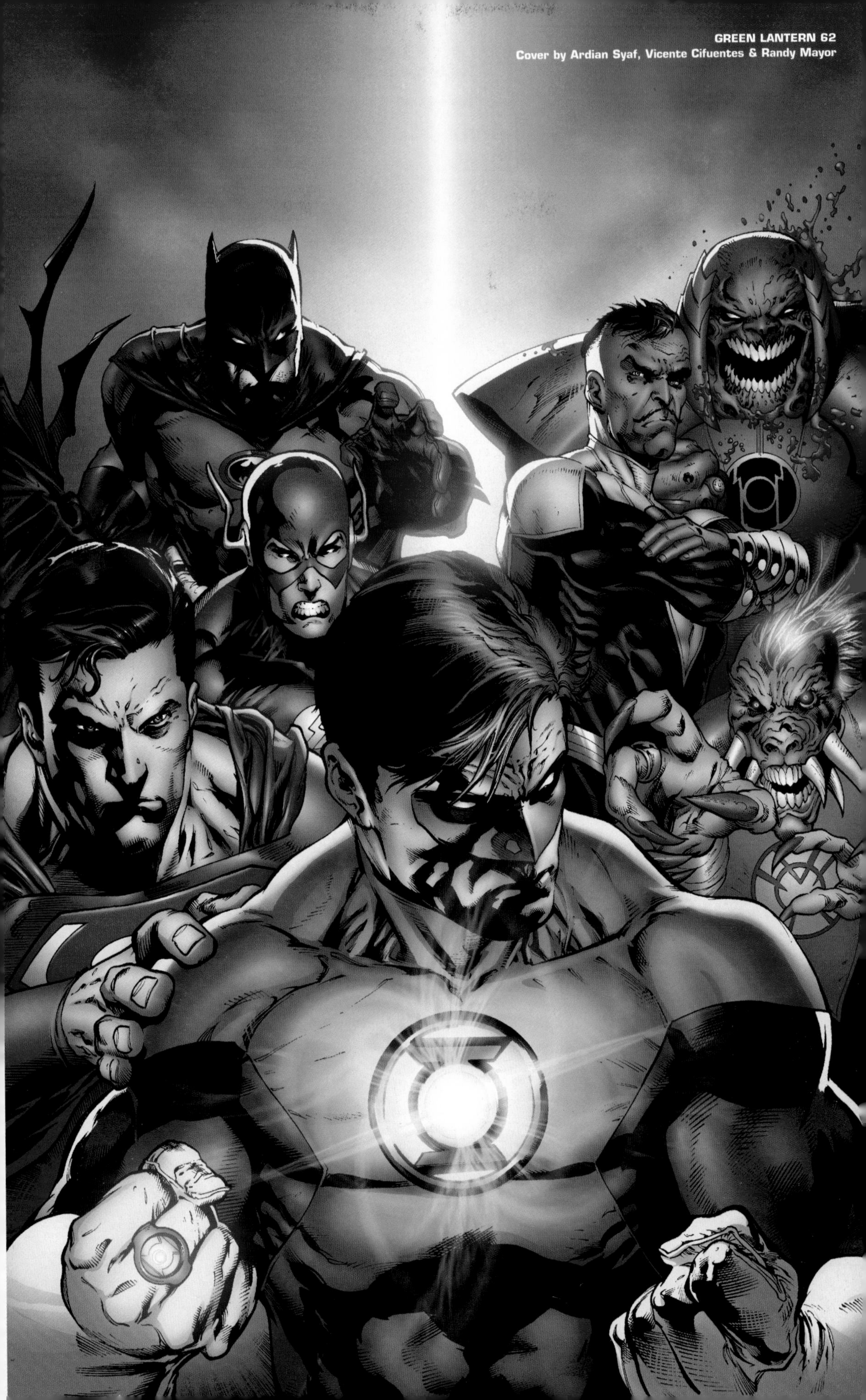

GREEN LANTERN 62
Cover by Ardian Syaf, Vicente Cifuentes & Randy Mayor

THE NEW GUARDIANS
CONCLUSION

Doug Mahnke Pencils

Keith Champagne, Christian Alamy & Tom Nguyen Inks

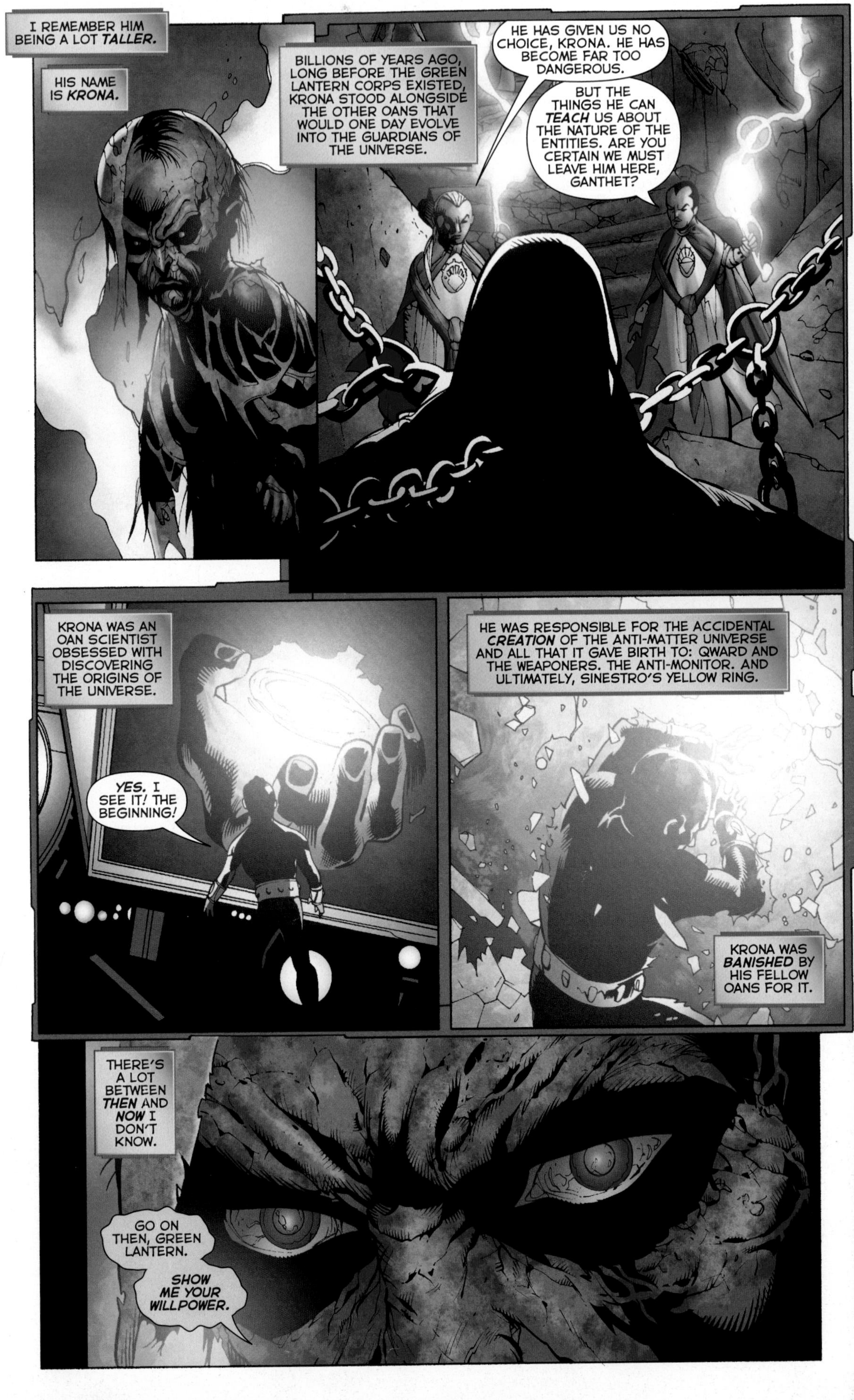
I REMEMBER HIM BEING A LOT TALLER.
HIS NAME IS KRONA.
BILLIONS OF YEARS AGO, LONG BEFORE THE GREEN LANTERN CORPS EXISTED, KRONA STOOD ALONGSIDE THE OTHER OANS THAT WOULD ONE DAY EVOLVE INTO THE GUARDIANS OF THE UNIVERSE.
HE HAS GIVEN US NO CHOICE, KRONA. HE HAS BECOME FAR TOO DANGEROUS.
BUT THE THINGS HE CAN TEACH US ABOUT THE NATURE OF THE ENTITIES. ARE YOU CERTAIN WE MUST LEAVE HIM HERE, GANTHET?
KRONA WAS AN OAN SCIENTIST OBSESSED WITH DISCOVERING THE ORIGINS OF THE UNIVERSE.
YES. I SEE IT! THE BEGINNING!
HE WAS RESPONSIBLE FOR THE ACCIDENTAL CREATION OF THE ANTI-MATTER UNIVERSE AND ALL THAT IT GAVE BIRTH TO: QWARD AND THE WEAPONERS. THE ANTI-MONITOR. AND ULTIMATELY, SINESTRO'S YELLOW RING.
KRONA WAS BANISHED BY HIS FELLOW OANS FOR IT.
THERE'S A LOT BETWEEN THEN AND NOW I DON'T KNOW.
GO ON THEN, GREEN LANTERN.
SHOW ME YOUR WILLPOWER.

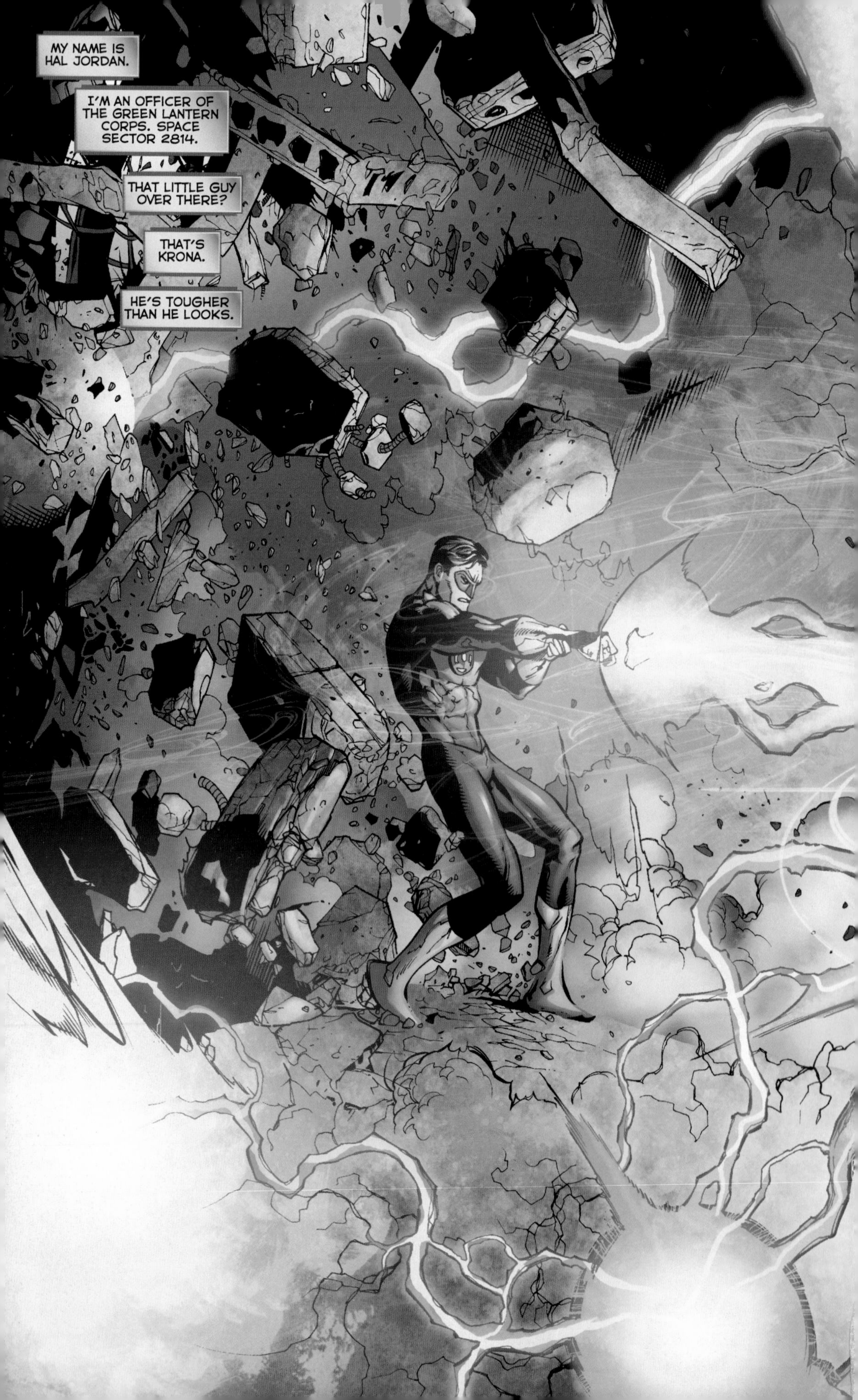
MY NAME IS HAL JORDAN.
I'M AN OFFICER OF THE GREEN LANTERN CORPS. SPACE SECTOR 2814.
THAT LITTLE GUY OVER THERE?
THAT'S KRONA.
HE'S TOUGHER THAN HE LOOKS.

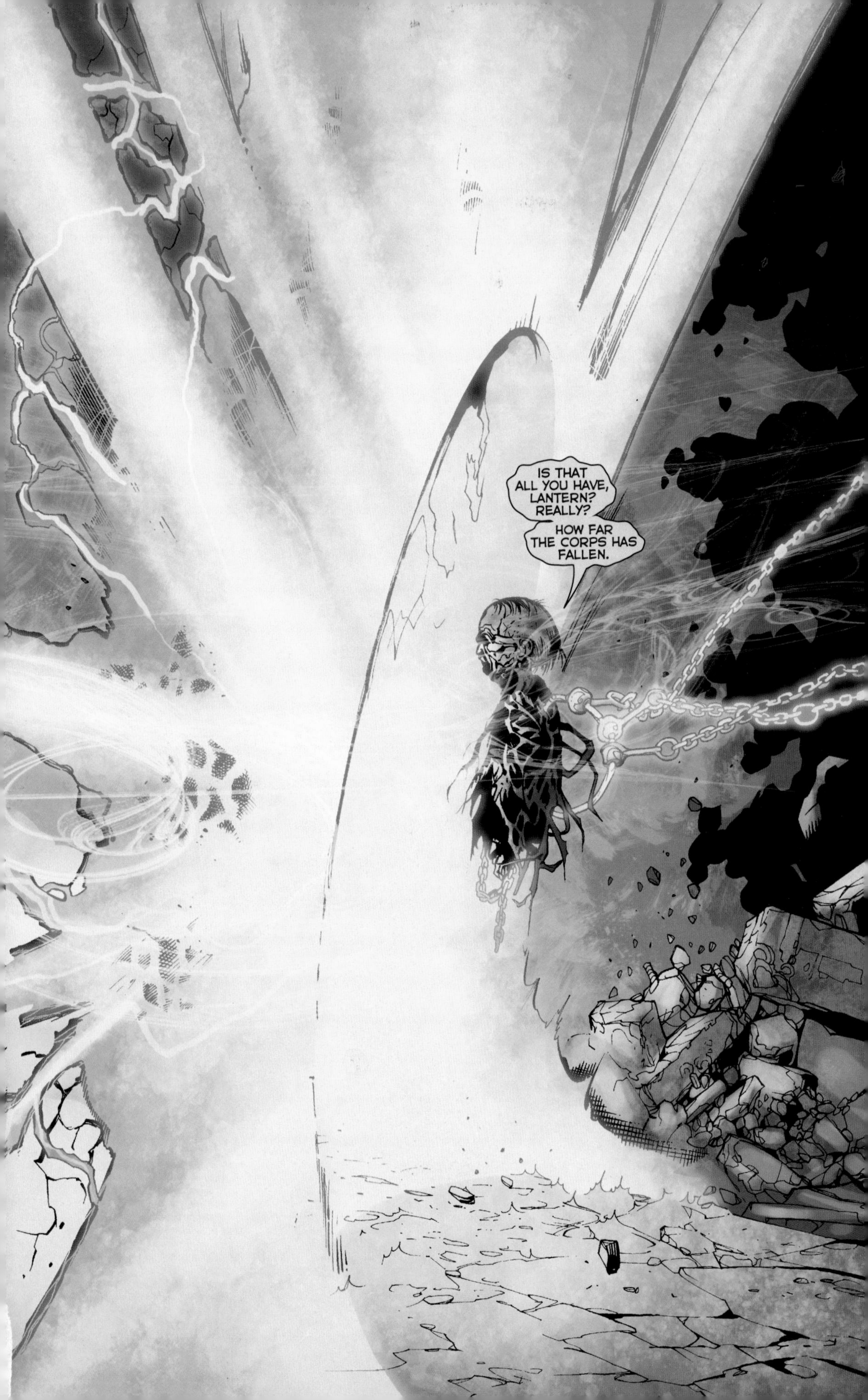
IS THAT ALL YOU HAVE, LANTERN? REALLY?
HOW FAR THE CORPS HAS FALLEN.

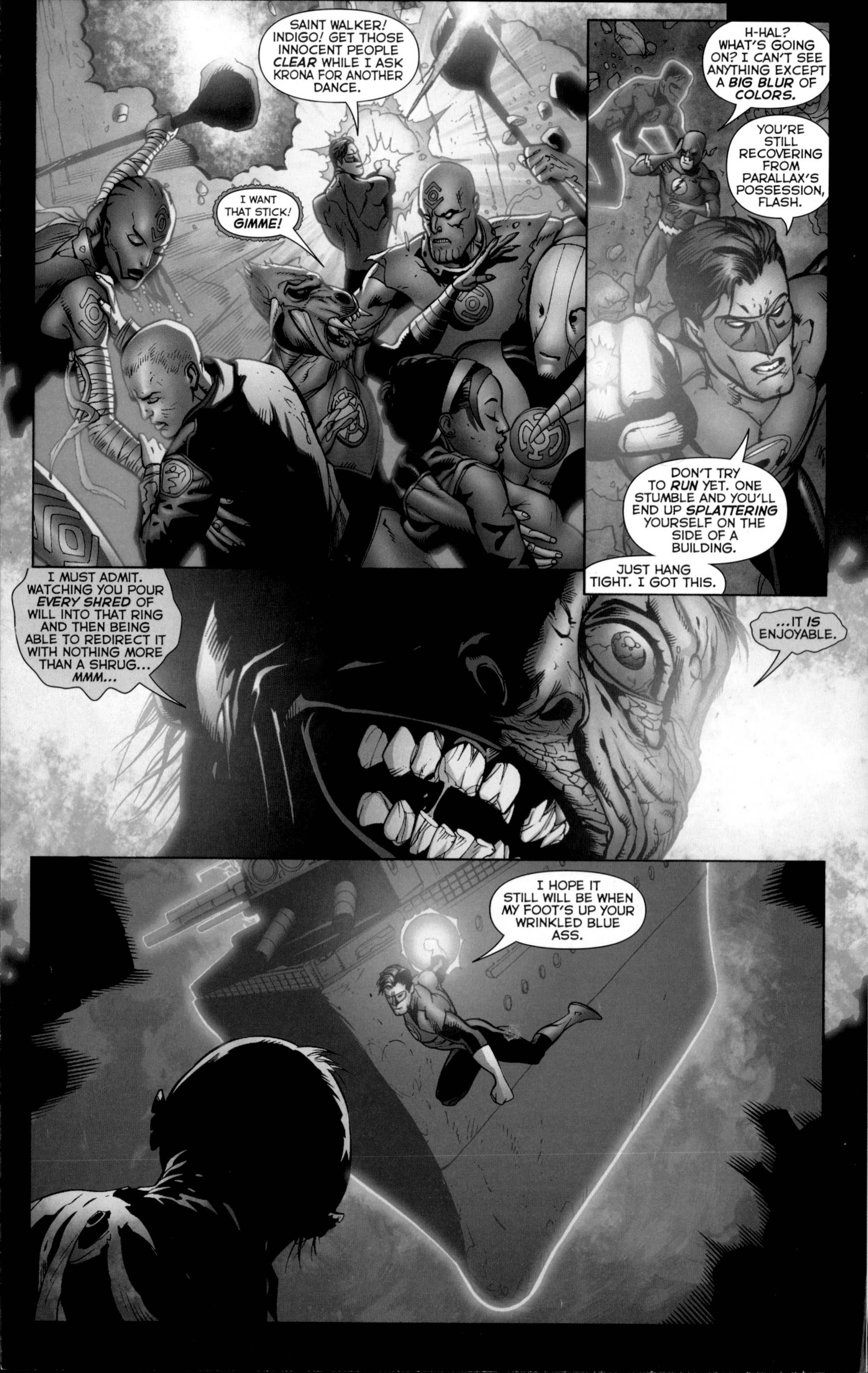
SAINT WALKER! INDIGO! GET THOSE INNOCENT PEOPLE CLEAR WHILE I ASK KRONA FOR ANOTHER DANCE.
I WANT THAT STICK! GIMME!
H-HAL? WHAT'S GOING ON? I CAN'T SEE ANYTHING EXCEPT A BIG BLUR OF COLORS.
YOU'RE STILL RECOVERING FROM PARALLAX'S POSSESSION, FLASH.
DON'T TRY TO RUN YET. ONE STUMBLE AND YOU'LL END UP SPLATTERING YOURSELF ON THE SIDE OF A BUILDING.
JUST HANG TIGHT. I GOT THIS.
I MUST ADMIT. WATCHING YOU POUR EVERY SHRED OF WILL INTO THAT RING AND THEN BEING ABLE TO REDIRECT IT WITH NOTHING MORE THAN A SHRUG... MMM...
...IT IS ENJOYABLE.
I HOPE IT STILL WILL BE WHEN MY FOOT'S UP YOUR WRINKLED BLUE ASS.

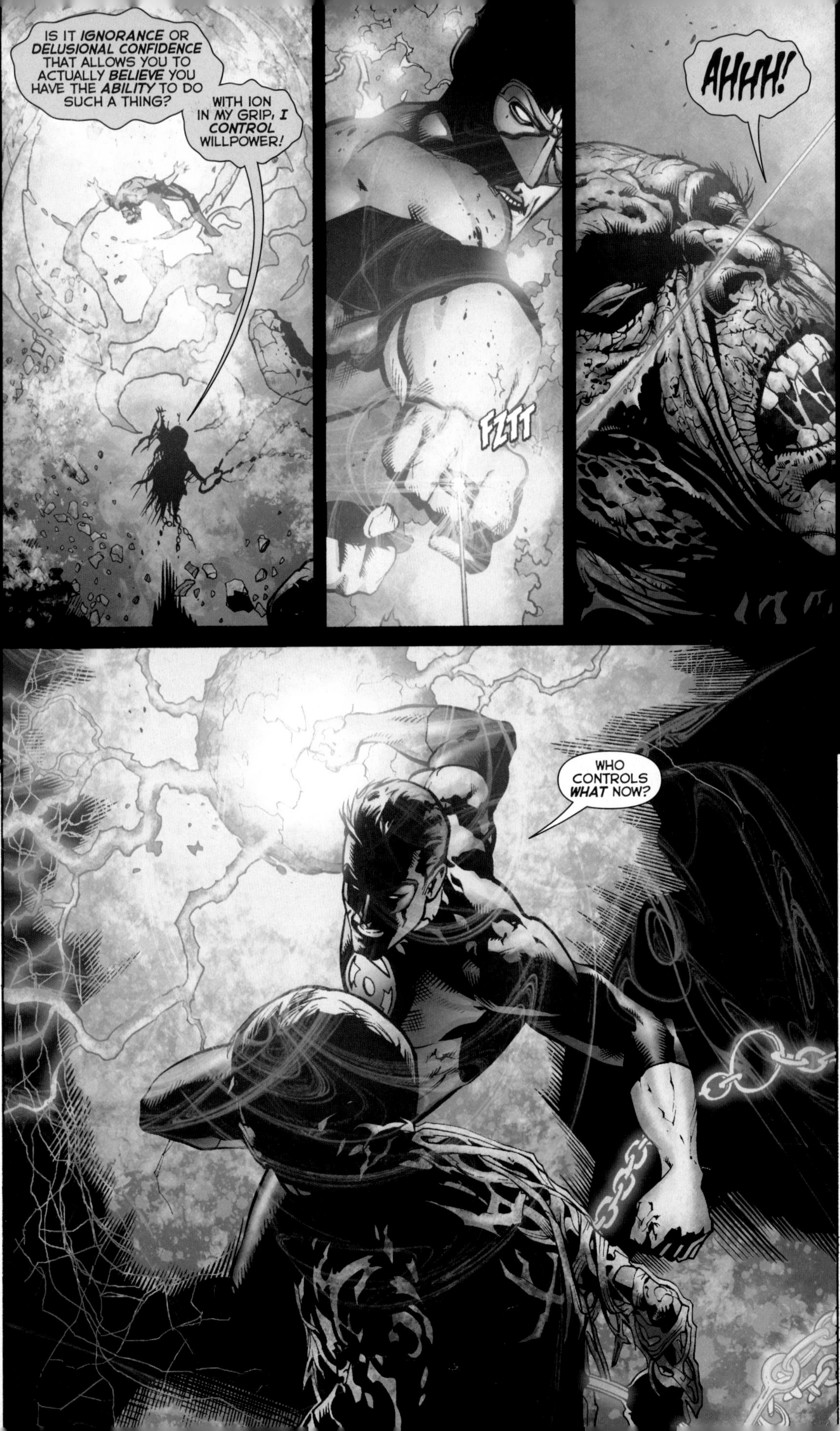
IS IT IGNORANCE OR DELUSIONAL CONFIDENCE THAT ALLOWS YOU TO ACTUALLY BELIEVE YOU HAVE THE ABILITY TO DO SUCH A THING?
WITH ION IN MY GRIP, I CONTROL WILLPOWER!
FZTT
AHHH!
WHO CONTROLS WHAT NOW?

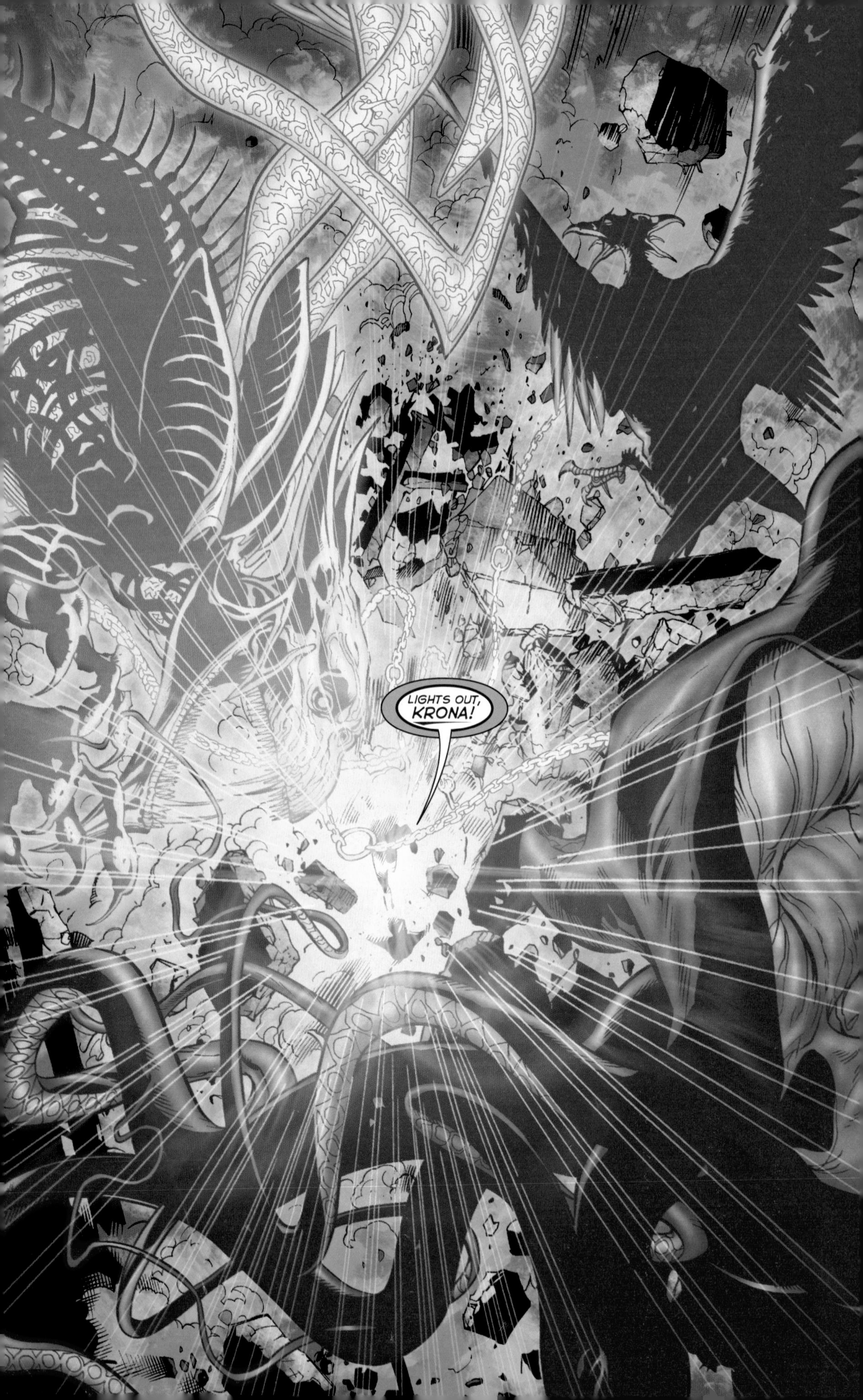
LIGHTS OUT, KRONA!

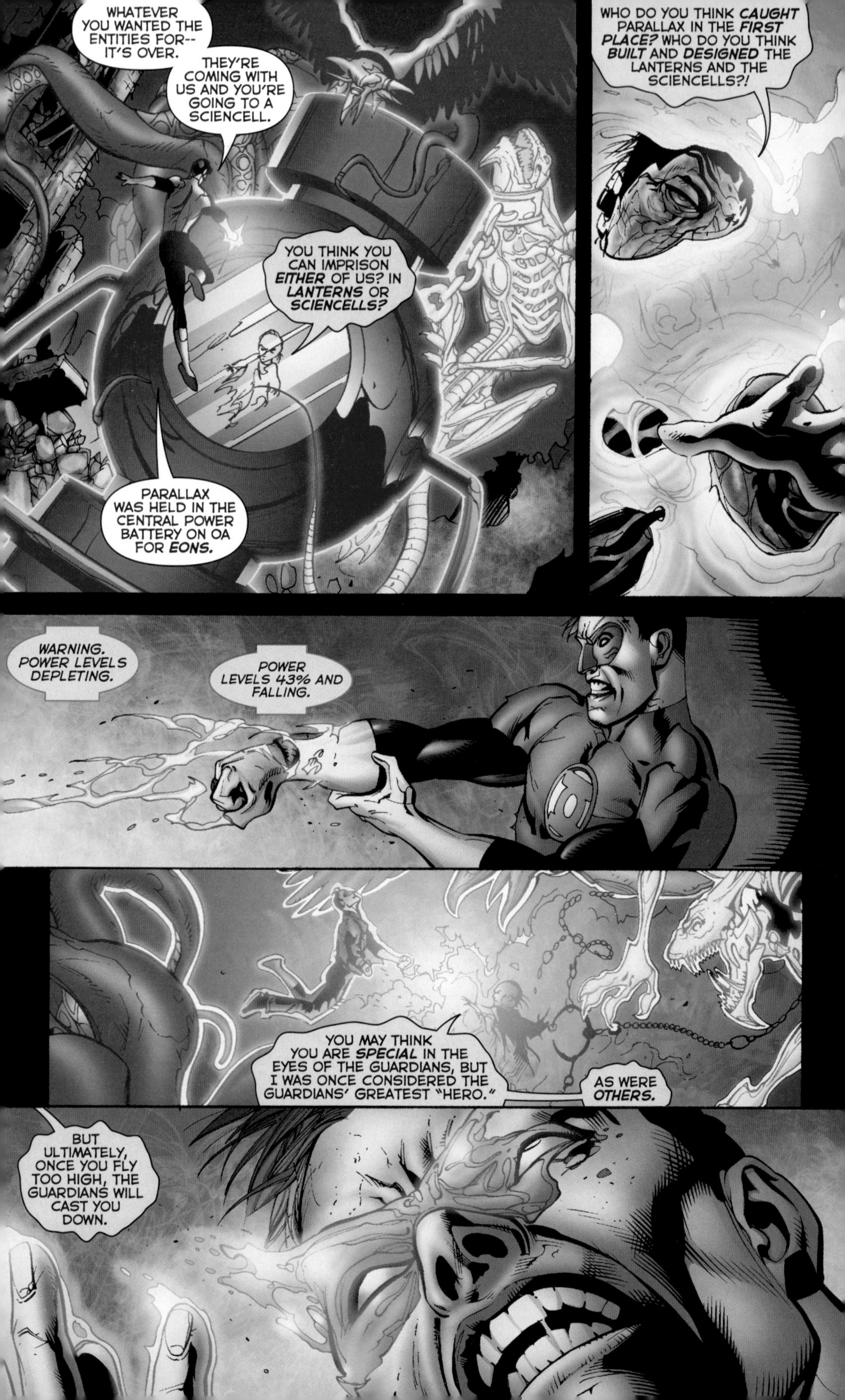
WHATEVER YOU WANTED THE ENTITIES FOR-- IT'S OVER.
THEY'RE COMING WITH US AND YOU'RE GOING TO A SCIENCELL.
WHO DO YOU THINK CAUGHT PARALLAX IN THE FIRST PLACE? WHO DO YOU THINK BUILT AND DESIGNED THE LANTERNS AND THE SCIENCELLS?!
YOU THINK YOU CAN IMPRISON EITHER OF US? IN LANTERNS OR SCIENCELLS?
PARALLAX WAS HELD IN THE CENTRAL POWER BATTERY ON OA FOR EONS.
WARNING. POWER LEVELS DEPLETING.
POWER LEVELS 43% AND FALLING.
YOU MAY THINK YOU ARE SPECIAL IN THE EYES OF THE GUARDIANS, BUT I WAS ONCE CONSIDERED THE GUARDIANS' GREATEST "HERO."
AS WERE OTHERS.
BUT ULTIMATELY, ONCE YOU FLY TOO HIGH, THE GUARDIANS WILL CAST YOU DOWN.

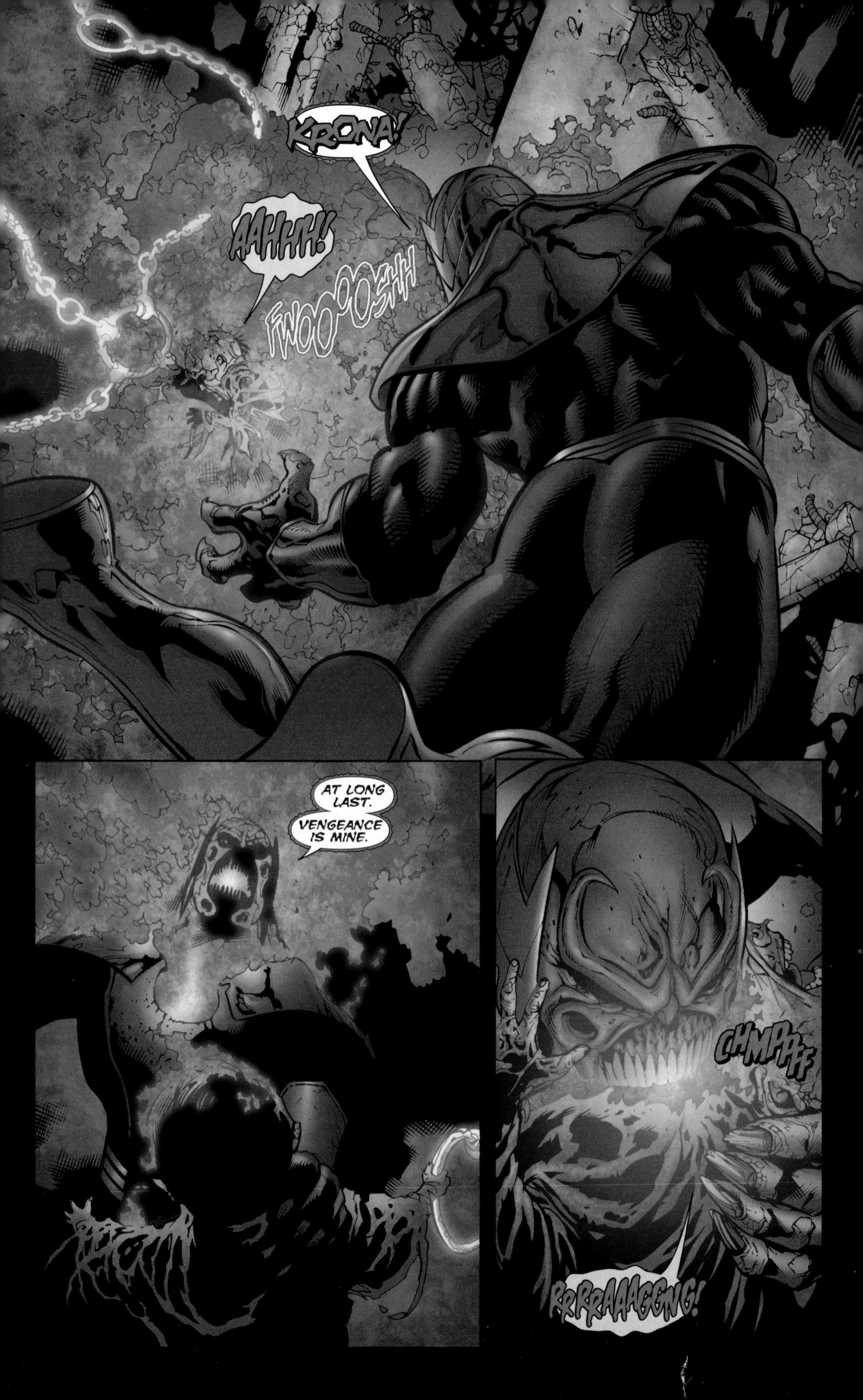
KRONA!
AAHHH!
FWOOOOSHH
AT LONG LAST.
VENGEANCE IS MINE.
CHMPFF
RRRRAAAGGNG!

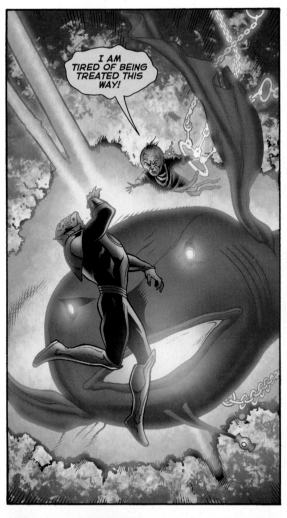

I AM TIRED OF BEING TREATED THIS WAY!

I AM NOT THE *ENEMY!* I WAS LABELED A PARIAH BECAUSE I *DARED* TO DISCOVER THE *SOURCE OF LIFE* AND CELEBRATE THE *JOY* OF IT!

BUT I ONLY WISHED TO *UNDER-STAND* EMOTION SO THAT WE COULD *CONTROL* IT, NOT *BURY* IT AWAY AS THE GUARDIANS DID!

BUT THEY WON'T HAVE THEM BURIED FOR *LONG!*

NO ONE CAN STOP ME FROM *CLEANSING* THIS UNIVERSE OF THE *EMOTIONALLY UNBALANCED!*

I THINK THE IRONY'S ESCAPING HIM.

HAL, THIS IS NO TIME FOR JOKES. YOUR RING--

HAS ENOUGH JUICE LEFT TO SEVER THOSE CHAINS AND FREE THE ENTITIES.

AND *THEN* WHAT? EVEN IF WE CAN GET THE ENTITIES *CLEAR* OF KRONA, WE STILL HAVE TO DEAL WITH *HIM.*

HOW DO WE DO THAT?

ALL THE HUMANS IN THE AREA HAVE BEEN EVACUATED, GREEN LANTERN.

HAVE SOME *FAITH,* BARRY.

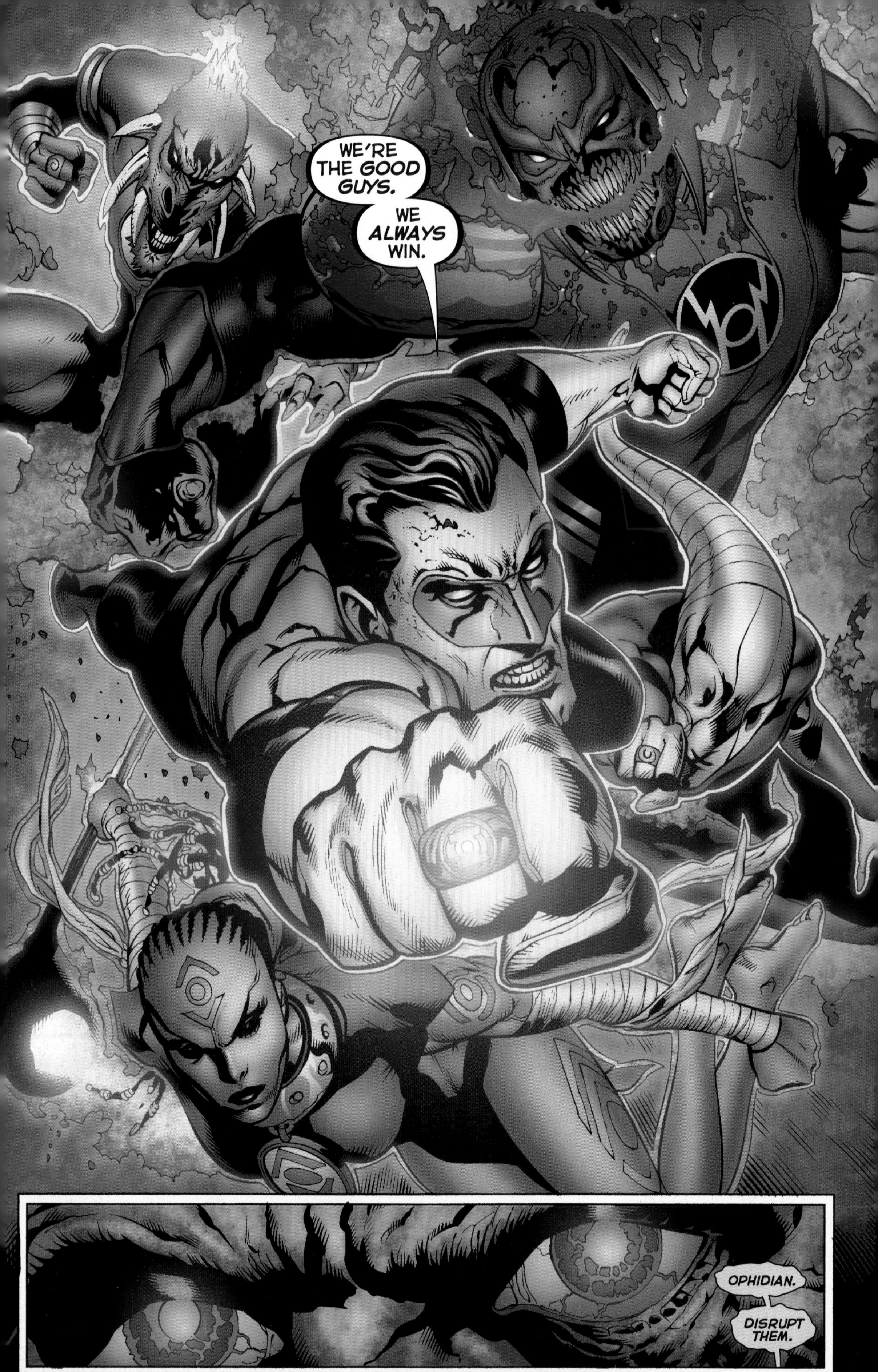
WE'RE THE GOOD GUYS.
WE ALWAYS WIN.
OPHIDIAN.
DISRUPT THEM.

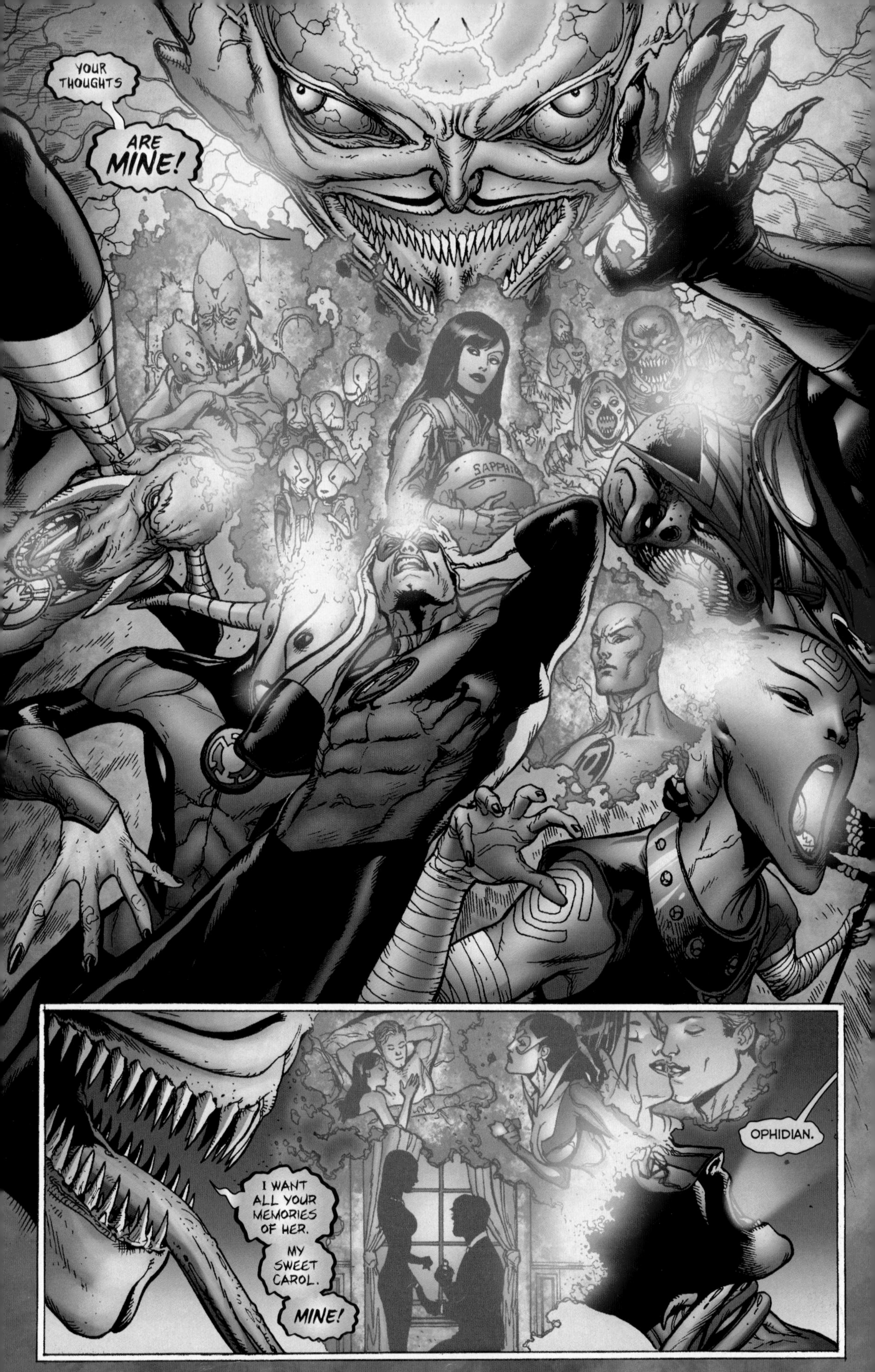
YOUR THOUGHTS
ARE MINE!
I WANT ALL YOUR MEMORIES OF HER.
MY SWEET CAROL.
MINE!
OPHIDIAN.

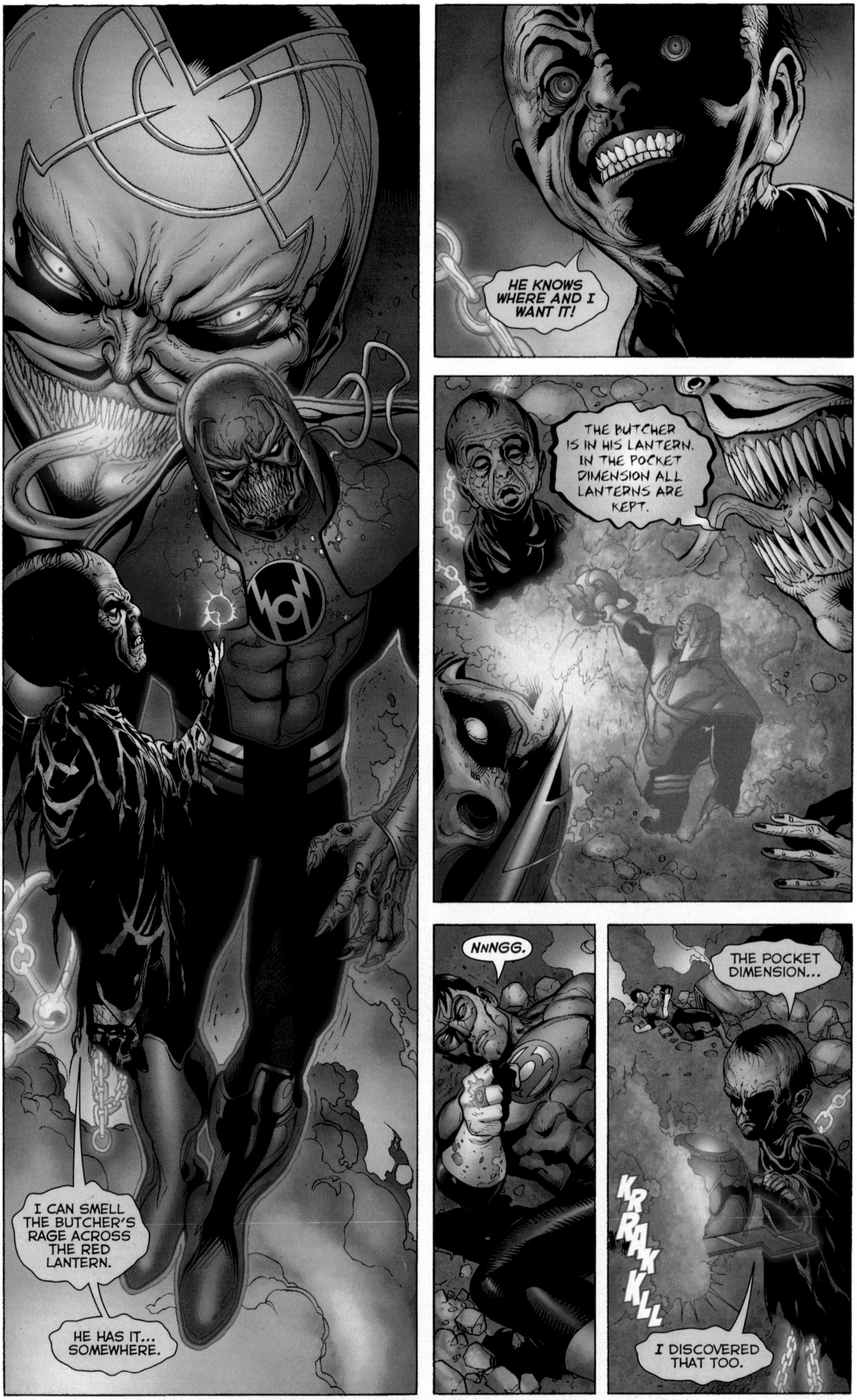
I CAN SMELL THE BUTCHER'S RAGE ACROSS THE RED LANTERN.
HE HAS IT... SOMEWHERE.
HE KNOWS WHERE AND I WANT IT!
THE BUTCHER IS IN HIS LANTERN. IN THE POCKET DIMENSION ALL LANTERNS ARE KEPT.
NNNGG.
THE POCKET DIMENSION...
KRAKKLL
I DISCOVERED THAT TOO.

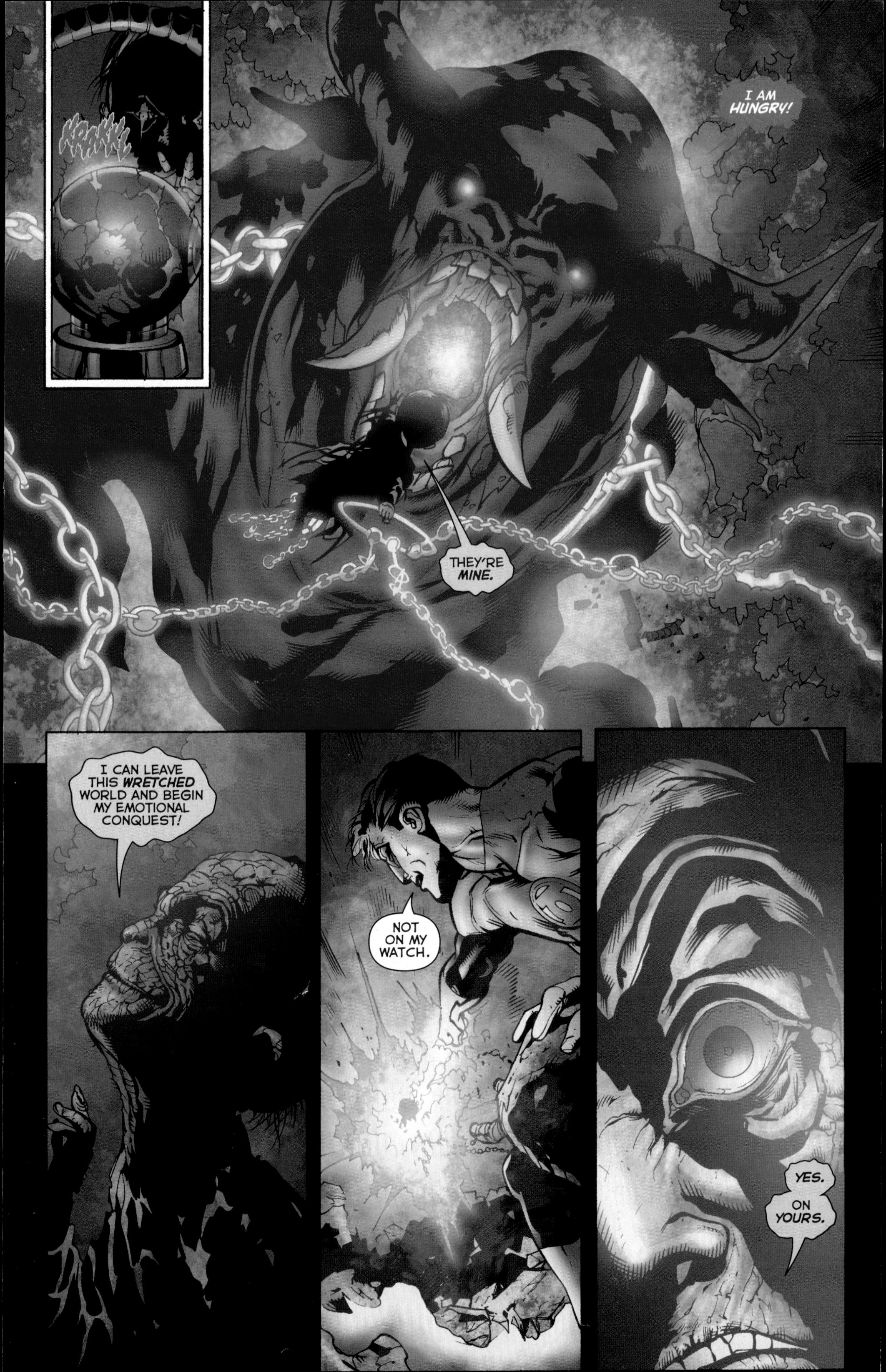
KRAKKL
I AM HUNGRY!
THEY'RE MINE.
I CAN LEAVE THIS WRETCHED WORLD AND BEGIN MY EMOTIONAL CONQUEST!
NOT ON MY WATCH.
YES.
ON YOURS.

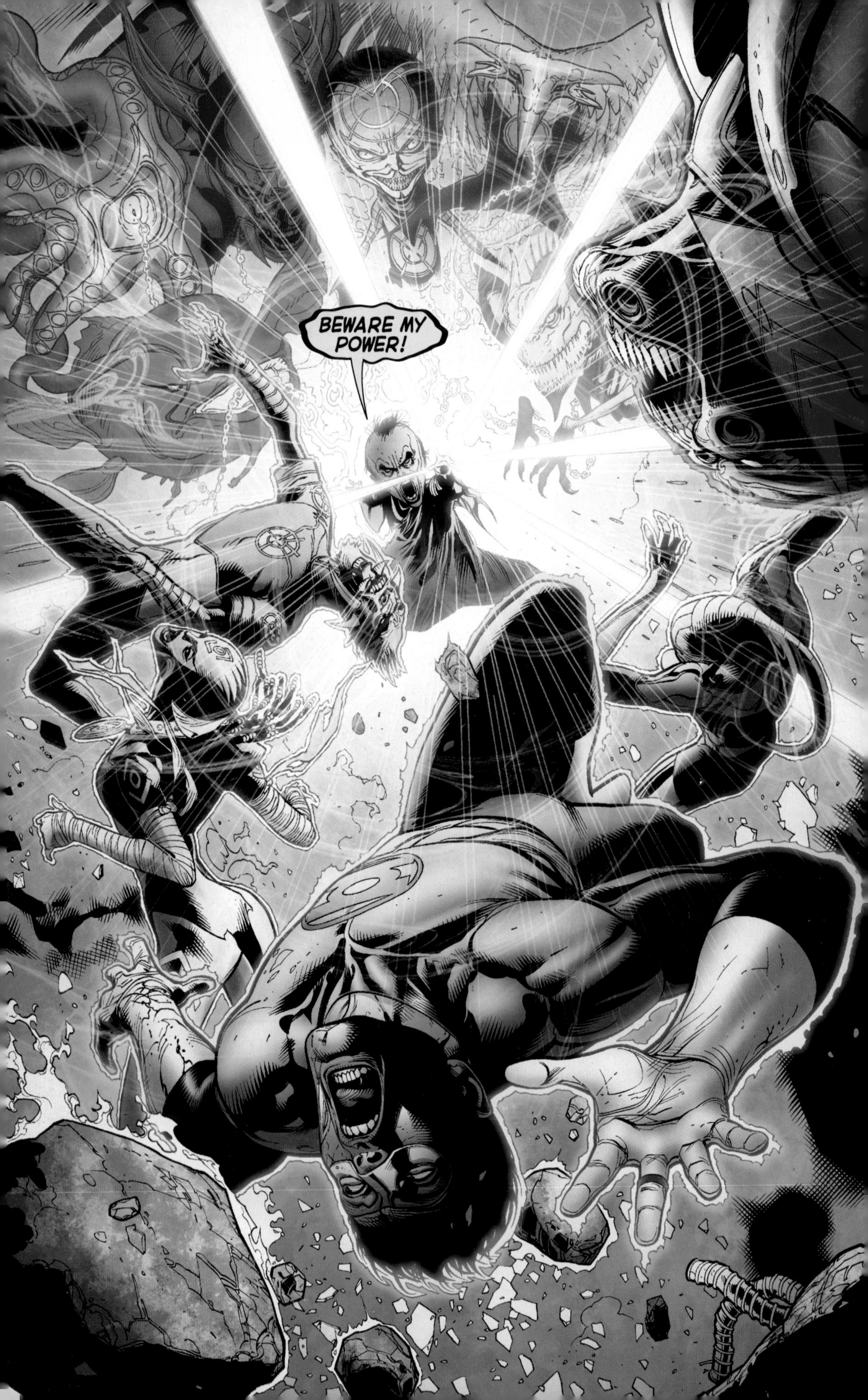
BEWARE MY POWER!

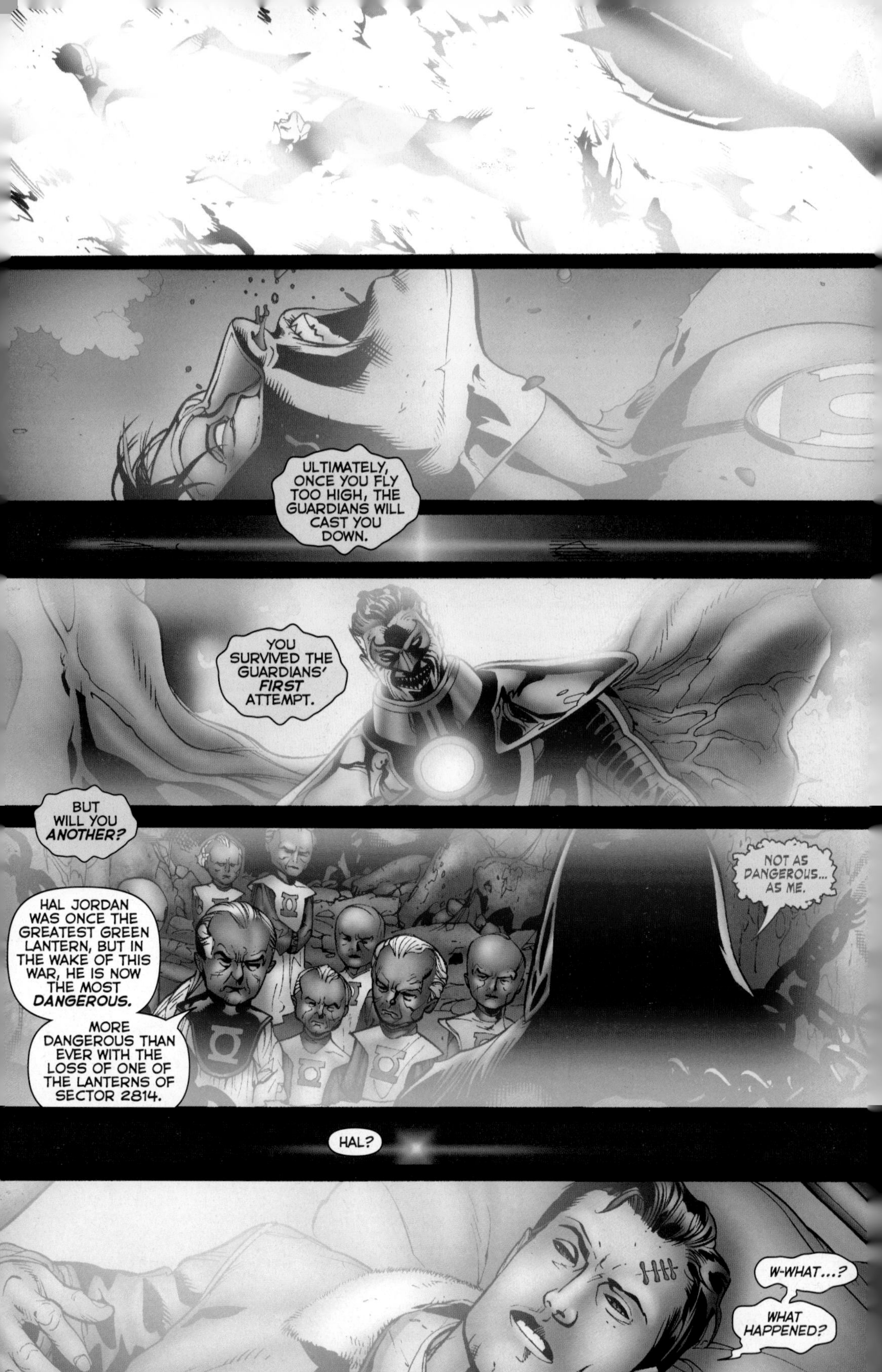
ULTIMATELY, ONCE YOU FLY TOO HIGH, THE GUARDIANS WILL CAST YOU DOWN.
YOU SURVIVED THE GUARDIANS' *FIRST* ATTEMPT.
BUT WILL YOU *ANOTHER?*
HAL JORDAN WAS ONCE THE GREATEST GREEN LANTERN, BUT IN THE WAKE OF THIS WAR, HE IS NOW THE MOST *DANGEROUS.*
MORE DANGEROUS THAN EVER WITH THE LOSS OF ONE OF THE LANTERNS OF SECTOR 2814.
NOT AS DANGEROUS... AS ME.
HAL?
W-WHAT...?
WHAT HAPPENED?

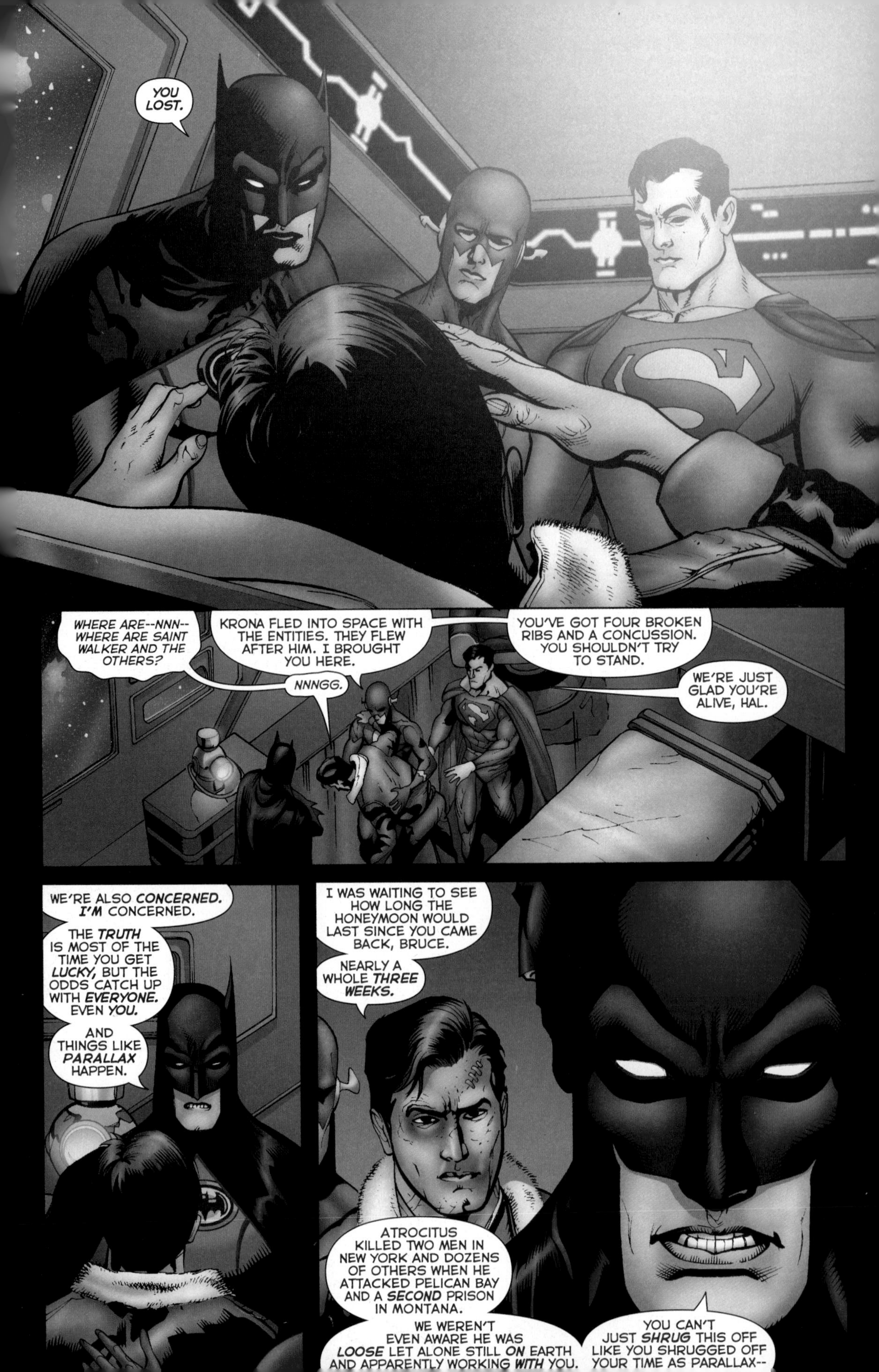
YOU LOST.
WHERE ARE--NNN-- WHERE ARE SAINT WALKER AND THE OTHERS?
KRONA FLED INTO SPACE WITH THE ENTITIES. THEY FLEW AFTER HIM. I BROUGHT YOU HERE.
NNNGG.
YOU'VE GOT FOUR BROKEN RIBS AND A CONCUSSION. YOU SHOULDN'T TRY TO STAND.
WE'RE JUST GLAD YOU'RE ALIVE, HAL.
WE'RE ALSO CONCERNED. I'M CONCERNED.
THE TRUTH IS MOST OF THE TIME YOU GET LUCKY, BUT THE ODDS CATCH UP WITH EVERYONE. EVEN YOU.
AND THINGS LIKE PARALLAX HAPPEN.
I WAS WAITING TO SEE HOW LONG THE HONEYMOON WOULD LAST SINCE YOU CAME BACK, BRUCE.
NEARLY A WHOLE THREE WEEKS.
ATROCITUS KILLED TWO MEN IN NEW YORK AND DOZENS OF OTHERS WHEN HE ATTACKED PELICAN BAY AND A SECOND PRISON IN MONTANA.
WE WEREN'T EVEN AWARE HE WAS LOOSE LET ALONE STILL ON EARTH AND APPARENTLY WORKING WITH YOU.
YOU CAN'T JUST SHRUG THIS OFF LIKE YOU SHRUGGED OFF YOUR TIME AS PARALLAX--

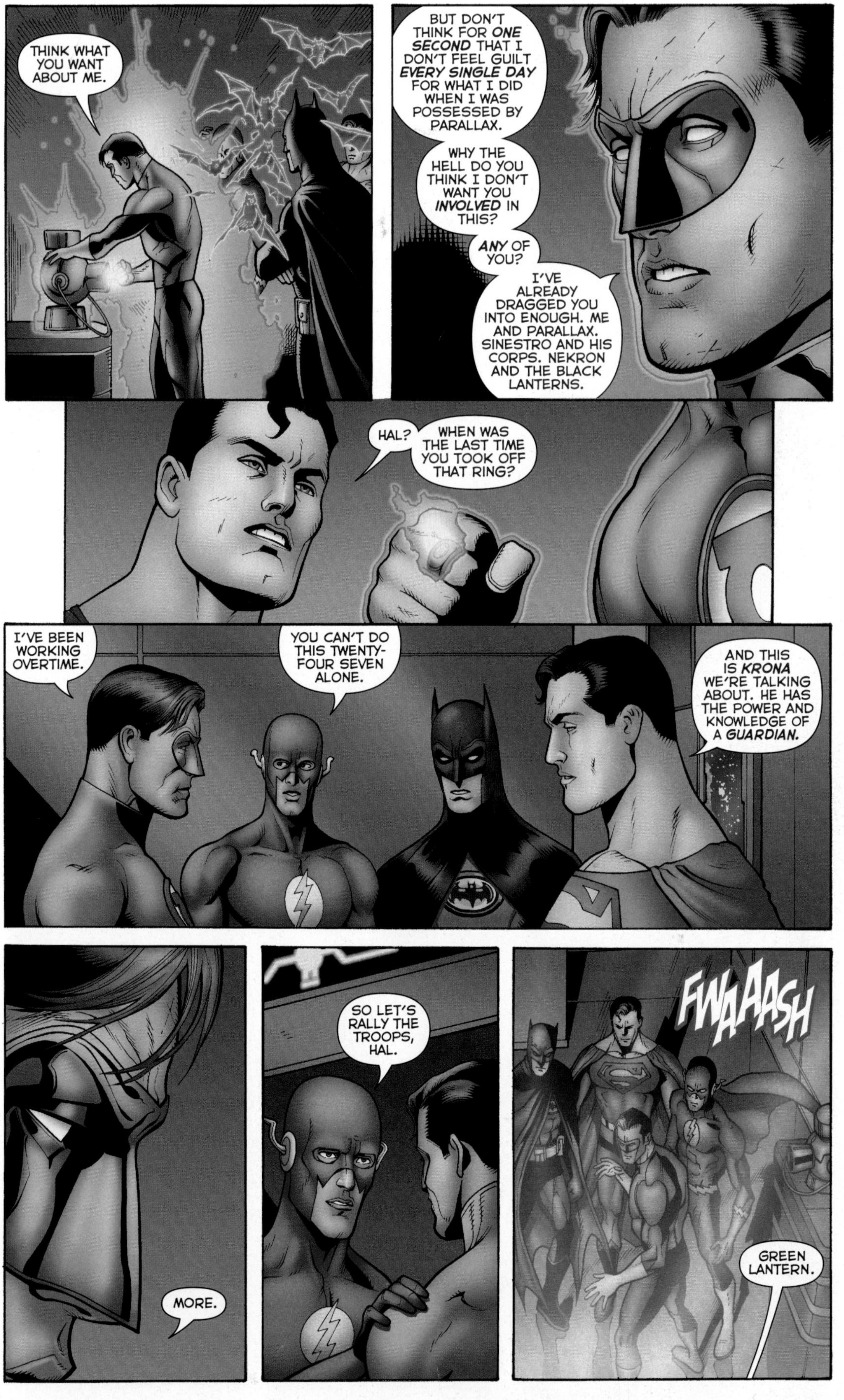
THINK WHAT YOU WANT ABOUT ME.
BUT DON'T THINK FOR ONE SECOND THAT I DON'T FEEL GUILT EVERY SINGLE DAY FOR WHAT I DID WHEN I WAS POSSESSED BY PARALLAX.
WHY THE HELL DO YOU THINK I DON'T WANT YOU INVOLVED IN THIS?
ANY OF YOU?
I'VE ALREADY DRAGGED YOU INTO ENOUGH. ME AND PARALLAX. SINESTRO AND HIS CORPS. NEKRON AND THE BLACK LANTERNS.
HAL?
WHEN WAS THE LAST TIME YOU TOOK OFF THAT RING?
I'VE BEEN WORKING OVERTIME.
YOU CAN'T DO THIS TWENTY-FOUR SEVEN ALONE.
AND THIS IS KRONA WE'RE TALKING ABOUT. HE HAS THE POWER AND KNOWLEDGE OF A GUARDIAN.
MORE.
SO LET'S RALLY THE TROOPS, HAL.
FWAAASH
GREEN LANTERN.

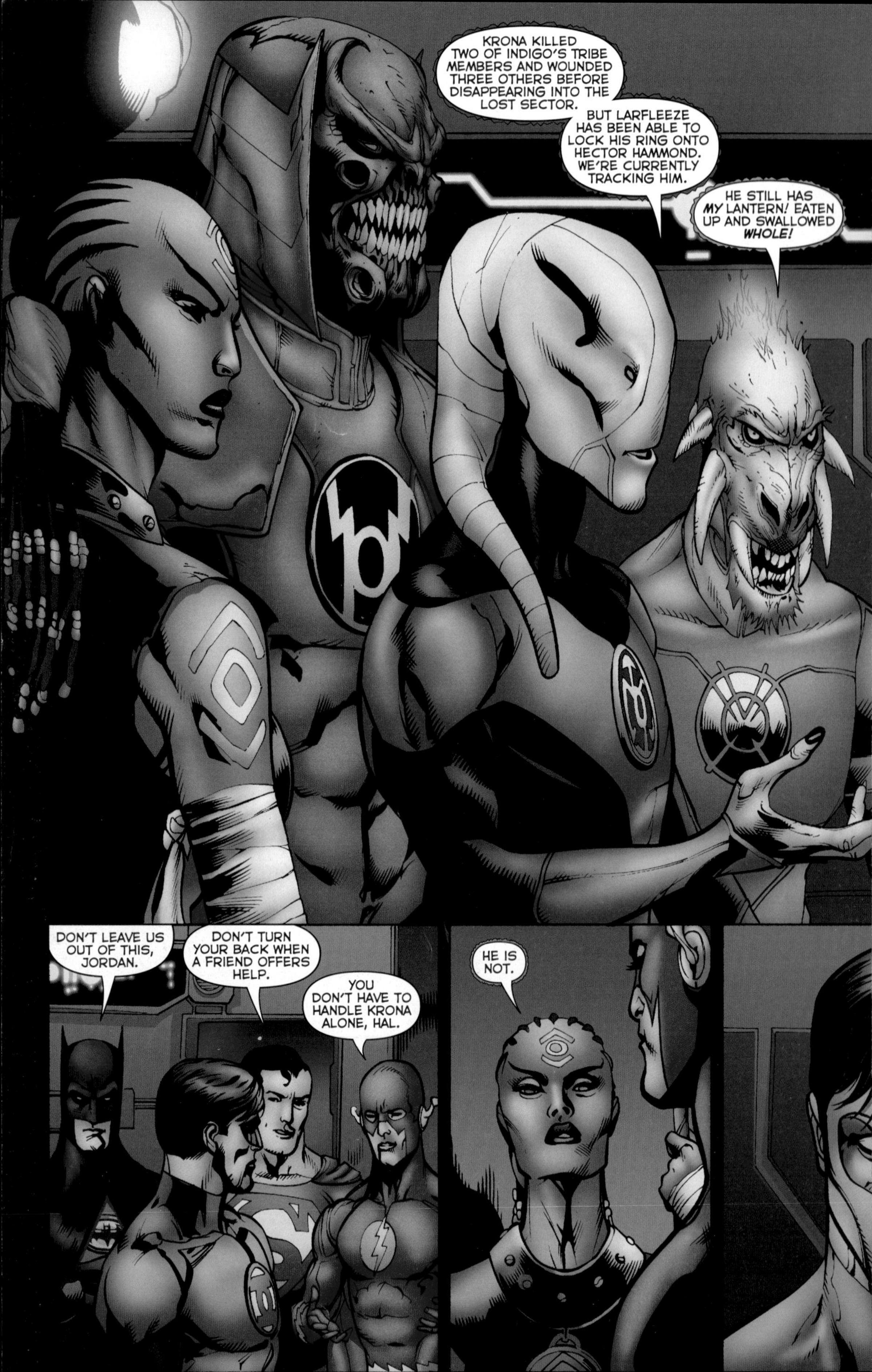
KRONA KILLED TWO OF INDIGO'S TRIBE MEMBERS AND WOUNDED THREE OTHERS BEFORE DISAPPEARING INTO THE LOST SECTOR.
BUT LARFLEEZE HAS BEEN ABLE TO LOCK HIS RING ONTO HECTOR HAMMOND. WE'RE CURRENTLY TRACKING HIM.
HE STILL HAS MY LANTERN! EATEN UP AND SWALLOWED WHOLE!
DON'T LEAVE US OUT OF THIS, JORDAN.
DON'T TURN YOUR BACK WHEN A FRIEND OFFERS HELP.
YOU DON'T HAVE TO HANDLE KRONA ALONE, HAL.
HE IS NOT.

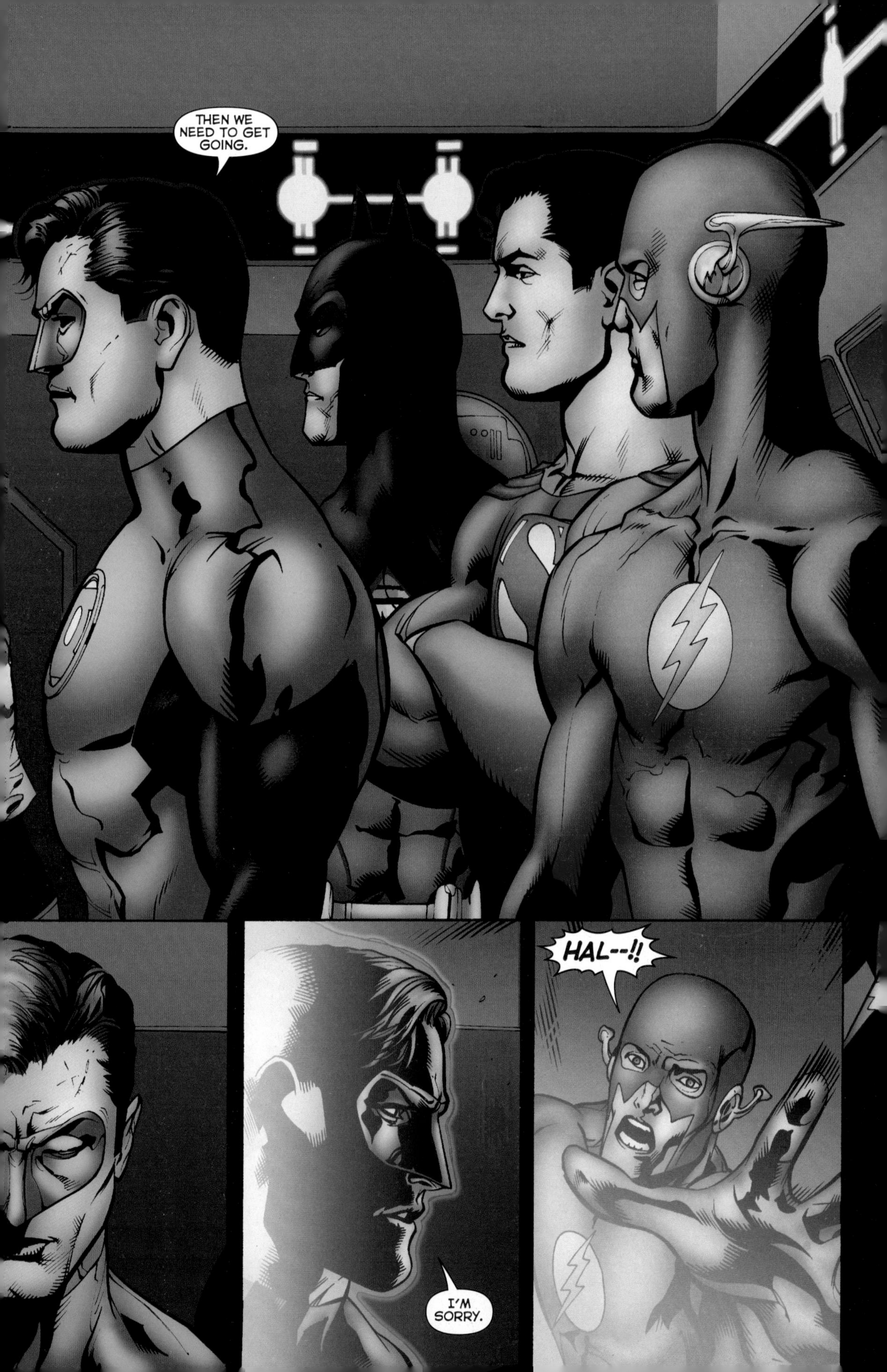
THEN WE NEED TO GET GOING.
I'M SORRY.
HAL--!!

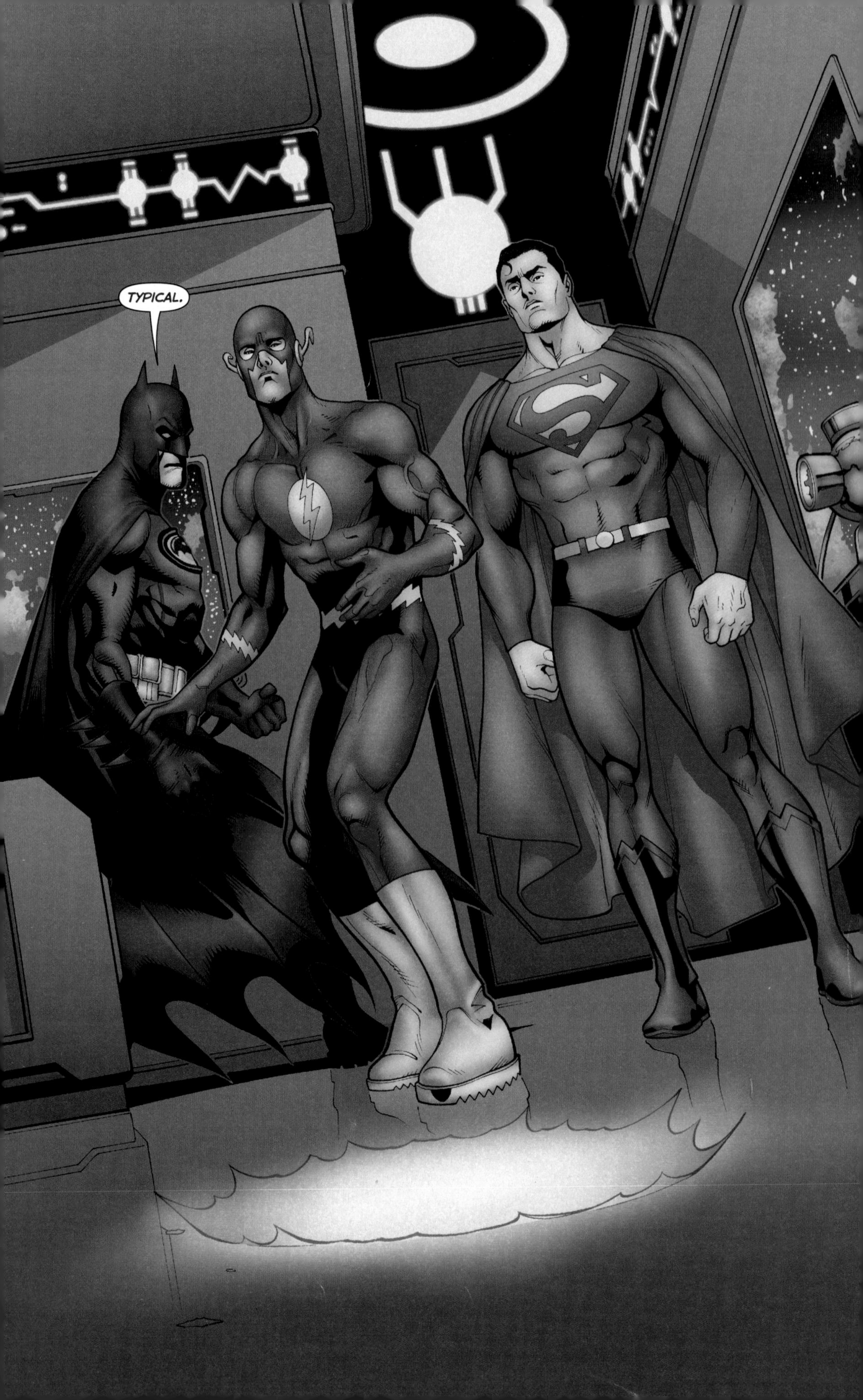
TYPICAL.

TALES OF THE RED LANTERN CORPS:
DEX-STARR

Shawn Davis Art
(with thanks to Jamie Grant)

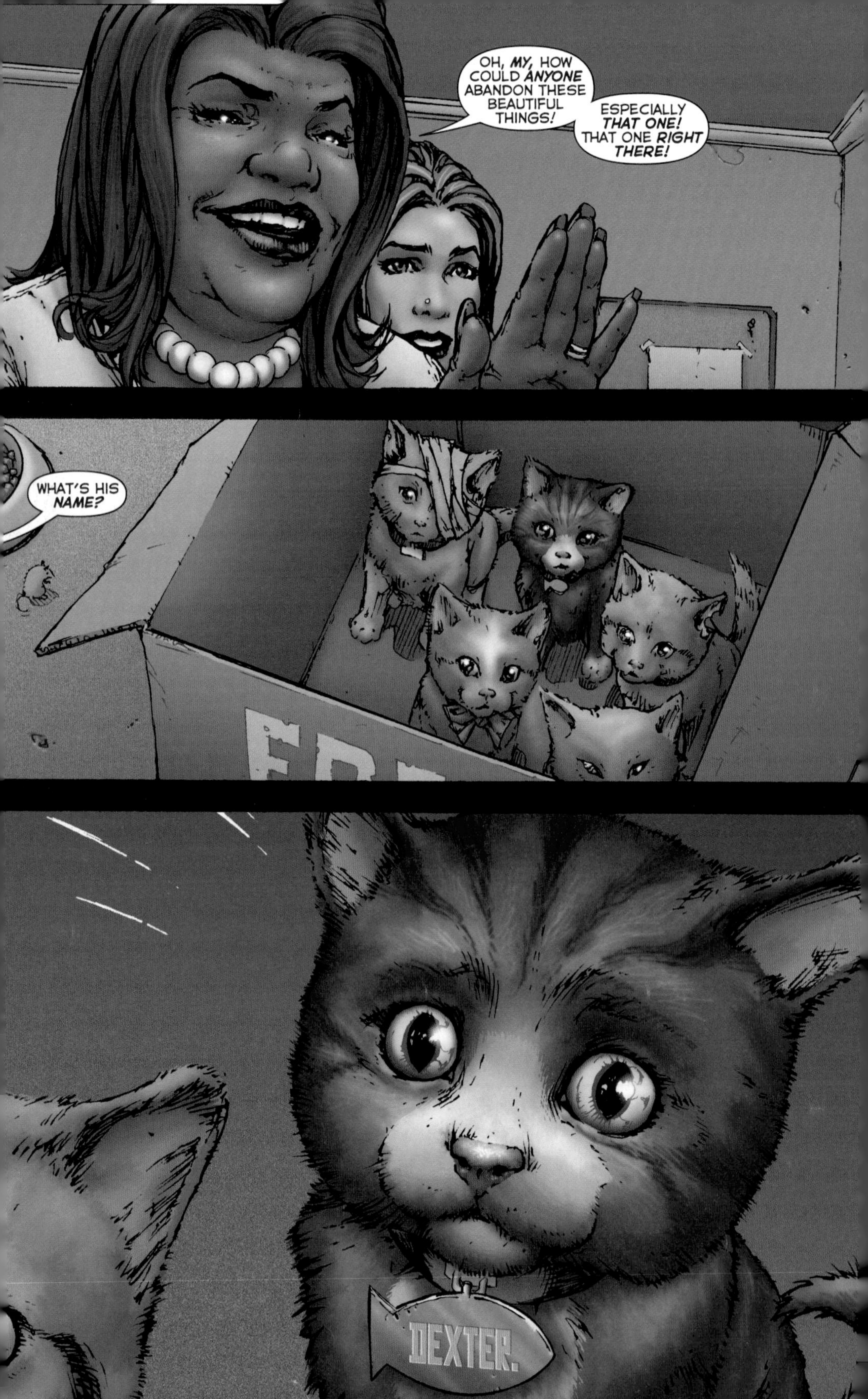
OH, MY, HOW COULD ANYONE ABANDON THESE BEAUTIFUL THINGS!
ESPECIALLY THAT ONE! THAT ONE RIGHT THERE!
WHAT'S HIS NAME?
DEXTER.

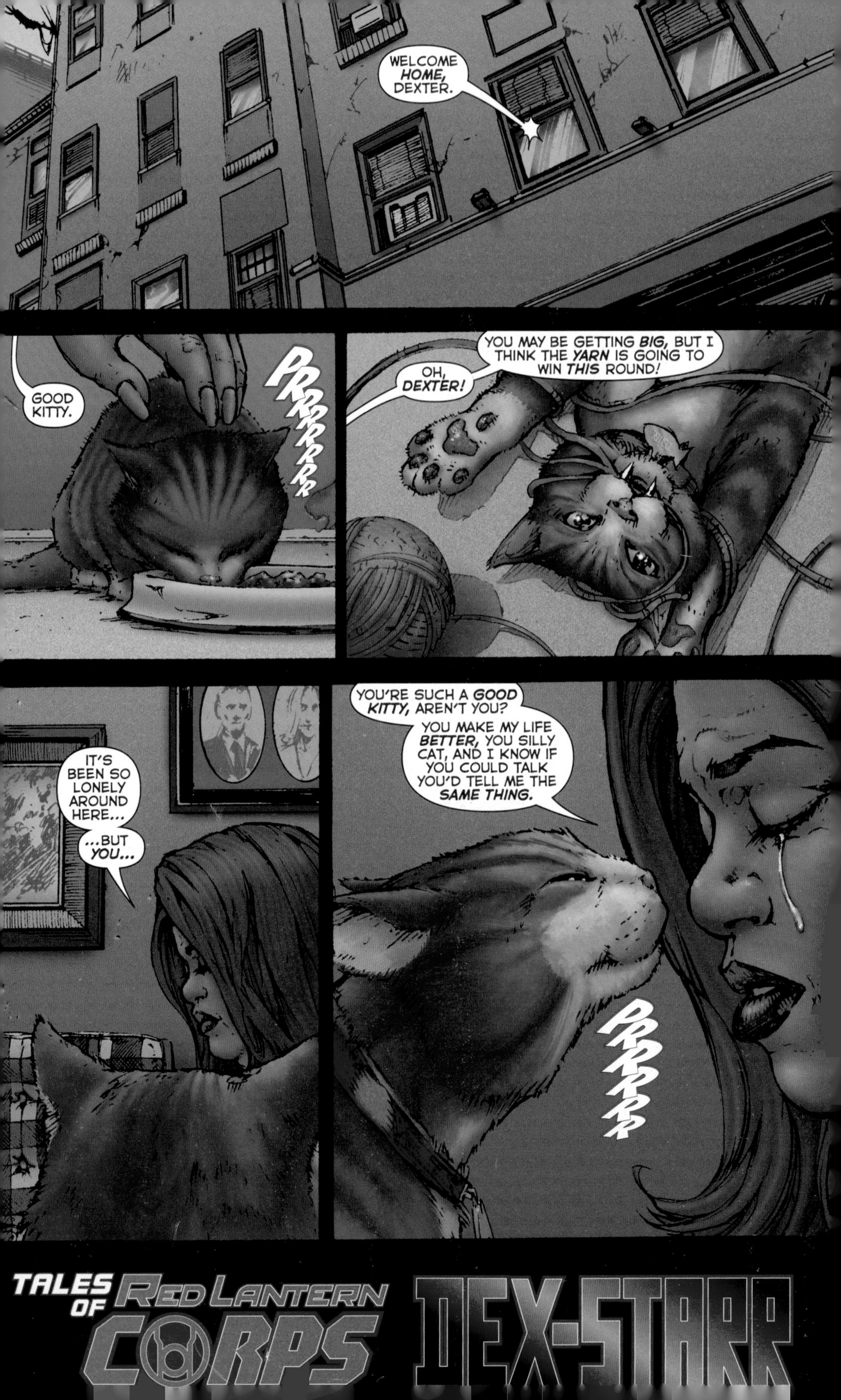

WELCOME HOME, DEXTER.
GOOD KITTY.
PRRRRRRR
OH, DEXTER!
YOU MAY BE GETTING BIG, BUT I THINK THE YARN IS GOING TO WIN THIS ROUND!
IT'S BEEN SO LONELY AROUND HERE...
...BUT YOU...
YOU'RE SUCH A GOOD KITTY, AREN'T YOU?
YOU MAKE MY LIFE BETTER, YOU SILLY CAT, AND I KNOW IF YOU COULD TALK YOU'D TELL ME THE SAME THING.
PRRRRR
TALES OF RED LANTERN CORPS
DEX-STARR

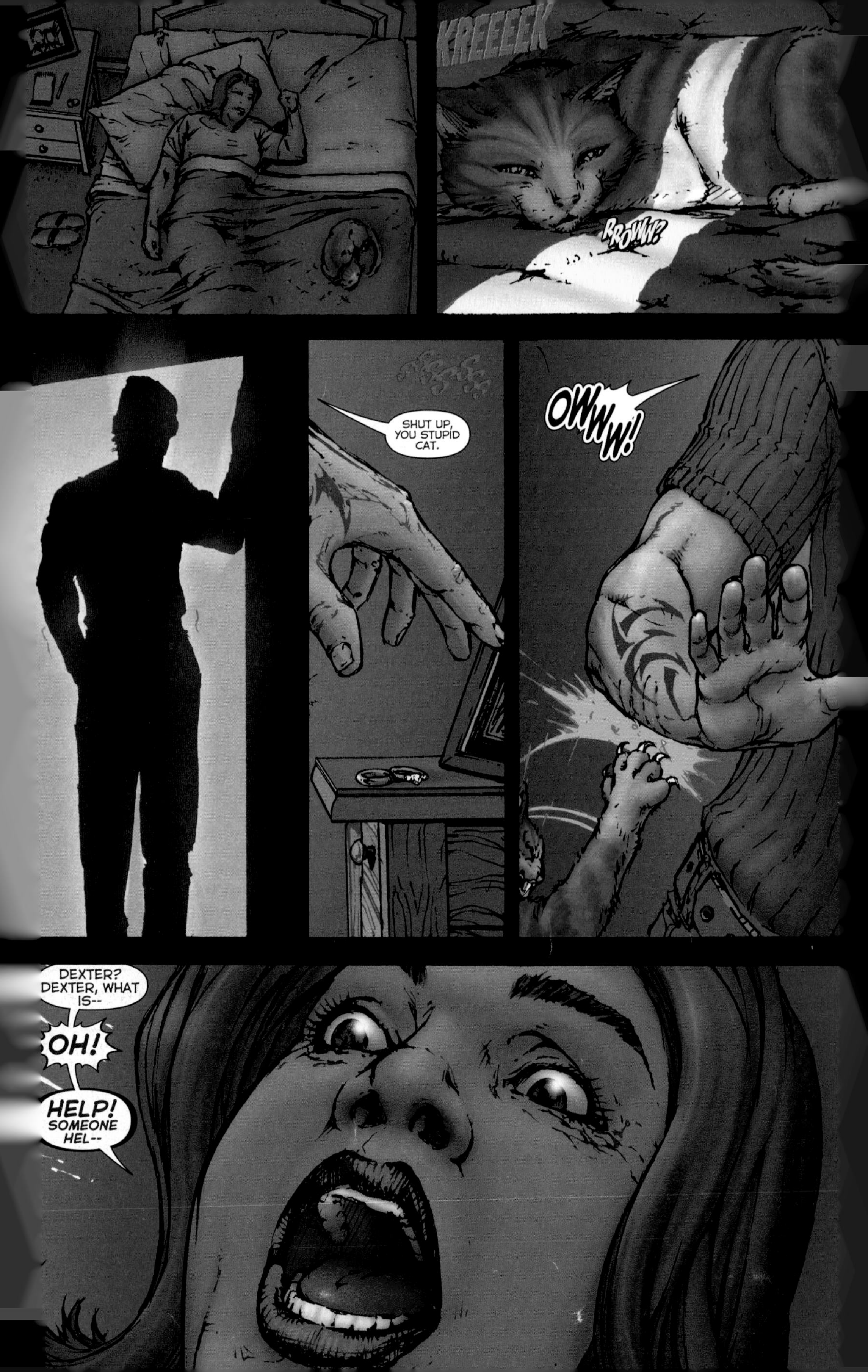
KREEEEK
BROWW?
SHUT UP, YOU STUPID CAT.
OWWW!
DEXTER? DEXTER, WHAT IS--
OH!
HELP! SOMEONE HEL--

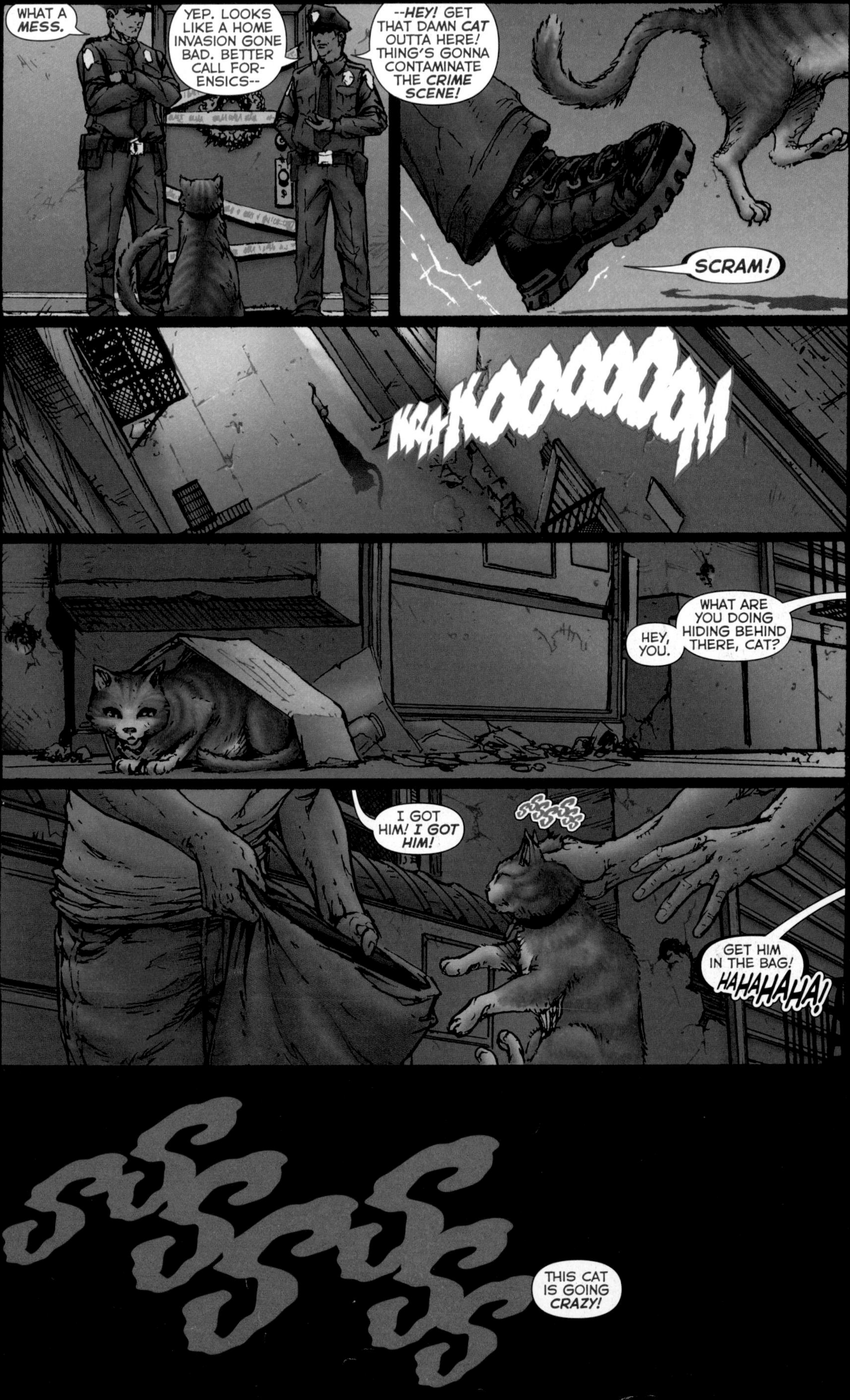

WHAT A *MESS.*
YEP. LOOKS LIKE A HOME INVASION GONE BAD. BETTER CALL FOR-ENSICS--
--*HEY!* GET THAT DAMN *CAT* OUTTA HERE! THING'S GONNA CONTAMINATE THE *CRIME SCENE!*
SCRAM!
KRA-KOOOOOOM
HEY, YOU.
WHAT ARE YOU DOING HIDING BEHIND THERE, CAT?
I GOT HIM! *I GOT HIM!*
GET HIM IN THE BAG! HAHAHAHA!
THIS CAT IS GOING *CRAZY!*

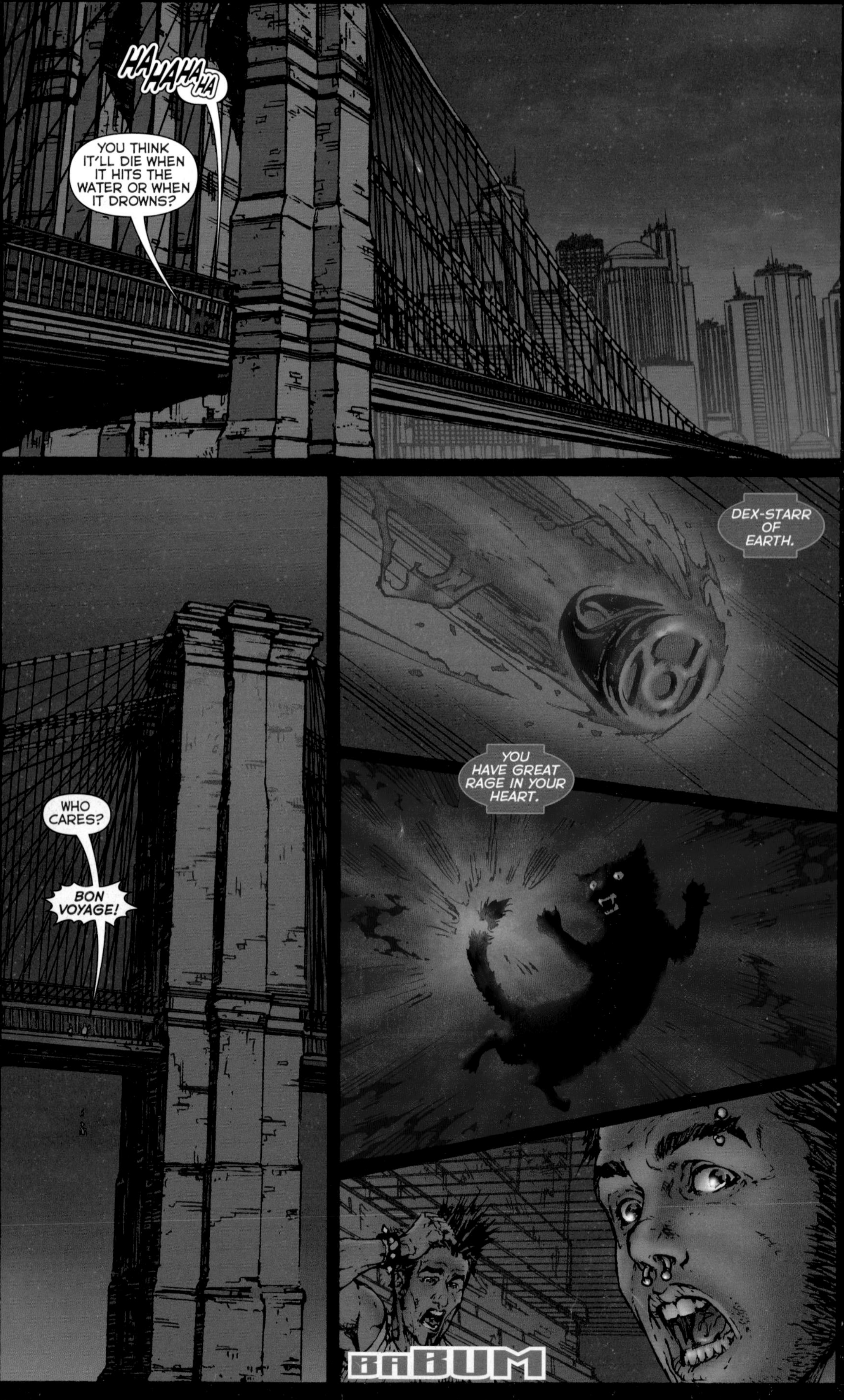
HAHAHAHAHA
YOU THINK IT'LL DIE WHEN IT HITS THE WATER OR WHEN IT DROWNS?
WHO CARES?
BON VOYAGE!
DEX-STARR OF EARTH.
YOU HAVE GREAT RAGE IN YOUR HEART.
BABUM

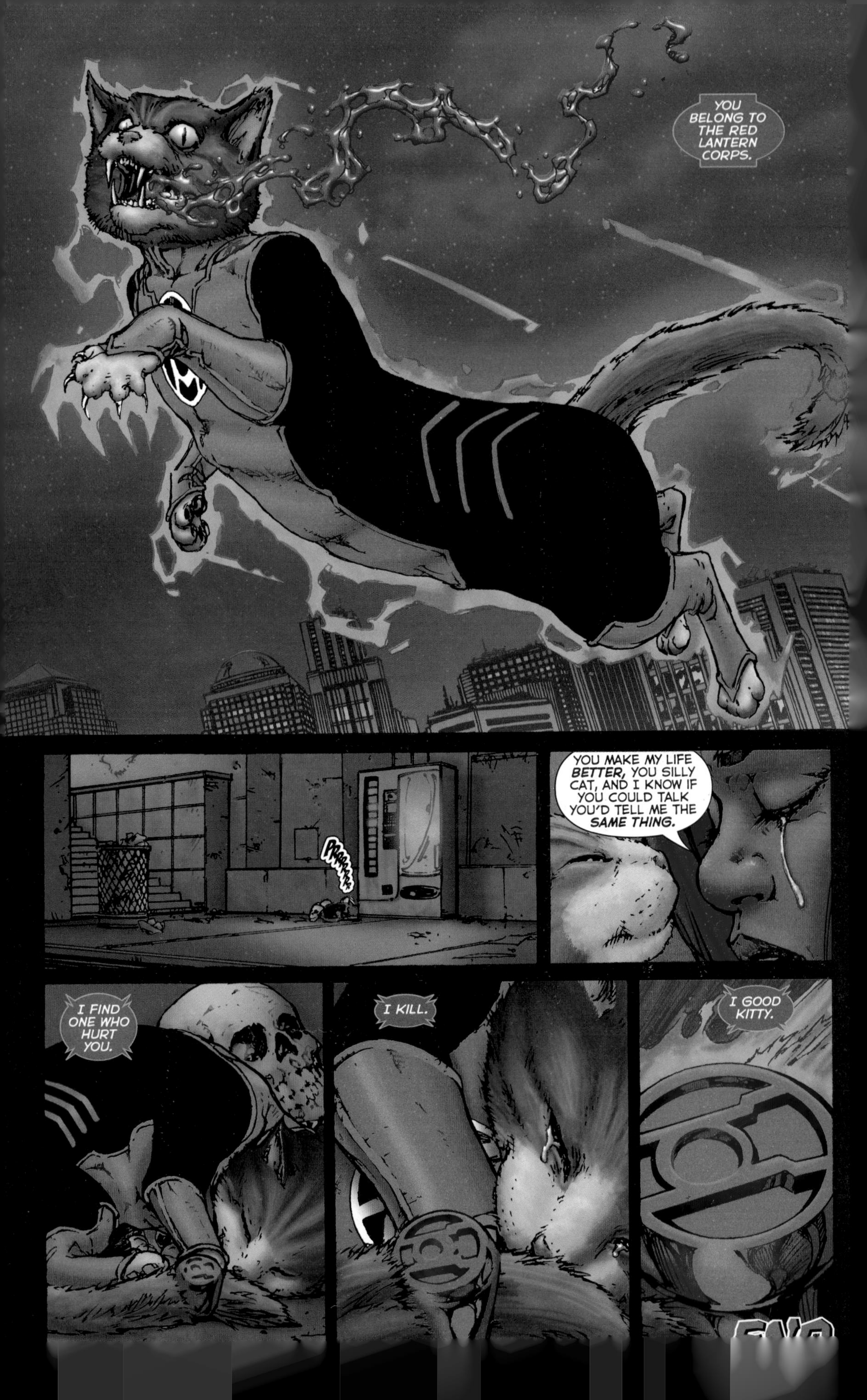
YOU BELONG TO THE RED LANTERN CORPS.
YOU MAKE MY LIFE BETTER, YOU SILLY CAT, AND I KNOW IF YOU COULD TALK YOU'D TELL ME THE SAME THING.
I FIND ONE WHO HURT YOU.
I KILL.
I GOOD KITTY.

GREEN LANTERN: BRIGHTEST DAY
VARIANT COVER GALLERY

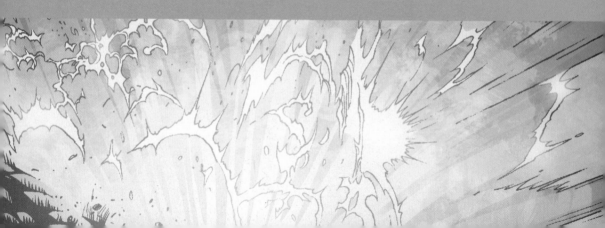

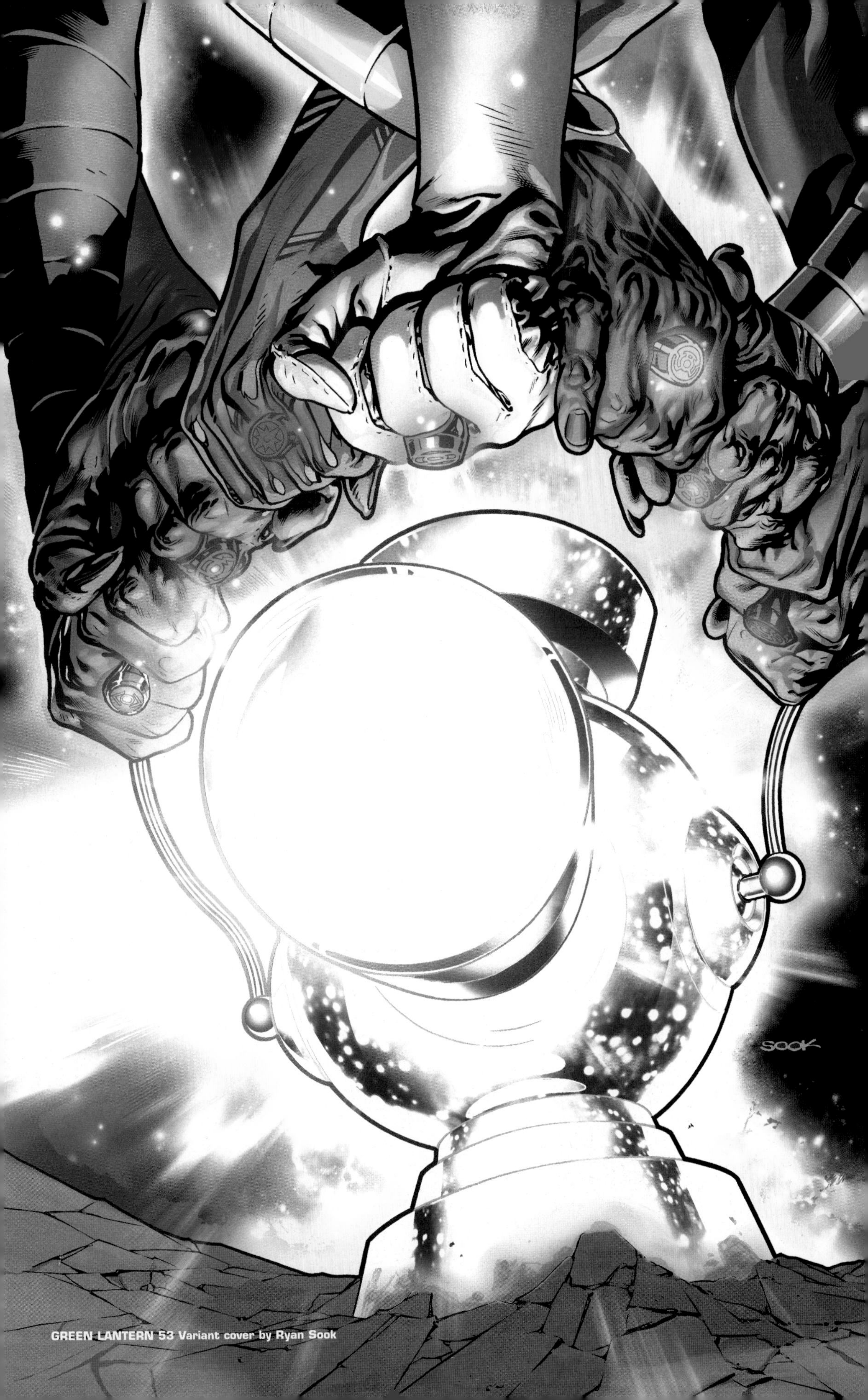
SOOK

GREEN LANTERN 53 Variant cover by Ryan Sook

GREEN LANTERN 54 Variant cover by Alex Garner

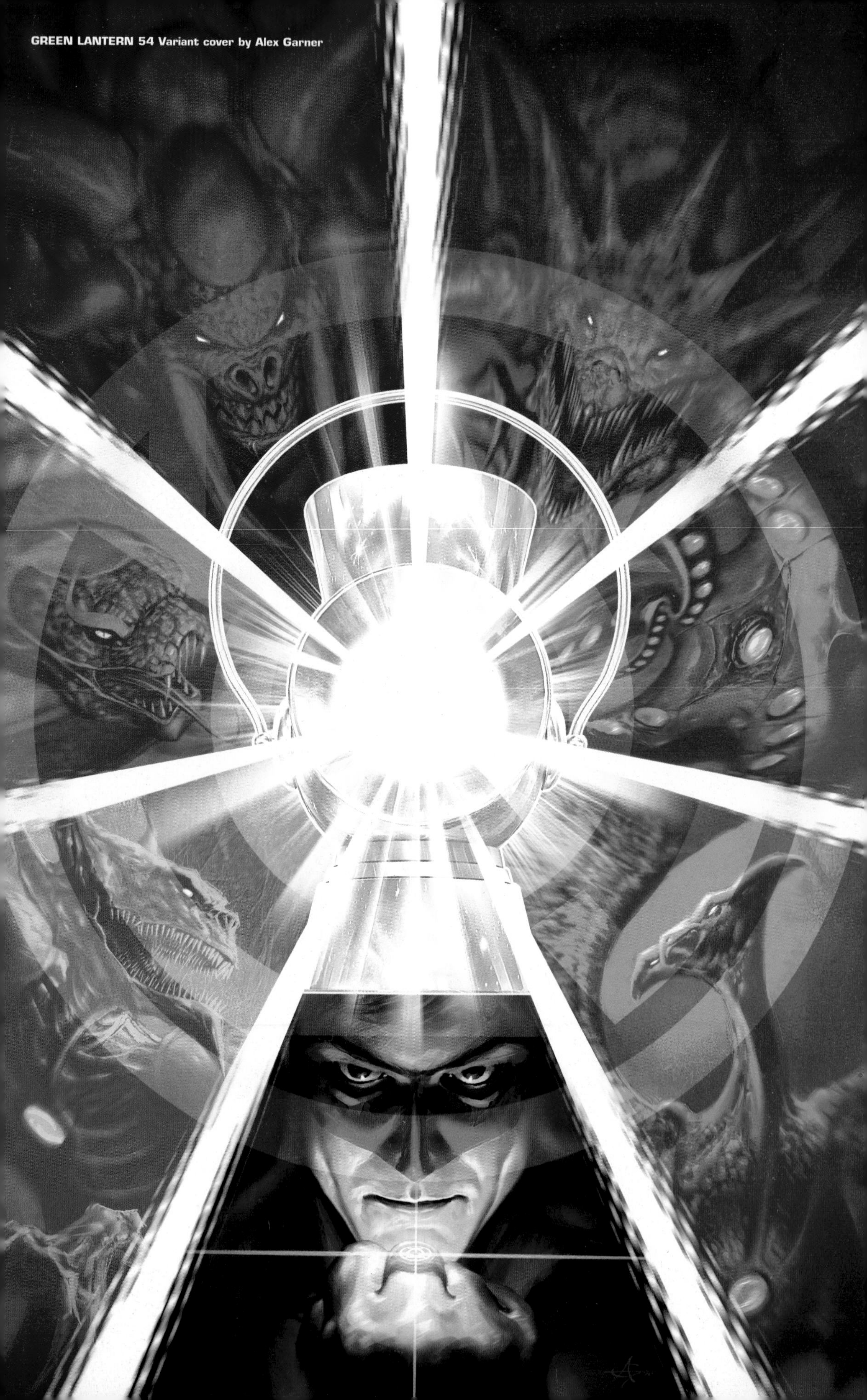

GREEN LANTERN 55 Variant cover by Doug Mahnke & Randy Mayor

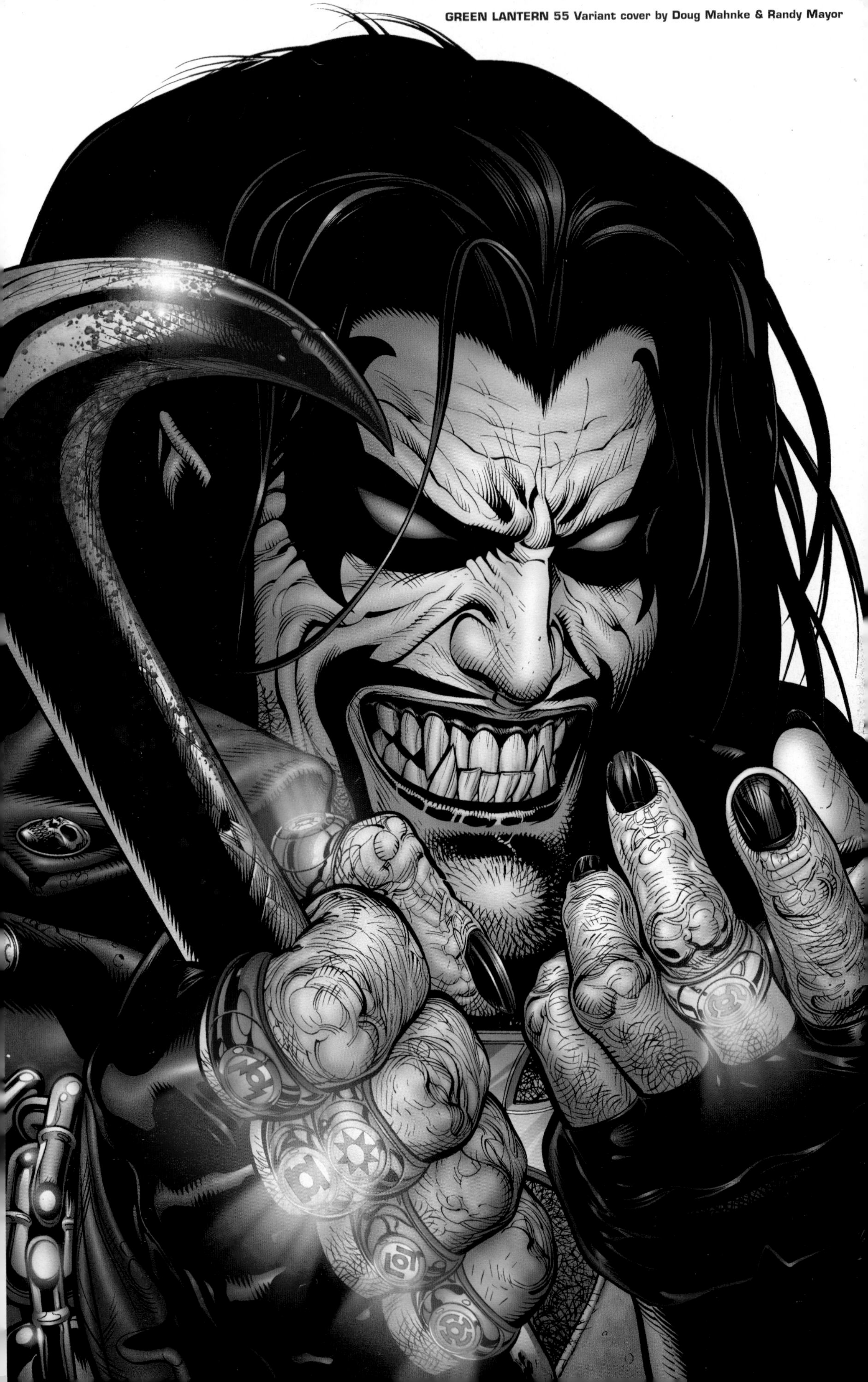

GREEN LANTERN 56 Variant cover by Art Germ

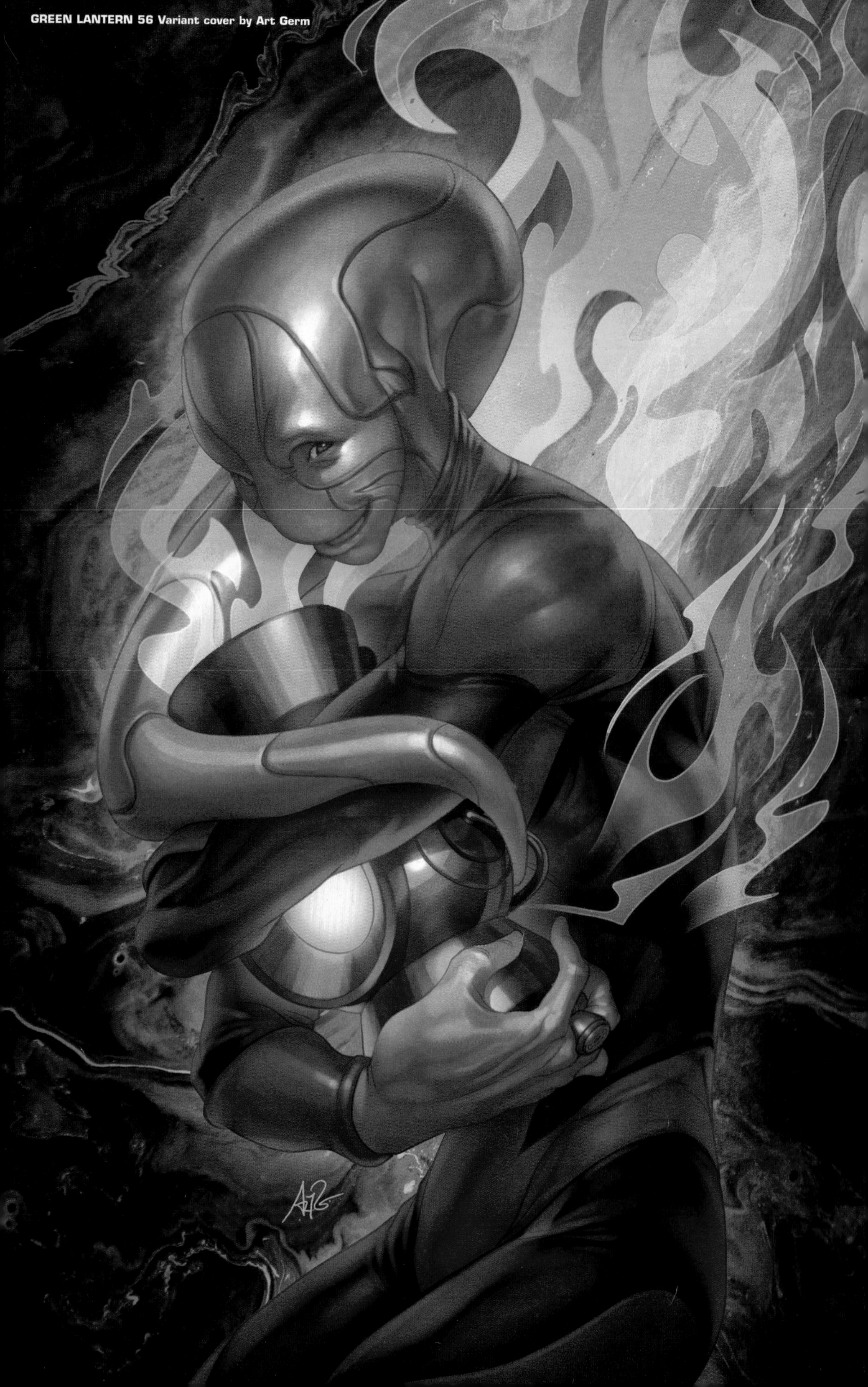

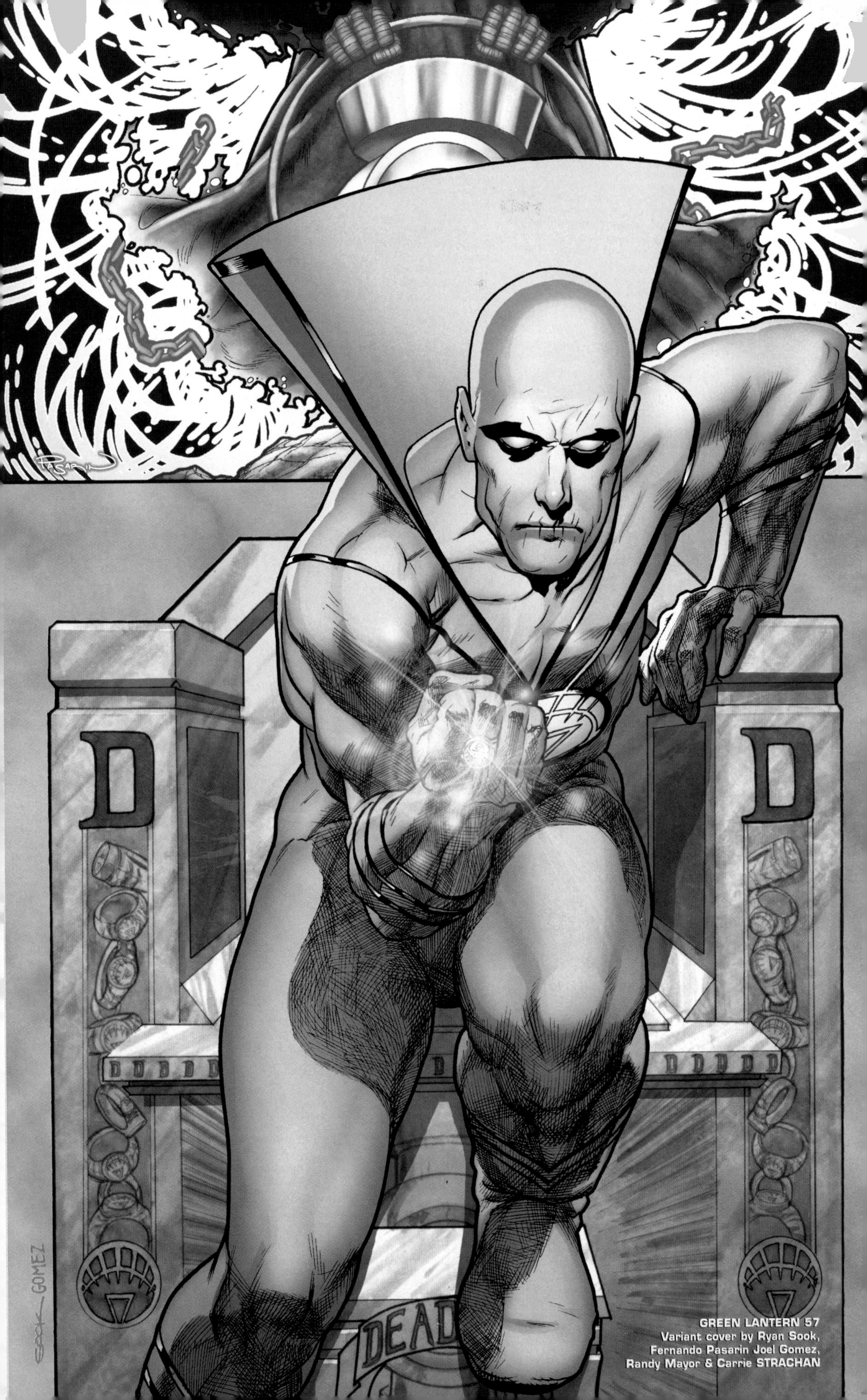
D
D
DEAD

GREEN LANTERN 57
Variant cover by Ryan Sook,
Fernando Pasarin Joel Gomez,
Randy Mayor & Carrie STRACHAN

GREEN LANTERN 58 Variant cover
by Gene Ha

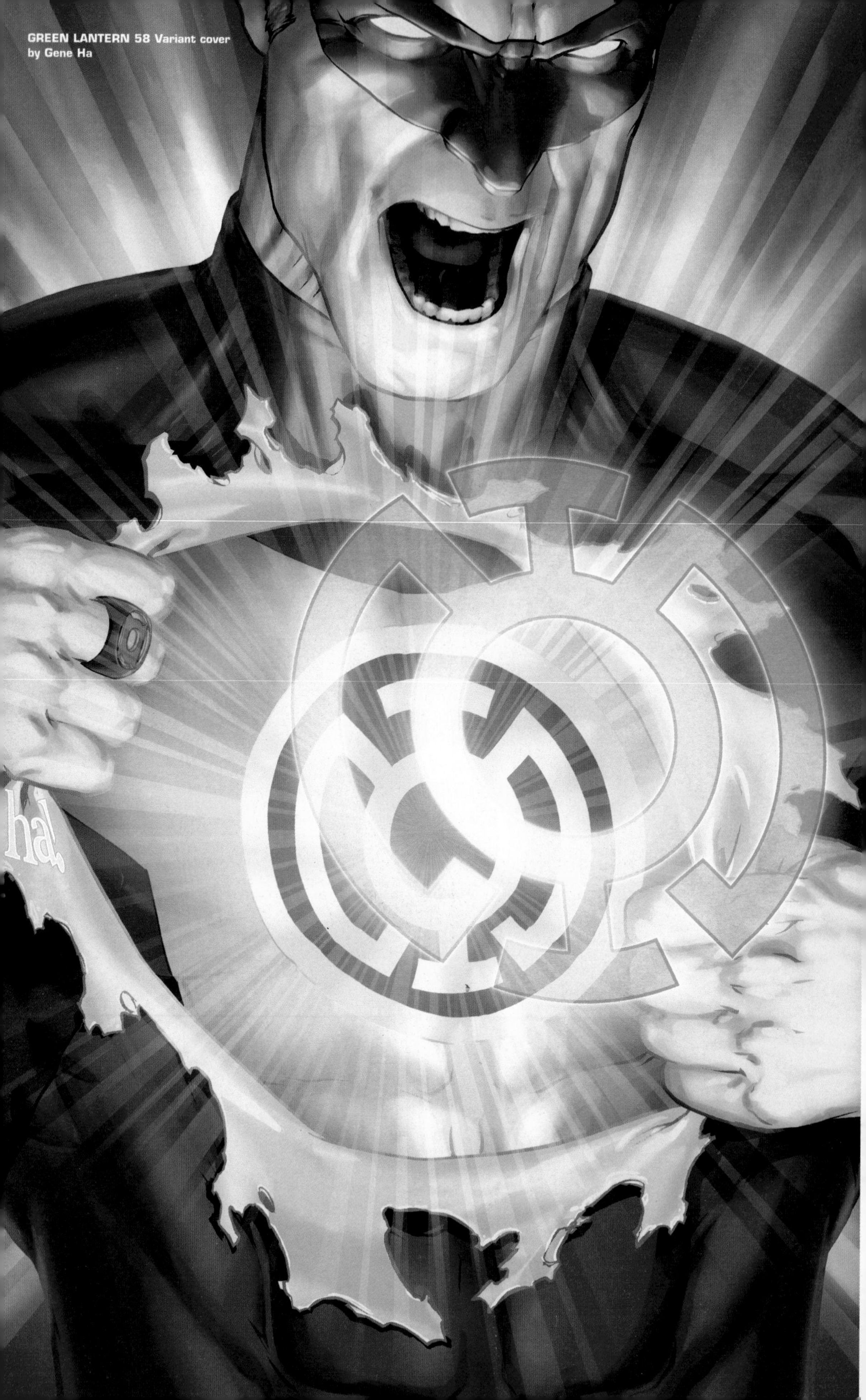
ha!

GREEN LANTERN 59 Variant cover by Gene Ha

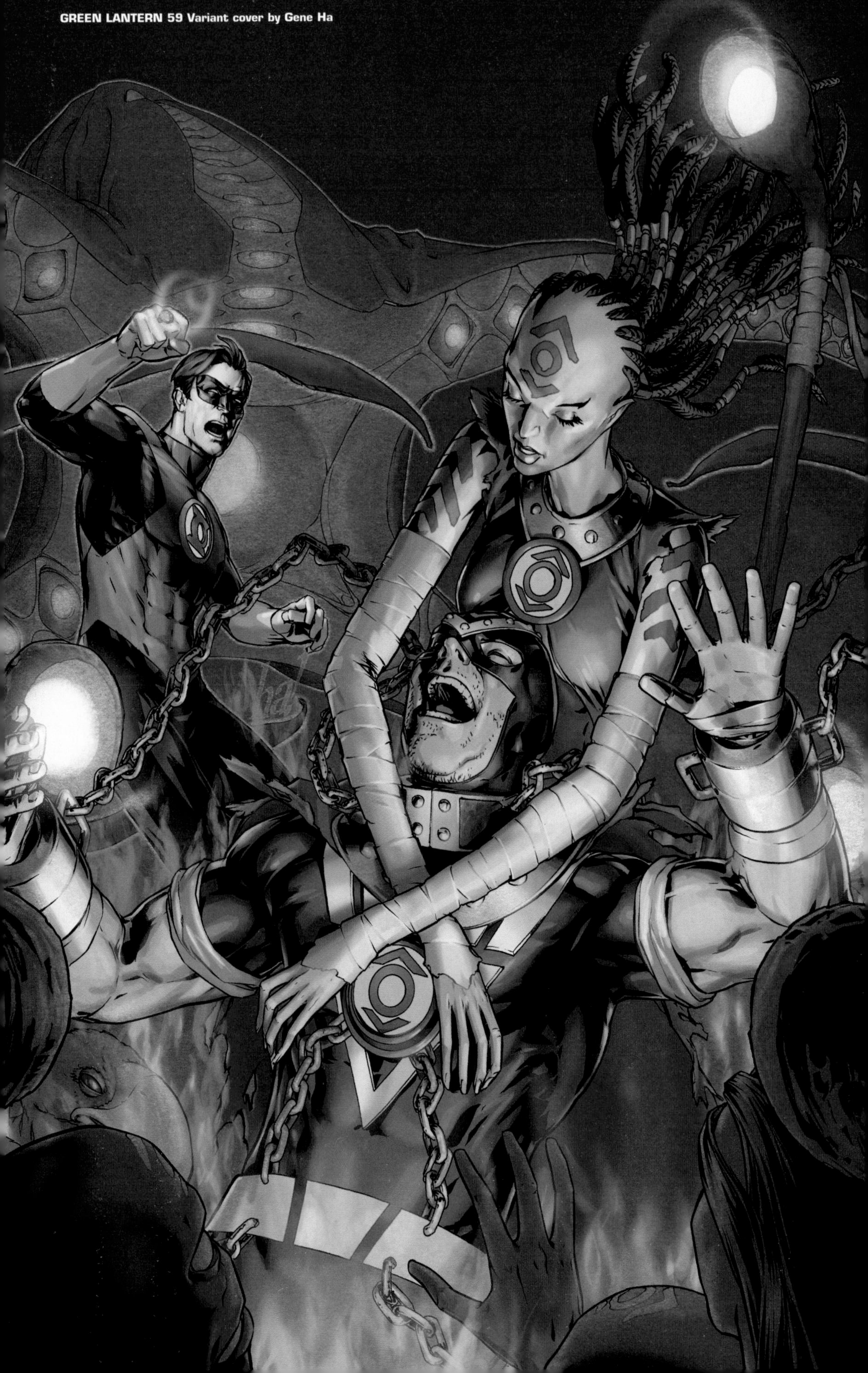

GREEN LANTERN 60 Variant cover by Frank Quitely

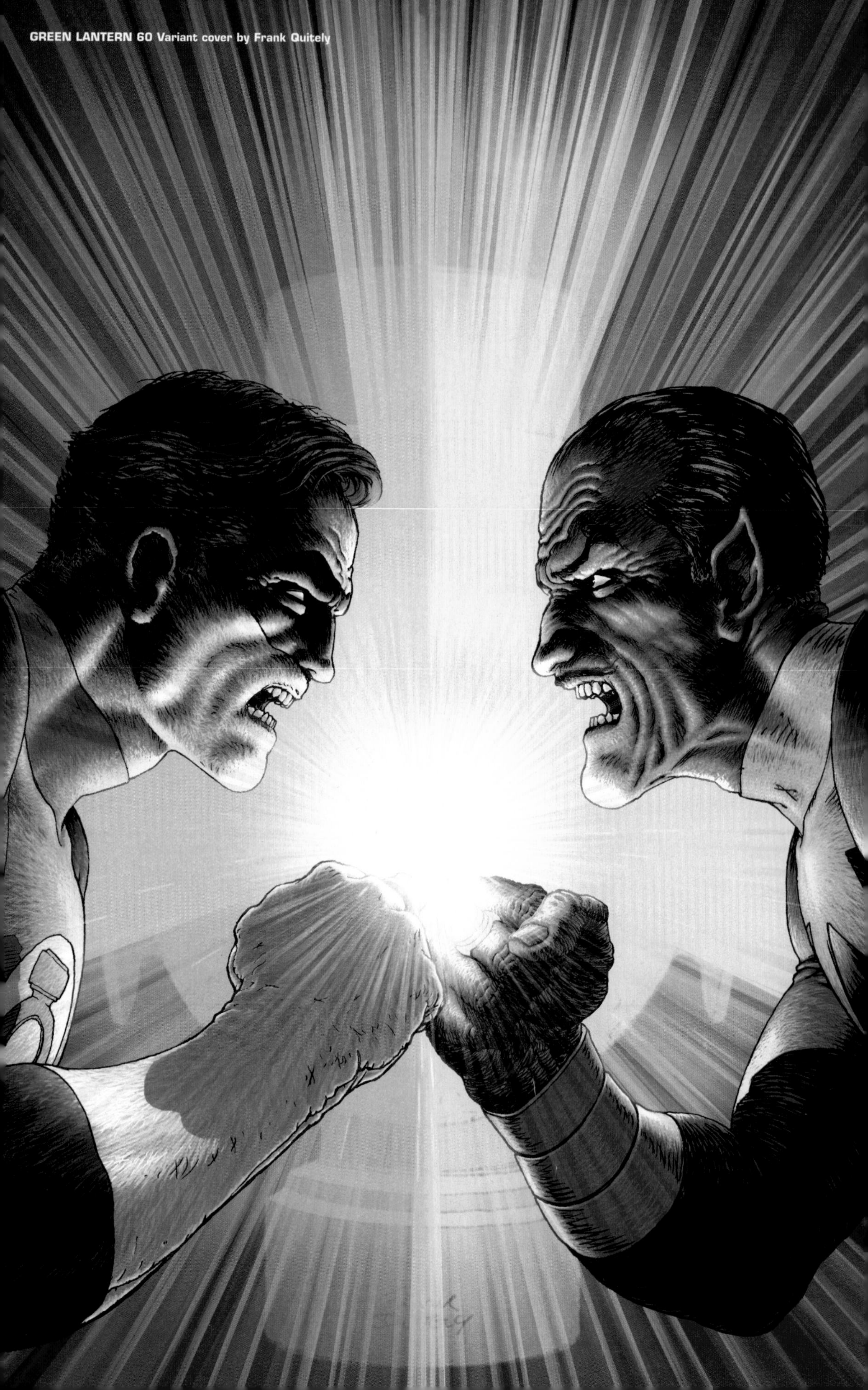

GREEN LANTERN 61 Variant cover by Alex Garner

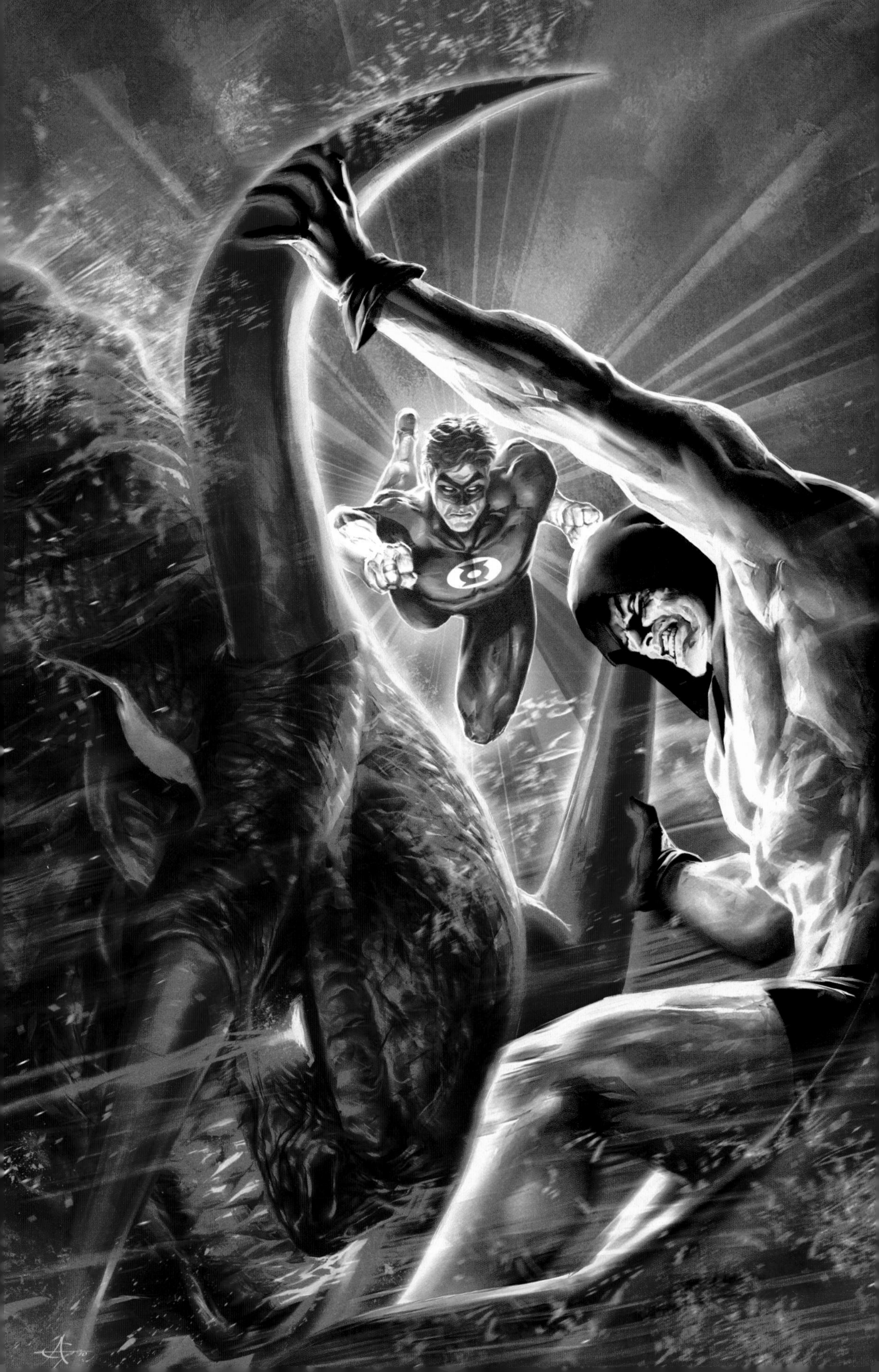

GREEN LANTERN 62 Variant cover by Doug Mahnke, Christian Alamy, Randy Mayor & Alex Sinclair

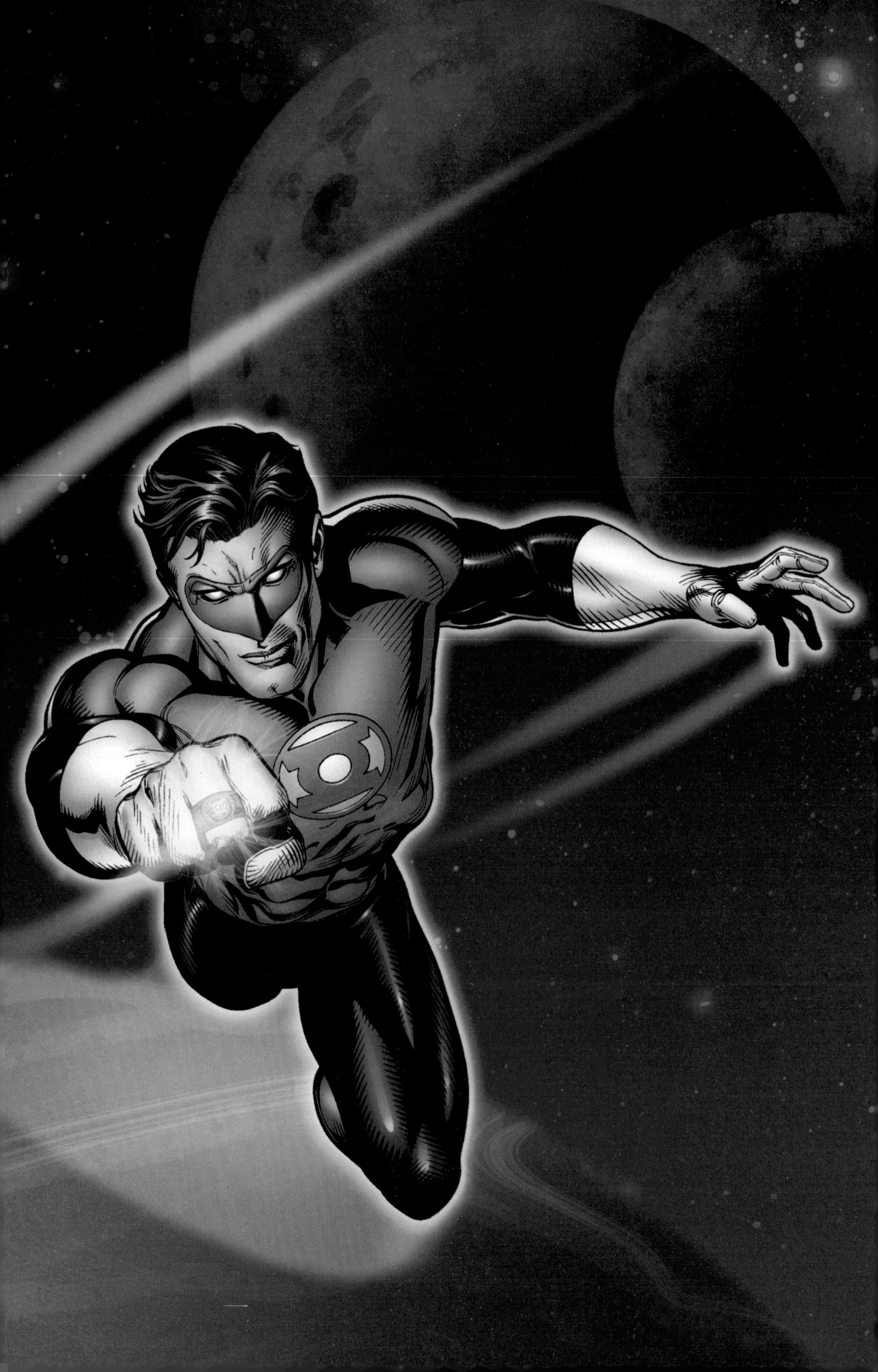

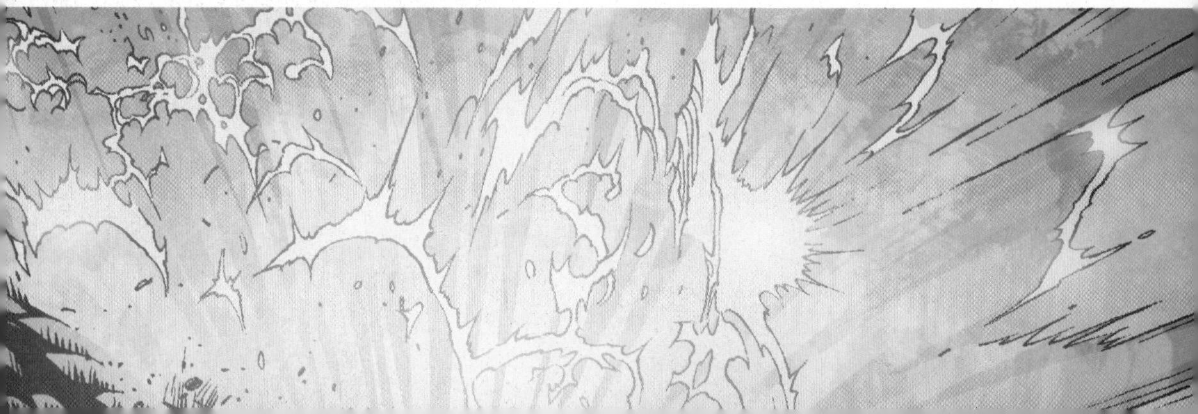

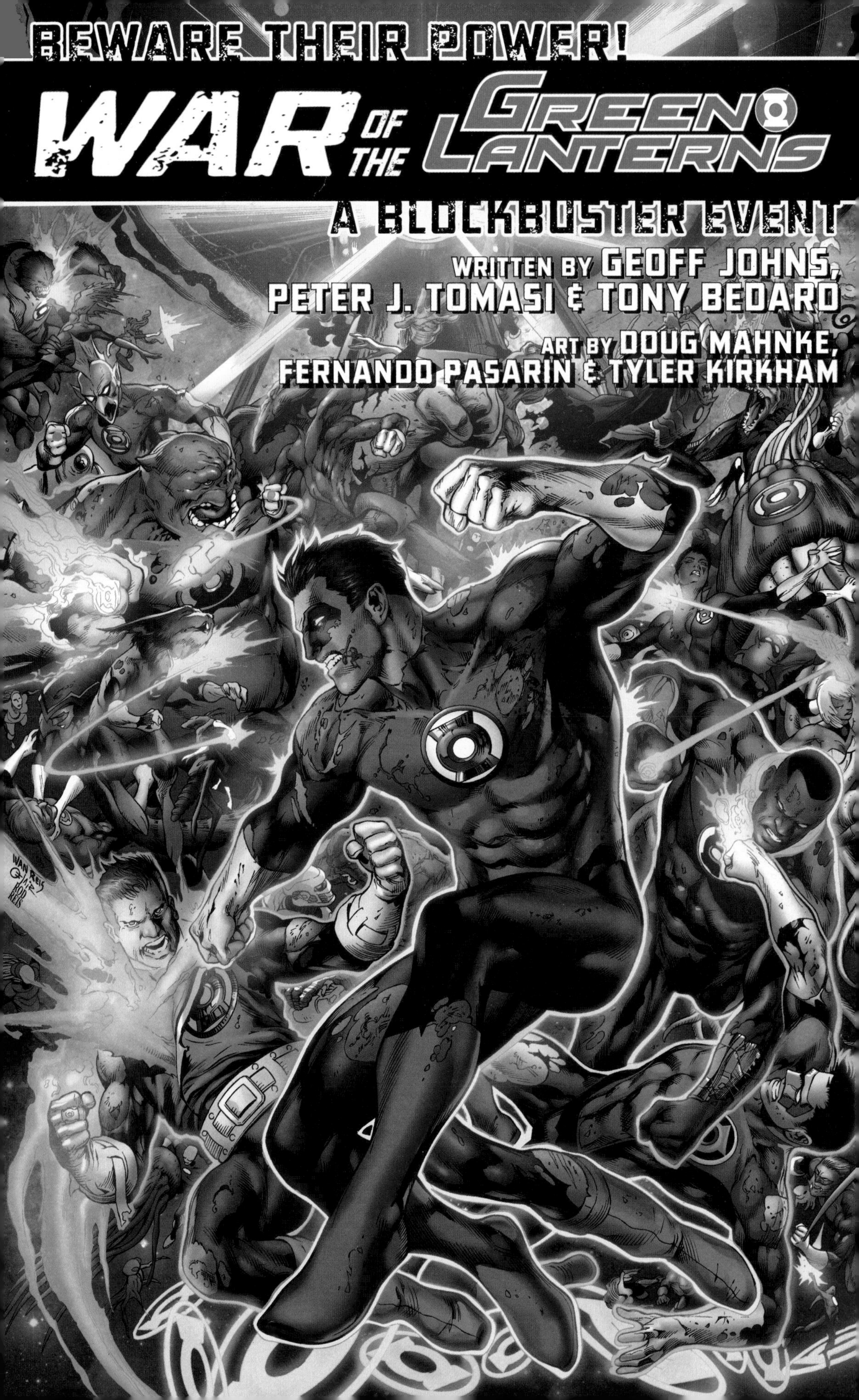
BEWARE THEIR POWER!
WAR OF THE GREEN LANTERNS
A BLOCKBUSTER EVENT
WRITTEN BY GEOFF JOHNS, PETER J. TOMASI & TONY BEDARD
ART BY DOUG MAHNKE, FERNANDO PASARIN & TYLER KIRKHAM

DO YOU STILL BELIEVE EMOTION IS *VITAL* TO LIFE, KRONA?

I STILL BELIEVE EMOTION *IS* LIFE, GANTHET. I ALWAYS WILL.

THEN YOU CONTINUE TO RISK YOUR IMPENDING INDUCTION INTO THE *GUARDIANS* OF THE *UNIVERSE.*

BUT IS *LIFE* NOT THE VERY THING THE SELF-APPOINTED "GUARDIANS" ARE DEVOTING THEMSELVES TO *PROTECTING?* THEY SPEAK IN *CONTRADICTIONS.*

MY FRIEND...YOU HAVE ALWAYS GIVEN ME YOUR SUPPORT AND I ASK FOR THAT SUPPORT *NOW* MORE THAN *EVER.*

I AM ON THE VERGE OF PEERING INTO THE *PAST* AND WITNESSING THE *BIRTH* OF THE *UNIVERSE* AND THEREFORE UNLOCKING THE *SECRETS* OF THE *EMOTIONAL SPECTRUM.*

WE DON'T HAVE TO BE *AFRAID--*

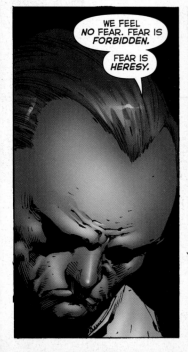

WE FEEL *NO FEAR.* FEAR IS *FORBIDDEN.*

FEAR IS *HERESY.*

PLEASE, GANTHET.

DO NOT *DENY* YOUR HEART LIKE THE OTHERS.

OUR HEARTS ARE FULL OF *CHAOS,* KRONA. WE MUST USE OUR MINDS AND *ONLY* OUR MINDS TO BRING *ORDER* TO THIS UNIVERSE.

I AM SORRY.

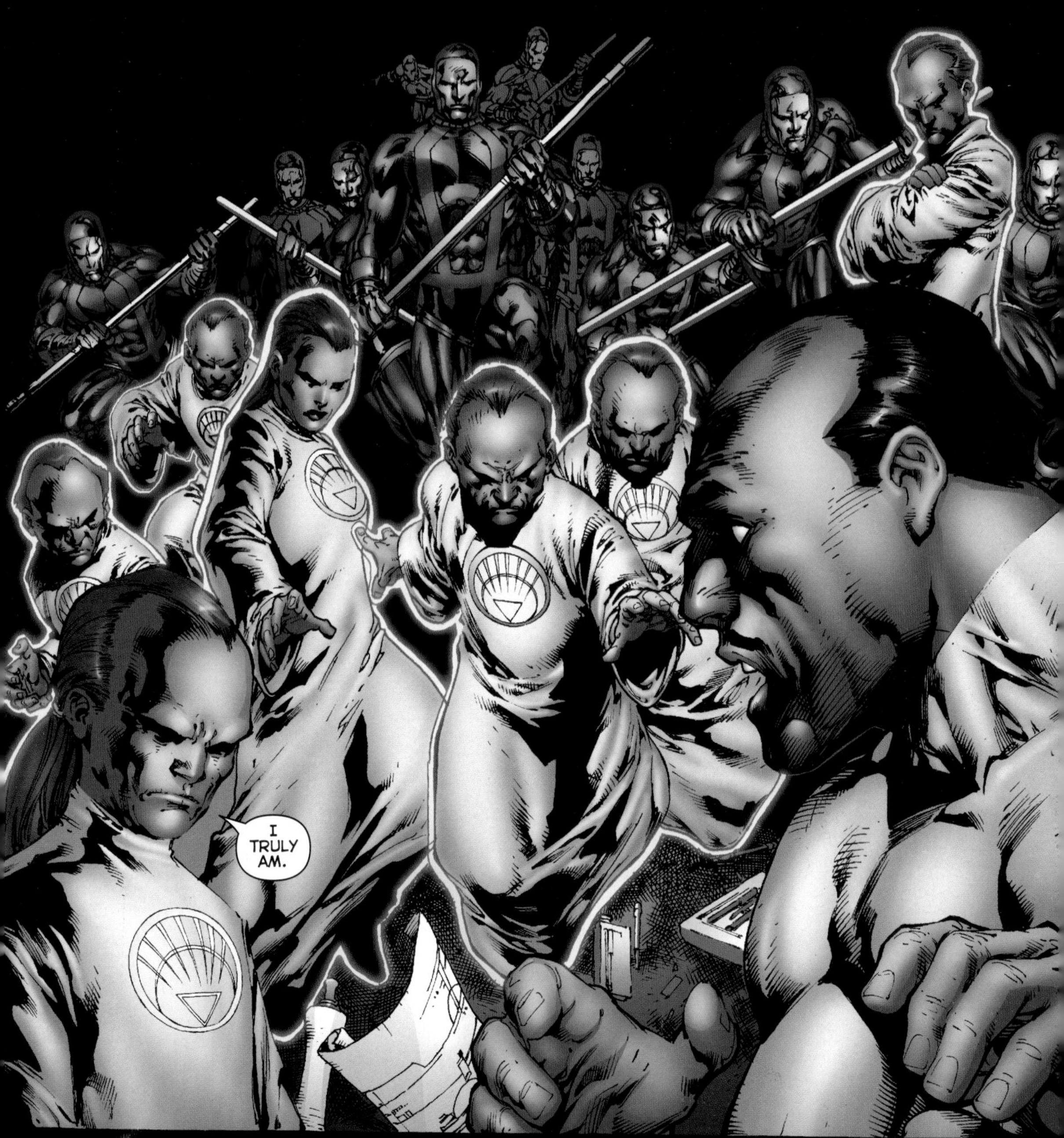
I TRULY AM.

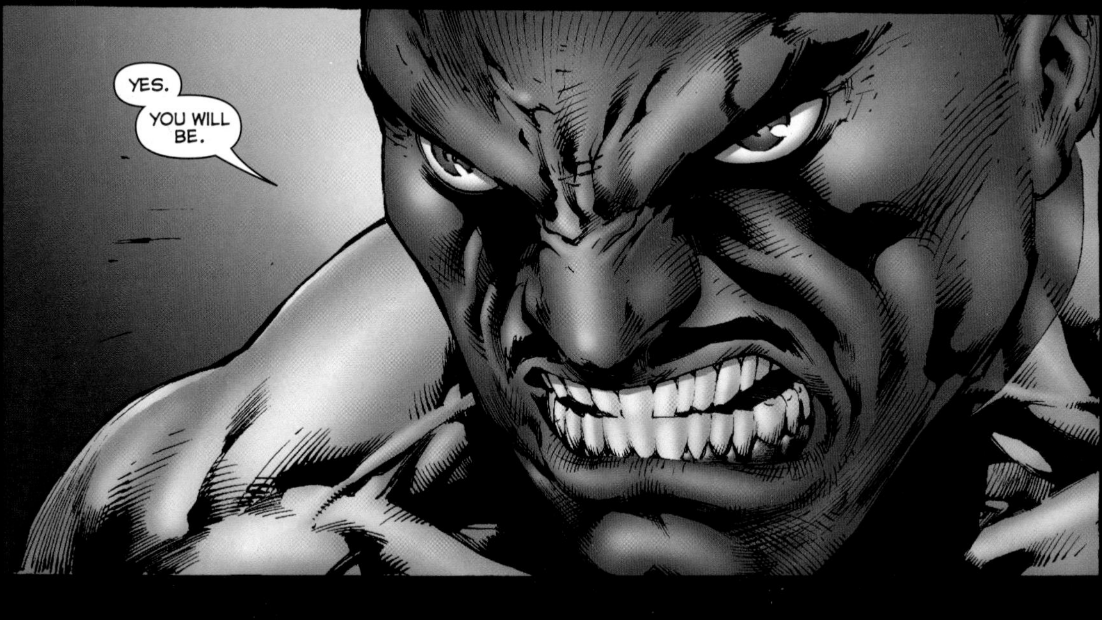
YES.
YOU WILL BE.

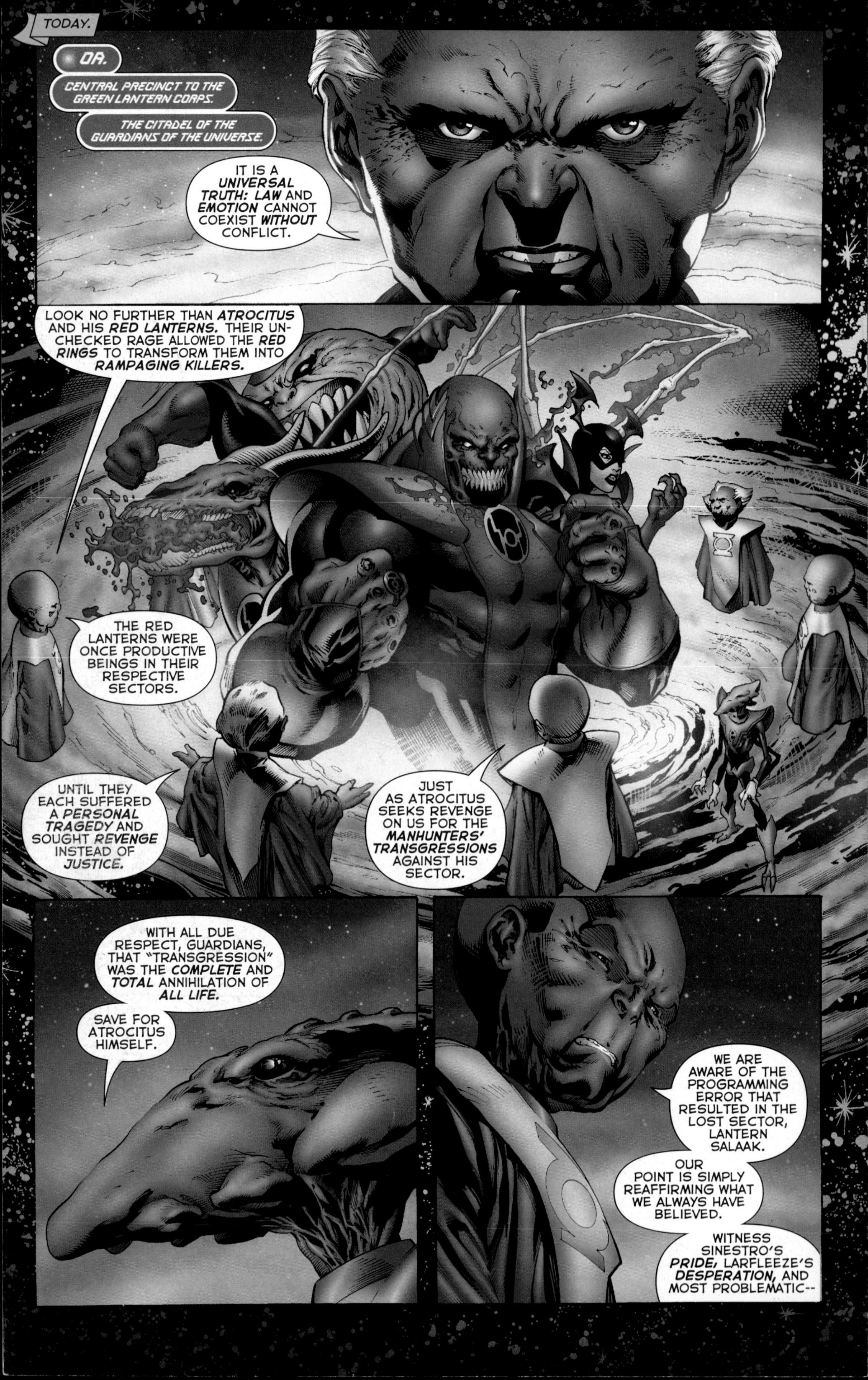
TODAY.
OA.
CENTRAL PRECINCT TO THE GREEN LANTERN CORPS.
THE CITADEL OF THE GUARDIANS OF THE UNIVERSE.
IT IS A UNIVERSAL TRUTH: LAW AND EMOTION CANNOT COEXIST WITHOUT CONFLICT.
LOOK NO FURTHER THAN ATROCITUS AND HIS RED LANTERNS. THEIR UNCHECKED RAGE ALLOWED THE RED RINGS TO TRANSFORM THEM INTO RAMPAGING KILLERS.
THE RED LANTERNS WERE ONCE PRODUCTIVE BEINGS IN THEIR RESPECTIVE SECTORS.
UNTIL THEY EACH SUFFERED A PERSONAL TRAGEDY AND SOUGHT REVENGE INSTEAD OF JUSTICE.
JUST AS ATROCITUS SEEKS REVENGE ON US FOR THE MANHUNTERS' TRANSGRESSIONS AGAINST HIS SECTOR.
WITH ALL DUE RESPECT, GUARDIANS, THAT "TRANSGRESSION" WAS THE COMPLETE AND TOTAL ANNIHILATION OF ALL LIFE.
SAVE FOR ATROCITUS HIMSELF.
WE ARE AWARE OF THE PROGRAMMING ERROR THAT RESULTED IN THE LOST SECTOR, LANTERN SALAAK.
OUR POINT IS SIMPLY REAFFIRMING WHAT WE ALWAYS HAVE BELIEVED.
WITNESS SINESTRO'S PRIDE, LARFLEEZE'S DESPERATION, AND MOST PROBLEMATIC--

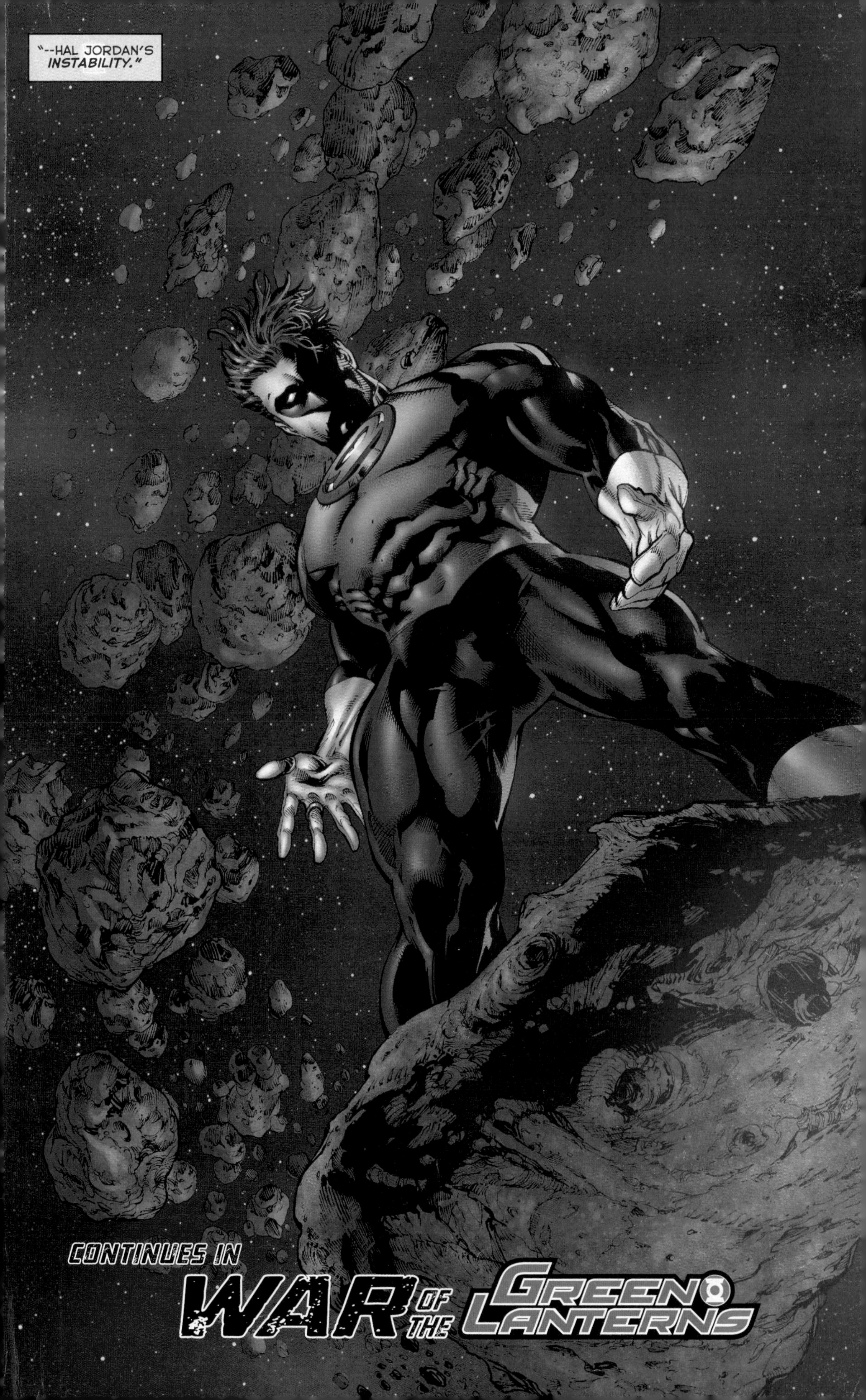
"--HAL JORDAN'S INSTABILITY."
CONTINUES IN
WAR OF THE GREEN LANTERNS

BIOGRAPHIES

GEOFF JOHNS

Geoff Johns is one of the most prolific and popular contemporary comic book writers. He has written highly acclaimed stories starring Superman, Green Lantern, the Flash, Teen Titans, and Justice Society of America. He is the author of the New York Times best-selling graphic novels GREEN LANTERN: RAGE OF THE RED LANTERNS, GREEN LANTERN: SINESTRO CORPS WAR, JUSTICE SOCIETY OF AMERICA: THY KINGDOM COME, and SUPERMAN: BRAINIAC.

Johns was born in Detroit and studied media arts, screenwriting, film production and film theory at Michigan State University. After moving to Los Angeles, he worked as an intern and later an assistant for film director Richard Donner, whose credits include *Superman: The Movie*, *Lethal Weapon 4* and *Conspiracy Theory*.

Johns began his comics career writing STARS AND S.T.R.I.P.E. and creating Stargirl for DC Comics. He received the Wizard Fan Award for Breakout Talent of 2002 and Writer of the Year for 2005, 2006, 2007 and 2008 as well as the CBG Writer of the Year 2003 through 2005 and 2007 and 2008, and CBG Best Comic Book Series for JSA 2001 through 2005.

After acclaimed runs on THE FLASH, TEEN TITANS and the best-selling INFINITE CRISIS miniseries, Johns co-wrote a run on ACTION COMICS with his mentor Donner. In 2006, he co-wrote 52: an ambitious weekly comic book series set in real time, with Grant Morrison, Greg Rucka and Mark Waid. Johns has also written for various other media, including the acclaimed "Legion" episode of SMALLVILLE and the fourth season of ROBOT CHICKEN. He is writing the story of the DC Universe Online massively multiplayer action game from Sony Online Entertainment LLC and has recently joined DC Entertainment as its Chief Creative Officer.

Johns currently resides in Los Angeles, California.

DOUG MAHNKE

Born in 1963 in the Year of the Rabbit, Doug Mahnke embarked on a love affair with comics at the age of five, having received a pile of Spider-Man issues from a rugby-playing college student named Mike who lived in his basement. A consistent interest in the medium, coupled with some art skill, landed Doug a job drawing comics for Dark Horse at the age of 24 (the date is known precisely, as it occurred just two weeks before he wed his lovely bride). His first gig was illustrating a moody detective one-shot entitled *Homicide*, written by John Arcudi. The two went on to collaborate on Dark Horse's *The Mask* and their creator-owned series MAJOR BUMMER, originally published by DC.

Since then Doug has worked on a wide variety of titles, including SUPERMAN: THE MAN OF STEEL, JLA, BATMAN, SEVEN SOLDIERS: FRANKENSTEIN, BLACK ADAM: THE DARK AGE and STORMWATCH: P.H.D. After contributing to 2009's FINAL CRISIS, he took over art chores on GREEN LANTERN. He resides in the midwest with his wife and seven kids, one dog, and a bunny named Suzie.